Please return / renew by date shown.
You can re... gov.uk
or by ... 6
Please have your library card & PIN ready.

KT-376-754

NORFOLK LIBRARY
AND INFORMATION SERVICE

NORFOLK ITEM
30129 077 032 507

THIS EDITION WRITTEN AND RESEARCHED BY

Becky Ohlsen,
Anna Kaminski, Josephine Quintero

PLAN YOUR TRIP

JOHN FREEMAN / GETTY IMAGES ©

MODERNA MUSEET MALMÖ P171

ANDERS BLOMQVIST / GETTY IMAGES ©

TURNING TORSO, MALMÖ P171

ON THE ROAD

Contents

Welcome to Sweden

Frozen wastelands, cosy cottages, virgin forest, rocky islands, reindeer herders and Viking lore – Sweden has all that plus impeccable style and to-die-for dining.

Swedish Style

In some ways, visiting Sweden feels like walking right into a fashion or home-decor magazine. There are no boring outfits on the streets of Stockholm, and the care with which houses, cottages, cafes and public spaces are decorated and kept up throughout the country is truly inspiring. But Swedish style is never too showy; form and function are tightly linked in this society known for valuing moderation, practicality, order, simple lines and clever designs. Whether you decide to shop for your own versions or just enjoy the scenery, it's hard not to fall for the cool aesthetics of this place.

Landscape

Truth be told, the best thing about Sweden is its natural beauty. To really appreciate this country's charms, you have to leave the city behind. Whether that means sailing across an archipelago to visit a lonely island or trekking along a trail through the northern wilderness just depends on your preferences – why not try both? Hiking, camping, cycling, skiing, boating, fishing and foraging for mushrooms and berries are all major Swedish pastimes, and it's easy to get in on the action from just about anywhere in the country.

The Sami

The northern part of Sweden is home to the indigenous Sami people, whose traditionally nomadic lifestyle is built around reindeer herding. Sami culture, including handicrafts, homes and villages, methods of transport and style of cooking, is one of the many things a visitor can become immersed in while spending time in Lappland. Don't miss the chance to learn about this unique group of people: spend a night or two in a Sami reindeer camp or take a dogsledding tour. If you're on a more limited schedule, have a meal in a Sami restaurant or pick up some handmade Sami woodwork or leather goods to take home as a souvenir.

Vikings & History

Ancient rune stones poke up out of the grass in parks all over Sweden; huge stone-ship settings and unobtrusive burial mounds are almost as common. Walled medieval cities and seaside fortresses are regular stops on the travellers circuit. Viking ruins and the stories surrounding them are very much a part of the modern Swedish landscape, and it's easy to feel as if you're walking through history. In fact, you are.

Why I Love Sweden

By Becky Ohlsen, Author

There's something so wholesome and healthy about Sweden. People here really know how to take advantage of their gorgeous country, from its scenic beauty to its edible bounty. My first trips here were to visit my grandparents, and no day was complete without a long walk on the forested trails around their apartments. Dinner was usually local fish and produce from one of Stockholm's market halls – and for dessert, Swedish strawberries from a Hötorget vendor. To this day, being in Sweden means being outdoors, camping or hiking or just happily wandering.

For more about our authors, see page 352

Above: Skärhamn, Tjörn (p151)

Sweden

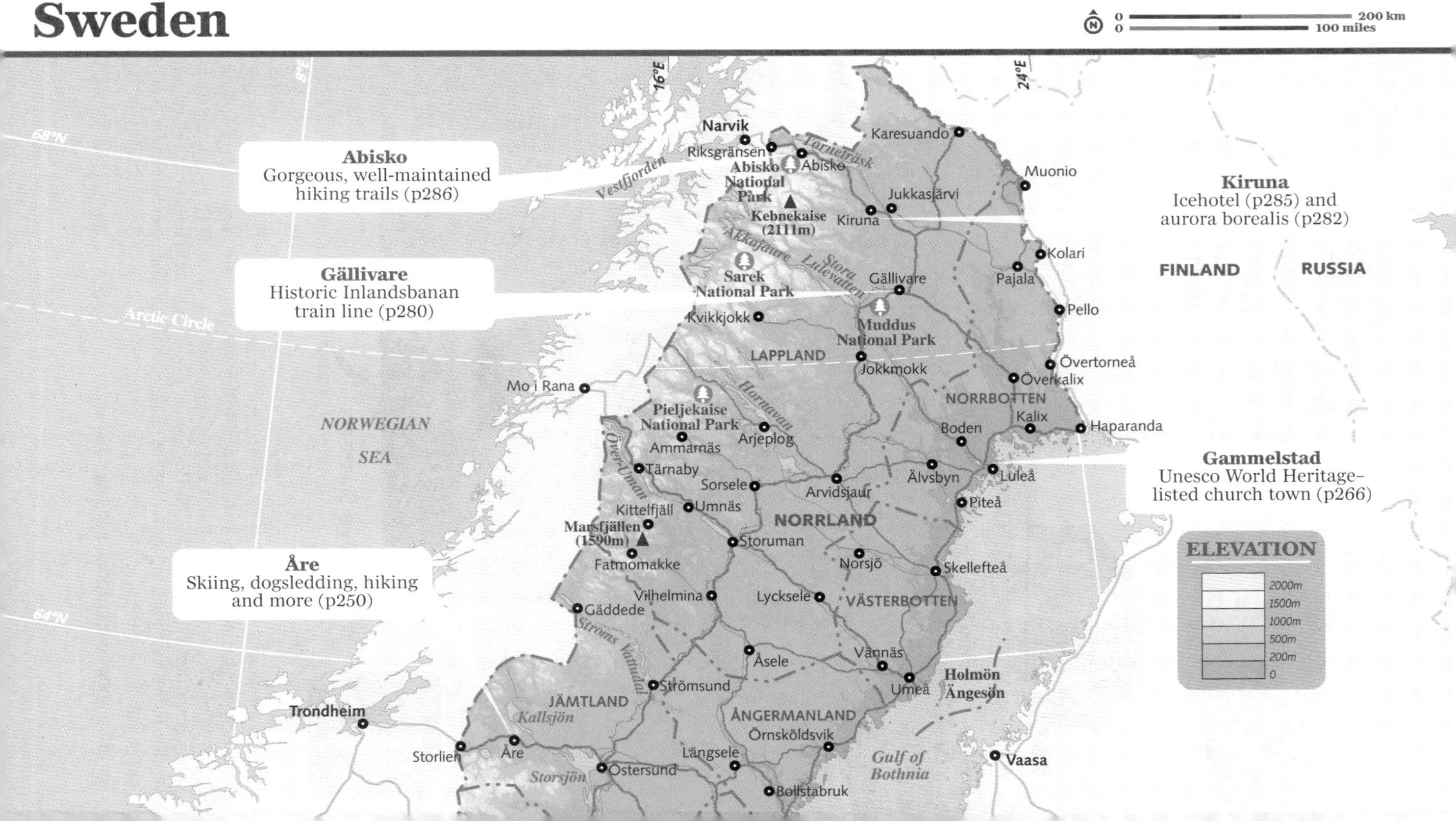

0 200 km
0 100 miles
Abisko
Gorgeous, well-maintained hiking trails (p286)
Gällivare
Historic Inlandsbanan train line (p280)
Åre
Skiing, dogsledding, hiking and more (p250)
Kiruna
Icehotel (p285) and aurora borealis (p282)
Gammelstad
Unesco World Heritage-listed church town (p266)
ELEVATION
2000m
1500m
1000m
500m
200m
0
68°N
64°N
8°E
16°E
24°E
Arctic Circle
NORWEGIAN SEA
FINLAND
RUSSIA
Narvik
Riksgränsen
Abisko
Abisko National Park
Torneträsk
Vestfjorden
Kebnekaise (2111m)
Kiruna
Jukkasjärvi
Karesuando
Muonio
Kolari
Pajala
Pello
Gällivare
Stora Lulevatten
Akkajaure
Sarek National Park
Kvikkjokk
Muddus National Park
LAPPLAND
Jokkmokk
Övertorneå
Överkalix
NORRBOTTEN
Kalix
Haparanda
Boden
Luleå
Mo i Rana
Pieljekaise National Park
Hornavan
Arjeplog
Ammarnäs
Tärnaby
Över-Uman
Sorsele
Arvidsjaur
Älvsbyn
Piteå
Kittelfjäll
Umnäs
NORRLAND
Marsfjällen (1590m)
Storuman
Norsjö
Skellefteå
Fatmomakke
Vilhelmina
Lycksele
VÄSTERBOTTEN
Gäddede
Ströms Vattudal
Åsele
Vännäs
Umeå
Holmön
Ängesön
Strömsund
JÄMTLAND
Kallsjön
ÅNGERMANLAND
Örnsköldsvik
Trondheim
Storlien
Åre
Storsjön
Östersund
Långsele
Bollstabruk
Gulf of Bothnia
Vaasa

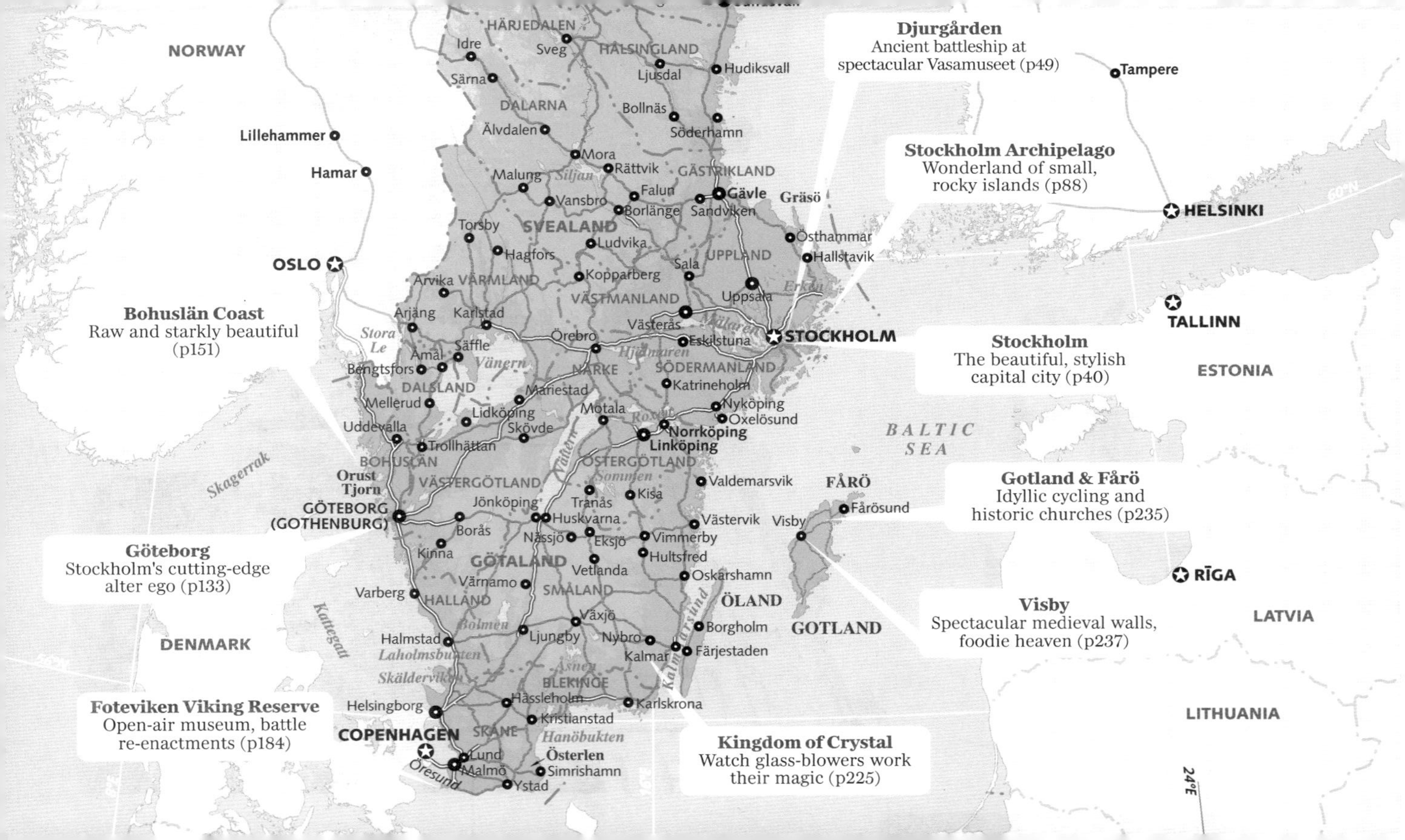
Djurgården
Ancient battleship at spectacular Vasamuseet (p49)
Stockholm Archipelago
Wonderland of small, rocky islands (p88)
Stockholm
The beautiful, stylish capital city (p40)
Gotland & Fårö
Idyllic cycling and historic churches (p235)
Visby
Spectacular medieval walls, foodie heaven (p237)
Kingdom of Crystal
Watch glass-blowers work their magic (p225)
Foteviken Viking Reserve
Open-air museum, battle re-enactments (p184)
Göteborg
Stockholm's cutting-edge alter ego (p133)
Bohuslän Coast
Raw and starkly beautiful (p151)
NORWAY
DENMARK
ESTONIA
LATVIA
LITHUANIA
HELSINKI
TALLINN
RĪGA
OSLO
COPENHAGEN
STOCKHOLM
GÖTEBORG (GOTHENBURG)
Tampere
Lillehammer
Hamar
BALTIC SEA
Skagerrak
Kattegatt
Öresund
Hanöbukten
Laholmsbukten
Skäldervíken
60°N
24°E
HÄRJEDALEN
HÄLSINGLAND
DALARNA
GÄSTRIKLAND
SVEALAND
UPPLAND
VÄRMLAND
VÄSTMANLAND
NÄRKE
SÖDERMANLAND
DALSLAND
BOHUSLÄN
VÄSTERGÖTLAND
ÖSTERGÖTLAND
GÖTALAND
SMÅLAND
HALLAND
BLEKINGE
SKÅNE
ÖLAND
GOTLAND
FÅRÖ
Idre
Sveg
Särna
Hudiksvall
Ljusdal
Bollnäs
Söderhamn
Älvdalen
Mora
Rättvik
Malung
Siljan
Falun
Gävle
Gräsö
Sandviken
Vansbro
Borlänge
Torsby
Hagfors
Ludvika
Östhammar
Hallstavik
Sala
Kopparberg
Arvika
Uppsala
Arjäng
Karlstad
Västerås
Mälaren
Stora Le
Säffle
Örebro
Eskilstuna
Åmål
Vänern
Hjälmaren
Bengtsfors
Katrineholm
Mariestad
Mellerud
Lidköping
Motala
Nyköping
Oxelösund
Uddevalla
Skövde
Norrköping
Linköping
Trollhättan
Vättern
Orust
Tjorn
Valdemarsvik
Tranås
Kisa
Jönköping
Huskvarna
Västervik
Visby
Fårösund
Borås
Nässjö
Eksjö
Vimmerby
Hultsfred
Kinna
Vetlanda
Oskarshamn
Värnamo
Varberg
Växjö
Borgholm
Bolmen
Ljungby
Nybro
Halmstad
Kalmar
Färjestaden
Kalmarsund
Karlskrona
Helsingborg
Hässleholm
Kristianstad
Lund
Österlen
Malmö
Simrishamn
Ystad

Sweden's Top 15

1

Stockholm

1 The nation's capital (p40) calls itself 'beauty on water', and it certainly doesn't disappoint in the looks department. Stockholm's many glittering waterways reflect slanted northern light onto spice-hued buildings, and the crooked cobblestone streets of Gamla Stan are magic to wander. Besides its aesthetic virtues, Stockholm also has top-notch museums, first-class dining and all the shopping anyone could ask for. Its clean and efficient public transport, and multilingual locals, make it a cinch to navigate, and at the end of the day you can collapse in a cushy designer hotel. Left: Stortorget, Gamla Stan (p43)

Norrland Hiking, Abisko

2 Sweden has some absolutely gorgeous hiking trails, most of which are well maintained and supplied with conveniently located mountain huts along the way. The season is relatively short, but it's worth a bit of extra planning to get out into the wilderness: the natural landscape is one of Sweden's best assets. A good place to start your venture is the Norrland village of Abisko (p286), at the top of the Kungsleden long-distance trail – it's a hiker headquarters and easily reached by train. Right: Abisko National Park (p286)

MATTI NIEMI / GETTY IMAGES ©

2

SABINE LUBENOW / GETTY IMAGES ©

Northern Delights, Kiruna

3 The twin phenomena that have made the north of Sweden so famous – one natural, one artificial – are both found beyond the Arctic Circle. No other natural spectacle compares to the aurora borealis (p274) – the shape-shifting lights that dance across the night sky during the Arctic winter (October to March). The Icehotel (p285), humble igloo turned ice palace just outside Kiruna, takes its inspiration from the changeable nature of the northern lights, and is recreated in a slightly different form every winter.

Ambitious Menus, Stockholm

4 Traditionally, basic Swedish cuisine is a humble, healthy enterprise based on fish, potatoes and preserved meat. But in recent years the country's top chefs have pushed the boundaries, so that alongside classic everyday dishes such as fried herring or meatballs, or even more exotic northern fare like Arctic char or reindeer with wild berries, you'll find innovative, experimental dishes that are fiercely global in influence and ambition. Dining out (p71) in Sweden can be an adventure and an experience.

3

Medieval Visby

5 It's hard to overstate the beauty of the Hanseatic port town of Visby (p237), in itself justification for making the ferry trip to Gotland. Inside its thick medieval walls are twisting cobblestone streets, fairy-tale cottages draped in flowers, and gorgeous ruins atop hills with stunning Baltic views. The walls themselves, with 40-plus towers and the spectacular church ruins within, are a travel photographer's dream, and the perimeter makes an ideal scenic stroll. The city is also a food-lover's heaven, packed with top-notch restaurants accustomed to impressing discriminating diners. Left: St Nicolai Kyrka (p237)

Göteborg

6 The edgy alter ego to Stockholm's confident polish, Göteborg (133)is a city of contrasts, with slick museums, raw industrial landscapes, pleasant parks, can-do designers and cutting-edge food. Try delectable shrimp and fish – straight off the boat or at one of the city's five Michelin-rated restaurants. There's the thrill-packed chaos of Sweden's largest theme park, the cultured quiet of the many museums, and you can't leave without window-shopping in Haga and Linné. You can even jump on a boat and wander the 190km of the Göta Canal. Top: Kungsparken (King's Park)

Bohuslän Coast

7 Caught between sky and sea, the coast of Bohuslän is raw and starkly beautiful, its skerries thick with birds and its villages brightly painted specks among the rocks. Choose from myriad quaint seaside bolt-holes. Film star Ingrid Bergman loved pretty Fjällbacka, the bargain-hunting Norwegians flock to Strömstad, and every sailor knows Tjörn is the place to be in August for the round-island regatta. For a real taste of Swedish summer, spread your beach blanket on a smooth rock and tuck into a bag of peel-and-eat shrimp. Bottom: Smögen (p155)

6

7

NIKLAS BERNSTONE / GETTY IMAGES ©

JOHNER IMAGES / GETTY IMAGES ©

Gotland & Fårö

8 Merchants in the 12th and 13th centuries dotted the beautiful island of Gotland (p235) with fabulous churches. Today, Gotland's lovely ruins, remote beaches, idyllic bike- and horse-riding paths, peculiar rock formations, excellent restaurants and rousing summer nightlife attract visitors from all over the world. The event of the season is Medeltidsveckan (Medieval Week; p237), which brings Visby's old town alive with costumes, re-enactments and markets. Film buffs and nature lovers will want to head north to visit Ingmar Bergman's stomping ground of Fårö (p242).

Kingdom of Crystal

9 In the Glasriket (Kingdom of Crystal; p225) a rich mix of skill and brawn combine to produce stunning (and often practical) works of art. Watch local glass-blowers spin bubbles of molten crystal into fantastic creatures, bowls, vases and sculptures. Choose something for the mantelpiece or try glass-blowing for yourself at the well-stocked centres in Kosta and Orrefors. . For background on the 500-year-old industry there's Smålands Museum in Vaxjo, and for the ultimate finish enjoy a cocktail at Kjell Engman's cobalt-blue bar at the Kosta Boda Art Hotel.

Stockholm Archipelago

10 Scattered between the city and the open Baltic Sea, this archipelago (p88) is a mesmerising wonderland of small rocky isles, some no more than seagull launch-pads, others studded with deep forests and fields of wildflowers. Most are within easy striking distance of the city, with regular ferry services in summer and several organised tours for easy island-hopping. Hostels, campgrounds and more upmarket slumber options make overnighting a good option, as does the growing number of excellent restaurants.

ANDERS BLOMQVIST / GETTY IMAGES ©

Vikings Village – Foteviken

11 There are still real, live Vikings, and you can visit them at one of Sweden's most absorbing attractions. An evocative 'living' reconstruction of a late–Viking Age village, Foteviken Viking Reserve (p184) was built on the coast near the site of the Battle of Foteviken (1134) and contains some 22 reed-roofed houses. You can tour all of these, check out the great meeting hall, see a war catapult and buy Viking-made handicrafts. It's all admirably legit, too – the reserve's residents hold to old traditions, laws and religions.

Gammelstad

12 There is an abundance of Unesco World Heritage–recognised treasures in Sweden. A fine example is Gammelstad church town (p266) near Luleå. The largest church town in the country, it was the medieval centre of northern Sweden; visiting feels a bit like time travel. The stone Nederluleå Church (built in 1492) has a reredos worthy of a cathedral and choir stalls for a whole church council, and there are 424 wooden houses where rural pioneers stayed overnight on their weekend pilgrimages.

Inlandsbanan to Gällivare

13 Take a journey through Norrland along this historic train line (p251; summer only), which passes small mining towns, deep green forests, herds of reindeer and, if you're lucky, the occasional elk (moose). Built during the 1930s and rendered obsolete by 1992, the line has more than enough charm and historical appeal to make up for its lack of speed – you'll have plenty of time to contemplate the landscape, in other words. It's a beautiful, oddball means of transport, best suited to those for whom adventure trumps efficiency.

Winter Sports, Åre

14 Winter sports in Lappland are a major draw. To go cross-country skiing, just grab a pair of skis and step outside; for downhill sports, be it heliskiing or snowboarding, Åre (p250) is your best bet. Few pastimes are as enjoyable as rushing across the Arctic wasteland pulled by a team of dogs, the sled crunching through crisp snow – but if you want something with a motor, you can test your driving (and racing) skills on the frozen lakes instead.

Vasamuseet

15 Stockholm's unique Vasamuseet (p51) is a purpose-built preservation and display case for an ancient sunken battleship. The ship was the pride of the Swedish Crown when it set out in August 1628, but pride quickly turned to embarrassment when the top-heavy ship tipped and sank to the bottom of Saltsjön, where it would await rescue for 300 years. The museum explains – in fascinating multimedia – how it was found, retrieved and restored, why it sank in the first place, and what it all means to the Swedish people.

14

15

Need to Know

For more information, see Survival Guide (p321)

Currency
Krona (Skr)

Languages
Swedish, Finnish, Sami dialects

Visas
Americans don't need a visa to enter Sweden; some nationalities will need a Schengen visa, good for 90 days.

Money
ATMs widely available. Credit cards accepted in most hotels and restaurants.

Mobile Phones
Most mobile phones work in Sweden, though often with hefty roaming fees. Local SIM cards also work in most phones.

Time
Central European Time (GMT/UTC plus one hour)

When to Go

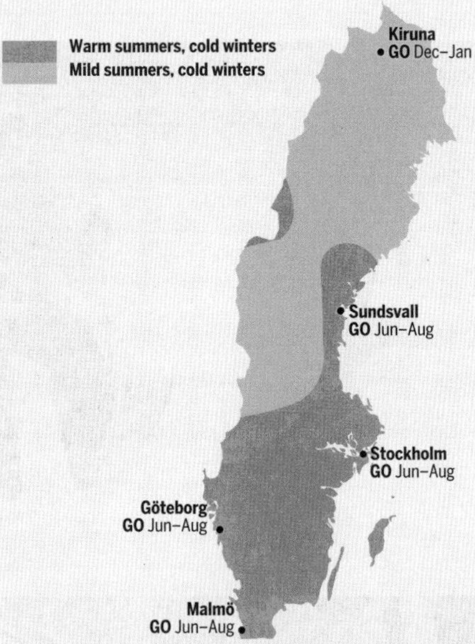

High Season
(mid-Jun–Aug)

- Season starts at Midsummer; expect warm weather and most sights and accommodation to be open.
- Some restaurants and shops close in July or August as Swedes take their own holidays.

Shoulder
(Sep–Oct)

- Weather is still good, even if no one's around to enjoy it.
- Many tourist spots are closed, but you'll have the rest all to yourself.
- Hotel rates return to normal but drop at weekends.

Low Season
(Nov–May)

- Best season for winter-sports adventures, the northern lights and holiday markets.
- Book accommodation and winter activities in advance.
- Many campgrounds and hostels close for the winter.

Useful Websites

Visit Sweden (www.visitsweden.com) Official tourist-bureau website.

Swedish Institute (www.si.se/English) Scholarly info on Swedish culture.

The Local (www.thelocal.se) News from Sweden in English.

Smorgasbord (www.sverigeturism.se/smorgasbord) A searchable info database.

Lonely Planet (www.lonelyplanet.com/sweden) For planning and inspiration.

Important Numbers

Country code	☎46
International access code	☎00
International directory assistance	☎118 119
Directory assistance within Sweden	☎118 118
Emergency	☎112

Exchange Rates

Australia	$1	Skr6.44
Canada	$1	Skr6.32
Europe	€1	Skr9.16
Japan	¥100	Skr6.65
New Zealand	$1	Skr6.07
UK	£1	Skr11.46
US	$1	Skr6.92

For current exchange rates see www.xe.com.

Daily Costs

Budget: Less than Skr1000

- Dorm bed or tent site: Skr200-300
- Fast-food meal (kebab, quiche, sandwich): Skr55-85
- 24-hour bus and metro ticket: Skr115
- Admission to museum: Skr100

Midrange: Skr1000–2000

- Double room in midrange hotel: Skr800-1600
- Happy-hour beer: Skr35-75
- Meal at a midrange restaurant: Skr100-200
- 72-hour bus and metro ticket: Skr230

Top End: More than Skr2000

- Double room in top-end hotel: Skr1600-2600
- Dinner with drinks at a nice restaurant: Skr350-600
- Taxi from airport: Skr520

Opening Hours

Except where indicated, we list hours for high season (mid-June to August). Expect more limited hours the rest of the year.

Banks 9.30am to 3pm Monday to Friday; some city branches open to 5pm or 6pm

Bars and pubs 11am or noon to 1am or 2am

Government offices 9am to 5pm Monday to Friday

Restaurants lunch 11am to 2pm, dinner 5pm to 10pm, often closed on Sunday and/or Monday, high-end restaurants often closed for a week or two in July or August

Shops 9am to 6pm Monday to Friday, to 1pm Saturday

Arriving in Sweden

Stockholm Arlanda airport (p330) Arlanda Express trains run every 10 to 15 minutes from 5am to 12.30am (every half-hour after 9pm); the trip takes 20 minutes and one-way tickets are Skr260. Taxis cost Skr475 to Skr520. Flygbuss airport shuttles from the airport to Cityterminalen run every 10 to 15 minutes, take about 50 minutes and cost Skr119 one way.

Getting Around

Transport in Sweden is reliable and easy to navigate. Roads are generally in good repair, and buses and trains are comfortable, with plenty of services on board and in stations. There's a good trip planner at http://reseplanerare.resrobot.se.

Train Affordable and extensive; speed depends on whether the route is local, regional or express.

Bus More thorough coverage than trains, and often equally quick and cheap (if not more so).

Car Expensive but ideal if you want to explore smaller roads and remote places, especially for camping and outdoor activities.

For much more on **getting around**, see p330

If You Like...

Hiking

Sweden is an awesome place to hike, with its springy, well-kept trails and excellent network of huts and campgrounds.

Kungsleden The 'King's Trail', a popular, accessible northern route (p288)

Höga Kusten Leden Awesome views from high coastal cliffs (p262)

Sarek National Park Challenging terrain for expert hikers (p279)

Skåneleden Lush path along Sweden's southern coast (p192)

Arctic Trail An 800km joint development of Sweden, Norway and Finland, above the Arctic Circle.

Kebnekaise Sweden's tallest peak is a highlight of hiking in Norrland (p284)

European long-distance paths E1 and E6 run from Varberg to Grövelsjön (1200km) and from Malmö to Norrtälje (1400km).

Finnskogleden A 240km route along the border between Norway and the Värmland region in Sweden (p119)

Alpine Adventures

Norrland in winter is home to all manner of exciting cold-weather activities.

Åre A fabulous ski resort in a chic little town (p250)

Riksgränsen Primarily for expert skiers, this resort nestles right up against the Norwegian border (p287)

Tärnaby A fun town at the edge of a gorgeous lake, with a growing ski resort that's more laid-back than its neighbour at Hemavan (p271)

Båtsuoj Sami Camp If you've never had a chance to meet a reindeer before (p276)

Jokkmokk Winter Market Apart from great shopping and street theatre, this huge market also features reindeer races (p277)

Abisko At this well-equipped national park you can go hiking, snowmobiling, dogsledding, or just kick back and gaze at the northern lights (p286)

Small Villages

The country is dotted with tiny masterpieces: red cottages, cobblestone town squares or windswept fishing huts clinging to the coastline.

Eksjö One of Sweden's best-preserved wooden towns (p219)

Vadstena A rewarding end for pilgrims visiting St Birgitta (p213)

Skanör An idyllic summer beach town (p184)

Höga Kusten The tiny fishing villages here are to die for (p260)

Tällberg A lovely collection of red-painted wooden buildings set along a twisty scenic road (p124)

Nora Not only gorgeous but also a premier source of ice cream (p111)

Sigtuna Within easy reach of Stockholm and Uppsala, this adorable village boasts numerous church ruins and Sweden's oldest main street (p93)

Vaxholm A photogenic harbour and a famous fortress entice flocks of visitors to this archipelago town (p88)

Cycling

Most towns have a place where visitors can rent or borrow a bicycle to ride around. Plus, not only is cycling a greener mode of transport, it forces you to slow the pace and really take in your surroundings.

Gotland Wide bike paths and sea views make for lovely island cycling (p235)

Öland Cycle between farmers markets and nature reserves on this peaceful island (p230)

Göta Canal Cycle alongside the locks en route to Vättern (p218)

Örebro Everyone in this college town rides a bicycle (p112)

Top: Sami man with reindeer, Lappland (p269)
Bottom: Sigtuna (p93)

Stockholm Sure, car traffic can be hectic here, but the shared-bike program and lots of bike paths make it cycle-friendly (p40)

Åre The mountain-bike park here delivers an amped-up cycling experience (p250)

Boat Trips

Don't forget, this is the land of 100,000 lakes (maybe even a few more). Go ahead and get your feet wet.

Stockholm Archipelago Sailing around the archipelago is what Stockholmers wish they had time to do on holiday (p88)

Göta Canal Float between locks and lakes on a tour of this peaceful canal (p218)

Bohuslän ferries Hop from ferry to ferry in Bohuslän (p150)

Luleå Archipelago The northern archipelago is well worth exploring (p266)

Tiveden National Park Hire a canoe and explore the wilderness (p115)

Under the Bridges of Stockholm Strömma Kanalbolaget offers a number of good tours of Stockholm's waterways, including this two-hour canal tour (p61)

Fine Dining

Given the number of superstar chefs in the media, the focus on organic and sustainably procured ingredients, and a devotion to great atmosphere, it's no surprise Sweden has some fantastic places to fill up.

Mathias Dahlgren The celebrated chef's double-Michelin-starred restaurant fits right in at the uberclassy Grand Hôtel (p75)

Wasa Allé Tuck into gourmet Swedish slow cuisine (p145)

Finnhamns Café & Krog Improbably good restaurant on a pastoral archipelago island (p91)

Länsmansgården A historic building near Sunne that appears in Selma Lagerlöf's *Gösta Berling's Saga*, and a picturesque place for a fine, traditionally Swedish lunch (p118)

Mariakyrkan (p93), Sigtuna

Swedish Design

Gorge yourself on the sleek and spartan, the rounded corner, the clever tool, the vividly printed fabric and the inventive glasswork that define Swedish design – from established artists now part of the canon to new talents making a name for themselves.

Nordiska Museet Huge building filled with objects illustrating the evolution of Swedish design, arranged by theme for various changing exhibitions (p51)

Svenskt Tenn Home of Josef Frank's stunning signature fabrics and other iconic pieces (p81)

DesignTorget Great selection of clever gadgets and decor from up-and-coming designers (p81)

Velour by Nostalgi Chic jeans, knits and jumpsuits from a savvy Göteborg designer (p147)

Kosta outlets Stock up on gorgeous glass in the heart of the Glasriket (Crystal Kingdom) (p225)

Shopping

Shopping in Sweden is easy to do – almost too easy. Look for crystal and glassware, authentic handicrafts marked with the *slöjd* (handicraft) sticker, fine linens, chic designer clothing and funky gadgets Ikea doesn't have yet.

Stockholm's shopping streets The pedestrian thoroughfares of Biblioteksgatan, Drottninggatan and Västerlånggatan are retail heaven (p80)

Svensk Slöjd Authentic handicrafts and high-quality gifts made by Swedish artists who are part of a strictly regulated crafts guild (p81)

Prickig Katt Retro hats and vintage frocks at a hipster Göteborg boutique (p146)

Gotländsk Konst & Form Cool local artwork and handicrafts, from textiles to glassware (p241)

Formargruppen Cooperative designer shop and gallery in Malmö (p179)

Sami Duodji Gallery and shop with authentic Sami handicrafts (p277)

Sami Culture

The Sami, Sweden's indigenous population, have a rich, often embattled culture that fascinates visitors and locals alike. There are many opportunities to learn more, be it a visit to an absorbing museum or an overnight (or longer) stay in a traditional Sami reindeer camp.

Ájtte Museum A stellar museum presenting the history and current status of the Sami people in Sweden (p277)

Båtsuoj Sami Camp Stay overnight with traditional reindeer herders at this forest camp (p276)

Visit Sápmi A gateway for visitors interested in learning about Sami culture (p280)

Arjeplog Silvermuseet This museum in a former nomad school has a stunning collection of Sami silver objects (p276)

Nutti Sami Siida Take a reindeer-sled excursion with this ecotourism expert (p282)

Month by Month

TOP EVENTS

Midsummer, June

Jokkmokk Winter Market, February

Gamla Stan Christmas Market, November–December

Vasaloppet, February

Stockholm International Film Festival, November

January

This is the peak of winter, with freezing temperatures and snow in most regions. Winter-sports activities draw the crowds.

Snöfestivalen

Based on a snow-sculpting competition, this annual fest (otherwise known as the Kiruna Snow Festival; www.snofestivalen.se) draws artists from all over to carve elaborate shapes out of the snow. It also features reindeer-sled racing, with Sami traditions emphasised.

Göteborg International Film Festival

Sweden's 'second city' hosts this annual festival that draws some 200,000 visitors each year, with short films, documentaries and features, plus seminars and parties.

February

It's still peak winter weather, with snow sports the main draw.

Jokkmokk Winter Market

A large gathering of Sami people from across Scandinavia, this festival (www.jokkmokksmarknad.se) includes a market, craft shows, performances and more.

Vasaloppet

This huge ski race (www.vasaloppet.se) between Sälen and Mora, started in 1922, commemorates Gustav Vasa's history-making flight on skis in 1521; it has grown into a week-long ski fest.

March

The winter season begins to wind down in the southern half of the country, though winter sports are still going strong in Norrland.

Liljevalchs Spring Salon

The Djurgården gallery's annual springtime launch of the new year in art brings to the fore up-and-coming artists as well as new work from established names.

April

The weather's still cold, but the days are longer and brighter.

Walpurgis Night

This public holiday, a pagan holdover to celebrate the arrival of spring, involves lighting bonfires, singing songs and forming parades; parties are biggest in the student towns, such as Uppsala.

May

Spring tourism starts to pick up as the days get longer and warmer; summer-only hostels and campgrounds start to open for the season.

May Day

Traditionally a workers' marching day in industrial towns and cities, it's observed with labour-movement events, brass bands and marches.

June

Midway through June is the official beginning of summer. The weather is perfect, hotel rates are low and travelling is effortless.

Sweden Rock Festival

This large three-day rock festival (www.swedenrock.com) is held in Sölvesborg and features huge metal and hard-rock acts like Judas Priest, Rob Zombie and Ozzy Osbourne.

Swedish National Day

Known merely as Swedish Flag Day until 1983, the public holiday (6 June) commemorates the crowning in 1523 of King Gustav Vasa and Sweden's independence from the Danish-led Kalmar Union.

Smaka På Stockholm

Taste samples from some of Stockholm's top kitchens in manageable quantities, and watch cooking duels at this week-long food fest (www.smakapastockholm.se) held in Kungsträdgården.

Midsummer's Eve

Arguably the most important Swedish holiday, Midsummer's Eve traditionally falls on the Friday between 19 and 25 June; revellers head to the countryside to raise the maypole, sing and dance, drink, and eat pickled herring. Midsummer Day is primarily spent recovering from the long night.

Öjebyn Church Market

This market near Piteå (www.pitea.se) attracts some 20,000 visitors each year.

July

July is peak summer-tourism season: the weather is fine, attractions are open and everyone is cheerful.

Piteå Dansar

One of Sweden's biggest street festivals, the PDOL (www.pdol.se) draws some 120,000 visitors for music, dance, food and a carnival.

Musik vid Siljan

A midsummer music festival (www.musikvidsiljan.se), it takes place in the towns around Lake Siljan, and includes chamber, jazz and folk music; tourist offices for Mora, Leksand and Rättvik will have up-to-date schedules.

Storsjöyran

Östersjön hosts this annual three-day music festival (www.storsjoyran.se), which features international artists and crowds of up to 55,000 people.

Classic Car Week

Rättvik hosts this gathering of motorheads and the objects of their devotion (www.classiccarweek.com); there are monster-truck battles, drive-in movies, laid-back cruising and lots of chrome.

Stockholm Pride

This annual parade and festival (www.stockholmpride.org/en) is dedicated to creating an atmosphere of freedom and support for gay, lesbian, bisexual and transgender people.

August

The weather is as nice as in July, but many Swedes (especially Stockholmers) are out of town on their own holidays, and some restaurants are closed for most of the month.

Medeltidsveckan

Find yourself an actual knight in shining armour at this immensely popular event. Visby Medieval Week (www.medeltidsveckan.se) puts Gotland's medieval city to great use with a market, games, costumes and a banquet. Be sure to reserve accommodation and transport to the island in advance.

Kräftskivor (Crayfish Parties)

Swedes celebrate the end of summer by wearing bibs and party hats while eating lots of crayfish and drinking *snaps* (usually aquavit). In the north, parallel parties take place but with *surströmming* (strong-smelling fermented Baltic herring).

September

Days begin to grow shorter and cooler, and many seasonal tourist facilities (campgrounds, some hostels, outdoor cafes) close for the season, but the weather can still be gorgeous.

Tjejmilen

Sweden's biggest sporting event for women (www.tjejmilen.se) features 24,000 runners of all ages in a race that begins at Gärdet, in Stockholm.

Göteborg International Book Fair

Scandinavia's biggest book fair, this event (www.bok-bibliotek.se) brings together authors, readers, publishers, agents, teachers, librarians and the media.

Öland's Harvest Festival

This celebration of the local harvest (www.skordefest.nu) takes place each autumn in Borgholm, Öland.

Lidingöloppet

Enshrined in the *Guinness World Records* as the world's largest terrain race, this annual event (www.lidingoloppet.se) takes place on Lidingö, just northeast of Stockholm.

October

Though the travel infrastructure can feel abandoned, autumn is a lovely time of year; and you'll essentially have the place to yourself.

Stockholm Jazz Festival

Held in clubs all over town, this internationally known jazz fest (www.stockholmjazz.com) brings big names like Van Morrison and Mary J Blige; evening jam sessions at famed Stockholm jazz club Fasching are a highlight.

Stockholm Open

A huge event among the international tennis crowd, this tournament (www.ifstockholmopen.se) draws its share of top-100 players.

Hem & Villa

This is the country's largest interior decor and design fair, with furniture trends, textiles, lighting schemes, and arts and crafts. The event (www.hemochvilla.se), held in Stockholm and Göteborg, includes displays, lectures and shopping.

Uppsala Short Film Festival

For the past 33 years, this film festival (www.shortfilmfestival.com) has screened more than 300 short films a year at four cinemas in central Uppsala.

Umeå International Jazz Festival

International jazz musicians have filled Umeå's stages for this event (www.umeajazzfestival.se) for more than 40 years running.

November

Grey winter is here, but the holiday season has yet to begin.

Stockholm International Film Festival

Screenings of new international and independent films, director talks and discussion panels draw cinephiles to this important festival (www.stockholmfilmfestival.se); tickets go quickly, so book early.

Gamla Stan Christmas Market

Usually opening in mid-November, this adorable Stockholm market (www.stortorgetsjulmarknad.com) in Gamla Stan's main square (Stortorget) can almost singlehandedly lift the spirits on a cold winter night. Shop for handicrafts and delicacies, or just wander with a mug of cocoa and a saffron bun.

St Martin's Day

In Sweden November 10 is St Martin's Eve, and, regardless of how the tradition originally began, these days the holiday is all about the goose. That means that, ideally, you'll see the traditional dinner of roasted goose on your plate.

December

The month in which Sweden cheerfully rages against the dying of the light, aided by hot spiced wine, delicious seasonal treats and loads of candles everywhere.

Luciadagen (St Lucia Day)

On 13 December, wearing a crown of lit candles, 'Lucia' leads a white-clad choir in traditional singing in a celebration that seems to merge the folk tradition of the longest night and the story of St Lucia of Syracuse. Look for free performances in churches.

Julafton (Christmas Eve)

The night of the smörgåsbord and the arrival of *jultomten* (the Christmas gnome), carrying a sack of gifts, this is the biggest celebration at Christmas time.

Itineraries

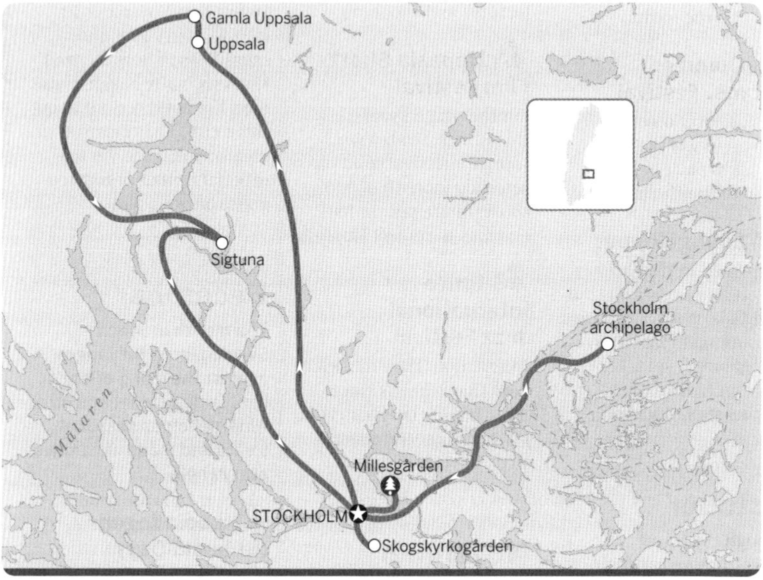

1 WEEK Stockholm & Its Surrounds

This itinerary brings you the highlights of the area around the capital, including ruins from early Swedish history and a few suburban delights.

Start in **Stockholm**, where mandatory attractions include the Kungliga Slottet (Royal Palace), the lovely Gamla Stan (Old Town) and Skansen (a family-friendly open-air museum that's basically Sweden in miniature). Kick off with a short boat tour of the city's waterways. You can do all of those in a couple of days, which leaves an evening for enjoying some nightlife in Södermalm; try the clubs and bars in the SoFo district. On day three, visit a museum or two.

The next day, check out the cathedral and palace at **Uppsala** and delve into early Swedish history via the burial mounds and museum at **Gamla Uppsala**. On the way back, explore **Sigtuna**, with its old-fashioned buildings, adorable cafes and atmospheric church ruins. The following day, visit the sculpture museum at **Millesgården**, or make a pilgrimage to Greta Garbo's memorial at Unesco-recognised cemetery **Skogskyrkogården**. Finally, take a leisurely boat ride out into the **Stockholm archipelago**, hopping off to explore one of the islands or even staying overnight if time allows.

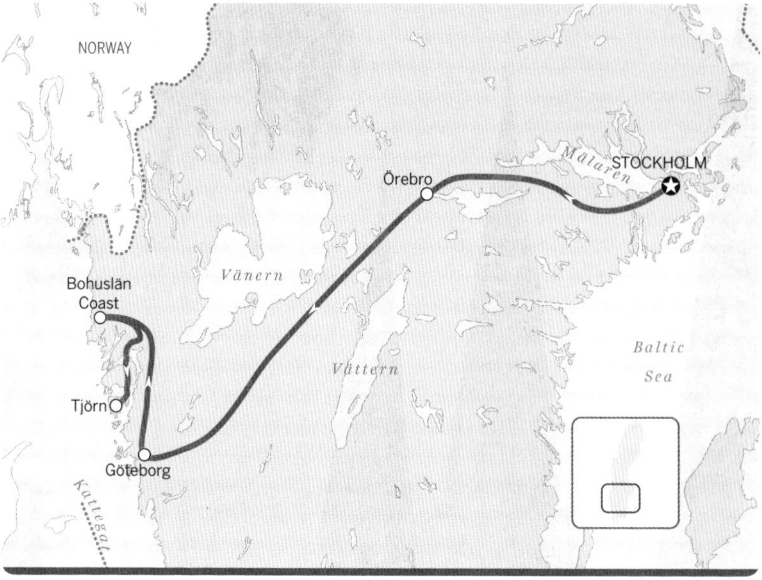

2 WEEKS Stockholm & Göteborg

You can see a good stretch of Sweden in just two weeks. This itinerary makes its way through the heart of the country, taking in lush landscape as well as the relics of industry.

To get a sense of the things that make the place so quintessentially Swedish, we suggest spending the first week of your trip as outlined in the Stockholm & Its Surrounds itinerary, exploring the sights in and around stylish capital **Stockholm**. Then, make your way west toward **Göteborg**, Sweden's so-called 'second city', a worthy destination in its own right. Take your time getting there – you'll want to stop along the way to visit the lively college town of **Örebro**, tour its moat-protected castle and wander through the nearby Stadsparken, one of Sweden's most beautiful city parks.

Continue heading southwest, between the huge inland lakes Vänern and Vättern, and into **Göteborg**. This engaging city is easily worth a few days of exploration – visit its theme park and museums, notably the art and design collection at Röhsska Museet, but don't neglect to do some Michelin-star dining and trend-focused shopping, perhaps in the attractive and well-preserved Haga district, Göteborg's oldest suburb. Take the whole clan along for the rides at the huge amusement park that is Liseberg, one of Sweden's most visited tourist attractions. Pick up some picnic supplies at Feskekörka, a fish market shaped like a church, or settle in for some locally sourced, gourmet 'slow food' at chef Mats Nordström's Wasa Allé. And don't miss the cool, retrofitted art space at Röda Sten, a gritty power-station-turned-gallery that exhibits some of the edgiest artwork around and has a wild range of evening events to boot.

Spend the rest of week two exploring the craggy coastline and rickety fishing villages of the **Bohuslän Coast**. Check out the Bronze Age rock carvings on the Tanum plain, then have a go at making sense of them with the help of the Vitlycke Museum. Cross the bridge from Stenungsund (on the Swedish mainland) to the island of **Tjörn**, a favourite of landscape artists and sailors alike. Wander the tiny villages admiring sailboats, have a summer barbecue on the deck of a youth hostel, or make a meal of smoked fish from Åstols Rökeri.

WAYNE WALTON / GETTY IMAGES ©

Top: Domkyrka (p100), Uppsala

Bottom: *Angel Musicians*, by Carl Milles, at Millesgården (p59), Stockholm

2 WEEKS Stockholm to Kiruna

The journey from Stockholm to the northernmost city in Sweden is epic. You'll cross vast stretches that seem populated by nothing but reindeer. You'll also see the fertile, forested breadbasket of the country.

From **Stockholm** head toward the **Lake Siljan** region, home to carved wooden Dala horses, red-painted huts and hobbitlike villages. Spend a day hopping between **Mora**, **Rättvik** and **Leksand**.

Continue north toward the **Höga Kusten** region, for scenery and cliffside hiking. From there, it's an easy journey up to the urban centres of Norrland: **Umeå** and **Luleå**. From Luleå, jag inland to **Arvidsjaur** for a dogsledding or snowmobile tour, and then on to **Jokkmokk**, whose Sami museum, Ájtte, mustn't be missed.

Continue to **Kiruna** to explore some of the world's last truly wild landscapes. Start with a hike in the vast and untamed **Abisko National Park**, a short train ride from Kiruna. From Kiruna, zip over to **Jukkasjärvi** for a look at the famed Icehotel and a chance to visit a Sami reindeer camp. Completists might opt to visit **Karesuando**, the northernmost village in Sweden.

3 WEEKS Stockholm to Malmö

You can cover a lot of the southern part of Sweden in three weeks, including two of the most dynamic urban centres in Scandinavia – Malmö and Göteborg – as well as some gorgeous coastline and fishing villages.

Start your journey in **Stockholm**. The wonderful capital city will hold your attention for as many days as you can devote to it. When it's time to move on, head toward dynamic **Göteborg**, and its surrounding coastline, whose charms include pretty fishing villages and spectacular, otherworldly light. Make your way along the coast, jagging north to enjoy the eye candy in upscale **Marstrand**, then edging south to dodge mopeds in beachy **Brännö**.

Stop in at **Varberg** and see the preserved body of Bocksten Man displayed in its medieval fortress. Continue south to **Lund**, Sweden's second-oldest town, with a striking cathedral and the great cafe culture that goes along with a large student population. Just south of here is **Malmö**, a diverse and lively city that sometimes feels more a part of neighbouring Denmark – no surprise, really, as Copenhagen is only a bridge away.

Plan Your Trip

Outdoor Adventures

Sweden is ideal for outdoor activities: it has thousands of square kilometres of forest with hiking and cycling tracks, vast numbers of lakes connected by mighty rivers, and a range of alpine mountains. And its concentrated population means you're likely to have the wildest places all to yourself.

Best Outdoors

Winter Sports

Abisko Has dogsledding and weekend multiactivity stays; the snowmobile track in Abisko National Park lets you drive along part of the Kungsleden.

Kiruna Offers dogsledding under the northern lights, snowmobiling trips and three-day wilderness excursions with camping and ice fishing.

Arvidsjaur Has over 600km of snowmobile tracks.

Hiking

Kungsleden The country's best-known and most accessible long-distance trail.

Sarek National Park Offers 2000 sq km of rugged hiking terrain; Kvikkjokk is a good entry point.

Padjelanteleden Offers easier hiking in gorgeous wilderness.

Cycling

Örebro An urban centre in central Sweden, seemingly built with bikes in mind.

Skåne Offers lovely weather, pastoral scenery and flat terrain, and plenty of services and facilities.

Gotland Mostly flat, with excellent cycling trails, comfortable hostels and stunning scenery.

Hiking

Swedes love their hiking, and there are many thousands of kilometres of marked trails that make most of the country a trekker's dream.

European long distance paths E1 and E6 run from Varberg to Grövelsjön (1200km) and from Malmö to Norrtälje (1400km), respectively. But the Kungsleden, in Lappland, is the best-known and most user-friendly trail in Sweden. Finnskogleden is a 240km-long route along the border between Norway and the Värmland region in Sweden. The Arctic Trail (800km) is a joint development of Sweden, Norway and Finland and is entirely above the Arctic Circle; it begins near Kautokeino in Norway and ends in Abisko, Sweden. The 139km Padjelantaleden is a generally easy route, with long sections of duckboards and bridged rivers. The mountainous part of western Jämtland is also one of Sweden's most popular hiking areas.

Mountain trails in Sweden are marked with cairns, wooden signposts or paint on rocks and trees. Marked trails have bridges across all but the smallest streams, and wet or fragile areas are crossed on duckboards. Overnight huts and lodges along these trails are maintained by Svenska Turistföreningen (STF).

The best hiking time is between late June and mid-September, when trails are mostly snow free. After early August the mosquitoes have gone.

Mountaineering & Rock Climbing

Mountaineers head for Sylarna, Helagsfjället, Sarek National Park and the Kebnekaise region.

The complete traverse of Sylarna involves rock climbing up to grade 3. The ridge traverse of Sarektjåhkkå (2089m; the second-highest mountain in Sweden) in Sarek, is about grade 4. There are lots of other glacier and rock routes in Sarek. The Kebnekaise area has many climbing routes (grades 2 to 6), including the north wall of Kaskasapakte (2043m), and the steep ridges of Knivkammen (1878m) and Vaktposten (1852m).

For qualified guides, contact **Svenska Bergsguideorganisation** (Swedish Mountain Guide Association; ☎098-01 26 56; www.utsidan.se/sbo). The website is in Swedish, but under *medlemmar* there's a list of guides and their contact details.

Rock climbers can practise on the cliffs around Stockholm and Göteborg – there are 34 climbing areas with 1000 routes around Göteborg, and some 200 cliffs around the capital. For further information, try the helpful **Svenska Klätterförbundet** (Swedish Climbing Federation; ☎08-618 82 70; www.klatterforbundet.se).

Cycling

Sweden is perfect for cycling, particularly in Skåne and Gotland. It's an excellent way to look for prehistoric sites, rune stones and quiet spots for free camping. The cycling season is from May to September in the south, and July and August in the north.

You can cycle on all roads except motor ways (marked by a green sign with two lanes and a bridge on it) and roads for motor vehicles only (green sign with a car symbol). Highways often have a hard shoulder, which keeps cyclists well clear of motor vehicles. Secondary roads are mostly quiet and safe by European standards, and many roads have dedicated cycle lanes.

You can take a bicycle on some regional trains and buses. Long-distance buses usually don't accept bicycles; Sveriges Järnväg (SJ) allows them only if they're foldable and can be carried as hand luggage. Bikes are transported free on some ferries.

THE RIGHT OF PUBLIC ACCESS

Allemansrätten, the right of public access to the countryside, is not a legal right but a common-law privilege. It includes national parks and nature reserves, although special rules may apply. Full details in English can be found on www.allemansratten.se.

You're allowed to walk, ski, boat or swim on private land as long as you stay at least 70m from houses and keep out of gardens, fenced areas and cultivated land. You can pick berries and mushrooms, provided they're not protected species. Generally you should move on after one or two nights' camping.

Don't leave rubbish or take live wood, bark, leaves, bushes or nuts. Fires fuelled with fallen wood are allowed where safe, but not on bare rocks (which can crack from the heat). Use a bucket of water to douse a campfire even if you think that it's completely out. Cars and motorcycles may not be driven across open land or on private roads; look out for the sign *ej motorfordon* (no motor vehicles). Dogs must be kept on leads between 1 March and 20 August. Close all farm gates and don't disturb farm animals or reindeer. Off-limits areas where birds are nesting are marked with a yellow or red-and-yellow sign containing the words *fågelskydd – tillträde förbjudet*.

If you have a car or bicycle, look for free camping sites around unsealed forest tracks leading from secondary country roads. Make sure your spot is at least 50m from the track and not visible from any house, building or sealed road. Bring drinking water and food, and don't pollute any water sources with soap or food waste.

Above all, remember the mantra: 'Do not disturb, do not destroy'.

RESPONSIBLE HIKING

Rubbish

Carry out all your rubbish, and make an effort to carry out rubbish left by others. Never bury your rubbish. Sanitary napkins, tampons, condoms and toilet paper should be carried out despite the inconvenience, as they burn and decompose poorly.

Human-Waste Disposal

Contamination of water sources by human faeces can lead to the transmission of all sorts of nasties. Where there is a toilet, please use it. Where there is no toilet, bury your waste. Dig a small hole 15cm (6in) deep and at least 100m (320ft) from any watercourse. Cover the waste with soil and a rock. In snow, dig down to the soil.

Washing

Don't use detergents or toothpaste in or near watercourses, even if they are biodegradable. For personal washing, use biodegradable soap and a water container (or even a portable basin) at least 50m (160ft) away from the watercourse. Wash cooking utensils at a similar distance using a scourer, sand or snow instead of detergent.

Erosion

Hillsides and mountain slopes, especially at high altitudes, are prone to erosion. Stick to existing trails and avoid short cuts.

Fires & Low-Impact Cooking

Don't depend on open fires for cooking or warmth. The cutting of wood for fires in trekking areas can cause rapid deforestation. Cook on a light-weight kerosene, alcohol or Shellite (white gas) stove and avoid those powered by disposable butane gas canisters.

Equipment

Hikers should be well equipped and prepared for snow in the mountains, even in summer. Prolonged bad weather in the northwest isn't uncommon – Sarek and Sylarna are the most notorious areas. In summer you'll need good boots, waterproof jacket and trousers, several layers of warm clothing (including spare dry clothes), warm hat, sun hat, mosquito repellent (a mosquito head-net is also highly advisable), water bottle, maps, compass and sleeping bag. Basic supplies are often available at huts, and most lodges serve meals (but check first, especially outside high season). If you're going off the main routes you should, obviously, take full camping equipment.

Information

The best source for hiking information is the youth-hostel organisation **Svenska Turistföreningen** (STF; ☎08-463 21 00; www.svenskaturistforeningen.se), one of Sweden's largest tour operators.

STF lodges sell up-to-date maps, but it's a good idea to buy them in advance. Fjällkartan (Skr127 each) is the best series for hikes. Try Kartbutiken (p326).

The best source of information on conservation is the Swedish environmental protection agency, Naturvårdsverket (p314).

You can hire bicycles from campgrounds, hostels, bike workshops and sports shops; the cost is usually around Skr150 a day or Skr500 a week.

Some country areas, towns and cities have special cycle routes; contact local tourist offices for information and maps. Kustlinjen (591km) runs from Öregrund (Uppland) southwards along the Baltic coast to Västervik, and Skånespåret (800km) is a fine network of cycle routes. The well-signposted 2600km-long Sverigeleden extends from Helsingborg in the south to Karesuando in the north, and links points of interest with suitable roads (mostly with an asphalt surface) and bicycle paths.

Brochures and maps are available from **Svenska Cykelsällskapet** (Swedish Cycling Association; ☎08-751 6204; www.svenska-cykel sallskapet.se).

Boating & Sailing

Boating and sailing are hugely popular in Sweden. The 7000km-long coastline, with its 60,000 islands, is a sailor's paradise, but look out for the few restricted military areas off the east coast. (They're quite obvious, and marked on maps.)

Inland, lakes and canals offer pleasant sailing in spring and summer. The main canals are the Göta Canal, the Kinda Canal and the Dalsland Canal. Various companies offer short canal cruises; contact local tourist offices for details.

Those with private boats will have to pay lock fees and guest harbour fees (around Skr150 per night, although some small places are free). A useful guide is the free, annual *Gästhamnsguiden*, which is published in Swedish by **Svenska Kryssarklubben** (Swedish Cruising Club; ☎08-448 28 80; www.sxk.se). It contains comprehensive details of 500 guest harbours throughout the country and is available from tourist offices.

Canoeing & Kayaking

With its countless lakes and rivers, and long coastlines, Sweden is a paradise for canoeists and kayakers. The national canoeing body is **Svenska Kanotförbundet** (Swedish Canoe Federation; ☎0155-20 90 80; www.kanot.com). It provides general advice and lists approved canoe centres that hire out canoes (per day/week from around Skr350/1600).

Fishing

There are national and local restrictions on fishing in many of Sweden's inland waters, especially for salmon, trout and eel. Before dropping a line, check with local tourist offices or councils.

Local permits *(fiskekort)* can be bought from tourist offices, sports or camping shops and typically cost Skr50 to Skr200 per day, depending on season and location.

Summer is the best fishing time with bait or flies for most species, but trout and pike fishing in southern Sweden is better in spring or autumn. Salmon fishing is best in late summer. Ice fishing is popular in winter.

An excellent web resource for fishing in Sweden is www.cinclusc.com/spfguide, or contact **Sportfiskeförbundet** (Angling Federation; ☎08-704 44 80; info@sportfiskarna.se).

Skiing

Large ski resorts cater mainly to downhill (alpine and telemark) skiing and snowboarding, but there's also scope for cross-country touring. For cross-country (Nordic) skiing, the northwest often has plenty of snow from December to April. The Kungsleden and other long-distance hiking tracks provide great skiing. You can also ski along parts of the Vasaloppet ski-race track in Dalarna (the town of Mora is a good starting point). Most towns have illuminated skiing tracks.

Take the usual precautions: don't leave marked routes without emergency food, a good map, local advice and proper equipment including a bivouac bag. Temperatures of -30°C or lower (including wind-chill factor) are possible; check daily forecasts. Police and tourist offices have information on local warnings. In mountain ski resorts, where there's a risk of avalanche (*lavin*), susceptible areas are marked by yellow, multilingual

SAFETY GUIDELINES

- Be aware of local laws, regulations and etiquette about wildlife and the environment.
- Pay any fees and possess any permits required by local authorities.
- Obtain reliable information about physical and environmental conditions along your intended route (eg from park authorities).
- Walk only in regions and on trails within your realm of experience.
- Be sure you are healthy and feel comfortable walking for a sustained period.
- Even if visiting in winter, bring a good pair of sunglasses to protect you from the glare of snowy surfaces.

ANDERS EKHOLM / GETTY IMAGES ©

Top: Dogsledding, Kiruna (p282)

Bottom: Sarek National Park (p279)

signs and buried-skier symbols. Make sure your travel insurance covers skiing.

Skating

When the Baltic Sea freezes (once or twice every 10 years), fantastic tours of Stockholm's archipelago are possible. The skating season usually lasts from December to March. Less ambitiously, there's skating all winter on many city parks and ponds, including Kungsträdgården in Stockholm, with skate-rental booths nearby.

Dogsledding

Sweden's Sami have readily adopted dogsledding as a means of winter transport, following in the footsteps of the indigenous people of Siberia, and excursions are available in most northern towns. Apart from being the most ecofriendly means of exploring the Arctic regions, it's also one of the most enjoyable ways of getting around, allowing you to bond with your own husky team and to slow down and appreciate the surrounding wilds as the mood takes you. Most operators offer anything from a two-hour taster to fairly demanding multiday expeditions, staying overnight in rustic forest cabins or Sami winter tents.

Snowmobile Safaris

While some may argue that snowmobiles are noisy and not terribly ecofriendly, they are the Arctic equivalent of an all-terrain vehicle, essential for travel within isolated areas, not to mention for rounding up reindeer. Travelling by snowmobile allows you to access difficult terrain and cover more ground than by dog- or reindeer sled. Snowmobile safaris (including night rides to see the northern lights) are offered by operators in all major northern towns. It's cheaper to ride as a passenger behind an experienced driver, though snowmobiles are available for hire to those with a valid driver's license (get a snowmobile permit from the nearest tourist office). Trails are marked with red crosses on poles.

ADRENALIN JUNKIES

One of the fastest-growing activities for summer is downhill mountain biking. The sport takes over ski resorts after the snow melts; fully armoured, riders carry their sturdy little bikes up the hill on chairlifts, then barrel down along rough mountain trails at dizzying speeds. Åre Bike Park (p250) is the mother lode, with 35km of slopes, 17 trails and a potential vertical drop of almost 900m. Multiday packages are available.

Golf

Sweden has about 500 golf courses, open to everyone, and many hotel chains offer golf packages. Björkliden, near Abisko, is a golf course 240km above the Arctic Circle, and at the Green Line golf course at Haparanda, playing a round means crossing the Swedish–Finnish border four times. Green fees range from Skr550 to Skr1450 per day, depending on the season and the kind of course (prices are higher near metro areas); for more information, contact **Svenska Golfförbundet** (Swedish Golf Federation; ☎08-622 15 00; sgf.golf.se).

Birdwatching

There are many keen ornithologists in Sweden, and there are birdwatchers' towers and nature reserves everywhere. For further information, contact Sveriges Ornitologiska Förening (p313).

Horse Riding

Sweden's multitude of tracks, trails, forests, shorelines and mountains make for some fantastically varied riding. Everything from short hacks to full-on treks are on offer (two hours/half day/full day start around Skr400/650/950) on Swedish or Icelandic horses. Trips can be arranged through local tourist offices.

Plan Your Trip

Travel with Children

Sweden is a fantastically fun and easy place to travel with children, from infants up to teens. Most sights and activities are designed with kids in mind, with free or reduced admission for under 18s and plenty of hands-on exhibits. Dining, accommodations and transport are also well accustomed to handling families.

Best Regions for Kids

Stockholm & Around

Museums, a petting zoo and an amusement park make the capital city a delight for kids.

Uppsala & Central Sweden

A great water park, zoo, ski slopes and camping.

Göteborg & the Southwest

The country's biggest amusement park, plus great museums and public parks.

Malmö & the South

One of Sweden's best open-air museums, plus a rad skatepark.

The Southeast & Gotland

Take an easy, round-island bicycle trip on Gotland, or visit Astrid Lindgrens Värld in Vimmerby.

Östersund & the Bothnian Coast

A legendary sea monster, a great zoo, an open-air museum and several kid-friendly hostels.

Lappland & the Far North

Hit the ski slopes or go on a dogsledding adventure, or a good long hike in summer.

Sweden for Kids

If you've got kids, you're guaranteed an easy ride in Sweden. As a general tip, get the kids involved in your travel plans – if they've helped to work out where you're going, chances are they'll still be interested when you arrive! Remember, don't try to cram too much in. Lonely Planet's *Travel with Children* is a useful source of information.

Swedes treat children well, and domestic tourism is largely organised around children's interests. Many museums have a kids' section with toys, hands-on displays and activities, and there are numerous public parks for kids, plus theme parks, water parks and so on. Most attractions allow free admission for young children – up to about seven years of age – and in many cases up to about 18. Tours and hostel beds are usually half-price for kids. Family tickets are often available.

High chairs and cots (cribs) are standard in most restaurants and hotels. Menus usually feature a couple of children's meals at a reasonable price. (These are generally along the lines of Swedish meatballs or pancakes with lingonberries and cream – a fairly easy sell even for fussy eaters.) Supermarkets offer a wide choice of baby food, infant formulas, soy and cow's milk, disposable nappies (diapers) etc. There are nappy-changing facilities in most toilets (men's and women's), and breastfeeding in public is not an issue.

Children's Highlights

Theme Parks

➡ **Liseberg** Sweden's most popular tourist attraction, for good reason (p133)

➡ **Gröna Lund Tivoli** Fun rides and concerts in the heart of Stockholm, with views of the capital from the more gravity-defying rides (p54)

➡ **Junibacken** Pretend you're Pippi Longstocking at this book-based theme park (p53)

Open-Air Museums

➡ **Skansen** A miniature Sweden (p49)

➡ **Himmelsberga** A farm village with quaint cottages (p234)

➡ **Kulturen** A vast museum with buildings from all points in history (p180)

➡ **Fredriksdals Friluftsmuseum** An old manor house, a farm, lovely gardens and a French baroque theater (p195)

➡ **Vallby Friluftsmuseum** A farmyard and several craft workshops (p108)

➡ **Jamtli** The north's answer to Skansen (p247)

➡ **Murberget** A traditional shop, smithy, church and school, in typical Norrland style (p260)

Museums

➡ **Tekniska Museet** Thrill tiny nerds with science and gadgetry (p55)

➡ **Naturhistoriska Museet** The forest comes to life in this diorama-filled museum (p137)

➡ **Medeltidsmuseet** Go back in time and underneath Stockholm for the gripping story of the city's foundations (p45)

➡ **Värmlands Museum** Everything there is to know about the region, plus great contemporary art (p116)

➡ **Ájtte Museum** Sami culture gets the attention it deserves, with beautiful multimedia presentations (p77)

Rainy-Day Activities

➡ **Kulturhuset** Crafts in Stockholm (p47)

➡ **Science Fiction Bookshop** In Stockholm's Gamla Stan (p82)

➡ **Cinemas** Catch a Hollywood blockbuster film.

Planning

When to Go

Parents will find that travel in the summer tourist season (mid-June to August) is easier than outside those times, simply because more visitor facilities, sights and activities are up and running. Be sure to book ahead, though, as this is also when accommodation tends to fill up.

If your family is interested in outdoor activities, winter is also a great time to visit; several ski hills (including the world-class Åre) have family-friendly facilities, bunny slopes, ski schools, day care and so on.

Accommodation

Campgrounds have excellent facilities and are overrun with ecstatic, energetic children. They get very busy in summer, so book tent sites or cabins well in advance.

Hotels and other accommodation options often have 'family rooms' that sleep up to two adults and two children for about the price of a regular double. Cots for young children are available in most hotels and hostels, usually either free of charge or for a nominal fee.

Hotel staff are accustomed to serving families and should be able to help you with anything you need, from heating bottles to finding a babysitter for a parents' night out.

Transport

Car-rental companies will hire out children's safety seats at a nominal cost, but it's essential that you book them in advance. Long-distance ferries and trains may have play areas for children.

Ask about free rides on public transport for young children; this is offered at certain times of day in many cities (for instance, kids under 12 ride free at weekends in Stockholm). Buses are nicely set up for strollers/prams, and most of the time you'll be swarmed by locals trying to help you get the stroller on and off the bus.

Regions at a Glance

Stockholm & Around

Food
Museums
Shopping

World-Class Cuisine

Stockholm is a world-class foodie destination, with multiple Michelin stars to its name and a number of celebrity chefs known for transcending expectations with their bold takes on locally sourced, traditionally rooted dishes. You can eat as well here as in most any European capital.

Multimedia Museums

There's no chance you'll be bored in a Stockholm museum: this city does them right. Stockholm's museums present the best of the country's art and historical treasures in an inviting atmosphere. Exhibition rooms are as well planned and well lit as the rest of the city's stylish spaces.

Ready, Set, Shop

From tucked-away thrift shops to big-name retail boutiques, from fine linens and handicrafts to cleverly designed kitchen gadgets, nearly every type of shopper will find plenty to pick through here.

p40

Uppsala & Central Sweden

History
Industry
Museums

Historical Relics

Uppsala is a treat for history buffs: from pre-Viking grave mounds to a hillside castle whose pink walls concealed decades of royal intrigue, plus the odd rune stone or stone-ship setting, and a stash of museum treasures from art and artefacts to ancient manuscripts.

Industrial Artefacts

Central Sweden is the country's industrial workhorse, plying the rich landscape for iron, copper and silver. Many of these places have been transformed into quaint and atmospheric historical sites well worth a visit.

Regional Museums

Great museums are spread throughout the region, from Örebro's regional art museum to the ambitious Värmland Museum in Karlstad to the homes of beloved Swedish artists Carl Larsson and Anders Zorn and author Selma Lagerlöf.

p86

Göteborg & the Southwest

Coastline
Food
Culture

Southwest Shore

From kitesurfing in Halland to island-hopping in Bohuslän, there are unlimited options for ocean lovers in the southwest. Spend the night on one of the coast's remote skerries or join the crowds to watch summertime round-island regattas.

Fresh Seafood

Local chefs boast that seafood arrives first in Göteborg and second in Stockholm, so if you want to experience truly fresh prawns, oysters, lobster or cod, look no further. Select your own dockside, or indulge in top-tier restaurants.

Urban Edge

Göteborg's industrial roots make its artists practical – less talk, more action – and there's a gritty refinement to design, music and art across the region. Distinctive venues abound: restored power stations, basement boutiques and castle lawns.

p131

Malmö & the South

Variety
Outdoors
Mystery

A Bit of Everything

A thorough experience of southern Sweden may include sailing on a restored Viking ship, taking in avant-garde architecture, climbing fortress steps and finishing up with a 5am felafel after a night out in Malmö. The best option is to try it all.

Outdoor Activities

Whether it's with apple picking, gorgeous beaches or some especially nice coastal hikes, southern Sweden is perfect for taking advantage of the great outdoors. More off beat options include seal safaris, scuba diving and pony trekking.

Secrets of the South

Ancient and present-day mysteries thrive in southern Sweden. Come face to face with (hopefully fictional) crime scenes in Kurt Wallander's Ystad or puzzle over Bronze Age relics at Kivik and Ales Stenar.

p168

The Southeast & Gotland

Outdoor Activities
World Heritage
History

Ports, Roads & Trails

The southeast is paradise for the outdoorsy person, with grand ports for sailors, quiet lakeside roads for cyclists and miles of glorious woodland trails.

National Treasures

A wander through Visby's cobblestone streets, past fairy-tale cottages and haunting church ruins, and the gasp-inducing view of sky, sea and rock at Öland's southernmost point will make it clear why both have earned Unesco distinction.

Canals, Castles & Churches

Steeped in tales of industry and migration, boasting the engineering triumph of the Göta Canal and with some seriously impressive castles, the southeast has plenty of history to share. Not to mention Gotland's stunning churches and the pilgrim's route to St Birgitta's abbey.

p206

Östersund & the Bothnian Coast

Wildlife
Activities
Islands

Mammals & Monsters

Quite apart from the musk oxen, elk and reindeer that you may meet in the wild (or pet at Järvzoo), the waters of Lake Storsjön hide the most elusive creature of all – Östersund's answer to the Loch Ness Monster.

Year-Round Adventure

Åre is adventure central, where you can try your hand at hillcarting, heliskiing, zorbing and mountain biking. The mountains west of Östersund and the Bothnian Coast offer varied terrain for some superb hiking in summer and skiing in winter.

Jagged Coast

The waters of the Gulf of Bothnia are dotted with myriad forested islands. While some allow you to play out your Robinson Crusoe fantasies, others introduce you to traditional fishing culture and that devil of a delicacy, *surströmming* (fermented herring).

p245

Lappland & the Far North

Wildlife
Hiking
Sami Culture

Elusive Creatures

There are few places in the world where it's easier to see reindeer, elk and foxes. If you're lucky, you may even spot a brown bear, lynx or wolverine, though they are nocturnal and shy.

Top Trails

The Kungsleden is the most celebrated hiking trail, although Padjelanta and Stora Sjöfjallet offer trails that are no less picturesque. The ascent of Kebnekaise provides exceptional views, while Sarek National Park will challenge even the most experienced of hikers.

Sami Way of Life

Explore the past and present of Europe's only indigenous people: admire Sami silver jewellery through the ages at Áttje Museum or the Silvermuseet, stay with Sami reindeer herders at Båtsuoj Sami Camp and visit the Jokkmokk Winter Market.

p269

On the Road

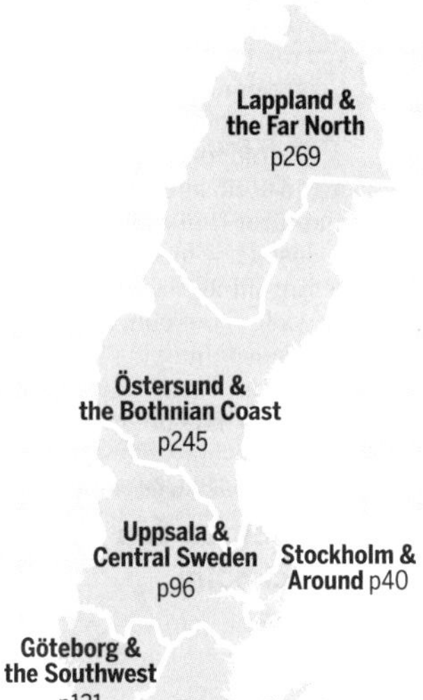

Lappland & the Far North p269
Östersund & the Bothnian Coast p245
Uppsala & Central Sweden p96
Stockholm & Around p40
Göteborg & the Southwest p131
The Southeast & Gotland p206
Malmö & the South p168

Stockholm & Around

☎08 / POP 881,235

Includes ➡

Best Places to Eat

- Kryp In (p72)
- Rosendals Trädgårdskafe (p75)
- Hermans Trädgårdscafé (p76)
- Grands Verandan (p74)
- Vurma (p72)

Best Places to Stay

- Rival Hotel (p70)
- Vandrarhem af Chapman & Skeppsholmen (p68)
- Hotel Hellsten (p67)
- Hotel Anno 1647 (p69)
- STF Fridhemsplan (p66)

Why Go?

Stockholm's good looks and fashion sense could almost be intimidating. But this city is an accessible beauty, as easy to explore as it is to love. Though spread across 14 islands, connected by 57 bridges, it is compact and walkable. Each neighbourhood has a distinct character, yet they're so close together you can easily spend time in several areas. In each, you'll find trend-setting design, inventive cuisine, unbeatable museums, great shopping, pretty parks and loads of atmosphere.

The old town, Gamla Stan, is one of Europe's most arresting historic hubs, all storybook buildings, imposing palaces and razor-thin cobblestone streets.

Just a few metres from this time capsule, the modern city centre shines like the pages of a magazine. Downtown is a catwalk, showroom and test kitchen. Everything here is the very latest thing.

And it's surrounded by pristine forests and a vast archipelago. What's not to love?

When to Go

Stockholm

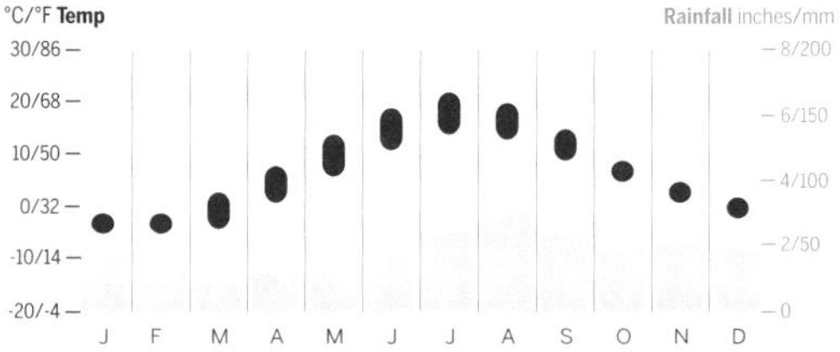

Mid-Jun–mid-Aug Stockholm's long days, uncannily pretty light and mild weather are dreamy.

Dec–Feb The city is a frosted cake, with holiday markets and mugs of *glögg* around every corner.

Sep & Oct Cooler weather, minimal crowds and beautiful autumn colours.

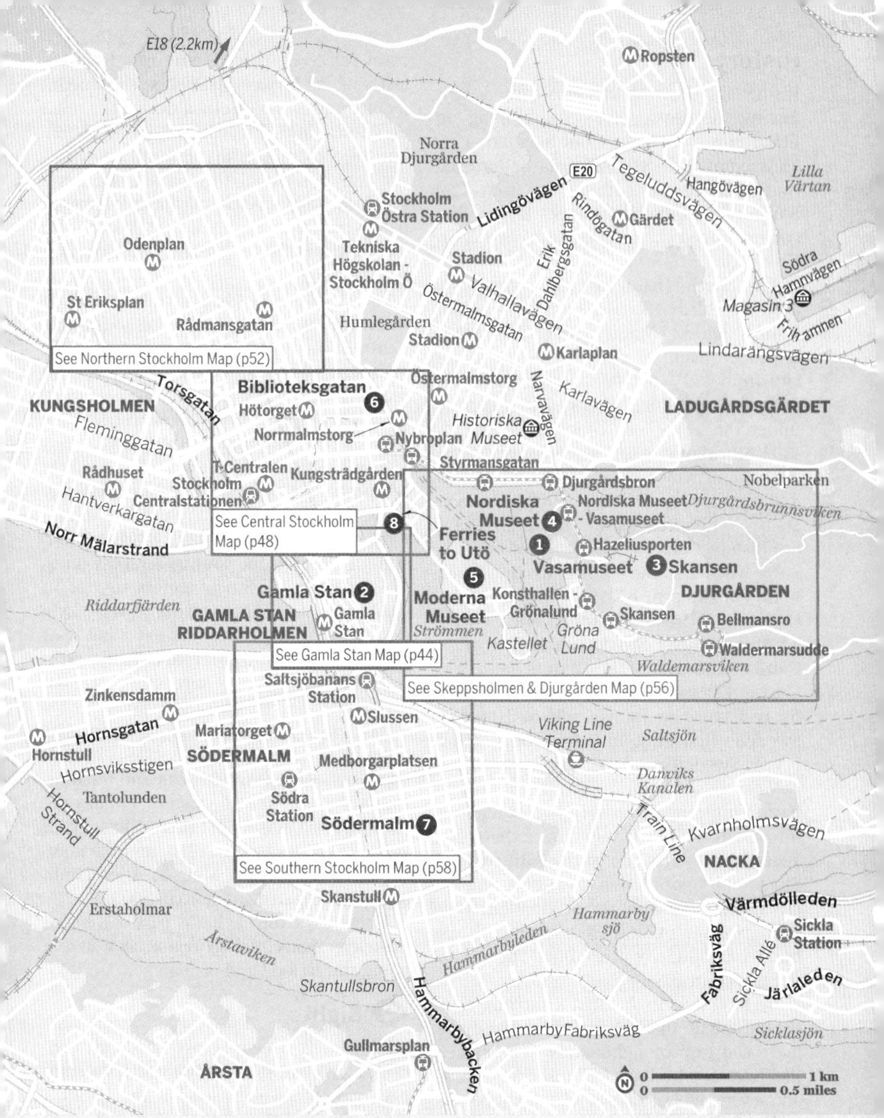

Stockholm & Around Highlights

1. Studying a shipwreck – and Swedish history – at **Vasamuseet** (p51).
2. Wandering atmospheric **Gamla Stan** (p43) and the Royal Palace.
3. Visiting Sweden in miniature at **Skansen** (p49) open-air museum.
4. Exploring Swedish culture, art and daily life at **Nordiska Museet** (p51).
5. Seeing cutting-edge international artwork at **Moderna Museet** (p55).
6. Shopping at big-name boutiques along **Biblioteksgatan** (p80).
7. Bar-hopping with the lively crowd in **Södermalm** (p77).
8. Taking a boat to **Utö** (p90) for a taste of the Stockholm archipelago.

History

Rising land drove Stockholm's early destiny, forcing the centre of Swedish Viking political power to move from northern Lake Mälaren to the lake's outlet for better trade routes. The town charter dates from 1250. Stockholm's official founder, Birger Jarl, commissioned the original royal castle, Tre Kronor, in 1252.

The Black Death of 1350 wiped out around a third of Sweden's population; then Danish Queen Margrethe Valdemarsdotter added insult to injury by besieging the city from 1391 to 1395, amalgamating the crowns of Sweden, Norway and Denmark under the unpopular Union of Kalmar in 1397. Stockholm was a key piece in control of the lands covered by the Kalmar Union, and from 1397 to the early 1500s it was constantly embattled as various Danish and Swedish factions struggled for power.

In what became known as the Stockholm Bloodbath of 1520, Danish King Christian II tricked, trapped and beheaded 82 rebellious Swedes on Stortorget in Gamla Stan. One of the victims had a son, Gustav Ericsson Vasa, who led a successful resistance to Danish rule and became Sweden's first king on 6 June 1523, which is now Sweden's national day.

Vasa's sons continued their father's nation-building, transforming Stockholm into a major military hub during the Thirty Years War. By the end of the 16th century, Stockholm's population was 9000, and the city had spread from the original old town onto Norrmalm and Södermalm. Stockholm was officially proclaimed the capital of Sweden in 1634.

By 1650 the city boasted a thriving artistic and intellectual culture and a grand new look, courtesy of father-and-son architects the Tessins, who built Drottningholms Slott and several other iconic Stockholm buildings.

The following decades weren't so kind to the capital. A devastating famine brought starving hordes to the city in 1696, and the beloved Tre Kronor went up in flames the following year. Russian military victories shrunk the Swedish empire, and a plague engulfed the city in 1711.

A now-fragile Stockholm traded state-building for character-building. Botanist Carl von Linné (1707–78) developed the template for the classification of plants and animals, Anders Celsius (1701–44) came up with the centigrade temperature scale, and royal palace Kungliga Slottet rose from the ashes of Tre Kroner. Swedish science, architecture and arts blossomed during the reign of Francophile King Gustav III (1771–92), but the theatre buff's tyrannical tendencies saw him assassinated by parliament member Jacob Johan Anckarström at a masked ball in the Opera House in 1792. The murder formed the basis of Giuseppe Verdi's opera *A Masked Ball*.

When Sweden's northern and southern train lines were connected via Stockholm's Centralstationen and Riddarholmen in 1871, an industrial boom kicked in. The city's population reached 245,000 in 1890 (an increase of 77,000 in 10 years), and new districts like Östermalm expanded the city limits.

Stockholm hosted the 1912 summer Olympics, but the resulting elation quickly dissipated when Sweden refused to uphold a blockade against Germany during WWI. Britain attacked the country's supply lines, causing starving Stockholmers to riot in Gustav Adolfs Torg. During WWII Sweden's official neutrality made it a hot spot for Jewish, Scandinavian and Baltic refugees, the first of many successive waves of migrants.

The city's postwar economic boom saw the advent of Eastern Bloc–style suburban expansion. Along with growth and modernisation came increased violence, notably the still-unsolved murder of Prime Minister Olof Palme on Sveavägen in 1986, and the stabbing death of Foreign Minister Anna Lindh at the NK department store in 2003.

These days, the capital is part of a major European biotechnology region, as well as a rising star in food and fashion.

Sights

Stockholm is strewn across 14 islands connected by more than 50 bridges. It's a compact, easily walkable city, but the layout – more pinwheel than grid, with water on all sides – can be disorienting. Neighbourhoods are closer together than they seem; it's often quicker to walk somewhere than it would be to catch a bus or navigate the tunnelbana (underground metro) system. The best approach is to allow for a bit of meandering, since you never know when you'll stumble across a delightful surprise.

Very few museums in Stockholm are open before 10am – often not until 11am. Plan to *ta det lugnt* (take it easy).

Gamla Stan

The old town is Stockholm's historic and geographic heart. Here, cobblestone streets wriggle past Renaissance churches, baroque palaces and medieval squares. Spice-coloured buildings sag like wizened old men, and narrow lanes harbour everything from dusty toy shops to candlelit cafes.

Västerlånggatan is the area's nerve centre, a bustling thoroughfare lined with galleries, eateries and souvenir shops. Step off the main drag and into the tinier alleyways for a surprisingly quiet chance to explore.

Kungliga Slottet PALACE

(Royal Palace; Map p44; ☎08-402 61 30; www.kungahuset.se; Slottsbacken; adult/child Skr150/75, valid for 7 days; ⊙10am-5pm mid-May–mid-Sep, closed Mon rest of year; 🚌43, 46, 55, 59 Slottsbacken, Ⓜ Gamla Stan) Kungliga Slottet was built on the ruins of Tre Kronor castle, which burned down in 1697. The north wing survived and was incorporated into the new building. Designed by court architect Nicodemus Tessin the Younger, it took 57 years to complete. Free 45-minute tours in English start at 11am and 2pm mid-May to mid-September, and at 2pm and 3pm the rest of the year. The apartments are occasionally closed for royal business; closures are noted on the website.

With 608 rooms, this is the world's largest royal castle still used for its original purpose. The first royal family moved here in 1754. Guided tours emphasise that the palace is not a museum, with rooms preserved in amber, but rather a working government building. It contains fine examples of baroque and rococo furnishings and interiors, while each room also bears the fingerprints of the many generations who have lived there.

Highlights include the decadent Karl XI Gallery, inspired by Versailles' Hall of Mirrors and considered the finest example of Swedish late baroque. And don't miss Queen Kristina's silver throne in the Hall of State, one of the few items rescued from the Tre Kronor fire.

Admission to the palace also includes the **Museum Tre Kronor**, devoted to Stockholm's original castle; the **Royal Treasury**; and **Gustav III's Antikmuseum** (the museum of antiquities).

In the basement of Museum Tre Kronor, you can see the foundations of 13th-century defensive walls and items rescued from the medieval castle during the 1697 fire. The museum also describes how the fire started (a fire watcher was off flirting with a kitchen maid, it seems) and explains rather vividly the meaning of 'run the gauntlet' (which in 1697 was how the court punished watchmen for flirting with kitchen maids while fire destroys a castle).

The Royal Treasury contains ceremonial crowns, sceptres and other regalia of the Swedish monarchy, including a 16th-century sword that belonged to Gustav Vasa.

Gustav III's Antikmuseum (closed mid-September to mid-May) displays Italian sculptures collected by King Gustav III in the 1780s.

It's worth timing your visit to see the **Changing of the Guard**, which takes place in the outer courtyard at 12.15pm Monday to Saturday and 1.15pm Sunday and public holidays from May through August, and 12.15pm Wednesday and Saturday and 1.15pm Sunday and public holidays from September to May.

Riksdagshuset BUILDING

(Swedish Parliament; Map p48; ☎08-786 48 62; www.riksdagen.se; Riksgatan 3; ⊙1hr tours in English noon, 1pm, 2pm & 3pm Mon-Fri mid-Jun–Aug, 1.30pm Sat & Sun Oct–mid-Jun) FREE Technically situated on Helgeandsholmen, the little island in the middle of Norrström, rather than on Gamla Stan, the Swedish Parliament building is an unexpected pleasure to visit. The building consists of two parts: the older front section (facing downstream) dates from the early 20th century, but the other more modern part contains the current debating chamber. Tours of the building offer a compelling glimpse into the Swedish system of consensus-building government.

Nobelmuseet MUSEUM

(Map p44; http://nobelmuseet.se; Stortorget; adult/child Skr100/70; ⊙10am-8pm; Ⓜ Gamla Stan) Nobelmuseet presents the history of the Nobel Prizes and their recipients, with a focus on the intellectual and cultural aspects of invention. It's a slick space with fascinating displays, including short films on the theme of creativity, interviews with laureates like Ernest Hemingway and Martin Luther King, and cafe chairs signed by the visiting prize recipients (flip them over to see!). The free guided tours are recommended (in English at 10.15am, 11.15am, 1pm, 3pm, 4pm and 6pm in summer).

The museum is housed in the Börsen building – the old Stock Exchange – which

Gamla Stan

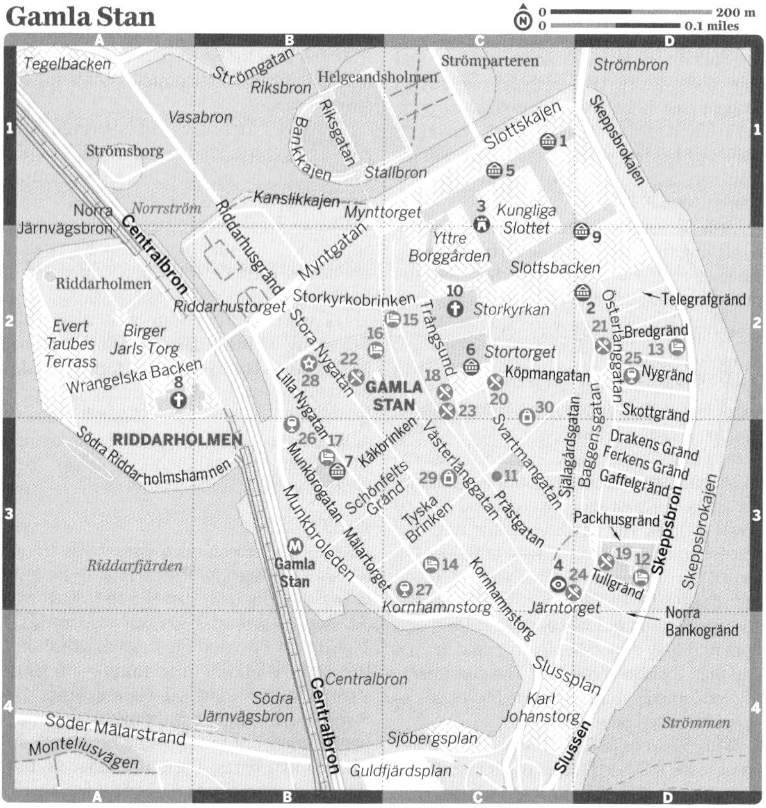

forms the north side of Stortorget, the historic main square in Gamla Stan.

Royal Armoury MUSEUM

(Livrustkammaren; Map p44; ☎08-402 30 30; www.livrustkammaren.se; Slottsbacken 3; adult/child Skr90/free; ⏰10am-5pm; 🚌43, 46, 55, 59 Slottsbacken, Ⓜ Gamla Stan) Livrustkammaren is housed in the cellar vaults of the palace but has a separate admission fee. It's a family attic of sorts, crammed with engrossing memorabilia spanning more than 500 years of royal childhoods, coronations, weddings and murders. Meet Gustav II Adolf's stuffed battle steed, Streiff; see the costume Gustav III wore to the masquerade ball on the night he was shot, in 1792; or let the kids try on a suit of armour in the playroom.

There's a fairy-tale collection of coronation coaches in the basement, including the outrageously rococo number used for the crowning of Adolf Fredrik and Ulrika Eleonora in 1751. Temporary exhibitions draw interesting connections between royal history and modern pop culture. Free guided tours in English at 3pm.

Riddarholmskyrkan CHURCH

(Riddarholmen Church; Map p44; ☎08-402 61 30; www.kungahuset.se; Riddarholmen; adult/child Skr50/free; ⏰10am-5pm mid-May–mid-Sep; 🚌3, 53 Riddarhustorget, Ⓜ Gamla Stan) The strikingly beautiful Riddarholmskyrkan, on the equally pretty and undervisited islet of Riddarholmen, was built by Franciscan monks in the late 13th century. It has been the royal necropolis since the burial of Magnus Ladulås in 1290, and is home to the armorial glory of the Seraphim knightly order. There's a guided tour in English at noon (included with admission) and occasional concerts. Holiday closures are frequent; check the website for updates. Admission fee is by credit card only.

Wall plates display the coats of arms of the knights. Look for the marble sarcopha-

Gamla Stan

Sights

1 Gustav III's Antikmuseum........C1
2 Kungliga Myntkabinettet........D2
3 Kungliga Slottet........C1
4 Mårten Trotzigs Gränd........C3
5 Museum Tre Kronor........C1
6 Nobelmuseet........C2
7 Postmuseum........B3
8 Riddarholmskyrkan........A2
9 Royal Armoury........D2
10 Storkyrkan........C2

Activities, Courses & Tours

11 Stockholm Ghost Walk........C3

Sleeping

12 2kronor Hostel Old Town........D3
13 First Hotel Reisen........D2
14 Hotel Scandic Gamla Stan........C3
15 Lady Hamilton Hotel........C2
16 Lord Nelson Hotel........B2
17 Victory Hotel........B3

Eating

Cafe Järntorget........(see 24)
18 Chokladkoppen........C2
19 Den Gyldene Freden........D3
20 Grillska Husets Konditori........C2
21 Hairy Pig Deli........D2
22 Hermitage........B2
23 Kryp In........C2
24 Sundbergs Konditori........C3

Drinking & Nightlife

25 Le Rouge........D2
26 Monks Porter House........B3
27 Torget........C3

Entertainment

28 Stampen........B2

Shopping

29 Science Fiction Bookshop........C3
30 Studio Lena M........C2

gus of Gustav II Adolf, Sweden's mightiest monarch, who died in 1632. Riddarholmen is easy to reach by footbridge from the Gamla Stan tunnelbana station.

Storkyrkan CHURCH

(Great Church; Map p44; www.stockholmsdomkyrkoforsamling.se; Trångsund 1; adult/child Skr40/free; 9am-4pm; Gamla Stan) The one-time venue for royal weddings and coronations, Storkyrkan is both Stockholm's oldest building (consecrated in 1306) and its cathedral. Behind a baroque facade, the Gothic-baroque interior includes extravagant royal-box pews designed by Nicodemus Tessin the Younger, as well as German Berndt Notke's dramatic sculpture *St George and the Dragon*, commissioned by Sten Sture the Elder to commemorate his victory over the Danes in 1471. Keep an eye out for posters and handbills advertising music performances here.

Medeltidsmuseet MUSEUM

(Medieval Museum; Map p48; www.medeltidsmuseet.stockholm.se; Strömparterren; adult/child Skr100/free; noon-5pm Tue-Sun, to 7pm Wed; ; 62, 65, Gustav Adolfs torg) Tucked beneath the bridge that links Gamla Stan and Norrmalm, this child-friendly museum was established when construction workers preparing to build a car park here in the late 1970s unearthed foundations from the 1530s. The ancient walls were preserved as found, and a museum was built around them. The circular plan leads visitors through faithful reconstructions of typical homes, markets and workshops from medieval Stockholm. Tickets are valid for one year and will also get you into Stockholms Stadsmuseum (p59).

As with most Stockholm museums, there are plenty of hands-on and multimedia elements here to bring history to life and keep the yawns at bay. Highlights include the 1520s-era ship *Riddarsholm*, a display about Gallows Hill, and a mysterious gated tunnel that leads through many kilometres of brick wall to the castle.

Kungliga Myntkabinettet MUSEUM

(Royal Coin Cabinet; Map p44; 08-519 553 04; www.myntkabinettet.se; Slottsbacken 6; adult/child Skr70/free, Mon free; 11am-5pm; Gamla Stan) Across the plaza from the Royal Palace, Kungliga Myntkabinettet gleams with a priceless collection of currency spanning 2600 years. Treasures include Viking silver and the world's oldest coin (from 625 BC), largest coin (a Swedish copper plate weighing 19.7kg) and first banknote (issued in Sweden in 1661).

Postmuseum MUSEUM

(Map p44; 08 781 17 59; www.postmuseum.posten.se/museng/; Lilla Nygatan 6; adult/child Skr60/free; 11am-4pm Wed-Sun; Gamla Stan) Examining almost four centuries of Swedish postal history, the Postmuseum is not as mind-numbing as it sounds. It's actually rather evocative, featuring old mail

PENNY-PINCHING PACKAGES

Depending on your plans and energy levels, getting your money's worth out of a visit to Stockholm can be easier with a discount package. The **Stockholm Card** (www.visitstockholm.com; adult 24/48/72/120hr Skr450/625/750/950, accompanying child Skr215/255/285/315) is available from tourist offices, Storstockholms Lokaltrafik (SL) information centres, some museums, and some hotels and hostels, or online at www.visitstockholm.com. It gives you entry to 80 museums and attractions, travel on SL's public-transport network, sightseeing by boat, some walking tours, and various other discounts. It is valid for one, two, three or five days and costs Skr525/675/825/1095 (or Skr235/275/315/350 for accompanying children, maximum two children per adult).

Students and seniors get discounted admission to most museums and sights without the card, so you'll need to work out if it's cheaper for you to just get a transport pass and pay admission charges separately. The one-day pass demands an athletic level of sightseeing energy; you may be better off paying admission at a couple of sights and walking between them. To get maximum value out of the multiday cards, plan ahead and be sure to note opening hours; for example, Skansen remains open until late, whereas royal palaces are only open until 3pm or 4pm.

Destination Stockholm (08-663 00 80; www.destination-stockholm.com) offers the Stockholm Pass, a similar discount package that includes free SL transit, sightseeing tours and admission to 75 attractions. Cards for two, three or four days cost Skr695/845/1035 (half-price for ages six to 15). Purchase the card online and you can choose to have it shipped to you or to pick it up on arrival in Stockholm. The website also has a hotel booking engine with about 40 participating hotels, which can be added onto your discount package (be aware that many are located in the suburbs or outskirts of town).

carriages, kitsch postcards and a cute children's post office for budding postal workers. There's also a great cafe and a philatelic library with 51,000 books on stamps and postal history.

Central Stockholm

Some of the city's best museums are smack in the middle of town, within easy walking distance of each other.

Historiska Museet MUSEUM
(08-5195 56 00; www.historiska.se; Narvavägen 13-17; adult/child Skr100/free; 10am-6pm, closed Mon Sep-May; 44, 56, Karlaplan, Östermalmstorg) The national historical collection awaits at this enthralling museum. From Iron Age skates and a Viking boat to medieval textiles and Renaissance triptychs, it spans over 10,000 years of Swedish history and culture. There's an exhibit about the medieval Battle of Gotland (1361), an excellent multimedia display on the Vikings, a room of altarpieces from the Middle Ages, a vast textile collection and a section on prehistoric culture.

An undisputed highlight is the subterranean Gold Room, a dimly lit chamber gleaming with Viking plunder and other treasures, including the jewel-encrusted Reliquary of St Elisabeth (who died at 24 and was canonised in 1235). The most astonishing artefact, however, is the 5th-century seven-ringed gold collar discovered in Västergötland in the 19th century. Weighing 823g, it is decorated with 458 symbolic figures.

Stadshuset NOTABLE BUILDING
(City Hall; Map p48; www.stockholm.se/stadshuset; Hantverkargatan 1; adult/child Skr100/free, tower Skr40/free; 9.30am-4pm, admission by tour only; 3, 62 Stadshuset, Rådhuset) The mighty Stadshuset dominates Stockholm's architecture. Topping off its square tower is a golden spire and the symbol of Swedish power: the three royal crowns. Entry is by guided tour only; tours in English take place every 30 minutes from 9.30am until 4pm in summer, less frequently the rest of the year. The **tower** is open for visits every 40 minutes from 9.15am to 4pm or 5pm from May to September; it offers stellar views and a great thigh workout.

Punctured by two courtyards, the building's interior includes the glittering, mosaic-lined **Gyllene salen** (Golden Hall), Prins Eugen's own fresco re-creation of the lake view from the gallery, and the very hall used for the annual Nobel Prize banquet. Part of the tour involves walking down the same stairs you'd use if you'd won the big prize.

Hallwylska Museet MUSEUM

(Hallwyl Collection; Map p48; ☎08-402 30 99; www.hallwylskamuseet.se; Hamngatan 4; adult/child Skr80/free; ⏰10am-4pm Tue-Sun; Ⓜ Östermalmstorg) A private palace completed in 1898, Hallwylska Museet was once home to compulsive hoarder Wilhelmina von Hallwyl, who collected items as diverse as kitchen utensils, Chinese pottery, 17th-century paintings, silverware, sculpture and her children's teeth. In 1920 she and her husband donated the mansion and its contents to the state. Guided tours (Skr100, including admission) in English take place at 12.30pm Tuesday through Sunday June through August (weekends only the rest of the year). The museum is not wheelchair accessible.

Armémuseum MUSEUM

(Artillery Museum; ☎08-51 95 63 00; www.armemuseum.se; Riddargatan 13; adult/child Skr80/free; ⏰10am-7pm Jun-Aug, 11am-8pm Tue, to 5pm Wed-Sun Sep-May; Ⓜ Östermalmstorg) Delve into the darker side of human nature at Armémuseum, where three levels of engrossing exhibitions explore the horrors of war through art, weaponry and life-size reconstructions of charging horsemen, forlorn barracks and starving civilians. You can even hop on a replica saw horse for a taste of medieval torture.

Nationalmuseum MUSEUM

(National Art Museum; Map p48; www.nationalmuseum.se; Södra Blasieholmshamnen; ⏰closed until 2017) Sweden's largest art museum, home to the nation's collection of painting, sculpture, drawings, decorative arts and graphics from the Middle Ages to the present, is closed for renovations until 2017. Until then, you can see highlights from the collection at the Konstakademien.

Konstakademien MUSEUM

(Royal Academy of Fine Arts; Map p48; ☎08-23 29 25; www.konstakademien.se; Fredsgatan 12; adult/child Skr100/free; ⏰10am-6pm, to 8pm Tue & Thu) While the Nationalmuseum is closed for renovations, highlights and temporary exhibitions from the collection will be displayed here, in the smaller but very lovely Konstakademien building. The museum has thousands of works to choose from, including painting and sculpture, design objects, prints and drawings from late medieval to current times, so the temporary space is well worth looking into.

The temporary exhibits are well conceived and entertaining. A recent exhibition of highlights from the collection was organised around the theme of the 'selfie', tracing a line from a Rembrandt self-portrait to today's obsession with the likes of Instagram.

Medelhavsmuseet MUSEUM

(Museum of Mediterranean Antiquities; Map p48; ☎010-456 12 98; www.medelhavsmuseet.se; Fredsgatan 2; adult/child Skr80/free; ⏰noon-8pm Tue-Fri, to 5pm Sat & Sun; Ⓜ Centralen, Kungsträdgården) Housed in an elegant Italianate building, Medelhavsmuseet lures history buffs with its Egyptian, Greek, Cypriot, Roman and Etruscan artefacts. Swoon over sumptuous Islamic art and check out the gleaming gold room, home to a 4th-century-BC olive wreath made of gold. There's also a well-regarded cafe (open 11.30am to 1.30pm).

Strindbergsmuseet MUSEUM

(Map p52; ☎08-411 53 54; strindbergsmuseet.se; Drottninggatan 85; adult/child Skr60/free; ⏰10am-4pm Tue-Sun; Ⓜ Rådmansgatan) The small but evocative Strindbergsmuseet in the Blue Tower is the well-preserved apartment where writer and painter August Strindberg (1849–1912) spent his final four years. Peep into his closet, scan his study and library (containing some 3000 volumes), do a round of the dining room, and take in the often absorbing temporary exhibits.

Dansmuseet MUSEUM

(Map p48; ☎08-441 76 51; www.dansmuseet.se; Drottninggatan 17; adult/child Skr60/free; ⏰11am-5pm Tue-Sun; Ⓜ Centralen) Having relocated onto a heavily trafficked pedestrian shopping street and added a chic cafe, Dansmuseet (or the Rolf de Maré Dance Museum, after its founder) focuses on the intersections between dance, art and theatre. Collection highlights include traditional dance masks from Africa, India and Tibet, avant-garde costumes from the Russian ballet, Chinese and Japanese theatre puppets and one of the finest collections of early-20th-century Ballets Russes costumes.

Kulturhuset ARTS CENTRE

(Map p48; ☎tickets noon-5pm 08-506 20 200; http://kulturhusetstadsteatern.se; Sergels Torg; ⏰11am-5pm, some sections closed Mon; 👪; 🚌52, 56, 59, 69, 91 Sergels Torg, Ⓜ T-Centralen, 🚊7 Sergels Torg) This architecturally divisive building, opened in 1974, is an arts hub, with

Central Stockholm

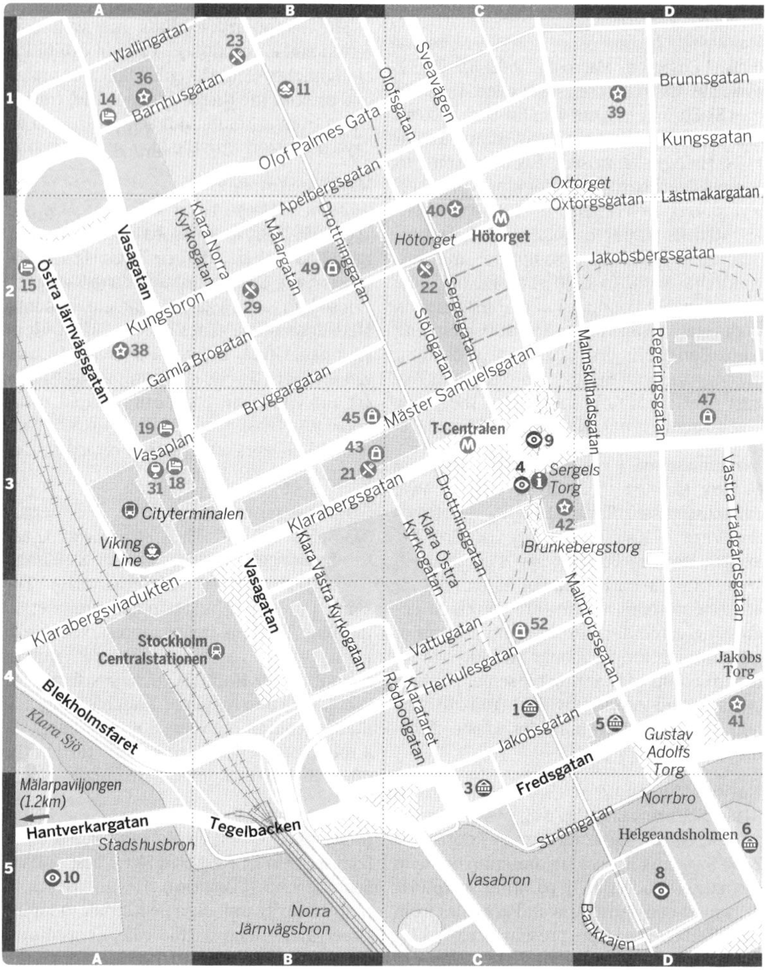

a couple of galleries and workshops, a cinema, three restaurants, and libraries containing international periodicals, newspapers, books and an unusually good selection of graphic novels in many languages. Mainly, though, it's home to Stadsteatern (the City Theater), with dance and theatre performances in various-sized venues (mostly in Swedish). The 5th-floor Cafe Panorama has good meals and a stellar view.

Stadsbiblioteket LIBRARY

(Map p52; ☎ 50 83 10 60; Sveavägen 73; ⏲ 9am-7pm Mon-Fri, noon-4pm Sat; Ⓜ Odenplan) **FREE** The main city library is just north of the city centre. Designed by architect Erik Gunnar Asplund and sporting a curvaceous, technicolour reading room, it's the finest example of Stockholm's 1920s neoclassicist style.

Bonniers Konsthall GALLERY

(Map p52; ☎ 08-736 42 55; www.bonnierskonsthall.se; Torsgatan 19; adult/child Skr80/free; ⏲ noon-8pm Wed, to 5pm Thu-Sun; Ⓜ St Eriksplan) This ambitious gallery keeps culture fiends busy with a fresh dose of international contemporary art, as well as a reading room, a fab cafe and a busy schedule of art seminars

and artists-in-conversation sessions. The massive, transparent flat-iron building was designed by Johan Celsing. There are discussions about the exhibitions in English at 1pm, 3pm, 5pm and 7pm Wednesdays, and 1pm and 4pm Thursday to Sunday. Sunday at 2pm there are free guided tours by the museum's curators.

Sven-Harrys Konstmuseum MUSEUM

(Map p52; ☎08-5116 00 60; www.sven-harrys.se; Eastmansvägen 10-12; adult/child Skr100/free; ⏲11am-7pm Wed-Fri, to 5pm Sat & Sun; Ⓜ Odenplan) This slick new building houses an art gallery with interesting temporary exhibitions (recently a survey of Swedish fashion from 2000 to 2010), as well as a re-creation of the former Lidingö home of owner and art collector Sven-Harry Karlsson. Access to the home is by guided tour (Skr150, 40 minutes, currently in Swedish only). There's also an award-winning restaurant with terrace seating facing the park.

Östermalms Saluhall MARKET

(Map p48; www.saluhallen.com; Östermalmstorg; ⏲9.30am-6pm Mon-Thu, to 7pm Fri, to 4pm Sat, closed Sun & holidays; Ⓜ Östermalmstorg) FREE Östermalms Saluhall is a must-see for both the architecture and for the gourmet food-hall atmosphere. Outdoors it's a many-spired brick confection; indoors it's a sophisticated take on the traditional market, with fresh produce, sparkling fish counters, baked goods, butcher shops and tea vendors as well as some of the city's favourite places to grab a meal. For best results, arrive hungry and curious.

Djurgården

This parklike island is a museum-goer's dream. Not only are many of Stockholm's top museums gathered here but the setting is sublime: gardens, greenery, a lazy river, cycle paths, picnic places, and all of it just one footbridge away from the centre of town.

★ **Skansen** MUSEUM

(Map p56; www.skansen.se; Djurgårdsvägen; adult/child Skr160/60; ⏲10am-10pm late Jun-Aug; 👪; 🚌44, ⛴Djurgårdsfärjan, 🚋7, Djurgården) The world's first open-air museum, Skansen was founded in 1891 by Artur Hazelius to give visitors an insight into how Swedes lived once upon a time. You could easily spend a day here and still not see it all (note that prices and hours vary seasonally). Around 150 traditional houses and other exhibits from across the country dot the hilltop – it's meant to be 'Sweden in miniature', complete with villages, nature, commerce and industry.

The glass-blowers' cottage is a popular stop; watching the intricate forms emerge from glowing blobs of liquid glass is transfixing. The Nordic Zoo, with elk, reindeer, wolverines and other native wildlife, is a highlight, especially in spring when baby critters scamper around.

Buildings in the open-air museum represent various trades and areas of the country. Most are inhabited by staff in period

Central Stockholm

Sights
1 Dansmuseet C4
2 Hallwylska Museet E3
3 Konstakademien C5
4 Kulturhuset C3
5 Medelhavsmuseet D4
6 Medeltidsmuseet D5
7 Nationalmuseum F5
Östermalms Saluhall .... (see 25)
8 Riksdagshuset D5
9 Sergels Torg C3
10 Stadshuset A5

Activities, Courses & Tours
11 Centralbadet B1
12 Strömma Kanalbolaget F3
Thousand Island Cruise .... (see 12)

Sleeping
13 Berns Hotel E3
14 City Backpackers A1
15 Clarion Hotel Sign A2
16 Grand Hôtel Stockholm F4
17 Hotel Stureplan E1
18 Nordic 'C' Hotel A3
19 Nordic Light Hotel A3

Eating
20 Bakfickan E4
Grands Verandan .... (see 16)
21 Hemköp B3
22 Hötorgshallen C2
23 La Neta B1
Lisa Elmqvist .... (see 25)
Mathias Dahlgren .... (see 16)
24 Operakällaren E4
25 Östermalms Saluhall F1
26 Pontus! E1
27 Sturehof E1
28 Sturekatten F2
29 Vetekatten B2
30 Vivo T-Jarlen F2

Drinking & Nightlife
31 Absolut Icebar A3
32 Berns Salonger E3
Café Opera .... (see 24)
33 Lilla Baren at Riche F2
34 Spy Bar E1
35 Sturecompagniet E1

Entertainment
36 Dansens Hus A1
37 Dramaten F3
38 Fasching A2
39 Glenn Miller Café D1
40 Konserthuset C2
41 Operan D4
42 Stockholms Stadsteatern C3

Shopping
43 Åhléns B3
44 Hedengrens E1
45 Kartbutiken B3
46 Naturkompaniet E1
47 NK D3
48 Nordiska Galleriet F2
49 PUB B2
50 Svensk Slöjd F1
51 Svenskt Tenn F3
52 Systembolaget C4

costume, often creating handicrafts, playing music or churning butter while cheerfully answering questions about the folk whose lives they're re-creating. Part of the pharmacy was moved here from Drottningholm castle; two little garden huts came from Tantolunden in Södermalm.

There's a bakery (still operational, serving coffee and lunch), a bank/post office, a machine shop, botanical gardens and Hazelius' mansion. There are also 46 buildings from rural areas around Sweden, including a Sami camp, farmsteads representing several regions, a manor house and a school. There's an aquarium (with a separate admission fee: Skr100/60 per adult/child). A map and an excellent booklet in English are available to guide you around. It's also worth noting that the closing times for each workshop can vary, so check times online to avoid disappointment.

There are cafes, restaurants and hot-dog stands throughout the park. Carrying water isn't a bad idea in summer, and it's not cheating to take the escalator to the top of the hill and meander down from there.

Daily activities take place on Skansen's stages, including folk dancing in summer and an enormous public festival at Midsummer's Eve. If you're in Stockholm for any of the country's other major celebrations, such as Walpurgis Night, St Lucia Day and Christmas, it's a great (if crowded) place to watch Swedes celebrate.

From mid-June through August, Waxholmsbolaget ferries (p88) run from Slussen to Djurgården; the route is part of the regular Storstockholms Lokaltrafik (SL) transit system, so you can use your SL pass to board.

Tobaks & Tändsticksmuseum MUSEUM
(Tobacco & Matchstick Museum; Map p56; ☎08-442 80 26; www.tobaksochtandsticksmuseum.se;

with Skansen admission free; ⏲11am-5pm, closed Mon Oct-Apr) Inside the vast open-air park of Skansen are several other museums, including the Tobaks & Tändsticksmuseum, which traces the history and culture of smoking and the manufacture of those iconic Swedish matches.

Skansen Akvariet AQUARIUM

(Map p56; ☎08-442 80 39; www.skansen.se; adult/child Skr100/60; ⏲from 10am, closing times vary by season) The Skansen Aquarium is worth a wander, its residents including piranhas, lemurs and pygmy marmosets (the smallest monkeys in the world). Intrepid visitors are allowed into the cages of some of the animals.

★Vasamuseet MUSEUM

(Map p56; www.vasamuseet.se; Galärvarvsvägen 14; adult/child Skr130/free; ⏲8.30am-6pm; ; 44, Djurgårdsfärjan, 7 Nordiska museet/Vasa) A good-humoured glorification of some dodgy calculations, Vasamuseet is the custom-built home of the massive warship *Vasa*. The ship, a whopping 69m long and 48.8m tall, was the pride of the Swedish crown when it set off on its maiden voyage on 10 August 1628. Within minutes, the top-heavy vessel tipped and sank to the bottom of Saltsjön, along with many of the people on board. Guided tours are in English every 30 minutes in summer.

Tour guides explain the extraordinary and controversial 300-year story of its death and resurrection, which saw the ship painstakingly raised in 1961 and reassembled like a giant 14,000-piece jigsaw. Almost all of what you see today is original.

On the entrance level is a model of the ship at scale 1:10 and a cinema screening a 25-minute film (in English at 9.30am and 1.30pm daily in summer) covering topics not included in the exhibitions. There are four other levels of exhibits covering artefacts salvaged from the *Vasa*, life on board, naval warfare, and 17th-century sailing and navigation, plus sculptures and temporary exhibitions. The bottom-floor exhibition is particularly fascinating, using modern forensic science to re-create the faces and life stories of several of the ill-fated passengers.

The bookshop is worth a browse and there's a restaurant for a well-earned pit stop.

Nordiska Museet MUSEUM

(Map p56; ☎08-5195 47 70; www.nordiskamuseet.se; Djurgårdsvägen 6-16; adult/child Skr100/free; ⏲10am-5pm; 44, 69, Djurgårdsfärjan, 7) The epic Nordiska Museet is Sweden's largest cultural-history museum and one of its largest indoor spaces. The building itself (from 1907) is an eclectic, Renaissance-style castle designed by Isak Gustav Clason, who also drew up Östermalms Saluhall. Inside you'll find a sprawling collection of all

STOCKHOLM IN...

Two Days

Beat the crowds to the labyrinthine streets of **Gamla Stan** (p43), the city's historic old town. Watch St George wrestle the dragon inside Storkyrkan (p45), the old-town cathedral, and join a tour of the royal palace, Kungliga Slottet (p43). Then trek to **Södermalm** (p57) for dizzying views from the Söder heights. See what's on at the photography gallery Fotografiska (p57) – you can grab a bite here, too. If the weather's nice, party on the terrace at Mosebacke Etablissement (p79) or the bars in Medborgarplatsen. Spend the next day exploring the outdoor museum Skansen (p49), before a seafood dinner at Sturehof (p75).

Four Days

On day three take a guided boat tour (p61) of Stockholm's **waterways**. Visit the impressive Vasamuseet (p51), then stroll up to Hötorgshallen (p73) for a big bowl of fish soup and speciality-food browsing. Next day, head to Millesgården (p59) for sculptures in a dreamy setting, then spend the afternoon doing what Stockholmers do best: shopping (p80). Start with pedestrianised **Biblioteksgatan** off Stureplan, then transition to **Drottninggatan** for souvenirs.

A Week

A week gives you time to visit the royal palace of Drottningholm (p85), then take a boat to an island on the **archipelago** (p88) for a quiet, pastoral overnight stay.

Northern Stockholm

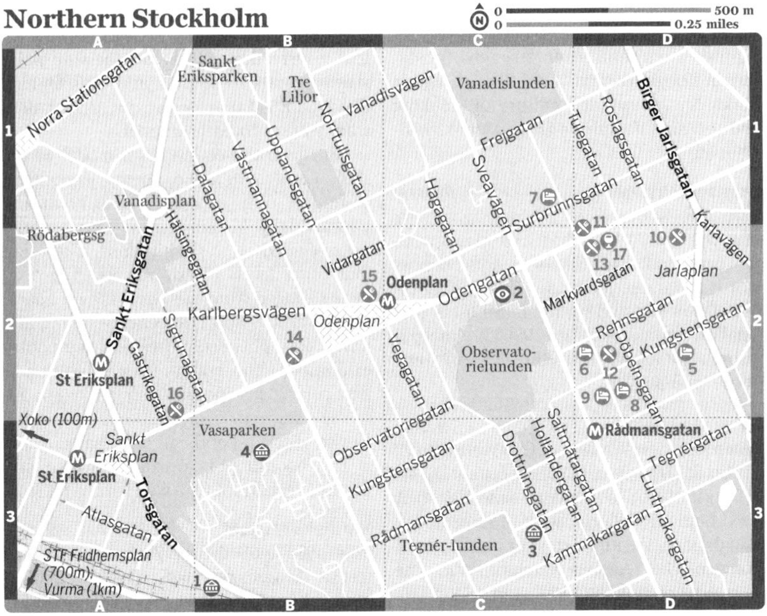

Northern Stockholm

Sights

1 Bonniers Konsthall B3
2 Stadsbiblioteket C2
3 Strindbergsmuseet C3
4 Sven-Harrys Konstmuseum B3

Sleeping

5 Birger Jarl Hotel D2
6 Hostel Bed & Breakfast D2
7 Hotel Hansson C1
8 Hotel Hellsten D2
9 Rex Hotel D2

Eating

10 Caffé Nero D2
11 ICA Baronen D2
12 Lao Wai D2
13 Storstad D2
14 Tennstopet B2
15 Tranan B2
16 Vurma A2

Drinking & Nightlife

17 Olssons D2

things Swedish, from sacred Sami objects to fashion, shoes, home interiors and even table settings.

The museum boasts the world's largest collection of paintings by August Strindberg, as well as a number of his personal possessions. In all, there are over 1.5 million items dating from 1520 to the present day. Topping it off are the often dynamic temporary exhibitions. The insightful audio guide (free with admission) offers several hours of English commentary.

Spritmuseum MUSEUM

(Museum of Spirits; Map p56; 08-12 13 13 00; http://spritmuseum.se; Djurgårdsvägen 38; admission Skr100; 10am-5pm, to 8pm Tue; 44, 69, Djurgårdsfärjan, 7) The surprisingly entertaining Museum of Spirits is dedicated to Sweden's complicated relationship with alcohol, as mediated over the years by the state-run monopoly System Bolaget. The slick space, in two 18th-century naval buildings, covers the history, manufacture and consumption of all kinds of booze, plus holiday traditions, drinking songs, food pairings and so on. Best of all, you can combine your visit with a tasting kit (Skr200), including various flavours of liquor to be sampled at specified points.

There's a 'hangover room' with a head-throbbing soundtrack and painful light, as well as a small theater in which the seating angle and first-person-perspective film make you feel slightly drunk. Multimedia displays dispense titbits about the alcohol industry ('The first entirely Swedish whiskey was a thundering fiasco', for example). There are also well-staged temporary exhibits (recently, a display of record-sleeve art and 'Swedish Sin', about varying cultural attitudes toward sex). The Absolut Art gallery displays collected works on the obvious theme by the likes of Damien Hirst, Andy Warhol and Keith Haring. Guided tours in English are available daily at 3pm.

Junibacken — AMUSEMENT PARK

(Map p56; www.junibacken.se; Djurgården; adult/child Skr145/125; 10am-5pm or 6pm; ; 44, 69, Djurgårdsfärjan, 7) Junibacken whimsically re-creates the fantasy scenes of Astrid Lindgren's books for children. Catch the flying Story Train over Stockholm, shrink to the size of a sugar cube, and end up at Villekulla cottage, where kids can shout, squeal and dress up like Pippi Longstocking. The bookshop is a treasure trove of children's books, as well as a great place to pick up anything from cheeky Karlsson dolls to cute little art cards with storybook themes.

ABBA: The Museum — MUSEUM

(Map p56; 08-1213 28 60; www.abbathemuseum.com; Djurgårdsvägen 68; adult/child Skr195/50; 10am-8pm, shorter hours in winter; 44, Djurgårdsfärjan, 7) A sensory-overload experience that might appeal only to devoted Abba fans, this long-awaited and wildly hyped cathedral to the demigods of Swedish pop is almost aggressively entertaining. It's packed to the gills with memorabilia and interactivity – every square inch has something new to look at, be it a glittering guitar, a vintage photo of Benny, Björn, Frida or Agnetha, a classic music video, an outlandish costume or a tour van from the band members' early days.

The museum even has the actual helicopter from the cover of Abba's 1976 album *Arrival*, in which visitors can pose for photos. You can also hang out in the reassembled Polar recording studio, shake your booty on stage alongside silhouettes of the rest of the band, and even create your own chart topper in a mini recording booth. Don't miss the roomful of amazing costumes or the player piano that is somehow linked to a piano in Benny's house; it plays whenever he plays.

Audio guides (Skr40, available in English) feature the members of Abba themselves narrating stories about their lives.

The museum is paired with the Swedish Music Hall of Fame, which occupies a separate gallery space and provides an efficient tutorial in the history of the country's pop music.

No cash accepted (cards only).

Prins Eugens Waldemarsudde — MUSEUM

(Map p56; 08-5458 37 07; www.waldemarsudde.com; Prins Eugens väg 6; adult/child Skr100/free; 11am-5pm Tue-Sun, to 8pm Thu, gardens 8am-9pm; 7) Prins Eugens Waldemarsudde, at the southern tip of Djurgården, is a soul-perking combo of water views and art. The palace once belonged to the painter prince (1865–1947), who favoured art over typical royal pleasures. In addition to Eugen's own work, it holds his impressive collection of Nordic paintings and sculptures, including works by Anders Zorn and Carl Larsson. The buildings and galleries, connected by tunnels, are surrounded by soothing gardens (free to wander) and an old windmill from the 1780s.

Thielska Galleriet — GALLERY

(08-662 58 84; www.thielska-galleriet.se; Sjötullsbacken 8; adult/child Skr100/free; noon-5pm Tue-Sun; 69) Thielska Galleriet, at the far eastern end of Djurgården, is a must for Nordic art fans, with a savvy collection of late-19th- and early-20th-century works from Scandinavian greats like Carl Larsson, Anders Zorn, Ernst Josephson and Bruno Liljefors, plus a series of Edvard Munch's etchings of vampiric women and several paintings from a bridge you'll recognise from *The Scream*. (Ernest Thiel, a banker and translator, was one of Munch's patrons.) Free tours in English happen at 2pm Friday in summer.

There's also a plaster cast of Nietzsche's death mask in the top-floor turret, if you're into that sort of thing. (Thiel translated some of Nietzsche's work into Swedish.) The 1905 building, designed for Thiel by prominent Swedish architect Ferdinand Boberg, is on the small, worn-in side; it feels more like walking through a home (which, of course, it was) than a museum.

Aquaria Vattenmuseum — MUSEUM

(Map p56; 08-660 90 89; http://aquaria.se; Falkenbergsgatan 2; adult/child Skr130/85; 10am-4.30pm Tue-Sun; ; 44, 69, Djurgårdsfärjan, 7) This conservation-themed aquarium, complete with sea horses, sharks, piranhas and clownfish, takes you through various environmental zones – from tropical jungle and coral reef to sewer systems – with an emphasis on ecology and the fragility of the marine environment. If that sounds a bit of a drag, it's not – there's enough to do and see to keep the family entertained. Time your visit to coincide with a feeding, daily at 11am, 1.30pm and 2.30pm.

Gröna Lund Tivoli AMUSEMENT PARK

(Map p56; www.gronalund.com; Lilla Allmänna gränd 9; adult/child under 7 Skr110/free, unlimited ride pass Skr310; 10am-11pm summer, shorter hours rest of year; ; 44, Djurgårdsfärjan, 7) Crowded Gröna Lund Tivoli has some 30 rides, ranging from the tame (a German circus carousel) to the terrifying (the Free Fall, where you drop from a height of 80m in six seconds after glimpsing a lovely, if brief, view over Stockholm). There are countless places to eat and drink in the park, but whether you'll keep anything down is another matter entirely. The Åkband day pass gives unlimited rides, or individual rides range from Skr20 to Skr60.

Big-name concerts are often staged here in summer. Gröna Lund is a stop on the Slussen–Djurgården ferry.

Biologiska Museet MUSEUM

(Museum of Biology; Map p56; 08-442 82 15; www.biologiskamuseet.com; Hazeliusporten; adult/child Skr65/25; 11am-4pm, closed Mon Oct-Mar; 44, 69, 7) As notable for its creaky wooden building as for its collection of critters, the 1893 Biologiska Museet charms visitors with two circular floors of stuffed wildlife in nature dioramas.

Rosendals Slott CASTLE

(Map p56; 08-402 61 30; www.kungahuset.se; Rosendalsvägen 49; adult/child Skr100/free; hourly noon-3pm Tue-Sun Jun-Aug; 44, 69, 7) On the northern side of Djurgården, Rosendals Slott was built as a palace for Karl XIV Johan in the 1820s. One of Sweden's finest examples of the Empire style, it sparkles with sumptuous royal furnishings. Admission is by guided tour only. While you're out this way don't miss the wonderful nearby Rosendals Trädgårdskafe (p75), set among lush gardens and greenhouses and serving tasty organic grub.

Liljevalchs Konsthall GALLERY

(Map p56; 08-5083 13 30; www.liljevalchs.se; Djurgårdsvägen 60; adult/child Skr80/free; 11am-5pm Jun-Aug, shorter hours rest of year; 44, 69, Djurgårdsfärjan, 7) Opened in 1916, Liljevalchs puts on at least four major exhibitions a year of contemporary Swedish and international art, including the popular Spring Salon.

STOCKHOLM FOR CHILDREN

Stockholm is well set up for travelling with children. There are baby-changing tables in almost every public bathroom, and even top-end restaurants have high chairs and children's menus. Hotel and hostel staff are accustomed to catering to families. Public transport is no problem: your fellow passengers might elbow each other out of the way to help you lift your stroller onto the bus. Speaking of strollers, they trundle along in huge numbers, which means the pavements and paths are adapted to handle them. Stairs usually have a stroller lane, so you can wheel Junior up or down without jarring. Public playgrounds are numerous and well maintained.

In terms of entertainment, many of Stockholm's best attractions are targeted specifically at children and families. Junibacken (p53) draws young readers into Swedish author Astrid Lindgren's fantastic world, home to Pippi Longstocking and her friends. Naturhistoriska Riksmuseet (p59) offers a child's-eye view of the natural world, with an entire section for hands-on science experiments. Medeltidsmuseet (p45) provides multimedia displays that transport visitors back in time to the city's earliest days. The Postmuseum (p45) includes a miniature post office for children who want to see how it all works. For slightly older kids and teens, Gröna Lund Tivoli (above) offers carnival-ride entertainment. Tekniska Museet (right) will entertain inquisitive brains for hours. And Skansen (p49) is essentially a children's paradise, with dozens of mini-exhibits to explore, snacks everywhere, a petting zoo, singalongs, and guides in old-timey costumes.

Even if they aren't particularly geared toward children, most of the city's museums have family playrooms available. Nobelmuseet (p43), for instance, has a 'childrens club' ('Barnens Nobelklubb') where kids aged between seven and 10 years can share ideas and be creative; other museums have rooms set aside for kid-friendly hands-on learning activities, such as painting, clay modelling or costume making.

Skeppsholmen

This small island is home to a couple of major museums. To get here, take the footbridge from the city centre or hop on the Djurgården ferry from Slussen.

Moderna Museet MUSEUM

(Map p56; ☎08-52 02 35 01; www.modernamuseet.se; Exercisplan 4; adult/child Skr120/free, 6-8pm Fri free; ⏰10am-6pm Wed, Thu, Sat & Sun, to 8pm Tue & Fri, closed Mon; 🚌65, ⛴Djurgårdsfärjan) Moderna Museet is Stockholm's modern-art maverick, its permanent collection ranging from paintings and sculptures to photography, video art and installations. Highlights include work by Pablo Picasso, Salvador Dalí (*The Enigma of William Tell*), Andy Warhol, Damien Hirst and Robert Rauschenberg (*Monogram* affectionately known as 'the goat in a tyre'). There are important pieces by Francis Bacon, Marcel Duchamp and Matisse, as well as their Scandinavian contemporaries, and plenty of work by not yet household names.

The museum also stages well-conceived temporary exhibits and career retrospectives (sometimes with a separate admission fee). Don't overlook the small viewing rooms in various corners and downstairs, where you can watch old Buñuel or Chaplin films or newer experimental videos. Bibliophiles and design fans will adore the well-stocked gift shop.

There's a fabulous and very popular restaurant (daily lunch Skr120, 11am to 2pm) with a great view over the water, an espresso bar in the foyer, and a small, casual cafe in a nice secluded courtyard, with salads and sandwiches (Skr115 to Skr125).

Arkitektur- och Designcentrum MUSEUM

(Map p56; ☎08-5872 70 00; www.arkdes.se; Exercisplan 4; adult/child Skr80/free, 4-6pm Fri free, combination ticket with Moderna Museet Skr180; ⏰10am-8pm Tue, to 6pm Wed-Sun; 🚌65, ⛴Djurgårdsfärjan) Adjoining Moderna Museet and housed in a converted navy drill hall, the architecture and design centre has a permanent exhibition spanning 1000 years of Swedish architecture and an archive of 2.5 million documents, photographs, plans, drawings and models. Temporary exhibitions also cover international names and work. The museum organises occasional themed architectural tours of Stockholm; check the website or ask at the information desk.

Östasiatiska Museet MUSEUM

(Museum of Far Eastern Antiquities; Map p56; www.ostasiatiska.se; Tyghusplan; adult/child Skr80/free; ⏰11am-8pm Tue, to 5pm Wed-Sun; 🚌65) This long, narrow building displays Asian decorative arts, including one of the world's finest collections of Chinese stoneware and porcelain from the Sing, Ming and Qing dynasties. The museum also houses the largest and oldest Asian library in Scandinavia, from which several notable specimens are displayed. The often refreshing temporary exhibitions cover a wide range of themes, with past shows including a look at Japanese anime characters and Chinese video art.

Ladugårdsgärdet

This wide-open, parklike area is a former military training ground. From the small pink pavilion on the hillside, Borgen, the royalty could enjoy leisurely banquets while watching the troops perform their exercises. It hasn't been used as a training ground since the 1860s; these days the smooth fields of Ladugårdsgärdet are popular for strolls and trail runs, volleyball games, football matches and hot-air-balloon rides. Reached by bus 69 from Centralstationen or Sergels Torg, the area boasts three fine museums, an art gallery and one of Stockholm's loftiest views.

Tekniska Museet MUSEUM

(Museum of Science & Technology; Map p56; www.tekniskamuseet.se; Museivägen 7; adult/child Skr120/40, 5-8pm Wed free; ⏰10am-5pm Mon-Fri, 10am-8pm Wed, 11am-5pm Sat & Sun; 🚌69 Museiparken) Tekniska is a sprawling wonderland of interactive science and technology exhibits. One of its biggest drawcards is **Cino4** (adult/child Skr80/40), Sweden's first '4D', multisensory cinema. The 'Teknorama' is a vast room of kinetic experiments and stations designed to do things like test your balance, flexibility and strength. In one corner is a dark and genuinely scary mining exhibit. There's also a model railroad, a survey of inventions by women, and a climate-change game.

Etnografiska Museet MUSEUM

(Museum of Ethnography; Map p56; www.etnografiska.se; Djurgårdsbrunnsvägen 34; adult/child Skr80/free; ⏰11am-5pm Tue-Sun, to 8pm Wed; 👪; 🚌69 Museiparken) The Museum of Ethnography stages evocative displays on various aspects of non-European cultures,

Skeppsholmen & Djurgården

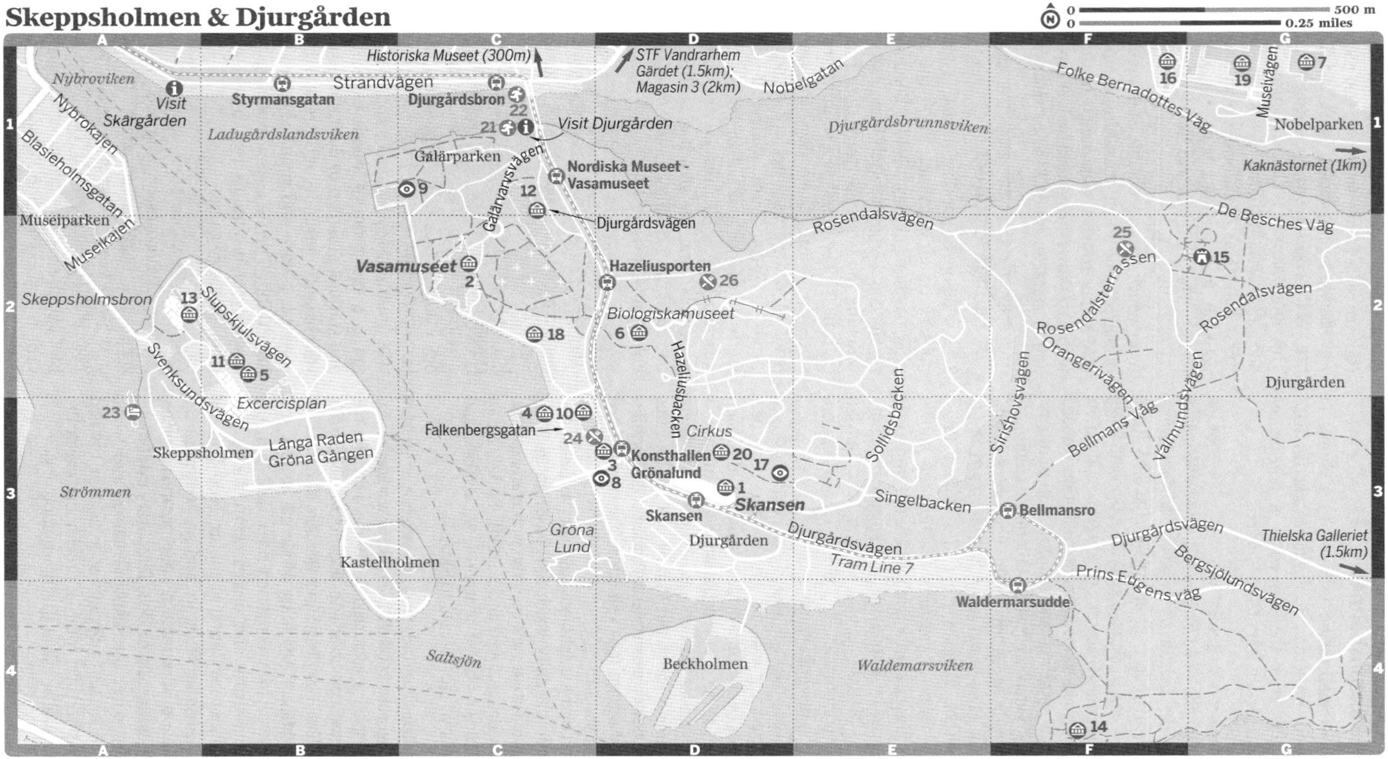

Skeppsholmen & Djurgården

Top Sights
1 Skansen ... D3
2 Vasamuseet ... C2

Sights
3 ABBA: The Museum ... D3
4 Aquaria Vattenmuseum ... C3
5 Arkitektur- och Designcentrum ... B2
6 Biologiska Museet ... D2
7 Etnografiska Museet ... G1
8 Gröna Lund Tivoli ... D3
9 Junibacken ... C1
10 Liljevalchs Konsthall ... C3
11 Moderna Museet ... B2
12 Nordiska Museet ... C1
13 Östasiatiska Museet ... A2
14 Prins Eugens Waldemarsudde ... F4
15 Rosendals Slott ... G2
16 Sjöhistoriska Museet ... F1
17 Skansen Akvariet ... D3
18 Spritmuseum ... C2
19 Tekniska Museet ... G1
20 Tobaks & Tändsticksmuseum ... D3

Activities, Courses & Tours
21 Sjöcaféet ... C1
22 Strandbryggan ... C1

Sleeping
23 Vandrarhem af Chapman & Skeppsholmen ... A3

Eating
24 Blå Porten Café ... C3
25 Rosendals Trädgårdskafe ... F2
26 Wärdshuset Ulla Winbladh ... D2

including dynamic temporary exhibitions and frequent live performances. Recent examples include a display about the cultural treasures of Afghanistan, Russian holiday traditions, and 'real-life' voodoo. If there's a dance or musical performance scheduled, don't miss it. The cafe is a treat, with great music, imported sweets and beverages, and authentic global dishes.

Sjöhistoriska Museet MUSEUM
(National Maritime Museum; Map p56; Djurgårdsbrunnsvägen 24; 10am-5pm Tue-Sun; 69 Museiparken) FREE A must for fans of model ships (there are over 1500 mini vessels in the collection). The museum's exhibits also explore Swedish shipbuilding, sailors and life on deck.

Kaknästornet VIEWPOINT
(www.kaknastornet.se; Mörka Kroken 28-30; adult/child Skr55/20; 9am-10pm Mon-Sat, to 7pm Sun; 69 Kaknästornet) A handy landmark for navigating this part of town, the 155m-tall Kaknästornet is the automatic operations centre for radio and TV broadcasting in Sweden. Opened in 1967, it's among the tallest buildings in Scandinavia. There's a small visitor centre (mainly a gift shop) on the ground floor and an elevator up to the observation deck, restaurant and cafe near the top, from where there are stellar views of the city and archipelago.

Magasin 3 GALLERY
(08-54 56 80 40; www.magasin3.com; Elevator 4, Magasin 3 Bldg, Frihamnen; adult/child Skr40/free; 11am-7pm Thu, to 5pm Fri-Sun, closed Jun-Aug & Christmas holidays; 1, 76, M Ropsten) Though it's a bit out of the way and hours are limited, Magasin 3 is one of Stockholm's best contemporary-art galleries and well worth seeking out. Located in a dockside warehouse northwest of Kaknästornet, its six to eight annual shows often feature specially commissioned, site-specific work from the likes of Pipilotti Rist or American provocateur Paul McCarthy.

Södermalm

Stockholm's southern island is known as the edgy, arty part of town. It's here that you'll find the coolest secondhand shops, art galleries, bars and espresso labs. The hills at the island's northern edge provide stunning views across Gamla Stan and the rest of the central city. Plus there are a couple of museum heavyweights to seek out.

Fotografiska GALLERY
(Map p58; www.fotografiska.eu; Stadsgårdshamnen 22; adult/child Skr120/90; 9am-9pm Sun-Wed, to 11pm Thu-Sat; M Slussen) A chic, upmarket photography museum, Fotografiska is a must for shutterbugs. Its temporary exhibitions are huge, interestingly chosen and well presented; examples have included a Robert Mapplethorpe retrospective and portraits by indie filmmaker Gus Van Sant. Recently the museum showed an enormous collection of black-and-white photos by Sebastião Salgado. There's also a strong permanent collection of photos from international and Swedish photographers. Follow signs from the Slussen tunnelbana stop to reach the museum.

Southern Stockholm

Southern Stockholm

Sights
1 Fotografiska D2
2 Stockholms Stadsmuseum C1

Sleeping
3 Bed & Breakfast 4 Trappor D4
4 Columbus Hotell D2
5 Den Röda Båten – Mälaren/Ran B1
6 Hilton Stockholm Slussen B1
7 Hotel Anno 1647 .... C1
8 Mosebacke Hostel C2
9 Rival Hotel B2

Eating
10 Chutney C3
11 Coop Konsum C1
12 Crêperie Fyra Knop C2
13 Eriks Gondolen C1
14 Hermans Trädgårdscafé D2
15 Koh Phangan D3
16 Nystekt Strömming C1
17 Östgöta Källaren C3
18 Pelikan C4
19 Söderhallarna B3
20 String D3

Drinking & Nightlife
21 Akkurat B1
22 Kvarnen C3
23 Lady Patricia A1
24 Marie Laveau A1
25 Pet Sounds Bar D4
26 Side Track A2
Vampire Lounge .... (see 17)

Entertainment
27 Debaser C3
28 Folkoperan A2
29 Mosebacke Etablissement C2

Shopping
30 10 Swedish Designers B2
31 Chokladfabriken D2
32 DesignTorget C2

Stockholms Stadsmuseum MUSEUM

(City Museum; Map p58; www.stadsmuseum.stockholm.se; Ryssgården, Slussen; adult/child Skr100/free; 11am-5pm Tue-Sun, to 8pm Thu; ; Slussen) Evocative exhibits cover Stockholm's development from fortified port to modern metropolis via plague, fire and good old-fashioned scandal. The museum is housed in a late-17th-century palace designed by Nicodemus Tessin the Elder. Temporary exhibitions are fresh and eclectic, focused on the city's ever-changing shape and spirit. Admission gets you a card good for one year here and at Medeltidsmuseet (p45). Note that the museum is to be closed for renovations until late 2016.

Spårvägsmuseet MUSEUM

(Transport Museum; 08-686 17 60; www.sparvagsmuseet.sl.se; Tegelviksgatan 22; adult/child Skr50/free; 10am-5pm Mon-Fri, 11am-4pm Sat & Sun; 2, 66 Spårvägsmuseet) In a former bus depot near the Viking Line terminal, Stockholm's charmingly old-school transport museum is an atmospheric spot to spend a rainy afternoon. An impressive collection of around 40 vehicles includes several very pretty antique horse-drawn carriages, vintage trams and buses, and a retro tunnelbana carriage (complete with original advertisements). Kids can play tunnelbana driver (there's video from the driver's seat). Displays about the construction of the tunnelbana system starting in 1933 are pretty mind-blowing.

The museum shares a space and entrance with Leksaksmuseet (one admission covers both).

Leksaksmuseet MUSEUM

(Toy Museum; 08-641 61 00; www.leksaksmuseet.se; Tegelviksgatan 22; with Spårvägsmuseet ticket free; 10am-5pm Mon-Fri, 11am-4pm Sat & Sun; 2, 66 Spårvägsmuseet) Sharing an entrance with Spårvägsmuseet (p59), the Toy Museum is packed with everything you probably ever wanted as a child (and may still be hankering for as an adult). If anybody in your family just happens to be crazy about model trains, model aeroplanes, toy soldiers, toy robots, Barbie dolls or stuffed animals, don't miss it.

Suburbs

It's well worth venturing beyond the city centre. In the surrounding suburbs you'll find some of Stockholm's most inviting attractions, from museums to parks to castles and even a cemetery. Thanks to a smooth-as-butter transit system, all of these places are easy to reach.

Millesgården MUSEUM

(08-446 75 90; www.millesgarden.se; Herserudsvägen 32; adult/child Skr100/free; 11am-5pm, closed Mon Oct-Apr; Ropsten, then bus 207) Beautiful Millesgården was the home and studio of sculptor Carl Milles, whose delicate water sprites and other whimsical sculptures dot the city landscape. The grounds include a crisp modern gallery for changing exhibitions of contemporary art, Milles' elaborately Pompeiian house and an exquisite outdoor sculpture garden where items from ancient Greece, Rome, medieval times and the Renaissance intermingle with Milles' own creations. There's also a museum shop and a cafe.

Skogskyrkogården CEMETERY

(08-508 31 730; www.skogskyrkogarden.se; Söckenvagen; 24hr; Skogskyrkogården) FREE One of Stockholm's more unusual attractions, Skogskyrkogården (the Woodland Cemetery) is an arrestingly beautiful graveyard set in soothing pine woodland. Designed by the great Erik Gunnar Asplund and Sigurd Lewerentz, it's on the Unesco World Heritage list and famed for its functionalist buildings. Famous residents include Stockholm screen goddess Greta Garbo. A visitor guide is available on the website in several languages. Guided tours (Skr100) in English are available at 10.30am Sunday July to September.

Naturhistoriska Riksmuseet MUSEUM

(Swedish Museum of Natural History; 08-51 95 40 00; www.nrm.se; Frescativägen 40; adult/child Skr100/free; 10am-6pm Tue-Fri, 11am-6pm Sat & Sun, closed Mon in winter; ; Universitetet) Naturhistoriska Riksmuseet was founded by Carl von Linné in 1739. There are hands-on displays about nature and the human body, as well as whole forests' worth of taxidermied wildlife, dinosaurs, marine life and the hardy fauna of the polar regions. Temporary exhibits keep things fresh and current. The museum is located 300m north of T-Universitetet tunnelbana stop. Cosmonova planetarium shares an entrance.

Cosmonova PLANETARIUM, CINEMA

(08-51 95 51 30; www.nrm.se; Frescativägen 40, at the Naturhistoriska Riksmuseet; adult/child Skr100/50, no children under 5yr; 10am-6pm

Tue-Fri, 11am-6pm Sat & Sun; ; T-Universitetet) Adjoining the Naturhistoriska Riksmuseet (p59) is Cosmonova, a combined planetarium, IMAX and 3D theatre with themes ranging from mummies and dinosaurs to the deep sea and prehistoric sea monsters. Films are screened on the hour (check the latest schedules online), and reservations by phone are recommended. Combination tickets are available, covering both Naturhistoriska Riksmuseet and Cosmonova (adult/child Skr150/50).

Hagaparken PARK

(Haga Park; www.visithaga.se; 24hr; 52, 515, 607 Haga Norra, 59 Haga Södra) FREE Another of Stockholm's lovely green pleasure gardens, Haga Park also happens to have a royal pedigree. Begun by Gustav III, it is Sweden's purest version of an 'English park', and the surrounding area contains three royal palaces. Crowning the hilltop is the peculiar **Koppartälten** (Copper Tent; 08-27 42 52; www.koppartalten.se; Hagaparken; 10am-5pm mid-May–Sep, 10am-3pm Fri-Sun rest of year), built in 1787 as barracks for Gustav III's personal guard. It now contains a cafe and a restaurant, as well as **Haga Parkmuseum**. Catch buses to Haga at Odenplan or Sergels torg.

Also in the park, **Gustav III's Paviljong** (Gustav III's Pavilion; 08-402 61 30; Hagaparken; entry by guided tour only adult/child Skr100/50; tours hourly noon-3pm Tue-Sun Jun-Aug) is a superb example of late-neoclassical style; the furnishings and decor reflect Gustav III's interest in all things Roman after his Italian tour in 1782.

The steamy **Fjärilshuset** (Butterfly House; 08-730 39 81; www.fjarilshuset.se; Hagaparken; adult/child Skr135/70; 10am-5pm) recreates a tropical environment, complete with free-flying birds and butterflies and some very friendly fish. It's a fascinating and lovely place any time of year, but it's an especially delightful retreat on a cold winter day.

Ulriksdals Slott CASTLE

(08-402 61 30; www.kungahuset.se; Slottsallén, Ulriksdal, Solna; adult/child Skr100/free; noon-4pm Tue-Sun Jun-Aug; Bergshamra, then bus 503) The 17th-century royal pad Ulriksdals Slott was home to King Gustaf VI Adolf and his family until 1973. Several of their exquisite apartments, including the Carl Malmsten–designed drawing room from 1923, are open to the public. The **stables** house Queen Kristina's magnificent 17th-century coronation carriage, while the **Orangery** contains Swedish sculpture and Mediterranean flora.

REGIONAL TOURS

From Stockholm it's easy to arrange various day or half-day tours, whether your interests run toward ancient history, royal palaces or seaside picnics. For something more ambitious, book a multiday journey along the **Göta Canal** (www.stromma.se; 4 days from Skr9775; May-early Sep) from coast to coast.

In just under two hours, the **Archipelago 'Race'** (www.stromma.se; tours Skr290; tours at 11.15am, 1.15pm & 3.15pm mid-Jun–Aug) whips you along on a guided tour among the islands nearest the city.

Just 25 minutes away by boat, the **Fjäderholmarna** (Feather Islands; www.fjaderholmslinjen.se; adult/child round trip Skr130/65; hourly 10am-10pm May-early Sep) make for an easy escape from the city and are a favourite swimming spot for locals.

Other options include an atmospheric all-day trip from Stockholm to the Unesco World Heritage Site of Birka (p93) on the island of Björkö; and a romantic jaunt to Drottningholm (p85) via turn-of-the-century steam ship.

Activities

One thing visitors will notice about Stockholm, particularly during the summer months, is how fit and active the majority of locals are. Outdoor activity is a well-integrated part of the city's healthy lifestyle, and there are numerous ways in which a visitor can get in on the action.

Cycling

Stockholm is a very bicycle-friendly city. Cycling is best in the parks and away from the busy central streets and arterial roads, but even busy streets usually have dedicated cycle lanes. There's also a separate network of paved walking and cycling paths that reach most parts of the city; these can be quite beautiful, taking you through green fields and peaceful forested areas. Tourist offices carry maps of cycle routes.

Stockholm City Bikes BICYCLE RENTAL

(www.citybikes.se; 3-day/season card Skr165/300) City Bikes has around 90 self-service bicycle-hire stands across the city. Bikes can be borrowed for three-hour stretches and returned at any City Bikes stand. You'll need to purchase a bike card online or from the tourist office, a Storstockholms Lokaltrafik (SL) centre, or most hotels (see the website for a list). Rechargeable season cards are valid April to October.

Sjöcaféet BICYCLE RENTAL, CANOEING
(Map p56; ☎08-660 57 57; www.sjocafeet.se; Djurgårdsvägen 2; bicycles per hour/day Skr80/275, canoes Skr150/400, kayaks Skr125/400; ⏲9am-9pm Apr-Sep; 🚊7) Rent bicycles from the small wooden hut below this huge cafe-and-tourist-info center beside Djurgårdsbron, which also offers canoes and kayaks for hire.

Sailing & Boating

Water surrounds and permeates the city, and it's hard not to want to get out there if you're walking around on a warm, sunny day. Fortunately, getting out there is easy to do. The city canals are mostly gentle and easily navigable, even for novices; if you're unsure, discuss your level of experience with staff before you rent equipment. Some places also offer guides.

Strandbryggan YACHTING
(Map p56; ☎070-564 93 58, 08-660 37 14; www.strandbryggan.se; Strandvägskajen 27, Strandvägen; ⏲10am-dusk Apr-Sep; 🚊7) Across the water from Sjöcaféet, floating restaurant-bar Strandbryggan offers yachts for charter for up to 12 passengers. Prices start at around Skr2000 per hour (minimum 2½ hours), and you can add catering from the restaurant.

Swimming

Swimming is permitted just about anywhere people can scramble their way to the water. Popular spots include the rocks around Riddarfjärden and the leafy island of Långholmen, the latter also sporting a popular gay beach.

Eriksdalsbadet SWIMMING
(☎08-50 84 02 58; www.eriksdalsbadet.se; Hammarby Slussväg 8; adult/child Skr90/40; ⏲9am-8pm Mon-Thu, to 7pm Fri, to 5pm Sat & Sun; Ⓜ Skanstull) At the southern edge of Södermalm is this sprawling complex, with both indoor and outdoor pools (and all the trimmings). The outdoor pools are open from 6.30am Monday to Friday.

Centralbadet SWIMMING, SPA
(Map p48; ☎08-54 52 13 00; www.centralbadet.se; Drottninggatan 88; admission Skr220, Sat Skr320; ⏲7am-9pm Mon-Fri, 9am-9pm Sat, 9am-6pm Sun) Worth exploring for its art nouveau building and gardenlike atmosphere alone, Centralbadet is almost literally a relaxing oasis in the middle of the busy city. Entry includes pool, sauna and gym access. Treatments available for an additional fee include massage, facials and body wraps; these are best booked two weeks ahead. You can also hire towels (Skr30) and robes (Skr50).

Rock Climbing

Climbers will find around 150 cliffs within 40 minutes' drive of the city, plus a large indoor climbing centre in Nacka.

Klätterverket ROCK CLIMBING
(☎08-641 10 48; klatterverket.se; Marcusplatsen 17, Nacka; adult/child Skr110/80; ⏲10am-10pm Mon-Fri, to 8pm Sat & Sun) One of Sweden's largest indoor climbing centres, with around 1000 sq metres of artificial climbing, this place also rents shoes (Skr35) and harnesses (Skr25). Next to the J-train Sickla stop.

Tours

Taking a tour can be an efficient way of getting a handle on Stockholm's highlights. For a unique perspective, try seeing the city from the water or from up in the air.

Strömma Kanalbolaget BOAT TOUR
(Map p48; ☎08-12 00 40 00; www.stromma.se; Strandvägen 8) This ubiquitous company offers tours large and small, from a 50-minute cruise around Djurgården (Skr170) to a three-hour 'brunch cruise' including a decadent buffet (Skr450). There are also hop-on, hop-off tours by bus (from Skr260), boat (Skr160) or both (Skr350).

Best bet: 'Under the Bridges of Stockholm' (Skr225), a two-hour canal tour running daily 10am to 7pm mid-April to October. Book tickets ahead if possible, as this tour sometimes sells out.

Millennium Tour WALKING TOUR
(www.stadsmuseum.stockholm.se; per person Skr130; ⏲11.30am Sat) Fans of Stieg Larsson's madly popular crime novels (*The Girl with the Dragon Tattoo* etc) will enjoy this walking tour pointing out key locations from the books and films. Buy tickets or a self-guided tour map (Skr40) at the Stadsmuseum (p59) gift shop. From July to September there's also a tour at 6pm on Thursday.

1

EDDIE GRANLUND / GETTY IMAGES ©

2

1. Globen arena (p80), Stockholm
Stockholm skyline at dusk.

2. Swedish cuisine
Stockholm's dining scene (p71) has plenty to offer, from the traditional to the innovative.

3. Buskers, Drottninggatan (p81)
This lively pedestrian thoroughfare offers many shopping opportunities.

4. Stockholm
Stockholm is an accessible beauty, easy to explore.

4

3

MERTEN SNIJDERS / GETTY IMAGES ©

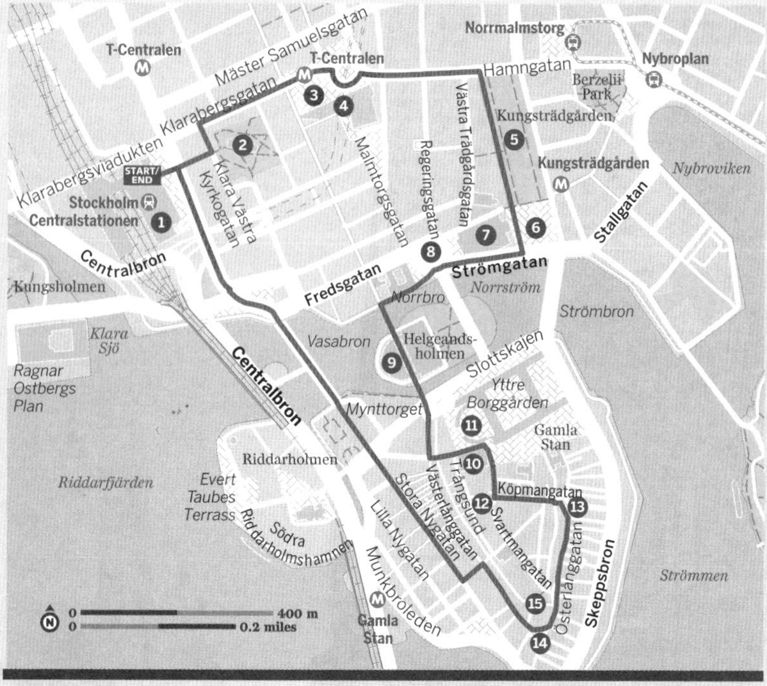

City Walk
Walking Tour Central Stockholm

START CENTRALSTATIONEN
END CENTRALSTATIONEN
LENGTH 3KM; TWO HOURS

Starting at ❶ **Centralstationen**, cross Vasagatan and enter side street Klara Vattugränd. Turn left onto Klara Västra Kyrkogatan, past the church ❷ **Klara Kyrka**. Follow Klarabergsgatan to ❸ **Sergels Torg**, home to commuters, shoppers and the odd demonstration. Pop into arts hub ❹ **Kulturhuset** (p47), with its exhibitions, theatres and cafes.

Continue a short way along Hamngatan before turning right into the grand ❺ **Kungsträdgården**. Originally the kitchen garden for the Royal Palace, this park is now a popular spot for sun soaking in the warmer months and ice skating in the colder ones.

At ❻ **Karl XII's Torg** there's a statue of King Karl XII. On your right is ❼ **Operan**, the Royal Opera House (opened in 1896), and across the road you'll see the Norrström, the outflow from Lake Mälaren. Continue along the waterfront, past ❽ **Gustav Adolfs Torg**, then turn left and cross the Riksbron bridge. Continue across the islet ❾ **Helgeandsholmen**, between the two parts of Sweden's parliament building, Riksdagshuset. Cross Stallbron bridge to reach Stadsholmen, Stockholm's medieval core.

Cross Mynttorget, follow Västerlånggatan for a block, then turn left (east) into Storkyrkobrinken to reach the city's oldest building, ❿ **Storkyrkan** (p45). Facing the cathedral across the square is ⓫ **Kungliga Slottet** (p43). Källargränd leads southward to ⓬ **Stortorget**, the cobblestone square where the Stockholm Bloodbath took place in 1520.

Head east along Köpmangatan to small square ⓭ **Köpmantorget** and the statue of St George and the Dragon. Turn right into Österlånggatan and pass shops and galleries until you reach ⓮ **Järntorget**, where metals were bought and sold in days long past. From there, keep right and turn into Västerlånggatan, looking out for ⓯ **Mårten Trotzigs Gränd**, (Stockholm's narrowest lane), by No 81.

Turn left (northwest) into Stora Nygatan before crossing over Vasabron to head back to Centralstationen.

Stockholm Ghost Walk WALKING TOUR
(Map p44; ☎07-61 46 66 00; www.stockholmghostwalk.com; Tyska Brinken 13; adult/child Skr200/100; ⊙6.45pm) This 90-minute walking tour features tales of murder, mayhem, hauntings and executions, narrated with gusto by multilingual costumed guides. The walk starts at Järntorget in Gamla Stan. Dinner packages available (from Skr575 per person). Check online for tour availability on particular days.

Far & Flyg BALLOONING
(☎08-645 77 00; www.farochflyg.se; per person Skr2345; ⊙flights late May–mid-Sep) Float over Stockholm in a hot-air balloon for up to an hour and see the city from a rare vantage point.

Festivals & Events

There's a bounty of festivals, concerts and other happenings on Sergels Torg and Kungsträdgården throughout the summer, and the major museums exhibit temporary exhibitions on a grand scale. The official tourism website Visit **Stockholm** (visitstockholm.com) lists daily events.

Stockholm Marathon SPORTS
(www.stockholmmarathon.se) A marathon run in late May or early June, with about 21,000 runners.

Smaka På Stockholm FOOD
(www.smakapastockholm.se) This five-day celebration of the Stockholm area's food scene is held in late May or early June. The program includes gourmet food stalls (including representatives from several archipelago restaurants) and entertainment on Kungsträdgården.

Stockholm Pride GAY & LESBIAN
(www.stockholmpride.org/en/) In late July or early August, Stockholm goes pink with a week of parties and cultural events plus a pride parade.

Stockholms Kulturfestival CULTURAL
(www.kulturfestivalen.stockholm.se) This mid-August festival is one big party week, with everything from pavement opera to street theatre and dancing in and around Sergels Torg. Free admission.

Lidingöloppet SPORTS
(www.lidingoloppet.se) The world's largest cross-country foot race, with 30,000 participants, is held in late September in Lidingö, on Stockholm's outskirts.

Stockholm Jazz Festival JAZZ
(www.stockholmjazz.com) One of Europe's premier jazz festivals is held in October, headquartered at Fasching (p79).

Stockholm Open SPORTS
(www.ifstockholmopen.se) Over a week of international tennis and courtside celebrity-spotting, held in October.

Stockholm International Film Festival FILM
(www.stockholmfilmfestival.se) Held in November, this is a major celebration of local and international cinema; its guest speakers include top actors and directors.

Sleeping

Whether you choose youth hostels, B&Bs, boutique digs or big-name chains, you can expect high-quality accommodation in Stockholm. The trade-off is that it can be expensive. But deals exist. Major hotel chains are invariably cheaper booked online and in advance, and most hotels offer discounted rates on weekends and in summer (mid-June to August), sometimes up to 50% off the listed price. Prices included here are the lowest available rate in high season; at other times, you could be paying twice as much.

Hotel prices typically include a large buffet breakfast. Wireless internet is nearly always available, and usually free. Some places have a computer available for guest use. Parking usually comes with a hefty fee (Skr150 to Skr250 per night).

Keep in mind that rooms in central Stockholm can be very tiny, especially the budget rooms in midrange hotels.

A number of services, including **Guestroom B&B** (☎070-206 71 69; www.gastrummet.com/eng/) and **Bed & Breakfast Agency** (☎070-739 05 15; www.bba.nu), can arrange apartment or B&B accommodation from around Skr400 per person per night, usually with a two-night minimum stay.

Stockholm's Svenska Turistföreningen (STF) hostels are affiliated with Hostelling International (HI), and a membership card yields a Skr50 discount. At Sveriges vandrarhem i förening (SVIF) hostels and independent hostels, no membership cards are required. Many have options for single, double or family rooms. Generally, you'll pay extra to use the hostel's linen and towels; bring your own to save Skr50 to Skr80 per night. Many hostels have breakfast available, usually for an additional Skr75 to Skr90.

Hostels tend to fill up during the late-afternoon in peak summer season, so arrive early or book in advance. They can also be busy in May, when Swedish school groups typically visit the capital. Many hostels have limited reception-desk hours; make arrangements in advance if arriving outside of those hours.

Gamla Stan

Ideal for romantics, though generally pricier than other parts of the city, Stockholm's medieval nexus has several atmospheric hotels that put you in easy reach of other neighbourhoods.

2kronor Hostel Old Town HOSTEL €
(Map p44; ☎08-22 92 30; www.2kronor.se; Skeppsbron 40; dm/s/d Skr220/495/595; check-in 3-6pm; M Gamla Stan, Slussen) This small, quiet, family-run hostel has a fantastic location and a friendly vibe. Rooms are on the basement level, slightly cavelike but pretty and well kept (and there are windows). Shared bathrooms are down the hall. Breakfast isn't available, but there's a guest kitchen and dining area by the reception upstairs. Dorms (six- and eight-bed rooms with bunks) are mixed.

First Hotel Reisen HOTEL €€
(Map p44; ☎08-22 32 60; www.firsthotels.com; Skeppsbron 12; s/d from Skr1195/1495; M Gamla Stan) Stockholm's oldest hotel once hummed with sailors. These days the impressive waterfront building draws passersby with a slinky restaurant-bar. Some rooms have exposed-brick walls, others are light and open in classic Scandi style; several have French doors with sea views. There's also a gym in the 16th-century vault-ceilinged basement, as well as a candlelit plunge pool and spa.

Lady Hamilton Hotel HOTEL €€
(Map p44; ☎08-506 401 00; www.ladyhamiltonhotel.se; Storkyrkobrinken 5; s/d Skr1050/1550; M Gamla Stan) Expect old-style luxury (with modern touches where it counts, such as in the bathrooms). The building dates back to the 1470s, and is packed with antiques and portraits of Lady Hamilton herself. If you're not a fan of church bells, request a room away from Storkyrkobrinken.

Hotel Scandic Gamla Stan HOTEL €€
(Map p44; ☎08-723 72 50; www.scandichotels.com; Lilla Nygatan 25; s/d Skr1490/1590; M Gamla Stan) The former Rica chain has been absorbed by Scandic, and this is one of the most atmospheric hotels in its vast collection. Each of the smallish 52 rooms is individually decorated in classic Swedish style – think powder blue wallpaper and vintage chandeliers. The 17th-century building has up-to-the-minute modern amenities, and the location is perfect for soaking up Gamla Stan's history.

Victory Hotel HOTEL €€€
(Map p44; ☎08-50 64 00 00; www.victoryhotel.se; Lilla Nygatan 5; s/d from Skr1090/1790; M Gamla Stan) Nautical antiques, art and model ships define the wonderfully quirky Victory. Most rooms are fairly small (though perfectly comfy), while the museum-like suites (from Skr2300) are larger. There are also four apartments available for long-term rentals (three nights or more).

Lord Nelson Hotel HOTEL €€€
(Map p44; ☎08-50 64 01 20; www.lordnelsonhotel.se; Västerlånggatan 22; s/d from Skr890/1890; M Gamla Stan) Yo-ho-ho, me scurvy barnacles! It's a tight squeeze, but this pink-painted, glass-fronted building feels like a creaky old ship loaded with character. At just 5m wide, the 17th-century building is Sweden's narrowest hotel. Its nautical theme extends to brass and mahogany furnishings, antique sea-captain trappings and a model ship in each of the small rooms.

Central Stockholm

The handiest area for Centralstationen and Cityterminalen, Stockholm's bustling, 'downtown' Norrmalm district is awash with shops and is an easy walk to most major sights. Just to the north, Vasastan harbours some top-notch eating and drinking spots.

★ **STF Fridhemsplan** HOSTEL €
(☎08-653 88 00; www.fridhemsplan.se; S:t Eriksgatan 20; s/d Skr550/650, hotel s/d from Skr750/850; M Fridhemsplan) This modern, inviting hostel near the Fridhemsplan tunnelbana stop on Kungsholmen has nice, modern, hotel-style rooms with shared bathrooms (the hotel-standard rooms are en suite). Some rooms have windows with city views. There's a cool lounge in the lobby to hang out in, and a vast and stylish breakfast room (with a better-than-average breakfast buffet, Skr70 for hostel guests).

Sheets, towels and cleaning are included. There's also a well-equipped kitchen for self-caterers, and free wi-fi and cable TV in each room. The location, on a lively street on Kungsholmen, is handy to lots of good eateries and the waterfront walking path along Norr Mälarstrand.

★City Backpackers HOSTEL €
(Map p48; ☎08-20 69 20; www.citybackpackers.org; Upplandsgatan 2a; dm Skr190-280, s/d/tr Skr500/650/870; ; T-Centralen) The closest hostel to Centralstationen has clean rooms, friendly staff, free bike hire and excellent facilities, including sauna, laundry and kitchen (with a free stash of pasta). En suite private rooms are also available. Bonus for female guests: there are four- and eight-bed female-only dorms if you prefer, and you can borrow a hairdryer from reception.

The hostel also has six-bed apartments (from Skr1740) for rent, with bunks, their own kitchens and bathrooms – a great option if you're in town for a while and want to cook your own meals.

Hostel Bed & Breakfast HOSTEL €
(Map p52; ☎08-15 28 38; www.hostelbedandbreakfast.com; Rehnsgatan 21; dm/s/d Skr320/550/780; reception 9am-8pm; ; Rådmansgatan) Located only a few steps from the T-Rådmansgatan tunnelbana station, in an up-and-coming neighbourhood full of great restaurants and pretty parks, this pleasant, informal basement hostel has modern bathrooms, floral wallpaper, a tidy guest kitchen and a laundry for guests (Skr50 including detergent). Breakfast is included in the prices; sheets can be rented.

★Hotel Hellsten HOTEL €€
(Map p52; ☎08-661 86 00; www.hellsten.se; Luntmakargatan 68; s/d from Skr1090/1490; ; Rådmansgatan) Hip Hellsten is owned by anthropologist Per Hellsten, whose touch is evident in the rooms and common areas, which are furnished and decorated with objects from his travels and life, including Congan tribal masks and his grandmother's chandelier. Rooms are supremely comfortable and individually styled, with themes ranging from rustic Swedish to Indian exotica; some even feature original tile stoves.

The sleek bathrooms sport phones and hand-cut Greek slate. Hotel extras include a sauna and a small fitness room, as well as live jazz in the lounge on Thursday evening. And the location is especially great for adventurous foodies.

Hotel Hansson HOTEL €€
(Map p52; ☎08-15 04 20; www.hotelhansson.se; Surbrunnsgatan 38; r from Skr695, design s/d from Skr995/1195; ; Rådmansgatan) This friendly, family-run boutique hotel is in a quiet but vibrant part of town and is loaded with atmosphere. The standard rooms are basic and spacious, with all the trimmings; a step up are the design rooms, with intense wallpaper, sumptuous fabrics and chandeliers. There's a beautiful lounge area and a fabulous breakfast buffet.

Nordic 'C' Hotel HOTEL €€
(Map p48; ☎08-50 56 30 00; www.nordicchotel.com; Vasaplan 4; s/d from Skr784/824; ; T-Centralen) A fantastic deal if you time it right and book ahead, this sister hotel to the slightly more upmarket Nordic Light has smallish but sleek rooms, great service and a cool lobby lounge area with an impressive 9000L aquarium in the foyer. The cheapest rooms are windowless and very tiny but efficiently designed and totally comfortable.

One of the two hotel bars is the famous Absolut Icebar (p78), newly redesigned and expanded. The breakfast buffet is enormous. The **Arlanda Express** (www.arlandaexpress.com; one-way Skr260) is just steps from the lobby, and you can buy tickets at the front desk.

Birger Jarl Hotel HOTEL €€
(Map p52; ☎08-674 18 00; www.birgerjarl.se; Tulegatan 8; cabin r Skr690, s/d from Skr890, studios from Skr1890; ; 43 Tegnérgatan, Rådmansgatan) One of Stockholm's original design hotels, the Birger Jarl has recently had a full renovation and update of the lobby, plus about 30 new rooms and suites. Standard rooms are all done up in ultramodern Swedish style, but each of the superior rooms is put together by a different Swedish designer, and they're well worth the price upgrade.

Students of vintage interior design should book the Retro Room, which was 'forgotten' during a major renovation and hence has been preserved in all its 1974 glory. (You can request it through the website.) The hotel also offers budget 'cabin' rooms, tiny and windowless but well designed, comfortable and equipped with all the mod cons. There's a sauna, a top-floor gym and a chic lobby bar with some outdoor seating.

Nordic Light Hotel HOTEL €€
(Map p48; ☎08-50 56 30 00; www.nordiclighthotel.com; Vasaplan 7; s/d from Skr1088/1288; ; T-Centralen) Extremely convenient to Central

Station, the Nordic Light is a minimalist Scandi design hotel, with modern, well-equipped rooms. The signature 'mood rooms' ditch conventional artwork for custom-designed light exhibits, which guests can adjust to suit their mood. Additional perks include mini gym, sauna and chic lobby bar, plus a new restaurant with fancy cocktails and DJs most nights.

Rex Hotel
HOTEL €€

(Map p52; ☑ 08-16 00 40; www.rexhotel.se; Luntmakargatan 73; s/d from Skr890/1290; ☞ ✳ @ ☜; Ⓜ Rådmansgatan) While a little less luxe than its sibling Hotel Hellsten across the street, Rex has small but stylish rooms with flat-screen TVs, rich colour schemes and Greek-stone bathrooms. Ultrabudget rooms on a lower level are recommended only if you don't plan to spend much time there – they are *very* tiny and windowless. Breakfast is in the lovely, exposed-brick atrium.

Crystal Plaza Hotel
HOTEL €€

(☑ 08-406 88 00; www.crystalplazahotel.se; Birger Jarlsgatan 35; s/d from Skr660/960; ☞ @ ☜; Ⓜ Östermalmstorg) Housed in an 1895 building with an eight-storey tower and neoclassical columns, this friendly hotel offers wonderfully cosy (albeit smallish) rooms, decorated in homey Swedish traditional style. There's also a sauna, a gym and a tiny lobby bar.

Grand Hôtel Stockholm
HOTEL €€€

(Map p48; ☑ 08-679 35 00; www.grandhotel. se; Södra Blasieholmshamnen 8; s/d/ste from Skr1900/3300/6400; Ⓟ ☞ ✳ @ ☜; ⬚ 2, 43, 55, 62, 65, 76 Karl XII's torg, ⛴ Strömkajen, Ⓜ Kungsträdgården, T-Centralen) This is where the literati, glitterati and nobility call it a night. A waterfront landmark, with several exclusive restaurants and a see-and-be-seen piano bar, it remains Stockholm's most sumptuous lodgings. Room styles span royal Gustavian to contemporary chic.

Room 701 (the Flag Suite) occupies a turret with a 360-degree view and a jacuzzi open to the sky; room 702 is the astounding Nobel Room, where the literature prizewinner slumbers overnight; and the Bernadotte suite is fit for royalty. All rooms include access to the Nordic Spa and Fitness centre, plus all the little luxuries that accompany five-star accommodation.

Berns Hotel
HOTEL €€€

(Map p48; ☑ 08-56 63 22 00; www.berns.se; Näckströmsgatan 8; s/d from Skr1490/1790; Ⓟ ☞ @ ☜; Ⓜ Kungsträdgården, ⬚ 7 Kungsträdgården) The rooms at Berns come equipped with entertainment systems and styles ranging from 19th-century classical to contemporary sleek. Some are more impressive than others (the balcony rooms get our vote); room 431 was once a dressing room used by Marlene Dietrich and Ella Fitzgerald. The cheapest rooms don't include breakfast, but it can be added for Skr195.

Hotel Stureplan
HOTEL €€€

(Map p48; ☑ 08-440 66 00; www.hotelstureplan. se; Birger Jarlsgatan 24; s/d from Skr1390/1790; ☞ ✳ @ ☜; Ⓜ Östermalmstorg) An ideally situated boutique hotel, Stureplan offers individually designed rooms with pared-back Gustavian decor (high ceilings, chandeliers, antique tile stoves) and high-tech touches like flat-screen TVs. Some rooms face the inner courtyard, others the busy Birger Jarlsgatan, so request the former if you're a light sleeper.

If you *really* want it quiet, ask for one of the cosy, yacht-inspired, windowless rooms (from Skr1000). There are also super-modern loft rooms and lovely, airy suites in varying degrees of luxury.

Skeppsholmen

Connected to the city centre by bridge and to Djurgården by ferry, this leafy island is home to some marvellous museums and views.

★Vandrarhem af Chapman & Skeppsholmen
HOSTEL €

(Map p56; ☑ 08-463 22 66; www.stfchapman. com; Flaggmansvägen 8; dm/r from Skr260/590; ☞ @ ☜; ⬚ 65 Skeppsholmen) The *af Chapman* is a storied vessel that has done plenty of travelling of its own. It's anchored in a superb location, swaying gently off Skeppsholmen. Bunks are in dorms below deck. Apart from showers and toilets, all facilities are on dry land in the Skeppsholmen hostel, including a good kitchen, a laid-back common room and a TV lounge.

Staff are friendly and knowledgable about the city and surrounding areas. Laundry facilities and 24-hour internet access are available.

Ladugårdsgärdet

This parklike area is home to one of the city's nicest hostels, a little out of the way but convenient to several great museums and walking trails.

STF Vandrarhem Gärdet HOSTEL €
(08-463 22 99; www.svenskaturistforeningen.se; Sandhamnsgatan 59; s/d from Skr495/760; P; 1 Östhammarsgatan, M Gärdet) Surrounded by forested trails and open fields in quiet Gärdet, this efficient hostel works more like a no-frills hotel. Rooms are tiny but well planned, and all have their own bathroom and TV. Towels, sheets and cleaning are included in the price; breakfast can be had for an extra Skr80, and there's a good guest kitchen.

Everything is sleek and modern with an office feel, though the lobby has some designer touches: red pin chairs, sheepskins, flat-screen TVs. There are no dorms, just private rooms of varying configurations (some lack windows, some have sofa beds, most have refrigerators). Reception is open 24 hours.

Södermalm

The Södermalm district is only a 15-minute walk or quick subway ride from Viking Line boats and Centralstationen; it's also the most happening section of Stockholm and is your best bet for interesting budget or midrange accommodation.

Långholmen Hotell & Vandrarhem HOSTEL, HOTEL €
(08-720 85 00; www.langholmen.com; Långholmsmuren 20; hostel dm from Skr260, cell s/d Skr620/750, hotel r from Skr1075; P; 4, 40, 77, 94 Högalidsgatan, M Hornstull) Guests at this hotel-hostel, in a former prison on Långholmen island, sleep on bunks in a cell, with either shared or private baths. (The friendly, efficient staff promise they will not lock you in.) The kitchen and laundry facilities are good, the restaurant serves meals all day, and Långholmen's popular summertime bathing spots are a towel flick away.

Hotel-standard rooms are also in cells but spruced up with textured wall coverings and mod fixtures; some of the budget doubles are in bunks, so be sure to clarify the room configuration you want. The hostel functions as a mini museum as well, with titbits of information about the prison's history scattered throughout the rooms and common areas. If you're really keen on the prison idea, you can also book a 'prisoner for a day' package – a two-hour competitive game that ends in a three-course meal (Skr886 per person).

Mosebacke Hostel HOSTEL €
(Map p58; 08-641 64 60; www.mosebackehostel.se; Högbergsgatan 26; s/d from Skr575/690; reception 8am-11pm; M Slussen) This hostel in the Söder Heights is a cool spot with a great location. The design is edgy and modern; there's a slick, Ikea-catalogue kitchen for guests, and there are plenty of common areas to hang out in. You can choose shared-bath or en suite rooms. Breakfast is included in the price. Laundry machines are available (Skr70).

★ **Hotel Anno 1647** HOTEL €€
(Map p58; 08-442 16 80; www.anno1647.se; Mariagränd 3; budget s/d from Skr570/740, standard s/d from Skr890/990; P; M Slussen) Just off buzzing Götgatan, this historical hotel in two beautiful buildings has labyrinthine hallways, gorgeous wooden floors and spiral staircases, affable staff, and budget as well as standard rooms – both are recommended. The latter have antique rococo wallpaper, all modern amenities and the odd chandelier. The location and reduced high-season rates make this a fantastic deal.

Economy rooms are simple but clean and comfy, with sinks in the rooms, almost comically tiny shared bathrooms and some noise from the street at night – a fair trade for sea views from the bay windows. Both price categories include the stellar buffet breakfast, a notch or two above the usual. Limited parking is available nearby.

Zinkensdamm Hotell & Vandrarhem HOTEL, HOSTEL €€
(08-616 81 00; www.zinkensdamm.com; Zinkens väg 20; dm Skr320, d without/with bathroom Skr700/950, hotel r from Skr1495; P; M Zinkensdamm) In a cheery yellow building next to the adorable Tantolunden park, the Zinkensdamm STF is fun, attractive and well equipped – complete with a sleek guest kitchen and personal lockers in each room – and caters for families with kids as well as pub-going backpackers. It can be crowded and noisy, but that's the trade-off for an upbeat vibe.

There are laundry facilities (Skr45) and a sauna. Guests can hire bicycles for Skr50 per hour. The hostel breakfast buffet isn't spectacular, but the cafe in the lobby sells good coffee and pastries as well as other meals throughout the day. Hotel-standard rooms are in a separate section and are spacious and comfortable.

Clarion Hotel HOTEL €€
(08-462 10 00; www.clarionstockholm.com; Ringvägen 98; budget/standard r from Skr980/1180; P ⊖ ❄ @ ≋; M Skanstull) This designer darling feels like a modern-art museum, its wide ramp leading into the foyer dotted with ubercool furniture and modelled on the Tate Modern. Standard rooms are compact but uncluttered and ultramodern, with 'deluxe' options and suites available for those wanting more space. The several bars and restaurants are their own draw.

The foyer features a huge wall mural and sculptures by Kirsten Ortwed, as well as funky lighting fixtures and fish-scale tiles at the front desk. There's a gym and sauna, as well as a spa where you can book ayurvedic treatments.

Bed & Breakfast 4 Trappor B&B €€
(Map p58; 08-642 31 04; www.4trappor.se; Gotlandsgatan 78; s/d Skr925/1250; P ≋; 3, 53, 76, 96 Gotlandsgatan, M Medborgarplatsen) This great little apartment has a cosy, polished-floorboard bedroom (maximum two guests), a modern bathroom and a kitchen (with its own espresso machine). Note that there's no lift; you'll be climbing four flights of stairs. There's a two-night minimum stay, and the place is a huge hit, so book months ahead. Breakfast is served in the owners' apartment next door.

Den Röda Båten – Mälaren/Ran HOSTEL, HOTEL €€
(Söder Mälarstrand; Map p58; 08-644 43 85; www.theredboat.com; Kajplats 10; dm from Skr300, hostel s/d Skr550/900, hotel r from Skr1350; ⊖ @ ≋; M Slussen, Gamla Stan) The 'Red Boat' is a hotel and hostel on two vessels, *Mälaren* and *Ran*. The hostel section is the cosiest of Stockholm's floating accommodation: lots of dark wood, nautical memorabilia and friendly staff. Linens are included in the price. Hotel-standard rooms are bigger, with blond wood, maritime paintings and breakfast; sea-view rooms are worth the extra Skr200 or so.

★ **Rival Hotel** HOTEL €€€
(Map p58; 08-54 57 89 00; www.rival.se; Mariatorget 3; s/d from Skr1895/2495; ⊖ ❄ @ ≋; M Mariatorget) Owned by ABBA's Benny Andersson and overlooking leafy Mariatorget, this ravishing design hotel is a chic retro gem, complete with vintage 1940s movie theatre and art-deco cocktail bar. The supercomfy rooms feature posters from great Swedish films and a teddy bear to make you feel at home. All rooms have good-size bathrooms and flat-screen TVs with Blu-ray players.

The tasty bakery-cafe and restaurant-bar attached to the hotel are prime spots from which to ogle Stockholm's beautiful people. In summer splurge on a deluxe room with a balcony for even better views.

Columbus Hotell HOTEL €€€
(Map p58; 08-50 31 12 00; www.columbushotell.se; Tjärhovsgatan 11; s/d from Skr1595/1795; P ⊖ @ ≋; M Medborgarplatsen) Columbus is inches from the beating heart of Södermalm, near lively Medborgarplatsen and a short walk from the city centre. The decor is classic homestyle Swedish, with linens and light-wood floors and spare, elegant furnishings. Rooms are all en suite with TVs, phones and comfy beds – many have views over Katarina churchyard or a pretty, central courtyard.

Hilton Stockholm Slussen HOTEL €€€
(Map p58; 08-517 353 00; www.hilton.com; Guldgränd 8; r from Skr1600; P ⊖ ❄ @ ≋; M Slussen) Perched between the chaotic Slussen interchange and Södermalm's underground highway, Stockholm's unmissable Hilton sports modern, comfortable rooms with swirly marble bathrooms and everything you'd expect in a top-notch business hotel. Several rooms have stunning city views. There's a nice terrace bar, and the vast lobby is well suited to meeting up with friends before a night exploring Söder.

Clarion Hotel Sign HOTEL €€€
(Map p48; 08-676 98 10; www.clarionsign.com; Östra Järnvägsgatan 35; s/d from Skr1380/1580; P ⊖ ❄ @ ≋ ≈; M T-Centralen) Stockholm's largest hotel is also among its most stylish. Behind the striking granite-and-glass facade, trendsetters lounge on Arne Jacobsen egg chairs, dine at chef Marcus Samuelsson's American Table Brasserie, and recharge at the rooftop spa, complete with 35°C plunge pool. The high-concept rooms showcase design objects from across Scandinavia, with each floor dedicated to a particular Nordic nation's designers.

Suburbs

If things get desperate in town, there are more than 20 hostels around the county easily reached by SL buses, trains or archipelago boats within an hour or so. There are also numerous summer campsites, many offering cheap cabin accommodation.

Bredängs Vandrarhem & Camping HOSTEL, CAMPGROUND €
(☎08-97 62 00; www.bredangvandrarhem.se; Stora Sällskapetsväg 51; sites Skr265, dm/s/d Skr220/420/590; ⏲campsites early Apr-early Oct; P ⊜ @ ☜; M Bredäng) This is a lakeside option 10km southwest of central Stockholm, with good public-transport connections. It's a well-equipped campground, with a hostel and modern cabins (Skr990). There's free wi-fi, free parking, minigolf, multiple guest kitchens and laundry facilities. It's about a 700m walk from the Bredäng tunnelbana station; if you're driving, it's well signposted from the E4/E20 motorway.

Hotel J HOTEL €€€
(☎08-601 30 00; www.hotelj.com; Ellensviksvägen 1, Nacka Strand; r from Skr1790; P ⊜ @ ☜; M Slussen, then bus 404, 443) This upscale hotel with a breezy, blue-and-white Hamptons vibe is a popular weekend getaway for Stockholmers. Initially a summer house built in 1912, it's named after the boats used in the America's Cup. The scent of nonchalant wealth wafts unmistakably through the air here. Rooms are decorated with comfortable furniture and fine linens; several have balconies.

Eating

Stockholm is a city of foodies. The relatively small city has more than half a dozen Michelin-starred restaurants. Top chefs are veritable celebrities, and getting a table at the restaurant of the moment can take some planning. Admittedly, Stockholm's epicurean highlights don't come cheap, but it's a world-class food scene, and you can eat as well here as in any major European city.

Keep in mind that some of the city's top restaurants close for a week or two in July or August ('*sommarstängt*'); check ahead to avoid disappointment.

In case you don't plan on five-star dining every day, Stockholm's many cafes and coffee shops offer a good range of standard fare, from enormous salads made with pasta or quinoa to quiches and baguettes.

Most of the top eating spots offer trendy takes on humble *husmanskost* (classic Swedish home cooking). There's also an ever-growing number of ethnic eateries; it's no longer any trouble to find authentic Ethiopian, Thai, Middle Eastern, Indian or Japanese food in Stockholm. A fun way to explore a range of flavours is to hit up one of the market halls. And the many vegetarian buffets strewn across the city might be the best way to snag a bargain.

For a quick, inexpensive snack, it's hard to beat a *grillad korv med bröd* – your basic grilled hot dog on a bun – available for between Skr25 and Skr40 from carts all over town. Options for decorating your dog include shrimp salad and curried potatoes, and the adventurous can opt for a *korv* roll with the lot.

Between meals, take time to investigate Stockholm's vibrant cafe culture. Just about every Stockholmer takes part in a daily *fika*, or midafternoon coffee break. Look for signs saying *konditori*, and feast your eyes on the always-amazing display cases of cakes and pastries.

Gamla Stan

Grillska Husets Konditori BAKERY, CAFE €
(Map p44; ☎08-68 42 33 64; www.stadsmissionen.se/matochkonferens/grillska-huset/; Stortorget 3; sandwiches Skr25-75; ⏲9am-6pm Mon-Fri, 10am-6pm Sat & Sun; M Gamla Stan) The cafe and

SELF-CATERING

Supermarkets in Stockholm are plentiful and easy to find; here are a few handy ones, but you'll see branches in almost every neighbourhood. Don't forget that you'll need to purchase a plastic grocery bag (Skr5) if you haven't brought along your own.

Hemköp (Map p48; Klarabergsgatan 50; ⏲7am-9pm Mon-Fri, from 10am Sat & Sun) The handiest central supermarket, located in the basement of Åhléns department store.

Coop Konsum (Map p58; Katarinavägen 3-7; ⏲7am-9pm Mon-Fri, from 9am Sat & Sun) A central supermarket near the Slussen tunnelbana stop.

ICA Baronen (Map p52; Odengatan 40; ⏲8am-10pm) Large outlet of a reliably good chain near Odenplan.

Vivo T-Jarlen (Map p48; Östermalmstorg tunnelbana station; ⏲7am-9pm Mon-Fri, 10am-7pm Sat, 11am-7pm Sun) Busy store inside the Östermalmstorg tunnelbana station.

bakery run by Stockholms Stadsmission, the chain of secondhand charity shops, is a top-notch spot for a sweet treat or a sandwich, especially when warm weather allows for seating at the outdoor tables in Gamla Stan's main square. There's a bakery shop attached, selling goodies and rustic breads to take away.

Hairy Pig Deli DELI €
(Håriga Grisen; Map p44; ☎073-800 26 23; www.hairypigdeli.se; Österlånggatan 9; tapas Skr45-55, mains Skr65-100; ⏲5-9pm Tue-Fri, noon-10pm Sat; Ⓜ Gamla Stan) Follow your nose to this cute little corner deli, where the personable owners make all their own sausages and serve beer brewed by a family friend. Try the sausage of the day (Skr65), a salami and cheese baguette (Skr85), a charcuterie plate, an assortment of tapas or the excellent salad with house-made salami and cheese from the Stockholm archipelago.

Chokladkoppen CAFE €
(Map p44; www.chokladkoppen.se; Stortorget 18; cakes Skr40-80; ⏲9am-11pm summer, shorter hours rest of year; Ⓜ Gamla Stan) Arguably Stockholm's best-loved cafe, hole-in-the-wall Chokladkoppen sits slap bang on the old town's enchanting main square. It's a gay-friendly spot, with cute waiters, a look-at-me summer terrace and yummy grub such as broccoli-and-blue-cheese pie and scrumptious cakes.

Cafe Järntorget ICE CREAM €
(Map p44; Västerlånggatan 81; ice cream Skr27-78; ⏲8am-6pm Mon-Fri, 10am-6pm Sat & Sun, open late in summer; Ⓜ Gamla Stan) If you make no other snack stops in Gamla Stan, at least make it to this ice-cream shop. It's the one place in town that reliably offers such outlandishly Swedish flavours as *lakrits* (black licorice), *hjörtron* (cloudberry), and the ambrosia that is saffron-and-honey ice cream.

Sundbergs Konditori CAFE €
(Map p44; ☎08-10 67 35; Järntorget 83; mains Skr55-85; ⏲9am-8pm; Ⓜ Gamla Stan) Dating from 1785, this is Stockholm's oldest bakery-cafe, complete with chintzy chandeliers, regal oil paintings and a copper samovar full of self-serve coffee. Mix and match with gleaming pastries and a soothing selection of bagels, ciabattas and quiches.

★ **Hermitage** VEGETARIAN €€
(Map p44; Stora Nygatan 11; lunch/dinner & weekends Skr110/120; ⏲11am-8pm Mon-Sat, noon-4pm Sun; ✎; Ⓜ Gamla Stan) Herbivores love Hermitage for its simple, tasty, vegetarian buffet, easily one of the best restaurant bargains in Gamla Stan. Salad, homemade bread, tea and coffee are included in the price. Pro tip: don't miss the drawers of hot food hiding under the main buffet tabletop.

★ **Kryp In** SWEDISH €€€
(Map p44; ☎08-20 88 41; www.restaurangkrypin.nu; Prästgatan 17; starters Skr135-195, mains Skr195-285; ⏲5-11pm Mon-Fri, 12.30-4pm & 5-11pm Sat & Sun; Ⓜ Gamla Stan) Small but perfectly formed, this spot wows diners with creative takes on traditional Swedish dishes. Expect the likes of salmon carpaccio or smoked reindeer salad followed by a gorgeous, spirit-warming saffron aioli shellfish stew. The service is seamless and the atmosphere classy without being stuffy. The brief weekend lunch menu (Skr119 to Skr158) is a bargain. Book ahead.

Den Gyldene Freden SWEDISH €€€
(Map p44; ☎08-24 97 60; www.gyldenefreden.se; Österlånggatan 51; lunch Skr165-265, dinner mains Skr180-370; ⏲lunch Mon-Fri, dinner Mon-Sat; Ⓜ Gamla Stan) Open since 1722, this venerable barrel-vaulted restaurant is run by the Swedish Academy, where (rumour has it) its members meet to decide the winners of the Nobel Prize. Personally, we think it should go to the chefs, whose sublime offerings include civilised *husmanskost* dishes like roast lamb with chanterelles, cabbage and country cheese, or old-school Swedish meatballs.

Central Stockholm

★ **Vurma** CAFE €
(www.vurma.se; Polhemsgatan 15-17; sandwiches Skr60-80, salads Skr108; ⏲7am-7pm Mon-Fri, 8am-7pm Sat & Sun; ☰✎👪; Ⓜ Rådhuset) Squeeze in among the locals at this friendly cafe-bakery, a reliably affordable place to get a healthy and substantial meal in an unfussy setting. The scrumptious sandwiches and salads are inspired, with ingredients like halloumi, felafel, cured salmon, avocado and greens over quinoa or pasta. The homemade bread that comes with your order is divine.

You'll find other branches in **Vasastan** (Map p52; www.vurma.se; Gästrikegatan 2; salads Skr109; ⏲9am-7pm Mon-Sat, 10am-7pm Sun; ✎; Ⓜ St:Eriksplan) and elsewhere around town.

Café Saturnus CAFE €
(☎08-611 77 00; Eriksbergsgatan 6; sweetrolls Skr50, salads & sandwiches Skr68-138; ⏲8am-

8pm Mon-Fri, 9am-7pm Sat & Sun; 2 Eriksbergsgatan) For velvety caffè latte, Gallic-inspired baguettes and perfect pastries, saunter into this casually chic bakery-cafe. Sporting a stunning mosaic floor, silky striped wallpaper and a few outdoor tables, it's a fabulous spot to flick through the paper while tackling what has to be Stockholm's most enormous sweetroll (cinnamon or cardamom, take your pick).

Östermalms Saluhall MARKET €
(Map p48; www.ostermalmshallen.se/en/; Östermalmstorg; mains from Skr85; 9.30am-6pm Mon-Thu, to 7pm Fri, to 4pm Sat; M Östermalmstorg) Stockholm's historic gourmet food market feeds all the senses with fresh fish, seafood and meat, fruit, vegetables and hard-to-find cheeses, as well as cafes for a quick lunch or snack. The 1885 building, a Stockholm landmark, is showing its age and will be closed for renovations from 2015 to 2017, with a temporary market set up in the square.

For a quick lunch, belly up to the bar at Sushibaren; for a real treat, grab a table at Lisa Elmqvist, one of the city's top seafood eateries. There's a clean, free, well-hidden toilet in the far corner opposite the market entrance.

Hötorgshallen FOOD HALL €
(Map p48; Hötorget; 10am-6pm Mon-Thu, to 6.30pm Fri, to 6pm Sat, closed Sun; M Hötorget) Located below Filmstaden cinema, Hötorgshallen is Stockholm at its multicultural best, with stalls selling everything from fresh Nordic seafood to fluffy hummus and fragrant teas. Ready-to-eat options include Lebanese spinach parcels, kebabs and vegetarian burgers. For the ultimate feed, squeeze into galley-themed dining nook Kajsas Fiskrestaurang for a huge bowl of soulful *fisksoppa* (fish stew) with aioli (Skr95).

While you're here, don't neglect to buy some produce from the vendors in the square outside – they're entertainers as much as they are retailers, and it's a fun way to get a good deal on some nice locally grown fruit and veggies.

Xoko BAKERY €
(08-31 84 87; www.xoko.se; Rörstrandsgatan 15; pastries from Skr25, breakfast Skr59-95; 7am-7pm Mon-Fri, 8am-6pm Sat & Sun; M S:t Eriksplan) Famous for making the desserts served at the Nobel Prize banquet, Xoko looks like a jewellery store, with row after row of gorgeous-looking edible gems on display. The cakes, sweets and truffles are crazy inventive, but you can also get outstanding versions of more humble and traditional fare – simple breads, sandwiches and cinnamon buns. Staff are entertaining and helpful.

La Neta MEXICAN €
(Map p48; http://laneta.se; Barnhusgatan 2; 1/5 tacos Skr22/95; 11am-9pm Mon-Fri, noon-9pm Sat, noon-4pm Sun; M Hötorget) Competition for the title of 'Stockholm's Best Taqueria' is not fierce, but La Neta wins hands down. Fast-food pseudo-Mexican eateries are all over town, but this is the real deal, with homemade corn tortillas, nuanced flavors, and zero frills in the dining area (unless you count the bowls of delicious salsa). It's great value for money.

The kitchen is bigger than the dining area, and there's a perpetual line halfway around the block from the minute the place opens. Cheap beer and soda are available, and the daily specials are worth trying.

Sturekatten CAFE €
(Map p48; 08-611 16 12; www.sturekatten.se; Riddargatan 4; pastries from Skr35; 9am-7pm Mon-Fri, 10am-6pm Sat, 11am-6pm Sun; M Östermalmstorg) Looking like a life-size doll's house, this vintage cafe is a fetching blend of antique chairs, oil paintings, ladies who lunch and waitresses in black-and-white garb. Slip into a salon chair, pour some tea and nibble on a piece of apple pie or a *kanelbulle* (cinnamon bun).

Vetekatten CAFE €
(Map p48; www.vetekatten.se; Kungsgatan 55; pastries from Skr25, salads Skr65-100; 7.30am-7.30pm Mon-Fri, 9.30am-5pm Sat & Sun; M Hötorget) A cardamom-scented labyrinth of cosy nooks, antique furnishings and oil paintings, Vetekatten is not so much a cafe as an institution. Wish back the old days over filling sandwiches, heavenly scrolls and warming cups of tea.

Lisa Elmqvist SEAFOOD €€
(Map p48; 08-55 34 04 10; www.lisaelmqvist.se; Östermalmstorg, Östermalms Saluhall; mains from Skr170; 9.30am-6pm Mon-Thu, to 6.30pm Fri, to 4pm Sat; M Östermalmstorg) Seafood fans, look no further. This Stockholm legend, suitably snug inside historic Östermalms Saluhall, is never short of a satisfied lunchtime crowd. The menu changes daily, so let the waiters order for you; whether it's lobster pancakes or seared Sichuan pepper char fillets, you

won't be disappointed. Classics include shrimp sandwiches (Skr170) and a gravadlax plate (Skr185).

In the warmer months, dine outdoors at sister bistro Lisa på Torget, on the square outside.

Tennstopet SWEDISH, PUB FOOD €€
(Map p52; ☎08-32 25 18; www.tennstopet.se; Dalagatan 50; dagens lunch Skr129; 11.30am-1am Mon-Fri, 1pm-1am Sat & Sun; Odenplan) Had there been a Swedish version of *Cheers*, it would've been filmed here. Oil paintings, gilded mirrors and winter candlelight set the scene for a lovable cast of wizened regulars, corner-seat scribes and melancholy dames. Watch the show with a soothing *öl* (beer) and a serve of soulful *husmanskost*. Try the traditional herring platter (Skr179).

Mälarpaviljongen SWEDISH, AMERICAN €€
(☎08-650 87 01; www.malarpaviljongen.se; Norr Mälarstrand 63; mains Skr168-235; 11am-1am; Rådhuset) When the sun's out, few places beat this alfresco waterside spot for some Nordic dolce vita. Its glassed-in gazebo, vast floating terrace and surrounding herb gardens are only upstaged by the lovely and supremely welcoming service. Both food and cocktails are beautified versions of the classics: huge burgers, pretty salmon salads, strawberry mojitos etc. Opening times are at the weather's mercy.

Lao Wai VEGETARIAN €€
(Map p52; ☎08-673 78 00; www.laowai.se; Luntmakargatan 74; dagens lunch Skr100, dinner mains Skr195-215; 11am-2pm Mon-Fri, 5.30-9pm Tue-Sat; ; Rådmansgatan) Tiny, herbivorous Lao Wai does sinfully good things to tofu and vegetables, hence the faithful regulars. Everything here is vegan and gluten free. A different lunch special is served each weekday; the dinner menu is more expansive, offering virtuous treats like Sichuan-style smoked tofu with shitake, chillies, garlic shoots, snow peas and black beans.

Caffé Nero CAFE €€
(Map p52; www.nerostockholm.se; Roslagsgatan 4; dagens lunch Skr100, mains Skr100-145; 7am-5pm Mon-Fri, 9am-5pm Sat & Sun; Odenplan, Rådmansgatan) Packed with local hipsters during the busy lunch hour, this stylish but casual neighbourhood cafe serves substantial meals (fish, pasta, salads) at good prices, plus sublime coffee drinks and pastries. There's also a Saturday brunch from noon to 3pm. Next door is a sleek bar-restaurant, Buco Nero, open late with DJs and an upscale dinner menu (mains Skr195 to Skr295).

★ **Grands Verandan** SWEDISH €€€
(Grand Hôtel Stockholm; Map p48; ☎08-679 35 86; www.grandhotel.se; Södra Blasieholmshamnen 8; mains Skr185-275, smörgåsbord Skr445; noon-3pm & 6-10pm Mon-Fri, 1-4pm & 6-10pm Sat & Sun; Kungsträdgården) Head here, inside the Grand Hôtel, for the famous smörgåsbord – especially during the Christmas holidays, when it becomes even more elaborate (reservations recommended). Arrive early for a window seat and tuck into both hot and cold Swedish staples, including gravadlax with almond potatoes, herring, meatballs and lingonberry jam. It's like a belt-busting crash course in classic Nordic flavours.

Operakällaren FRENCH, SWEDISH €€€
(Map p48; ☎08-676 58 00; www.operakallaren.se; Karl XII's Torg 10; tasting menus Skr995-2750; 6-10pm Tue-Sat, closed mid-Jul–mid-Aug Kungsträdgården) Inside Stockholm's show-off Opera House, the century-old Operakällaren is a major gastronomic event. Decadent chandeliers, golden mirrors and exquisitely carved ceilings set the scene for French-meets-fusion adventures like seared scallops with caramel, cauliflower purée, *pata negra* ham and brown-butter emulsion. Book at least two weeks ahead.

Tranan SWEDISH €€€
(Map p52; ☎08-52 72 81 00; www.tranan.se; Karlbergsvägen 14; starters Skr95-285, mains Skr195-345; 5-11pm; Odenplan) Locals pack this former beer hall, now a comfy but classy neighbourhood bistro with a seafood-heavy menu and red-checked tablecloths. The food combines Swedish *husmanskost* with savvy Gallic touches; don't miss the fried herring. In summer choose an outdoor table and watch the human dramas across Odenplan. On the weekends, DJs and live bands perform in the basement bar.

Bakfickan SWEDISH €€€
(Map p48; ☎08-676 58 00; www.operakallaren.se; Karl XII's Torg, Opera House; mains Skr170-275; 11.30am-11pm Mon-Fri, noon-10pm Sat; Kungsträdgården) The small, casual 'hip pocket' of Operakällaren, this comfy restaurant is crammed with opera photographs and deco lampshades. Dexterous old-school waiters serve comforting Swedish *husmanskost*, and the counter seats make it a perfect spot for solo dining. Late at night, rumour has it, this is where the opera singers hang out.

Mathias Dahlgren INTERNATIONAL €€€
(Map p48; 08-679 35 84; www.mathiasdahlgren.com; Grand Hôtel Stockholm, Södra Blasieholmenshamnen 6; Matbaren mains Skr145-295, Matsalen 5-/8-course menu Skr1500/1900; Matbaren noon-2pm Mon-Fri & 6pm-midnight Mon-Sat, Matsalen 7pm-midnight Tue-Sat, both closed mid-Jul–Aug; M Kungsträndsgården) Celebrity chef Matthias Dahlgren has settled in at the Grand Hôtel with a two-sided restaurant: there's the formal, elegant Matsalen (Dining Room), which has been awarded two Michelin stars, and the bistro-style Matbaren (Food Bar), boasting its own Michelin star. Both focus on seasonal ingredients, so menus change daily. Reservations are crucial.

Pontus! SWEDISH €€€
(Map p48; 08-54 52 73 00; Brunnsgatan 1; lunch Skr185, dinner mains Skr155-525; 11.30am-2pm & 6-10pm Mon-Fri, 6-10pm Sat, closed Sun; M Östermalmstorg) This Östermalm favourite has reconfigured its space, thankfully keeping the beloved library wallpaper and huge round booths in the main dining room. Indulge in set menus (Skr425 to Skr795) or à la carte mains featuring French-influenced treatments of seasonal ingredients – a chanterelle brioche with sorrel and onion, perhaps, or smoked *matjes* herring with new potatoes and egg-yolk confit.

Pontus' little sibling restaurant, Pocket, serves a more casual but no less tantalising menu (Skr125 to Skr195) and is open noon to 10pm Tuesday to Friday, and from 5pm Saturday. There's also a cute, tiny, white-tiled deli that offers breakfast and takeaway meals.

Storstad FRENCH, SWEDISH €€€
(Map p52; www.storstad.se; Odengatan 41; herring plates Skr65-165, mains Skr165-275; 4pm-1am Mon-Wed, to 3am Fri & Sat, closed Sun; M Odenplan) This attractive bistro near Odenplan, which shares a corner (and owners) with Olssons bar (p78), serves Scandi classics like *toast skagen* (toast with bleak roe, crème fraiche and chopped red onion), or Swedish meatballs alongside traditional French favourites like *moules frites* (mussels and fries) and tarte Tatin. It transforms into a lively cocktail bar later in the evening.

Sturehof SEAFOOD €€€
(Map p48; 08-440 57 30; www.sturehof.com; Stureplan 2; starters Skr155-265, mains Skr185-495; 11am-2am Mon-Fri, noon-2am Sat & Sun; M Östermalmstorg) Superb for late-night sipping and supping, this convivial brasserie sparkles with gracious staff, celebrity regulars and fabulous seafood-centric dishes (the bouillabaisse is brilliant). Both the front and back bars are a hit with the eye-candy brigade and perfect for a post-meal flirt.

Djurgården

★ **Rosendals Trädgårdskafe** CAFE €€
(Map p56; 08-54 58 12 70; www.rosendalstradgard.se; Rosendalsterrassen 12; mains Skr85-145; 11am-5pm Mon-Fri, to 6pm Sat & Sun May-Sep, closed Mon Feb-Apr & Oct-Dec; P; 44, 69, 76 Djurgårdsbron, 7) Set among the greenhouses of a pretty botanical garden, Rosendals is an idyllic spot for heavenly pastries and coffee or a meal and a glass of organic wine. Lunch includes a brief menu of eco-friendly soups, sandwiches (such as ground-lamb burger with chanterelles) and gorgeous salads. Much of the produce is biodynamic and grown on site.

The next-door bakery and shop sells everything from preserved lemons and freshly baked bread to Rosendals' very own cookbook. Follow signs from Djurgårdsbron; it's about a 15-minute walk. Closed in January and on Midsummer weekend.

Blå Porten Café CAFE €€
(Map p56; 08-663 87 59; www.blaporten.com; Djurgårdsvägen 64; mains Skr85-155; 11am-9pm Mon-Thu, to 7pm Fri-Sun; ; 47 Liljevalc Gröna Lund, 7 Liljevalc Gröna Lund) Blissful on sunny days, when you can linger over lunch or *fika* in a garden reminiscent of a Monet painting, this cafe next to Liljevalchs Konsthall boasts an obscenely tempting display of baked goods, as well as lip-smacking Scandi and global meals. Mercifully, many of Djurgården's museums are within rolling distance.

Wärdshuset Ulla Winbladh SWEDISH €€€
(Map p56; 08-53 48 97 01; www.ullawinbladh.se; Rosendalsvägen 8; starters Skr125-265, mains Skr155-295; 11.30am-10pm Mon, 11.30am-11pm Tue-Fri, 12.30-11pm Sat, 12.30-10pm Sun; Djurgårdsfärjan, 7) Named after one of Carl Michael Bellman's lovers, this villa was built as a steam bakery for the Stockholm World's Fair (1897) and now serves fine food in intimate rooms and a blissful garden setting. Sup on skilfully prepared upscale versions of traditional Scandi favourites, mostly built around fish and potatoes; try the herring plate with homemade crispbread.

Roxette fans should ask the staff to point out the artwork of singer Marie Fredriksson. Book ahead in summer.

Södermalm

Chutney
VEGETARIAN €

(Map p58; ☑08-640 30 10; www.chutney.se; Katarina Bangata 19; dagens lunch Skr80; ⊙11am-10pm Mon-Sat, noon-9pm Sun; ✔; ⓜMedborgarplatsen) Sitting among a string of three inviting cafes along this block, Chutney is one of Stockholm's many well-established vegetarian restaurants, offering excellent value and great atmosphere. The daily lunch special is usually a deliciously spiced, curry-esque heap of veggies over rice, and includes salad, bread, coffee and a second helping if you can manage it.

Huddle on the pillowed benches indoors and sample the vaguely Middle Eastern– and Asian-themed veggie delights, or just hang out with a beer and watch the Söder crowds filter by.

Nystekt Strömming
SWEDISH €

(Map p58; Södermalmstorg; combo plates Skr35-75; ⊙11am-8pm Mon-Fri, to 6pm Sat & Sun, closing times vary; ⓜSlussen) For a quick snack of freshly fried herring, seek out this humble cart outside the tunnelbana station at Slussen. Large or small combo plates come with big slabs of the fish and a selection of sides and condiments, from mashed potato and red onion to salads and hardbread; more portable wraps and the delicious herring burger go for Skr55.

String
CAFE €

(Map p58; ☑08-714 85 14; www.cafestring.com; Nytorgsgatan 38; sandwiches Skr50-65, salads Skr80; ⊙9am-8pm Mon-Thu, to 7pm Fri, 10am-7pm Sat & Sun; ⓜMedborgarplatsen) This retro-funky SoFo cafe does a bargain weekend brunch buffet (Skr80; 10.30am to 1pm Saturday and Sunday). Load your plate with everything from cereals, yoghurt and fresh fruit to pancakes, toast and amazing homemade hummus. Fancy that '70s chair you're plonked on? Take it home; almost everything you see is for sale.

Crêperie Fyra Knop
CAFE €

(Map p58; ☑08-640 77 27; Svartensgatan 4; crêpes Skr64-84, gallettes Skr100-118; ⊙5-11pm Mon-Fri, noon-11pm Sat & Sun; ⓜSlussen) Head here for perfect crêpes in an intimate setting, plus a hint of shanty-town chic – think reggae tunes and old tin billboards for Stella Artois. A good place for a quiet tête-à-tête before you hit the clubs down the street.

Söderhallarna
FOOD HALL €

(Map p58; Medborgarplatsen 3; ⊙10am-6pm Mon-Wed, to 7pm Thu & Fri, to 4pm Sat; ✔) This food hall on Medborgarplatsen contains a cinema as well as shops selling everything from cheese and smallgoods to decent vegetarian grub.

★ Hermans Trädgårdscafé
VEGETARIAN €€

(Map p58; ☑08-643 94 80; www.hermans.se; Fjällgatan 23A; buffet Skr175, desserts from Skr35; ⊙11am-9pm; ✔; 🚌2, 3, 53, 71, 76 Tjärhovsplan, ⓜSlussen) ✔ This justifiably popular vegetarian buffet is one of the nicest places to dine in Stockholm, with a glassed-in porch and outdoor seating on a terrace overlooking the city's glittering skyline. Fill up on inventive, flavourful veggie and vegan creations served from a cozy, vaulted room – you might need to muscle your way in, but it's worth the effort.

The desserts (sold separately) are mostly vegan, gluten-free, or both, and they look amazing, though it's a challenge to save room. If you have a valid student ID, you may be able to get a two-for-one deal on the buffet. Worth asking!

Pelikan
SWEDISH €€

(Map p58; ☑08-55 60 90 90; www.pelikan.se; Blekingegatan 40; mains Skr172-285; ⊙5pm-midnight or 1am; ⓜSkanstull) Lofty ceilings, wood panelling and no-nonsense waiters in waistcoats set the scene for classic *husmanskost* at this century-old beer hall. The herring options are particularly good (try the 'SOS' plate, an assortment of pickled herring, Skr124 to Skr138) and there's usually a vegetarian special to boot. There's a hefty list of aquavit, too.

Östgöta Källaren
SWEDISH €€

(Map p58; ☑08-643 22 40; Östgötagatan 41; mains Skr155-225; ⊙5pm-1am Mon-Fri, 3pm-1am Sat, 5pm-1am Sun; ⓜMedborgarplatsen) The regulars at this soulful pub-restaurant range from multipierced rockers to blue-rinse grandmas, all smitten with the dimly lit romantic atmosphere, amiable vibe and hearty Swedish, Eastern European and French-Mediterranean grub. Try the saffron shellfish casserole (Skr198).

The restaurant shares an entrance with the underworldy Vampire Lounge (p77).

Koh Phangan
THAI €€

(Map p58; ☑08-642 50 40; www.kohphangan.se; Skånegatan 57; starters Skr85-95, mains Skr155-285; ⊙4pm-1am Mon-Fri, noon-1am Sat & Sun; ⓜMedborgarplatsen) Best at night, this outrageously kitsch Thai restaurant has to be seen to be believed. Tuck into your *kao pat gai* (chicken fried rice) in a real *tuk-tuk* to the accompanying racket of crickets and tropical thunder, or kick back with beers in a bamboo hut. DJs occasionally hit the decks and it's best to book ahead.

Eriks Gondolen SWEDISH €€€
(Map p58; ☎08-641 70 90; www.eriks.se; Stadsgården 6; mains Skr215-340; ⏰11.30am-11pm Mon, 11.30am-1am Tue-Fri, 4pm-1am Sat; Ⓜ Slussen) Perched above Slussen atop the antique lift Katarinahissen, this place is known for top-notch Swedish food, refined service, perfect cocktails and endless views. There's a formal dining room (reservations recommended), or you can keep it a little more casual in the bar area. In summer there's seating outdoors (not ideal for the acrophobic).

It's a fantastic place to relax over fine food and drinks and ogle the lovely Stockholm skyline at your leisure. If there are a few of you, try the shellfish platter (Skr545).

Drinking & Nightlife

Stockholm is a stylish place to drink, whether you're after cocktails or coffee. (Most coffee shops also do great food; it's the rare Swede who sips a cup of coffee without a little something to nibble on.) In fact, just about the only kind of place you'll have trouble finding here is a dive bar with bad lighting, frumpy regulars and cheap swill on tap.

The coolest and most casual drinking holes are on Södermalm, the bohemian island in the southern part of town. (And if you *are* looking for a cheap dive, this would be a good place to start; try near the corner of Tjärhovsgatan and Östgötagatan.) For a moneyed, glamorous scene, head to Östermalm's late-night clubs. Even the hotel bars draw an ultrachic cocktail crowd.

Note that many places charge a mandatory Skr30 to Skr50 coat-check fee.

Locals often save money by meeting for drinks at home before they go out. To do the same, hit up a **Systembolaget** (liquor store; Map p48; www.systembolaget.se; Drottninggatan 22; ⏰10am-7pm Mon-Fri, to 3pm Sat), the state-owned alcohol monopoly, to buy booze to take away. (Supermarkets also sell low-alcohol beer, up to 3.5%.)

Stockholm is home to some mighty clubs, with DJ royalty regularly on the decks. You'll find the slickest spots in Östermalm, especially on and around Stureplan. Expect an entry charge of Skr150 to Skr200 at the trendiest venues, and plan on dressing up if you want to get in. Södermalm offers a more varied scene, with club nights spanning local indie to salsa, and a more denim-friendly crowd.

Pet Sounds Bar BAR
(Map p58; www.petsoundsbar.se; Skånegatan 80; beer Skr72, cocktails Skr118; Ⓜ Medborgarplatsen) A SoFo favourite, this jamming bar pulls in music journos, indie culture vultures and the odd goth rocker. While the restaurant serves decent Italian-French grub, the real fun happens in the basement. Head down for a mixed bag of live bands, release parties and DJ sets. Hit happy hour (2pm to 6pm) for drink specials.

Akkurat BAR
(Map p58; ☎08-644 00 15; www.akkurat.se; Hornsgatan 18; beers Skr59-95; ⏰11am-1am Mon-Fri, 3pm-1am Sat, 6pm-1am Sun; Ⓜ Slussen) Valhalla for beer fiends, Akkurat boasts a huge selection of Belgian ales as well as a good range of Swedish-made microbrews, including Nynäshamn's Ångbryggeri. It's one of only two places in Sweden to be recognised by a Cask Marque for its real ale. Extras include a vast wall of whisky, and mussels (half/full order Skr155/215) on the menu.

Kvarnen BAR
(Map p58; ☎08-643 03 80; www.kvarnen.com; Tjärhovsgatan 4; ⏰11am-1am Mon-Tue, 11am-3am Wed-Fri, 5pm-3am Sat, 5pm-1am Sun; Ⓜ Medborgarplatsen) An old-school Hammarby football-fan hang-out, Kvarnen is one of the best bars in Söder. The gorgeous beer hall dates from 1907 and seeps tradition; if you're not the clubbing type, get here early for a nice pint and a meal (mains Skr139 to Skr195). As the night progresses, the nightclub vibe takes over. Queues are fairly constant but justifiable.

Vampire Lounge BAR
(Map p58; www.vampirelounge.se; Östgötagatan 41; ⏰5pm-1am Mon-Fri, 7pm-1am Sat; Ⓜ Medborgarplatsen) The name says it all: this dark basement bar is bloodsucker-themed all the way through. There are perspex 'windows' in the floor showing buried caches of anti-vamp supplies such as holy water, crosses and garlic – just in case. Locals recommend the ice-cream cocktails. The lounge shares an entrance with Östgöta Källaren (p76) restaurant.

Marie Laveau BAR
(Map p58; www.marielaveau.se; Hornsgatan 66; ⏰11am-3am; Ⓜ Mariatorget) In an old sausage factory, this kicking Söder playpen draws a

boho-chic crowd. The designer-grunge bar (think chequered floor and subway-style tiled columns) serves killer cocktails, while the sweaty basement hosts club nights on the weekend. Its known for its monthly 'Bangers & Mash' Britpop night; check online for dates.

Monks Porter House PUB
(Map p44; 08-23 12 12; www.monkscafe.se; Munkbron 11; from 6pm Tue-Sat; M Gamla Stan) This cavernous brewpub has an epic beer list, including 56 taps, many of which are made here or at the Monks microbrewery in Vasastan. Everything we tried was delicious, especially the Monks Orange Ale – your best bet is to ask the bartender for a recommendation (or a taste). Check online for beer-tasting events.

Berns Salonger BAR
(Map p48; www.berns.se; Berzelii Park; club 11pm-4am Thu-Sat, also Wed & Sun occasionally, bar from 5pm daily) A Stockholm institution since 1862, this glitzy entertainment palace remains one of the city's hottest party spots. While the gorgeous ballroom hosts some brilliant live-music gigs, the best of Berns' bars is in the intimate basement, packed with cool creative types, top-notch DJs and projected art-house images. Check the website for a schedule of events; some require advance ticket purchase.

Le Rouge BAR
(Map p44; 08-50 52 44 30; Österlånggatan 17; 11.30am-2pm & 5pm-1am Mon-Fri, 5pm-1am Sat) Fin de siècle Paris is the inspiration for this decadent lounge in Gamla Stan, a melange of rich red velvet, tasselled lampshades, inspired cocktails and French bistro grub. (The adjoining restaurant is run by two of Stockholm's hottest chefs, Danyel Couet and Melker Andersson.) DJs hit the decks Thursday to Saturday.

Olssons BAR
(Map p52; 08-673 38 00; Odengatan 41; 9pm-3am Wed-Sat) The blue neon sign outside this bar tips you off to its former life as a shoe store. These days, it serves as the back bar to Storstad (p75), forming a busy corner of activity along this neighbourhoody street.

Lilla Baren at Riche BAR
(Map p48; 08-54 50 35 60; Birger Jarlsgatan 4; 5pm-2am Tue-Sat) A darling of Östermalm's hip parade, this pretty, glassed-in bar mixes smooth bar staff, skilled DJs and a packed crowd of fashion-literate media types; head in by 9pm to score a seat.

Absolut Icebar BAR
(Map p48; 08-50 56 35 20; www.icebarstockholm.se; Vasaplan 4, Nordic 'C' Hotel; prebooked online/drop in Skr185/195; 11.15am-midnight Sun-Thu, to 1am Fri & Sat) It's touristy. Downright gimmicky! And you're utterly intrigued, admit it: a bar built entirely out of ice, where you drink from glasses carved of ice on tables made of ice. The admission price gets you warm booties, mittens, a parka and one drink. Refill drinks cost Skr95.

Café Opera CLUB
(Map p48; 08-676 58 07; www.cafeopera.se; Karl XII's Torg; admission from Skr160; 10pm-3am Wed-Sun; M Kungsträdsgården) Rock stars need a suitably excessive place to schmooze, booze and groove, one with glittering chandeliers, ceiling frescoes and a jet-set vibe. This bar-club combo fits the bill, but it's also welcoming enough to make regular folk *feel* like rock stars. If you only have time to hit one primo club during your visit, this is a good choice.

Sturecompagniet CLUB
(Map p48; 08-54 50 76 00; www.sturecompagniet.se; Stureplan 4; admission Skr120; 10pm-3am Thu-Sat; M Östermalmstorg) Swedish soap stars, flowing champagne and look-at-me attitude set a decadent scene at this glitzy, mirrored and becurtained hallway. Dress to impress and flaunt your wares to commercial house. Big-name guest DJs come through frequently.

Spy Bar CLUB
(Map p48; Birger Jarlsgatan 20; admission from Skr160; 10pm-5am Wed-Sat; M Östermalmstorg) No longer the superhip star of the scene it once was, the Spy Bar (aka 'the Puke' because *spy* means 'vomit' in Swedish) is still a landmark and fun to check out if you're making the Östermalm rounds. It covers three levels in a turn-of-the-century flat (spot the tile stoves).

☆ Entertainment

For most concerts and events, the tourist office can sell you tickets or tell you where to get them. (Call 508 28 508 to check.) For an up-to-date calendar visit www.visitstockholm.com. Another good source if you can navigate a little Swedish is the Friday 'På Stan' section of *Dagens Nyheter* newspaper (www.dn.se). **Ticnet** (077-170 70 70; www.

GAY & LESBIAN STOCKHOLM

Stockholm is a dazzling spot for queer travellers. Sweden's legendary open-mindedness makes homophobic attitudes rare, and party-goers of all persuasions are welcome in any bar or club. As a result, Stockholm doesn't really have a gay district, although you'll find most of the queercentric venues in Södermalm and Gamla Stan. For club listings and events, pick up a free copy of street-press magazine *QX*, found at many clubs, shops and cafes around town. Its website (www.qx.se) is more frequently updated and has listings in English. *QX* also produces a free, handy *Gay Stockholm Map*, available at the tourist office. The national organisation for gay and lesbian rights, **RFSL** (08-50 16 29 50; www.rfsl.se/stockholm; Sveavägen 59; M Rådmansgatan), is another good source of information, with a library and cafe to boot.

Good bars and clubs include the following:

Lady Patricia (Map p58; 08-743 05 70; www.patricia.st; Söder Mälarstrand, Kajplats 19; 5pm-midnight Wed & Thu, to 5am Fri-Sun) This is a perennial Sunday-night favourite – two crowded dance floors, drag shows and *schlager*-loving crowd. It's all aboard a docked old royal yacht (now open five nights a week, in a new spot on Söder Mälarstrand).

Side Track (Map p58; 08-641 16 88; www.sidetrack.nu; Wollmar Yxkullsgatan 7; 6pm-1am Wed-Sat; M Mariatorget) This establishment is a particular hit with down-to-earth guys, with a low-key, publike ambience.

Torget (Map p44; www.torgetbaren.com; Mälartorget 13; 5pm-midnight, to 1am Sun; M Gamla Stan) In Gamla Stan, this is Stockholm's premier gay bar-restaurant, with mock-baroque touches and a civilised salon vibe.

ticnet.se) is a frequently used online ticket outlet for big concerts and sporting events.

Live Music

Stockholm's music scene is active and varied. On any one night you can catch emerging indie acts, edgy rock, blues and Balkan pop. Jazz and blues have a particularly strong presence, with several legendary venues saxing it up and an annual jazz festival held in mid-July.

Ticket prices for live music range from Skr150 to Skr400, but they'll vary widely depending on who's performing. Generally, you'll want to buy tickets well in advance.

Debaser LIVE MUSIC
(Map p58; 08-694 79 00; www.debaser.se; Medborgarplatsen 8; 7pm-1am Sun-Thu, 8pm-3am Fri & Sat; M Medborgarplatsen) This mini-empire of entertainment has its flagship rock venue (Debaser Medis) on Medborgarplatsen. Emerging or bigger-name acts play most nights, while the killer club nights span anything from rock-steady to punk and electronica. (There are also a couple of restaurants around town and a location in Malmö.)

Mosebacke Etablissement LIVE MUSIC
(Map p58; www.mosebacke.se; Mosebacketorg 3; tickets Skr80-400; 6pm-late; M Slussen) Eclectic theatre and club nights aside, this historic culture palace hosts a mixed line-up of live music. Tunes span anything from home-grown pop to antipodean rock. The outdoor terrace (featured in the opening scene of August Strindberg's novel *The Red Room*) combines dazzling city views with a thumping summertime bar.

Glenn Miller Café JAZZ, BLUES
(Map p48; 08-10 03 22; Brunnsgatan 21A; 5pm-1am Mon-Thu, to 2am Fri & Sat) Simply loaded with character, this tiny jazz-and-blues bar draws a faithful, fun-loving crowd. It also serves excellent, affordable French-style classics like mussels with white wine sauce.

Fasching JAZZ
(Map p48; 08-53 48 29 60; www.fasching.se; Kungsgatan 63; 6pm-1am Mon-Thu, to 4am Fri & Sat, 5pm-1am Sun; M T-Centralen) Music club Fasching is the pick of Stockholm's jazz clubs, with live music most nights. DJs take over with either Afrobeat, Latin, neo-soul or R&B on Friday night and retro-soul, disco and rare grooves on Saturday.

Stampen JAZZ
(Map p44; 08-20 57 93; www.stampen.se; Stora Nygatan 5; admission free-Skr200; 5pm-1am Mon-Thu, 8pm-2am Fri & Sat, blues jam 2-6pm Sat) Stampen is one of Stockholm's music-club

stalwarts, swinging to live jazz and blues six nights a week (and sometimes on Sunday). The free blues jam, at 2pm on Saturday, pulls everyone from local noodlers to the odd music legend.

Globen LIVE MUSIC
(☎077-131 00 00; www.globen.se; Arenavägen; Ⓜ Globen) This huge white spherical building (it looks like a giant golf ball) just south of Södermalm hosts regular big-name pop and rock concerts, as well as sporting events and trade fairs. Even if nothing's going on inside, you can take a ride up and over the building inside SkyView, a miniglobe with glass walls that great views across town.

Concerts, Theatre & Dance

Stockholm delivers outstanding dance, opera and music performances; for an overview, see the calendar section on visitstockholm.com or ask at the tourist office. Most ticket sales are handled by the tourist office as well. Alternatively, you can buy some tickets direct from Ticnet (p78)

Operas are usually performed in their original language, while theatre performances are invariably in Swedish.

Konserthuset CLASSICAL MUSIC
(Map p48; ☎08-50 66 77 88; www.konserthuset.se; Hötorget; tickets Skr80-325; Ⓜ Hötorget) Head to this pretty blue building for classical concerts and other musical marvels, including the Royal Philharmonic Orchestra.

Operan OPERA
(Map p48; ☎08-791 44 00; www.operan.se; Gustav Adolfs Torg, Operahuset; tickets Skr100-750; Ⓜ Kungsträndsgården) The Royal Opera is the place to go for thunderous tenors, sparkling sopranos and classical ballet. It has some bargain tickets in seats with poor views, and occasional lunchtime concerts for less than Skr200 (including light lunch).

Folkoperan THEATRE
(Map p58; ☎08-616 07 50; www.folkoperan.se; Hornsgatan 72; tickets Skr145-455; Ⓜ Zinkensdamm) Folkoperan gives opera a thoroughly modern overhaul with its intimate, cutting-edge and sometimes controversial productions. The under-26s enjoy half-price tickets.

Dramaten THEATRE
(Kungliga Dramatiska Teatern; Map p48; ☎08-667 06 80; www.dramaten.se; Nybroplan; tickets Skr90-390; 👪; Ⓜ Kungsträndsgården) The Royal Theatre stages a range of plays in a sublime art nouveau environment. You can also take a guided tour in English at 4pm most days (adult/child Skr30/60), bookable online.

Stockholms Stadsteatern THEATRE
(Map p48; ☎08-50 62 02 00; www.stadsteatern.stockholm.se; Kulturhuset, Sergels Torg; tickets Skr200-350; Ⓜ T-Centralen) Regular performances are staged at this theatre inside Kulturhuset, as well as guest appearances by foreign theatre companies.

Dansens Hus DANCE
(Map p48; ☎08-50 89 90 90; www.dansenshus.se; Barnhusgatan 12-14; tickets around Skr300, under 20yr half-price) This place is an absolute must for contemporary-dance fans. Guest artists have included everyone from British choreographer Akram Khan to Canadian innovator Daniel Léveillé.

Sport

Bandy matches, a uniquely Scandinavian phenomenon, take place all winter at Stockholm's ice arenas.

For the ultimate Scandi sport experience, head to an ice-hockey game. Contact Globen for details; matches take place at Hovet, the arena inside the Globen complex, up to three times a week from September to April. There are regular football fixtures, too.

Impromptu public ice-skating areas spring up during the winter at Kungsträdgården in Norrmalm and at Medborgarplatsen in Södermalm. Skate-rental booths next to the rinks hire out equipment (per hour adult/child around Skr50/30).

Zinkensdamms Idrottsplats SPECTATOR SPORT
(www.svenskbandy.se/stockholm; Ringvägen 16; tickets around Skr130; Ⓜ Zinkensdamm) Watching a bandy match is great fun. The sport, a precursor to ice hockey but with more players (11 to a side) and less fighting, has grown massively popular since the rise of the Hammarby team in the late '90s. The season lasts from November to March; you can buy tickets at the gate.

There's a round vinyl ball instead of a puck, and the rules are similar to football, except that you hit the ball with a stick instead of kicking it. Bring a thermos of *kaffekask* – a warming mix of coffee and booze.

Shopping

Stockholm is a seasoned shopper's paradise. It's practically a sport here. For big-name Swedish and international retail outlets like Diesel, Urban Outfitters, Whyred and Face Stockholm, hit the pedestrianised Biblioteksgatan from Östermalm to Norrmalmstorg, as well as the smaller streets that branch off it. Östermalm is generally good for browsing at high-end boutiques.

For the slightly funkier and artier stores and galleries, head to Södermalm. And for souvenirs and postcards, Gamla Stan has the most stores per square inch, but pedestrian thoroughfare Drottninggatan offers supercheap Viking hats and Absolut Swede T-shirts in mass quantities.

Svenskt Tenn ARTS, HOMEWARES
(Map p48; www.svenskttenn.se; Nybrogatan 15; 10am-6.30pm Mon-Fri, 10am-5pm Sat, noon-4pm Sun) As much a museum of design as an actual shop, this iconic store is home to the signature fabrics and furniture of Josef Frank and his contemporaries. Browsing here is a great way to get a quick handle on what people mean by 'classic Swedish design' – and it's owned by a foundation that contributes heavily to arts funding.

Svensk Slöjd ARTS, HANDICRAFTS
(Map p48; Nybrogatan 23; 10am-6pm Mon-Fri, 11am-6pm Sat; M Östermalmstorg) If you like the traditional Swedish wooden horses but want one that looks a little unique (or maybe you'd prefer a traditional wooden chicken instead?), check out this shop. It's crammed with quirky hand-carved knick-knacks as well as luxurious woven textiles, handmade candles, ironwork, knitted clothing and other high-quality gifts.

Studio Lena M GIFTS
(Map p44; www.lenamdesign.se; Kindstugan 14; M Gamla Stan) This tiny, dimly lit shop is crammed with adorable prints and products featuring the graphic design work of Lena M, as well as other likeminded artists. It's a great place to find a unique – and uniquely Swedish – gift to bring home, or even just a cute postcard.

Papercut BOOKS
(08-13 35 74; www.papercutshop.se; Krukmakargatan 24; 11am-6.30pm Mon-Fri, 11am-5pm Sat, noon-4pm Sun, closed Sun Jul; M Zinkensdamm) This artfully curated shop sells books, magazines and DVDs with a high-end pop-culture focus. Pick up a new Field Notes journal and a decadent film journal or a gorgeous volume devoted to one of the many elements of style.

Nordiska Galleriet ARTS, CRAFTS
(Map p48; www.nordiskagalleriet.se; Nybrogatan 11; 10am-6pm Mon-Fri, 10am-5pm Sat, noon-4pm Sun; M Östermalmstorg) This sprawling showroom is a design freak's El Dorado – think Hannes Wettstein chairs, Hella Jongerius sofas, Alvar Aalto vases and miniature Verner Panton chairs for style-sensitive kids. Luggage-friendly options include designer coathangers, glossy architecture books and bright Marimekko paper napkins.

Chokladfabriken CHOCOLATE
(Map p58; www.chokladfabriken.com; Renstiernas Gata 12; 10am-6.30pm Mon-Fri, 10am-5pm Sat;

SWEDISH DESIGN

Now that Ingvar Kamprad's unmistakably huge blue-and-yellow Ikea stores are sprouting up all over the world, Swedish design may have lost some of its exotic appeal. But that just means more people can know the sleek, utilitarian joy of invisible drawers, paper chandeliers and round squares.

Most of the clever designs Ikea brings to the masses originated among Stockholm's relentlessly inventive designers, and you can see these artifacts in their undiluted form all over the city in museums, shops, and a few shops that are so exclusive they may as well be museums.

Functional elegance defines Swedish design, although in recent decades a refreshing tendency towards the whimsical has lightened the mood. For a good collection of design objects arranged chronologically and by theme, head to Nordiska Museet (p51). You can also find examples of both historic and contemporary design at upmarket shops like Svenskt Tenn (above), home to floral fabric prints by design legend Josef Frank, and Nordiska Galleriet (above), with its dizzying array of neat things to look at.

Södermalm's main drag, Götgatan, is home to democratically priced **DesignTorget** (Map p58; Götgatan 31) as well as the iconic **10 Swedish Designers** (Tiogruppen; Map p58; 08-643 25 04; Götgatan 25). Known in Swedish as Tiogruppen, 10 Swedish Designers started in 1970 when a band of young textile designers (notably Tom Hedqvist) introduced unapologetically bold, geometric patterns. These days, their eye-catching graphics cover tote bags, wallets, cushions, plates and napkins.

M Medborgarplatsen, Slussen) For an edible souvenir, head to this chocolate shop, where seasonal Nordic ingredients are used to make heavenly treats. In addition to chocolate boxes and hot-cocoa mix in gift boxes, there's a cafe for an on-the-spot fix, occasional tastings, and a stash of speciality ingredients and utensils for home baking.

Science Fiction Bookshop BOOKS

(Map p44; www.sfbok.se; Västerlånggatan 48; 10am-7pm Mon-Fri, to 5pm Sat, noon-5pm Sun; M Gamla Stan) In some ways this seems an unlikely location for a science fiction–fantasy comic bookshop, but in other ways it makes perfect sense. Regardless, this is the place to come for comics and graphic novels both mainstream and obscure (in English and Swedish), as well as books, games, toys and posters. Friendly staff will help you find obscure treasures.

Hedengrens BOOKS

(Map p48; 08-611 51 32; Sturegallerian Shopping Centre; 10am-7pm Mon-Fri, 10am-5pm Sat, noon-5pm Sun; M Östermalmstorg) Inside this upmarket Östermalm shopping mall is this great bookstore, with a huge selection of new fiction and nonfiction books in English.

Kartbutiken MAPS

(Map p48; 08-20 23 03; www.kartbutiken.se; Mäster Samuelsgatan 54; 10am-6pm Mon-Fri, 10am-4pm Sat, noon-4pm Sun; M T-Centralen) This huge, helpful store has all kinds of maps and guidebooks for Scandinavia and elsewhere, from urban centres to remote hiking areas, plus a variety of gifts and gadgets.

Naturkompaniet OUTDOOR EQUIPMENT

(Map p48; www.naturkompaniet.se; Kungsgatan 4; 10am-6.30pm Mon-Fri, 10am-5pm Sat, noon-4pm Sun; M Östermalmstorg) Find everything you might need for an excursion into the Swedish wilderness here, from backpacks and sleeping bags to woolly socks, headlamps, cooking stoves and compasses. There are several other locations across the city.

PUB DEPARTMENT STORE

(Map p48; Drottninggatan 72-6; 10am-7pm Mon-Fri, 10am-6pm Sat, 11am-5pm Sun; M T-Hötorget) Historic department store PUB is best known as the former workplace of Greta Garbo, and advertisements still work that angle pretty strongly. It's a major fashion and lifestyle hub, carrying fresh Nordic labels like Stray Boys, House of Dagmar and Baum & Pferdgarten. Refuel at the slinky cafe-bar.

Åhléns DEPARTMENT STORE

(Map p48; 08-676 60 00; Klarabergsgatan 50; 10am-9pm Mon-Fri, 10am-7pm Sat, 11am-7pm Sun; M T-Centralen) For your all-in-one retail therapy, scour department-store giant Åhléns.

NK DEPARTMENT STORE

(Map p48; 08-762 80 00; www.nk.se; Hamngatan 12-18; 10am-8pm Mon-Fri, 10am-6pm Sat, 11am-5pm Sun; M T-Centralen) An ultraclassy department store founded in 1902, NK (Nordiska Kompaniet) is a city landmark – you can see its rotating neon sign from most parts of Stockholm. You'll find top-name brands and several nice cafes, and the basement levels are great for stocking up on souvenirs and gourmet groceries. Around Christmas, check out its inventive window displays.

Information

EMERGENCY

24-Hour Medical Advice (08-32 01 00)

24-Hour Police Stations Kungsholmen (08-401 00 00; Kungsholmsgatan 37); Södermalm (08-401 03 00; Torkel Knutssonsgatan 20).

AutoAssistans (020-53 65 36) Roadside assistance for vehicle breakdowns.

Emergency (112) Toll-free access to the fire service, police and ambulance.

INTERNET ACCESS

Nearly all hostels and most hotels have a computer or two with internet access for guests, and most offer wi-fi in rooms (though occasionally hotels charge a fee). There is also wi-fi in Centralstationen (requiring a paid account), and most coffee shops offer free wi-fi to customers. Those without their own computer have fewer options, but most public libraries offer internet access (you may need to sign up for a free membership card).

MEDIA

Dagens Nyheter (www.dn.se) Daily paper with a great culture section and a weekend event listing ('På Stan'). The website (in Swedish) is a good place to look for bar and restaurant news.

Nöjesguiden (www.nojesguiden.se) Entertainment and pop-culture news and event listings.

Svenska Dagbladet (www.svd.se) Daily news, in Swedish.

MEDICAL SERVICES

Apoteket CW Scheele (www.apoteket.se; Klarabergsgatan 64; M T-Centralen) A 24-hour pharmacy located close to T-Centralen.

CityAkuten (☎ 020-150 150; www.cityakuten.se; Apelbergsgatan 48; ⏲ 8am-6pm Mon-Thu, to 5pm Fri, 10am-3pm Sat) Emergency health and dental care.

Södersjukhuset (☎ 08-616 10 00; www.soderjukhuset.se; Ringvägen 52) The most central hospital.

MONEY

ATMs are plentiful, with several at Centralstationen and all the airports; expect queues on Friday and Saturday evenings in the downtown area.

The exchange company Forex has over a dozen branches in the capital and charges Skr15 per travellers cheque.

Forex-Vasagatan (Vasagatan 16; ⏲ 5.30am-10pm Sun-Fri, to 6pm Sat) Near the tourist office and Centralstationen. There's also a branch in Terminal 2 at Arlanda airport.

POST

You can buy stamps and send letters at most newsagents and supermarkets – keep an eye out for the Swedish postal symbol (yellow on a blue background). There's a convenient outlet next to the Hemköp supermarket in the basement of central department store Åhléns (p82).

TELEPHONE

Smartphones are ubiquitous in Stockholm; hence, coin-operated public telephones are virtually nonexistent. The few remaining payphones are operated with phonecards purchased from Pressbyrån newsagents (or with a credit card, although this is ludicrously expensive). Ask for a *telefon kort* for Skr50 or Skr120, which roughly equates to 50 minutes or 120 minutes of local talk time, respectively. (Be sure to specify you're using the card on a payphone, not refilling a mobile phone.) For mobile phones, check with your service provider to ensure your network is compatible with Sweden's. In many cases you can buy a local SIM card to use in your own phone. Barring that, it may be worthwhile to buy a cheap mobile phone you can load with prepaid minutes and use as needed.

TOURIST INFORMATION

Stockholm Visitors Center (Map p48; ☎ 08-508 28 508; www.visitstockholm.com; Kulturhuset, Sergels Torg 3; ⏲ 9am-7pm Mon-Fri, to 6pm winter, 9am-4pm Sat, 10am-4pm Sun; Ⓜ T-Centralen) The main visitors centre occupies a space inside Kulturhuset on Sergels Torg.

Visit Djurgården (Map p56; ☎ 08-667 77 01; www.visitdjurgarden.se; Djurgårdsvägen 2; ⏲ 9am-dusk) With tourist information specific to Djurgården, this office at the edge of the Djurgården bridge is attached to Sjöcaféet (p61), so you can grab a bite or a beverage as you plot your day.

> **PAY TO PEE**
>
> Most public toilets charge Skr5 or Skr10, payable with Skr5 or Skr10 coins, so keep a few handy.

Getting There & Away

AIR

Stockholm's main airport, **Stockholm Arlanda** (☎ 10-109 10 00; www.swedavia.se/arlanda), is 45km north of the city centre and can be reached from central Stockholm by both bus and express train. It has self-service **lockers** for luggage storage (small/medium/large locker for 24 hours Skr40/50/80), payable with a credit card. There's also a **baggage counter** (☎ 08-797 62 28; ⏲ 6am-11pm).

Bromma Airport (☎ 797 68 00; Ⓜ Brommaplan) is 8km west of Stockholm and is used for some domestic flights. Skavsta Airport (p330), 100km south of Stockholm, near Nyköping, is mostly used by low-cost carriers like Ryanair.

BOAT

Both **Silja Line** (☎ 22 21 40; www.tallinksilja.com; Silja & Tallink Customer Service Office, Cityterminalen) and Viking Line (p332) run ferries to Turku and Helsinki. Tallink (p332) ferries head to Tallinn (Estonia) and Riga (Latvia).

BUS

Most long-distance buses arrive at and depart from **Cityterminalen** (Map p48; www.cityterminalen.com; ⏲ 7am-6pm), which is connected to Centralstationen. The main counter sells tickets for several bus companies, including Flygbussarna (airport coaches).

CAR & MOTORCYCLE

The E4 motorway passes through the city, just west of the centre, on its way from Helsingborg to Haparanda. The E20 motorway from Stockholm to Göteborg via Örebro follows the E4 as far as Södertälje. The E18 from Kapellskär to Oslo runs from east to west and passes just north of central Stockholm.

TRAIN

Stockholm is the hub for national train services run by **Sveriges Järnväg** (SJ; ☎ 0771-75 75 75; www.sj.se). Luggage can be stored in the **lockers** on the lower level of **Central Station** (Ⓜ T-Centralen) .

Getting Around

TO/FROM THE AIRPORT

The Arlanda Express (p67) train service from Centralstationen takes 20 minutes to reach Arlanda; trains run every 10 to 15 minutes from about 5am to 12.30am (less frequently after 9pm). In peak summer season (mid-June to August), two adults can travel together for Skr280.

The same trip in a taxi costs around Skr520; agree on the fare first and don't use taxis without a contact telephone number displayed. Taxi Stockholm is one reputable operator. **Airport Cab** (☎ 08-25 25 25; www.airportcab.se) goes from Stockholm to Arlanda for a flat fee of Skr365 to Skr390, and in the opposite direction for Skr475.

A cheaper option is the **Flygbuss** (www.flygbussarna.se) service between Stockholm Arlanda and Cityterminalen. Buses (Skr119, 50 minutes, every 10 or 15 minutes) leave from stop 11 in Terminal 5. Tickets can be purchased online, at Cityterminalen or at the Flygbuss self-service machine in Terminal 5.

BICYCLE

Bicycles can be carried free on SL local trains as foldable 'hand luggage' only. They're not allowed in Centralstationen or on the tunnelbana, although you'll occasionally see some daring souls.

Stockholm City Bikes (p60) has self-service bicycle-hire stands across the city. Bikes can be borrowed for three-hour stretches and returned at any City Bikes stand. Purchase a bike card online or from the tourist office. Rechargeable season cards are valid April to October.

BOAT

Djurgårdsfärjan city ferry services connect Gröna Lund Tivoli on Djurgården Nybroplan (summer only) and Slussen (year-round) as frequently as every 10 minutes in summer (and less frequently at other times); a single trip costs Skr36 (free with an SL transport pass).

CAR & MOTORCYCLE

Driving in central Stockholm is not recommended. Skinny one-way streets, congested bridges and limited parking all present problems; note that Djurgårdsvägen is closed near Skansen at night, on summer weekends and some holidays. Don't attempt driving through the narrow streets of Gamla Stan.

Parking is a hassle, but there are *P-hus* (parking stations) throughout the city; they charge up to Skr100 per hour, though the fixed evening rate is usually lower.

PUBLIC TRANSPORT

Storstockholms Lokaltrafik (SL; ☎ 08-600 10 00; www.sl.se; Centralstationen, Sergels Torg; single trip Skr25-50, unlimited 24hr/72hr/7-day pass Skr115/230/300, students & seniors half-price) SL runs all tunnelbana (metro) trains, local trains and buses within Stockholm county. You can buy tickets and passes at SL counters, ticket machines at tunnelbana stations, and Pressbyrå kiosks. Tickets cannot be bought on buses. Fines are steep (Skr1200) for travelling without a valid ticket. Refillable SL travel cards (Skr20) can be loaded with single-trip or unlimited-travel credit.

The Stockholm Card (p46) covers travel on all SL trains and buses. International rail passes (eg Scanrail, Interrail) aren't valid on SL trains. Kids under age seven travel free with an adult.

Inner-city buses radiate from Sergels Torg, Odenplan, Fridhemsplan (on Kungsholmen) and Slussen. Bus 47 runs from Sergels Torg to Djurgården, and bus 69 from Centralstationen and Sergels Torg to the Ladugårdsgärdet museums and Kaknästornet. Useful buses for hostellers include bus 65 (Centralstationen to Skeppsholmen) and bus 43 (Regeringsgatan to Södermalm).

Pendeltåg (local trains) are most useful for connections to Nynäshamn (for ferries to Gotland), Märsta (for buses to Sigtuna) and Uppsala (requires supplemental fee).

The historic No 7 tram (and its sleek modern siblings) runs between Norrmalmstorg and Skansen, passing most attractions on Djurgården. SL passes are valid.

TAXI

Taxis are readily available but expensive, so check for a meter or arrange the fare first. The flag fall is around Skr45, then Skr10 to Skr13 per kilometre. (A 10km ride that takes 15 minutes should cost around Skr230 to Skr250.) At night, women travelling alone should ask about *tjej-taxa*, a discount rate offered by some operators. Use one of the established, reputable firms, such as **Taxi Stockholm** (☎ 08-15 00 00; www.taxistockholm.se), **Taxi 020** (☎ 020-20 20 20; www.taxi020.se) or **Taxi Kurir** (☎ 0771-86 00 00; www.taxikurir.se).

AROUND STOCKHOLM

With royal palaces, vintage villages and Viking traces, the greater Stockholm county is certainly worth a venture or three. Conveniently, SL travel passes allow unlimited travel on all buses and local trains in the area. Free timetables are available from the SL office in Centralstationen, most tunnelbana stations and the SL website.

Just to the east of Stockholm, the magical islands of the Stockholm archipelago have inspired the likes of writer August Strindberg and artist Anders Zorn. Ferry services aren't expensive and there's a travel pass available if you fancy a spot of island-hopping.

Drottningholm

The royal residence and parks of Drottningholm on Lovön are justifiably popular attractions and easy to visit from the capital.

Sights

Drottningholm Slott PALACE

(☎08-402 62 80; www.kungahuset.se; adult/child Skr120/free, combined ticket incl Chinese Pavillion Skr180/free; ⏰10am-4.30pm May-Aug, 11am-3.30pm rest of year, closed mid-Dec–Jan; P; M Brommaplan, then bus 301-323 Drottningholm, ⛴ Stadshuskajen summer only) Home to the royal family for part of the year, Drottningholm's Renaissance-inspired main **palace** was designed by architectural great Nicodemus Tessin the Elder and begun in 1662, about the same time as Versailles. You can roam on your own, but it's worth taking a one-hour guided tour (Skr10; in English at 10am, noon, 2pm and 4pm June to August, noon and 2pm other months). Guides are entertaining, and provide insight into the cultural milieu that influenced some of the decorations.

The Lower North Corps de Garde was originally a guard room, but it's now replete with gilt-leather wall hangings, which used to feature in many palace rooms during the 17th century. The Karl X Gustav Gallery, in baroque style, depicts this monarch's militaristic exploits, though the ceiling shows classical battle scenes. The highly ornamented State Bedchamber of Hedvig Eleonora is Sweden's most expensive baroque interior, decorated with paintings that feature the childhood of Karl XI. The painted ceiling shows Karl X and his queen, Hedvig Eleonora.

Although the bulk of Lovisa Ulrika's collection of 2000 books has been moved to the Royal Library in Stockholm for safe keeping, her library here is still a bright and impressive room, complete with most of its original 18th-century fittings.

The palace's elaborate staircase, with statues and trompe l'œil embellishments at every turn, was the work of both Nicodemus Tessin the Elder and the Younger. The geometric gardens, angled to impress, are well worth exploring.

Drottningholms Slottsteater & Teatermuseum MUSEUM

(Court Theatre & Museum; www.dtm.se; entry by tour adult/child Skr100/free; ⏰tours hourly noon-3.30pm Fri-Sun Apr & Oct, 11am-4.30pm May-Aug,

Drottningholm

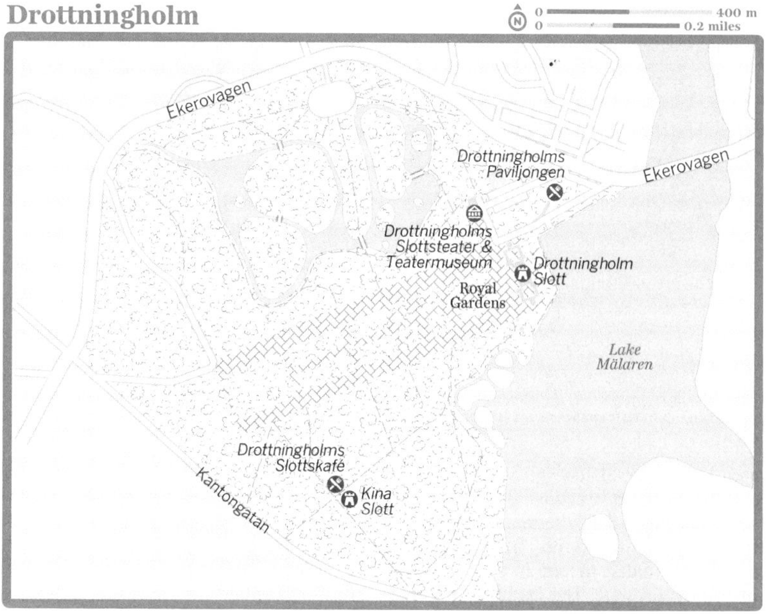

Around Stockholm

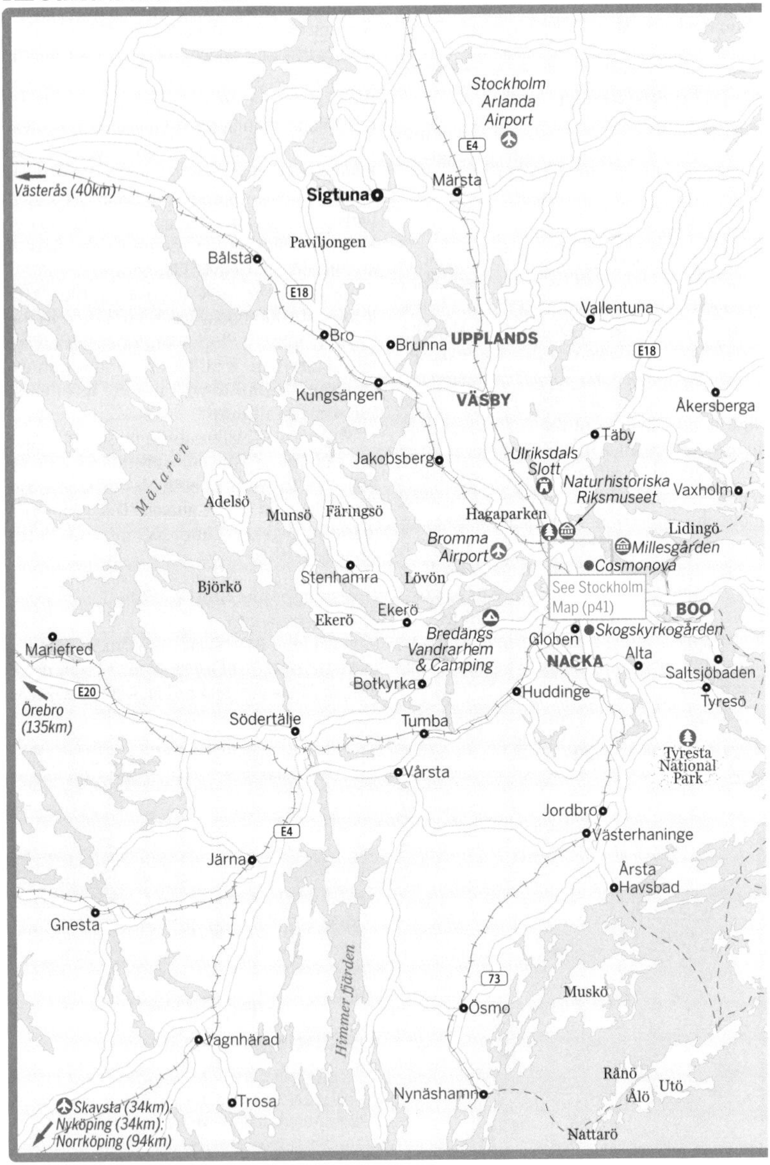

noon-3.30pm Sep) Slottsteater was completed in 1766 on the instructions of Queen Lovisa Ulrika. Remarkably untouched from the time of Gustav III's death (1792) until 1922, it's now the oldest theatre in the world still in its original state. The fascinating guided tour takes you into other rooms in the building, where highlights include hand-painted 18th-century wallpaper and an Italianate room (*salon de déjeuner*) with fake three-dimensional wall effects and a ceiling that looks like the sky.

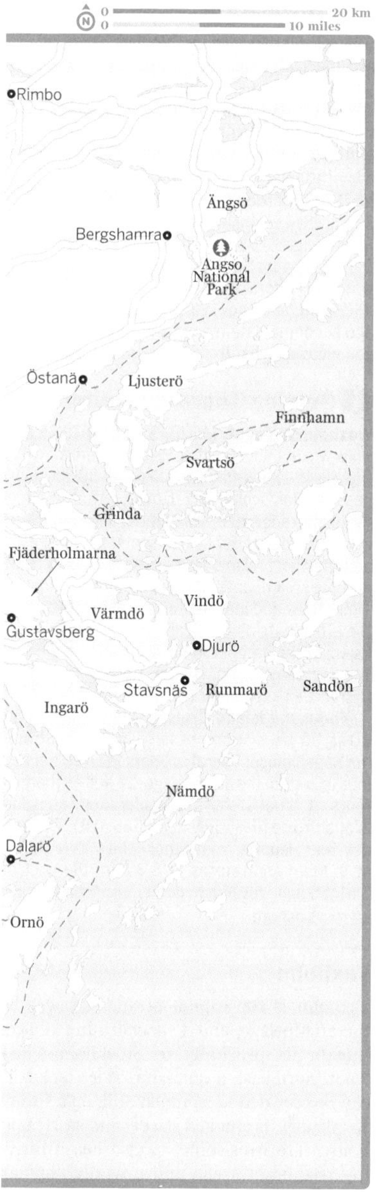

Performances are held at **Drottningholms Slottsteater** (www.dtm.se; tickets Skr300-995) in summer using 18th-century machinery, including ropes, pulleys, wagons and wind machines. Scenes can be changed in less than seven seconds! Illusion was the order of the day, and accordingly the theatre makes use of fake marble, fake curtains and papier mâché viewing boxes. Even the stage was designed to create illusions regarding size.

Kina Slott CASTLE

(Chinese Pavilion; adult/child Skr100/free, combined ticket incl royal palace Skr180/free; ⌚11am-4.30pm) At the far end of the royal gardens is Kina Slott, a lavishly decorated Chinese pavilion built by King Adolf Fredrik as a birthday surprise for Queen Lovisa Ulrika in 1753. Restored between 1989 and 1996, it boasts one of the finest rococo chinoiserie interiors in Europe. The admission price includes guided tours, which run at 11am, 1pm and 3pm daily from June to August (fewer in May and September). There's a cafe on the premises serving good waffles.

On the slope below Kina Slott, the carnivalesque **Guards' Tent** was erected in 1781 as quarters for the dragoons of Gustav III, but it's not really a tent at all (another illusion).

Eating

Bring a picnic with you and enjoy lunch out in the gardens, or munch away at one of the restaurants by the palace.

Drottningholms Paviljongen CAFE €€

(☎08-759 04 25; light meals Skr85-120, mains Skr155-250; ⌚lunch & dinner) Close to the boat dock, this cafe offers light meals like sandwiches and heartier mains, as well as coffee and cakes. Outdoor seating lends the place a garden-party vibe.

Drottningholms Slottskafé SWEDISH €€

(☎08-759 00 35; Drottningholm; mains Skr110-265; ⌚9.30am-5pm May-Aug, 11am-4pm rest of year) Within the palace grounds, this cafe-restaurant serves coffee and pastries as well as full meals, with both indoor and outdoor seating for plenty of atmosphere.

Getting There & Away

If you're not short of time you can cycle out to the palace along a well-marked path. Otherwise, take the tunnelbana to Brommaplan and change to any bus numbered between 301 and 323 (SL passes are valid). For a more scenic and leisurely approach, Strömma Kanalbolaget (p61) will take you to the palace by boat (about an hour one way, Skr145; round trip Skr195). Frequent services depart from Stadshusbron (Stockholm) daily between May and mid-September, with less frequent departures in September and October. A combined ticket (Skr375) includes return travel and admission to the palace and Chinese Pavilion.

Stockholm Archipelago

Mention the archipelago to Stockholmers and prepare for gushing adulation. Buffering the city from the open Baltic Sea, it's a mesmerising wonderland of rocky isles carpeted with deep forests and fields of wildflowers, dotted with yachts and little red wooden cottages. Exactly how many islands there are is debatable, with headcounts ranging from 14,000 to 100,000 (the general consensus is 24,000). Whatever the number, it's an unmissable area and much closer to the city than many visitors imagine, with regular ferry services and various tours.

There are essentially two ways to visit the archipelago, depending on your preferred travel style: if time is short, take a boat tour of anywhere from a few hours to a full day, passing several islands and making brief stops at one or two. Otherwise, you can arrange your own longer, slower self-guided trip with overnight stays. The area's many comfortable hostels, campsites and cushy hotels – plus some excellent restaurants – make the latter option dreamy if you have a few days to spare.

(Keep in mind that most of the island villages are very remote, with limited options for dining and groceries; bring some provisions along. There are also bar-restaurants on the boats.)

If you're not on an organised tour, it can be tricky to figure out how to reach a particular island. Confusion is augmented by the fact that summer boat schedules aren't published until a week before they take effect, which makes it challenging to plan travel between islands. Planning is essential, though, as you'll want to book accommodation well in advance. Luckily, though the timetables change, the routes are consistent year to year.

Waxholmsbolaget (p88), the main provider for island traffic, divides the archipelago into three sections: middle, north and south. Within each section, several numbered routes go out and back, usually once a day, calling at various ports along the way. (Think of them as rural bus routes, but on water.) The Waxholmsbolaget office in Stockholm has maps and timetables for all routes and helpful staff to answer questions. And there's a useful trip planner on its website.

Information

Skärgårdsstiftelsen (Archipelago Foundation; archipelagofoundation.se) With a focus on conservation and sustainable development more than tourism, the foundation manages the nature reserves within the archipelago. It owns and oversees a number of hostels and historic sites throughout the islands.

Visit Skärgården (Map p56; ☎08-52 22 27 22; www.visitskargarden.se; Kajplats 18, Strandvägen; ⏲9am-5pm Mon-Fri, 10am-4pm Sat, 11am-4pm Sun; Ⓜ T-Ropsten) This new waterside information centre in Stockholm can advise on (and book) various types of archipelago accommodation and tours, as well as give you ideas on what to see and do.

Getting There & Around

Waxholmsbolaget (Map p48; ☎08-679 58 30; www.waxholmsbolaget.se; Strömkajen; single trip Skr45-130, 5-day pass Skr440, 30-day pass regular/senior Skr770/470; ⏲8am-6pm; Ⓜ Kungsträdgården) Waxholmsbolaget is the main provider of public transportation in the archipelago. It also operates tours on beautiful antique steamboats; check schedules online. Timetables and information are available from the office outside the Grand Hôtel on Strömkajen, at the harbour in Vaxholm and online. The company also runs ferries to and from Djurgården in summer (SL passes are valid).

Thousand Island Cruise (Map p48; ☎08-12 00 40 00; www.stromma.se; Nybrokajen) Strömma Kanalbolaget operates boats to and from various islands in the archipelago, as well as themed tours. If time is short, consider the Thousand Island Cruise (daily July to mid-August). The full-day tour departs from Stockholm's Nybrokajen at 9.30am and returns at 8.30pm; the cost of Skr1150 includes lunch, dinner, drinks and guided tours ashore.

Vaxholm

Vaxholm is the capital of and gateway to the archipelago, and it's a charming village, though its proximity to Stockholm (just 35km northeast, a quick bus ride) means it can be crowded in summer. Still, on a sunny spring day, its crooked streets and storybook houses are irresistible. It also has a thriving restaurant scene and a wildly popular Christmas market. Boat fiends should plan to check out Archipelago Boat Day on the first Wednesday in June (book ahead). If you plan an overnight stay, the tourist office keeps a list of private B&Bs.

The town of Vaxholm was founded in 1647 and has about 11,000 inhabitants. The oldest buildings are in Norrhamn, a few minutes' walk north of the town hall. Equally photogenic is Hamngatan, awash with interesting architecture, galleries, boutiques and souvenir shops. Vaxholm's most prominent feature, however, is its hulking fortress, built in 1548 to defend the northern sea approach to Stockholm. (It worked, too: when the Russian navy attacked in 1719, nearly all archipelago settlements were burned to the ground, but the invasion never reached the Swedish capital.)

Sights

Vaxholm Fortress Museum HISTORIC SITE, MUSEUM
(☎08-54 17 18 90; www.vaxholmsfastning.se; Vaxholm Kastellet; adult/child Skr60/free; ⌚12.15-4pm Jun, 11.15am-5pm Jul & Aug) King Gustav Vasa ordered the construction of Vaxholm Fortress in 1544 to protect the Swedish capital and mainland. It repelled an attack by the Danes in 1612 and the Russians in 1719, among others. It was a prison from the mid-18th century until 1842. Occupying an islet just east of town, it's now home to a museum and a B&B. The ferry to the island leaves Vaxholm harbour every 20 minutes from 11am to 5pm and costs Skr50 return.

Hembygdsgård MUSEUM
(☎08-54 13 19 80; Trädgårdsgatan 19; ⌚11am-4pm Sat & Sun May-Aug) FREE The Hembygdsgård preserves the finest old houses in Norrhamn. The **fiskarebostad** is an excellent example of a late-19th-century fisherman's house, complete with typical Swedish fireplace. The award-winning cafe here is open daily from mid-May to mid-September.

Sleeping & Eating

Supermarkets and a liquor store are on Hamngatan.

Vaxholm/Bogesunds Slottsvandrarhem HOSTEL €
(☎08-54 17 50 60; www.bogesundsslottsvandrarhem.se; Bogesunds Gård; beds from Skr205; P @ ; 681 Bogesunds Gård) Behind Bogesunds Castle 5.5km southwest of Vaxholm, this pleasant STF hostel has a pretty, farm-like setting. There's a nice guest kitchen, but you'll need to get groceries in Vaxholm. Bus service to the hostel is infrequent even in summer; buses depart Vaxholm's Söderhamnsplan at 11am, 2.12pm, 5.20pm and 6.40pm Monday to Friday, and 11.40am, 2.40pm and 5.40pm on weekends.

Vaxholms Bakery BREAKFAST €
(Vaxholmsbagarna; ☎08-54 13 18 72; Söderhamnen 6; breakfast buffet Skr70, pastries from Skr20; ⌚6am-8pm Mon-Sat, 8am-6pm Sun) This comfy bakery-cafe at the edge of the harbour serves an excellent-value breakfast buffet, simple but filling, as well as good coffee, sandwiches and other baked goods. It's an obvious neighborhood favourite, with steady traffic throughout the morning.

Waxholms Hotell SWEDISH €€
(☎08-54 13 01 50; www.waxholmshotell.se; Hamngatan 2; dagens lunch Skr105, mains Skr159-355; ⌚noon-10.30pm, to 9pm Sun) In a historic building opposite the harbour, grand Waxholms offers fine dining and unbelievable views. Grab a pint in the vaguely British woodsman-esque lobby bar or head upstairs to the formal dining room. In summer stop for lunch on the popular outdoor terrace at Kabyssen bar-cafe – the fish dishes are highly recommended (Baltic herring is a speciality).

Discounted rooms with half and full board are available here in July and on weekends year-round (singles/doubles with half board from Skr1150/1425, with full board Skr1500/2125).

Melanders Fisk SEAFOOD €€
(☎08-54 13 34 66; Hamngatan 2; mains from Skr130; ⌚10am-6pm Mon-Fri, to 3pm Sat & Sun) On the waterfront, Melanders Fisk is a seafood market that includes a cafe serving quality grub. If there's a fish stew on the day's menu, don't miss it, but any seafood dish here is bound to be satisfying.

Information

Banks, ATMs and other services are on Hamngatan.

Tourist office (☎08-54 13 14 80; www.vaxholm.se; Rådhuset; ⌚10am-6pm Mon-Fri, to 4pm Sat & Sun) The tourist office is located inside the *rådhus* (town hall), off Hamngatan; look for the onion dome, a product of the *rådhus* rebuilding in 1925.

Getting There & Away

Bus 670 from the Tekniska Högskolan tunnelbana station runs regularly to Vaxholm's town centre and harbour. (SL passes valid.)

Waxholmsbolaget (p88) boats sail at least hourly between Vaxholm and Strömkajen in Stockholm from 8am to 7.15pm (50 to 70 minutes, Skr75 one way).

Strömma Kanalbolaget (p61) sails between Strandvägen (berth 16) and Vaxholm at noon and 3pm daily from April to December (three hours, Skr250 round trip).

Utö

Star of the archipelago's southern section, Utö has it all: sublime sandy beaches, lush fairy-tale forests, sleepy farms, abundant bird life and a highly rated restaurant. Dining and accommodation are in Gruvbryggan, the island's northernmost village and its main ferry stop, but exploring further afield is rewarding. At 13km long and up to 4km wide, Utö's network of roads and tracks make for heavenly cycling sessions; ask at the guest harbour about cycle hire.

⊙ Sights & Activities

Most of the activity happens at the northern end of the island, near Gruvbryggan. Follow signs from the harbour to the various attractions. The well-preserved, 18th-century miners' houses on Lurgatan are worth a peek, while the Dutch-style windmill has beautiful coastal views. And there are some impressive glaciated rock slabs a 20-minute walk along a forest path toward Rävstavik.

Iron Mine MINE

(⊙24hr) The most unusual of Utö's sights is the remains of Sweden's oldest iron mine, which opened in 1150 but closed in 1879. The three pits are now flooded – the deepest is Nyköpingsgruvan (215m). They're an atmospheric and impressive sight. The mining museum (in a wooden cottage opposite the Värdshus hotel) keeps variable hours (roughly 11am to 3pm in summer), so check locally.

Stora Sand BEACH

The best sandy beach is Stora Sand on the south coast; it's a gorgeous 40-minute bike ride from the Värdshus hotel. Routes to the beach are occasionally closed due to military training exercises; ask at the tourist office or Värdshus front desk for updates.

⊨ Sleeping & Eating

Utö Värdshus HOTEL, HOSTEL, CABINS €€€

(☑08-50 42 03 00; www.utovardshus.se; Gruvbryggan; hostel s/d Skr425/850, 2-person chalets incl breakfast per person from Skr995, hotel s/d Skr1750/2300) This is the only hotel on the island, with good facilities and a sterling gourmet restaurant (closed January; mains from Skr200). It also runs the very pretty STF

hostel, with comfy bunks in smallish rooms overlooking the picturesque harbour. (Note there's no lift, and rooms on four floors.) Hostelers can purchase the hotel's elaborate breakfast buffet (Skr150).

Utö Bageri BAKERY €€

(breakfast Skr80-120, lunch Skr140, sandwiches Skr40-70; ⊙8am-5pm) This adorable bakery in a cottage by the harbour serves what might be the best cup of coffee in Sweden, as well as champion baked goods (don't pass up the cardamom *bulle*), delicious and filling sandwiches, fruit smoothies and hot meals. Show up before 9am or so to beat the crowds.

Nya Dannekrogen EUROPEAN €€

(☑08-50 15 70 79; www.nyadannekrogen.se; Bygatan 1; mains Skr150-250; ⊙May-Sep) Near the Gruvbryggan harbour, this lively restaurant looks formal but has a young, casual vibe, with grub ranging from hearty fish stew to polenta. The fried herring (Skr175) with lingonberries and mashed potatoes is recommended; weirdly, pizza seems to be the most popular thing on the menu.

ⓘ Information

Tourist office (☑08-50 15 74 10; ⊙10am-4pm May-Sep) You can get a map of the island from the tourist office, found in a small cabin by the guest harbour at Gruvbryggan (the northernmost village). When the tourist office is closed, ask at the Värdshus hotel, just up the hill.

ⓘ Getting There & Away

There are two options to reach Utö:

➡ Waxholmsbolaget (p88) – departs Strömkajen at 8.45am daily in summer (Skr130, four hours); return trip departs Gruvbryggan at 3.30pm.

➡ SL *pendeltåg* – Stockholm Centralstationen to Västerhaninge (30 minutes, frequent), then bus 846 to Årsta brygga (15 minutes, frequent), then Waxholmsbolaget ferry to Utö (Skr75, 45 minutes, eight times daily in summer). Check that your boat stops at Gruvbryggan. Return ferries leave Gruvbryggan for Årsta brygga eight times daily from 6.45am to 8.30pm.

Arholma

Arholma is a quiet, idyllic island in the archipelago's far north. Everything was burnt down during a Russian invasion in 1719. The landmark lighthouse was rebuilt in the 19th century and is now an art gallery with impressive views. A popular resort in the early 20th century, Arholma has a moneyed yet agricultural feel. There are green pastures, walking trails, sandy beaches and rocky bathing spots.

The hike up to the lighthouse (called Båkan) is a bit challenging; it's a steep path cut into the stone. The old chapel (open 10am to 8pm) is more easily reachable. For more great views, check out **Batteri Arholma** (tours in English at 10am, 11.15am, 1.30pm, 2.45pm and 4pm in summer, tours Skr100/50 per adult/child), adjoining the Archipelago Lodge (access to the viewpoint itself is free). There's also a 5km walking path through the forested northern section of the island; ask for a map at either hostel.

Sleeping & Eating

★ **Bull-August Vandrarhem** HOSTEL €
(☎0176-560 18; www.bullaugust.se; Arholma Södra Byväg 8; s/d from Skr340/575) This sweet, comfortable hostel is a treat. Rooms are in a refurbished old homestead about 1km from the harbour, some in the main house and some in rustic wooden side buildings. The guest kitchen is huge and modern, and there's a comfy TV room, as well as laundry, bicycle rental, a sunny grassy courtyard and an exceptionally nice hostess.

Breakfast, served in a lovely tent in the grassy yard, is easily worth the extra Skr75.

Arholma Nord Archipelago Lodge HOSTEL €€
(☎08-017 65 62 40; www.arholmanord.se; Riddarviken; s/d from Skr550/980; ⏲year-round; P 📶) This hotel-hostel complex offers a variety of accommodation, most in simple bunk rooms but also a few really nice cabins. Price includes breakfast and bedding. There's a sauna, outdoor grill, bicycle and kayak rentals (from Skr50/250), small restaurant, and access to a little swimming beach. Tours to Arholma's Cold War defence battery are booked here. It's about 1.2km from the harbour, well signposted.

Arholma Dansbana SWEDISH €€
(☎073-521 55 01; Norra Bryggan 7; mains Skr155-185; ⏲from 5pm) The only dining option near the harbour, this hilltop restaurant offers amazing views from its glassed-in dining room as well as a few outdoor tables. Seating is arranged around a dance floor (hence the name), which can get lively on summer weekend nights. The menu is brief but well executed; try the seafood stew or the vegetarian special.

Getting There & Away

➡ Waxholmsbolaget (p88) – line 27 from Stockholm, via Vaxholm, Norrsund and Tjockö, is the long, scenic route to Arholma (Skr130, 4½ hours). Departs Strömkajen at 10am Monday to Friday, 8.45am weekends in summer. Return boat departs Arholma at 4.20pm Monday to Friday, 3.10pm Saturday, 4.15pm Sunday.

➡ SL – from Danderyds Sjukhus tunnelbana stop, take bus 676 to Norrtälje, then bus 636 to Simpnäs (three to six daily), and then make a 20-minute Waxholmsbolaget ferry crossing to the island (Skr45).

Finnhamn

This 900m-long island, northeast of Stockholm, combines lush woods and meadows with sheltered coves, rocky cliffs and visiting eagle owls. It's a popular summertime spot, but there are enough quiet corners to indulge your inner hermit.

There's a sauna (Skr100 per person per hour) near the beach that can be booked through the hostel. You can also rent kayaks there. Walking trails cover most of the island, taking in awesome panoramic views at various points. At the harbour there's a little shop (open until 7pm) where you can pick up basic groceries and snacks.

Sleeping & Eating

STF Vandrarhem Utsikten HOSTEL €
(☎08-54 24 62 12; www.finnhamn.se; dm/s/d Skr320/520/640; ⏲year-round; @ 📶) This hostel in a large wooden villa has a killer view ('Utsikten' means 'view'), tiny rooms and cheerful staff who go above and beyond. It's an old building, which means no lift and no soundproofing; if crowded it can get noisy. But it's fun and lively and an excellent base for exploring the island. Advance booking is essential.

The hostel is about 1km along a rough dirt track, well signposted from the harbour. It also has four-bed 'sea cabins' available just outside the hostel (from Skr1095). Campsites nearby cost Skr120 per night. Breakfast is available at the hostel for Skr90. And you can rent kayaks and rowboats – ask at reception about availability.

★ **Finnhamns Café & Krog** SWEDISH €€€
(☎08-54 24 62 12; www.finnhamn.se; Ingmarsö; starters Skr98-185, mains Skr175-265; ⏲11am-9pm Jun-Aug, weekends only rest of year) It may be the only game in town, but Finnhamns Krog doesn't use that as an excuse for slacking.

The kitchen and service are top notch: classy yet comfortable, and capable of transforming seafood into gold. Try the Finnhamns *tallrik* (Skr185), with several kinds of local fish, potatoes and all the fixin's. Sustainable ingredients are a priority. Reservations recommended for dinner.

There's also a rooftop bar here in summer, with live music weekend nights and a good selection of Swedish beers.

❶ Getting There & Away

➠ Waxholmsbolaget (p88) – Strömkajen to Finnhamn via Vaxholm (Skr130, three hours), three times daily in summer (twice on Saturday).

➠ Strömma Kanalbolaget (p61) – Strandvägen to Finnhamn (Skr165, two hours 10 minutes), twice daily May to September, with reduced services mid-April to early May.

Siaröfortet

The tiny island of Kyrkogårdsön, in the important sea lane just north of Ljusterö (40km due northeast of Stockholm), is one of the archipelago's most fascinating islands, and easy to visit on a day trip.

After the outbreak of WWI, military authorities decided that the Vaxholm fortress just didn't cut it, so construction of a new fort began on Kyrkogårdsön in 1916. Dubbed Siaröfortet, it's now a fascinating museum (www.blidosundsbolaget.se/siarofortet/; adult/child Skr50/30; ⊙10.30am-2pm Mon-Fri, to 5pm Sat & Sun May-Aug), where you can check out the officers' mess, kitchen, sleeping quarters and tunnels, plus two impressive 15.2cm cannons (they're trained on passing Viking Line ferries!). Fixed opening times vary by demand and season but are roughly 10am to 2pm; guided tours are available (Skr15 extra) through the STF hostel at 1pm Monday to Thursday, 12.30pm Friday and Saturday, and 3.30pm Sunday.

STF Vandrarhem Siaröfortet (☑08-24 30 90; kontoret@blidosundsbolaget.se; dm/s/d from Skr200/395/520; ⊙late Apr–mid-Oct) is an excellent hostel in the old soldiers' barracks. Canoe hire and breakfast are available; advance booking is recommended.

Blidösundsbolaget (☑08-24 30 90; www.blidosundsbolaget.se) ferries to Siaröfortet depart from Strömkajen in Stockholm and sail to Siaröfortet via Vaxholm around three times daily in the peak summer season (mid-June to mid-August), with greatly reduced services the rest of the year. The journey takes one hour and 45 minutes

from Stockholm (Skr100) and 50 minutes from Vaxholm (Skr50). The island is also a stop on the Waxholmsbolaget route toward Finnhamn.

Kapellskär

Kapellskär is so tiny it can't really even be described as a village – there's little to it except for a campsite, a hostel and a large ferry terminal. The coastline, however, is spectacular, dotted with small, still-working fishing villages, and the surrounding countryside is delightfully pastoral. Most people come here for ferry connections to Finland and Estonia.

There's also a small memorial for the 852 passengers killed in the Estonia ferry disaster of September 1994; it's up the hill across the main road from the ferry terminal.

An STF hostel (☑0176-441 69; Riddersholm; dm/s/d from Skr 220/340/600) sits off the E18, 2km west of the ferry terminal; book in advance outside of the peak summer season (mid-June to mid-August). There's no restaurant, so bring provisions.

Viking Line's direct bus from Stockholm Cityterminalen to meet the ferries costs Skr65, but if you have an SL pass take bus 676 from Tekniska Högskolan tunnelbana station to Norrtälje and change to bus 631, which runs every two hours or so weekdays (three times Saturday and once Sunday).

Tyresta National Park

Some of the best hiking and wilderness scenery in the area can be found in the 4900-hectare Tyresta National Park, only 20km southeast of Stockholm. Established in 1993, the park is noted for its two-billion-year-old rocks and virgin forest, which includes 300-year-old pine trees. It's a beautiful area, with rocky outcrops, small lakes, marshes and a wide variety of bird life.

At the southwestern edge of the park is Naturum Nationalparkernas Hus (National Parks Visitors Centre; ☑08-745 33 94; www.tyresta.se; ⊙9am-4pm Tue-Fri, 10am-5pm Sat & Sun) FREE. Here you can discover all of Sweden's 29 national parks through exhibitions and slide shows. Be sure to check out the centre itself: it's built in the shape of Sweden, complete with all 41 corners! There are even 'lakes' on the floor, indicated by different stones.

Ask for the national park leaflet in English and the *Tyresta Nationalpark och Naturreservat* leaflet in Swedish, which

A VIKING VISIT IN BIRKA

The historic Viking trading centre of **Birka** (www.stromma.se; return trip Skr360; ⊙ May-Sep), on Björkö in Lake Mälaren, makes a fantastic day trip. A Unesco World Heritage Site, it was founded as a village around AD 760 with the intention of expanding and controlling trade in the region.

The village attracted merchants and craft workers, and the population quickly grew to about 700. A large defensive fort with thick dry-stone ramparts was constructed next to the village. In 830 the Benedictine monk Ansgar was sent to Birka by the Holy Roman Emperor to convert the heathen Vikings to Christianity; he hung around for 18 months. Birka was abandoned in the late 10th century when Sigtuna took over the role of commercial centre.

The village site is surrounded by the largest Viking-age cemetery in Scandinavia, with around 3000 graves. Most people were cremated, then mounds of earth were piled over the remains, but some Christian coffins and chambered tombs have been found. The fort and harbour have also been excavated. A cross to the memory of St Ansgar can be seen on top of a nearby hill.

Exhibits at the brilliant **Birka Museum** (☑ 08-56 05 14 45; ⊙ 11am-3pm Mon-Fri, 10am-4pm Sat & Sun) include finds from the excavations, copies of the most magnificent objects, and an interesting model of the village in Viking times.

Round-trip cruises to Birka on Strömma Kanalbolaget's *Victoria* from Stadshusbron in central Stockholm make for a full day's outing (and are the only way to reach the site). The cruise price (Skr360) includes a visit to the Birka Museum and a guided tour in English of the settlement's burial mounds and fortifications. Ferries run from early May to mid-September, departing from Stadshusbron in Stockholm at 10am. (No ferries run during the Midsummer holidays.)

includes an excellent topographical map at 1:25,000 scale. From the visitor centre there are various trails into the park. Sörmlandsleden track cuts across 6km of the park on its way to central Stockholm.

Access to the park is easy. Take the *pendeltåg* to Haninge centrum (also called Handen station) on the Nynäshamn line, then change to bus 834. Some buses run all the way to the park, while others stop at Svartbäcken (2km west of Tyresta village).

Sigtuna

Just 40km northwest of Stockholm, Sigtuna is one of the cutest, most historically relevant villages in the area. Founded around AD 980, it's the oldest surviving town in Sweden, and the main drag, Storagatan, is very likely Sweden's oldest main street.

Around the year 1000, Olof Skötkonung ordered the minting of Sweden's first coins in the town, and ancient church ruins and rune stones are scattered everywhere. Indeed, there are about 150 runic inscriptions in the area, most dating from the early 11th century and typically flanking ancient roads.

Most of Sigtuna's original buildings went up in flames in devastating late-medieval fires, but the main church survived and many of the quaint streets and wooden abodes still follow the medieval town plan.

◉ Sights

Mariakyrkan CHURCH
(⊙ 9am-5pm) During medieval times, Sigtuna boasted seven stone-built churches, though most have since crumbled. Mariakyrkan is the oldest brick building in the area: it was a Dominican monastery church from around 1250 but became the parish church in 1529 after the monastery was demolished by Gustav Vasa. Pop in for restored medieval paintings and free weekly concerts in summer.

The adjacent St Olof church was built in the early 12th century, but by the 17th century it was a ruin. Nearby, the ruins of St Per and St Lars can be seen off Prästgatan.

Sigtuna Museum MUSEUM
(☑ 08-59 12 66 70; www.sigtunamuseum.se; Storagatan 55; adult/child Skr20/free; ⊙ noon-4pm Tue-Sun) This museum looks after several attractions in the town and has a small exhibition area; it's currently closed for

renovations, but you can see some of the exhibits at the *rådhus*.

Sigtuna Rådhus HISTORIC BUILDING
(noon-4pm Tue-Sun) FREE The smallest town hall in Scandinavia, Sigtuna *rådhus* dates from 1744 and was designed by the mayor himself. It's on the town square opposite the tourist office. The main museum building has displays of gold jewellery, runes, coins and loot brought home from abroad.

Rosersbergs Slott CASTLE
(08-59 03 50 39; www.kungahuset.se; adult/child Skr100/free; tours hourly 11am-4pm daily Jun-Aug, Sat & Sun only May & Sep) Rosersbergs Slott is on Lake Mälaren about 9km south-east of Sigtuna. Built in the 1630s, it was used as a royal residence from 1762 to 1860; the interior boasts exquisite furnishings from the Empire period (1790–1820), and is noted for its textiles. Highlights include the lavishly draped State Bedchamber and Queen Hedvig Elisabeth Charlotta's conversation room. The palace cafe serves delicious light meals and cakes in regal surrounds. Rosersberg is off the E4 motorway, or take the *pendeltåg* from Stockholm.

Sleeping & Eating

Stora Brännbo HOTEL €€
(08-59 25 75 00; www.storabrannbo.se; Stora Brännbovägen 2-6; s/d Skr600/900; P @; 570) Just north of central Sigtuna, this large hotel and conference centre offers small, contemporary rooms in soothing neutral hues with flat-screen TVs and fluffy bathrobes. There's sauna, jacuzzi and gym for guests, and the bountiful breakfast includes waffles and freshly squeezed orange juice.

Sigtunastiftelsens Gästhem HOTEL €€
(08-59 25 89 00; www.sigtunastiftelsen.se; Manfred Björkquists allé 2-4; s/d from Skr700/900; P) This attractive, imposing place is run by a Christian foundation. It might look like a cross between a cloister and a medieval fortress, but its 62 unique rooms – each named for a historical figure and decorated accordingly – are much cosier than you'd think. As is usual, rates go up outside peak summer season.

Tant Brunn Kaffestuga CAFE €
(08-59 25 09 34; Laurentii gränd; coffees & cakes from Skr35; 10am-7pm) In a small alley off Storagatan, this delightful 17th-century cafe is set around a pretty courtyard. It's well worth seeking out for its home-baked bread and pastries (the apple pie is divine); just watch your head as you walk in, as the roof beams sag precariously (did we mention it's adorable?).

Farbror Blå Café & Kök CAFE €€€
(08-59 25 60 50; Storatorget 14; dagens lunch Skr95, mains Skr265-298; 11am-midnight Mon-Fri, noon-midnight Sat, noon-4pm Sun) Adjacent to the town hall, this cosy nosh spot is the 'uncle' *(farbror)* to the 'aunt' of Tant Brunn cafe; both names are taken from a popular children's story. Head in for bistro-style meals like veal cutlet with honey-roasted potatoes, tomato-basil cream cheese and black pepper sauce.

Information

Tourist office (08-59 48 06 50; destinationsigtuna.se/turistbyra; Storagatan 33; 10am-6pm Mon-Sat, 11am-5pm Sun, shorter hours winter) The tourist office inhabits an 18th-century wooden house in Drakegården, on the main street.

Getting There & Around

Travel connections from Stockholm are easy. Take a local train to Märsta, from where there are frequent buses (570 or 575, Skr72, SL pass is valid) to Sigtuna.

Mariefred

Tiny, lakeside Mariefred is a pretty little village that pulls in the crowds with its grand castle, Gripsholm Slott.

Sights

Gripsholm Slott CASTLE
(0159-101 94; www.gripsholmslott.se; adult/child Skr120/free; 10am-4pm mid-May–mid-Sep, shorter hours rest of year) Gripsholm Slott is the epitome of castles, with its round towers, spires, drawbridge and creaky wooden halls. Originally built in the 1370s, the castle had passed into royal hands by the early 15th century. In 1526 Gustav Vasa took over and ordered the demolition of the adjacent monastery. A new castle with walls up to 5m thick was built using materials from the monastery; extensions continued for years. The oldest 'untouched' room is Karl IX's bedchamber, from the 1570s.

The castle was abandoned in 1715 but renovated and extended during the reign of Gustav III (especially between 1773 and 1785). The moat was filled in and, in 1730 and later in 1827, two 11th-century rune stones were found. These stones stand by the access road and are well worth a look; one has a Christian cross, while the other describes an expedition against the Saracens. Gripsholm Slott was restored again in the 1890s; the moat was cleared and the drawbridge rebuilt.

The castle contains some of the state portrait collection, which dates from the 16th century. There are guided tours in English at 3pm daily in summer.

Grafikens Hus MUSEUM

(☎0159-231 60; www.grafikenshus.se; Storgatan 15; ⏲noon-6pm Tue-Fri, 11am-4pm Sat & Sun) FREE Grafikens Hus is a centre for contemporary graphic art and printmaking, offering art classes and staging several exhibitions throughout the year.

Information

Tourist office (☎0159-297 90; www.strangnas.se/turism; Rådhustorget; ⏲10am-6pm Mon-Fri, 11am-3pm Sat & Sun Jun-Aug, by telephone only Sep-May) The tourist office has a map and notes (in English) for a self-guided walking tour of the idyllic village centre, filled with cobblestone streets and 18th-century buildings.

Getting There & Away

Mariefred isn't on the main railway line – the nearest station is at Läggesta, 3km to the west, with trains from Stockholm every two hours in summer. A **museum railway** (☎0159-210 06; www.oslj.nu; one-way/return from Skr60/80) from Läggesta to Mariefred runs on weekends from early May to late September (daily from Midsummer to mid-August), roughly every hour during the day; call or go online to check the schedule. Bus 303 runs hourly from Läggesta to Mariefred.

The steamship **S/S Mariefred** (☎08-669 88 50; www.mariefred.info; one-way/return Skr200/290) departs from Stadshusbron in Stockholm for Mariefred four times daily from Tuesday to Sunday mid-June to August, and weekends only from late May to mid-June and in early September.

Uppsala & Central Sweden

Includes ➡

Best Places to Eat

- Kopparhatten Café & Restaurang (p122)
- Jons-Andersgården (p126)
- Kalle på Spangen (p109)
- Nora Glass (p112)
- Hälls Konditori Stallbacken (p114)

Best Places to Stay

- Hotell Hackspett (p108)
- Behrn Hotell (p114)
- STF Vandrarhem Leksand (p123)
- Mora Parken (p127)
- STF Nora Tåghem (p112)

Why Go?

A wonderland of painted wooden horses marching across green hills dotted with little cabins, central Sweden is such a perfect distillation of all the Swedish highlights it could almost be one of those Las Vegas theme parks. It's an easily explored area right in the middle of the country, so travellers on a tight schedule can see a lot of what makes Sweden so Swedish.

The Lake Siljan area, with its idyllic villages and evergreen forest, represents the country's heartland. Further north, the landscape gets wilder and more rugged, a teaser offering hints of Lappland and the far north. In between lies Sweden's industrial core – perhaps not glamorous, but illuminating and important.

Uppsala and Örebro are lively cultural centres with well-preserved historical buildings and great museums, dining, shopping and nightlife. Outdoorsy types will have plenty to do, too, from skiing and hiking to birdwatching and canoeing.

When to Go

Uppsala

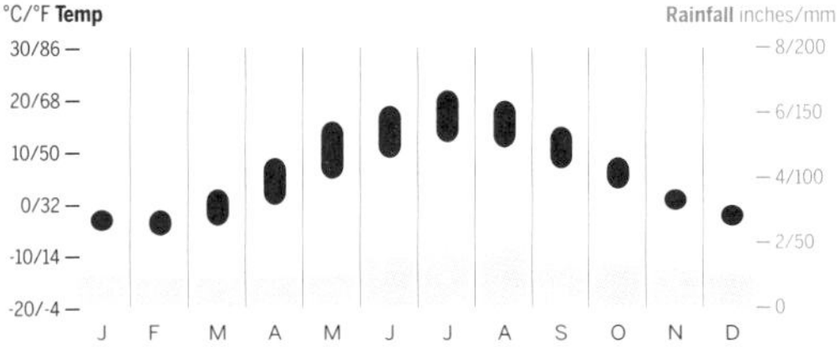

Mid-Jun–Aug The weather's fine, accommodation prices are low and attractions are open.

Sep & Oct Many sights are closed, but the weather's fair and autumn leaves mean gorgeous scenery.

Dec–Feb Winter means bundling up, but central Sweden during the Christmas holidays is lovely.

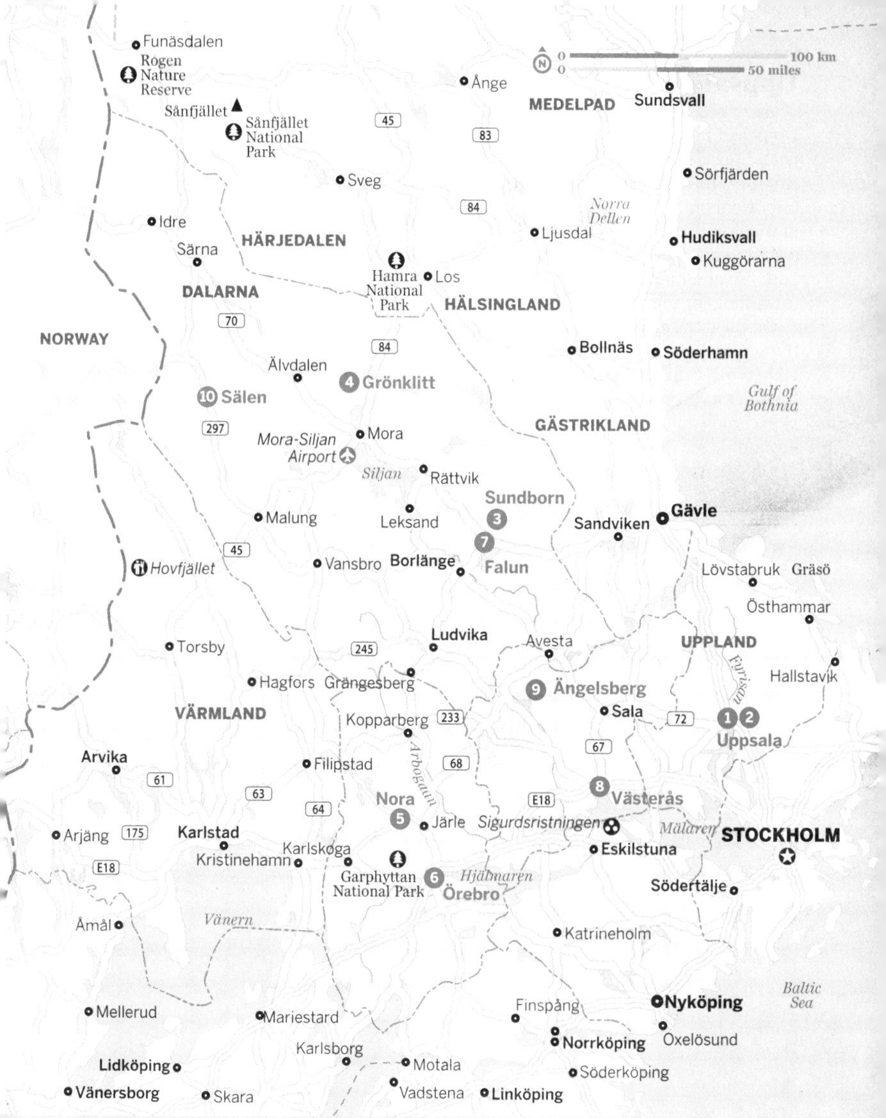

Uppsala & Central Sweden Highlights

1. Pondering the ancient burial mounds at **Gamla Uppsala** (p98).
2. Soaking up antique science and wonder at Uppsala's **Museum Gustavianum** (p100).
3. Visiting Carl Larsson's inspiring **family home** (p121) in Sundborn.
4. Watching roly-poly bears at play in **Grönklitt** (p129).
5. Stopping for **ice cream** (p112) in Nora.
6. Wandering the city park and historic **Wadköping village** (p113) in Örebro.
7. Seeing regional art and history in **Dalarnas Museum** (p121), Falun.
8. Sleeping underwater, or in a treehouse, in **Västerås** (p107).
9. Exploring an atmospheric old mine at **Ängelsberg** (p109).
10. Hitting the ski slopes at **Sälen** (p129).

Uppsala

☎018 / POP 156,000 (CITY)

Drenched in history but never stifled by the past, Uppsala has the party vibe of a university town to balance out its large number of important buildings and general atmosphere of weighty cultural significance. It's a terrific combination, and one that makes the town both fun and functional, not to mention very rewarding for the interested traveller.

On the city's edge is Gamla (Old) Uppsala, the original site of the town – once a flourishing 6th-century religious centre where human sacrifices allegedly were made to the Norse gods, and home to an ancient burial ground.

On 30 April, students dressed in white gather to celebrate the **Walpurgis Festival**. Traditionally, this includes a student boat race on the river at 10am and a run down Carolinabacken at 3pm, as well as various processions and singing. Perhaps less charming are the traditional early-summer graduation parties, in which cheerfully inebriated students are driven around town in the backs of large trucks, singing to loud pop music and saluting passersby.

Sights

Gamla Uppsala ARCHAEOLOGICAL SITE

(www.arkeologigamlauppsala.se; 24hr; P; 2) **FREE** One of Sweden's largest and most important burial sites, Gamla Uppsala (4km north of Uppsala) contains 300 mounds from the 6th to 12th centuries. The earliest are also the three most impressive. Legend has it they contain the pre-Viking kings Aun, Egil and Adils, who appear in *Beowulf* and Icelandic historian Snorre Sturlason's *Ynglingsaga*. More recent evidence suggests the occupant of Östhögen (East Mound) was a woman, probably a female regent in her 20s or 30s.

Uppsala

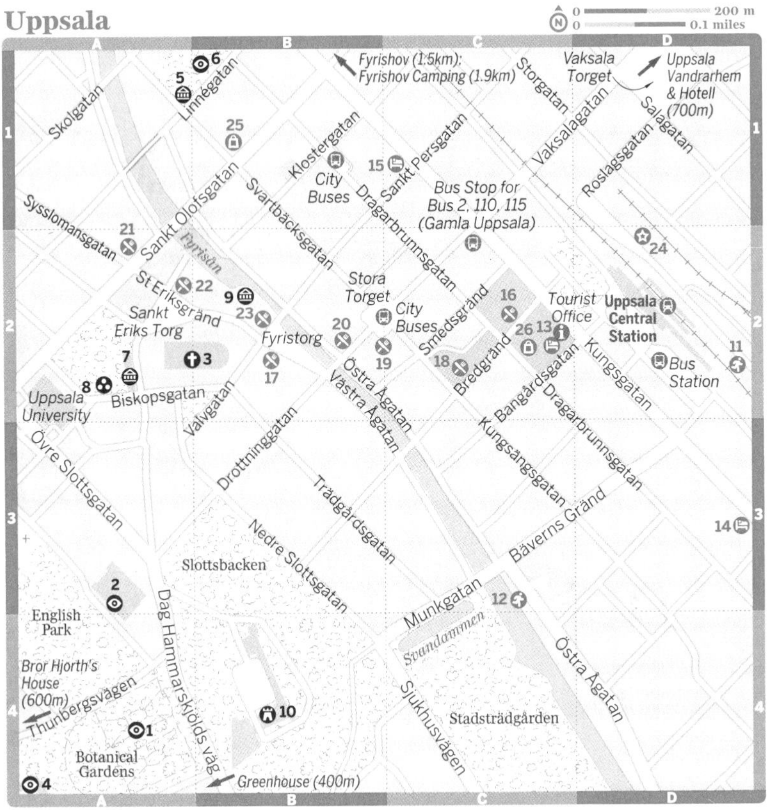

According to Olof Rudbeck's 1679 book *Atlantica*, Gamla Uppsala was the seat of Western culture. Rudbeck (1630–1702), a scientist, writer and all-around colourful character, amassed copious evidence proving that Old Uppsala was, in fact, the mythical lost city of Atlantis. In retrospect, this seems unlikely. But the area is a fascinating attraction nevertheless. You can learn more in the adjoining museum, or wander on your own.

Speculation has surrounded the burial site from the beginning. Early press reports include that of medieval chronicler Adam of Bremen – who never actually visited – describing a vast golden temple in Gamla Uppsala in the 10th century. Allegedly, animal and human sacrifices were strung up in a sacred grove outside.

When Christianity arrived around 1090, Thor, Odin and the other Viking gods began to fade. From 1164, the archbishop of Uppsala had his seat in a cathedral on the site of the present church.

If you feel like a stroll or a bicycle ride, **Eriksleden** is a 6km 'pilgrims path' between the cathedral in Uppsala and the church in Gamla Uppsala. Its namesake, Erik the Holy, was king of Sweden from around 1150 until the Danes beheaded him 10 years later. The story is that his head rolled down the hill, and where it stopped a spring came up. The main trail also provides access to a ridged wilderness area called **Tunåsen**, with a panoramic viewpoint (follow signs along Eriksleden just south of Gamla Uppsala to '*utsiktsleden*').

Uppsala

Sights

1	Botanical Gardens	A4
2	Carolina Rediviva	A3
3	Domkyrka	A2
4	Linnaeum Orangery	A4
5	Linnémuseet	A1
6	Linnéträdgården	B1
7	Museum Gustavianum	A2
8	Rune Stones	A2
	Treasury	(see 3)
9	Upplandsmuseet	B2
	Uppsala Art Museum	(see 10)
10	Uppsala Slott	B4

Activities, Courses & Tours

11	Lennakatten	D2
12	M/S Kung Carl Gustaf	C3

Sleeping

13	Best Western Hotel Svava	C2
14	Samariterhemmets Gästhem	D3
15	Uppsala City Hostel	C1

Eating

16	Amazing Thai	C2
17	Hambergs Fisk	B2
18	Hemköp Supermarket	C2
19	Jalla	B2
20	Magnussons Krog	B2
21	Ofvandahls	A2
22	Saluhallen	A2
23	Tzatziki	B2

Drinking & Nightlife

	O'Connor's	(see 19)

Entertainment

24	Katalin & All That Jazz	D2

Shopping

25	English Bookshop	B1
26	Systembolaget	C2

Gamla Uppsala Museum MUSEUM

(www.raa.se/gamlauppsala; adult/child Skr70/free; 11am-5pm Apr-Sep, noon-4pm Mon, Wed, Sat & Sun rest of year; P) Gamla Uppsala Museum contains finds from the cremation mounds, a poignant mix of charred and melted beads, bones and buckles. More intact pieces come from various **boat graves** in and around the site. The museum is arranged as a timeline – useful for re-creating the history of the area.

Follow signs from the grave mounds to **Disagården** (018-16 91 80; guided tours Skr30; 10am-5pm Jun-Aug, tours 1pm) FREE, a 19th-century farming village turned open-air museum consisting of 26 timber buildings and a platform stage that serves as the focal point for Uppsala's Midsummer celebrations.

Next to the unexcavated flat-topped mound Tingshögen is **Odinsborg** (018-32 35 25; www.odinsborg.nu; dagens lunch Skr85, mains Skr90, waffles Skr45; 10am-6pm), a restaurant known for its horns of mead and Viking feasts (although daintier refreshments are offered at the summer cafe downstairs).

Uppsala Slott CASTLE

(www.uppsalaslott.se; admission by guided tour only, adult/child Skr90/15; tours in English 1pm & 3pm Tue-Sun late Jun-Sep) Uppsala Slott was built by Gustav Vasa in the 1550s. It contains the state hall where kings were enthroned and Queen Kristina abdicated. It was also the scene of a brutal murder in 1567, when King Erik XIV and his guards killed Nils Sture and his two sons, Erik and Svante, after accusing them of high treason. The castle burned down in

1702 but was rebuilt and took on its present form in 1757.

At the castle entrance marked E, the **Uppsala Art Museum** (☑ 018-727 24 82; www.uppsala.se/konstmuseum; adult/child Skr40/free, 4-8pm Wed free; ☺ noon-4pm Tue, Thu, Fri, to 8pm Wed, to 4.30pm Sat & Sun Jun-Aug) displays Swedish and international contemporary art and ceramics as well as the art-study collection of Uppsala University.

Domkyrka
CHURCH
(Cathedral; www.uppsaladomkyrka.se; Domkyrkoplan; ☺ 8am-6pm) **FREE** The Gothic Domkyrka dominates the city, just as some of those buried here, including St Erik, Gustav Vasa and the scientist Carl von Linné, dominated their country. Tours are available in English at 11am and 2pm Monday to Saturday, 4pm Sunday, in July and August.

Gustav's funerary sword, silver crown and shiny golden buttons are kept in the **treasury** (Domkyrkan; ☺ 10am-5pm Mon-Sat, 12.30-5pm Sun May-Sep) **FREE** in the cathedral's north tower, along with a great display of medieval textiles. Particularly fine are the clothes worn by the three noblemen who were murdered in the castle: they're the only example of 16th-century Swedish high fashion still in existence. Tours in English start at 3pm Monday to Saturday in July and August.

Botanical Gardens
GARDENS
(www.botan.uu.se; Villavägen 6-8; ☺ 7am-9pm) **FREE** The Botanical Gardens, below the castle hill, show off more than 10,000 species and are pleasant to wander through. Attractions include the 200-year-old **Linnaeum Orangery** (☺ 9am-3pm Tue-Fri) and a tropical **greenhouse** (admission Skr40).

Museum Gustavianum
MUSEUM
(www.gustavianum.uu.se; Akademigatan 3; adult/child Skr50/40; ☺ 10am-4pm Tue-Sun Jun-Aug, from 11am rest of year) The Museum Gustavianum rewards appreciation of the weird and well organised. The shelves in the pleasantly musty building hold case after case of obsolete tools and preserved oddities: stuffed birds, astrolabes, alligator mummies, exotic stones and dried sea creatures. A highlight is the fascinating 17th-century **Augsburg Art Cabinet** and its thousand ingenious trinkets. Don't miss Olof Rudbeck's vertiginous **anatomical theatre**, where executed criminals were dissected. Admission includes a tour in English at 1pm Saturday and Sunday.

Carolina Rediviva
LIBRARY
(www.ub.uu.se; Dag Hammarskjölds väg 1; ☺ exhibition hall 9am-8pm Mon-Fri, 10am-5pm Sat) **FREE** Rare-book and map fiends should go directly to Carolina Rediviva, the university library. In a small, dark gallery, glass cases hold precious maps and manuscripts, including illuminated Ethiopian texts and the first book ever printed in Sweden. The star is the surviving half of the *Codex Argentus* (AD 520), aka the Silver Bible, written in gold and silver ink on purple vellum; aside from being pretty, it's linguistically important as the most complete existing document written in the Gothic language.

Upplandsmuseet
MUSEUM
(www.upplandsmuseet.se; Sankt Eriks Torg 10; ☺ noon-5pm Tue-Sun) **FREE** Upplandsmuseet, in an 18th-century watermill, houses county collections of folk art, music and the history of Uppsala from the Middle Ages onwards, as well as more modern displays. (Temporary installations have included photographs from the life of author Astrid Lindgren.) In particular, kids will find the inventive dioramas and reconstructions engrossing.

Linnémuseet
MUSEUM
(www.linnaeus.se; Svartbäcksgatan 27; adult/under 16yr Skr60/free; ☺ 11am-5pm Tue-Sun May-Sep) No matter how many times the brochures refer to the 'sexual system' of classification, the excitement to be had at Linnémuseet is primarily intellectual; still, botanists and vegetarians will enjoy a visit to the pioneering scientist's home and workshop, where he lived with his wife and five kids (1743–78). The adjoining **Linnéträdgården** (☑ 018-471 25 76; adult/child Skr60/free, admission with Linnémuseet ticket free; ☺ shop & exhibit 11am-5pm Tue-Sun May-Sep, park 11am-8pm Tue-Sun May-Sep) is a reconstructed version of Sweden's oldest botanical garden – Linné's playground – with more than 1300 species arranged according to the system he invented.

Bror Hjorth's House
GALLERY
(☑ 018-56 70 30; www.brorhjorthshus.se; Norbyvägen 26; adult/child Skr40/free; ☺ noon-4pm Thu-Sun, plus Tue & Wed in summer; 🚌 6, 7) Bror Hjorth's House, the studio of beloved local artist Bror Hjorth (1894–1968), is jam-packed with Hjorth's charming paintings and sculptures, and hosts temporary exhibitions.

Rune Stones
RUIN
FREE In the grassy, sloping park between Domkyrkan and the main Uppsala Univer-

sity building are nine typical Uppland rune stones. There's another row of them propped in the grass just outside the entrance to the Domkyrka.

Activities

Lennakatten TRAIN RIDES

(018-13 05 00; www.lennakatten.se; Stationsgatan 11, track 10; all-day ticket adult/child Skr220/110; 9am-5pm Wed-Thu, Sat & Sun) You can ride the narrow-gauge steam train 33km into the Uppland countryside. Schedules vary, so check online for updates. The trains depart from the Uppsala Östra museum station, in Bergsbrunnaparken, toward the east side of Uppsala Central Station.

M/S Kung Carl Gustaf CRUISE

(070-293 81 61; www.mskungcarlgustaf.se; Islandsbron bridge; adult/child return Skr580/380, Skokloster admission Skr90) Slow down the pace with a boat cruise to the baroque castle of Skokloster. M/S *Kung Carl Gustaf*, a 19th-century ex-steamship, sails Tuesday to Sunday from mid-May to mid-August. Tours leave Islandsbron at 11am and return at 4.15pm, allowing about two hours at Skokloster.

There are also evening river cruises at 7pm Tuesday to Saturday from mid-May to mid-September; the cruise plus buffet and entertainment costs Skr580 per person.

Fyrishov WATER PARK

(018-727 49 50; www.fyrishov.se; Idrottsgatan 2; adult/child Skr100/80; park 9am-9.30pm, pool from 6.15am; 1, 13, 42, 111) Families with water-loving children should head for Fyrishov, one of Sweden's largest water parks. It features the full complement of slides, jacuzzis, waterfalls and wave machines.

Sleeping

STF Vandrarhem Sunnersta Herrgård HOSTEL €

(018-32 42 20; www.sunnerstaherrgard.se; Sunnerstavägen 24; dm Skr245, s/d incl breakfast from Skr650/770; Jan–mid-Dec; P; 20) In a historic manor house about 6km south of the city centre, this hostel has a parklike setting at the water's edge and a good restaurant on site. You can rent bikes (Skr50/200 per day/week) or borrow a boat, and there's free wi-fi. Hotel-standard rooms include breakfast; hostel guests can add it for Skr85.

Uppsala Vandrarhem & Hotell HOSTEL €

(018-24 20 08; www.uppsalavandrarhem.se; Kvarntorget 3; dm Skr190, s/d hostel Skr445/550, s/d hotel Skr750/895; P; 3 Kvarntorget) This hostel, attached to Hotell Kvarntorget, is away from the action but walkable from Uppsala Central Station. Spacious rooms, some with double beds, face an enclosed courtyard that works as a breakfast room; a newly designed dividing wall has greatly reduced the resulting noise. There's a guest kitchen and laundry. Bedding is included; towels (Skr30) and breakfast (Skr69) are extra.

Uppsala City Hostel HOSTEL €

(018-10 00 08; http://uppsalacityhostel.se/en/; Sankt Persgatan 16; dm/s/d from Skr220/400/500; reception 8am-11pm; @) The no-nonsense Uppsala City Hostel is recommended for its sheer convenience – you really can't stay anywhere more central for these prices. Rooms, all named after famous Uppsala landmarks, are small but decent (although dorms suffer from traffic and level-crossing noise). There's wi-fi access in parts of the hostel. Breakfast costs Skr50, and a kitchen is available.

Samariterhemmets Gästhem GUESTHOUSE €

(018-56 40 00; www.samariterhemmet.se; Samaritergränd 2; s/d Skr500/715) Run by a Christian charity, this clean and inviting guesthouse shares a building with a church. Old-style rooms with separate bathrooms are decorated in cool creams and antique furniture.

Fyrishov Camping CAMPGROUND €

(018-727 49 60; www.fyrishov.se; Idrottsgatan 2; sites Skr130, 4-bed cabins from Skr895) This campsite, 2km north of the city, is great for families with water babies: it's attached to water park Fyrishov, with discounted swim-and-stay packages (from Skr995 for cabins). Take bus 1 from Dragarbrunnsgatan.

Best Western Hotel Svava HOTEL €€

(018-13 00 30; www.bestwestern.se; Bangårdsgatan 24; s/d Skr1350/1450; P) Named after one of Odin's Valkyrie maidens, Hotel Svava, right opposite the train station, is a very comfortable top-end business-style hotel with summer and weekend discounts that make it a smashing deal.

Eating

There's a centrally located **supermarket** (Stora Torget; 8am-10pm).

Ofvandahls CAFE €

(Sysslomansgatan 3-5; cakes Skr35, snacks Skr55-75; 8am-6pm Mon-Fri, 9am-5pm Sat, 11am-5pm Sun) Something of an Uppsala institution, this classy but sweet *konditori* (bakery-cafe) dates back to the 19th century and is a cut above your average coffee-and-bun shop. It's been endorsed by no less a personage than the king, and radiates old-world charm – somehow those faded red-striped awnings just get cuter every year.

Jalla FAST FOOD €
(Stora Torget 1; mains Skr65-89; 10am-9pm) Get your fix of cheap and (relatively) healthful felafel, kebabs and meze platters at this efficient fast-food joint right on the main square, with some outdoor tables for watching the action. The meals are enormous and tasty.

Saluhallen MARKET €
(Sankt Eriks Torg; 10am-6pm Mon-Thu, to 7pm Fri, to 4pm Sat, restaurants 11am-4pm Sun) Stock up on meat, fish, cheese and fancy chocolate at this indoor market, or hit one of the restaurant corners for a bite; a couple stay open late for dinner, with pleasant terrace bars available in summer.

Hambergs Fisk SEAFOOD €€
(www.hambergs.se; Fyristorg 8; mains Skr125-295; 11.30am-10pm Tue-Sat) Let the aromas of dill and seafood tempt you into this excellent fish restaurant, in a tiny storefront facing the river. Self-caterers should check out the adjoining fresh-fish counter.

Magnussons Krog SWEDISH €€
(www.magnussonskrog.se; Drottninggatan 1; dagens lunch Skr109, mains Skr175-225; 11am-late) Try any of the specials on the chalkboard at this sleek corner hang-out. Late-night bar snacks (Skr109 to Skr129) help soak up delicious cocktails, which you can enjoy at outdoor tables on a busy riverside corner in fair weather. Great for people-watching.

Amazing Thai THAI €€
(Bredgränd 14; buffet Skr159; lunch & dinner) This small, family-friendly spot inside a shopping centre is popular for its good-value buffet (both lunch and dinner) and welcoming atmosphere. The evening menu features a good selection of fragrant stir-fries, noodle dishes and curries.

Tzatziki GREEK €€€
(018-15 03 33; Fyristorg 4; starters Skr69, mains Skr145-197;) Tzatziki will supply all your moussaka and souvlaki needs. There's cosy seating in the 16th-century interior, and in summer the outside tables by the riverside thrum with diners. Service is fast, the food is tasty and there are several veggie options.

Drinking & Entertainment

In the evenings local students converge on the university bars on Sankt Olofsgatan (hard to get into if you're not an Uppsala student, but worth a go). Just follow the crowds to find out which ones are currently primo.

O'Connor's PUB
(018-14 40 10; Stora Torget 1; 4pm-3am Mon-Thu, from 2pm Fri, from noon Sat & Sun) Upstairs on the main square is this friendly Irish pub and restaurant, with live music six nights a week and a selection of over 30 beers on tap, plus bottles from around the world.

Katalin & All That Jazz LIVE MUSIC
(018-14 06 80; Godsmagasinet, Östra Station; mains Skr130-175; from 2pm Mon-Thu, from 1pm Fri & Sat) Katalin, in a former warehouse behind the train station, hosts regular live jazz and blues, with occasional rock and pop bands. There's a good restaurant too, and in summer the sun-splashed back patio is jammed with great-looking people acting like they're not checking each other out.

Shopping

English Bookshop BOOKS
(http://bookshop.se; Svartbäcksgatan 19; 10am-4pm Mon-Fri, noon-3pm Sat) Stop by this friendly corner store to stock up on new releases and get recommendations on a huge selection of books in English.

Systembolaget DRINK
(Dragarbrunnsgatan 50; 10am-7pm Mon-Fri, to 3pm Sat) For alcohol, Systembolaget is inside the Svava shopping centre.

Information

EMERGENCY

Police (114 14; www.polisen.se/english; Svartbäcksgatan 49)

MEDICAL SERVICES

Apoteket Kronan (Svartbäcksgatan 8; 10am-7pm Mon-Fri, to 3pm Sat) Pharmacy chain; one of several city-centre locations.

Uppsala University Hospital (Akademiska sjukhuset; 018-611 22 97; Uppsala Care, Entrance 61, Sjukhusvägen) Has an urgent-care facility for foreign visitors, as well as an after-hours pharmacy.

MONEY

Head over to Stora Torget to find banks and ATMs. Next door to the tourist office is a **Forex** (10-211 16 37; Kungsgatan 59; 9am-7pm

OUTDOOR ACTIVITIES

Getting out into nature is one of the most rewarding things to do in this part of Sweden. And it's easy. Outdoors enthusiasts have a number of options within easy reach, for all types of weather.

Skiers are spoiled for excellent choices, as sleepy little **Sälen** transforms itself in winter into a major destination for skiers of all abilities. There's also good skiing at the smaller, slightly more remote **Grönklitt** and at the bustling, snowboard-friendly **Sunne**. At Hovfjället (p119) you can opt for downhill or cross-country skiing, or choose something more unusual, like snowshoeing, dogsledding or wolf-watching.

Torsby and its surrounds are also a good base for warm-weather activities like hiking and cycling. Finnskogleden (p119) is a well-marked 240km trekking path that roughly follows the Norwegian border. Dalarna has **Siljansleden**, a 300km network of walking and cycling paths surrounding the scenic Lake Siljan. And near Sälen it's easy to hop onto the southern section of **Kungsleden**, the popular walking trail through Norrland. Walking trails are also plentiful in and around Tiveden National Park (p115), which is a good place to enquire about fishing as well.

For a good summary of fishing in this part of Sweden, visit www.sportfiskeguide.se; the website has information on where to go, what's required, where to stay, and how to find a guide, in Swedish and English. Fishing generally requires you to purchase a Fiskekort, which must be bought locally where you intend to fish. Anglers will find some great fishing in and around **Grövelsjön**, along with excellent skiing, hiking, rock climbing, river paddling and most other outdoor activities. The village is inside a nature reserve.

Mon-Fri, to 3pm Sat), offering currency-exchange services.

POST

You can buy stamps at the tourist office, most supermarkets and Pressbyrån shops. There are mailboxes at Stora Torget and Uppsala Central Station.

TOURIST INFORMATION

Tourist Office (☎018-727 48 00; www.destinationuppsala.se; Kungsgatan 59; ⏰10am-6pm Mon-Fri, to 3pm Sat, plus 11am-3pm Sun Jul & Aug) Relocated to a prime spot directly in front of the train station, the tourist office has helpful advice, maps and brochures for the whole county.

ℹ Getting There & Away

- Flygbuss (bus 801) to Arlanda Airport (every 30 minutes, 45 minutes, adult/child Skr125/75) from Uppsala train station.
- Swebus Express to Stockholm (Skr59, one hour, at least hourly), Västerås (via Stockholm, Skr139, 3½ hours, six daily), Örebro (via Stockholm, from Skr179, 4½ hours, four to seven daily) and Falun (change in Stockholm and Börlange, Skr259, nine hours, daily).
- SJ trains to/from Stockholm (Skr70 to Skr110, 35 to 55 minutes one way), Gävle (from Skr143, 50 minutes, at least seven daily), Östersund (Skr560, five hours, two daily) and Mora (Skr213, 3¼ hours, two daily).
- For car hire, try **Statoil** (☎20 91 00; Gamla Uppsalagatan 48) or **OKQ8.** (☎29 04 96; Årstagatan 5-7)

ℹ Getting Around

Upplands Lokaltrafik (☎0771-14 14 14; www.ul.se) runs public transport within the city and county. City buses depart from Stora Torget and the nearby streets. Tickets for 90 minutes of unlimited bus travel can be purchased for Skr25.

Lövstabruk

☎0294

Tiny Lövstabruk (Leufsta Bruk), 71km north of Uppsala, is perhaps the prettiest of the many historic Vallonbruk villages in the Northern Uppland area. Once a centre of industry, the region is now a lush green landscape dotted with picturesque industrial leftovers, mainly ironworks and mines. To learn more about the area's heritage, ask at the tourist offices for the free booklet *Valonbruk in Uppland*, or check out www.svetur.se/vallonbruken.

The word *bruk*, part of many local place names, means an industrial village that processed raw materials, such as iron ore. Most appeared in the 17th century and were owned, run and staffed by Dutch and Walloon (Belgian) immigrants – hence the local name for the forges, *wallonbruk*. The profits were used to build fine mansions, surrounded by humble workers' homes.

In 1627 the Dutchman Louis de Geer came to Lövstabruk, and the mansion was built for his grandson, Charles de Geer, around 1700. The house and its factories were destroyed by a Russian attack in 1719, but everything was rebuilt and iron production continued until 1926.

The *bruk* buildings are open to visitors from 11am to 4pm or 5pm daily June to August. If you like what you see here, consider also visiting the nearby towns of **Forsmark** (www.visitforsmark.se) and **Österbybruk** (http://gammeltammen.se).

Sleeping & Eating

Gamla Brukshandeln B&B B&B €
(☎070-676 59 94; leufstabruk.com/b-b-rum.html; Stora gatan 48; s/d Skr495/795; P) B&B Läkarvillan is a cosy house on the ironworks grounds that has whitewashed rooms decorated with pretty antiques and those classic Swedish ceramic stoves, and a nice view over the *bruk*. It's small, so book ahead.

Lövstabruk Wärdshus SWEDISH €€
(☎0294-311 22; www.leufstabrukswardshus.se; Stora gatan 33; lunch buffet Skr90; noon-5pm Sun-Wed, to 9pm Thu-Sat mid-Jun–mid-Aug) This pretty restaurant with outdoor garden seating serves a hearty buffet lunch on weekdays, and a menu of Swedish classics on weekends and evenings.

Information

Tourist Office (☎0294-310 70; 11am-5pm mid-Jun–mid-Aug, noon-4pm Sat & Sun mid-Aug–mid-Jun) The tourist office is inside the Stora Magasinet building, next to the Wärdshus (p104) restaurant. Buy tickets here (adult/child Skr70/45) for a one-hour guided tour of the mansion and grounds (2pm Saturday and Sunday May to June).

Getting There & Away

Take bus 811 from Uppsala to Östhammar, then change to bus 835 (about two hours, four to eight daily, Skr80 one way).

Nyköping

☎0155 / POP 53,038

Once the setting for one of Swedish royalty's greatest feuds, Nyköping these days is a pretty, mellow town where the big activities include strolling along the river and sitting by the harbour.

Sights & Activities

By Stora Torget, there's the old **rådhus** (town hall) and **St Nicolai Kyrka**, with a splendid pulpit; free guided tours of the church run at 3pm Monday to Friday, and at 2pm Sunday. Two rune stones and 700 Bronze Age rock carvings decorate **Släbroparken**, about 2.5km northwest of town.

Take a walk along the river: 'Sweden's longest museum', or so the publicity goes. For longer hikes, the 1000km-long **Sörmlandsleden** (☎355 64; www.sormlandsleden.se) passes through town on its way around the county. In summer you can also explore the nearby **archipelago**; enquire at the tourist office, or via Trosa Rederi (www.trosarederi.se).

Sörmlands Museum MUSEUM
(☎0155-24 57 20; www.sormlandsmuseum.se; 11am-7pm Jun-Aug, to 5pm Sun & with scheduled programs rest of year) FREE Inside the grounds of Nyköpingshus, Sörmlands Museum includes **Kungstornet** (King's Tower), a whitewashed four-storey castle tower; **Gamla Residenset**, the old governor's residence; and the neighbouring **Konsthallen**, with interesting art exhibitions and a collection of 19th-century boathouses. Free guided tours of Kungstornet take place in English at 2pm Tuesday, Thursday, Saturday and Sunday in summer.

Nyköpingshus CASTLE
(24hr) FREE The ruined castle Nyköpingshus hosted some violent times in the Swedish monarchy. The bickering among King Birger and his two brothers, Erik and Valdemar, peaked in 1317 when Birger invited them to a 'peace banquet'. When they arrived, he hurled them into the dungeon and threw the keys in the river, letting them starve to death. (It didn't do Birger much good, as he was driven to exile in Denmark the following year.)

This cheerful episode is re-created each summer as *The Nyköping Banquet*, a traditional play; ask for a schedule at Sörmlands Museum.

Sleeping & Eating

There are supermarkets on Västra Storgatan, running west from Stora Torget.

Nyköpings Vandrarhem HOSTEL €
(☎070-679 56 08; http://nykopingsvandrarhem.se; Brunnsgatan 4; dm/s/d Skr200/390/470; P)

So close to the castle that you'd feel threatened if there were a siege, this independent hostel is homely and casual. The kitchen is great, there are picnic tables in the yard, and the folks in charge are accommodating and helpful. Mainly, though, the riverside location is hard to beat.

Strandstuviken Camping CAMPGROUND €
(☎0155-978 10; www.strandstuviken.se; sites Skr250, 4-bed cabins Skr500-600; ⏲May-Sep; P) The nearest camping ground is this beachside family-friendly place, just off the Sörmlandsleden walking trail. Has 10 cabins, some tent sites and dorms; there's also a sauna, minigolf, and canoe and bicycle hire. It's a good 9km southwest of town, though, with no public transport.

Clarion Hotel Kompaniet HOTEL €€
(☎0155-28 80 20; cc.kompaniet@choice.se; Folkungavägen 1; r from Skr1080; P@≋) This enormous structure near the harbour features stylish modern rooms – not huge, but intelligently arranged, and many with nice views – in a building that was once home to a furniture factory. Prices vary seasonally, but all include breakfast and a dinner buffet (or a sandwich for those who arrive late).

Café Hellmans CAFE €
(☎0155-21 05 25; Västra Trädgårdsgatan 24; mains Skr75-125; ⏲8am-6pm Mon-Fri, 9am-5pm Sat, 11am-4pm Sun) A charming cafe with a boutique shop attached, Hellmans is a nice spot for lunch, with soups, salads, lasagne and focaccia. Also has good coffee and excellent cakes to enjoy in the summer courtyard.

Aktersnurran CAFE €
(Skeppsbron 7; ice cream 1/2/3 scoops Skr25/35/45, sandwiches Skr45-65) Aktersnurran is one of several casual bar-restaurants along the harbour; the crowds shift from one terrace to the other according to time of day and availability of live music. This is the simplest in the line-up, with basic meals like pizza, meatballs and burgers, as well as sweet-smelling waffle cones.

Information

Banks and other services can be found on Västra Storgatan.

Tourist office (☎0155-24 82 00; www.nykopingsguiden.se; Stadshuset, Stora Torget; ⏲8am-6pm Mon-Fri, 10am-4pm Sat & Sun) The tourist office is inside the town hall on the main square.

Getting There & Around

Nyköping's **Skavsta Airport** (☎0155-28 04 00; www.skavsta-air.se), 8km northwest of town, has flights to/from the UK and the European continent with Ryanair. Airport buses meet most flights and run to/from Stockholm (Skr139, 80 minutes). Local buses 515 and 715 run every 10 minutes from Nyköping to Skavsta (Skr25, 20 minutes); alternatively, a **taxi** (☎21 75 00) to Nyköping costs about Skr240.

The bus and train stations are roughly 800m apart on the western side of the central grid. Nyköping is on the regular **Swebus Express** (☎0200-21 82 18; www.swebusexpress.se) routes, including Stockholm–Norrköping–Jönköping–Göteborg/Malmö, and Stockholm–Norrköping–Kalmar. SJ trains run every hour or two to Norrköping (Skr93, 40 minutes), Linköping (Skr174, one to two hours) and Stockholm (Skr143, one hour). Most X2000 services don't stop in Nyköping.

The tourist office has bikes for rent (Skr50/200 per day/week).

Eskilstuna

☎016 / POP 100,000

If you're here from abroad, locals may very well ask you, 'Why Eskilstuna, of all places?' Although its suburban ordinariness doesn't exactly scream 'tourist destination', Eskilstuna has some family-friendly sights, primarily its famous zoo, and just northeast of town is one of the most extraordinary rock carvings in Sweden. The old town is also an attractive shopping district.

Sights & Activities

Sigurdsristningen ARCHAEOLOGICAL SITE
(www.illustrata.com/pages/sigurdsristning; ⏲24hr; 🚌225) FREE The vivid, 3m-long Viking Age rock carving Sigurdsristningen illustrates the story of Sigurd the Dragon Slayer, a hero whose adventures are described in *Beowulf* and the Icelandic sagas. The story inspired Wagner's *Ring Cycle*, and *The Hobbit* and *The Lord of the Rings* also borrow from it. Runes in the dragon's body, unrelated to the legend, explain that a woman named Sigrid raised a nearby bridge (the abutments can still be seen) in memory of her husband Holmger.

Carved into the bedrock around AD 1000, the carving shows Sigurd roasting the heart of the dragon Fafnir over a fire. Sigurd's stepfather Regin persuaded him to kill Fafnir for the dragon's golden treasure. Sigurd touches the heart to see if it's cooked, then sucks his finger, and voila – he tastes the dragon's blood and suddenly understands the language of birds. They warn him that Regin is plotting to kill him and keep the treasure, so Sigurd attacks first, chopping off his stepfather's head; the unfortunate fellow is shown in the left corner of the carving, among his scattered tools. Also depicted is Sigurd's horse Grani, a gift from Odin, tied to the tree where the birds perch.

A walking path along the river starts from the parking lot; ask at the tourist office about raft trips. The carving is situated near Sundbyholms Slott and Mälaren lake, 12km northeast of Eskilstuna.

Parken Zoo ZOO

(016-10 01 01; www.parkenzoo.se; adult/child Skr250/180, amusement park Skr195, swimming pool Skr50/40; 10am-6pm Jul–mid-Aug, shorter hours May, Jun & Sep, amusement park from noon, pool 10am-7pm Jun-Aug; P; 1) Parken Zoo is one of central Sweden's most popular family attractions. The 80-plus kinds of animals on show include monkeys, komodo dragons and beautiful white tigers that were successfully bred here. It's not a cheap day out: additional charges are levied for parking (Skr15 per hour), the **amusement park** and the **swimming pool**.

The zoo is 1.5km west of the town centre. The bus runs frequently from the train and bus stations.

Rademachersmedjorna MUSEUM

(Rademacher Forges; 016-710 13 71; Rademachergatan; 10am-4pm Mon-Fri year-round, plus some weekends in summer) FREE The Rademachersmedjorna (forges), contain the carefully preserved 17th-century remnants of Eskilstuna's ironworking past. Visitors can see workshops where the tradition continues: iron-, silver- and goldsmiths all still work here. Stay alert for sightings of 'Sundin of the Gab', a local craftsman who produced masterworks.

Eskilstuna Konstmuseum MUSEUM

(016-710 13 69; Portgatan 2, Munktellstaden; 11am-4pm Mon-Fri, to 8pm Thu, noon-4pm Sat & Sun) Eskilstuna Konstmuseum has an ambitious and very cool art collection in a beautiful space in the Munktell area. A chic little restaurant is attached.

Ebelingmuseet MUSEUM

(016-10 73 05; Eskilstunavägen 5; noon-4pm Tue-Sun; 2, 15 Torshälla) FREE The museum hosts bizarre steel sculptures by Allan Ebeling and paintings by his daughters, Marianne and Harriet, plus various temporary exhibitions. The old wooden houses and pretty riverside areas in Torshälla are also worth a look. It's about a 40-minute bus ride from Eskilstuna.

Sleeping & Eating

STF Hostel Eskilstuna HOSTEL €

(016-51 30 80; www.vilstasporthotell.se; hostel s/d from Skr350/520, hotel s/d from Skr695/890; P; 12) Inside the Vilsta nature reserve 2km south of town, this hostel is well provided for – all rooms have TV and ensuite bathroom. It's part of the Vilsta sport complex, with gym, jacuzzi and sports facilities on hand (for extra fees). Hotel rates include breakfast, linens and room cleaning. Sörmlandsleden, the long-distance walking trail, passes right through the grounds.

City Hotell Eskilstuna HOTEL €€

(016-10 88 50; www.cityhotell.se; Järnvägsplan 1; s/d Skr1045/1220; P) Right opposite the train station, this is among the better hotels. Rooms are spacious and comfortable, and some have balconies or cylindrical Swedish stoves, giving them a hint of the 19th century.

Café Kaka CAFE €

(016-13 10 94; www.cafekaka.se; Kyrkogatan 6; sandwiches Skr60, salads Skr70-100; 11am-6pm) Kaka is a funky, upbeat cafe and meeting place, serving sandwiches, wraps, and big, filling salads, with the occasional live DJ.

Restaurang Tingsgården SWEDISH €€

(016-51 66 20; Rådhustorget 2; dagens lunch Skr89, 2-course meal Skr210, mains Skr149-250; 11am-11pm Mon-Fri, noon-11pm Sat, noon-10pm Sun) This intimate restaurant, inside a wonderful wooden 18th-century house in the old town, is a treat. Its menu is heavy on the meat and fish, from lamb and steak to mountain trout. In summer you can sit out on a large deck overlooking the twinkling river.

Information

You'll find most services around Fristadstorget and the pedestrianised part of Kungsgatan.

Tourist office (016-710 70 00; www. eskilstuna.nu; Tullgatan 4; 10am-6pm Mon-Fri, 10am-2pm Sat & Sun, closed Sun winter) Dispenses helpful information.

Public library (016-10 13 51; Kriebsensgatan 4; 10am-7pm Mon-Thu, to 6pm Fri, to 2pm Sat)This central library has free internet access.

Getting There & Around

The bus station is located 500m east of the train station, beside the river. Local buses 701 and 801 go roughly hourly to Nyköping (Skr118, 1¾ hours). **Swebus Express** (0200-21 82 18; www.swebusexpress.se) operates up to six buses daily on its Stockholm–Eskilstuna–Örebro route, but SJ trains are best for destinations such as Örebro (Skr93, one hour, every two hours), Västerås (Skr73, 30 minutes, hourly) and Stockholm (Skr136, one hour, hourly).

Västerås

021 / POP 137,207

With its cobbled streets, higgledy-piggledy houses and flower gardens, Västerås' old town is an utter delight. But Sweden's sixth-largest city is a place of two halves: head just a few blocks southeast and you'll find modern shopping centres, large industries and sprawling suburbs that bear no resemblance to the teeny lanes and crafts shops you've left behind.

Västerås is also a handy base for exploring Mälaren lake and important pagan sites nearby.

Sights

★**Karlsgatan 2** MUSEUM
(Konstmuseum & Länsmuseum; 021-16 13 00; Karlsgatan 2; 10am-7pm Tue-Fri, to 8pm Thu, noon-4pm Sat & Sun) FREE This newly refurbished and expanded space in an old industrial block near the train station combines two museums that were each already noteworthy, making it a top destination. On one side is the Västmanland Länsmuseum (county museum), a huge and elaborate space that introduces the region's history (and prehistory) in kid-friendly, remarkably high-production-value fashion. In the opposite wing is the Västerås Konstmuseum, with a permanent collection of regional highlights (Bror Hjorth, Aguelí) and

Västerås

Top Sights
1 Karlsgatan 2 .... D2

Sights
2 Domkyrkan B1

Sleeping
3 Elite Stadshotellet B2
4 First Hotel Plaza C2
5 Klipper Hotel B2

Eating
6 Bill & Bobs B2
7 ICA C2
8 Kalle på Spangen B2

Västerås

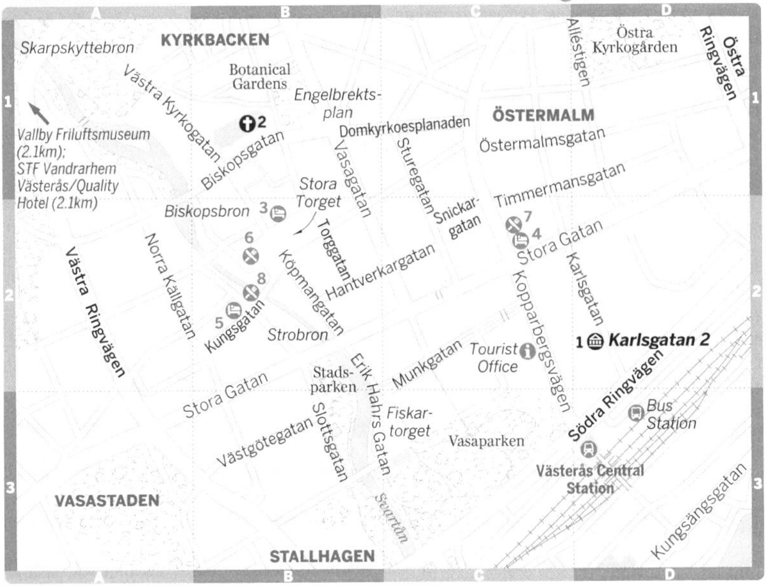

ARTY ALTERNATIVE LODGINGS

In addition to Västerås' normal, run-of-the-mill hotels, there are two unique accommodation possibilities in and around town. Both created by local artist Mikael Genberg, they are well worth investigating if you like your lodgings with a twist.

The **Hotell Hackspett** (Woodpecker Hotel; s/d per night incl breakfast Skr1250/2500) is a fabulous tree house in the middle of Vasaparken. The cabin is 13m above the ground in an old oak tree; guests (and breakfast) are hoisted up and down in a basket.

The second of Genberg's fascinating places to stay is the **Utter Inn** (Otter Inn; s/d per night incl breakfast Skr1250/2500): a small, red floating cabin in the middle of Mälaren lake, accessible only by boat. The bedroom is downstairs – 3m below the surface – and is complete with glass viewing panels to watch the marine life outside. There's room for two people, and a canoe is provided.

Both places can be booked through the Västerås tourist office (above). Genberg also has a website (www.mikaelgenberg.com); it's in Swedish, but the photographs will give you an idea of his creations.

ambitious, insightfully presented temporary displays.

Both museums have gallery spaces for temporary exhibitions, including vintage photographs, a recent survey of Swedish fashion design, contemporary Nordic painters, and interactive learning stations. In the central foyer there's a small gift shop and a cafe.

Vallby Friluftsmuseum MUSEUM
(☑021-39 80 70; www.vallbyfriluftsmuseum.se; Skerikesvägen 2; ☉10am-5pm; ℗; ⬚10,12) FREE
Vallby Friluftsmuseum, off Vallbyleden near the E18 interchange, 2km northwest of the city, is home to an extensive open-air collection of traditional huts and cottages. Among the 40-odd buildings, there's an interesting farmyard populated by adorable Jämtland goats, bunnies and draft horses, a cute cafe with outdoor seating, and craft workshops in old-school carpentry and glassmaking.

Domkyrkan CHURCH
(Cathedral; Biskopsgatan; ☉9am-5pm) FREE
The fine brick-built Domkyrka was begun in the 12th century, although most of what you see today is late-14th-century work. It contains carved floor slabs, six altarpieces and the marble sarcophagus of King Erik XIV, Gustav Vasa's son and successor, who died in 1577 after eating pea soup laced with arsenic. Ask about going into the **tower**; times vary, but it's generally open at 2pm Monday and Thursday and 10.30am Saturday (Skr30).

Behind the cathedral is the quaint old-town area **Kyrkbacken**. Once the student district and now a well-preserved portion of pre-18th-century Västerås, it's studded with artisans' workshops.

Anundshög ARCHAEOLOGICAL SITE
(☉24hr; ℗; ⬚12 Bjurhovda) FREE Västerås is surrounded by pre-Christian sites. The most interesting and extensive is Anundshög, the biggest *tumulus* (burial ground) in Sweden, 6km northeast of the city. It has a full complement of prehistoric curiosities, such as mounds, stone ship settings and a large 11th-century rune stone. The two main ship settings date from around the 1st century. The area is part of the Badelunda Ridge, which includes the 13th-century **Badelunda Church** (1km north) and the 16m-wide **Tibble Labyrinth** (1km south).

To get here from the bus stop walk 2km east. Ask at the tourist office for the handy map *Badelunda Forntids Bygd*.

🛏 Sleeping

STF Vandrarhem Västerås/Quality Hotel HOSTEL €
(☑021-30 38 00; q.vasteras@choice.se; Svalgången 1, Vallby; s/d from Skr300/600; ℗🚭🛜🛗) A couple of kilometres out of town, this hotel offers hostel accommodation in a dozen of its hotel rooms. The building is a suburban-industrial colossus with exterior and common areas in varying shades of white. Glass roofs over some rooms let in the long summer nights (if you want them to). There's a lobby restaurant, pool table and swimming pool.

Klipper Hotel HOTEL €
(☑021-41 00 00; www.klipperhotel.com; Kungsgatan 4; s/d incl breakfast Skr595/695; ℗) The attractive Klipper has one of the best locations in the city, near the river in the old town and 700m from the bus and train stations. The comfortable (if smallish) rooms are simple

and fresh. Budget rooms are available for Skr395 (no breakfast, and you make your own bed).

Västerås Mälarcamping CAMPGROUND €
(☎021-14 02 79; www.nordiccamping.se; Johannisbergsvägen; sites/cabins from Skr200/475; @ ; 25) The closest campground is this place 5km southwest of the city near Mälaren lake. It has up-to-date facilities including wi-fi and a pretty awesome miniature-golf course.

Elite Stadshotellet HOTEL €€
(☎021-10 28 00; info@vasteras.elite.se; Stora Torget; s/d Skr1050/1400; P @) Many of the rooms at the Elite, in a lovely art nouveau building, have prime views over the main square – request one if you like people-watching. The decor is tasteful (pale walls, leafy bedspreads and mahogany timber), the staff are obliging and there's a popular English-style pub attached. Parking is Skr90.

First Hotel Plaza HOTEL €€
(☎021-10 10 10; www.firsthotels.se; Karlsgatan 9A; r from Skr1000; P @) Bang in the centre of the modern city, this 25-storey skyscraper was built for gravity-defying lounge lizards: its cocktail bar surveys the city from the 24th floor. Some rooms have views over Mälaren lake, and there's a spa with masseurs, sauna and gym, and a restaurant churning out upscale Swedish favourites.

Eating & Drinking

The **ICA supermarket** (Kopparbergsvägen 15) is around the corner from the First Hotel Plaza.

Kalle på Spangen CAFE €
(☎021-12 91 29; www.kallepaspangen.se; Kungsgatan 2; lunch Skr65; ⏲10am-10pm Mon-Sat, 11am-10pm Sun) This great cafe, right by the river in the old part of town, inhabits several cosy, creaky-floored rooms filled with mismatched furniture and gilt-edged grandfather clocks. Lunch specials, such as the lasagne, are hefty and include salad, beverage, bread and coffee. There's nice riverside outdoor seating in summer.

Bill & Bobs SWEDISH €€
(☎021-41 99 21; www.billobob.se; Stora Torget 5; grill Skr199-350, mains Skr149-159, cocktails Skr98; ⏲5pm-2am) A diverse crowd settles down at this casual spot to drink and chatter at the outdoor tables on the square. Caesar salad and hamburger with bacon and bearnaise sauce are among Bill & Bobs' popular 'classic' dishes, though the focus is on the cook-your-own 'Black Rock' grill and its various combinations.

Information

Banks, ATMs and most services visitors will require can be found along Stora Gatan.

ÄNGELSBERG

Looking more like a collection of gingerbread houses than an industrial relic, **Engelsberg Bruk** (☎0223-444 64; engelsberg.se), a Unesco World Heritage Site in the tiny village of Ängelsberg, was one of the most important early-industrial ironworks in Europe. During the 17th and 18th centuries, its rare timber-clad **blast furnace** and **forge** (still in working order) were state-of-the-art technology, and a whole town sprang up around them. Today you can wander the perfectly preserved estate, made up of a mansion and park, workers' homes and industrial buildings. **Guided tours** (adult/child Skr65/free) run daily at 11am, 1.30pm and 3.30pm from June to August, and less frequently in May and September; call for details or head over to the tourist information hut near the parking area.

Nya Servering (☎0223-300 18; ⏲11.30am-2pm Mon-Fri, noon-5pm Sat & Sun) is not far from Ängelsberg train station, next to the tourist information hut, and serves fast food, coffee and simple sandwiches. There's a good view from here across to the island Barrön on Åmänningen lake, where the world's oldest surviving **oil refinery** is located – it was opened in 1875 and closed in 1902. You can take a ferry out to visit it in combination with Engelsberg Bruk (Skr110; departures at 11am, 1.30pm and 3.30pm in summer, check www.oljeon.se or fagersta.se/turism for updated schedules).

Ängelsberg is around 60km northwest of Västerås, from where regional trains run every hour or two (from Skr89, 45 minutes); from Ängelsberg train station it's a 1.5km walk north to the Engelsberg Bruk site. If you have your own wheels, it's a gorgeous drive from pretty much any direction.

Forex (☎021-18 00 80; Stora Gatan 18; ⏱9am-7pm Mon-Fri, to 3pm Sat) Currency-exchange office.

Tourist office (☎021-39 01 00; www.vasterasmalarstaden.se; Kopparbergsvägen 8; ⏱10am-6pm Mon-Fri, to 3pm Sat) Can help with visitor enquiries for the town and region.

Getting There & Around

Västerås airport (☎021-80 56 00; www.vasterasflygplats.se), 6km east of the city centre, is connected by bus L941. Budget carrier Ryanair flies here daily from the UK, and other budget airlines reach a variety of destinations, including Crete and Turkey (weekly). Check the airport website for an updated schedule.

The bus and train stations are adjacent, on the southern edge of Västerås. Regional bus 569 runs frequently to Sala (Skr74, 50 minutes, frequent), as do trains (Skr43, 25 minutes). **Swebus Express** (☎0200-21 82 18; www.swebusexpress.se) runs to Uppsala (via Stockholm, Skr149, three hours, five daily), Stockholm (Skr89, 1½ hours, eight daily) and Örebro (Skr89, 1¼ hours, seven daily).

SJ trains run frequently from Stockholm (Skr143, one hour) and to Örebro (Skr128, one hour), Uppsala (Skr97, 1½ hours) and Eskilstuna (Skr78, 30 minutes).

For taxis, call **Taxi Västerås** (☎021-18 50 00).

Sala

☎0224 / POP 12,289

The source of tiny Sala's parklike charm is distinctly unfrivolous. The local silver mine made Sweden rich in the 16th and 17th centuries, and its creation changed the face of the town: those small rivers, ponds and canals that weave so prettily through and around the neighbourhoods were actually built to power the mines.

For shops, banks and other services, head to Stortorget, the main square, and Rådmansgatan, the pedestrianised main street.

Sights & Activities

Sala Silvergruva MINE, MUSEUM

(☎0224-67 72 60; www.salasilvergruva.se; 60 Metersturen adult/child Skr160/85, 150 Metersturen Skr220/115; ⏱10am-5pm May-Sep, 11am-4pm Oct-Apr; Silverlinjen to Styrars) Even if you're reluctant to take the plunge, the above-ground parts of Sala Silvergruva, a mine about 2km south of the town centre, are nice to walk around. Beneath the surface are 20km of galleries, caverns and shafts. Tours go either 60m or 150m deep into the mines, every half-hour from 11am to 3pm. The descent involves walking down (and back up!) about 300 steps, and you'll want to bring a jacket as it gets cold in the mine.

The mine closed in 1908. The museum village contains artists' workshops, a restaurant (open from 11am to 4pm in summer, daily lunch Skr85) and a **museum** (admission free), with displays including a timeline of Swedish mining history and the barrel that was used to lower King Karl XI into the depths for his royal visit in 1687.

Both village and mine are off the Västerås road. It's a pretty walk along the Gröna Gången (Green Walk), which takes you southwest via the parks and the Mellandammen pond at Sofielund. Bring a camera – the weird landscape of mysterious, purpose-built structures in the area occasionally sprouts chimneys or falls away into deep holes.

Aguélimuseet MUSEUM

(☎0224-138 20; http://aguelimuseet.se; Vasagatan 17; ⏱11am-4pm Wed-Sun) FREE Aguélimuseet exhibits the largest display of oils and watercolours by local artist Ivan Aguéli (1869–1917) in Sweden, as well as work by some of his contemporaries. Aguéli was a pioneering Swedish modernist whose motto was 'One can never be too precise, too simple or too deep'. In summer there are also temporary exhibitions, usually of experimental young Scandinavian artists. The building is next door to the town library.

Väsby Kungsgård MUSEUM

(☎0224-106 37; www.vasbykungsgard.se; Museigatan 2; adult/child Skr25/free; ⏱1-4pm Mon-Fri; P) FREE In the main park in town is Väsby Kungsgård, a 16th-century royal farm where, according to a love letter from 1613, Gustav II Adolf met his mistress, Ebba Bruhe. Excitement for the traveller is confined to the beautifully preserved interiors, idyllic courtyard and 17th-century weapons collection.

Norrmanska Gården HISTORIC BUILDING

(Brunnsgatan 26) FREE The pretty wooden houses and courtyard called Normanska Gården were built in 1736; the area is now home to shops and a cafe (below).

Sleeping & Eating

STF Vandrarhem & Camping Sofielund HOSTEL €

(☎0224-127 30; http://sofielundsala.se; Sofielund; dm/s/d from Skr170/200/340; P) This haven of tranquillity is in the woods near the Mellandammen pond, 2km southwest of the town centre. It's a pet-friendly complex with camping, minigolf and a cafe (open June to August). Walk along Gröna Gången (25 minutes) or take the Silverlinjen bus to the water tower and walk the rest of the way. Reservations are necessary September to mid-May.

Hotell Svea HOTEL €
(☎0224-105 10; www.hotellsvea.com; Väsbygatan 19; s/d from Skr495/595) Friendly, 10-room Svea puts the emphasis on its personal service. Rooms are old-fashioned, with shared bathrooms, but it's clean and comfortable – and exceptionally handy for the train and bus stations.

Mat o Prat på Norrmanska CAFE €€
(☎0224-174 73; www.matoprat.nu; Brunnsgatan 26; dagens lunch Skr80, mains Skr109-230; 11am-2pm Mon & Tue, 11am-10pm Wed & Thu, noon-1am Fri & Sat) This restaurant, inside the rustic 18th-century wooden courtyard of Norrmanska Gården, has a great outdoor patio and includes a cute pub. On the menu you'll find everything from burgers and pasta to shrimp salad. It's a popular evening spot, too, with a decent happy-hour menu.

Information

The **tourist office** (☎0224-552 02; www.sala.se/turism; Stora Torget; 8am-5pm Mon-Fri year-round, plus 10am-2pm Sat May-Sep) inside the town hall faces the main square; it doesn't always stick to posted hours, but brochures are also available at the **library** (☎0224-555 01; Norra Esplanaden 5; 9.30am-7pm Mon-Thu, 9.30am-6pm Fri, 11am-3pm Sat). Internet access is available at both the tourist office and library. The free town map is useful if you want to use the walking paths.

Getting There & Around

Going to or from Uppsala, take regional bus 848 (Skr80 to Skr120, 1¼ hours, hourly). Regional trains go every two hours from Stockholm (Skr100, 30 to 90 minutes).

Ask about bike hire at the tourist office.

Nora

☎0587 / POP 6500

One of Sweden's most seductive old wooden towns, Nora sits snugly on the shores of a little lake, clearly confident in its ability to charm the pants off anyone. Slow your pace and take the time to succumb to its captivating features, such as quaint cobbled streets, old-world steam trains, mellow boat rides and decadent ice cream.

Sights & Activities

★**Kvarteret Bryggeriet** GALLERY
(www.norart.se; 11am-5pm Jun-Aug) FREE At the end of Prästgatan is a collection of buildings that once housed a brewery and now contain several art galleries and studios. A collective of locals puts on a knockout gallery show in the main building each summer, including work by established and rising Swedish artists. The building itself is a work of art, restored just enough to be functional without losing any of its original charm. Check online or ask at the main gallery for openings and evening events.

Göthlinska Gården HISTORIC BUILDING
(tours adult/child Skr80/free; 1pm Tue & Wed Jul & Aug, Sat May-Jun & Sep) The manor house, Göthlinska Gården, just off the main square, was built in 1739 and is now a museum featuring furniture, decor and accoutrements from the 17th century onward; entrance is by guided tour only.

Antique Railway TRAIN RIDES
(to Järle Skr120, to Pershyttan Skr 100; Tue-Thu, Sat & Sun mid-Jun–mid-Aug) From the train station down by the tourist office, a vintage train takes you 10km southeast to Järle (three times daily) or 2.5km southwest to the excellent old mining village at Pershyttan on an old steam train (once daily). The return trip is by bus (included in ticket price). Get tickets at the tourist office.

Alntorps Island CRUISE
(☎070-216 65 24; adult/child Skr20/10; 10am-6pm Jun-Aug;) Though it's technically a youngsters' activity, you don't need to be a child to appreciate the entertaining boat trips to Alntorps island. Boats depart roughly every half-hour from the jetty near the STF hostel. A walk around the island takes about an hour, and there are swimming spots, minigolf and a cafe. Tickets can be purchased at the tourist office.

Camping and cabins (from Skr1000) can be booked through the tourist office (but if you plan to stay, do bring supplies).

Sleeping & Eating

Self-caterers will find supermarkets on Prästgatan and near Nora Glass at the end of Storgatan.

STF Nora Tåghem HOSTEL €
(☎0587-146 76; www.norataghem.se; s/d Skr240/320; ⏲May–mid-Sep) Outdoing its home town in the cuteness department, this hostel lets you sleep in the tiny but adorable antique bunks of 1930s railway carriages. All compartments have great views over the lake, and there's a cafe that does breakfast, plus sandwiches and snacks in summer.

Trängbo Camping CAMPGROUND €
(☎0587-123 61; www.trangbocamping.se; sites Skr185, cabins from Skr325; ⏲May-Sep) This small campsite is by the lake 1.5km north of Nora (a lake-shore walking path leads from the train station/tourist office). Amenities are fine, if basic, and there's a place for swimming and beach volleyball. Guests can hire boats and canoes (Skr50/300 per hour/day).

Nora Stadshotell HOTEL €€
(☎0587-31 14 35; www.norastadshotell.se; Rådstugugatan 21; s/d from Skr790/1190) You can't miss this elegant building, planted smack on the main square, with 36 simple, white-furnitured rooms – some of them in a more modern annexe. There's a good-value lunch buffet (Skr85) at the restaurant, which can be eaten on the airy summer terrace, along with à la carte evening mains from Skr129 and a comfortable pub.

Nora Glass ICE CREAM €
(☎0587-123 32; Storgatan 11; ice creams Skr32-74; ⏲10.30am-6.30pm May-Aug) Nora is renowned for its incredible ice cream, made here for more than 80 years. You never know what flavours will be available – three or four different ones are churned out freshly each day – but you do know that they're worth queuing for. If hazelnut is among the day's selections, don't pass it up.

Strandstugan CAFE €
(☎0587-137 22; Storgatan 1; mains Skr35-86, sandwiches Skr45-55; ⏲10.30am-4.30pm summer) Down by the lake is this delightful wooden cottage, set in a flower-filled garden, where you can get coffee, sandwiches, quiches, desserts and other home-baked goodies, as well as Nora Glass ice-cream creations. If it's available, try the local speciality, *Bergslags paj*, a quiche made with venison, chanterelles and juniper berries.

Information

Tourist office (☎0587-811 20; Stationshuset; ⏲10am-6pm Mon-Sat, 10.30am-4pm Sun, shorter hours winter) At the train station by the lake, the tourist office books various guided tours (from June to August), including a town walk available in English. Alternatively, buy a brochure (Skr10) for self-guided walks.

Getting There & Around

Länstrafiken Örebro buses run every half-hour to Örebro (Skr64, 40 minutes) and other regional destinations. Ask at the tourist office about bike rental.

Örebro

☎019 / POP 140,000

A substantial, culturally rich city, Örebro buzzes around its central feature: the huge and romantic castle surrounded by a moat filled with water lilies. The city originally sprang up as a product of the textile industry, but it's now decidedly a university town – students on bicycles fill the streets, and other relaxed folk gather on restaurant patios and in parks. It's an ideal spot to indulge in standard holiday activities, like nursing a beer in a terrace cafe or shopping unhurriedly along a cobbled street.

Sights & Activities

Slottet CASTLE
(☎019-21 21 21; www.orebroslott.se; tours adult/child Skr60/30; ⏲daily Jun-Aug, 1pm Sat & Sun rest of year, history exhibition 10am-5pm daily May-Aug) The magnificent Slottet is now the county governor's headquarters. It was originally built in the late 13th century, but most of what you see today is from 300 years later. The outside is far more dramatic than the interior. To explore you'll need to take a tour; those in English start at noon, 2pm and 4pm daily in summer, and at 1pm weekends otherwise. Book through the tourist office (on the lower level). The northwestern tower holds a small **history exhibition**.

Länsmuseum MUSEUM
(County Museum; www.orebrolansmuseum.se; Engelbrektsgatan 3; ⏲9am-6pm Tue & Thu, noon-9pm Wed, noon-4pm Fri-Sun) FREE The Länsmuseum has strong and topical temporary exhibits; for example, a collection of protest posters from the '60s, or a consideration

Örebro

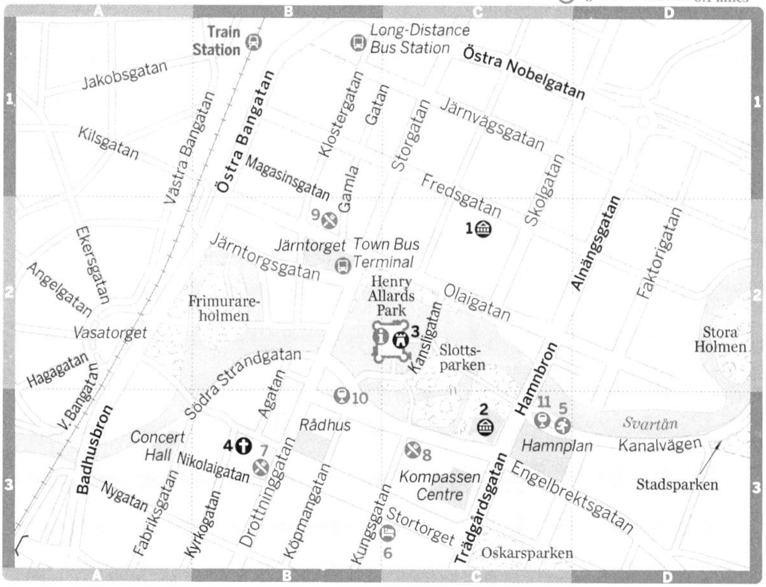

of the era's clothing and home furnishings as cultural indicators. It's also home to a permanent collection of artwork grouped by theme, and historical displays about the region (mostly in Swedish). The grounds are often dotted with sculptures or outdoor art installations.

Stadsparken PARK

(11am-5pm Tue-Sun; P) Stadsparken is an idyllic and kid-friendly park once voted Sweden's most beautiful. It stretches alongside Svartån (the Black River) and merges into the **Wadköping museum village** (admission Skr25; 11am-4pm or 5pm Tue-Sun, tours 1pm & 3pm Aug;). The village, named after what author Hjalmar Bergman called his hometown in his novels, is a cobblestone maze of workshops, cafes, a bakery and period buildings, including Kungsstugan (the King's Lodgings; a medieval house with 16th-century ceiling paintings) and Cajsa Warg's house (home of an 18th-century celebrity chef).

You can wander the village at any time; there are guided tours (Skr20) at 1pm and 3pm June to August. Most information is posted in Swedish, but there's a small tourist office with brochures in English. Ask about summer performances at the children's theater (tickets Skr50).

Örebro

Sights

1 Biologiska Museet C2
2 Länsmuseum C3
3 Slottet C2
4 St Nikolai Kyrka B3

Activities, Courses & Tours

5 M/S Gustaf Lagerbjelke C3

Sleeping

6 Behrn Hotell C3

Eating

7 Creperiet B3
8 Hälls Konditori Stallbacken C3
9 Pacos B2

Drinking & Nightlife

10 Bishops Arms B3
11 Harrys C3

Biologiska Museet MUSEUM

(19-21 65 16; Fredsgatan; adult/child Skr30/10; 11am-2pm Mon-Fri mid-Jun–mid-Aug) Many Swedish schools once had private natural history collections, but most were binned in the 1960s. Örebro's Biologiska Museet, in Karolinska Skolan, is a survivor; it's well worth a glance for its tier upon tier of stuffed birds. Outside peak summer hours, check with the tourist office for opening times.

St Nikolai Kyrka CHURCH
(10am-5pm) The 13th-century St Nikolai Kyrka has some historical interest: it's where Jean Baptiste Bernadotte (Napoleon's marshal) was chosen to take the Swedish throne.

Just opposite, on Drottninggatan, is the **Rådhus** (town hall); if you're around at the right time, stop to hear the chimes (12.05pm and 6.05pm year-round, plus 9pm June to September), when sculptures representing the city's past, present and future come wheeling out of a high arched window.

Svampen TOWER
(019-611 37 35; www.svampen.nu; Dalbygatan 4; 11am-4pm Sat & Sun, daily May-Aug; 11) FREE The first of Sweden's modern 'mushroom' water towers, Svampen was built in 1958 and now functions as a lookout tower. There are good views of lake Hjälmaren at the top, as well as a cafe (daily specials Skr100).

M/S Gustaf Lagerbjelke CRUISE
(019-760 93 00; www.lagerbjelke.com; Engelbrektsgatan 5; lunch cruise adult/child Skr250/125) Hop a boat here for a three-hour lunch cruise to Hjälmaren, including an on-board shrimp supper. Boats leave daily at noon in summer. There's also the special four-hour 'shrimp boat' (a reference to the menu, not the vessel), leaving at 7pm Monday and Wednesday to Saturday (Skr280/140 per adult/child). Order tickets by phone or online.

Sleeping

Gustavsvik Camping CAMPGROUND, CABIN €€
(019-19 69 50; www.gustavsvik.se; Sommarrovägen; sites/cabins from Skr325/890; year-round; 11) This camping facility is 2km south of the city centre, and it's attached to a family-oriented water park that can be a bit of a madhouse in summer. There are various swimming and soaking pools, minigolf, a cafe, a gym, a restaurant-pub and bike rental (Skr60 per day). Cabins have full kitchens, TV and wireless internet. Book ahead in summer.

Behrn Hotell HOTEL €€€
(019-12 00 95; www.behrnhotell.se; Stortorget 12; s/d Skr1375/1855;) Excellently situated on the main square, the Behrn goes the extra mile with individually decorated rooms, ranging from strictly business to farmhouse or edgy modern Scandinavian. Do it right and get a room with a balcony or a suite with old wooden beams, chandeliers and a jacuzzi. There's also a spa, and a restaurant serving dinner Tuesday to Friday.

Clarion Hotel Örebro HOTEL €€€
(019-670 67 00; http://choice.se/clarion/orebro; Kungsgatan 14; s/d from Skr1680/1880;) This modern hotel along a shopping street just a block from the main square has comfortable rooms with all the amenities, done up in chic Swedish fabrics and fixtures. There's a popular and attractive lobby lounge area, a gym and spa, and parking (Skr175). Its restaurant, Kitchen & Table, is by famed Swedish-New York chef Marcus Samuelsson.

Eating

Cheap eating options such as pizza and kebabs abound. For self-caterers there's a supermarket in the Kompassen Centre on Stortorget.

Hälls Konditori Stallbacken CAFE €
(www.hallsconditori.se; Engelbrektsgatan 12; pastries Skr20-45, lunch specials Skr79, brunch buffet Skr85; 7.30am-6pm Mon-Fri, 10am-4pm Sat;) One of two locations of this bakery-cafe (the other's in Järntorget), Hälls is a classic old-style *konditori* and a favourite hangout for locals. Go for *fika* (coffee and cake) or more substantial salads, quiche and sandwiches. If the weather's nice, sit out back in the hidden courtyard area – part of Stallbacken, the tiny Old Town block.

Creperiet CAFE €
(Nikolaigatan; mains Skr59-85; 11am-9pm Mon-Fri, 10am-5pm Sat & Sun;) This large underground space is extremely kid-friendly: a play area occupies about a third of the room. But it's no frumpy parental refuge; the long, low room is neatly designed, with subdued colours and well-chosen lighting. There are also tables outdoors on a terrace. The menu is mostly healthy salads and crêpes filled with fresh veggies.

Pacos TEX-MEX €€
(019-10 10 46; Olaigatan 13A; mains Skr85-189; 11am-10pm Mon-Fri, noon-11pm Sat, 2-9pm Sun) OK, maybe Tex-Mex isn't exactly what you expected to be eating in the middle of Sweden, but the fun decor and chirpy music at Pacos make for a nice change of pace, and the lunch specials are good value.

WORTH A TRIP

TIVEDEN NATIONAL PARK

Carved by glaciers, **Tiveden National Park** (activities 0584-47 40 83; www.tiveden.se; visitor centre 10am-4pm May-Sep, 11am-4pm Sat & Sun Apr & Oct) makes for wonderful wild walking. This trolls' home and former highwaymen's haunt 33km south of Askersund is noted for its ancient virgin forests, which are rare in southern Sweden, and has lots of dramatic bare bedrock, extensive boulder fields and a scattering of lakes.

Several self-guided walks, including the 6km Trollkyrka (Troll Church) trail, start from the visitor centre in the southeastern part of the park, 5km north of Rd 49 (turn off at Bocksjö).

There are also themed guided tours (Skr150), starting at 10am Wednesday through Sunday from the visitor centre from mid-June to August. You can pick up brochures and maps here, and there's a small shop.

A few kilometres north along Rd 49 is the turn-off to **Fagertärn**, a pretty lake that fills with blood-red water lilies in July. Legend says a fisherman called Fager traded his daughter to the fearsome water spirit Näcken in exchange for a good catch. On their wedding day, the daughter rowed out onto the lake alone and drove a knife into her heart, and the lilies have been stained red ever since.

The park is a bit out of the way, and there's no public transport, but if you have your own wheels it's worth a stop, especially for hikers.

The area is also good for **cycling** (the Sverigeleden trail passes nearby), **canoeing**, **fishing**, **cross-country skiing** and **horse riding**. The **tourist office** (0583-810 88; www.visitaskersund.se; Torget, Askersund; 10am-7pm daily, weekdays only winter) in Askersund or the Tiveden visitor centre can help make arrangements.

You can camp overnight in the park or stay in adorable little red huts at the **STF Tivedstorp Vandrarhem** (0584-47 20 90; www.tivedstorp.se; dm/s/d from Skr200/370/500, sites Skr100; Apr-Oct; P).

Drinking & Nightlife

Harrys PUB
(019-10 89 89; Hamnplan; beer from Skr60; 5pm-1am or 2am, from 2pm Sat) Though it's part of a sort of blah chain, this particular branch of Harrys has a good location in a cool old brick factory building by the river. It's popular and has a comprehensive menu of pub meals (snacks Skr65, mains Skr149-239), live music on a Thursday, and a nightclub on Friday and Saturday.

Bishops Arms PUB
(019-15 69 20; Drottninggatan 1; to at least midnight) Whether or not you're convinced by the 'authentic English pub' schtick, the bar's outdoor drinking area, with super castle views, is a swinging spot on a summer evening. There are also pub meals available.

Information

Banks can be found along Drottninggatan, south of the castle.

Library (21 10 00; Näbbtorgsgatan) The public library has brochures on tourist attractions in the area, plus free internet access.

Tourist Office (019-21 21 21; www.orebrotown.se; 10am-5pm summer, noon-4pm Sat & Sun rest of year) The tourist office is inside the castle on the lower level.

Getting There & Away

Long-distance buses leave from opposite the train station and run almost everywhere in southern Sweden. **Swebus Express** (0771-21 82 18; www.swebus.se) has connections to Norrköping, Karlstad and Oslo (Norway); Mariestad and Göteborg; Västerås and Uppsala; and Eskilstuna and Stockholm.

Train connections are also good. Direct SJ trains run to/from Stockholm (Skr219, two hours) every hour with some via Västerås (Skr128, one hour); and frequently to and from Göteborg (Skr410, three hours). Other trains run to Gävle (Skr240 to Skr430, three to four hours, five daily) and Borlänge (Skr296, 2¼ hours, twice daily), where you can change for Falun and Mora.

Getting Around

Town buses leave from Järntorget; tickets cost Skr26/13 per adult/child and are good for three hours.

Cykeluthyrning (019-21 19 09), at the Hamnplan boat terminal, rents bikes from May to September from Skr90 per day.

For a cab, call **Taxi Kurir** (019-12 30 30).

Karlstad

054 / POP 87,000

A pleasant and compact town centre wrapped in layers of perpetually snarled traffic, Karlstad makes itself useful as a base for travellers pursuing outdoor activities in Värmland. There are several sights worth seeing in town, and a large student population means it has a decent restaurant and bar scene.

Sights & Activities

★Värmlands Museum MUSEUM

(054-14 31 00; www.varmlandsmuseum.se; adult/child Skr80/free; 10am-6pm Mon-Fri, to 8pm Wed, 11am-4pm Sat & Sun) The award-winning and imaginative Värmlands Museum occupies two buildings on Sandgrundsudden (reclaimed land now converted into a pleasant park) near the library. Its multimedia displays cover local history and culture from the Stone Age to current times, including music, the river, forests and textiles. Some components of the museum are open-air, activity-based displays about local industry and working life, including a log-driving museum and a mineral mine, just outside of town; pick up brochures at the museum or tourist office.

Mariebergsskogen PARK

(054-29 69 90; www.mariebergsskogen.se; Stadspark; 7am-10pm; P; 1, 31) FREE For green spaces and picnic spots, seek out Mariebergsskogen, a combined leisure park, open-air museum and animal park in the southwestern part of town (about 1km from the centre). Also here is Naturum Värmland, with a cafe and shop, perched over Lake Vänern.

Domkyrka CHURCH

(10am-7pm Mon-Fri, to 4pm Sat, to 6pm Sun Jun-Aug, 10am-4pm daily Sep-May) It's worth peeking into the 18th-century domkyrka (cathedral), a soothing space with chandeliers and votive ships.

Old Town Prison MUSEUM

(Karlbergsgatan 3; 10am-5pm) FREE You can visit the small and creepy old town prison in the basement of Clarion Hotel Bilan, with original cells and prisoners' letters.

Gamla Stenbron BRIDGE

On the eastern river branch, find Gamla Stenbron – at 168m, it's one of Sweden's longest stone bridges.

Boat Cruises CRUISE

(054-046 18; www.karlstad.se; single trip Skr23) From Tuesday to Saturday late June to mid-August, there are regular two-hour boat cruises on Vänern lake, leaving from the harbour behind the train station. A cheaper option (Tuesday to Sunday, summer only) is the 'boat bus' – city 'buses' 91 to 97 circle Karlstad on the water, and you can use your regular city-bus ticket (good for one hour).

Sleeping

STF Vandrarhem Karlstad HOSTEL €

(054-56 68 40; karlstad.vandrarhem@swipnet.se; dm/s/d from Skr210/390/580; P; 100) The hostel, in an impressive, renovated military building on a hillside, is off the E18 at Kasernhöjden, 1km southwest of Karlstad's centre, and has good facilities. Reception hours are limited (8am to 10am and 4pm to 7pm), so call ahead.

CarlstadCity Hostel HOSTEL €

(054-21 65 60; www.carlstadcity.se; Järnvägsgatan 8; s/d hostel from Skr390/500, hotel from Skr580/800;) This very central hostel, with hotel-standard rooms also available, has bunks in simple, basic whitewashed rooms with shared bathrooms. There's a guest kitchen and a good breakfast buffet available (Skr60 for hostellers).

Skutbergets Camping CAMPGROUND €

(054-53 51 20; www.camping.se/s10; sites from Skr150, cabins from Skr390; P; 18) This big, friendly lakeside campsite, 7km west of town off the E18 motorway, is part of a large sports and recreation area, with beach volleyball, a driving range, minigolf, exercise tracks and a mountain-bike course. There are also sandy and rocky beaches nearby.

Clarion Hotel Bilan HOTEL €€

(054-10 03 00; cc.bilan@choice.se; Karlbergsgatan 3; r from Skr1050; P) The town's old jail cells have been converted into large, bright and cleverly decorated rooms with exposed-wood ceiling beams and funky shapes – and a display in the basement fills you in on the building's history. There's a guest sauna,complimentary afternoon tea, and a free dinner buffet and breakfast.

Eating & Drinking

Make tracks to the main square, Stora Torget, and its surrounds for good eating and drinking options – most have outdoor summer seating. There's a handy supermarket

(☎054-15 22 00; Fredsgatan 4) inside Åhléns and a **Systembolaget liquor store** (☎054 15 56 00; Drottninggatan 26) nearby.

Kebab House PIZZA, GRILL €€
(☎054-15 08 15; Västra Torggatan 9; kebabs Skr64-89, pizza Skr85-112, mains Skr99-249; ⏰from 4pm, lunch 11am-3pm Mon-Fri) Don't be fooled by the name – the Kebab House is a cut above your average fast-food place and serves good-value pizza, kebabs and salads as well as steaks and fish. Check out its fancy striped wallpaper and chandeliers if you don't believe us. In summer, stake out one of the popular outdoor tables, along the busy pedestrianised street.

Källaren Munken SWEDISH €€€
(☎054-18 51 50; restaurang@munken.nu; Västra Torggatan 17; starters Skr115-155, mains Skr195-295; ⏰closed Sun) Inspired gourmet meals, like roasted stag in lingonberry-chanterelle sauce, and French standards like *moules frites* (mussels & fries), are served up in this elegant but cosy 17th-century vaulted cellar, the oldest building in town.

Båten FLOATING RESTAURANT
(Magasin 1, Inre Hamn; ⏰5pm-late Mon-Sat Jun-Aug) The huge Båten ('the boat'), on a boat moored at the harbour, is a highly rated open-air restaurant and a very popular summer drinking (and eating) spot.

Information

Sharing the same building as the library at the edge of the town centre, the **tourist office** (☎054-540 24 70; www.visitkarlstad.se; Bibliotekshuset, Västra Torggatan 26; ⏰9am-7pm Mon-Fri, 10am-6pm Sat, 10am-3pm Sun) has lots of info on both town and county (including fresh-air escapes in the region's forests) and its rivers and lakes. Internet access is available in the library. Banks and ATMs line Storgatan.

Getting There & Around

Karlstad is the major transport hub for western central Sweden. The long-distance bus terminal is at Drottninggatan 43, 600m west of the train station.

Swebus Express (☎0200-21 82 18; www.swebusexpress.se) has daily services on a number of routes, including Karlstad–Falun–Gävle (Skr289, 10 hours), Karlstad–Göteborg (Skr199, two to three hours), Stockholm–Örebro–Karlstad–Oslo and Karlstad–Mariestad–Jönköping (Skr309, six hours).

Intercity trains to Stockholm (Skr420, two to three hours) run frequently. There are also several daily services to Göteborg (Sk210, three to four hours) and express services to Oslo (Skr358, three hours).

Värmlandstrafik (☎020-22 55 80) runs regional buses. Bus 250 travels to Sunne (Skr107, 1¼ hours, one to five daily) and Torsby (Skr144, two hours, one to three daily).

Free bikes are available from the city's two **Solacykeln** booths: **Stora Torget** (☎054-29 50 29; Stora Torget; ⏰7.30am-7pm Mon-Fri, 10am-3.30pm Sat May-Sep) and **outer harbour** (outer harbour; ⏰9.30am-5.30pm Mon-Fri, 10am-3.30pm Sat Jun-Aug). All you need is a valid ID.

Sunne

☎0565 / POP 4900

Sunne has the largest ski resort in southern Sweden. In summer it's a quiet spot with a number of cultural attractions. It also has a proud literary heritage, as the hometown of both Selma Lagerlöf and Göran Tunström. (The latter lived at Ekebyvägen 56 and is buried near the east gable of Sunne Church.)

Sights & Activities

Mårbacka MUSEUM
(☎0565-310 27; www.marbacka.s.se; admission Skr30; ⏰10am-4pm daily Jun-Aug, 11am-3pm Sat & Sun May & Sep, 11am-2pm Sat Oct-Dec & Feb-Apr, closed Jan; P; 🚌215 from Sunne) The main draw in the area is the house at Mårbacka, 9km from Sunne, where Swedish novelist Selma Lagerlöf (1858–1940) was born. She was the first woman to receive the Nobel Prize for Literature, and many of her tales are based in the local area. Seeing the interiors requires a 45-minute guided tour (Skr125), which leave on the hour from 11am to 3pm; a tour in English is given daily in summer at 2pm.

Rottneros Park PARK
(☎0565-602 95; www.rottnerospark.se; adult/child Skr120/40; ⏰10am-4pm May-Jun & Sep, to 6pm Jul & Aug; P 👪; 🚌200) Known as 'Ekeby' in *Gösta Berling's Saga*, Rottneros Park, 6km south of Sunne, soothes travel-weary adults with flower gardens, a tropical greenhouse and an arboretum. There's lots for kids, including the rope-swinging delights of Sweden's largest climbing forest. The attached warehouse has temporary exhibitions. Rottneros has its own train station.

Sundsbergs Gård MUSEUM
(☎0565-103 63; adult/child Skr50/free; ⏰noon-4pm Wed-Sun late Jun–mid-Aug) Sundsbergs

Gård, behind the Hotel Selma Lagerlöf, was featured in Lagerlöf's *Gösta Berling's Saga* and now contains a forestry museum, a furniture and textiles collection, an art exhibition, a cafe and a manor house.

Ski Sunne SNOW SPORTS
(☎0565-602 80; www.skisunne.se; day pass adult/child Skr295/240) Ski Sunne, the town's ski resort, has nine different descents, a snowboarding area and a cross-country skiing stadium, and night skiing in some areas, plus all the usual ski-area facilities (lodge, bar-restaurant, shop, equipment rentals). In summer the resort becomes a mountain-bike park.

Freya af Fryken CRUISE
(www.frejaaffryken.se; ⏲Jul–mid-Aug) The steamship *Freya af Fryken* sank in 1896, but it was raised and lovingly restored in 1994. Now you can sail along the lakes north and south of Sunne; departures are several times weekly in summer. Lunch and dinner cruises are also on the program. The boat was undergoing renovations when we visited; check with the tourist office for updates.

Sleeping & Eating

There are supermarkets on Storgatan.

STF Vandrarhem Sunne HOSTEL €
(☎0565-107 88; www.sunnevandrarhem.se; Hembygdsvägen 7; dm Skr200, s/d from Skr300/440) Part of a little homestead museum just north of town, this well-equipped hostel has beds in sunny wooden cabins. There's a futuristic kitchen, an antique dining room and outside tables and chairs for alfresco meals. Breakfast is available (Skr60) and bikes can be rented.

Sunne SweCamp Kolsnäs CAMPGROUND €
(☎0565-164 00; www.kolsnas.se; sites/2-/4-bed cabins Skr210/495/615;) This is a large, family-oriented campsite at the southern edge of town, with minigolf, a restaurant, a beach and assorted summer activities, plus bikes, boats and canoes for rent. There's a good restaurant attached. Book ahead in summer.

Länsmansgården INN €€
(☎0565-140 10; info@lansman.com; Ulfsby; s/d from Skr895/1195, buffet lunch Skr149, mains Skr195-225; ⏲buffet lunch noon-3pm, dinner from 6pm; P) This historic 'sheriff's house' features in Lagerlöf's *Gösta Berling's Saga*. It's a picturesque place for a fine lunch or restful evening in one of the romantic bedrooms, named after the book's characters. The highly rated restaurant specialises in Swedish cuisine from the Värmland region, using locally sourced pike, salmon, beef, reindeer and lamb and fresh seasonal ingredients.

Check the website for occasional hotel packages with steeply discounted room rates. The mansion is 4km north of Sunne centre, by Rd 45 (toward Torsby).

Saffran & Vitlök CAFE €
(☎0565-120 09; www.saffranvitlok.se; Stortorget; salads Skr85; ⏲11am-6pm Mon-Fri, to 3pm Sat) Having expanded and moved into the big, white library building on the main square, this cafe serves giant bowls of hefty salads to take away or dine in on (there's indoor or courtyard seating), plus excellent coffee, sandwiches, pastries and hot dishes. It lives up to the name (*vitlök* is garlic), so just follow your nose and you'll find it.

Nya Hembageriet BAKERY €
(Badhusgatan 12; pastries from Skr10; ⏲8am-6pm Mon-Fri) This tiny bakery in an old wooden building on a side street has a broad range of baked goodies, decadent pastries and hearty rustic breads to take away.

Strandcaféet CAFE €€
(☎0565-104 88; Strandpromenaden; lunch specials Skr79-99, mains Skr79-199; ⏲noon-6pm May-Sep) In the park is this appealing beach cafe, with outdoor seating over the water and live music on some summer evenings. Look for dinner specials (like pig roast or all-you-can-eat lobster) midweek.

Information

Banks and most other tourist facilities are on Storgatan.

Tourist office (☎0565-167 70; www.sunneturism.se; Kolsnäsvägen 4; ⏲9am-6pm Mon-Thu, to 8pm Fri, plus 10am-3pm Sat & Sun summer) Located at the campsite reception building next to a water park, the tourist office has brochures and internet access (Skr20 for 30 minutes).

Getting There & Around

Värmlandstrafik bus 202 runs to Torsby (Skr74, 45 minutes, one to three daily) and bus 200 goes to Karlstad (Skr107, 1¼ hours, one to five daily). Regional trains to Torsby and Karlstad (one to three daily) are faster than the bus but cost the same.

Torsby & Around

☎0560 / POP 12,000 (MUNICIPALITY)

Sleepy Torsby, deep in the forests of Värmland, is only 38km from Norway. The area's history and sights are linked to emigrants from Finland, who settled in western parts of Sweden in the mid-16th century and built their own distinctive farms and villages in the forests. These homesteads, many of which have been well preserved, are the main attraction for visitors to the area; public transport isn't great, and the sites are far apart, so it's easiest to explore if you have your own wheels.

Sights

★ Ritamäki Finngård MUSEUM

(☎073-849 61 66; hembygdsforeningen@lekvattnet.nu; Lekvattnet; ⏰11am-6pm Jun-Aug; 🚌310) FREE Known for its characteristic smokehouse, Ritamäki Finngård, 32km west of Torsby and 10km from Lekvattnet, is one of the best-preserved Finnish homesteads in the area. It was probably built in the late 17th century and was inhabited until 1964, making it the last permanently inhabited Finnish homestead in Sweden. It's surrounded by a nature reserve. Follow signs from Lekvattnet; from the Ritamäki parking lot it's a 1.5km walk along a forest path to the site.

Ritamäki is also one of the stops along the 8.2km-long 'Seven-torpsleden' (a 'torp' is a croft or homestead), a pretty walking trail that makes a loop among several of the homesteads in the Finn Forest. Ask for a map at the Finnskogscentrum.

★ Torsby Finnskogscentrum MUSEUM

(Torsby Finn Forest Centre; ☎0560-162 93; www.varmlandsmuseum.se; Lekvattnet 84; adult/child Skr40/free; ⏰11am-5pm mid-Jun–mid-Aug; P) The ingeniously designed Forest Centre, opened in June 2014 near Lekvattnet as part of Värmlands County Museum, covers the 17th-century Finnish settlement of the area, with displays on smokehouses, hunting, music, witchcraft and the settlers' trademark 'slash and burn' style of cultivating grain. (They planted rye in the ashes of burnt trees.) There's also a research library and a cafe. The centre is on the E16 road, 22km from Torsby, across from a small convenience shop.

Hembygdsgården Kollsberg MUSEUM

(☎0560-718 61; Levgrensvägen 36; adult/child Skr20/free, guided tours Skr40; ⏰noon-5pm Jun-Aug) Hembygdsgården Kollsberg, down beside Fryken lake, is a dinky homestead museum with several old houses, including a Finnish cabin. A cafe serves coffee and waffles (Skr40) and the traditional Finnish settlers' dish *motti och fläsk* (oat porridge with pork, Skr80).

Fordonsmuseum MUSEUM

(☎0560-712 10; Gräsmarksvägen 8; adult/child Skr40/free; ⏰10am-5.30pm Mon-Fri Jun-Aug, plus noon-5pm Sat & Sun May & Sep) At the edge of Torsby's town centre, the Fordonsmuseum will appeal to motorheads with its collection of rare and vintage cars, motorcycles and fire engines.

Activities

There are a number of summer activities and tours in the area, including fishing, canoeing, white-water rafting, rock climbing, mountain biking, and beaver and elk safaris. Contact the tourist office for information.

You can also catch boat trips on the *Freya af Fryken* from Torsby.

Finnskogleden HIKING

This easy and well-marked long-distance path roughly follows the Norwegian border for 240km, from near Charlottenberg to Søre Osen in Norway (passing the old Finnish homestead Ritamäki Finngård). A guidebook (Skr125, from tourist offices) has text in Swedish only but all the topographical maps you'll need. The best section, Øyermoen to Röjden, requires one or two overnight stops.

Bus 311 runs from Torsby to near the border at Röjdåfors (twice daily on weekdays), and bus 310 runs to Vittjärn (twice daily on weekdays), 6km from the border on Rd 239.

Fortum Ski Tunnel SKIING

(☎0560-270 00; www.skitunnel.se; Vasserudsvägen 11, Valberget; adult/child rental packet Skr200/130, 1hr pass Skr160/100; ⏰9am or 10am-7pm Mon-Fri, 9am-5pm Sat & Sun) Looking like something you might use to smash atoms, Sweden's first ski tunnel (1.3km) offers controlled conditions and a gentle incline, making it a great workout or equipment-testing track. It also contains the world's only indoor biathlon shooting range.

Hovfjället SKIING

(☎0560-313 00; www.hovfjallet.se; day pass adult/child Skr310/250, alpine ski hire per day from Skr255/210; ⏰Dec–mid-Apr) For skiing outdoors, check out Hovfjället, 20km north of Torsby. There are several ski lifts and a variety of runs. The resort also offers dog-sledding on weekends, plus other activities such as snowshoeing, mountain biking and wolf-viewing trips.

Sleeping & Eating

Vägsjöfors Herrgård B&B, HOSTEL €
(0560-313 30; www.vagsjoforsherrgard.com; sites Skr180, dm Skr210, B&B with shared/private bathroom Skr380/480) This large manor house is 20km north of Torsby, by a stunning lake. Rooms are individually and tastefully decorated, and there are hostel beds in little cabins and campsites on the grounds as well. Hostel breakfast is Skr65 extra. There's also a guest kitchen. Family-size groups can rent a self-catering apartment (Skr1200, sleeps up to six).

Torsby Camping CAMPGROUND €
(0560-710 95; www.torsbycamping.se; Bredviken; sites Skr190, cabins from Skr570; May–mid-Sep) With its child-friendly beach, playgrounds and minigolf, this large, well-equipped lakeside campsite (5km south of town along Rd 45) is a popular family spot. There's a variety of huts and chalets for rent, including a cool 'studio' cottage with a lake-facing picture window (Skr1190).

Hotell Örnen HOTEL €€
(0560-146 64; www.hotellornen.se; Östmarksvägen 4; s/d Skr895/1095; P) Cosy Örnen is a pretty lemon-coloured place set behind a white picket fence in the town centre. Cheerful, homey Swedish-style rooms practically vibrate with wholesomeness and folky charm.

Wienerkonditoriet CAFE €
(Järnvägsgatan 6; coffee Skr20, pastries from Skr17; 9am-6pm) This homey cafe on the main drag feels like an auntie's living room, complete with family portraits on the walls.

Information

Tourist office (0560-160 50; www.torsby.se; Gräsmarksvägen 12; 9am-6pm Mon-Fri, 10am-3pm Sat & Sun, shorter hours winter) In the large, grass-roofed Torsby Infocentre a couple of kilometres west of town, on Rd 45.

Getting There & Around

There are a few buses that run north of Torsby, but generally on weekdays only.

Falun

023 / POP 56,700

An unlikely combination of industrial and adorable, Falun is home to the region's most important copper mine and, as a consequence, the source of the deep-red paint that renders Swedish country houses so uniformly cute. It's the main city of Dalarna, putting it within easy striking distance of some of Sweden's best attractions, and the town itself is a pretty place to roam. Falu Kopparbergsgruva (Copper Mountain Mine) is unique enough to appear on Unesco's World Heritage list. Even more compelling is the nearby home of painter Carl Larsson, a work of art in itself and absolutely unmissable.

Sights & Activities

The Unesco World Heritage listing actually encompasses a much larger area than just the Kopparbergsgruva. The free brochure *Discover the Falun World Heritage Site* places Falun in historical context and pinpoints all the smelteries, slag heaps and mine estates within a 10km radius of the town; pick it up at the mine entrance or the tourist office.

Falu Kopparbergsgruva MINE
(023-78 20 30; www.falugruva.se; tours adult/child Skr210/80, above-ground only Skr80/40; tours hourly 10am-5pm Jun-Aug, less frequent rest of year; P; 53, 708 Timmervägen) Falun's copper mine was the world's most important by the 17th century; called 'Sweden's treasure chest', it drove the small country's international aspirations. Entrance to the mining complex is west of town at the top end of Gruvgatan. You can opt to take a one-hour underground tour of the mines or simply explore above ground. For the mine tour, bring warm clothing and good shoes. In summer tours in English happen hourly; from October to April you should book ahead.

Don't miss the dramatic **Stora Stöten** (Great Pit), a vast hole caused by a major mine collapse in the 17th century. By some miracle, the miners were on holiday that day and no one was harmed. There are lookouts around the crater edge, and numerous mine buildings, including a 15m waterwheel and shaft-head machinery.

Tradition says a goat called Kåre first drew attention to the copper reserves when he rolled in the earth and pranced back to the village with red horns. The first historical mention is in a document from 1288, when the Bishop of Västerås bought shares in the company. As a by-product, the mine produced the red paint that became a characteristic of Swedish houses – Falu Red is still used today. The mine finally closed in 1992.

When you buy your ticket, ask for a map of the walking routes around the area – there are some very pretty trails that follow the path of the water once used to power the mine. Suggested routes range from 1.5km to a nice 12.2km ramble.

If you're getting peckish, the pretty cafe Gjuthuset, serving coffee, sandwiches and cake, teeters on the edge of the Great Pit. Opposite the main reception is Geschwornergården Värdshus (☑ 023-78 26 16; lunch Skr85), which is a more stately affair and does excellent hot lunch specials.

Mine Museum MUSEUM
(www.falugruva.se; adult/child Skr80/40; ☉ 10am-5:30pm daily Jul & Aug, 10am-5:30pm Mon-Fri, noon-4pm Sat & Sun May, Jun & Sep) The mine museum, just behind the ticket-sales building at the entrance to the mining complex, contains everything you could possibly want to know about the history, administration, engineering, geology and copper production of the mine, plus displays about the miners' hospital, the world's biggest coin, and various myths and legends about the mine.

★ **Carl Larsson-gården** HISTORIC BUILDING
(☑ 023-600 53; www.clg.se; Sundborn; tours adult/child/family Skr160/60/550; ☉ frequent tours in English 10am-5pm May-Sep, 11am Mon-Fri & 1pm Sat & Sun Jan-Apr; ♿ ; ☐ 64) Whatever you do, don't miss Carl Larsson-gården, home of artist Carl Larsson and his wife, Karin, in the picturesque village of Sundborn. After the couple's deaths, their early-20th-century home was preserved in its entirety by their children, but it's no gloomy memorial. Lilla Hyttnäs is a work of art, full of brightness, humour and love.

Tours (45 minutes) run hourly; call in advance for the times of English tours (alternatively, borrow an English handbook and follow a Swedish tour).

Superb colour schemes and furniture fill the house: Carl's portraits of his wife and children are everywhere, and Karin's tapestries and embroidery reveal she was as skilled an artist as her husband. Even today, the modern styles throughout the house (especially the dining room) will inspire interi-

or decorators, and the way the family lived, suffused in art and learning, will inspire practically everyone.

Also worth a look is the **Kvarnen** (Mill) gallery, which focuses on Karin Larsson and hosts temporary exhibits (admission Skr50).

Dalarnas Museum MUSEUM
(www.dalarnasmuseum.se; Stigaregatan 2-4; ☉ 10am-5pm Tue-Fri, noon-5pm Sat-Mon, to 9pm Wed summer; ♿) **FREE** Dalarnas Museum is a super introduction to Swedish folk art, music and costumes. It's kid-friendly, too, with the opposite of the usual 'Do not touch' signs (these say 'Be curious! Please touch!'). Selma Lagerlöf's study is preserved here, and there are ever-changing art and craft exhibitions, including a great regional collection of textiles. Don't miss the graphic-arts hall, with a display on the history of Swedish sketching and engraving techniques, or the gallery of traditional costumes from all parts of Dalarna.

Kristine Kyrka CHURCH
(☑ 023-545 70; Stora Torget; ☉ 10am-4pm) A sea of baroque blue and gold hits you at Kristine Kyrka (built 1642–55), which shows off the riches brought to town by the 17th-century copper trade. In the **Stortorget** (main square) in front of the church is an impressive **statue** of the rebel warrior Engelbrekt, by Karl Hultström. The square has been used for various civic functions over the years – markets, beheadings – and is bordered by historic buildings, including the town hall, once a prison for suspected witches.

Stora Kopparbergs Kyrka CHURCH
(Kyrkbacksvägen 8; ☉ 10am-6pm Mon-Sat, 9am-6pm Sun) Falun's oldest building is Stora Kopparbergs Kyrka, dating from the late 14th century, with brick vaulting and folk-art flowers running round the walls.

🛏 Sleeping

Falu Fängelse Vandrarhem HOSTEL €
(☑ 023-79 55 75; www.falufangelse.se; Villavägen 17; dm/s/f Skr270/370/680; ☉ reception 8am-6pm; @ 🛜 🐾) This hostel really feels like what it is – a former prison. Dorm beds are in cells, with heavy iron doors, thick walls, concrete floors, and steel lockers for closets. The shower and toilet facilities are somewhat limited, so it's worth asking if a room with a bathroom is available.

The place is extremely friendly though, and common areas are spacious and full of well-worn, denlike furniture. There's a back deck in summer.

Hotel Falun HOTEL €
(023-291 80; Trotzgatan 16; s/d from Skr800/900; P @) There are some good hotel choices near the tourist office, including this place, which has comfortable modern rooms (cheaper rooms have private toilet but shared showers).

Lugnets Camping & Stugby CAMPGROUND €
(023-835 63; lugnet-anl@falun.se; sites Skr185, simple 2-bed huts Skr380, cabins Skr980; ; 705, 713) This long, thin campground is 2km northeast of town, in the skiing and sports area. Amenities are good: crazy golf, boules and a nearby outdoor swimming pool will keep kids amused.

Scandic Hotel Lugnet Falun HOTEL €€
(023-669 22 00; falun@scandic-hotels.com; Svärdsjögatan 51; s/d from Skr1100/1300; P @) This large, modern building stands out a mile with its ski-jump design. It has something of a college-dorm feel and heaps of facilities, including a restaurant, a bar and even a bowling hall in the basement. Steep summer and weekend discounts make it a smoking deal. The hotel is about 2km east of the centre off E16, close to Lugnet.

Eating & Drinking

There's a conveniently central **ICA grocery store** (Falugatan 1; 7am-9pm Mon-Fri, 10am-9pm Sat, 11am-9pm Sun), and a **Systembolaget liquor store** (Åsgatan 19; 10am-6pm Mon-Fri, to 2pm Sat & Sun) inside the Falun Galleria shopping mall.

Sandbergs Skafferi CAFE €
(023-176 70; Åsgatan 18; baguettes from Skr55, mains from Skr79; 11am-6pm Mon-Fri, 10am-6pm Sat, 10am-3pm Sun) This cute little shop selling gifts and speciality foods is also a deli, with everything from coffee and pastries to delicious baguette sandwiches and hot meals like quiche or lasagne. It's on a pedestrianised shopping street, with a handful of tables both inside and out.

Kopparhattan Café & Restaurang CAFE €€
(Stigaregatan 2-4; lunch buffet Skr89, mains Skr142-210;) An excellent choice is this funky, arty cafe-restaurant below Dalarnas Museum. Choose from sandwiches, soup or a good vegetarian buffet for lunch; and light veggie, fish and meat evening mains. There's an outside terrace overlooking the river, and live music on Friday nights in summer.

Banken Bar & Brasserie SWEDISH €€€
(023-71 19 11; www.bankenfalun.se; Åsgatan 41; mains Skr185-225; 11.30am-11pm Mon-Thu, 11.30am-midnight Fri, 1pm-midnight Sat) Based in a former bank, classy Banken has a splendid interior and matching service. The menu features decadent preparations of Swedish traditional meals, like reindeer carpaccio with truffles, or saffron-scented roast salmon; there's also a simpler daily lunch special available weekdays.

Information

Most services (such as banks) are on or just off Stortorget.

Library (023-833 35; Kristinegatan 15; 10am-7pm Mon-Thu, to 6pm Fri, 11am-3pm Sat) Sign in here for free internet access.

Tourist office (023-830 50; www.visit-sodradalarna.se; Trotzgatan 10-12; 10am-6pm Mon-Fri, to 4pm Sat) This tourist office has a nice gift shop and can book accommodation. Staff can help with questions about the whole region.

Getting There & Around

Falun isn't on the main train lines – change at Borlänge when coming from Stockholm or Mora – but there are direct trains to and from Gävle (Skr188, 1¼ hours, every two hours), or regional buses (Skr120, two hours) equally often.

Swebus Express (0200-21 82 18; www.swebusexpress.se) has buses on the Göteborg–Karlstad–Falun–Gävle route, and connections to buses on the Stockholm–Borlänge–Mora route.

Regional transport is run by **Dalatrafik** (0771-95 95 95; www.dalatrafik.se), which covers all corners of the county of Dalarna. Tickets cost Skr26 for trips within a zone, and Skr15 extra for each new zone. A 30-day *länskort* (county pass) costs Skr1350 and allows you to travel throughout the county; cards in smaller increments are also available. Regional bus 70 goes hourly to Rättvik (Skr56, one hour) and Mora (Skr86, 1¾ hours).

Lake Siljan Region

Typically, when you ask Swedes where in Sweden they would most like to go on holiday, they get melty-eyed and talk about Lake Siljan. It's understandable – the area combines lush green landscapes, outdoor activities, a rich tradition of arts and crafts, and some of the prettiest villages in the country. It's the loveliest part of the already lovely region of Dalarna, source of the ubiquitous painted-wooden-horse souvenirs.

Though Lake Siljan is the picture of tranquillity now, 360 million years ago it felt Europe's largest meteor impact. Crashing through the earth's atmosphere, the giant lump of rock hit with the force of 500 million atomic bombs, obliterating all life and creating a 75km ring-shaped crater.

The area is a very popular summer destination, with numerous outdoor festivals and attractions. Maps of **Siljansleden**, an excellent network of walking and cycling paths extending for more than 300km around Lake Siljan, are available from tourist offices for Skr20. Another way to enjoy the lake is by boat: in summer **M/S Gustaf Wasa** (☎070-542 10 25; www.wasanet.nu; tickets Skr125-150, with meal Skr300-400) runs a complex range of lunch, dinner and sightseeing cruises from the towns of Mora, Rättvik and Leksand. Ask at any tourist office or go online for a schedule.

The big summer festival **Musik vid Siljan** (www.musikvidsiljan.se) is held in venues around the lakeside towns in early July; look for schedules at tourist offices.

Check out the Siljan area website (www.siljan.se) for lots of good information.

Leksand

☎0247 / POP 15,289 (MUNICIPALITY), 5900 (TOWN)

Leksand's main claim to fame is its **Midsummer Festival**, the most popular in Sweden, in which around 20,000 spectators fill the bowl-shaped green park on Midsummer Eve (always a Friday between 19 and 25 June) to sing songs and watch costumed dancers circle the maypole. (Leksand is also the namesake of a popular brand of hardbread.) Norsgatan is the main pedestrian street, with shops and cafes.

Sights & Activities

Look for the unusual belltower near the bridge between Norsgatan and Kyrkallén.

Munthe's Hildasholm HISTORIC BUILDING
(☎0247-100 62; www.hildasholm.org; Klockaregatan 5; admission by guided tour only, adult/child Skr120/40, garden only Skr30; ⏲11am-5pm mid-Jun–mid-Aug, Sat & Sun mid-Aug–Sep) Built by Axel Munthe (1857–1949), who served as the Swedish royal physician and wrote the best-selling memoir *The Story of San Michele*, Munthe's Hildasholm is a sumptuously decorated National Romantic–style mansion, set in beautiful gardens with stunning views over Lake Siljan. Munthe built it for his second wife, an English aristocrat, in 1910–11; Munthe himself rarely visited the mansion as he spent most of his time attending to Queen Viktoria on the island of Capri.

Siljansnäs Naturum NATURE RESERVE
(☎010-22 50 329; www.naturumdalarna.se; Siljansnäs, on Björkberget; ⏲10am-6pm, shorter hours winter; 👪; 🚌84 Siljansnäs) FREE Siljansnäs Naturum, 14km northwest of Leksand, has information about the meteor that hit several millennium ago and local flora and fauna, with a slightly moth-eaten collection of 50 stuffed animals. Two-hour English-language guided tours of the nature reserve take place at 11am Monday and Friday in summer. There are activities for toddlers, nature walks and films; kids can even paint their own wooden horse. The highlight is the 22m-high **viewing tower**, with stunning 360-degree views around the lake.

Leksands Kyrka CHURCH
(Kyrkallén; ⏲10am-6pm Jun–mid-Aug) Leksands Kyrka, with its distinctive onion dome, dates from the early 13th century but has been extensively renovated and enlarged. The church contains extravagant baroque furnishings; check the posted schedules for evening concerts in summer. Guided tours run mid-June to mid-August at 10am and 1pm Monday to Friday, 10am Saturday and 1pm Sunday.

Sleeping & Eating

Quick eats surround the main square, where you'll also find branches of all the main supermarket chains.

★ **STF Vandrarhem Leksand** HOSTEL €
(☎0247-152 50; info@vandrarhemleksand.se; dm Skr200; ⏲summer only; P ⊖ 📶) It's a little out of the way (2km south of town), but this is a lovely wee hostel and Dalarna's oldest, with ultracute wooden huts built around a flowery courtyard. Bikes are available for rent (Skr70 per day). Breakfast is available, and there's a guest kitchen and laundry (Skr40). Reserve early, as it's popular with groups.

Hotell Leksand HOTEL €€

(☎0247-145 70; www.hotelleksand.com; Leksandsvägen 7; s/d from Skr980/1280; ⊙reception 7.30-11am & 3-9.30pm; P ⊖ @ ≋) This is a small, modern and conveniently situated hotel in the heart of town. The rooms are mostly nondescript, but the people here are friendly and it's not a bad place to lay your head. Phone in advance, as the reception keeps short hours.

Siljans Konditori BAKERY €

(☎0247-150 70; Sparbanksgatan 5; ice cream Skr28-39, sandwiches Skr40-75, buffet Skr85; ⊙8.30am-7pm Mon-Fri, 9am-5pm Sat, 10am-5pm Sun) This large and inviting bakery-cafe serves good sandwiches (on its own fresh bread) from a busy corner of Stora Torget.

Leksands Gårdcafeet CAFE €€

(☎0247-13 260; gardscafe.se; Norsgatan 19; sandwiches Skr69-99, dagens lunch Skr90, salads Skr109; ⊙9am-9pm) A cute old wooden house with front-patio and back-garden seating, this busy but friendly cafe serves tempting coffee and pastries as well as enormous, filling pasta salads and hot meals. The help-yourself *dagens* lunch buffet with a salad bar is a great deal; you can also order just the salad bar for Skr80.

Shopping

Leksands Hemslöjd CRAFTS

(www.leksandshemslojd.se; www.Kyrkallén 1; ⊙10am-6pm Mon-Sat, noon-4pm Sun) This shop sells high-quality textiles, knitted cloths, ceramics, and other local crafts including Dalahäst (wooden horses), candle-holders, linens, yarn and wooden knives.

Information

Banks line Sparbankgatan.

Library (☎0248-802 45; Kulturhuset, Kyrkallén) Across the street from the tourist office, the busy library has internet access (including wireless), regional information and art exhibitions.

Tourist office (☎0248-79 72 00; info@siljan.se; Norsgatan 27E; ⊙9am-6pm Mon-Fri, 10am-4pm Sat & Sun) The tourist office can help with information about the whole region.

Getting There & Around

Dalatrafik buses and local trains go frequently between Leksand and the rest of the region, including Mora (one hour, Skr71), Rättvik (30 minutes, Skr41) and Tällberg (20 minutes, Skr26).

Tällberg

☎0247 / POP 200

The main reason to visit Tällberg is that it's adorable: a whole village of precious little gingerbread houses, mostly painted Falu Red, sprinkled over a green hillside sloping toward a lake.

It knows it's cute, too – the town of 200 residents supports eight upmarket hotels and several chic boutiques. It's a tourist hot spot and an appealing place for lunch and a walk, but unless you're after a romantic countryside escape, it's perhaps better to stay in Rättvik or Leksand and visit for the afternoon.

Bus 58 between Rättvik and Leksand stops in the village regularly (two to six times daily, Skr26). Tällberg is also on the train line that travels around Lake Siljan; the train station is about 2km below the village proper.

Rättvik

☎0248 / POP 10,811

Rättvik is a totally unpretentious town in an area that sometimes borders on the precious. Nonetheless, it's a very pretty place, stretching up a hillside and along the shores of Lake Siljan. There are things to do year-round, for kids and adults alike, whether you like skiing, cycling, hiking or lolling on beaches.

A full program of special events in summer includes a **folklore festival** (www.folklore.se) in late July and **Classic Car Week** (www.classiccarweek.com) in late July or early August.

Sights & Activities

Scandinavia's longest wooden pier, the impressive 628m **Långbryggan**, runs out into the lake from just behind the train station. The 13th-century church has 87 well-preserved **church stables**, the oldest dating from 1470. The pseudo-rune **memorial** beside the church commemorates the 1520s uprising of Gustav Vasa's band against the Danes – the rebellion that created modern Sweden.

Kulturhuset CULTURAL CENTRE

(☎0248-701 95; Storgatan 2; ⊙11am-7pm Mon-Thu, to 4pm Fri, to 2pm Sat, 1-4pm Sun; ≋) FREE Central Kulturhuset houses the public library, art exhibitions and a display describing the Siljan meteor impact. The helpful staff go above and beyond to answer any questions you might have about the area. There's also free wi-fi and four computers available for internet use.

Hembygdsgård Gammelgård MUSEUM
(☎0248-514 45; ⏲11am-5pm mid-Jun–mid-Aug) FREE You can get your open-air-museum fix 500m north of the church at Hembygdsgård Gammelgård – it's a 1909 collection of buildings that were moved here during the '20s from villages around Rättvik parish (the oldest is from the 1300s). There's a good collection of furniture painted in the local style, and a unique *ullkorgen* (wool bin) from the 1200s. The grounds are always open for exploring, but the cafe and building interiors are open in summer only.

Vidablick Utsiktstorn TOWER
(adult/child Skr35/15; ⏲10am-6pm Jun-Aug) An enterprising 17-year-old built Vidablick Utsiktstorn, a viewing tower about 5km southeast of town, from where there are great panoramas of the lake, a good cafe and a summer-only youth hostel (dorm beds from Skr150). On your way up the tower, check out the miniature reconstruction of the village as it was at the turn of the century, made by a local carpenter in the 1930s.

SommarRodel ADVENTURE SPORTS
(☎073-671 00 10; www.rattviksbacken.se; 1/3 rides Skr60/150; ⏲10am-6pm Jun-Aug, closed when raining) The 725m-long SommarRodel, a sort of snowless bobsled chute, is lots of fun. You hurtle down a ski hill at 56km/h, which feels very fast so close to the ground. Now with paintball!

Ski Slopes SKIING
(www.rattviksbacken.se; day pass adult/child Skr260/200) The easy ski slopes are excellent; there are four lifts.

Sleeping

Summer accommodation in Rättvik disappears fast, so it's worth booking ahead – even for camp sites. Central places to stay are few and far between, but the STF hostel is tops.

STF Vandrarhem Rättvik HOSTEL €
(☎0248-561 09; Centralgatan; s/d from Skr400/500; ⏲reception 8-10am & 5-6pm; P@📶) Toward the edge of town is this comfortable hostel with cosy rooms in three wooden buildings clustered around a grassy courtyard. It's a quiet place with good facilities, including a nice kitchen with a large dining/TV room in the main building, and picnic tables on the lawn for alfresco meals. Reception is at the Enåbadet campground office.

Enåbadet CAMPGROUND €
(☎0248-561 00; www.enabadet.se; Furudalsvägen 1; sites from Skr240, cabins Skr555-1160) A large, bustling campground by the river off Centralgatan (1km from the train station), behind the STF hostel, this area includes a *fäbod* (summer livestock farm) and is built to echo the traditional, rustic look of old farmhouse buildings. The walking trail Siljansleden passes through the site.

Siljansbadets Camping CAMPGROUND €
(☎0248-561 18; www.siljansbadet.com; sites Skr285, cabins from Skr610) Near the train station, this shady, woodsy campground is on the lakeshore and boasts its own Blue Flag beach.

Jöns-Andersgården B&B €€
(☎0248-130 15; www.jonsandersgarden.se; Bygatan 4; r from Skr696, cabin from Skr1100; ⏲mid-Apr–mid-Oct; P🚭📶; 🚌74) Beds here are in traditional wooden houses dating from the 15th century, way up on the hill with superb views. Rooms are all in tip-top shape with modern interiors, and one suite has its own sauna. If you don't have transport the owners will pick you up from the train station by arrangement.

Stiftsgården Rättvik HOTEL €€
(☎0248-79 78 17; www.stiftsgarden.org; Kyrkvägen 2; s/d with shared bathroom from Skr530/930, with private bathroom Skr760/1070) This picturesque, church-run place is by the lake, away from the hustle and bustle of town but still within easy walking distance and near footpaths and outdoor activities. Rooms are simple but pleasant; a lunch (Skr90) and dinner (Skr130) buffet are available. Canoes and cycles can be hired.

Hotell Hantverksbyn HOTEL €€
(☎0248-302 50; vidablick@hantverksbyn.se; Faluvägen; s/d from Skr650/1150, breakfast Skr75) Vidablick is an excellent choice, with rustic hotel accommodation in grass-roofed huts, some with lake views. The hotel is behind the OKQ8 petrol station on the road to Leksand, about 3km south of town. The attached restaurant (open May to August; *dagens* lunch Skr89, coffee and cakes Skr35) has free wi-fi, a great view from its outdoor tables, and dance nights on Thursday.

Eating & Drinking

There are supermarkets and a Systembolaget liquor store on Storgatan.

Frick's Konditori CAFE €
(www.frickskonditori.se; Stora Torget; sandwiches from Skr45) An old-fashioned bakery-cafe with a casual, neighbourhood feel, Fricks offers sandwiches, quiches and salads but specialises in cakes and pastries. It's opposite the train station and is a local gossip hang-out.

Jöns-Andersgården SWEDISH, ITALIAN €€€
(☎0248-130 15; www.jonsandersgarden.se; Bygatan 4; mains Skr165-255; ⏲5-10pm late May-Aug; 🚌74) If you can stir your stumps and make it up the hill, you'll find this rather sweet restaurant tucked at the top, attached to the hotel of the same name. Dishes such as lemony chicken with gremolata potatoes, shellfish canneloni, or herb-and-parmesan roasted lamb over gnocchi bring a taste of Italy to this very Swedish establishment.

Entertainment

Dalhalla CONCERT VENUE
(☎0455-61 97 00; www.dalhalla.se; tickets Skr600-900) Dalhalla, an old limestone quarry 7km north of Rättvik, is used as an open-air theatre and concert venue in summer; the acoustics are incredible and the setting is stunning. Check online for schedule and ticket information (prices vary depending on the act). From July to October, on nonconcert days you can tour the theatre at 11am, 1pm and 2.30pm (Skr125).

Information

There are banks on Storgatan.

Library (☎0248-701 95; Storgatan 2) Attached to the Kulturhuset, the library offers free internet access.

Tourist office (☎0248-79 72 00; Riksvägen 40; ⏲9am-6pm Mon-Fri, 10am-4pm Sat & Sun) Located at the train station, the tourist office has info for the entire Siljan region.

Getting There & Around

Buses depart from outside the train station. Dalatrafik's bus 70 runs regularly between Falun, Rättvik and Mora. Swebus Express goes from Stockholm to Rättvik a few times a day (Skr219, four hours). A couple of direct intercity trains per day from Stockholm (Skr396, 3½ hours) also stop at Rättvik (otherwise you have to change at Borlänge).There are local trains every couple of hours between Rättvik and Mora (Skr56, 25 minutes).

Mora

☎0250 / POP 3500

Mora is spliced with Sweden's historic soul. Legend has it that in 1520 Gustav Vasa arrived here in a last-ditch attempt to start a rebellion against the Danish regime. The people of Mora weren't interested, and Gustav was forced to put on his skis and flee for the border. After he left, the town reconsidered and two yeomen, Engelbrekt and Lars, volunteered to follow Gustav's tracks, finally overtaking him in Sälen and changing Swedish history.

Today the world's biggest cross-country ski race, **Vasaloppet**, which ends in Mora, commemorates this epic chase, and involves 90km of gruelling Nordic skiing. Around 15,000 people take part on the first Sunday in March. In summer you can walk the route on the 90km **Vasaloppsleden**.

Sights & Activities

Vasaloppsmuseet MUSEUM
(☎0250-392 00; www.vasaloppet.se; Vasagatan; adult/child Skr50/25; ⏲8am-4.30pm Mon-Wed & Fri, to 3pm Thu, closed noon-1pm daily) Even if you have no interest in skiing, you may be pleasantly surprised by the excellent Vasaloppsmuseet, which really communicates the passion behind the world's largest cross-country skiing event. There's some fantastic crackly black-and-white film of the first race, a display about nine-times winner and hardy old boy Nils 'Mora-Nisse' Karlsson, and an exhibit of prizes. Outside the museum is the race finish line, a favourite place for holiday *snaps* (a distilled alcoholic beverage, such as vodka or aquavity).

Zornmuseet MUSEUM
(☎0250-59 23 10; www.zorn.se; Vasagatan 36; adult/child Skr60/free; ⏲9am-5pm Mon-Sat, 11am-5pm Sun mid-May–mid-Sep, noon-4pm Sep–mid-May) Zornmuseet displays many of the best-loved portraits and characteristic nudes of Mora painter Anders Zorn (1860–1920), one of Sweden's most renowned artists. His naturalistic depictions of Swedish life and landscapes are shown here, as is the Zorn family silver collection.

Zorngården HISTORIC BUILDING
(☎0250-59 23 10; Vasagatan 36; adult/child Skr90/40; ⏲by guided tour only 10am-4pm Mon-Sat, 11am-4pm Sun) The Zorn family house, Zorngården, is an excellent example of a wealthy artist's residence and reflects An-

VIKING BURIAL MOUNDS AT SOLLERÖN

Just 15km from Mora is the small island settlement of Sollerön, where you'll find the largest and best-preserved Viking burial ground in Dalarna. The site includes grave fields from the Iron Age with an estimated 50 to 140 graves, plus other evidence of habitation from the Stone Age (and, naturally, a cafe serving coffee and sandwiches).

Grab a pamphlet for a self-guided tour and follow the 3km walking trail (most of it wheelchair-accessible) among the burial mounds and other features. Points of interest include the Sacrificial Well, where ancient Vikings allegedly made sacrifices to the likes of Odin and Thor. Rumour has it that the well never runs dry in summer or freezes in winter.

Though it's well off the main drag now, and about as quiet as they come, this northern section of Lake Siljan was once an important part of the iron industry and home to a vibrant farming community. Initially, everyone assumed the grave mounds were left over from the island's days as farming country. But in 1928 a grave was discovered in one of the mounds, leading to another 10 graves being excavated, at which point locals understood the significance of their lumpy fields. Three of the swords found in the graves are now preserved at Stockholm's Museum of National Antiquities.

It's a scenic area even if you're not all that jazzed about ancient burial grounds: the cafe occupies one building in the old homestead museum, alongside a wooden Viking longship and some antique farm equipment. To get here, take bus 107 from Mora bus station (Skr26, 40 minutes, frequent departures Monday to Saturday).

ders Zorn's National Romantic aspirations (check out the Viking-influenced hall and entryway). Access to the house is by guided tour (on the hour and half-hour); you can request a tour in English when you buy tickets, at the Zornmuseet next door.

Sleeping

Mora Parken CAMPGROUND, CABINS €
(☎0250-276 00; www.moraparken.se; sites Skr195, 2-/4-bed cabins from Skr495/645, hotel s/d Skr995/1245; @) This extra-fancy campground and hotel are in a great waterside spot, 400m northwest of the church. There's a beach, laundry, kitchen, minigolf, bicycle rentals and more. A hodgepodge of camping cabins are well equipped and full of rustic charm. The Vasaloppet track and Siljansleden trail pass through the grounds, and you can hire canoes to splash about on the pond.

Hotel rooms (all ground floor in the main building) have wooden floors and a sleek, modern look.

STF Hostel Mora HOSTEL €
(☎0250-381 96; info@malkullan.se; Fredsgatan 6; dm/s/d from Skr210/370/520; ⏱check-in 8-10am & 5-7pm; P ⊖ @ ᯤ) This humble hostel occupies two buildings just a couple of blocks from the Vasaloppet museum. There's a guest kitchen, and rooms are simple but comfy, with mostly four- to six-bunk rooms in one building and hotel-standard beds with TVs in the other. Breakfast is Skr50 (book the night before). Free wi-fi and free sauna are available.

Mora Hotell & Spa HOTEL €€
(☎0250-59 26 50; www.morahotell.se; Strandgatan 12; r from Skr1195; P ⊖ ❄ ᯤ) There's been a hotel here since 1830, although the current version is as modern as it gets, with all the facilities you'd expect from a big chain (it's a Best Western) – plus personality. Rooms combine clean lines, wooden floors and earthy tones with bright folk-art accents. Head to the spa for steam rooms, jacuzzis, massage and body treatments.

Eating

For eats, head to Kyrkogatan, the pedestrianised shopping street in the town centre; there aren't a wealth of options to be found, but between bar snacks and substantial cafe fare (there are no fewer than three pizza-and-kebab joints) you're sure to find something. For self-caterers there are an ICA supermarket and a Systembolaget liquor store across from each other on Kyrkogatan.

Mora Kaffestuga CAFE €
(☎0250-100 82; Kyrkogatan 8; lunch specials Skr85; ⏱9am-7pm Mon-Fri, to 5pm Sat, 10am-4pm Sun) For a quick lunch – such as basic salads, quiches and sandwiches – or a coffee-and-pastry break, this popular, stylish little coffee shop has a grassy garden out back.

THE DALA HORSE

What do Bill Clinton, Elvis Presley and Bob Hope have in common? They've all received a Swedish Dalahäst as a gift. These iconic, carved wooden horses, painted in bright colours and decorated with folk-art flowers, represent to many people the essence of Sweden.

The first written reference to a Dalahäst comes from the 17th century, when the bishop of Västerås denounced such horrors as 'decks of cards, dice, flutes, dolls, wooden horses, lovers' ballads, impudent paintings', but it's quite likely they were being carved much earlier. Sitting by the fireside and whittling wood was a common pastime, and the horse was a natural subject – a workmate, friend and symbol of strength. The painted form that is so common today appeared at the World Exhibition in New York in 1939 and has been a favourite souvenir for travellers to Sweden ever since.

The best-known Dala horses come from Nusnäs, about 10km southeast of Mora. The two biggest workshops are **Nils Olsson Hemslöjd** (☎0250-372 00; www.nohemslojd.se; 8am-4pm Mon-Fri, 10am-4pm Sat) and **Grannas A Olsson Hemslöjd** (☎0250-372 50; www.grannas.com; 9am-6pm Mon-Fri, to 4pm Sat & Sun), where you can watch the carving and painting, then buy up big at the souvenir outlets. Wooden-horse sizes stretch from 3cm to 50cm high (with prices from around Skr100 to Skr3500).

Public transport to Nusnäs isn't great: bus 108 runs frequently from Mora but only Monday to Friday.

Helmers Konditori CAFE €
(☎0250-100 11; http://helmers.se; Kyrkogatan 10; sandwiches from Skr47; 8am-7pm) This highly recommended bakery-cafe on the main pedestrian street draws a devoted local crowd with plenty of homemade bread, sandwiches and delicious pastries.

Information

Library (☎0250-267 79; Köpmannagatan) Free internet access is available at the public library.

Tourist office (☎0250-59 20 20; mora@siljan.se; Köpmannagatan 3A; 9am-6pm Mon-Fri, 10am-4pm Sat & Sun) In a central location across from the library.

Getting There & Around

The Mora-Siljan Airport is 6km southwest of town on the Malung road. **Nextjet** (www.nextjet.se) has three flights to Stockholm Arlanda on weekdays and one on Sunday (50 minutes).

All **Dalatrafik** (www.dalatrafik.se) buses use the bus station at Moragatan 23. Bus 70 runs to Rättvik and Falun, and buses 103, 104, 105 and 245 run to Orsa. Once or twice daily, bus 170 goes to Älvdalen, Särna, Idre and Grövelsjön, near the Norwegian border.

Mora is the terminus for **SJ** (☎0771-75 75 75; www.sj.se) trains and the southern terminus of the Inlandsbanan (Inland Railway), which runs north to Gällivare (mid-June to mid-August). The main train station is about 1km east of town. The more central Mora Strand is a platform station in town, but not all trains stop there, so check the timetable. When travelling to Östersund, you can choose between Inlandsbanan (Skr494, 6¼ hours, one daily, mid-June to mid-August only) or bus 45 (Skr269, 5¼ hours, two daily).

Hire a car in Mora to see the best of the region, especially northwest Dalarna; for smaller budget models try **OKQ8** (☎139 58; Vasagatan 1). You can rent bikes at **Intersport** (☎59 39 39; Kyrkogatan 7).

Orsa & Grönklitt

☎0250 / POP 5300

Orsa, 16km north of Mora, is a natural stopping point on the way to the area's biggest attraction, the humongous bear park further north in Grönklitt. In winter there's a **ski area** (day ski pass adult/child Skr285/235; Dec-Mar) at Grönklitt.

Orsa Camping (☎0250-462 00; www.orsagronklitt.se; sites from Skr150, cabins per week from Skr5400;) is a big campsite beautifully situated on the shores of the lake in Orsa. Rates vary depending on length of stay. It's particularly suitable for families, with several playgrounds, a waterslide, canoe hire, minigolf and a beach to keep the kids happy. Another option is the **STF Hostel** (☎0250-421 70; Gillevägen 3; s/d from Skr350/550; P ; 103).

There's a **tourist office** (☎0250-55 25 50; orsa@siljan.se; 9am-6pm Mon-Fri, 10am-4pm Sat & Sun) in Orsa, with a bank about three blocks down Dalagatan and a grocery and Systembolaget both nearby.

Buses 103 and 104 run regularly between Mora and Orsa.

Sälen & Around

0280 / POP 650

A split-personality village, Sälen transforms itself completely from a quiet fishing paradise in summer into one of Sweden's largest and poshest ski resorts in winter. It's a tiny spot in the wilds of Dalarna, and in addition to its seven ski areas it's a good base for all kinds of outdoor activities, including canoeing, horse riding and wildlife safaris (ask at the tourist office).

Activities

The ski areas, with chalets, pubs and nightclubs, are strung out for 20km along the road running through the steep-flanked mountains west of Sälen. There are over 100 lifts, pistes of all degrees and guaranteed snow from 15 November to mid-April. For details visit www.skistar.com. About 45km north of Sälen, cheaper and quieter skiing is available at Näsfjället.

In summer the ski hills convert to mountain-bike parks; the ski area at Lindvallen (0771-84 00 00) has a whole summer season built around the sport, and you can rent helmets and gear at the lift or via the tourist office. The bike park is open Thursday to Sunday from mid-June to August.

There's some good hiking in summer, mainly north of the road. Buy a map (Skr20) of the southern section of the Kungsleden trail at the tourist office.

Sleeping & Eating

Winter visitors should contact their travel agent or the tourist office for accommodation, or SkiStar (0771-84 00 00; www.skistar.com) for packages. For self-caterers, the Centrumhuset complex has a Systembolaget liquor store; supermarkets are opposite the complex.

Kläppen HOTEL €
(0280-96 200; www.klappen.se; condos summer/winter from Skr595/1300) Some of the area's most luxurious resorts become very affordable in summer; condos at Kläppen, for instance, are a smoking deal in July and August, when the price of an average hostel room fetches you a fully equipped apartment with kitchenette, patio, jacuzzi and pool access.

The resort can also book guided canoe tours (adult/child from Skr280/220) and other activities.

STF Vandrarhem Sälens HOSTEL €
(0280-820 40; info@salensvandrarhem.se; Gräsheden; dm/s/d Skr180/310/460; P) This rustic hostel 27km north of Sälen is a fantastic hideaway. It's based in a peaceful nature reserve at Gräsheden (near Näsfjället), with some great walks nearby – and the southern section of the Kungsleden trail passes 2km from the hostel. Breakfast is available for Skr70 (order in advance).

Bullans CAFE €
(Centrumhuset; coffee Skr22, dagens lunch Skr85; 7am-5pm Mon-Fri, 8am-3pm Sat) This surprisingly chic cafe is located inside the shopping centre (which also doubles as the town centre). Service is extremely cheerful.

Information

Head first to the Centrumhuset complex, where you'll find a bank, doctor, pharmacy and most other facilities. Opposite the complex are shops where you can rent ski gear during winter, and in-line skates, boats and canoes in summer.

Tourist office (0280-187 00; info@salen.se; Centrumhuset; 9am-6pm Mon-Fri) Inside the Centrumhuset shopping centre.

GRÖNKLITT BJÖRNPARK

Fat-bottomed roly-poly bear cubs are the star attraction at Grönklitt Björnpark (0250-462 00; www.orsabjornpark.se; adult/child/ family Skr240/160/680; 9am-6pm mid-Jun–Aug, hours vary rest of year; P; 103 or 104, then 118), a wildlife reserve 16km from Orsa. Even if there are no cubs around during your visit, there's plenty to see: lynxes, wolves, red foxes, wolverines and a new snow leopard. The animals have a lot of space and natural surroundings, which is ideal for them, but it means there's plenty of room to hide, so you may not see the more skittish creatures. For the closest views, follow the posted feeding schedule. Summer activities such as fishing, canoeing and elk or beaver safaris can also be booked at the park, and on certain mornings you can do yoga on 'tiger hill' (check online for schedules). There are plans are to expand the park to nearly twice its current size. Bus 118 runs from Mora to Grönklitt, via Orsa (twice daily weekdays, once on Sunday).

Getting There & Around

Bus 95 runs all the way from the ski area to Mora via Sälen once daily in the ski season (otherwise you have to change buses at Lima). In winter jump on the ski bus (free with a ski pass), which tours around the ski area.

Idre & Grövelsjön

0253

Though part of the Swedish heartland, Idre and its surrounding wilderness feel utterly remote – the rugged landscape looks nothing like the rest of Dalarna. The skiing and hiking here are excellent.

Idre Fjäll ski centre (0253-410 00; www.idrefjall.se; day lift passes adult/child Skr400/300; Nov-Apr), 9km eastof Idre, has three chairlifts, 29 ski-tows and 42 downhill runs, including 11 black runs and 60km of prepared cross-country tracks.

The **tourist office** (0253-200 00; info@idreturism.se; Framgårdsvägen 1; 10am-5pm Mon-Fri) has brochures, hiking advice and internet access (Skr20 for 15 minutes). Staff can book accommodation and arrange activities such as dogsledding, skiing, hiking, canyoning, rock climbing, boat trips, elk and beaver safaris, horse riding, rafting and canoeing.

Grövelsjön, 38km northwest of Idre and close to the Norwegian border, lies on the edge of the wild 690-sq-km **Långfjällets Nature Reserve**, noted for its lichen-covered heaths, moraine heaps and ancient forests. Reindeer from Sweden's southernmost Sami community wander throughout the area.

Sörälvens Fiske Camping (0253-201 17; www.soralven-camping.com; Västanå 519; sites/cabins Skr200/550) has good fishing-themed shared facilities with well-maintained four-bed cabins in a riverside setting. It's just out of Idre, 2.5km toward Grövelsjön, and well signposted.

The excellent **STF Fjällstation Grövelsjön** (0253-59 68 80; grovelsjon@stfturist.se; 2-/4-bed r from Skr620/1200; Feb-Apr & mid-Jun–Sep) in Grövelsjön has lots of facilities, including a kitchen, a spa, a shop and outdoor-gear hire. The restaurant serves breakfast, lunch and dinner; ask about half and full board.

At the northern edge of town on the main drag is the appealing **Restaurang Njalla** (0253-204 11; www.idresamecentrum.se; Byvägen 30; mains Skr85-265; 10am-3pm Mon-Sat), serving traditional Sami cuisine. Fill up on a hearty reindeer burger or try the *renskavspanna*, a plate of sliced reindeer meat with crispy fried potatoes and lingonberry jam. You can also opt for a three-meat sampler or the lunch buffet.

Dalatrafik bus 170 travels on a route between Mora, Idre and Grövelsjön (2¼ hours from Mora to Idre, 3¾ hours to Grövelsjön). There are three services to Grövelsjön on weekdays, and one or two on weekends.

Göteborg & the Southwest

Includes ➡

Best Places to Eat

- Thörnströms Kök (p145)
- Brygghuset (p154)
- Albert Hotell (p161)
- Magasinet Härön (p151)
- Restaurang Sjöboden (p163)

Best Places to Stay

- IQ Suites (p143)
- Resö Gamla Skola (p156)
- Utpost Hållö (p160)
- Stora Hotellet (p156)
- Salt & Sill (p152)

Why Go?

Sweden's southwest is diversity personified. Heading the cast is Sweden's 'second city' of Göteborg and its kicking bars, cafes, museums and theme-park thrills. Just south, the Halland coast is home to sandy Blue Flag beaches and Sweden's top surfing, windsurfing and kitesurfing. Västergötland's attractions are low-key and eclectic, from Trollhättan's postindustrial museums and mighty gushing locks to Lidkoping's fairy-tale Läckö Slott.

North of Göteborg the Bohuslän coastline shatters into myriad granite islands with craggy cliffs and adorable red-and-white fishing villages. Yachts weave their way between uninhabited islets and skerries, while the area's mysterious Bronze Age rock carvings testify to the rich spiritual life of the region's early inhabitants.

Further inland, Dalsland, with its network of canals, locks and narrow lakes amid thick, dark forest, throws down the gauntlet to boating and kayaking enthusiasts.

When to Go

Göteborg

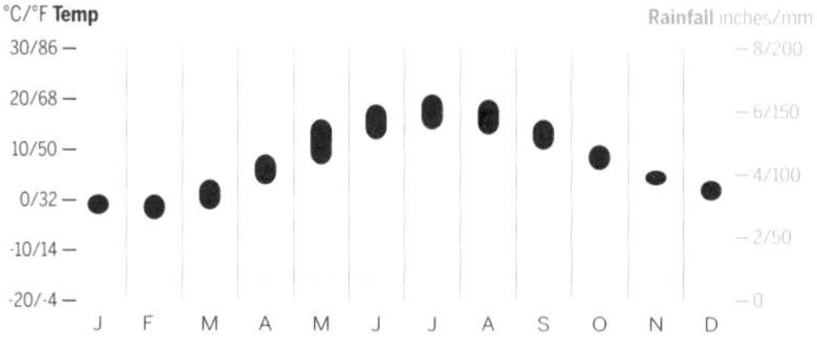

Jul & Aug Sailboat-loving Swedes beeline to Bohuslän. Gotebörg festivals run back to back.

May & Sep Ideal time for avoiding summer crowds and indulging in fine dining.

Dec & Jan Inland lakes and canals freeze over. Perfect skating and ice-fishing conditions.

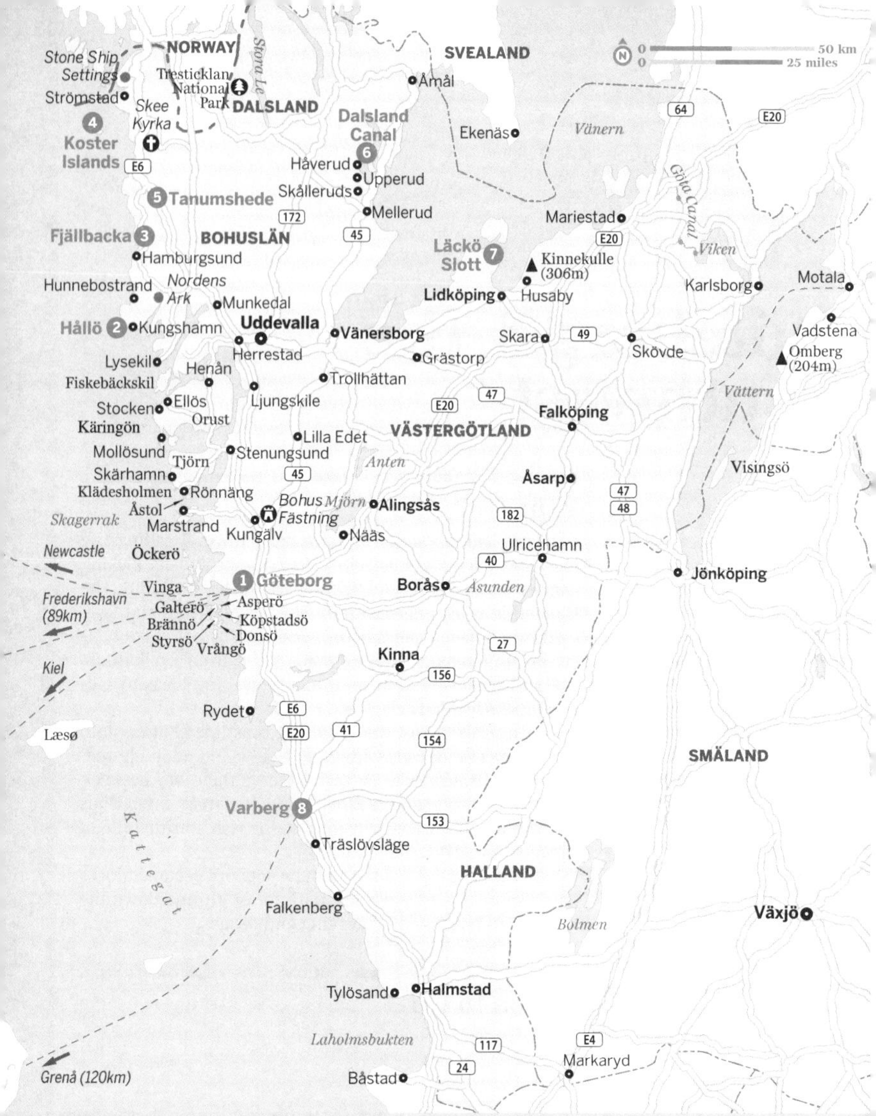

Göteborg & the Southwest Highlights

1 Plummeting down roller coasters and experiencing counterculture art and cutting-edge Swedish home cooking in **Göteborg** (p133).

2 Feasting on shrimp and archipelago views on the tiny island of **Hållö** (p155), a short ferry trip from Smögen.

3 Being charmed by **Fjällbacka** (p155), Ingrid Bergman's favourite summer haunt.

4 Pedalling your way around the **Koster Islands** (p156).

5 Decoding Bronze Age artwork at the Unesco World Heritage Site in **Tanumshede** (p152), Bohuslän.

6 Piloting a boat or paddling a kayak along the **Dalsland Canal** (p158).

7 Listening to opera staged on the lawns of **Läckö Slott** (p162), north of Lidköping.

8 Surfing at Apelviken and sunbathing in a Russian bathhouse in **Varberg** (p166).

GÖTEBORG (GOTHENBURG)

031 / POP 549,839

Though often caught in Stockholm's shadow, gregarious, chilled-out Göteborg actually has greater appeal for many visitors (and resident Swedes) than the fast-paced capital. Some of the country's finest talent hails from the streets of this cosmopolitan port, including music icons José González and Soundtrack of Our Lives. Neoclassical architecture lines its tram-rattled streets, grit-hip cafes hum with bonhomie, and there's always some cutting-edge art and architecture to grab your attention.

From Centralstationen at the northern end of town, shop-lined Östra Hamngatan leads southeast across one of Göteborg's few 17th-century canals, through verdant Kungsparken (King's Park) to the city's 'Champs-Élysées', the boutique- and upscale-bar-lined 'Avenyn' boulevard.

The waterfront abounds with all things nautical but nice, from ships, aquariums and sea-related museums to the freshest fish, and, to the west, the Vasastan, Haga and Linné districts buzz with creativity. Fashionistas design fair-trade threads, artists collaborate over mean espressos and street artists spice up forlorn facades. Stockholm may represent the 'big time', but many of the best ideas originate in this grassroots town.

History

Gamla Älvsborg fortress, standing guard over the river 3km downstream of the centre, is Göteborg's oldest significant structure and was a key strategic point in the 17th-century territorial wars. The Swedes founded Göteborg in 1621 to be free of the extortionate taxation rates imposed on Swedish ships by the Danes.

Fearful of Danish attack, the Swedes employed Dutch experts to construct a defensive canal system in the centre. The workers lived in what is now the revitalised Haga area: around a fifth of the original buildings are still standing. Most of Göteborg's oldest wooden buildings went up in smoke long ago – the city was devastated by no fewer than nine major fires between 1669 and 1804.

Once Sweden had annexed Skåne in 1658, Göteborg expanded as a trading centre. Boom time came in the 18th century, when merchants like the Swedish East India Company made huge amounts of wealth from trade with the Far East, their profits responsible for numerous grand houses that are still standing.

Göteborg was sustained largely by the shipbuilding industry until it went belly up in the 1980s. These days, the lifeblood of Scandinavia's busiest port is heavy industry (Volvo manufacturing in particular) and commerce.

Sights

★Liseberg AMUSEMENT PARK

(www.liseberg.se; Södra Vägen; 1-/2-day pass Skr415/595; 11am-11pm Jun–mid-Aug; ; 2, 4, 5, 6, 8, 10 Korsvägen) The attractions of Liseberg, Scandinavia's largest amusement park, are many and varied. Adrenalin blasts include: the venerable wooden roller coaster Balder; its 'explosive' colleague Kanonen, where you're blasted from 0km/h to 75km/h in under two seconds; AtmosFear, Europe's tallest (116m) free-fall tower; and the park's biggest new attraction, thrilling rollercoaster Helix that lets you experience weightlessness and loops the loop seven times. Softer options include carousels, fairy-tale castles, an outdoor dance floor, adventure playgrounds, and shows and concerts.

Day passes are the most popular method of entry and good value if you're planning on going on numerous rides. Allternatively, entry to the park grounds costs Skr90 for those taller than 90cm (the Göteborg Pass gets you into the park for free), and you pay for individual rides using coupons: each ride costs between one and four coupons (Skr20 each) per go. Opening hours are complex; check the website.

When it comes to refuelling in between rides, Lisberg is also the first theme park in the world to offer a very high-quality, delicious, exclusively vegetarian/vegan buffet lunch (Skr138) at the Green Room.

★Röda Sten GALLERY

(www.rodasten.com; Röda Sten 1; adult/under 21yr Skr40/free; noon-5pm Tue-Sun, to 7pm Wed; 3, 9 Vagnhallen Majorna) Occupying a defunct, graffitied power station beside the giant Älvsborgsbron, Röda Sten's four floors are home to such temporary exhibitions as edgy Swedish photography and cross-dressing rap videos by Danish-Filipino artist Lillibeth Cuenca Rasmussen that challenge sexuality stereotypes in Afghan society. The indie-style cafe hosts weekly live music and club nights, and offbeat one-offs like punk bike races,

Göteborg (Gothenburg)

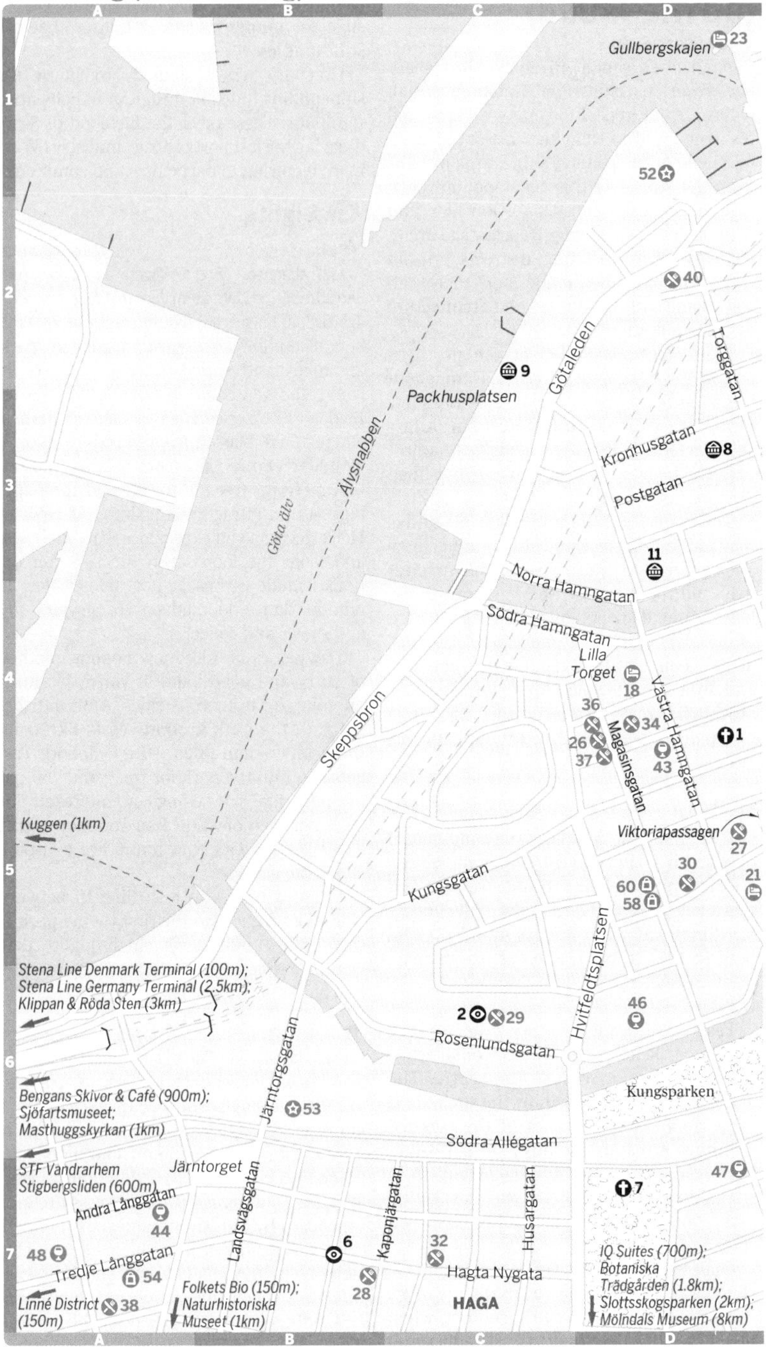

A
B
C
D
1
2
3
4
5
6
7
Gullbergskajen
23
52
40
Götaleden
Torggatan
9
Packhusplatsen
Kronhusgatan
8
Postgatan
Älvsnabben
Göta älv
11
Norra Hamngatan
Södra Hamngatan
Lilla Torget
18
Västra Hamngatan
36
34
1
26
37
Magasinsgatan
43
Skeppsbron
Viktoriapassagen
27
Kuggen (1km)
30
21
60
58
Kungsgatan
Hvitfeldtsplatsen
Stena Line Denmark Terminal (100m);
Stena Line Germany Terminal (2.5km);
Klippan & Röda Sten (3km)
2
29
46
Rosenlundsgatan
Järntorgsgatan
Kungsparken
Bengans Skivor & Café (900m);
Sjöfartsmuseet;
Masthuggskyrkan (1km)
53
Södra Allégatan
STF Vandrarhem
Stigbergsliden (600m)
Järntorget
47
Andra Långgatan
Landsvägsgatan
Kaponjärgatan
Husargatan
7
44
48
6
32
Tredje Långgatan
54
Hagta Nygata
IQ Suites (700m);
Botaniska
Trädgården (1.8km);
Slottsskogsparken (2km);
Mölndals Museum (8km)
28
Linné District
38
(150m)
Folkets Bio (150m);
Naturhistoriska
Museet (1km)
HAGA

0 200 m
0 0.1 miles
Göteborgs-Utkiken (150m); Taste of Peru (1.5km)
Götaleden
Sahlgrenska Universitetssjukhuset (5km); Kvibergs Vandrarhem & Stugby (5.5km); Bohus Fästning (15km)
Kruthusgatan
Lilla Bommen torg
Nils Ericson platsen
Swebus Express
Centralstationen
Flygbuss (to Landvetter Airport)
Flygbuss (to Göteborg City Airport)
Odinsgatan
Östra Hamngatan
Nordstantorget
Tourist Office
Drottningtorget
Stampgatan
Ullevigatan
Brunnsparken
Nya Ullevi (750m); Landvetter (20km)
Gustav Adolfs torg
Södra Hamngatan
Drottninggatan
Kyrkogatan
Korsgatan
Kungsgatan
Östra Larmgatan
Trädgårdsföreningen
Vallgatan
Kungsportsplatsen
Tourist Office
Nya Allén
Sten Sturegatan
Parkgatan
S Larmgatan
Kungstorget
Lilla Korsgatan
Gronsakstorget
Scandinavium (450m)
HEDEN
Kungsportsavenyn
Södra vägen
Lorensbergsgatan
Götabergsgatan
Parkgatan
Storgatan
Erik Dahlbergsg
Vasaplatsen
Linnéa Art (240m); Liseberg (500m); Universeum (600m); Världskulturmuseet (850m)
Engelbrektsgatan
Berzeliigatan
Vasagatan
VASASTAN
Vasaparken
Götaplatsen
Trattoria La Strega (200m)
Thörnströms Kök (550m)
Göteborgs Konserthuset (50m)

Göteborg (Gothenburg)

Sights

1 Domkyrkan ... D4
2 Feskekörka ... C6
3 Galleri Ferm ... E7
4 Galleri Nils Åberg ... F7
5 Galleri Thomassen ... G7
6 Haga District ... B7
7 Hagakyrkan ... D7
8 Kronhuset ... D3
9 Maritiman ... C2
10 Röhsska Museet ... F6
11 Stadsmuseum ... D3
12 Trädgårdsföreningen ... G4

Activities, Courses & Tours

13 Hop On Hop Off ... F5
14 Paddan City Boat Tour ... E5
15 Strömma Cruises ... E1

Sleeping

16 Avalon ... E4
17 Dorsia Hotel ... F4
18 Elite Plaza Hotel ... D4
19 First Hotel G ... F2
20 Gerdur Helga B&B ... E5
21 Hotel Flora ... D5
22 Hotel Royal ... F3
23 Hotell Barken Viking ... D1
24 STF Göteborg City ... F3
25 Vanilla Hotel ... E4

Eating

26 Beijing8 ... D4
27 Da Matteo ... D5
28 En Deli i Haga ... B7
29 Feskekörka ... C6
30 Gourmet Korv ... D5
31 Hemköp ... E2
32 Hemma Hos ... C7
33 Koka ... E7
34 Magnus & Magnus ... D4
35 Moon Thai Kitchen ... G7
36 Puta Madre ... D4
37 Restaurant 2112 ... D4
38 Saluhall Briggen ... A7
39 Saluhallen ... E5
40 Simba ... D2
41 Smaka ... E6
42 Wasa Allé ... E7

Drinking & Nightlife

43 Barn ... D4
44 Cafe Santo Domingo ... A7
45 Greta's ... E4
46 Nefertiti ... D6
47 NOBA Nordic Bar ... D7
48 Notting Hill ... A7
49 Ölhallen 7:an ... E5

Entertainment

50 Biopalatset ... E5
51 Göteborgs Stadsteatern ... H7
52 GöteborgsOperan ... D1
53 Pustervik ... B6

Shopping

54 Butik Kubik ... A7
55 DesignTorget ... E4
Fanny Michel ... (see 27)
56 J. Lindeberg ... E5
57 Nordiska Kompaniet ... E4
58 Prickig Katt ... D5
59 Systembolaget ... G6
60 Velour by Nostalgi ... D5

boxing matches and stand-up comedy. To get there, walk towards the Klippan precinct, continue under Älvsborgsbron and look for the brown-brick building.

Beside Röda Sten, check out work-in-progress *The Thing*, a communal 'sculpture' in the vein of Lars Vilks' Nimis. On weekends, families head here with hammers and nails to further its evolution.

★ Universeum MUSEUM

(www.universeum.se; Södra Vägen 50; adult/3-16yr Skr230/175; 10am-6pm; ; 2, 4, 5, 6, 8 Korsvägen) In what is arguably the best museum for kids in Sweden, you find yourself in the midst of a humid rainforest, complete with trickling water, tropical birds and butterflies flitting through the greenery, and tiny marmosets. On a level above, roaring dinosaurs maul each other, while next door, denizens of the deep float through the shark tunnel and venomous beauties lie coiled in the serpent tanks. In the 'technology inspired by nature' section, stick your children to the Velcro wall.

If that's not enough, go button crazy with the fantastically fun, hands-on science exhibitions, where themes range from nanotechnology and space travel to mixing music.

Konstmuseet GALLERY

(www.konstmuseum.goteborg.se; Götaplatsen; adult/under 25yr Skr40/free; 11am-6pm Tue & Thu, to 8pm Wed, to 5pm Fri-Sun; ; 4, 5, 7, 10 Berzeliigatan) Göteborg's premier art collection, Konstmuseet hosts works by the French Impressionists, Rubens, Van Gogh, Rembrandt and Picasso; Scandinavian masters such as Bruno Liljefors, Edvard Munch, Anders Zorn and Carl Larsson have pride of place in the **Fürstenburg Galleries**.

Other highlights include a superb sculpture hall, the **Hasselblad Center**, with its annual *New Nordic Photography* exhibition, and temporary displays of next-gen Nordic art.

The unveiling of the bronze **Poseidon** fountain out front scandalised Göteborg's strait-laced citizens, who insisted on drastic penile-reduction surgery.

Stadsmuseum MUSEUM

(City Museum; www.stadsmuseum.goteborg.se; Norra Hamngatan 12; adult/under 25yr Skr40/free; 10am-5pm Tue-Sun, to 8pm Wed; ; 1, 3, 4, 5, 6, 9 Brunnsparken) At Stadsmuseum, admire the remains of the *Äskekärrkeppet*, Sweden's only original Viking vessel, alongside silver treasure hoards, weaponry and jewellery from the same period in the atmospheric semigloom. Walk through the history of the city from its conception to the 18th century, spiced up with period wares, including an impressive booty of East Indian porcelain, and play 'Guess the Object!'. Temporary art and photography exhibitions are also worth a peek.

Sjöfartsmuseet MUSEUM

(www.sjofartsmuseum.goteborg.se; Karl Johansgatan 1-3; adult/under 25yr Skr40/free; 10am-5pm Tue-Sun, to 8pm Wed; ; 3, 9, 11 Stigbergstorget) Sjöfartsmuseet focuses on the city's maritime history through an entertaining collection of maps, model ships, re-created sailors' quarters, and period objects. Most compelling is the large darkened hall where you're surrounded by soaring figureheads – some regal, some pensive, some vicious. You may spot some scrimshaw and a tiny weaving loom in a bottle among the nautical booty.

The attached **aquarium** wriggles with goofy North Sea flatfish, lobsters and upside-down jellyfish, and you can find Nemo in the tropical fish tank.

Outside, the Sjömanstornet (Mariner's Tower), topped by a statue of a grieving woman, commemorates Swedish sailors killed in WWI.

Feskekörka MARKET

(Rosenlundsgatan; 9am-5pm Tue-Thu, to 6pm Fri, 10am-3pm Sat; 1, 3, 5, 6, 7, 9 Hagakyrkan) This peculiar fish market is shaped like a church. You may see the odd bride and groom posing with the shellfish; they're not lost – it's just that the market is also consecrated as a place of worship/matrimony.

Maritiman MUSEUM

(www.maritiman.se; Packhuskajen; adult/5-15yr Skr100/50; 11am-6pm Jun-Aug; ; 5, 10 Lilla Bommen) Near the opera house, the world's largest floating **ship museum** is made up of 20 historical crafts, including fishing boats, a light vessel and a firefighter, all linked by walkways. Shin down into the 69m-long submarine *Nordkaparen* for a glimpse into underwater warfare. Inside the labyrinthine 121m-long destroyer *Småland*, in service from 1952 to 1979, hunched figures listen to crackling radio messages, and the bunks look just-slept-in – you half expect to meet uniformed sailors in the dim, twisting passages...

Naturhistoriska Museet MUSEUM

(Natural History Museum; www.gnm.se; Museivägen 10; adult/under 25yr Skr40/free; 11am-5pm

GÖTEBORG DISCOUNT CARDS

Göteborg City Card (www.goteborg.com/en/Do/Gothenburg-City-Card/; 24/48/72hr Skr355/495/655) The brilliant Göteborg City Card is particularly worthwhile if you're into intensive sightseeing: it gives you free access to most museums and Liseberg amusement park, discounted and free city tours, unlimited travel on public transport and free parking in the city with the most dedicated traffic wardens.

The card is available at tourist offices, hotels, Pressbyrån newsagencies and online at www.goteborg.com.

Göteborgspaketet (http://butik.goteborg.com/en/package; adult from Skr635) The Göteborgspaketet is an accommodation-and-entertainment package offered at various hotels, with prices starting at Skr635 per person per night in a double room. It includes the Göteborg Pass for the number of nights you stay; book online in advance.

Museum Discount Card (adult Skr40) If you're looking to visit more than one of the following: Stadsmuseum, Konstmuseet, Röhsska Museet, Sjöfartsmuseet and Naturhistoriska Museet, ask for the discount card that allows you to visit all five for a total of Skr40 – the price of a single museum admission – within the space of a year. (It's available at any of the five museums.)

WORTH A TRIP

BOHUS FÄSTNING

Bohus Fästning (☎0303-23 93 03; www.bohusfastning.com; adult/7-16yr Skr75/35, cash only; ⏰10am-7pm daily May-Aug) Survivor of no fewer than 14 sieges, the hulking ruins of Bohus Fästning stand on an island in the Nordre älv, near Kungälv. Founded in 1308 by the Norwegian king to protect Norway's southern border, the fortress was inherited by Sweden at the Peace of Roskilde in 1658.

Take the Västtrafik Grön Express bus from Göteborg to Kungälv (30 minutes, every 10 to 15 minutes); get off at the Eriksdal stop and walk the remaining 500m.

Inside the castle, you can peer into the lightless dungeons of the rough-hewn round stone tower, Fars Hatt, where unfortunates were once imprisoned for witchcraft and heresy, and climb the battlements for a lofty view.

Tue-Sun; 👪; 🚋1, 2, 6 Linnéplatsen) The Natural History Museum is home to an incredible range of taxidermied wildlife, from the horned and hooved denizens of the savannah to all the big cats, the extinct Stellers sea cow, all manner of birds and pickled creatures of the deep. Its tour de force is the world's only stuffed blue whale. Visitors were allowed inside until an amorous couple was caught *in flagrante*, but Santa Claus still holds court here in the lead-up to Christmas.

Röhsska Museet MUSEUM
(www.designmuseum.se; Vasagatan 37; adult/under 25yr Skr40/free; ⏰noon-8pm Tue, to 5pm Wed-Fri, 11am-5pm Sat & Sun; 🚋3, 4, 5, 7, 10 Valand) Sweden's only art and design museum captures the style of different eras from 1851 to the present day. Exhibitions cleverly contrast the classic and the cutting edge, whether it's Josef Frank and Bruno Mathsson furniture or 18th-century porcelain and Scandi-cool coat stands, allowing you to see how the the idea of utility and beauty changed with each successive historical period. Temporary exhibitions often favour the offbeat – Pablo Picasso's porcelain efforts, for example.

Världskulturmuseet MUSEUM
(Museum of World Culture; www.varldskulturmuseet.se; Södra Vägen 54; adult/under 19yr Skr40/free; ⏰noon-5pm Tue-Sun; 🚋4, 5, 6, 7, 8 Korsvägen) In a striking building by London-based architects Cécile Brisac and Edgar Gonzalez, the Varldskulturmuseet sees ethnography, art and global politics collide in immersive multimedia exhibitions. Recent ones have included up-to-the-minute photography of Africa's cities and a special exhibition devoted to the Dark Continent's art.

Nya Älvsborgs Fästning CASTLE
At the mouth of the Göta älv, squat red **Elfsborgs Fortress** was built in the 17th century to keep out the marauding Danes and saw action again in the early 18th century during the Great Nordic War. Tours take in the church built for Karl XII's troops, the dungeons that discouraged escape by swimming and the original tower.

Strömma (www.stromma.se) runs boat trips and guided tours (adult/6-11yr Skr170/85) three to four times daily from May to mid-August from Lilla Bommen harbour.

Volvo Museum MUSEUM
(www.volvogroup.com; Arendal Skans; adult/6-12yr Skr60/25; ⏰10am-5pm Tue-Fri, to 6pm Wed, 11am-4pm Sat & Sun) Pay homage to one of Sweden's enduring icons at the Volvo Museum, which contains everything from the company's debut vehicle to its most experimental designs – including the first jet engine used by the Swedish Air Force.

The museum is about 8km west of the city centre at Arendal. Fittingly, it's tricky to get to without a car. Take tram 5 or 10 to Eketrägatan, then bus 32 to Arendal Skans.

Trädgårdsföreningen PARK
(www.tradgardsforeningen.se; Nya Allén; ⏰7am-8pm; 🚋3, 4, 5, 7, 10 Kungsportsplatsen) Laid out in 1842, the lush Trädgårdsföreningen is a large protected area off Nya Allén. Full of flowers and tiny cafes, it's popular for lunchtime escapes and is home to Europe's largest **rosarium**, with around 2500 varieties. The gracious 19th-century **Palmhuset** (⏰10am to 8pm) is a bite-size version of the Crystal Palace in London, with five differently heated halls: look out for the impressive camellia collection and the 2m-wide tropical lily pads.

Botaniska Trädgården GARDENS
(www.gotbot.se; Carl Skottsbergsgatan 22A; voluntary admission Skr20; ⏰9am-sunset; 🚋1, 2, 6, 7, 10 Linnéplatsen) Botaniska Trädgården, Sweden's largest botanical garden, breathes easy with around 16,000 plant species.

Masthuggskyrkan CHURCH
(Storebackegatan; ⏲9am-6pm daily Jun-Aug; 🚊1, 3, 5, 6, 9 Stigbergstorget) One of Göteborg's most distinctive buildings, this is a welcome landmark for sailors and is a smashing viewpoint over the western half of the city. Completed in 1914, its interior resembles an upturned boat.

Haga District NEIGHBOURHOOD
The Haga district is Göteborg's oldest suburb, dating back to 1648. A hardcore hippie hang-out in the 1960s and '70s, its cobbled streets and vintage buildings are now a gentrified blend of cafes, op shops and boutiques. During some summer weekends and at Christmas, store owners set up stalls along Haga Nygata, turning the neighbourhood into one big market.

Linné District NEIGHBOURHOOD
The Linné district holds fast to its grungy roots, especially along the Långgatan streets. Here, hip cafes, junk shops and street-smart boutiques mix it with seedy sex shops and eclectic locals. It's home to the kicking **Andra Långdagen block party**, a wild, one-day street bash organised by the street's traders and fans. Held annually between April and June (check Facebook for dates), it's a thumping concoction of DJ sets, film screenings, barbecues, clothes swaps and backyard B-boy battles.

Klippan Precinct HISTORIC SITE
(🚊3, 9 Vagnhallen Majorna) Once a bustle of industry (with glassworks, foundries, breweries and salting houses), the Klippan precinct has been revamped into a rather fetching heritage centre. It includes 18th-century sailors' cottages, the remains of Gamla Älvsborg fort (ransomed from the Danes in 1619), a brewery opened by the Scot David Carnegie (now a hotel) and St Birgittas kapell. Klippan is just off Oscarsleden, about 400m east of Älvsborgsbron.

Kronhuset HISTORIC BUILDING
(Postgatan 6-8; 🚊6, 13 Nordstan) The city's oldest secular building, Kronhuset is a former arsenal built between 1642 and 1654 in Dutch style. It was here that Karl X held the disastrous *riksdag* (parliament) in 1660 – he died while it was in session. Kronhusbodarna, across the courtyard from Kronhuset, houses workshops making and selling pottery, glass,

KVARNBYN: CREATIVE OUTSKIRTS

The tiny, creative hub of Kvarnbyn, a district of Mölndal 8km south of Göteborg, has long attracted architects, designers and artists looking to escape the high rents and pressures of the city. Here, a brooding landscape of roaring rapids gripped by grain mills and historic factories (Mölndal means 'valley of the mills') has been transformed into a dynamic yet low-key cultural centre.

The district's nexus is the smart, interactive **Mölndals Museum** (☎031-431 34; www.museum.molndal.se; Kvarnbygatan 12; ⏲noon-6pm Tue-Sun) FREE. Located in an old police station, the museum is like a vast warehouse, with a 10,000-strong booty of local nostalgia spanning a 17th-century clog to kitchen kitsch and a re-created 1930s worker's cottage. With a focus on memories and feelings, it's an evocative place where you can plunge into racks of vintage clothes, pull out hidden treasures and learn more about individual items on the digital catalogue. One particular highlight is the eclectic collection of chairs, including beautifully crafted pieces from the nearby village of Lindome, one of Sweden's most historic furniture-making areas. The temporary exhibitions are clever (a circus exhibit will skip from art to brain research and finish up with a bit of history) and the in-house cafe boasts summertime seating right by the rapids. The museum also hires out a brilliant, hand-held computer guide (in Swedish), which leads you through Kvarnbyn's industrial landscape using a lively mix of historical anecdotes, animation and soundscapes.

The town also hosts some noteworthy cultural events. On a Saturday in mid- to late April, **Kvarnbydagen** (Kvarnbyn Day; www.kvarnbydagen.se) sees local artists and designers open their studios to the public. In September **Kulturnatt** (www.mondal.se) is a starlit spectacle of open studios and art installations, as well as dance and music performances.

To reach Kvarnbyn from Göteborg, catch a Kungsbacka-bound train to Mölndal station, then bus 756 or 752 to Mölndals Museum.

DON'T MISS

CONTEMPORARY ART & ARCHITECTURE

Göteborg has imagination and creativity to spare. It seems that every time we're in town, new art galleries have opened, brimming with up-and-coming talent, and architectural flights of fancy made flesh have sprung up like mushrooms after the rain. In addition to the below, be sure to check out GöteborgsOperan (p146).

Galleri Ferm (www.galleriferm.se; Karl Gustavsgatan 13; ⌚11am-6pm Mon-Thu, to 5pm Fri, noon-3pm Sat & Sun; 🚊1, 2, 3, 7, 10 Viktoriagatan) Constant surprises, mainly from Scandinavian artists such as Per Cederbank, Emil Olsson and Yrjö Edelmann, plus works by internationally renowned contemporary artists.

Galleri Thomassen (www.gallerithomassen.se; Götabergsgatan 32; ⌚noon-6pm Tue-Thu, to 4pm Fri-Sun; 🚊1, 2, 3, 7, 10 Vasaplatsen) Showcases up-and-coming talent in its Lilla Galleriet and contemporary art from all over Scandinavia as well as Berlin.

Galleri Nils Åberg (www.gallerinilsaberg.se; Götabergsgatan 24; ⌚noon-6pm Wed-Fri, 11am-4pm Sat & Sun; 🚊1, 2, 3, 7, 10 Vasaplatsen) Works by fresh, young Scandinavian artists sit alongside established contemporary pieces by the likes of Picasso and Joan Miró.

Göteborgs-Utkiken (Lilla Bommen torg 1; adult/child Skr40/20; ⌚11am-4pm; 🚊6, 13 Nordstan) The red-and-white 'skyscraper' Göteborgs-Utkiken, nicknamed 'The Lipstick' for obvious reasons, has killer views of the harbour from the top.

Kuggen (Lindholmsplatsen) Across the river and next to the Science Park is the city's most exciting new building – the epitome of green engineering. Kuggen, or 'Cogwheel', resembles a bright red Colosseum, only with triangular windows that make maximum use of daylight and a host of eco-credentials that include adaptive ventilation and interactive heating and cooling systems. Take the Älvsn ferry from the Rosalund stop along Skeppsbron to Lindholmspiren.

textiles and silverware, as well as **Göteborgs Choklad & Karamellfabrik** (⌚11am to 5pm): its chocolate balls are enough to lead the purest of angels into sugar-filled temptation.

Slottsskogsparken PARK
(⌚24hr; 🚊1, 2, 6, 7, 10 Linnéplatsen) FREE Slottsskogsparken is an enormous park featuring dozens of walking trails and kid magnets **Barnens Zoo** and **Djurgårdarna**, an animal park with farm animals, elk, deer and other furry and feathered Swedish creatures.

Domkyrkan CHURCH
(Gustavi Cathedral; Västra Hamngatan; ⌚8am-6pm Mon-Fri, 10am-4pm Sat & Sun; 🚊1, 2, 5, 6, 9 Domkyrkan) The elegant Domkyrkan was consecrated in 1815, the two previous cathedrals on this site having both been destroyed by town fires. Although many of the cathedral's contents are relatively modern, seasoned features include an 18th-century clock and reredos.

Hagakyrkan CHURCH
(Haga Kyrkoplan; Haga Kyrkogata; ⌚11am-3pm Mon-Thu, to 1pm Sat; 🚊2, 7, 10 Handelshögskolan) The park behind the beautiful 19th-century Hagakyrkan is home to a simple yet moving **monument** to Swedish hero Raoul Wallenberg. A Nordic Schindler of sorts, Wallenberg is credited with saving the lives of around 15,000 Hungarian Jews during WWII. Wallenberg himself was arrested by the Russian government in 1945 as an alleged spy and executed sometime after.

Tours

Paddan City Boat Tour BOAT TOUR
(www.stromma.se; adult/6-11yr Skr160/72.50; ⌚Apr-Oct) Strömma runs 50-minute city tours on its Paddan boats from Kungsportsplatsen, right across from the tourist office. They're an information-packed way to get your bearings and are free with the Göteborg Pass.

Hop On Hop Off BUS TOUR, BOAT TOUR
(www.stromma.se; adult/6-11yr Skr300/150) Strömma runs the Hop On Hop Off bus-boat combo. A 24-hour ticket gives you access to the double-decker bus routes that take you past the city's main attractions, while the boats whisk you along the canals. You can also opt for separate bus (Skr185/90 per adult/child) and boat (Skr160/80) passes.

Strömma Cruises BOAT TOUR
(adult/6-11yr Skr170/85) The tour to Nya Älvsborgs Fästning departs Lilla Bommen torg daily from early May to August. Strömma also runs Archipelago cruises (Skr295) and a four-hour trip around the island of Hisingen (Skr195), among others.

Festivals & Events

Göteborg International Film Festival FILM
(www.giff.se) One of Scandinavia's major film festivals, with flicks spanning all continents and genres. It's usually held in late January.

Metaltown MUSIC
(www.metaltown.se) Metaltown is one of Sweden's biggest metal festivals. Taking place over a weekend in June, it attracts the likes of Slipknot, Korn, Napalm Death and Motörhead, as well as a large number of attendees featuring heavy black eyeliner and spike-adorned clothing.

Clandestino Festival MUSIC
(www.clandestinofestival.org) A hip-shaking line-up of world music, held in June.

Way Out West MUSIC
(www.wayoutwest.se) In early August, Way Out West is a mighty three-day music festival pulling in big guns like OutKast, Queens of the Stone Age, Röyksopp & Robin and Neneh Cherry.

Sleeping

Most hotels offer decent discounts at weekends and in summer. Check www.goteborg.com for hotel, breakfast and Göteborg Pass package deals (from Skr635) and www.goteborgsvandrarhem.se for the pick of budget digs.

Most hostels are clustered in the central southwestern area; all are open year-round.

★ **STF Göteborg City** HOSTEL €
(031-756 98 00; www.svenskaturistforeningen.se; Drottninggatan 63-65; s/d from 545/988; ; 1, 4, 6, 9, 11 Brunnsparken) Brand new and gleaming, this large supercentral hostel is all industrial chic in the cafe/dining area and lounge and plush comfort on each of its individually themed floors. All rooms are private, with en suite bathroom, plush carpeting and comfortable bed-bunks, and – rarity of rarities! – your bed linen and towels are provided for you.

Gerdur Helga B&B B&B €
(031-13 55 29; www.inomvallgraven.com; Södra Larmgatan 18; d/q Skr 800/1400; ; 1, 3, 5, 6, 9, 11 Grönsakstorget) This very central B&B consists of just two rooms – a quad and a twin – in a spacious apartment. Bed linen is included, and nothing is too much trouble for the friendly proprietress. Common spaces are shared with other guests and four adorable felines.

STF Vandrarhem Stigbergsliden HOSTEL €
(031-24 16 20; www.hostel-gothenburg.com; Stigbergsliden 10; dm/s/d/f from Skr185/475/675/875; reception 4-6pm; @; 3, 9, 11 Stigbergstorget) Rooms at Stigbergsliden have a certain monastic simplicity to them, in keeping with the hostel's history as a 19th-century seaman's institute. Staff are especially helpful, and besides the usual stuff (big kitchen, laundry, TV room) there is a pleasant sheltered garden. On the downside, the showers don't lock.

STF Vandrarhem Slottsskogen HOSTEL €
(031-42 65 20; www.sov.nu; Vegagatan 21; hostel dm/s/d from Skr195/395/540, hotel s/d Skr620/940; P@; 1, 2, 6 Olivedalsgatan) Like a good university dormitory, big, friendly Slottsskogen is a cracking place for meeting people. The facilities are top-notch, with comfortable beds, individual reading lights, lockable storage under the beds, a dressing table in the women's dorm and a good ratio of guests per bathroom. Proximity to the nightlife area is a bonus and the buffet breakfast (Skr70) is brilliant.

Kvibergs Vandrarhem & Stugby HOSTEL €
(031-43 50 55; www.vandrarhem.com; Kvibergsvägen 5; hostel d/tr/q Skr585/720/900, hotel d/tr/q Skr850/1050/1140, 5-person cabins Skr1350; P@; 6, 7, 11 Kviberg) This sterling Sveriges Vandrarhem i Förening (SVIF) hostel, a few kilometres northeast of the city centre, attracts families and travellers looking for a quiet spot with its extensive amenities that include a sauna and a pleasant outdoor area good for barbecuing. Hotel rooms throw in breakfast and bed linen and have their own bathrooms; dorm rooms don't. Cabins are particularly good value for groups.

Änggårdens Bed & Breakfast B&B €
(070-554 47 60, 031-41 97 06; Änggårdsplatsen 1; s/d Skr650/800; ; 1, 2, 6, 8, 10 Botaniska Trädgården) Across the street from the Slottsskogen city park and surrounded by greenery, this appealing yellow stone house

welcomes you with its homey atmosphere, four compact, cosy rooms (the largest double has its own bathroom) and a chill-out garden area.

Linné Vandrarhem
HOSTEL €

(☑031-12 10 60; www.linnehostel.com; Vegagatan 22; dm/s/d Skr280/490/680; @ 🛜; 🚊 1, 6, 7, 10 Prinsgatan) The helpful staff really brighten up this central, homey hostel. Make sure you have your door code if arriving after office hours and avoid the windowless 'economy' rooms (read: ovens) in summer.

Vanilla Hotel
BOUTIQUE HOTEL €€

(☑031-711 62 20; www.vaniljhotel.se; Kyrkogatan 38; s/d Skr1195/1345; P @ 🛜; 🚊 1, 3, 5, 6, 9 Domkyrkan) This petite slumber spot has the cosy, welcoming feeling of a Swedish home. The compact rooms are pleasantly light and decorated in sparing Scandinavian style, with wooden floors and furniture, crisp sheets and immaculate bathrooms, but they get rather hot in summer. Ask for a garden-view room, as the street gets noisy from early morning. Weekend rates drop sharply.

Hotel Flora
BOUTIQUE HOTEL €€

(☑031-13 86 16; www.hotelflora.se; Grönsakstorget 2; r from Skr840; @ 🛜; 🚊 1, 5, 6, 9, 10 Grönsakstorget) Fabulous Flora's slick, individually themed rooms flaunt black, white and a-dash-of-bright-colour interiors, designer chairs, flat-screen TVs and sparkling bathrooms, though lack of storage facilities may dismay those with extensive sartorial needs. The top-floor rooms have air-con and several rooms offer river views. Rooms overlooking the chic split-level courtyard are for night owls rather than early birds.

Hotel Royal
HOTEL €€

(☑031-700 11 70; www.hotelroyal.nu; Drottninggatan 67; s/d from Skr1165/1495; @ 🛜; 🚊 1, 2, 5, 6, 9 Domkyrkan) Göteborg's oldest hotel (1852) has aged enviably. The grand entrance has been retained, complete with its flowery, artnouveau painted ceiling and sweeping staircase, and the elegant, individually styled rooms make necessary 21st-century concessions such as flat-screen TVs and renovated bathrooms. There's also homemade cake for guests, and an excellent breakfast. Check the website for special offers.

Aprikosen B&B
B&B €€

(☑031-41 40 50; www.aprikosenbab.se; Muraregatan 5; s/d/f Skr695/895/1295; P 🛜; 🚊 2 Brunnsgatan) There's a pleasant contrast between the historic 1880s building this B&B is located in and the contemporary furnishings in the spacious rooms. The congenial hostess is happy to assist with the exploration of the city, there are tea- and coffee-making facilities in each room, and the breakfast spread is excellent.

Hotell Barken Viking
HOTEL €€

(☑031-63 58 00; www.barkenviking.com; Lilla Bommens torg 10; r from Skr1095; 🛜; 🚊 5, 10 Lilla Bommen) If staying aboard a schooner floats your boat, you mast try the *Barken Viking*, an elegant four-masted sailing ship converted into a stylish hotel. The wood-panelled rooms are cosy (read: small), with Hamptons-style linen, and designed for those who travel light. You won't run into any seamen, however, as there's no access to the upper deck.

Sankt Sigfrid B&B
B&B €€

(☑0735-51 52 80; www.sanktas.se; Sankt Sigfrids Plan 7; s/d/tr/q Skr650/870/1070/1270; P 🛜; 🚊 5 Sankt Sigfrids Plan) Particularly handy for hitting Liseberg or the Avenyn nightlife, this welcoming guesthouse in a quiet area offers all the perks of staying practically in the city centre, minus the city-centre prices. The rooms are snug, guests have access to a small kitchen, and the host couldn't be more attentive.

First Hotel G
HOTEL €€

(☑031-63 72 00; www.firsthotels.se; Nils Ericsonsplatsen 4; r/ste from Skr1098/1898; P ✳ 🛜; 🚊 1, 2, 3, 4, 9 Centralstationen) In a you-couldn't-be-more-central location on top of the train station, this high-tech business hotel is completely soundproof, and its spacious rooms boast laminated wooden floors and thoroughly comfortable beds. Extensive breakfast is thrown in, and there's an in-house spa for pre- or postjourney relaxation. Substantial discounts online.

Gothia Towers
HOTEL €€

(☑031-750 88 10; www.gothiatowers.com; Mässans Gata 24; budget s/d from Skr990/1090, s/d/ste from Skr1490/1590/2990; P @ 🛜 ♨; 🚊 2, 4, 5, 6, 7 Korsvägen) The 23-storey Gothia Towers looms right above Liseberg. Its rooms ooze Nordic cool: they're all sharp, with clean lines, and suites on floors 18 and 21. 'Gothia Limited' budget rooms are available and guests have access to the luxurious spa at sister hotel Upper House. More bird's-eye views await at Sky bar and restaurant Heaven 23.

★ IQ Suites APARTMENT €€€
(☎031-760 80 40; www.iqsuites.com; Besvärsgatan 3; s/d Skr1500/1800; P ; 2 Brunnsgatan) Short of scanning your retinas upon entry, these luxurious, industrial-chic apartments are as high-tech as they come and are within walking distance of the city's main attractions, to boot. The fully equipped Miele kitchens are a boon for self-caterers, while the smaller of the two apartments comes with its own sauna and jacuzzi, for the ultimate in pampering.

★ Dorsia Hotel BOUTIQUE HOTEL €€€
(☎031-790 10 00; www.dorsia.se; Trädgårdsgatan 6; s/d/ste from Skr1900/2500/5800; @ ; 3, 4, 5, 7, 10 Kungsportsplatsen) If heaven had a bordello, it would resemble this lavish, flamboyant establishment that combines old-world decadence with cutting-edge design. Rooms delight with their heavy velvet curtains, a purple-and-crimson colour scheme and opulent beds; thick carpet in the corridors muffles your footsteps; and the fine art adorning the walls comes from the owner's own collection.

A uniformed footman greets you upon entry, the seating on either side of the lobby resembles a theatre, and the new dining room will make you wonder whether you've inadvertently emerged in the middle of a Tim Burton movie.

★ Upper House BOUTIQUE HOTEL €€€
(☎031-708 82 00; www.upperhouse.se; Mässans Gata 24; P ; 2, 4, 5, 6, 7 Korsvägen) One of the highest hotels in Sweden, sumptuous Upper House takes up the top four floors of one of the Gothia Towers. The decor is cool Scandinavian chic, the beds are the ultimate in slumbering comfort, and the superlative spa comes with a *hammam* and a 19th-floor outdoor pool encased in glass, with killer views of the city.

Avalon HOTEL €€€
(☎031-751 02 00; www.avalonhotel.se; Kungstorget 9; r from Skr1211; @ ; 3, 4, 5, 7, 10 Kungsportsplatsen) Rooms at the design-conscious Avalon are packed with eye-popping Nordic design, bright colours, curvaceous furniture and flat-screen TVs. Some rooms feature a mini-spa or their own gym equipment, the hip resto-bar is an after-work hot spot, and there's a small rooftop pool. Downsides are the temperamental wi-fi and the below-par service. Book online for the best rates.

Elite Plaza Hotel HOTEL €€€
(☎0771-78 87 89; www.elite.se; Västra Hamngatan 3; s/d from Skr1400/1620; P @ ; 1, 3, 5, 6, 9 Domkyrkan) With stucco ceilings and lovely mosaic floors, the Elite Plaza is a grand, old-world establishment with all the modern trimmings. Most rooms are spacious and breakfast is ample (though chaotic when the hotel is full). The proximity to some of the city's best restaurants and bars is a boon, but the latter is also a bane if you're a light sleeper.

Eating

Göteborg isn't short on great epicurean experiences: the city's chefs are at the cutting edge of Sweden's Slow Food movement and there are no fewer than four Michelin-starred restaurants. Happily, there are more casual and less-expensive options for trying the country's best seafood and old-fashioned *husmanskost* (home cooking).

Cool cafes, cheap ethnic gems and foodie favourites abound in the Vasastan, Haga and Linné districts, often with lower prices than their tourist-trap Avenyn rivals. Many fine-dining establishments close between mid-July and mid-August, so if you have your heart set on haute cuisine, best plan your visit for a different time of year.

There's a **Hemköp** (Östra Hamngatan; 8am-9pm Mon-Fri, 10am-8pm Sat & Sun; 5, 6, 9, 13 Nordstan) supermarket in the Nordstan shopping complex.

Gourmet Korv SAUSAGES €
(www.gourmetkorv.se; Södra Larmgatan; mains Skr25-85; 10am-6pm Mon-Fri, to 4pm Sat, to 3pm Sun; 1, 6, 9) A sausage fest to sate the hungriest of the carnivorously inclined. Choose from the likes of *currywurst*, *bierwurst* and the immensely satisfying, cheese-squirting *käsekrainer* and have it in a bun or with a full spread of salad and mash.

Beijing8 DIM SUM €
(www.beijing8.se; Magasinsgatan 3; dim sum from Skr29; 11am-9pm Mon-Fri, noon-10pm Sat; 1, 3, 5, 6, 9 Domkyrkan) Take six imaginatively filled types of dumpling (duck and ginger, pork and shiitake, courgette and aubergine, chicken and peanut…), cook 'em four different ways, add a few veggie sides, four types of sauce, a couple of desserts and a few types of tea and you have a winning formula.

En Deli i Haga DELI €
(Haga Nygata 15; salad buffet from Skr75; 8am-7pm Mon-Fri, 10am-5pm Sat & Sun; ; 1, 3,

5, 6, 9 Järntorget) En Deli dishes out great Mediterranean-style salads and meze, as well as good soup and sandwiches. An extra perk is the locally brewed beer and organic wine to accompany your meal.

Taste of Peru PERUVIAN €
(www.tasteofperu.se; Gustaf Dalénsgatan 2; mains Skr70-99; 11am-6pm Mon-Fri, to 4pm Sat; 5, 6, 10, 13 Vågmästareplatsen) Well worth the short trip across the river, the city's only Peruvian eatery is found on the 1st floor of a market hall. Sate your cravings for ceviche (five types!) The weekday specials – *aji de gallina* (chicken in a creamy yellow sauce), *seco de carne* (beef stew) and *arróz con mariscos* (seafood rice) – are all present and correct.

Da Matteo CAFE €
(www.damatteo.se; Vallgatan 5; sandwiches & salads Skr50-95; 8am-7pm Mon-Fri, 9am-5pm Sat, 10am-5pm Sun; 1, 3, 5, 6, 9 Domkyrkan) The perfect downtown lunch pit stop and a magnet for coffee lovers, this cafe serves wickedly fine espresso, moreish mini *sfogliatelle* (Neapolitan pastries), sandwiches, pizza and great salads. There's a sun-soaked courtyard and a second branch on Viktoriapassagen.

Feskekörka MARKET €
(www.feskekörka.se; Rosenlundsgatan; salads Skr70; 9am-5pm Tue-Thu, to 6pm Fri, 10am-3pm Sat; 3, 5, 9, 11 Hagakyrkan) A market devoted to all things that come from the sea (except sailors), the 'Fish Church' is, erm, heaven for those who appreciate slabs of gravadlax, heaped shrimp sandwiches and seafood-heavy salads. The outdoor picnic tables are the ideal place to munch on them.

Saluhall Briggen MARKET €
(www.saluhallbriggen.se; Nordhemsgatan 28; sandwiches Skr60; 9am-6pm Mon-Fri, to 3pm Sat; ; 1, 6, 7, 10 Prinsgatan) This covered market will have you drooling over its bounty of fresh bread, cheeses, quiches, seafood and ethnic treats. It's particularly handy for the hostel district.

Saluhallen MARKET €
(Kungstorget; sandwiches Skr60; 9am-6pm Mon-Fri, to 3pm Sat; ; 3, 4, 5, 7, 10 Kungsportsplatsen) Göteborg's main central market is jammed with tasty budget eateries, delis, bakeries and food stalls, and it's the perfect place to stock up that picnic basket.

★ **Moon Thai Kitchen** THAI €€
(www.moonthai.se; Kristinelundsgatan 9; mains Skr129-298; 11am-11pm Mon-Fri, noon-11pm Sat & Sun; 4, 5, 7, 10) The owners have opted for a 'Thailand' theme and decided to run with it a few kilometres, hence the kaleidoscopic whirl of *tuktuks*, flowers and bamboo everything. Luckily, the dishes are authentic, the whimsical menu features such favourites as *som tum* (spicy papaya salad) and the fiery prawn red curry will make you weep with pleasure and gratitude.

Puta Madre MEXICAN €€
(031-711 88 38; www.putamadre.se; Magasinsgatan 3; mains Skr179-262; 6pm-midnight Mon-Thu, 5pm-2am Fri & Sat; 1, 3, 5, 6, 9 Domkyrkan) This tribute to a Mexican brothel madam serves fresh, imaginative takes on classic Mexican dishes, such as *chile en nogada* (stuffed chilli), fish tacos, shrimp and crab enchiladas and jicama salad. And haven't you always wanted to toast your friends with a 'Rusty Puta'?

Trattoria la Strega ITALIAN €€
(031-18 15 01; www.trattorialastrega.se; Aschebergsgatan 23B; mains Skr120-220; 5pm-late Tue-Fri, from 4pm Sat & Sun; ; 1, 2, 3, 7, 10 Vasaplatsen) A genuine rustic trattoria in the middle of Göteborg, La Strega has a limited but beautifully executed menu of regularly changing dishes, complemented by wines from different Italian regions. Feast on the likes of black-truffle risotto, buckwheat pasta with savoy cabbage and entrecôte with chestnut ragu, and leave room for the organic gelato.

Restaurant 2112 BURGERS €€
(031-787 58 12; Magasinsgatan; burgers Skr189-399; 4pm-1am, from 2pm Sat; 1, 3, 5, 6, 9 Domkyrkan) Appealing to refined rockers and metalheads, this upmarket joint serves only burgers and beer. But what burgers! These masterpieces range from the superlative Smoke on the Water with its signature Jack Daniels glaze to the fiery Hell Awaits Burger, featuring habanero dressing. The hungriest of diners will meet their match in the 666g monster Number of the Beast.

Linnéa Art SWEDISH €€
(031-16 11 83; www.linneaartrestaurant.se; Södra Vägen 32; mains Skr149-325, 7-course menu Skr1195; bistro 5-11pm Mon-Sat, fine dining 6-11pm Tue-Sat; 2, 4, 5, 6, 7 Korsvägen) Intimate Linnéa takes its 'food as art' concept seriously, with classic Swedish dishes presented in unusual forms and bold pairings of ingredients. Your taste buds will thank you for the likes of lobster with iced lingon-

berries, and the seven-course menu is an experience to savour.

Smaka SWEDISH €€
(www.smaka.se; Vasaplatsen 3; mains Skr130-225; 5pm-late; 1, 2, 3, 7, 10 Vasaplatsen) For top-notch Swedish *husmanskost*, like the speciality meatballs with mashed potato and lingonberries, it's hard to do better than this smart yet down-to-earth restaurant-bar. Mod-Swedish options might include hake with suckling pig cheek or salmon tartar with pickled pear.

Hemma Hos TAPAS €€
(031-13 40 90; Haga Nygata 12; small plates Skr69-159; 11.30am-mdnight; 1, 3, 5, 6, 9 Hagakyrkan) With a smooth black bar and comfortable tables, this Haga restaurant-bar manages to be both urbane and relaxed. Its selection of small plates is decidedly gourmet – slow-cooked pork with apple chutney or goat's cheese with honey and pine nuts – and there is a good variety of wine by the glass.

Simba AFRICAN €€
(www.restaurangsimba.se; Sankt Eriksgatan 3; mains Skr139-285; 4-10pm Tue-Thu, to late Fri & Sat; 5, 10 Lilla Bommen) Tuck into the likes of *domoda* (tender lamb with peanut butter) or springbok steak, or mop up *wat* (stew) with *injera* (spongy Ethiopian pancake) under the watchful eyes of the tribal masks surrounding you.

★**Thörnströms Kök** SCANDINAVIAN €€€
(031-16 20 66; www.thornstromskok.com; 3 Teknologgatan; mains Skr255-285, 4-/6-/9-course menu Skr625/825/1125; 6pm-1am Mon-Sat; 7, 10 Kapellplatsen) Specialising in modern Scandinavian cuisine, chef Håkan shows you how he earned that Michelin star through creative use of local, seasonal ingredients and flawless presentation. Feast on the likes of sweetbreads with hazelnut and cured perch with rhubarb; don't miss the remarkable milk-chocolate pudding with goat's-cheese ice cream. À la carte dishes are available if a multicourse menu overwhelms you.

Magnus & Magnus MODERN EUROPEAN €€€
(031-13 30 00; www.magnusmagnus.se; Magasinsgatan 8; 2-/3-course menus Skr455/555; from 6pm Mon-Sat; 1, 2, 5, 6, 9 Domkyrkan) Ever-fashionable Magnus & Magnus serves inspired and beautifully presented modern European dishes in an appropriately chic setting. It's an unpretentious place in spite of its popularity, with pleasantly down-to-earth waitstaff. The menu tantalises with its lists of dish ingredients (pork belly, king crab, melon, feta cheese) and the courtyard draws Göteborg's hipsters in summer.

Wasa Allé SWEDISH €€€
(031-13 13 70; www.wasaalle.se; Vasagatan 24; business lunch from Skr225, mains Skr195-225; 11.30am-2pm Mon-Fri & 6pm-late Tue-Sat; ; 1, 2, 3 Vasa Viktoriagatan) At Wasa Allé, the flagship restaurant of Mats Nordström, most ingredients come from within four hours of the restaurant, year-round. The result is 'modern, conscious Swedish food': choose between the lunchtime buffet (Skr145), seasonal business-lunch dishes, stomach-filling classics (pork with potato pancakes and lingonberries) at the attached Wasa Basement, and the surprise three- to seven-course *stolen* (chair) evening menu.

Koka MODERN SWEDISH €€€
(031-701 79 79; www.restaurangkoka.se; Viktoriagatan 12C; 3-/5-/7-course meals Skr400/600/800; from 6pm Wed-Sat; 1, 2, 3, 7, 10 Vasaplatsen) Stylish Koka is distinguished by its smart, contemporary decor – blond wood, clean lines, mood lighting – and a dedication to conjuring up inspired dishes from the seasonal ingredients of Sweden's west coast. Brace yourself for the likes of mackerel with gooseberries, pork with blackcurrant and chervil ice cream.

Drinking & Nightlife

Swedish licensing laws mean that bars must have a restaurant section, although in most cases, it's vice versa. While Kungsportsavenyn brims with beer-downing tourists, there are still some savvier options.

Clubs have minimum-age limits ranging from 18 to 25, and many may charge admission depending on the night.

Barn BAR
(www.thebarn.se; Kyrkogatan 11; beers from Skr50; 5pm-late Mon-Sat, from 2pm Sun; 1, 3, 5, 6, 9 Domkyrkan) As the name suggests, this bar is all roughly hewn wood and copper taps, and the beer/wine/cocktail selection is guaranteed to get you merry enough to, erm, raise the barn. The burgers make fantastic stomach-liners, too.

Cafe Santo Domingo BAR
(www.cafesantodomingo.se; Andra Långgatan 4; 9am-late; 1, 3, 5, 6, 9 Järntorget) Cafe-record

shop serving mean espressos by day turns into a bar with a great array of beers and rowdy live-music sets by night.

NOBA Nordic Bar BAR
(www.noba.nu; Viktoriagatan 1A; beers from Skr52; 4pm-1am Mon-Thu, to 3am Fri & Sat, 5pm-1am Sun; 1, 2, 3, 7, 10 Viktoriagatan) With ye olde maps of Scandinavia on the walls and a glassed-over beer patio with birch tree stumps for stools, this bar takes its Nordic beers very seriously. From Iceland's Freja to Denmark's K:rlek, you name it, this bar's got it. The free-flowing whiskies liven up the scene on weekends.

Notting Hill PUB
(www.nottinghill.se; Nordhemsgatan 19A; 4pm-late Mon-Fri, 2pm-late Sat & Sun; 1, 3, 5, 6, 9 Järntorget) Friendly local between the Haga and Linné districts, with a respectable selection of tipples, British and Swedish pub fare (meatballs, fish and chips) and football on the big screen.

Ölhallen 7:an BEER HALL
(Kungstorget 7; 4pm-late; 3, 4, 5, 7, 10 Kungsportsplatsen) This well-worn Swedish beer hall hasn't changed much in over 100 years. It attracts an interesting mix of bikers and regular folk with its homey atmosphere and friendly service. There's no food, wine or pretension, just beer, and plenty of choices.

Nefertiti CLUB
(www.nefertiti.se; Hvitfeldtsplatsen 6; admission Skr120-220; 1, 5, 6, 9, 11 Grönsakstorget) Named rather incongrously after an Egyptian goddess, this Göteborg institution is famous for its smooth live jazz and blues, as well as club nights spanning everything from techno and deep house to hip hop and funk. Saturday's BEAT is all about soul.

Greta's GAY
(031-13 69 49; Drottninggatan 35; 9pm-3am Fri & Sat; 1, 3, 4, 5, 6, 9 Brunnsparken) Decked out with Greta Garbo memorabilia, Greta's is Göteborg's only gay club, featuring flamboyant Tiki parties, DJs and other kitsch-a-licious fun on Friday and Saturday nights.

☆ Entertainment

Göteborgs Stadsteatern THEATRE
(031-708 71 00; www.stadsteatern.goteborg.se; Götaplatsen; tickets from Skr110) Stages theatre productions in Swedish.

Göteborgs Konserthuset CLASSICAL MUSIC
(Concert Hall; 031-726 53 10; www.gso.se; Götaplatsen; tickets Skr100-360; closed summer) Home to the local symphony orchestra, with top international guests and some sterling performances.

GöteborgsOperan OPERA
(031-13 13 00; www.opera.se; Christina Nilssons Gata; tickets Skr50-650; 5, 10 Lilla Bommen) Designed by architect Jan Izikowitz, the opera house is a striking contemporary glass building with a sloped roof overlooking Lilla Bommen harbour. It stages ballet and opera performances, too.

Pustervik LIVE MUSIC, THEATRE
(www.pusterviksbaren.se; Järntorgsgatan 12; 1, 3, 5, 9, 11 Järntorget) Culture vultures and party people pack this hybrid venue, with its heaving downstairs bar and upstairs club and stage. Gigs range from independent theatre and live music (anything from emerging singer-songwriters to Neneh Cherry) to regular club nights spanning hip hop, soul and rock.

Nya Ullevi STADIUM
(031-368 45 00; www.gotevent.se; Skånegatan) The city's outdoor stadium hosts rock concerts and sporting events.

Scandinavium CONCERT VENUE
(031-368 4500; www.gotevent.se; Valhallagatan 1) An indoor concert venue near Nya Ullevi stadium.

Biopalatset CINEMA
(08-562 600 00; Kungstorget) Multiscreen Biopalatset screens mainstream blockbusters.

Folkets Bio CINEMA
(031-42 88 10; www.hagabion.se; Linnégatan 21) For independent and art-house offerings.

Shopping

DesignTorget HOMEWARES
(www.designtorget.se; Vallgatan 14; 10am-7pm Mon-Fri, to 5pm Sat, noon-4pm Sun; 1, 2, 5, 6, 9 Domkyrkan) Cool, brightly coloured, affordable designer kitchenware, jewellery and more from both established and up-and-coming Scandi talent.

Prickig Katt CLOTHING
(www.prickigkatt.se; Magasinsgatan 17; 11am-6pm Mon-Fri, to 4pm Sat; 1, 5, 6, 9, 11 Grönsakstorget) The outrageous 'Spotted Cat' has retro-clad staff and idiosyncratic fashion from Dutch, Danish and home-grown labels,

as well as kitschy wares and out-there handmade millinery and bling.

Velour by Nostalgi CLOTHING
(www.velour.se; Magasinsgatan 19; 11am-6.30pm Mon-Fri, to 5pm Sat, noon-4pm Sun; 1, 6, 9, 11 Domkyrkan) Revamped flagship store of local label. Stocks slick, stylish streetwear for guys and girls.

Butik Kubik CLOTHING
(www.butikkubik.se; Tredje Långgatan 8; noon-8pm Tue-Fri, to 6pm Sat; 1, 6 Prinsgatan) Run by two young designers, this basement shop is a great place to check out local, bright, flowery threads.

Bengans Skivor & Café MUSIC
(031-14 33 00; www.bengans.se; Stigbergstorget 1; to 4pm Sat, noon-4pm Sun; 3, 9, 11 Stigbergstorget) Göteborg's mightiest music store is set in an old cinema, complete with retro signage and indie-cool cafe.

Nordiska Kompaniet MALL
(www.nk.se; Östra Hamngatan 42; 10am-8pm, to 6pm Sat, 11am-5pm Sun; 3, 4, 5, 7, 10 Kungsportsplatsen) A local institution since 1971, the four floors of this venerable shopping mall host the likes of Tiger, RedGreen, NK Boutique and Mayla amid its mix of Swedish and international designers.

J. Lindeberg CLOTHING
(www.jlindeberg.com; 17 Korsgatan; 11am-6pm Mon-Fri, to 5pm Sat; 1, 6, 9, 11 Domkyrkan) This established Stockholm designer offers slick knitwear, casual shirts and those perfect autumn/winter coats for the discerning gent.

Fanny Michel ACCESSORIES
(www.fannymichel.se; Vallgatan 19; 11am-6pm Mon-Fri, to 5pm Sat, noon-4pm Sun; 1, 6, 9, 11 Domkyrkan) Awash with lace, hats, scarves and other accessories. There are outlets in Haga and Viktoriapassagen too.

Shelta SHOES
(031-24 28 56; www.shelta.eu; Andra Långgatan 21; 11am-6.30pm Mon-Sat; 3, 9, 11 Masthuggstorget) Pimp your style with limited-edition and must-have sneakers and streetwear from big players and lesser-known labels.

Systembolaget DRINK
(Kungsportsavenyn 18; 3, 4, 5, 7, 10 Valand) Handy central branch for all your alcohol-related needs.

Information

EMERGENCY

Police station (077-114 14 00; Stampgatan 28) Handy police station.

INTERNET ACCESS

Sidewalk Express (www.sidewalkexpress.se; per hour Skr25) Sidewalk Express computers are found at Centralstationen and the 7-Eleven shop on Vasaplatsen. To log on, buy vouchers from the coin-operated machines and enter the username and password issued.

MEDICAL SERVICES

For 24-hour medical information, phone 1177.

Apotek Hjärtat (0771-45 04 50; Nils Eriksongatan; 8am-10pm) Late-night pharmacy inside the Nordstan shopping complex.

Sahlgrenska Universitetssjukhuset (031-342 00 00; www.sahlgrenska.se; 1) Major hospital about 5km northeast of central Göteborg, near the terminus at the end of tram line 1.

MONEY

Banks with ATMs are readily available, including inside the Nordstan shopping complex and along Kungsportsavenyn.

Forex (www.forex.se) Foreign-exchange office with branches at Centralstationen, Kungsportsavenyn 22, Kungsportsplatsen, Landvetter Airport and Norstan shopping complex.

POST

Postal services are mainly provided by kiosks, newsagents, petrol stations and supermarkets; look for the blue-and-yellow postal symbol.

Post office (Östra Hamngatan; 7am-7pm Mon-Fri) Main post office inside Nordstan shopping centre.

TOURIST INFORMATION

Cityguide Gothenburg (www.goteborg.com/en/Do/Artiklar/Mobileapp/) Info on the city's attractions, events and more, available as an Android and iPhone app. City map available offline.

RFSL (031-13 83 00; www.rfsl.se/goteborg) Comprehensive information on the city's gay scene, events and more.

Tourist office (www.goteborg.com; Nils Eriksongatan; 10am-8pm Mon-Fri, to 6pm Sat, noon-5pm Sun) Branch office inside the Nordstan shopping complex.

Tourist office (031-368 42 00; www.goteborg.com; Kungsportsplatsen 2; 9.30am-8pm) Central and busy; has a good selection of free brochures and maps.

Getting There & Away

Luggage lockers (small/large up to 24 hours Skr50/60) are available at both Centralstationen and the long-distance bus terminal Nils Ericson Terminalen.

AIR

Twenty-five kilometres east of the city, Sweden's second-biggest international airport, **Göteborg Landvetter Airport** (www.swedavia.se/landvetter), has up to 12 direct daily flights to/from Stockholm Arlanda and Stockholm Bromma airports (with SAS, Malmö Aviation and Norwegian), as well as weekday services to Umeå and several weekly services to Borlänge, Falun, Visby and Sundsvall.

Direct European routes include Amsterdam (KLM), Brussels (SAS), Copenhagen (SAS and Norwegian), Frankfurt (Lufthansa), Berlin (Air Berlin), Helsinki (Norwegian and SAS), London (British Airways and easyJet), Manchester (SAS), Munich (Lufthansa), Oslo (Norwegian) and Paris (Air France and SAS).

Göteborg City Airport (www.goteborgairport.se), some 15km north of the city at Säve, is used for budget Ryanair and Wizz Air flights to destinations including London Stansted, Edinburgh, Paris, Malaga and Budapest, as well as domestic flights to Visby with Gotlandsflyg.

BOAT

Göteborg is a major entry point for ferries, with several car/passenger services to Denmark and Germany.

For a special view of the region, jump on a boat for an unforgettable journey along the Göta Canal. Starting in Göteborg, you'll pass through Sweden's oldest lock at Lilla Edet, opened in 1607. From there the trip crosses the great lakes Vänern and Vättern through the rolling country of Östergötland and on to Stockholm.

Stena Line (Denmark) (www.stenaline.se; 3, 9, 11 Masthuggstorget) Nearest to central Göteborg, the Stena Line Denmark terminal near Masthuggstorget has around six daily departures for Frederikshavn in peak season (one way/return from Skr499/998).

Stena Line (Germany) (www.stenaline.se; 3, 9 Jaegardorffsplatsen) Services to Kiel in Germany (one way/return from Skr1699/2998) depart from near the Älvsborgsbron bridge. Departures are daily at 6.45pm and the journey takes 14 hours.

BUS

Västtrafik (0771-41 43 00; www.vasttrafik.se) and **Hallandstrafiken** (0771-33 10 30; www.hlt.se) provide regional transport links. If you're planning to spend some time exploring the southwest counties, a monthly pass or a *sommarkort* offers cheaper travel in the peak summer period (from late June to mid-August).

The bus station, Nils Ericson Terminalen, is next to the train station. There's a Västtrafik information booth here, providing information and selling tickets for all city and regional public transport within the Göteborg, Bohuslän and Västergötland area.

Swebus Express (0771-21 82 18; www.swebusexpress.com) operates frequent buses to most major towns and cities; nonrefundable advance tickets work out considerably cheaper than on-the-spot purchases. Services include the following:

- Copenhagen (Skr239, 4¾ to five hours, four daily)
- Halmstad (Skr109, 1¾ hours, four to five daily)
- Helsingborg (Skr139, 2¾ hours, five to eight daily)
- Stockholm (Skr389, 6½ to seven hours, four to five daily)
- Malmö (Skr159, 3½ to four hours, five to eight daily)
- Oslo (Skr189, 3½ hours, five to 10 daily)

CAR & MOTORCYCLE

The E6 motorway runs north–south from Oslo to Malmö just east of the city centre and there's also a complex junction where the E20 motorway diverges east for Stockholm.

International car-hire companies **Avis** (www.avisworld.com), **Europcar** (www.europcar.com) and **Hertz** (www.hertz-europe.com) have desks at Göteborg Landvetter and City Airports.

TRAIN

All trains arrive at and depart from Centralstationen, Sweden's oldest railway station and a listed building. The main railway lines in the west connect Göteborg to Karlstad, Stockholm, Malmö and Oslo. In the east, the main line runs from Stockholm via Norrköping and Linköping to Malmö. Book tickets online via **Sveriges Järnväg** (SJ; www.sj.se) or purchase from ticket booths at the station. Train services include the following:

- Copenhagen (Skr450, 3¾ hours, hourly)
- Kalmar (Skr192, four hours, four daily)
- Karlstad (Skr172, 2½ hours, seven daily)
- Luleå (Skr763, 17½ hours, daily)
- Malmö (Skr195, 2½ to 3¼ hours, hourly)
- Oslo (Skr299, four hours, three daily)
- Stockholm (Skr419, three to five hours, one to two an hour)
- Västerås (Skr405, 3¾ hours, seven daily)
- Östersund (Skr820, 12 hours, daily)

Getting Around

TO/FROM THE AIRPORT

Göteborg Landvetter Airport is located 25km east of the city, while Göteborg City Airport is 17km north of the city. Fixed taxi rates with Taxi

Göteborg from the city to Landvetter and City Airport are Skr405 and Skr355, respectively.

Flygbuss (to Göteborg City Airport) (www.flygbussarna.se; one way/return Skr79/145) Flygbuss services run from Nils Ericson Terminalen to Göteborg City Airport at least once an hour between 5.30am and 8.15pm on weekdays. There are seven buses on Saturday between 6.30am and 8pm and six buses on Sunday between 8am and 7.30pm. Buses from the airport are timed to meet flights. Online discounts available.

Flygbuss (to Landvetter Airport) (☎0771-51 51 52; www.flygbussarna.se; one way/return Skr99/185) Flygbuss services run to Landvetter Airport from Nils Ericsons Terminalen every 15 to 20 minutes from 4.20am to 9pm and from the airport to the city between 5am and 11.30pm. Discounts available for online bookings.

BICYCLE

Cyclists should ask the tourist office for the free map *Cykelkarta Göteborg*, covering the best routes.

Styr & Ställ (www.goteborgbikes.se; 1/2hr Skr10/70) Göteborg's handy city-bike system. A three-day pass (Skr25) can be purchased directly from docking stations around the city. All journeys under half an hour are free, making this ideal for quick trips.

Cykelkungen (☎031-18 43 00; www.cykelkungen.se; Chalmersgatan 19; 24hr/3 days/1 week Skr200/400/700) Reliable spot for hire of 24 hours and over.

PUBLIC TRANSPORT

Buses, trams and ferries run by Västtrafik (p148) make up the city's public-transport system; there are Västtrafik information booths selling tickets and giving out timetables inside Nils Ericson Terminalen, in front of the train station on Drottningtorget and at Brunnsparken.

The most convenient way to travel around Göteborg is by tram. Colour-coded lines, numbered 1 to 13, converge near Brunnsparken (a block from the train station). Trams run every few minutes between 5am and midnight; some lines run a reduced service after midnight on Friday and Saturday.

Holders of the Göteborg Pass travel free, including on late-night transport. Otherwise a city transport ticket costs Skr25/19 per adult/child (Skr45 on late-night transport). One- and three-day travel cards (from Västtrafik information booths, 7-Eleven minimarkets or Pressbyrån newsagencies) work out much cheaper than buying tickets each time you travel. A 24-hour Dagkort (day pass) for the whole city area costs Skr80, Skr160 for three days.

Västtrafik has regional passes for 24 hours/three days (adult Skr235/470) that give unlimited travel on all *länstrafik* (regional) buses, trains and boats within the Göteborg, Bohuslän and Västergötland area.

TAXI

Taxi Göteborg (☎031-65 00 00; www.taxigoteborg.se) One of the larger taxi companies. Taxis can be picked up outside Centralstationen, at Kungsportsplatsen and on Kungsportsavenyn.

AROUND GÖTEBORG

Southern Archipelago

☎031 / POP 4400

A car-free paradise, the southern archipelago is a short hop from Göteborg's hustle. Despite the summer crowds, you'll always find a quiet bathing spot or serene pocket of green.

There are nine major islands and numerous smaller ones. The largest island, Styrsö, is less than 3km long, while Brännö is the most popular for overnight stays.

The best information about the islands can be found in the English-language booklet *Excursions in the Southern Archipelago*, published by Västtrafik and available from the tourist offices or Västtrafik information booths.

Brännö

Brännö's beaches and outdoor dance floor are its biggest attractions. On Thursday night you can boogie on down at the Husvik pier, a 1km walk from the main ferry terminal in Rödsten.

From the church in the centre of the island, day trippers can follow the cycling track through the woods towards the west coast. A 15-minute walk from the end of the track leads to a stone causeway and the island **Galterö** – a strange treeless landscape of rock slabs, ponds, deserted sandy beaches and haunting bird calls.

Get away from it all at **Pensionat Bagge** (☎031-97 38 80; www.baggebranno.se; s/d/f Skr595/990/1295), a simple, friendly place about a kilometre south of the ferry quay. The same owners operate **Brännö Värdshus** (www.baggebranno.se; Husviksvägen; mains Skr185-255; ⏲11am-11pm), which houses a cosy restaurant, cafe and bakery and serves

GETTING OUT TO THE ARCHIPELAGO

Take tram 11 or 9 (summer only) from central Göteborg to Saltholmen, from where an excellent 16-destination passenger-only **ferry network** (www.styrsobolaget.se) runs round the islands (with the exception of Marstrand). The Göteborg Pass is valid, or you can buy a ticket (one way Skr25 per adult) to the island of your choice. Bicycles are allowed on the ferries free of charge if there is space, but they're not allowed on city trams.

Boats run frequently to Asperö (nine minutes), Brännö (20 minutes) and Styrsö (30 minutes) from around 5.30am to 1am (less frequently at weekends); services to the other islands are more limited. Departures are most frequent between mid-June and mid-August.

excellent meals, including the local speciality *rödtunga* (plaice). It also hosts regular live jazz and folk gigs in summer.

Other Islands

Just southeast of Brännö, **Köpstadsö** is a small island with a quaint village of pretty painted houses and narrow streets. Wheelbarrows parked at the quay are what pass for transport in these parts.

In the central part of the archipelago, **Styrsö** has two village centres (Bratten and Tången, both with ferry terminals), and a history of smuggling.

The southern island of **Vrångö** has a good swimming beach on the west coast, about 10 minutes' walk from the ferry. The northern and southern ends of the island are part of an extensive nature reserve.

Tiny **Vinga**, 8km west of Galterö, has impressive rock slabs and decent swimming, and has been home to a lighthouse since the 17th century. The writer, composer and painter Evert Taube was born here in 1890 – his father was the lighthouse-keeper.

Marstrand

☎0303 / POP 1319

Looking like a Tommy Hilfiger ad, this former spa town and island is a Swedish royal favourite. Boasting the country's most popular *gästhamn* (guest harbour), it's *the* weekend destination for yachting types.

Looming over the town is doughty **Carlstens Fästning** (www.carlsten.se; adult/7-15yr Skr80/40; ⌚11am-6pm late Jun-late Jul, to 4pm rest of Jun & Aug), a fortress constructed in the 1660s after the Swedish takeover of Bohuslän; later building work was completed by convicts sentenced to hard labour. There are smashing archipelago views from the top of its round tower; you can also explore the secret tunnel and in the prison cells learn the story of Lasse Maja, a cross-dressing thief and local Robin Hood figure.

The most reasonably priced place to stay is **Marstrands Varmbadhus Båtellet** (☎0303-600 10; www.xn--btellet-exa.se; Kungsplan; dm/d Skr300/750; @ 🏊), a private hostel with associated pool and sauna. Turn right after disembarking from the ferry and follow the waterfront for 400m.

Located at the northern end of the harbour, the renovated yet overpriced **Hotell Nautic** (☎0303-610 30; www.nautichotell.se; Långgatan 6; d/f Skr1600/1800; 📶) has bright, simple rooms; a couple have balconies with great sea views.

Marstrand's numerous eating options include century-old local institution **Bergs Konditori** (www.bergskonditori.com; Hamngatan 9; sandwiches from Skr69; ⌚7am-5pm May-Aug), a dockside bakery selling fresh bread, cakes, quiches and sandwiches, while Johan the chef tantalises with the likes of king crab paired with pickled carrot and entrecôte with roasted beef marrow and port reduction at **Johan's Krog** (☎0303-612 12; www.johanskrogmarstrand.se; Kungsgatan 12; mains Skr265-345; ⌚6.30pm-late), the best of Marstrand's fine-dining options.

The **tourist office** (☎0303-600 87; www.marstrand.se; Hamngatan 33; ⌚10am-6pm Mon-Fri, 11am-5pm Sat & Sun) is opposite the ferry terminal.

From Göteborg, take the **Marstrands Expressen** (www.vasttraffik.se) directly to Marstrand passenger-only ferry terminal (50 minutes). The ferry crosses over to the island every 15 minutes (Skr25).

BOHUSLÄN

Dramatic, stark and irrepressibly beautiful, the Bohuslän Coast is one of Sweden's natural treasures. The landscape here is a grand mix of craggy islands and rickety fishing villages caught between sky and sea. Island-hopping is a must, as is lounging on broad, sun-warmed rocks and gorging on the region's incredible seafood.

Bohuslän Coast

If you're heading north from Göteborg, stop at the **tourist office** (☎0303-833 27; www.bastkusten.se; Kulturhuset Fregattan; 9am-6pm Mon-Fri, 11am-3pm Sat) in Stenungsund to pick up brochures and maps of the surrounding area.

Transport connections are generally good: the E6 motorway runs north from Göteborg to Oslo via the larger towns of Stenungsund, Ljungskile, Herrestad, Munkedal and Tanumshede, passing close to Strömstad before crossing the Norwegian border. Local trains run frequently from Göteborg to Strömstad, via much the same towns as the E6 route.

Tjörn & Around

☎0304 / POP 15,050

A large bridge swoops from Stenungsund (on the Swedish mainland) to the island of Tjörn, a magnet for artists thanks to its striking landscapes and cutting-edge watercolour museum. Sailors are equally smitten, with one of Sweden's biggest sailing competitions, the **Tjörn Runt** (www.stss.se), taking place here in August.

Skärhamn and **Rönnäng**, in the southwest, are the island's main settlements; the small **tourist office** (☎0304-60 10 16; Södra Hamnen; noon-5pm Mon-Fri, 11am-3pm Sat & Sun Jun-Aug) is located in Skärhamn.

Skärhamn's proudest feature is the superb **Nordiska Akvarellmuseet** (☎0304-60 00 80; www.akvarellmuseet.org; Södra Hamnen 6; adult/under 25yr Skr80/free; 11am-6pm mid-May–mid-Sep), a sleek waterside building housing changing exhibits by the likes of Julie Nord, whose ink drawings bring to mind a darker, more nightmarish Alice in Wonderland, and Lars Lerin's compelling cityscapes, seemingly illuminated from within. The five ultramodern cubes right over the water are guest cabins for the artistically inclined or those looking for a quiet retreat (artists/public Skr500/1000), and the legendary fish dishes at the adjacent gourmet cafe-restaurant **Vatten** (☎0304-67 00 87; www.restaurangvatten.com; Södra Hamnen 6; lunches Skr160-180, 2-course dinner Skr245; from noon Jul–mid-Aug, shorter hours rest of year) are a perfect match with the archipelago backdrop.

Rönnängs Vandrarhem (☎0304-67 71 98; www.ronnangsvandrarhem.se; Nyponvägen 5; s/d Skr330/650; P @), an SVIF hostel in Rönnäng, about 1km from the ferry, is good and spacious, with one sizeable kitchen and a rambling, country-home feel. There's a leafy terrace for lazy summer barbecues.

Magasinet Härön (☎0304-66 40 20; www.magasinetharon.com; 2-/3-course lunch Skr275/350, 5-course dinner Skr595; 11.30am-4pm & 5pm-late mid-Jun–mid-Aug), at the northwest end of Tjörn, is the summer home of Göteborg chef Mats Nordström. His restaurant here, within a stone's throw of the sea in an 1847 fisherman's *magasinet* (depot), becomes a bustling hub in summer. Meals are appropriately seafood intensive and served with all the care of Norström's established Wasa Allé (p145). Take the passenger-only ferry from Kyrkesund to get there.

The Tjörn-Express bus runs up to six times on weekdays from Göteborg's bus terminal to Tjörn, calling at Skärhamn, Klädesholmen and Rönnäng. Bus 355 from Stenungsund crosses the island to Rönnäng.

KLÄDESHOLMEN

The 'herring island' of Klädesholmen, reachable via the bridge from the south of Tjörn, is a mash-up of red and white wooden cottages. Its activity is fairly subdued due to the departure of the herring (there were once 30 processing factories here, today just a handful), but the tiny **herring museum** (☎0304-67 33 08; Sillgränd 8; 3-7pm Jul–mid-Aug) FREE tells you all you need to know about Sweden's enduring love for its favourite fish.

Waterside **Salt & Sill** (☎0304-67 34 80; www.saltosill.se; lunch mains Skr159-185, dinner mains Skr195-335; May-Sep & Dec, call ahead

PUBLIC TRANSPORT ON THE COAST

Using public transport to get to some of the Bohuslän Coast's remoter islands or quiet corners can be a bit of a fool's errand, particularly out of peak season. The coast is best suited to independent exploration on your own two or four wheels, but if you're reliant on buses and boats, it's best to use the Travel Planner feature on the **Västtrafik** (www.vasttrafik.se) website to avoid long connection times.

other times) is one of the region's best seafood restaurants (which is saying something!), with a changing, innovative menu. The herring board is legendary, with herring prepared in six ways (Skr159). Summer lunches may include grilled catch of the day and rye-bread-fried mackerel, while evenings bring more sophisticated fare. Not content with culinary fame, Salt & Sill is also Sweden's first **floating hotel** (☎0304-67 34 80; www.saltosill.se; s/d Skr1790/2290; 📶). The row of slick cubic buildings houses 23 light, bright, contemporary rooms, each featuring the hues of its namesake herb or spice. A floating sauna is available for pampering purposes.

Åstol

Tiny Åstol looks straight out of a curious dream – think a tiny, barren chunk of rock dotted with rows of gleaming white houses that seem perched on top of each other from the sea. Amble round the car-free streets, soak up the views of the other islands, and feast on the likes of fish stew and their very own smoked salmon at **Åstols Rökeri** (www.astolsrokeri.se; lunch from Skr150, dinner mains Skr179-245; ⏲noon-10pm Apr-Sep), a fish smokery with summer restaurant attached.

ROCK CARVINGS UNVEILED

Bohuslän's Bronze Age dwellers did not have a written language, but they were prolific rock carvers and, like all humans since the beginning of time, possessed of the need to leave their mark on the world, to record their beliefs, rituals, triumphs and tragedies – in this case, by etching them into granite slabs. Many of these 3000-year-old *hällristningar* (rock carvings) survive to this day. The Tanum plain, around Tanumshede, is particularly rich in carvings, and the entire 45-sq-km area has been placed on the Unesco World Heritage list. At the time of carving, the sites would have been close to the water, as the sea was 15m higher.

The interactive **Vitlycke Museum** (☎0525-209 50; www.vitlyckemuseum.se; ⏲10am-6pm daily mid-Apr–Aug) FREE is an excellent introduction to the carvings, explaining their origins, offering interpretations of what each particular carving meant, and delving into the typical daily life of the carvers. There's a re-created Iron Age farm out the back for the little ones, and worthwhile English-language tours held at 11.30am and 2.30pm in peak season; longer themed tours are also available. Bicycles are available for rent (Skr100) if you want to pedal your way to the rock-carving sites around the museum.

From the museum, a series of paths and boardwalks run through pine forest to the most important of the rock-carving grounds, though dozens of lesser sites are scattered throughout the area. Cross the road, and you reach the splendid 22m Vitlycke Rock that forms a huge canvas for 500 carvings of 'love, power and magic'. You may spot some of Sweden's most famous rock-art images, including *The Lovers* – a male and female figure, joined; a horned god riding a chariot; a whale; a grieving woman; a man running away from a giant snake; and a fertility goddess.

Further south is Aspeberget, the site with the heaviest concentration of carvings. You can tell that Bronze Age lives were dominated by two things: boats, and violence in the shape of men with hefty axes.

Towards the coast lies the third large site, Litsleby. A nautical theme prevails, but the boats are eclipsed by the huge image of a (very obviously male) god, believed to be Odin, brandishing a spear. You may also spot dogs, a pair of bare feet and a spearman on horseback.

In case you're wondering, the carvings are all red not because 3000-something-year-old paint is remarkably well preserved but because modern-day archaeologists wanted to make the images easier to see and study.

The enlightening book *The Rock Carving Tour* (Skr50), available only from Bohusläns Museum, contains thoughtful interpretations and detailed maps showing you how to find the best Bohuslän sites.

To get to Vitlycke by public transport, take bus 870 or 945 from Tanumshede bus station to Hoghem. From there it's a five- to 10-minute walk. Regional buses on the Göteborg–Uddevalla–Strömstad route stop at Tanumshede.

You can reach Åstol by ferry from Rönnäng (once or twice every hour between 5.30am and 11.30pm).

Orust

0304 / POP 15,221

Sweden's third-biggest island, Orust boasts lush woodlands and some breathtakingly pretty fishing villages. It also has a thriving boat-building industry, with over half of Sweden's sailing craft made here. A bridge connects Orust to Tjörn, its southern neighbour.

Orust's tourist office (0304-33 44 94; www.orust.se; Kulturhuset Kajutan, Hamntorget; noon-4pm Tue-Fri, 10am-2pm Sat) is in the same building as the library in the town of Henån.

There's an outstanding STF hostel, Tofta Gård (0304-503 80; www.toftagard.se; s/d/tr Skr360/640/550; P), near Stocken in the island's west, about 5km from the larger village of Ellös. It's located in an old farmhouse and surrounding little cottages in a blissfully bucolic setting, with good walking, swimming and canoeing nearby. The restaurant serves a nightly tapas buffet (Skr245) in peak season, and there's also a hot tub.

MOLLÖSUND

Supercute Mollösund, in the island's southwest, is the oldest fishing village on the Bohuslän Coast. There's a picture-perfect harbour and several scenic walking paths for a gentle pick-me-up.

Emma's Café, Grill & Vinbar (0304-211 75; www.cafeemma.com; Hamnvägen 4; lunches Skr59-185, dinner mains Skr139-215; restaurant 11am-midnight Jun–mid-Aug), another Bohuslän establishment co-owned by Göteborg chef Mats Nordström, is the red house right on the harbour with a small, welcoming hostel (doubles from Skr950). The cosy cafe-restaurant serves hearty dishes created from local (mostly fishy) and organic ingredients – anything from open shrimp sandwiches to exceptional fish soup.

Mollösunds Wärdshus (0304-211 08; www.mwhus.se; Kyrkvägen 9; d from Skr1295; Easter-Dec;) is an upmarket 19th-century inn featuring 10 well-turned-out rooms (available from Easter to December) with funky wallpaper, and a slinky, sun-soaked terrace for lazy wining and dining on local fish and seafood. Enquire here about island-hopping, adrenalin-pumping RIB boat tours, and ask staff to fire up the hot tub for extra pampering.

Bus 975 runs to Henån on weekdays at 7.30am, while bus 372 connects Mollösund to the small town of Varekil (Monday to Friday only). The Orustexpressen bus runs several times on weekdays direct from Göteborg to Henån; otherwise change in Stenungsund or Lysekil.

Lysekil & Around

0523 / POP 14,521

With its air of faded grandeur, the 19th-century spa resort of Lysekil feels oddly like an English seaside town. It pampers summer visitors less than other Bohuslän towns do, but there's something strangely refreshing about this unfussed attitude.

Sights & Activities

The town retains some interesting architecture from its spa days, such as old bathing huts and Curmans villor, the wooden seafront houses built in romantic 'Old Norse' style. Carl Curman was the resort's famous physician, who was able to persuade visitors that Lysekil's sea bathing was a complete cure-all. Crooked street Gamla Strandgatan has a too-cute collection of painted wooden abodes.

Havets Hus AQUARIUM

(www.havetshus.se; Strandvägen 9; adult/5-17yr Skr110/60; 10am-6pm mid-Jun–mid-Aug;) Havets Hus is an excellent aquarium with sea life from Gullmar, Sweden's only true fjord, which cuts past Lysekil. Peer at such cold-water beauties as wolffish, lumpsuckers, anglerfish, cranky-looking flatfish, rays, and ethereal jellyfish; watch a magnified shark's embryo grow; walk through an underwater tunnel; and learn about the pirate history of the area.

Stångehuvud Nature Reserve NATURE RESERVE

Out at the tip of the Stångenäs peninsula, the Stångehuvud Nature Reserve, crammed with coastal rock slab, is worth a stop for its secluded bathing spots and the wooden lookout tower.

Fiskebäckskil ISLAND

Passenger/cyclist-only ferry 847 (Skr25) crosses the Gullmarn fjord roughly hourly to Fiskebäckskil, of the cute cobbled streets and wood-clad houses. The interior of its church recalls an upturned boat, with votive ships and impressive ceiling and wall

A GLIMPSE OF THE WILD

Nordens Ark (0523-795 90; www.nordensark.se; Åby säteri; adult/5-17yr Skr230/90; 10am-7pm daily mid-Jun–mid-Aug, shorter hours rest of year;) Snow leopards, wolves and lynxes prowl Nordens Ark, a well-conceived safari park 12km northeast of Smögen. It shows off animals and plants from countries with a similar climate to Sweden's and has breeding programs for critically endangered species, such as the Amur tiger and Amur leopard. A 3km path allows visitors a glimpse of the wild beasts as it runs past the spacious enclosures, and guided tours are available daily in peak season (included in entry price).

paintings. Fiskebäckskil is also reachable by road from the E4 and Tjörn.

Käringön ISLAND

This picture-perfect island boasts plenty of good swimming holes, some complete with floats and trampolines for the enjoyment of those frolicking in the water. The plenitude of flat, broad rocks makes Käringön an ideal location for picnicking on a summer's day. Regular ferry 381 runs roughly hourly from Tuvesvik (on the northwestern coast of Orust island); check up-to-date timetables at www.vasttrafik.se.

Seal Safaris CRUISE

(0523-66 81 61; adult/5-17yr Skr200/110; 1pm Jul–mid-Aug) Seal safaris lasting 1½ hours leave from near the aquarium; buy tickets at Havets Hus.

Sleeping

Siviks Camping CAMPGROUND €

(0523-61 15 28; www.sivikscamping.nu; sites Skr310; end Apr–mid-Sep; P) Built on large pink-granite slabs by a sandy beach 2km north of town, Siviks is the best-located campground in the area and particularly popular with RVs.

Strand Vandrarhem & Hotell HOSTEL, HOTEL €€

(0523-797 51; www.strandflickorna.se; Strandvägen 1; hostel dm/s/d Skr350/850/950, hotel s/d Skr1095/1440; P) Not far from Havets Hus aquarium, this large, rambling wooden house resembles a mansion from the Deep South, and you can almost see the guests sipping bourbon on the porch. All of the prettily wallpapered rooms are en suite, even the hostel rooms, though the hotel rooms (some with sea views) are rather plusher.

Strandlickorna Havshotell HOTEL €€

(0523-797 50; www.strandflickorna.se; Turistgatan 13; s/d from Sk1295/1595; P) Run by the same people who run the Strand Hotel, this more upmarket option is based in a sensitively renovated turn-of-the-20th-century house. The atmospheric rooms feature a seafaring/historical theme and there's a sauna and hot tub overlooking the sea.

Eating

★ **Brygghuset** SEAFOOD €€

(0523-222 22; www.brygghusetkrog.com; Fiskebäckskilsvägen 28; lunch buffet Skr125, mains 205-305; noon-midnight; P) Across the estuary from the Fiskebäckskil ferry terminal, this celebrated waterfront restaurant is lauded for its superb fish dishes that taste so fresh that the fish may as well have just leapt out of the harbour onto your plate. At lunchtime, have your herring eight – count 'em! – ways at the self-service buffet or grab a seafood soup.

Pråmen SEAFOOD €€

(0523-145 42; www.pramen.nu; Södra Hamnen; mains Skr158-255; noon-3.30pm & 6pm-late;) Crabs, mussels, prawns, halibut, salmon: if it swims, scuttles or sticks to rocks in the sea, this popular floating restaurant-bar will have it on the menu.

Old House Inn INTERNATIONAL €€

(www.theoldhouseinn.se; Kungsgatan 36; mains Skr129-189; noon-late;) The menu of this quaint restaurant on the little main square runs the gamut from pulled-pork sandwiches to pastas, while its chilli-chocolate *pannacotta* targets those with a sweet tooth. Live music most nights in summer.

Information

Tourist office (0525-130 50; Södra Hamngatan 6; 9.30am-5pm Mon-Fri, to 3pm Sat & Sun Jul–mid-Aug) Offers information on various summer boat tours, including island-hopping swimming trips to fishing jaunts.

Getting There & Away

Express buses 840 and 841 run hourly from Göteborg to Lysekil via Uddevalla (Skr148, one hour 50 minutes). You can also take one of the regular passenger ferries from Fiskebäckskil, just south of Lysekil (15 minutes).

Smögen

0523 / POP 1329

Another seaside star, Smögen sports a buzzing waterside boardwalk, rickety fishermen's houses, and steep steps leading up into a labyrinth of lovingly restored cottages and pretty summer gardens.

Dubbed **Smögenbryggan** and famous throughout Sweden as a hip, youthful destination, the boardwalk heaves with bars and shops around the harbour; head in early or out of season if you're seeking solitude. Fishing boats unload their catches of prawns, lobsters and fish at the harbour. You can score some uberfresh shellfish if you get to the small **fish auction** (www.smogens-fiskauktion.com; Fiskhall; 8am Mon-Fri, plus 4pm Thu) early enough: the big one happens online these days.

From Smögen harbour, the **Hållö Färjan** (0706-91 36 33; www.hallofarjan.se; adult/under 12yr return Skr90/45) leaves every half-hour or so from 9.30am in summer for the nature reserve on the nearby island of **Hållö**. The island's smooth granite boulders, bizarre potholes and deep fissures are the result of thousands of years of glacial carving. Perched on top is a red-and-white 19th-century lighthouse, as well as a small church (ask at the hostel if you want to take a peek inside). Terns and other seabirds nest in the surrounding oat grass, and delicate wild pansies dot the island. It's pristine and remote, an ideal haunt for those keen to capture the true essence of Bohuslän. Utpost Hållö (p160) is the island's gloriously out-of-the-way hostel.

SVIF-affiliated **Makrillvikens Vandrarhem** (0523-315 65; www.makrillviken.se; Makrillgatan; dm/d Skr300/800; P), in the yellow former spa bathing house with smashing views of the archipelago, is a sterling, hugely popular budget choice – 500m from the boardwalk crowds, bathing spots just metres from your room and an old seaside sauna for guest use. For more watery action, there are canoes for hire. Book ahead!

Hotel Smögens Havsbad (0523-66 84 50; www.smogenshavsbad.se; Hotellgatan 26; s/d from Skr1095/1395; P) is an architectural haystack with a rather tacked-on-looking prosthetic extension that is (thankfully for guests) beautiful on the inside, with light Scandi-style rooms, many with sea views. The on-site restaurant celebrates local seafood, with dishes like wolffish with blue-mussel froth and sautéed new potatoes.

Right above the water, the friendly **Hallo Bar** (Fiskhamnsgatan 32; dishes from Skr79; 11.30am-10pm) serves small plates of seafood dishes (so you can really go to town here!), as well as beautifully battered fish and chips and overflowing prawn sandwiches. **Coffee Room** (Sillgatan; bagels & wraps Skr75-99; 9am-11pm daily Jun-Aug), arguably the nicest cafe for miles around, is your pit stop for moreish milkshakes, stuffed bagels and fresh wraps. As you walk along the boardwalk, you're likely to be lured into **Hamnen 4** (0523-708 50; www.hamnen4.se; Sillgatan 14-16; mains Skr165-275; 6pm-3am Mon-Fri, noon-3am Sat) by the bewitching smells emanating from the grill. Hamnen 4 woos piscatareans with its coley with blue mussels and brown-butter cod, but carnivores are also well catered for with expertly seared steaks and hamburgers. The well-stocked bar keeps the sea salts entertained into the wee hours.

The **tourist office** (0523-66 55 50; www.sotenasturism.se; Bäckevikstorget 5; 10am-6pm Mon-Fri, to 5pm Sat & Sun) is in Kungshamn. During summer there's a second branch in the parking lot of the ICA shopping centre directly over the Smögenbron.

Bus 841 runs regularly from Göteborg to Torp, where you switch to the 860 to Smögen (Skr175, 2¼ to 2½ hours, five daily). From Lysekil, take bus 850 and switch to 860 in Hallinden (Skr65, 1¼ hours, five daily).

Fjällbacka

0525 / POP 859

Film star Ingrid Bergman spent her summer holidays at Fjällbacka (the main square is named after her), though you can bet that in her day the waterfront wasn't utterly clogged up with sun-worshipping crowds and the main street wasn't chock-a-block with classic Chevvies and Pontiacs on fine summer days. Despite that, the tiny town is utterly charming, its brightly coloured houses squashed between steep cliffs and placid sea.

The **tourist office** (0525-321 20; www.fjallbacka.com; Ingrid Bergmanstorg; mid-Jun–Aug) can advise on boat trips to the popular, rocky island of Väderöarna.

A block off the waterfront, steep wooden staircases lead to the top of the **Vetteberget** cliff for unforgettable 360-degree views of the village, the sea and the skerries, and several paths cross the rocky plateau for longer strolls. From July to mid-August,

WORTH A TRIP

RESÖ

This tiny island, 10km south of Strömstad, is reachable via an appealing narrow road that winds its way through the forest and crosses a couple of bridges. The main reason for coming here is to stay at the **Resö Gamla Skola** (0525-259 00; www.resogamlaskola.se; s/d Skr600/1000), the loveliest of the Bohuslän Coast's many budget lodgings. This cheerful yellow house, a former school (you can check out the old gym upstairs) feels like a friend's home: its cosy rooms are nautically themed and guests have access to a library, a spacious kitchen and outdoor terraces on which to linger. The breakfast is superb, as are the hosts.

Vadero Express runs 1½-hour island boat trips, including a tour that takes in the local **seal colony** (per person Skr375; 3pm). Boats depart from Ingrid Bergmanstorg.

On a teeny little island just off the harbour, **Badholmens Vandrarhem** (0525-321 50; www.hamburgsundbokning.se; r/tr/q Skr750/1050/1350; Apr-Oct) is a hostel reached by a causeway. Four plain bunk-bedded huts named after creatures of the deep look out to sea, and there's a cafe, laundry, sauna and hot tub for guests nearby. Behind the huts is a great spot for sunbathing and diving.

A whimsical hotel offering a trip 'around the world in 23 rooms', **Stora Hotellet** (0525-310 60; www.storahotellet-fjallbacka.se; Galärbacken; s/d/ste Skr1490/1990/2750; @) was originally owned by a ship's captain who decorated it with exotic souvenirs. He named each room after his favourite ports and explorers (and girls!), and each tells its own story. Extras include five dining venues that range from tapas bar to fine dining.

With its killer waterside location, **Bryggan Fjällbacka** (0525-310 60; www.storahotelletbryggan.se; Ingrid Bergmanstorg; lunch mains Skr125-150, dinner mains Skr265-365; cafe 11am-10pm, restaurant 6.30pm-late) gives you two dining options: the informal Bryggan Cafe & Bistro, where you can grab an open shrimp sandwich, salad and cold beer, and the refined Restaurant Matilda, where you may feast on such fare as grilled scallops and seared tuna steak.

The best way to reach Fjällbacka from Göteborg is either to take bus 871 to Håby and then switch to bus 875 (Skr175, 2¼ hours in total, two daily), or else to take a train to Dingle station, then transfer to Hamburgsund-bound bus 875 to Fjällbacka (Skr175, 2½ hours, two to three daily).

Uddevalla

0522 / POP 31,212

Bohuslän's capital, Uddevalla, is handy for transport connections but little else. Trains run to Strömstad (Skr120, 1¼ hours, five daily) and Göteborg (Skr120, one hour 10 minutes, hourly). **Swebus Express** (www.swebusexpress.com) runs to Oslo (Skr169, 2½ hours) up to six times daily. Buses drop off and pick up from the bus station on the E6 motorway, rather than in the town centre.

Strömstad

0526 / POP 6288

A sparky resort, fishing harbour and spa town, Strömstad is laced with ornate wooden buildings echoing those of nearby Norway. There are several fantastic Iron Age remains in the area, and some fine **sandy beaches** at Capri and Seläter. Boat trips run to the most westerly islands in Sweden, popular for cycling and swimming.

Sights & Activities

Stone Ship Settings ARCHAEOLOGICAL SITE
(24hr) FREE One of Sweden's largest, most magnificent stone-ship settings (an oval of stones, shaped like a boat) lies 6km northeast of Strömstad. There are 49 stones in total, with the stem and stern stones reaching over 3m in height; the site has been dated to AD 400 to 600. Across the road is a huge site containing approximately 40 **Iron Age graves**. The tourist office can help with transport. Alternatively, there's a gorgeous walking path from the north of town.

Koster Islands ISLAND
(www.kosteroarna.com) Boat trips (adult Skr130 return) run from Strömstad's north harbour to the beautiful cluster of forested Koster Islands every 30 minutes from July to mid-August, less frequently at other times. Tiny North Koster is hilly and has good beaches. Larger South Koster is flatter and better for cycling, with bike-rental facilities,

numerous restaurants scattered about and two large beaches at Rörvik and Kilesand.

Skee Kyrka
CHURCH

Open by appointment only (contact the tourist office), the Romanesque stone Skee Kyrka is about 6km east of Strömstad and has a 10th-century nave. There's also a painted wooden ceiling and an unusual 17th-century reredos with 24 sculptured figures. Nearby lie Iron Age graves, a curious bell tower and a mid-Neolithic passage tomb (c 3000 BC).

Strömstads Museum
MUSEUM

(www.stromstadsmuseum.se; Södra Hamngatan 26; ⊙10am-1pm & 2-4pm Tue-Fri, 11am-2pm Sat) **FREE** In town; housed in an old power station, this museum displays local photography and objects from its nautical history.

Selin Charter Boat Tours
CRUISE

(www.selincharter.se; tours from Skr200; ⊙Jun-Aug) Boat tours out to Ursholmen, Sweden's most westerly lighthouse and seal safaris are on offer, as well as mackerel fishing (June) and lobster safaris (autumn). Trips leave from Strömstad's southern harbour.

🛏 Sleeping & Eating

Strömstad Camping
CAMPGROUND €

(☑0526-611 21; www.stromstadcamping.se; Uddevallavägen; sites Skr340, 2-bed cabins from Skr540; ⊙mid-Apr–Aug) In a lovely, large park at the southern edge of town, the campground also has shady cabins for rent.

★Emma's Bed and Breakfast
B&B €€

(☑0916-65 046; www.emmasbedandbreakfast.se; Kebal 2; s/d from Skr700/1400; P 🤶) A 10-minute walk from central Strömstad, this stately house, dating back to 1734, sits amidst quiet wooded grounds. The rooms are bright and airy and the friendly hostess whips up a full Scandinavian spread at breakfast time.

Heat
THAI, SUSHI €€

(www.heat.nu; Ångbåtskajen 6; mains Skr109-189; ⊙11.30am-11pm Mon-Fri, from noon Sat, from 1pm Sun) Dockside Heat packs some authentic, erm, heat with its Thai curries. Though we're normally wary of places that claim to offer two seprate cuisines, the sushi here is as good as the dishes from Siam: the samurai sushi rolls stand out, and if you're in a group the 'deluxe sashimi' (Skr399) is a worthy splurge.

Rökeri i Strömstad
SEAFOOD €€

(dnn.rokerietistromstad.se; Torksholmen; lunch mains Skr130-180, dinner mains Skr209-359; ⊙noon-5pm Tue-Sat, 5pm-late Fri & Sat) This family-run dockside restaurant dishes out deep bowls of fish soup, catch of the day and seafood-filled baguettes at lunch. Dinner is more refined; the smokehouse platter is a real treat. However, continents may drift before you get served when the restaurant is busy. The adjacent smokehouse is a great place to pick up slabs of gravadlax for a picnic.

❶ Information

Tourist office (☑0526-623 30; www.stromstad.se; Ångbåtskajen 2; ⊙9am-8pm Mon-Sat, 10am-7pm Sun Jun-Aug) Sits just opposite the boat landing for the Koster Islands.

❶ Getting There & Around

Buses and trains both use the train station near the southern harbour. **Västtrafik** (www.vasttrafik.se) runs bus 871 to Göteborg (Skr170, 2¼ hours, three to four daily). Direct trains connect Strömstad to Göteborg (Skr180, 2¼ to three hours, one to two hourly).

Color Line ferries run from Strömstad to Sandefjord in Norway (2½ hours).

DALSLAND

Northern Dalsland is an introspective mix of long lakes, still forests and quiet little towns, quite rightly described as 'Sweden in miniature'.

To the west, sleepy Dals-Ed is sparsely populated – about seven people for every square kilometre – making it ideal for the outdoorsy. You can paddle north from the town of Ed on the fjordlike Stora Le lake all the way to Norway, passing verdant islands and quiet woodlands. Be sure to enjoy a dip in one of the municipality's 400 or so crystal-clear lakes. Walkers can enjoy miles of quiet trails and, in the later summer, may even be lucky to find mushrooms or berries along the way. Contact Canodal (☑0534-618 03; www.canodal.com; Gamla Edsvägen 4; 2-person canoes per day/week Skr290/1375) for details. The company also supplies equipment for wilderness camping.

❶ Getting There & Away

Transport hub Mellerud is on the main Göteborg–Karlstad train line, and Swebus Express buses between Göteborg and Karlstad stop here

❶ 'DOING' THE DALSLAND CANAL

The scenic Dalsland Canal crosses the eastern half of the Dalsland region and, while the canal itself is only 10km long, it links a series of narrow lakes between Vänern and Stora Le, providing a watery playground 250km long for boat enthusiasts and kayakers during the summer months.

If you wish to captain your own boat, Harry Potter fans (and others!) can rent a Nimbus 2600 from **Dalslands Kanal AB** (☑ 0530-447 50; www.dalslandscanal.se; per week Skr14,999) and chug gently through tranquil rural scenery, negotiating locks en route; weekly rental only. Want to be a passenger? M/S *Storholmen* (below) and M/S *Dalslandia* (right) run short passenger trips along the canal from Håverud.

Want to paddle in glorious solitude? There are 10 locations along the Dalsland Canal network where you can rent kayaks and canoes and all necessary equipment and get advice on routes, including **Kajaklodge** (☑ 0531-125 40; www.kajaklodge.se; Bengtsfors; per day from Skr220), where you can also find accommodation. Not challenging enough? Then join the **Dalsland Kanot Maraton** (www.kanotmaraton.se) endurance race that sees competitors racing their canoes over a gruelling 55km course here in mid-August.

once daily (except Saturday) in either direction. Local bus 720 runs a circular route to/from Mellerud via Upperud, Håverud and Skållerud.

Håverud

☑ 0530

An intriguing triple transport pile-up occurs at tiny Håverud, where a 32m **aqueduct** carries the Dalsland Canal over the river, a railway passes above the aqueduct and a road bridge crosses above them both.

The area around the aqueduct is a chilled-out spot, with folks strolling along the sides of the canal or sitting with a beer and watching the water gush out from between the lock gates as boats navigate their way up the canal. At the Tardis-like **Kanalmuséet** (adult/under 15yr Skr30/free; ◷ 10am-6pm Jun-Aug) you can be initiated into the history and mystery of the canal, designed by engineer Nils Ericson and inaugurated in 1868; or hop on a vessel yourself. Turn-of-the-century canal boat **M/S Storholmen** (☑ 0531-106 33; www.storholmen.com; adult/7-12yr Skr300/150) runs along the canal to Långbron and Bengtsfors (one-way adult/seven to 12 years Skr300/150) and can be combined with a return trip on the historic **Dalsland-West Värmland Railway** (☑ 0531-106 33; www.dvvj. se; adult/7-12yr Skr360/180). These mainly run from late June to late August, and can be booked at the tourist office.

The Dalslands Center is the main venue for **Bokdagar i Dalsland** (www.bokdagari-dalsland.se), a three-day literature festival held annually in late July or early August, with readings, seminars and book launches

focusing on Nordic writers. The **tourist office** (☑ 0530-189 90; www.haverud-upperud.se; Dalslands Center; ◷ 10am-7pm Jul–mid-Aug), also based here, can organise fishing licences and canoe hire.

The **STF Hostel Håverud** (☑ 0530-302 75; Museivägen 3; dm/s/d Skr195/275/390; 🅿 🛜) could use a coat of paint but has a winning location overlooking the canal. Rooms are pleasant but can feel rather like a pressure cooker during summer heat waves. Outside May to August, book ahead.

Based in an old paper mill and part of the Dalslands Center, **Håfveruds Brasseri** (Dalslands Centre; mains Skr169-249; ◷ 9am-6pm daily Jun & Jul, 9am-6pm Sat & Sun only May & Aug), with shaded lockside tables, serves everything from smoked salmon with new potatoes to hamburgers. The attached smokery is the place to stock up on fishy goodies or grab a shrimp baguette (Skr59).

Around Håverud

About 3km south of the aqueduct is **Upperud**, home to the savvy **Dalslands Museum & Konsthall** (☑ 0530-300 98; www.dalslands-museum.se; ◷ 11am-6pm daily Jul–mid-Aug) **FREE**. Pop in for a compact collection of local art, woodwork (including a shell-shocked wooden cat), ceramics, ironware and Åmål silverware, as well as thought-provoking photography exhibitions. The small sculpture park in the grounds features an anarchic wooden tower by eccentric artist Lars Vilks. The on-site Bonaparte cafe (so-called because Napoleon's niece Christine once lived there) combines yummy coffee and snacks with soothing lake views.

Another few kilometres south at **Skållerud** is a beautiful, shiny-red, 17th-century wooden **church** (9am-7pm Sat & Sun Apr-Oct), with well-preserved paintings and baroque fittings.

Atmospheric **Högsbyn Nature Reserve**, about 8km north of Håverud near Tisselskog, has woodland walks and a shallow bathing spot. Best of all are its impressive Bronze Age **rock carvings** *(hällristningar)*: 50 overgrown slabs feature animals, boats, labyrinths, sun signs, and hand and foot marks. The **M/S Dalslandia** (070-665 96 03; www.dalslandia.com; adult/6-12yr Skr300/150; 10.50am Sun Jul–mid-Aug) does a 40-minute stop here on its Sunday trip between Håverud and Bengtsfors. Call ahead to arrange weekday visits.

VÄSTERGÖTLAND

Home to Sweden's film-industry hub of Trollhäten, Västergötland is a pleasant mix of stylish manor houses, royal hunting grounds and cultural attractions. Castle buffs and opera lovers flock to Läckö Slott in July, Göta Canal tours abound and the woods are perfect for spotting gangly elk, berry picking or simply strolling.

Vänersborg

0521 / POP 21,699

Vänersborg, at the southern outlet of Vänern lake, was once known as 'Little Paris', most likely by someone who has never seen the real thing. The one thing you'll take away from the main attractions is just how much the Swedish royal family enjoys hunting elk.

Eight kilometres out of town, the **Hunneberg & Hanneberg Nature Reserve** covers two dramatic, craggy plateaus; its deep ravines and primeval forest also make great hiding places for wild elk, and this area has been a favourite royal hunting ground for over 100 years. If you're not too trigger-happy you can enjoy walking the 50km of walking trails instead. You can learn everything there is to know about the noble horned creatures at the **Kungajaktmuseet Älgens Berg** (www.algensberg.com; adult/child Skr60/30; 10am-6pm), the royal hunting museum, which also organises **elk-spotting safaris** (0521-135 09; adult/5-16yr Skr325/175; tours Mon-Thu Jul & Aug) leaving from either the Trollhätten (6.30pm) or Vänersborg (6.45pm) train station for those who wish to get up close and personal; book in advance. To get to Hunneberg, catch the frequent bus 62 from Vänersborg town square to Vägporten, then walk 2km uphill.

For dining out, your best options are in nearby Trollhättan, with the exception of fine dining (three-course dinner from Skr350) at the stately **Ronnums Herrgård** (0521-26 00 00; www.ronnums.se; Vargön; s/d/ste from Skr895/995/1650; P) mansion, set amidst gorgeous grounds and good enough for Nicole Kidman during the filming of *Dogville*. Here you can also lay your weary head in lavish surroundings, complemented by contemporary touches, such as iPad docks, or else take refuge in the large old manor house near the cliffs of Hunneberg that houses **Hunnebergs Vandrarhem & Kursgård** (0521-22 03 40; www.hunnebergsgard.se; Bergagårdsvägen 9B, Vargön; dm/s Skr250/300; P), a large, well-equipped SVIF hostel. Take bus 62 from the town square to Vägporten, then walk 500m.

The helpful **tourist office** (0521-135 09; www.visittrollhattanvanersborg.se; Järnvägsbacken 1C; 9am-6pm Mon-Fri, 10am-3pm Sat & Sun) is located at the train station. Local buses 61, 62 and 65 run from the town square to Trollhättan every half-hour, with onward bus connections to Göteborg (Skr89, 1½ hours).

SJ trains to Göteborg (Skr120, 50 minutes) run at least hourly.

Trollhättan

0520 / POP 46,457

'Trollywood', as it's colloquially known, is home to Sweden's film industry. A number of local and foreign flicks have been shot in and around the town, including Lebanese-Swedish director Josef Fares' Oscar-nominated *Jalla! Jalla!* (2000) and Danish director Lars von Trier's *Dancer in the Dark* (1999), *Dogville* (2002) and *Manderlay* (2005). Trollhättan itself has the air of a surreal film set: looming warehouses, foggy canals, crashing waterfalls and a futuristic cable car all give it a bizarre and thrilling edge. The locks and canals have been the town's lifeblood for centuries, and Trollhättan has made the most of its industrial heritage, with red-brick warehouses housing everything from crowd-pleasing museums to the odd art installation.

DON'T MISS

CANDLE ON THE WATER

Balanced atop the windswept skerries of Västra Götaland, bright at the country's southernmost tip or acting as sturdy wardens of Gotland's sandy shores: the *fyr* (lighthouses) of southern Sweden are as varied as they are beautiful.

Staying in a lighthouse is one of southern Sweden's quintessential experiences, as you find yourself amidst pristine and unique surroundings on the edge of civilisation.

Utpost Hållö (☎0703-53 68 22; www.utposthallo.se; d/q/f Skr1000/1300/1500; ⏲mid-May–Aug) Treeless, rocky Hållö feels remote and raw. The lovely red and white-trimmed cabins of the Utpost Hållö are perched on broad granite slabs within 100m of the sea and the lighthouse. It's a great place to take in the ocean, birds and crisp blue skies. Hållöfärjan ferry runs here from Smögenbryggan, while Hållöexpressen goes to and from Kungshamn.

Stora Karlsö (☎0498-24 05 00; www.storakarlso.se; hostel s/d Skr200/500, old lighthouse r from Skr800; ⏲May-Aug) At the island of Stora Karlsö off the coast of Gotland, you can stay in rooms still decorated with the antique furniture left by the lighthouse-keeper. There's a small restaurant if you don't fancy cooking and it's a fantastic place to birdwatch or go fossil-hunting. The island is reachable by two to three ferries daily.

Smygehuk (☎0410-245 83; www.smygehukhostel.com; s/d/f Skr375/520/790; ⏲mid-May–mid-Sep) Sweden's southernmost hostel, the shipshape Smygehuk lighthouse in Skåne, is about an hour out of Malmö and within an easy walk of Skåne's excellent fish smokehouse.

Kullens Fyr (☎0705-82 23 72; www.kullensfyr.se; adult/6-12yr Skr30/15; ⏲11am-5pm mid-Jun–mid-Aug, weekends only mid-Aug–Nov) If living in a lighthouse is not your thing, you can still visit what's arguably Scandinavia's oldest lighthouse (there's been a light of some kind here for over 1000 years) on the Kullaberg Peninsula. Kullens Fyr also shines the strongest lighthouse light, guiding ships to safety from 50km away.

Festivals & Events

Waterfall Days MUSIC
(www.fallensdagar.se) A thumping three-day celebration held in mid-July with live bands, circus performances, fireworks and some impressive waterworks.

Sights

Saab Bilmuseum MUSEUM
(www.saab.com; Åkerssjövägen 10; adult/4-19yr Skr90/40; ⏲9am-5pm) Saab Bilmuseum is a must for car fanatics and Swedish design buffs. At this warehouse-showroom, gleaming Saab car models span the first (a sensational 1946 prototype) and the Sonnet Super Sport, of which only six were made between '55 and '57, to the futuristic Aero X – the Bio-Power Hybrid Concept that's the first car in the world to run on bioethanol and produce no emissions whatsoever.

Innovatum Science Center MUSEUM
(www.innovatum.se; adult/7-19yr Skr90/50; ⏲9am-5pm) Innovatum Science Center, next door to the Saab Bilmuseum, is a fantastic science centre with all sorts of whacky interactive gadgets for kids of all ages – from weird skateboards you sit on, gyroscopes, whirlpool machines and a machine that allows you to control a ball with your brain waves to oversized Lego blocks for little ones. Why wasn't physics fun like this when we were kids?

Galleri Nohab Smedja GALLERY
(☎0520-28 94 00; Åkerssjövägen 10; admission varies; ⏲9am-5pm Mon-Fri Jun-Aug during exhibitions) Galleri Nohab Smedja, an old smithy's workshop now used for temporary art exhibitions, such as metal art by local and international smiths, is managed by Innovatum Science Center. The gallery is opposite the museum, just behind the tourist office.

Innovatum Linbana CABLE CAR
(per person Skr20; ⏲9am-5pm mid-Jun–Aug) The Innovatum Linbana sweeps you over the canal to the hydroelectricity area, giving you a great overview of the city's locks and waterways. Once you're on the far side of the canal, follow the stairs down to the river, where you'll find one of Sweden's most unusual industrial buildings, the potent-looking **Olidan**

power station, which supplied much of the country's electricity in the early 20th century.

Slussområde PARK

Take a wander southwest to Slussområde, a lovely waterside area of parkland and ancient lock systems. Here you'll find cafes and the Kanalmuseet, which runs through the history of the canal as well as exhibiting over 50 model ships.

Waterfall WATERFALL

(3pm daily Jul & Aug, 3pm Sat May, Jun & Sep) Northeast near the Hojum power station crowds gather on the bridge in anticipation of a mighty cascade of unleashed water. Normally the water is diverted through the power station, but at set times the sluice gates are opened and 300,000L per second thunders through. For an even more magnificent sight, wait for the night-time illuminated waterfall, which usually occurs during the Waterfall Days festival in mid-July.

Tours

Canal Tours BOAT TOUR

(www.stromkarlen.se) Two- to three-hour canal tours on the M/S *Elfkungen* (adult/under 15 yrs Skr220/60) leave at noon from the Slussområde or at 12.30pm from the pier behind the Scandic Swania Hotel (Storgatan 47) in central Trollhätten. Buy tickets on board.

Sleeping & Eating

Gula Villan HOSTEL €

(0520-129 60; www.svenskaturistforeningen.se; Tingvallavägen 12; dm/s/d Skr190/270/380; P) The cheery STF hostel, in a pretty old yellow villa, is about 200m from the train station. The walls are on the thin side, but there's a good communal vibe and breakfast and bikes are available.

First Hotel Kung Oscar HOTEL €€

(0520-470 470; www.kungoscar.se; Drottninggatan 17; s/d from Skr614/702; P) Comfortable, contemporary business hotel – all charcoals and creams with bold splashes of colour, in an enviable central location. A lavish breakfast spread and the helpfulness of the staff seal the deal, but get here early to snag one of the prized parking spots.

Strandgatan EUROPEAN €

(www.strandgatan.com; Strandgatan 34; lunch buffet Skr89; 10am-11pm;) Trendy canal-side bistro that sells everything from filled paninis, quinoa salad and juices to quiches, fish and chips, muffins and good coffee.

★ **Albert Hotell** SWEDISH €€€

(0520-129 90; www.alberthotell.se; Strömsberg; 6-course dinner Skr795; lunch & dinner Mon-Fri, dinner Sat; P) This restaurant-hotel combo is based in a splendid 19th-century wooden villa. Superb, modish Nordic dishes might include steak with bone marrow or crème brûlée with roasted white chocolate. The hotel itself offers 27 contemporary rooms (singles/doubles from Skr795/995), as well as a vintage suite (Skr2900). The place is an easy 10-minute walk across the river from central Trollhättan.

Drinking

Majo Bar BAR

(www.majobar.se; Polhemsgatan 6; 6pm-1am Mon-Sat) Pulled pork, grilled chorizo and platters of Spanish cold cuts rub (pork) shoulders with Sweden's own Västerbottenpaj at this stylish tapas bar. Tipple wise, choose from an extensive selection of beer and cocktails, imbibed to the accompaniment of local and international DJ talent on weekends.

Information

Tourist office (0520-135 09; www.visit-trollhattanvanersborg.se; Åkerssjövägen 10; 10am-5pm Mon-Fri, to 3pm Sat & Sun) The tourist office is about 1.5km south of the town centre, next to the museum cluster. The two-day *sommarkortet* (travel pass; from Skr200) available here from late June to late August includes cable-car trips and museum admissions. The tourist office also sells a handy *Guidebook to Trollhättan's Falls & Locks*, which details walking routes in the mazelike industrial areas.

Getting There & Around

To reach the attractions in Trollhättan from the train station or the Drottningtorget bus station, walk south along Drottninggatan, then turn right into Åkerssjövägen, or take town bus 21 – it runs most of the way.

Local buses 61, 62 and 65 run from the Drottningtorget bus station to Vänersborg and bus 1 connects the town to Lidköping. From the train station, a couple of blocks north of the city centre, trains run to Göteborg (Skr120, 38 minutes) at least once hourly.

Lidköping

0510 / POP 25,644

It might be short on wow factor, but cheery Lidköping – set on Vänern lake – is deeply likeable. Its handsome main square, Nya Stadens Torg, is dominated by the curious, squat old courthouse and its tower (it's actually a replica – the original burnt down in 1960). A previous fire in 1849 destroyed most of the town, but the cute 17th-century houses around Limtorget still stand.

Lidköping's finest attractions lie some distance out of town.

Sights & Activities

★Läckö Slott CASTLE
(☎0510-103 20; www.lackoslott.se; adult/under 26yr Skr80/free; ⏱10am-6pm daily mid-Jun–Aug) An extraordinary example of 17th-century Swedish baroque architecture, with cupolas, towers and ornate plasterwork, Läckö Slott lies 23km north of Lidköping. The first castle on the site was constructed in 1298, but it was improved enormously by Count Magnus Gabriel de la Gardie after he acquired it in 1615.

Admission includes 40-minute guided tours. From mid-June to mid-August, bus 132 runs three times daily from Lidköping to the castle (Skr32, 50 minutes).

The lakeside castle has 240 rooms, with the most impressive being the King's Hall, with 13 angels hanging from the ceiling and nine epic paintings depicting the Thirty Years War. Most rooms are largely unadorned, with the exception of their spectacularly painted ceilings.

Tours run on the hour and give you access to the most interesting rooms, including the representative apartments, the count's private chambers, the Banquet Hall where guests sat down for their 55-course meals and the chamber with the German double-headed eagle, perhaps intended as mockery of the enemy. From mid-June to August there are English-language tours at 11.30am, 1.30pm and 3.30pm daily. Otherwise you're free to bumble about in the kitchen, dungeon, armour chamber, chapel and the terraced castle gardens that overlook the lake. The lower floors contain shops and the atmospheric castle restaurant, Fataburen, which uses vegetables and herbs from the castle garden.

Classical-music and opera events are held in the courtyard several times in July and August; enquire at Lidköping tourist office.

Vänermuseet MUSEUM
(www.vanermuseet.se; Framnäsvägen 2; adult/under 18yr Skr50/free; ⏱10am-5pm Mon-Fri, 11am-4pm Sat & Sun) Vänermuseet boasts a 20-cu-metre aquarium, home to all manner of aquatic wildlife from its namesake lake, Europe's third largest (5650 sq km). A variety of other exhibits highlight the lake's nature and culture.

Husaby Kyrka CHURCH
(⏱8am-8pm Mon-Fri, 9am-8pm Sat & Sun) Husaby (15km east of Lidköping) is inextricably linked to Sweden's history. King Olof Skötkonung, the country's first Christian king, was converted and baptised here by the English missionary Sigfrid in 1008. Husaby Kyrka dates from the 12th century, but the base of the unusual three-steeple tower may well be that of an earlier wooden structure. Lurking inside are medieval paintings, as well as a 13th-century font and triumphal cross. Nearby, **St Sigfrid's Well** is where Olof's royal dunking took place.

Kinnekulle MOUNTAIN
The scenic 'flowering mountain' Kinnekulle (306m), 18km northeast of Lidköping, features unusually diverse geology and plant life, including mighty ancient oaks. It's also home to rare creatures, including the greater crested newt and short-horned grasshopper. There are numerous short nature trails, or you could explore it on the 45km-long **Kinnekulle vandringsled** (walking trail). The tourist office provides a map and the informative *Welcome to Götene and Kinnekulle* brochure. Local trains run to Källby, Råbäck and Hällekis, with access to the trail.

Sleeping & Eating

STF Vandrarhem Lidköping HOSTEL €
(☎0510-664 30; www.lidkopingsvandrarhem.com; Gamla Stadens Torg 4; dm/s/d/tr/Skr250/350/550/850; 📶) Just a couple of minutes' walk from the train station, this large yellow hostel sits in a tree-shaded spot in the old town. Rooms are spartan but spacious, bathrooms institutional-looking but spotless, and you can cook up a storm in the guest kitchen while washing your dirties in the laundry room.

Krono Camping CAMPGROUND €
(☎0510-268 04; www.kronocamping.com; Läckögatan; sites Skr200, 2-person cabins Skr500; 🏊) Huge, family-oriented lakeside campsite, 1.5km northwest of town beside the road to Läckö Slott, with a plethora of facilities and activities.

★Hotell Läckö HOTEL €€
(☎0510-230 00; www.hotellacko.se; Gamla Stadens Torg 5; s/d/tr/ste Skr795/1095/1595/1895; 📶) Our favourite in town is this old-school,

family-run charmer. The spacious rooms boast high ceilings, solid wooden furniture and crisp linen, while breakfast is served on dainty antique porcelain. There's a cosy little reading room with comfy leather armchairs, and quirky touches like bright bed-curtains, four-poster beds and whimsical hanging millinery.

Naturum Vanerskargarden HOTEL €€
(☎0510-48 46 60; www.naturum.lackslott.se; s/d/f Skr950/1490/1990;) Imagine that you can see a castle overlooking a tranquil lake from your window. Actually, you don't have to: the 15 stylish rooms above Naturum are practically on top of Läckö Slott and the archipelago of Lake Vänern, the on-site cafe is fabulous and the design of the futuristic nature centre lives up to its eco-credentials.

Mellbygatans Ost & Delikatesser SWEDISH €
(☎0510-280 80; www.mellbygatansdelikatesser.com; Mellbygatan 10; mains Skr59-85; 10am-3pm & 6pm-late Mon-Sat;) A block from the main square, this sweet cafe and deli has been delighting locals with its fresh, changing menu for years. You might be greeted with the likes of cheese and courgette pie with onion marmalade, pulled-pork sandwiches, and smoked-salmon salad.

★**Restaurang Sjöboden** SEAFOOD €€
(☎0510-104 08; www.sjoboden.se; Spikens Fiskehamn; lunch buffet Skr 225, mains Skr175-295; noon-4pm & 5-10pm early Jun–Sep) Six kilometres south of Läckö Slott, the tiny village of Spiken is home to this unmissable harbourside restaurant that wins our vote for the best buffet on Sweden's west coast. Feast on salmon smoked umpteen ways, take your pick of the herrings and don't miss the smoked lamb's shoulder. Dinner is seafood heaven, too. Take bus 132.

Pirum SWEDISH €€
(☎0510-615 20; www.restaurangpirum.se; Skaragatan 7; mains Skr145-295; from 5pm Mon-Sat;) The menu at restaurant–wine bar Pirum in central Lidköping is short, sweet and classic. Bleak roe, beef carpaccio and shrimp salad are present and correct, there's a good balance of fishy and meaty mains, and meals finish on the comforting sweet note that is white-chocolate mousse and apple pie. White linen tablecloths and seamless service complete the experience.

Information

Tourist office (☎0510-200 20; www.lackokinnekulle.se; Nya Stadens Torg; 10am-6pm Mon-Fri, to 3pm Sat, noon-4pm Sun) Situated in the old courthouse on the main square.

Getting There & Around

Town and regional buses stop on Nya Stadens Torg. The train station is centrally located off Rörstrandsgatan. Bus 1 runs roughly hourly between Trollhättan and Lidköping. The quickest way to get to Stockholm (Skr432, 3½ to 4¼ hours) is by bus to Skövde and then change to a train service. There are three direct trains to Göteborg daily (Skr180, 1¾ hours); you can also take a bus to Trollhättan, Skövde or Herrljunga and hop on a Göteborg-bound train there.

HALLAND

Sea, sun and surf are the name of the game in Halland, with the populations of the most desirable beach destinations often tripling during the summer months. The long white-sand beaches at Tylösand and Varberg are ideal for lounging, swimming and all manner of watersports. Firmly on dry land, there are museums and an an imposing fortress to explore.

Halmstad

☎035 / POP 58,577

Danish until 1645, Halmstad served as an important fortified border town. Its street plan was laid out by the Danish king Christian IV after a huge fire wiped out most of the buildings in 1619 (apart from a few merchants' houses along Storgatan). He also awarded Halmstad its coat of arms: you'll see the three crowns and three hearts motif dotted all over the place.

While in-town attractions are a bit ho-hum, the town's proximity to some of southern Sweden's best beaches and the many places to eat, drink and be merry make Halmstad a good place to linger in summer.

Sights & Activities

★**Halmstad's Beaches** BEACH
Packed with tanned sun worshippers in the summer, Blue Flag–designated Tylösand, 8km west of town, is Halmstad's most popular beach, with a perpetual party vibe courtesy of the surrounding bars and restaurants. Head to the signposted Tjuvahålan smuggler's cove

Halmstad

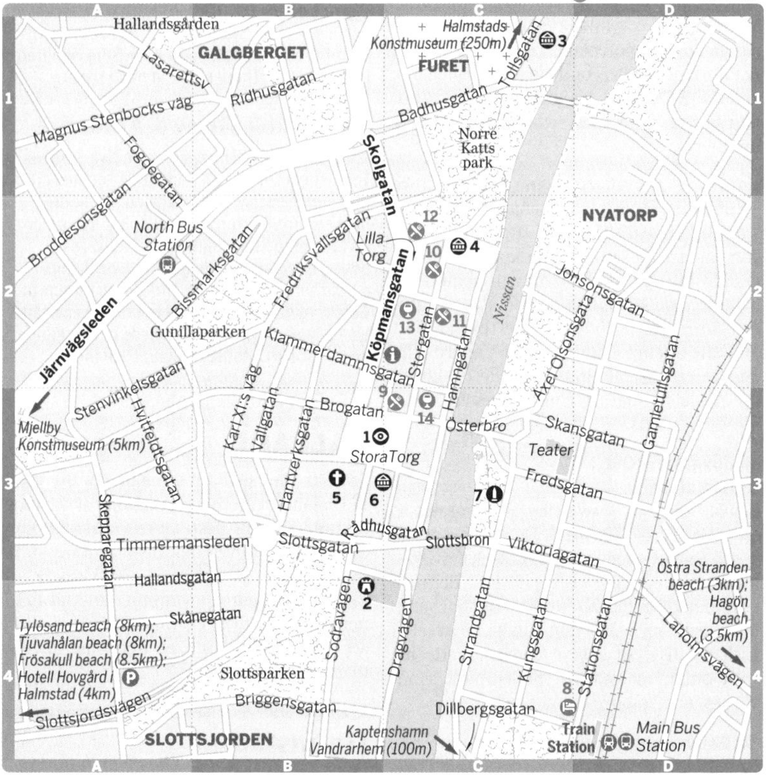

Halmstad

Sights

1 Europa and the Bull B3
2 Halmstad Slott B4
3 Halmstads Konstmuseum C1
4 Norre Port C2
5 St Nikolai Kyrka B3
6 Tre Hjärtan B3
7 Woman's Head C3

Sleeping

8 Best Western Plus Grand Hotel C4

Eating

9 Indian Kitchen C3
10 Pio & Co C2
11 Skånska C2
12 Spis & Deli C2

Drinking & Nightlife

13 Bulls Pub C2
14 Harrys C3

to search for pirate treasure, and walk north from Tjuvahålan to Frösakull for some peace and quiet.

East of town, the shallow, calm waters of Östra Stranden are particularly family friendly, while nudists can bronze their behinds at secluded Hägon further south.

Halmstads Konstmuseum MUSEUM
(www.hallandskonstmuseum.se; Tollsgatan; noon-4pm Tue-Sun, to 8pm Wed) FREE Besides the modest permanent collection of works by the Halmstad Group (p165), Halmstads Konstmuseum hosts some impressive temporary exhibitions. Recent ones have included *Africa Is a Great Country* by acclaimed photographer Jens Assur.

Medieval Attractions HISTORIC SITES
Christian IV built **Halmstad Slott** and the town walls. The latter were demolished in the 18th century, although fragments like north gate **Norre Port** remain at the north-

ern end of Storgatan. Other medieval attractions include the lovely 14th-century church **St Nikolai Kyrka** (Kyrkogatan 4; ⊙ 8.30am-6pm Jun-Aug, to 3pm Sep-May), and the half-timbered **Tre Hjärtan** building on Stora Torg.

Halmstad's Sculptures SCULPTURE

In Stora Torg, the main square, stands Carl Milles' sculptural fountain **Europa and the Bull**, with the characteristically buff mermen with somewhat scary faces. Picasso's **Woman's Head** is down by the river, in Picassoparken off Strandgatan.

Mjellby Konstmuseum MUSEUM

(www.mjellbykonstmuseum.se; Mjällby; adult/under 20yr Skr60/free; ⊙ 11am-5pm Jul & Aug, from noon Sep-Jun) The main focus of Mjellby Konstmuseum, 5km from town, is a changing exhibition of works by the Halmstad Group – six local artists who pushed the boundaries with French Cubism in the 1920s and Surrealism in the 1930s, influenced by Magritte and Dalí. Not only were their pieces controversial at the time, but these six artists collaborated with each other on various projects.

Take bus 300 to the Mjällby stop.

🛏 Sleeping

Kaptenshamn Vandrarhem HOSTEL, HOTEL €

(☑ 035-12 04 00; www.halmstadvandrarhem.se; Stuvaregatan 8; hostel dm/s Skr350/500, hotel s/d/q Skr850/1100/2200; P🛜) This hostel-hotel is in a pleasant brick building about 100m south of the train station and then west on Dillbergsgatan by the river. Rooms are fairly basic, but spacious and quiet, and friendly staff, a leafy back patio and a nearby playground jazz things up.

Hotell Hovgård i Halmstad HOTEL €€

(☑ 035-12 35 77; www.hovgard.se; Gamla Tylösandsvägen 102; s/d/tr Skr1190/1390/1990; P🛜) Appealing family-run hotel halfway between Halmstad and Tylosänd. The rooms are decked out in soothing creams, with the odd wrought-iron bedstead, the breakfast buffet is excellent and guest bicycles are available so that you can cycle from the hotel to the beach.

Best Western Plus Grand Hotel HOTEL €€

(☑ 035-280 81 00; www.grandhotel.nu; Stationsgatan 44; s/d Skr1095/1250; P🛜🞧) Across from the train station, this hotel has well-kept rooms decorated in traditional style with the odd modern touch. There's a decent restaurant and bar, too.

Tylebäck RESORT €€

(☑ 035-19 18 00; www.tyleback.com; Kungsvägen 1; sites Skr250, hostel s/d 750/950, hotel s/d Skr1000/1400; P🛜) Accommodation to suit all travellers – camping, hostel, hotel – is offered at Tylebäck, in an attractive forested setting.

Hotel Tylösand HOTEL €€

(☑ 035-305 00; www.tylosand.se; Tylöhusvägen; d incl breakfast & spa from Skr795; P🛜🞧🞤) Plusses: ideal if you're into beaches, clubbing, spa treatments, good breakfasts and/or Roxette (it's part-owned by Per Gessle). It's a large, upmarket complex on the beach, with a good spa and a foyer full of art. Fusses: can be noisy, the windows only open a little, and woe betide you if you're housed in the yet-to-be-refurbished part of the hotel.

🍴 Eating

The best dining options in Halmstad are along and around the pedestrianised Storgatan. On summer nights head to the after-beach parties at Tylösand.

Spis & Deli DELI €

(www.spisdeli.se; Tyghusgatan 4; mains from Skr79; ⊙ 10am-7pm Mon-Fri, 9am-5pm Sat, noon-4pm Sun; 🞠) Half health food shop, half deli, Spis is all about eco-friendly, organic food. As you might have guessed, that's good news for vegans and vegetarians, who'll find a few items to sate them among the wraps, salads, meatless burgers and energy smoothies.

Skånska BAKERY €

(Storgatan 40; sandwiches Skr59; ⊙ 9am-6pm Mon-Fri, to 4pm Sat, noon-4pm Sun) This is a good old-fashioned bakery with cafe attached. As well as chunky sandwiches, there's a tempting stock of chocolates and cakes to crank up the calories.

★ Pio & Co EUROPEAN €€

(☑ 035-21 06 69; Storgatan 37; mains Skr188-315; ⊙ from 6pm) Award-winning Pio is an upmarket brasserie with an extensive menu of both Swedish and continental favourites – think Halland pork with roasted garlic and potatoes au gratin, fish 'planks' and moreish gnocchi with bok choy.

Indian Kitchen INDIAN €€

(www.indiankitchenhalmstad.se; Nygatan 8; mains Skr85-145; ⊙ 11am-10pm; 🞠) Authentic Indian restaurant specialising mostly in nothern Indian dishes. Dishes of the day are a good deal; we're particularly fond of Goan fish curry and Acher lamb.

Drinking

Harrys PUB
(☎035-10 55 95; Storgatan 22; ⊙5pm-midnight Mon-Thu, to 2am Fri, noon-2am Sat, 4-11pm Sun) American-style pub complete with a great alfresco terrace and the likes of pulled-pork sandwiches, felafel burgers and baby back ribs to back up your beer.

Bulls Pub PUB
(☎035-14 09 21; Bankgatan 5; ⊙5pm-late Mon-Thu, noon-2am Fri & Sat, 3-11pm Sun) Popular English bar in a former fire station, with live music on weekends and light meals.

Information

Tourist office (☎035-12 02 00; www.destinationhalmstad.se; Köpmansgatan 20; ⊙10am-7pm Mon-Fri, to 5pm Sat, to 2pm Sun) Well-stocked office.

Getting There & Away

From the **train station** (Stationsgatan), regular trains between Göteborg (Skr206, 1¼ hours, twice hourly) and Malmö (Skr159, 1½ to 1¾ hours) stop in Halmstad and call in at Helsingborg (Skr128, one hour) and Varberg (Skr115, 32 minutes).

Swebus Express (www.swebusexpress.com) buses run from the **main bus station** (Stationsgatan) to Malmö (Skr159, 2¼ hours, six daily), Helsingborg (Skr89, one hour, six daily) and Göteborg (Skr129, 1¾ hours, seven daily).

Getting Around

Local **Hallandstrakiken** (www.hallandstrafiken.se) bus 10 runs half-hourly (hourly in the evenings) to the clubs and beaches at Tylösand.

Varberg

☎0340 / POP 27, 602

The 19th-century bathing resort of Varberg lies by the side of a 60km stretch of beautiful white-sand beaches: its population triples in the summer months. The town's sights, restaurants and hotels are largely clustered around its other main attraction, its fortress.

Sights & Activities

Varberg Fortress CASTLE
(www.lansmuseet.varberg.se; adult/under 20yr Skr120/free; ⊙10am-6pm daily mid-Jun–mid-Aug) Varberg's star attraction is this imposing medieval prison fortress overlooking the sea. Its museum is home to the 14th-century Bocksten Man, a garrotted, impaled and drowned murder victim, dug out of a peat bog at Åkulle in 1936. His 14th-century costume is the most perfectly preserved medieval clothing in Europe and his full head of red-blond hair is intact. You can also delve into the still-unsolved mystery of King Karl XII's murder.

Nudist Beaches BEACH
Varberg has three nudist beaches just a short walk south from the fortress along the Strandpromenaden. Don't expect white sand; these beaches all consist of large, smooth rocks, all with easy access to the water. Beaches are segregated by gender: the first two, Kärringhålan and Skarpe Nord, are women-only beaches; a few minutes further south is Goda Hopp, the men's bathing spot.

Getterön Nature Reserve NATURE RESERVE
Getterön Nature Reserve is just 2km north of the town and its abundant bird life (mostly waders and geese) attracts twitchers.

Grimeton Radio Station MUSEUM
(☎0340-67 41 90; www.grimeton.info; Grimeton; adult/under 18yr Skr90/free; ⊙10am-5pm daily late Jun-Aug) On the Unesco World Heritage list, Grimeton Radio Station lies about 10km east of Varberg. Once part of the interwar transatlantic communication network, it's now the world's only surviving long-wave radio station. Two English-language tours at 1pm and 3pm in June, July and August initiate you into its mysteries.

Kallbadhuset SPA
(www.kallbadhuset.se; Otto Torels gata 7; adult/under 15yr Skr65/30; ⊙10am-6pm daily, to 8pm Wed Jun–mid-Aug) After you've finished sunbathing next to all the bronzed Nordic bodies at Kallbadhuset, a Moorish-style outdoor bathhouse on stilts above the sea just north of the fort, have a dip in the bracing waters. The sunbathing areas (nudity is the norm) are divided into male and female sections, with steps leading down into the water (facing away from the beach).

Fahlén Surfshop SURFING, KITESURFING
(www.fahlensurf.se; Birger Svenssons väg 38; ⊙10am-6pm Mon-Fri, to 2pm Sat Jun-Aug) A few minutes' walk north from the train station, these guys cater to all your surfing, kitesurfing, windsurfing and paddleboarding needs with equipment rental and watersports

courses. Two hours of paddleboarding instruction costs Skr 400, while an eight-hour introduction to kitesurfing will set you back Skr2000.

Apelviken SURFING
Apelviken, 2km south of Varberg, is Sweden's best spot for windsurfing and kitesurfing. At the southern end of Apelviken, Surfers Center (☑0340-67 70 55; www.surferscenter.se; surfboards per hour/day Skr100/300, windsurfing Skr150/500; ⊘10am-6pm) rents boards and also gives surfing and windsurfing lessons from late May to August.

🛏 Sleeping & Eating

★ Fästningens Vandrarhem HOSTEL €
(☑0340-868 28; www.fastningensvandrarhem.se; Varbergs fästning; s/d/tr/q from Skr300/600/1100/1440) Within Varberg Fortress, this SVIF hostel can lock you up inside its gnarly single and double prison cells. If that's too 'authentic' an experience, opt for one of the large, bright rooms in surrounding buildings. Miracle of miracles: linen is included and so is breakfast (in high season).

Getteröns Camping CAMPGROUND €
(☑0340-168 85; www.getteronscamping.se; sites/ cabins from Skr280/490; ⊘May–mid-Sep; ℗) On a sandy beach on the Getterön peninsula, tent spaces sit cheek by jowl with caravan spots and rows of self-contained summer cabins. It does get busy during high season, when most cabins are available only on a weekly basis (from Skr2450).

★ Hotell Gästis HOTEL €€€
(☑0340-180 50; www.hotellgastis.nu; Borgmästaregatan 1; s/d Skr1495/1750; ℗ 🛜 ⛲) This one-of-a-kind hotel is bursting with quirky details that include an elevator shaft covered in pulp-fiction covers and the basement Lenin Baths (open to nonguests) – a bathhouse that's a replica of the 19th-century St Petersburg version inside a former girls' boarding

school, featuring hot and cold pools, a massage area and an anachronistic giant candle-lit jacuzzi.

Cosy rooms come with shelves full of books and a dinner buffet is included.

Värdshuset i Varberg SWEDISH €€
(www.varbergsvardshus.com; Kungsgatan 14; mains Skr149-215; ⊘11.30am-10.30pm; 🖫) The speciality at this appealing central restaurant is the 'plank': a sizzling platter of fish or grilled meat, surrounded by ringlets of mashed and baked potato. Salads, banana splits and a terrace for people-watching are among its other lures.

★ Vin & Skafferi Hus No. 13 SWEDISH €€€
(☑0340-835 94; www.hus13.se; Varbergs fästning; mains Skr245-275; ⊘11am-2pm & 6pm-late Wed-Sat) Next door to the fortress hostel, this friendly wine bar and restaurant dishes up great lunches for Skr125 (freshly fried mackerel, meatballs), with more sophisticated gourmet dishes – veal with hazelnuts, hake with beets and capers – tantalising diners' tastebuds in the evenings. Watch tourists stream up to the *fästning* (fortress) from the pleasant outdoor patio.

🛈 Information

Tourist office (☑0340-868 00; www.visitvarberg.se; Brunnparken; ⊘10am-7pm Mon-Sat, to 9pm Thu, 11am-4pm Sun) Well-stocked tourist office in the centre of town; most facilities are nearby.

🛈 Getting There & Around

Stena Line (www.stenaline.se; Färjeläget Hamnen) ferries run twice daily (Skr99, 4¼ hours) between Varberg and the Danish town of Grenå; the ferry dock is next to the town centre.

From the **train station** (Östra Hamnvägen), regular services run to Halmstad (Skr115, 36 minutes, twice hourly), Göteborg (Skr109, 45 minutes, twice hourly) and Malmö (Skr246, 2½ hours, hourly).

Malmö & the South

Includes ➡

Best Places to Eat

- Atmosfär (p177)
- Salt & Brygga (p177)
- Holy Greens (p197)
- Gärdens Café & Vedugn (p191)
- St Jakobs Stenugnsbageri (p182)

Best Places to Stay

- Kivik Strand Logi & Café (p192)
- Mäster Johan Hotel (p176)
- Sekelgården Hotel (p187)
- Sjöbacka Gård (p191)
- Hotel Duxiana (p181)

Why Go?

Artists love southern Sweden. Here, the light seems softer, the foliage brighter and the shoreline more dazzling. Skåne (Scania) was Danish property until 1658 and still flaunts its differences: the strong dialect (*skånska*), the half-timbered houses and the region's hybrid flag: a Swedish yellow cross on a red Danish background. Copenhagen is a mere bridge away from vibrant Malmö, the region's largest city.

South of Malmö is a bona fide Viking settlement, while, just to the north, erudite Lund with its cycling students is Sweden's answer to Cambridge. Pottery studios, manors and dramatic cliffs dot Skåne's northwestern coast, while its southern shore is home to medieval showpiece Ystad, as well as Bronze Age remains and the rosy apple-orchard landscapes of Österlen.

Northeast of Skåne lies the forested county of Blekinge, splashed with fish-filled lakes, and once home to Sweden's 17th-century sea power. Topping its crown is handsome Karlskrona, a Unesco World Heritage–listed site.

When to Go

Malmö

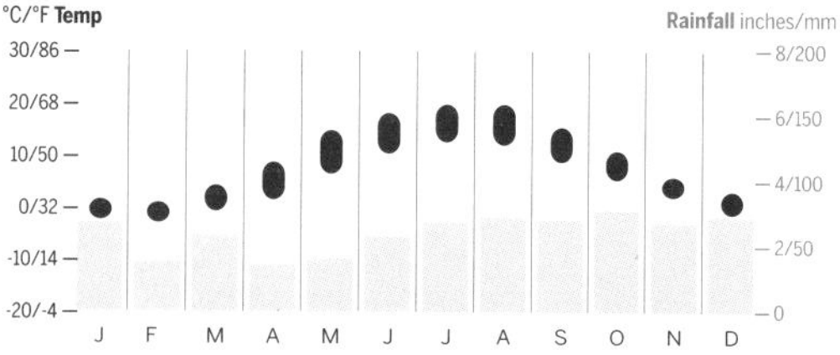

Jul & Aug Warmest and busiest months; tourists flock to the coast and the fabulous Malmö Festival.

May & Sep Cool, clear and peaceful. Autumn weather is ideal for apple harvesting and hikes.

Nov–Feb Expect the country's mildest winter, although it tends to be wet with snow inland.

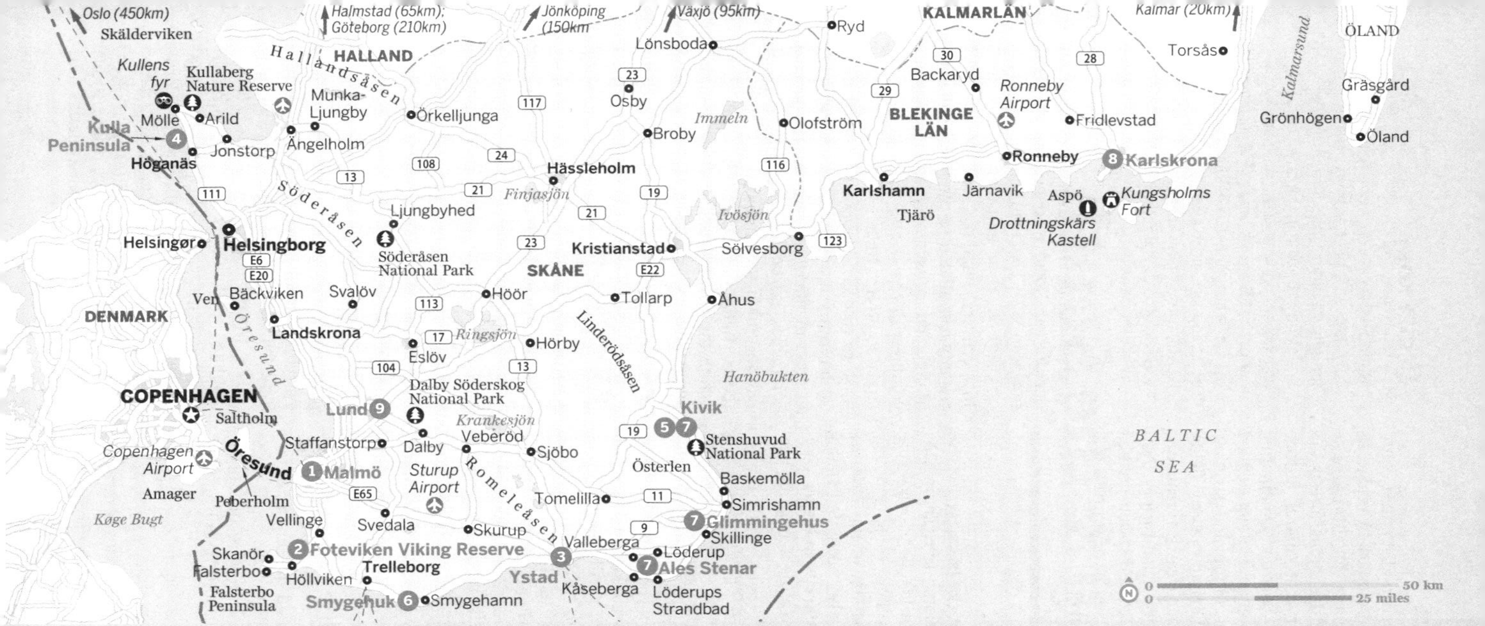

Malmö & the South Highlights

1. Dancing late into the night at fashionable clubs like **Debaser** (p178) in Malmö.
2. Hanging out with verified Vikings at the **Foteviken Viking Reserve** (p184).
3. Walking in the footsteps of fictional Inspector Wallander at Ystad's **Cineteket** (p187).
4. Galloping through the Kulla Peninsula with **Kullabergs Islandshäster** (p199).
5. Picking apples in the sweet-smelling orchards of **Kiviks Musteri** (p192).
6. Playing lighthouse-keeper at **Captain Brinck's Cabin** (p186).
7. Cycling past stone ships, graves and castles at **Ales Stenar** (p191), **Kivik** (p192) and **Glimmingehus** (p191).
8. Marching alongside Swedish marines and checking out impenetrable fortresses like **Kungsholms Fort** (p201).
9. Listening to the marvellous **Domkyrkan** (p180) clock strike up *In Dulci Jubilo*.

SKÅNE

Skåne (Scania) is Sweden at its most continental. Connected to Denmark by bridge, its trademark mix of manors, gingerbread-style abodes and delicate, deciduous forests are a constant reminder that central Europe is just beyond the horizon. Dominating the scene is metropolitan Malmö, defined by its cosmopolitan culture and striking, twisting tower. Further out, velvety fields, sandy coastlines and stoic castles create one of Sweden's most bucolic landscapes. Add to this the fact that Skåne is often dubbed Sweden's larder and you have yourself one scrumptious Scandi treat.

Malmö

040 / POP 300,000

Sweden's third-largest city has a progressive contemporary feel. Home to Scandinavia's tallest building, beautiful parks, edgy contemporary museums and some seriously good cuisine, the opening of the Öresund bridge in 2000 has also been undeniably positive, connecting the city to bigger, cooler Copenhagen and creating a dynamic new urban conglomeration.

Such a cosmopolitan outcome seems only natural for what is Sweden's most multicultural metropolis – 150 nationalities make up Malmö's head count. Here, exotic Middle Eastern street stalls, urbane Italian coffee culture and hipster skateboard parks counter the town's intrinsic Nordic reserve.

Even the city's lively historic core echoes its multicultural past. The showpiece square of Stortorget evokes Hamburg more than it does Stockholm, while nearby Lilla Torg is a chattering mass of alfresco supping and half-timbered houses that give away the Danish connection.

Gamla Staden (Old Town) is Malmö's heart, encircled by a canal. There are three principal squares here: Stortorget, Lilla Torg and Gustav Adolfs Torg. The castle, Malmöhus Slott, in its leafy park setting, guards the western end of Gamla Staden. Across the canal on the northern side is the snazzy redeveloped harbour precinct, home to some excellent cafes and restaurants.

History

Malmö really took off in the 14th century with the arrival of the Hanseatic traders, when grand merchants' houses were erected, followed by churches and a castle. The greatest medieval expansion occurred under Jörgen Kock, who became the city's mayor in 1524. The town square, Stortorget, was laid out then, and many of the finest 16th-century buildings still stand. After the city capitulated to the Swedes in 1658, Malmö found its groove as an important commercial centre and its castle was bolstered to protect trade.

More recently, Malmö has traded in its 20th-century heavy industries, like car and aircraft manufacture, for cleaner, greener companies, particularly in the service, financial and IT sectors. Since its founding in the late 1990s, the university has also helped define the city, creating a thriving student population.

> **CITY KORT**
>
> Malmö's **City Kort** (www.malmocity.se) has over 600 offers and discounts for entertainment, restaurants, attractions and shopping in the city. The card also covers parking in the multistorey car park at **Bagers plats** (24hr) near the Centralstationen. The discount card costs Skr100 and is on sale at the tourist office and many hotels and shops. You can also download City Kort as a smartphone app.

Sights

★Malmö Museer MUSEUM

(www.malmo.se/museer; Malmöhusvägen; adult/child Skr40/free; audio guides Skr20; 10am-4pm Jun-Aug, shorter hours rest of year;)
Various museums with diverse themes, including handicrafts, military materiel, art and transport, are located in and around Malmöhus Slott and make up the so-called Malmö Museer. There are gift shops and cafe-restaurants inside all the museums and plenty to keep the tots interested, including an **aquarium**. Renovated in 2014, don't miss the nocturnal hall here, wriggling with everything from bats to electric eels, plus local swimmers like cod and pike.

The **Malmö Konstmuseum** boasts a fabulous collection of Swedish furniture and handicrafts, as well as Scandinavia's largest collection of 20th-century Nordic art, while the **Stadsmuseum** (City Museum) combines exhibitions on the region's cultural history with more international themes. The **Knight's Hall** contains various late-medieval and Renaissance exhibits, such as the regalia of the order of St Knut. The northwest **cannon tower** is an atmospheric mix of cannons and shiny armour.

A short distance to the west of Malmöhus Slott, the technology and maritime museum **Teknikens och Sjöfartens Hus** is home to aircraft, vehicles, a horse-drawn tram, steam engines, and the amazing 'U3' walk-in submarine, outside the main building. The submarine was launched in Karlskrona in 1943 and decommissioned in 1967. Upstairs, a superb hands-on experiment room will keep kids (of all ages) suitably engrossed.

The old **Kommendanthuset** (Commandant's House) arsenal, opposite the castle, hosts regular photography exhibitions.

★Malmöhus Slott CASTLE

FREE The addition of red-brick, Functionalist buildings in the 1930s might make it look slightly factory like, but Malmöhus Slott has an intriguing history and houses some of the superb Malmö Museer.

After the Swedish takeover of Skåne in 1648, the Danes made a futile attempt to recapture the castle in 1677. When peace was restored, most of it became derelict and a devastating fire in 1870 left only the main building and two gun towers intact; these sections were revamped in 1930.

Erik of Pomerania built the first fortress here in 1436 to control the growing medieval town and Öresund shipping. This castle was destroyed between 1534 and 1536 during a popular uprising in Skåne. Immediately after the rebellion, King Christian III of Denmark had the castle rebuilt in forbidding late-Gothic and early-Renaissance styles.

Malmöhus Slott's most famous prisoner (from 1567 to 1573) was the Earl of Bothwell. Bothwell married Mary, Queen of Scots, but was forced to flee from Scotland after she was deposed. On reaching Europe, he was detained by the Danes until his death in 1578.

★Moderna Museet Malmö MUSEUM

(www.modernamuseet.se; Gasverksgatan 22; admission Skr70; ⏲11am-6pm Tue-Sun) Architects Tham & Videgård chose to make the most of the distinct 1901 Rooseum, once a power-generating turbine hall, by adding a contemporary annexe, complete with a bright, perforated orange-red facade. Venue aside, the museum's galleries are well worth visiting, with their permanent exhibition including works by such modern masters as Matisse, Dalí and Picasso.

Form/Design Center ARTS CENTRE

(www.formdesigncenter.com; Lilla Torg 9; ⏲11am-5pm Tue-Sat, noon-4pm Sun) FREE Form/Design Center showcases cutting-edge design, architecture and art. The central cobbled courtyard is a remnant of the late-medieval town, while the historic half-timbered houses are now home to galleries and boutiques selling Scandi-cool art, fashion, crafts, toys and homewares. Pore over design magazines in the cafe and pick up one of the bicycle maps designed to guide you to design and architectural hot spots in the city.

OUTSTANDING & UNUSUAL BUILDINGS

The northwest harbour redevelopment is home to the **Turning Torso**, a striking skyscraper that twists through 90 degrees from bottom to top. Designed by Spaniard Santiago Calatrava, the 190m-high building is Sweden's tallest.

For vintage veneers, head for the statue of King Karl X Gustav in the centre of Stortorget and spin around (clockwise from the northwestern corner) to see the following buildings. **Kockska Huset** (1524) is a stately pile that mayor Jörgen Kock had built for himself; it's where Gustav Vasa stayed when he popped into town. The **County Governor's Residence** is a grand, stuccoed masterpiece built in the 19th century but with a deceptively Renaissance style. Next door, the **Rådhuset** (city hall) was originally built in 1546 but has since been altered. At the southeastern corner of the square, the city's oldest pharmacy, **Apoteket Lejonet**, flaunts an exquisite art-nouveau interior, with carved wooden shelves, antique medicine bottles and a glass-plated ceiling. Founded in 1571, the business originally occupied **Rosenvingeskahuset** on Västergatan.

Just off Östergatan, **St Gertrud Quarter** is a cute cluster of 19 buildings from the 16th to 19th centuries, with the mandatory mix of cobbled walkways, restaurants and bars. Across the road, **Thottska Huset** is Malmö's oldest half-timbered house (1558). It's now a restaurant, so peek inside.

Malmö

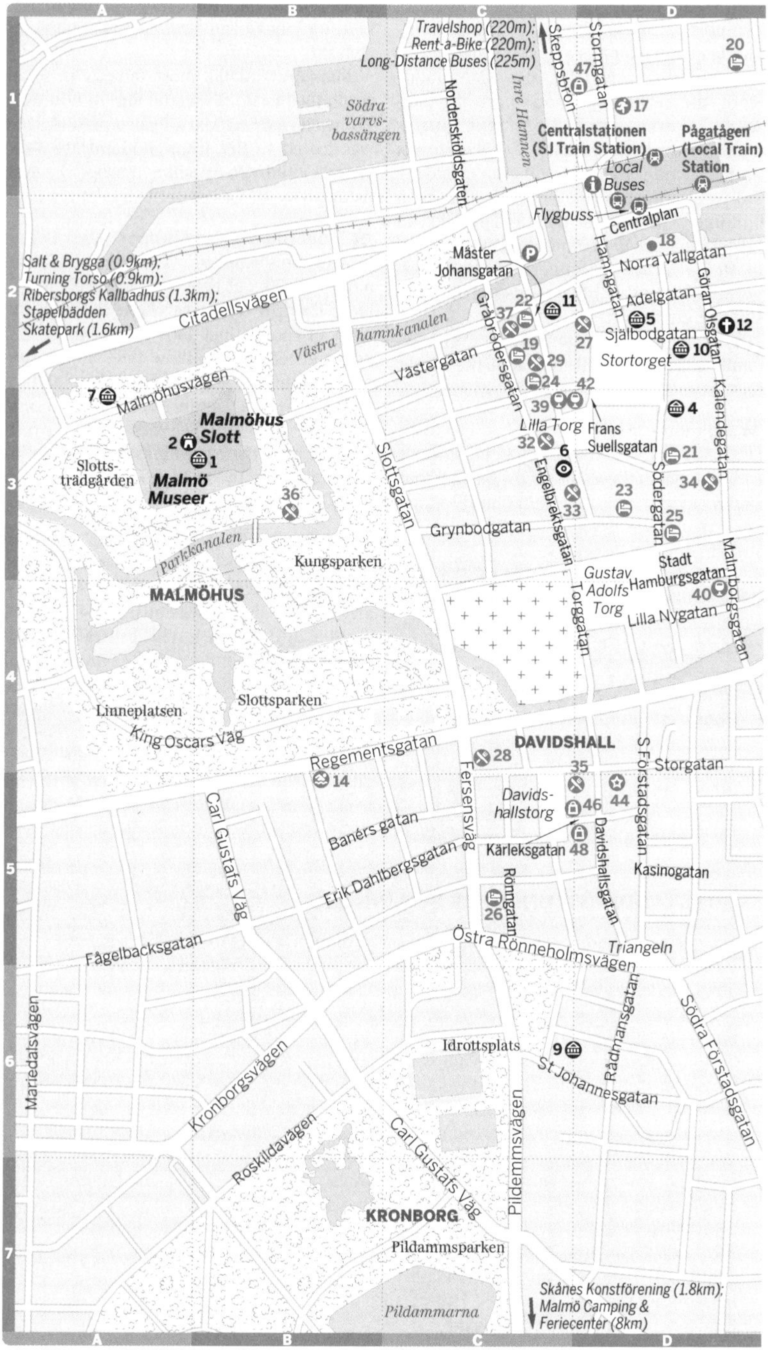

A
B
C
D
1
2
3
4
5
6
7
Travelshop (220m);
Rent-a-Bike (220m);
Long-Distance Buses (225m)
Skeppsbron
Stormgatan
Nordenskiöldsgatan
Inre Hamnen
Södra varvs-bassängen
47
20
17
Centralstationen (SJ Train Station)
Pågatågen (Local Train) Station
Local Buses
Flygbuss
Centralplan
18
Mäster Johansgatan
Hamngatan
Norra Vallgatan
Salt & Brygga (0.9km);
Turning Torso (0.9km);
Ribersborgs Kallbadhus (1.3km);
Stapelbädden Skatepark (1.6km)
Citadellsvägen
Västra hamnkanalen
Gråbrödersgatan
22
11
37
Adelgatan
Göran Olsgatan
5
12
Själbodgatan
27
19
29
Stortorget
10
Västergatan
24
42
Kalendegatan
7
Malmöhusvägen
39
4
Malmöhus Slott
2
1
Lilla Torg
Frans Suellsgatan
32
6
21
Slottsträdgården
Malmö Museer
Engelbrektsgatan
Södergatan
34
36
Slottsgatan
33
23
25
Grynbodgatan
Parkkanalen
Kungsparken
Gustav Adolfs Torg
Stadt Hamburgsgatan
Malmborgsgatan
MALMÖHUS
40
Torggatan
Lilla Nygatan
Linneplatsen
Slottsparken
King Oscars Väg
DAVIDSHALL
Regementsgatan
28
S Förstadsgatan
Storgatan
14
35
Carl Gustafs Väg
Fersensväg
Davidshallstorg
46
44
Banérs gatan
48
Kärleksgatan
Davidshallsgatan
Kasinogatan
Erik Dahlbergsgatan
26
Rönngatan
Östra Rönneholmsvägen
Triangeln
Fågelbacksgatan
Rådmansgatan
Södra Förstadsgatan
Mariedalsvägen
Idrottsplats
9
St Johannesgatan
Kronborgsvägen
Roskildavägen
Carl Gustafs Väg
Pildammsvägen
KRONBORG
Pildammsparken
Skånes Konstförening (1.8km);
Malmö Camping & Feriecenter (8km)
Pildammarna

Sankt Petri Kyrka CHURCH

(Göran Olsgatan; 10am-6pm) FREE This red-brick Gothic beast is Malmö's oldest church, built in the early 14th century. Protestant zealots whitewashed the medieval frescoes in 1555, but the original wall paintings in the **Krämarekapellet** have been successfully restored. There's a magnificent altarpiece dating from 1611 and a votive ship in the south aisle, dedicated to all who died at sea in WWII.

Malmö Konsthall GALLERY

(www.konsthall.malmo.se; St Johannesgatan 7; 11am-5pm, to 9pm Wed) FREE Malmö Konsthall, south of central Malmö, is one of Europe's largest contemporary-art spaces, with exhibitions spanning both Swedish and foreign talent. The museum cafe **Smak** (040-50 50 35; www.smak.info; mains from Skr80; 11am-5pm) serves an excellent weekend brunch.

Malmö Chokladfabrik MUSEUM

(Chocolate Museum; www.malmochokladfabrik.se; Möllevångsgatan 36; adult/child Skr100/50; 10am-6pm Mon-Fri, to 3pm Sat) Watch heavenly cocoa concoctions being made, wander through the mini museum and devour the finished product at the chocolate-scented cafe. Dating from 1888, Malmö Chokladfabrik produces famous organic chocolates that have won several international chocolatiers' awards. The tours take around an hour and include an audiovisual presentation and a 20% discount in the choc shop.

Skånes Konstförening GALLERY

(040-10 33 80; www.skaneskonst.se; Bragegatan 15, entrance at Ystadvägen 22; 2-6pm Wed-Fri, 1-4pm Sat & Sun during exhibitions) FREE Concentrates on emerging and lesser-known, mainly Scanian artists. Located 1km south of Möllevångstorget.

Folkets Park AMUSEMENT PARK, OUTDOORS

(www.malmofolketspark.se; Norra Parkgatan 2A; park 7am-9pm Mon-Fri, 8am-9pm Sat & Sun, to 11pm Jun-Aug, attractions noon-7pm May–mid-Aug, shorter hours rest of year) FREE Family-friendly Folkets Park boasts pony rides, a funfair, mini golf, a wading pool (transformed into an ice rink in winter), a reptile house and (phew, something for the grown-ups) – a beer garden. Entrance is free, but some attractions have a minimal cost.

Malmö

Top Sights
1 Malmö Museer B3
2 Malmöhus Slott A3
3 Moderna Museet Malmö E3

Sights
4 Apoteket Lejonet D3
Aquarium .... (see 1)
5 County Governor's Residence D2
6 Form/Design Center C3
7 Kommendanthuset A3
8 Malmö Chokladfabrik E7
9 Malmö Konsthall C6
Malmö Kontsmuseum .... (see 1)
10 Rådhuset D2
11 Rosenvingeskahuset C2
12 Sankt Petri Kyrka D2
Stadsmuseum .... (see 1)
13 Thottska Huset E2

Activities, Courses & Tours
14 Aq-va-kul B5
15 City Boats Malmö E4
16 Folkets Park F6
17 Rent-a-Bike D1
18 Rundan D2

Sleeping
19 Astoria C2
20 Comfort Hotel Malmö D1
21 Hotel Baltzar D3
22 Hotel Duxiana C2
23 Hotel Noble House D3
24 Mäster Johan Hotel C2
25 Scandic Hotel St Jörgen D3
26 STF Vandrarhem Malmö City C5

Eating
27 Årstiderna i Kockska Huset D2
28 Atmosfär C4
29 Bastard Restaurant C2
30 Dolce Sicilia F2
31 Falafel No. 1 .... F2
32 Izakaya Koi C3
33 Johan P C3
34 Lilla Kafferosteriet D3
35 Mrs. Brown D5
36 Slottsträdgårdens Kafé B3
37 Surf Shack C2

Drinking & Nightlife
38 Club Wonk F5
39 Drumbar C3
Mello Yello .... (see 42)
40 Pickwick Pub D4
41 Tempo Bar & Kök E7
42 Victors C3

Entertainment
43 Debaser F6
44 Filmstaden Malmö D5
Inkonst .... (see 8)
45 Kulturbolaget E6

Shopping
Formargruppen .... (see 32)
46 Love Street Vintage C5
47 Malmö Modern D1
48 Tjallamalla D5

Activities

Ask the tourist office for the free cycling map *Cykla i Malmö*. **Rent-a-Bike** (☎0707-49 94 22; www.travelshop.se; Carlsgatan 4; per 24hr Skr150), near the tourist office, and Rundan (p175) both rent bikes.

Aq-va-kul SWIMMING
(☎040-30 05 40; www.aqvakul.se; Regementsgatan 24; adult/child Skr80/30; ⊙9am-8.30pm Mon, Wed & Thu, 7am-8.30pm Tue, 9am-7.30pm Fri, 9am-6pm Sat & Sun) Aq-va-kul is a water park with heated indoor and outdoor pools, a water slide, wave machine, sauna, solarium and Turkish bath.

Ribersborgs Kallbadhus SWIMMING
(☎040-26 03 66; www.ribersborgskallbadhus.se; adult/child Skr55/free; ⊙9am-8pm Mon, Tue & Thu, to 9pm Wed, to 6pm Fri-Sun May-Sep, shorter hours rest of year) Ribersborg is a fetching sandy beach backed by parkland, about 2km west of the town centre. Off the beach, at the end of a 200m-long pier, is an open-air naturist saltwater pool, with separate sections for men and women, and a wood-fired **sauna** dating from 1898. There is also a pleasant cafe.

City Boats Malmö BOATING
(☎0704-71 00 67; www.cityboats.se; Amiralsbron, Södra Promenaden; per 30/60min Skr90/150; ⊙11am-7pm May-Aug) To scoot round Malmö's canals in a pedal boat, head to City Boats Malmö, just east of Gustav Adolfs Torg.

Stapelbädden Skatepark SKATE PARK
(www.stpln.se; Stapelbäddsgatan 1) Swing by this intense urban jungle near the Turning Torso, at the northwestern harbour redevelopment, to gasp at skaters – local and international – sliding, flying and occasionally tumbling from dizzying heights. Check out www.bryggeriet.org for more details on the city's vibrant skateboarding scene.

Tours

Rundan BOAT TOUR
(040-611 74 88; www.stromma.se; adult/child Skr130/65; 10.30am-9pm May-Sep, tours run less frequently other times) To experience Malmö by water, visit Rundan, opposite Centralstationen. Fifty-minute boat tours of the canals run regularly from May to September. It also rents bicycles (Skr170 per day).

Malmö Bike Tours BICYCLE TOUR
(0708-46 25 40; www.malmobiketours.se; 2hr tour Skr275, rental day/week Skr150/650) Starting from Stortorget, Malmö Bike Tours runs two-hour and 3½-hour cycling trips around the city, covering major landmarks and lesser-known neighbourhoods. It also rents bicycles if you'd rather tour on your own. Book online, by phone or through the tourist office.

Malmö By Foot WALKING TOUR
(0708-43 50 20; www.malmobyfoot.com; 1¼hr tour Skr80; 11am & 12.45pm Jul & Aug) A guided walk covering the history of Malmö from the Middle Ages to today. Tours go twice a day from Sankt Petri Kyrka. Book online, by phone or through the tourist office.

Festivals & Events

Malmö Festival MUSIC
(www.malmofestivalen.se; mid-Aug) Malmö's premier annual event – with an average of some 1.5 million visitors – is the week-long Malmö Festival. The mostly free events include theatre, dance, live music, fireworks and sizzling food stalls.

Regnbågsfestivalen GAY & LESBIAN
(late Sep) The week-long Regnbågsfestivalen (Rainbow Festival) is Malmö's main gay celebration, packed with exhibitions, films, parties and a pride parade. Contact **RFSL-Malmö** (040-611 99 62; www.rfsl.se/malmo; Monbijougatan 15), Malmö's gay and lesbian centre, for details.

Sleeping

The city has a good range of accommodation.

STF Vandrarhem Malmö City HOSTEL €
(040-611 62 20; www.svenskaturistforeningen.se; Rönngatan 1; dm/d from Skr230/560; @) Don't be put off by the exterior; this is a sparkling hostel right in the city centre with a bright and airy communal kitchen and an outdoor patio. Staff are enthusiastic and helpful.

Comfort Hotel Malmö HOTEL €
(040-33 04 40; www.choice.se; Carlsgatan 10C; s/d Skr690/800; P @) Not the right choice if you want an intimate place to propose: there are 293 rooms here, making it the largest hotel in the city. That said, the aesthetically revamped rooms are bright, airy and contemporary with massive black-and-white photos (with a music theme) covering an entire wall. The facilities are excellent and include a gym.

The company is planning to build three more similar-calibre hotels in Malmö around 2015–16.

Scandic Hotel St Jörgen HOTEL €
(040-693 46 00; www.scandichotels.com; Stora Nygatan 35; s/d Skr750/800; P @) A sleek, minimalist foyer reflects the contemporary, well-equipped and spacious rooms at this friendly, upmarket chain. Most rooms have bathtub-shower combos and look out onto Gustav Adolfs Torg. There are a few windowless 'cabin' rooms. Book online for the best rates.

Malmö Camping & Feriecenter CAMPGROUND €
(040-15 51 65; www.firstcamp.se; Strandgatan 101; sites Skr320, 2-bed cabins Skr700; P) By the beach, this campground has a great view of

BRIDGING THE GAP

Opened in 2000, the **Öresund bridge** (www.oresundsbron.com; motorcycle/car/minibus Skr225/440/880) is the planet's longest cable-tied road and rail bridge, measuring 7.8km from Lernacken (on the Swedish side, near Malmö) to the artificial island of Peberholm (Pepper Island), south of Saltholm (Salt Island). From the island, a further 3km of undersea tunnel finally emerges just north of Copenhagen airport.

Local commuters pay via an electronic transmitter, while tolls for everyone else are payable by credit card, debit card or in euros, Danish or Swedish currency at the Lernacken toll booths.

An alternative option is to catch a commuter train to Copenhagen (Skr105), an easy 35-minute trip from Malmö and a good excuse to explore Denmark's so-hip capital.

the Öresund bridge. It's about 5km southwest of the centre of town: take bus 4 from Gustav Adolfs Torg (Skr16).

★**Hotel Duxiana** HOTEL €€
(☎040-607 70 00; www.malmo.hotelduxianacom; Mäster Johansgatan 1; s/d/ste from Skr795/1090/2140; P @) Close to Centralstationen, ubersleek Hotel Duxiana is one for the style crew. In a palate of white, black and gunmetal grey, design features include Bruno Mattheson sofas and the same heavenly beds supplied to the world's first seven-star hotel in Dubai. Single rooms are small but comfy, while the decadent junior suites feature a claw-foot bathtub facing the bed.

Astoria HOTEL €€
(☎040-786 60; www.astoriahotel.se; Gråbrödersgatan 7; s/d from Skr800/900; @) At this family-owned older hotel located a short suitcase trundle from Centralstationen, rooms are spacious, comfortable and conservatively furnished – aside from the in-your-face brightly coloured paintings, that is. There is a delightful shady patio.

Hotel Baltzar HISTORIC HOTEL €€
(☎040-665 57 00; www.baltzarhotel.se; Södergatan 20; s/d standard Skr590/855, superior Skr950/1050; @) Located smack in the heart of town (though it's remarkably quiet) and in an imposing listed building, the hotel's public areas could do with brightening up, but the rooms are superb. The superior rooms are flamboyantly decked out with antique furniture, brass mirrors and oriental rugs, while the standard rooms are marginally less chintzy but just as spacious.

Hotel Noble House HOTEL €€
(Best Western; ☎040-664 30 00; www.hotelnoblehouse.se; Per Weijersgatan 6; s/d Skr995/1195; ❄ @) These rooms may lack wow factor, but they are eminently comfortable and classically furnished with parquet floors, tasteful wallpaper and the quirky addition of stuffed toys on the bed. Breakfast is a superb spread; apparently a local celeb chef has had some influence on the Best Western buffets – and it shows.

★**Mäster Johan Hotel** HOTEL €€€
(☎040-664 64 00; www.masterjohan.se; Mäster Johansgatan 13; r/ste from Skr1290/1790; P @) Just off Lilla Torg is one of Malmö's finest slumber spots, with spacious, elegantly understated rooms featuring beautiful oak floors and snowy white matched with cobalt blue fabrics. Bathrooms flaunt Paloma Picasso-designed tiles, there's a sauna and gym, and the faultless breakfast buffet is served in a glass-roofed courtyard.

Eating

Malmö isn't short on dining experiences, whether it's vegan grub enjoyed in a grungy left-wing hang-out or designer supping on contemporary Nordic flavours. You can even eat well at the foodie kiosks in Centralstationen. But for sheer atmosphere, head to the restaurant-bars on Lilla Torg.

The best **produce market** (Mon-Sat) is on Möllevångstorget.

★**Lilla Kafferosteriet** CAFE €
(☎040-48 20 00; www.lillakafferosteriet.se; Baltzarsgatan 24; sandwiches from Skr35; 8am-7pm Mon-Fri, 10am-5pm Sat, 11am-5pm Sun) Have a mosey around the warren of atmospheric rooms here before you bag your table, or head out to the pretty patio. This is a serious-about-coffee cafe with freshly ground (Fairtrade) beans, plus plenty of sweet and savoury goodies. You may just stay for a while; it's that kind of place.

Surf Shack BURGERS €
(☎0761-76 40 18; Västergatan 8; burgers from Skr59; 10.30am-8pm Mon-Thu, to 11pm Fri-Sun;) Enjoy a surfing-dude theme and a menu of top-range burgers, including a veggie option of tofu and black beans, 'no roll' (wrapped in lettuce) and healthy extra toppings like avocado, feta and grilled mushrooms. There are also sodas and shakes, including double chocolate and peanut butter if you are determined to sink that board.

Slottsträdgårdens Kafé CAFE €
(☎040-30 40 34; www.slottstradgardenskafe.se; Grynbodgatan 9; sandwiches from Skr50; 11am-5pm Apr-Sep) There is no better way to enjoy summertime Malmö than to settle down under a white umbrella at this quaint cafe, tucked in the middle of the Slottsträgården. Savour the aromas of fennel, herbs and baking while enjoying a delicious sandwich or square of rhubarb crumble with organic vanilla ice cream.

Dolce Sicilia ICE CREAM €
(☎040-611 31 10; www.dolcesicilia.se; Drottningtorget 6; ice cream from Skr27; noon-5pm Mon, 11am-7pm Tue-Sun) Head to Dolce Sicilia, run by certified Sicilians, for fresh, organic Italian-style gelato with flavours ranging

from chilli chocolate to liquorice or forest berry. There's another location near the Turning Torso, at Västra Varvsgatan 37.

Falafel No. 1 FELAFEL €
(☎ 040-84 41 22; www.falafel-n1.se; Österportsgatan 2; felafel from Skr35) Malmö residents are so fond of felafel that it even features in songs by local rapper Timbuktu. Falafel No. 1 (also known as the Orient House) is a long-standing favourite, or check out the website Everything About Falafel (www.alltomfalafel. se) for details on other venues.

★Atmosfär SWEDISH €€
(☎ 040-12 50 77; www.atmosfar.com; Fersensväg 4; mains from Skr125; ⊙ 11.30am-11pm Mon-Fri, to 2am Sat) This classy neighbourhood restaurant changes its menu regularly depending on what's in season, but you can depend on flavourful, innovative combinations like salads topped with young nasturtium leaves and veal with truffles, green peas and horseradish. The cocktails (Skr105) are similarly irresistible. Elderflower fizz, anyone?

Salt & Brygga SWEDISH €€
(☎ 040-611 59 40; www.saltobrygga.se; Sundspromenaden 7; lunch mains from Skr110, dinner mains from Skr145; ⊙ 11am-2pm & 5-11pm Mon-Fri, 12.30-4pm & 5-11pm Sat; ♫) ✔ With an enviable view overlooking the Öresund bridge and the small harbour, this stylish slow-food restaurant presents updated Swedish cuisine with a clear conscience. Everything is organic (including the staff's uniforms), waste is turned into biogas, and the interior is allergy free. Flavours are clean and strictly seasonal.

Johan P SEAFOOD €€
(☎ 040-97 18 18; www.johanp.nu; Hjulhamnsgatan 5; mains from Skr175, set menu Skr375, *pintxos* Skr38; ⊙ 11.30am-11pm Mon-Fri, noon-11pm Sat, 1-10pm Sun) With brand-new premises (in 2014) but the same high standards, Johan P continues to enthrall diners with its fresher-than-fresh seafood. Choose your fishy favourite from the market-style counter out back or go for the set menu. There are lovely bisques, *moules meunière* (mussels cooked in wine) and chilled shellfish platters. For snacks, Basque-style *pintxos* (tapas) are available.

Izakaya Koi ASIAN €€
(☎ 040-757 00; www.koi.se; Lilla Torg 5; mains from Skr109; ⊙ 6pm-late Mon-Sat) On heaving Lilla Torget, Koi attracts crowds with excellent cocktails, sushi and other Asian-inspired nibbles. You'll find Malmö's trendsetters in the upstairs lounge, mingling on the dance floor or perched on white leather banquettes looking gorgeous well into the early hours.

★Bastard Restaurant EUROPEAN €€€
(☎ 040-12 13 18; www.bastardrestaurant.se; Mäster Johansgatan 11; mains from Skr200; ⊙ 5pm-midnight Tue-Thu, to 2am Fri & Sat) ✔ This hipster restaurant is about as close as you'll get to a gastro-pub in Sweden. Meals here are both hearty and distinctive, ranging from gourmet meat platters to blackened grilled chicken for two or pizza with snails. The bar is a popular choice with well-heeled locals.

Mrs. Brown SWEDISH €€€
(☎ 040-97 22 50; www.mrsbrown.nu; Storgatan 26; mains from Skr200; ⊙ noon-3.30pm & 5-10.30pm Mon-Fri, 6-10.30pm Sat; ♫) ✔ Demure little Mrs. Brown is the kind of neighbourhood place you dream will open up near you. The open kitchen churns out modern Scandinavian home cooking using local and organic ingredients like Greenland prawns in chilli sauce. Service is attentive but not overbearing and the dining room is decorated in a minimalist fashion that is both comforting and modish.

A vegetarian menu is available.

Årstiderna i Kockska Huset SWEDISH €€€
(☎ 040-23 09 10; www.arstiderna.se; Frans Suellsgatan 3; mains Skr235-325; ⊙ 11.30am-midnight Mon-Fri, 5pm-midnight Sat) This top-notch restaurant serves meals in the vaults beneath Kockska Huset. Food is upscale Swedish and the atmosphere is classic with crisp white tablecloths and quietly professional service.

🍸 Drinking & Nightlife

Bars in Malmö generally stay open until around 1am, although some close later on Friday and Saturday evenings. The heaving bars around Möllevångstorget tend to pull a more student, indie crowd.

The bars on Lilla Torg are great spots, with affable service, alfresco summer seating (you may have to wait for a table), tasty meals and everything from Chilean whites to sex-on-the-beach-style cocktails.

Clubs generally stay open until around 1am, and to 3am, 4am or 5am on Friday and Saturday. The minimum age requirements (20 to 25) vary according to the venue, so bring ID. Entry usually costs between Skr100 and Skr200.

Victors COCKTAIL BAR
(www.victors.se; Lilla Torg 1; ☺3-6.30pm Mon-Thu,
noon-1am Fri & Sat) Glam cocktails on Lilla
Torg with light late-night snacks available to
accompany your tipple.

Drumbar BAR
(Lilla Torg 9; ☺4-11pm Mon-Thu, to 1am Fri & Sat)
Popular Scottish-themed pub with a pretty
outside garden and a traditional och-aye
atmosphere.

Mello Yello BAR
(www.melloyello.se; Lilla Torg 1; ☺3.30pm-1am
Mon-Fri, from noon Sat & Sun) Located on Lilla
Torg, with nice nibbles and an animated atmosphere. It serves decent burgers if you're
peckish.

Pickwick Pub PUB
(www.pickwickpub.se; Stadt Hamburgsgatan 12;
☺4-10.30pm Mon-Thu, to 1.30am Fri & Sat, to
9.30pm Sun) Friendly, traditional pub with
Chesterfield chairs and a cosy fireplace.

Tempo Bar & Kök LOUNGE
(☑040-12 60 21; www.tempobarokok.se; Södra
Skolgatan 30; ☺5pm-1am Mon-Sat) Funky neighbourhood lounge for the student and indie
crowd with occasional DJ sets.

Club Wonk GAY
(☑040-23 93 03; www.wonk.se; Amiralsgatan 23;
before/after midnight Skr50/100; ☺11.30pm-5am
Sat) Malmö's best bet for gay clubbers, Wonk
works up the crowd with three bars, two
dance floors and a karaoke lounge.

☆ Entertainment

Pick up (or check online) local newspaper
Sydsvenskan (www.sydsvenskan.se) on a
Friday, when it contains the listings mag
Dygnet Runt (which covers Lund as well as
Malmö). Also, scan the weekly street press
Nöjesguiden (www.nojesguiden.se). They're
both in Swedish, but the club and film infor-
mation is decipherable. Alternatively, take
the regular train to Copenhagen for a huge
array of options.

MOVING ON?

For tips, recommendations and reviews,
head to shop.lonelyplanet.com to purchase a downloadable PDF of the
Copenhagen chapter from Lonely Planet's *Denmark* guide.

Debaser LIVE MUSIC
(www.debaser.se; Norra Parkgatan 2; ☺7pm-3am
Wed-Sun Apr-Sep; 🚌5, 32 Malmö Folkets park)
After a temporary closure, Debaser opened
again in mid-2014 with live gigs and club
nights spanning anything from indie, pop
and hip-hop to soul, electronica and rock.
There's a buzzing outdoor bar-lounge overlooking Folkets Park.

Kulturbolaget LIVE MUSIC
(www.kulturbolaget.se; Bergsgatan 18; ☺varies)
Some pretty big names have performed
here, but even if there's no one playing, 'KB'
has a kicking bar and nightclub (usually Friday and Saturday).

Inkonst LIVE MUSIC
(www.inkonst.com; Bergsgatan 29; ☺11pm-3am)
This cultural hang-out serves up some brilliant club nights, pumping out anything
from underground UK grime and garage to
hip hop and rhythm and blues. It also stages
theatre and dance performances.

Filmstaden Malmö CINEMA
(☑040-660 20 90; Storgatan 22) Hollywood
releases.

🛍 Shopping

The current hot spot for up-and-coming designers and vintage threads are the streets
around Davidshallstorg, south of Gamla
Staden.

Tjallamalla FASHION
(☑040-791 90; www.tjallamalla.co; Davidshallsgatan 15; ☺10.30am-6pm Tue-Fri, to 4pm Sat)
Stockholm's legendary purveyor of new and
emerging designers now feeds local trendsetters on cult labels like Stylein, Ida Sjöst-
edt and Diana Orving.

Love Street Vintage VINTAGE
(Kärleksgatan 15; ☺noon-6pm Tue-Fri, to 4pm
Sat) A glorious packed-to-the-rafters shop
selling everything from beaded bags to den-
im jackets, boas, jewellery and '50s-style
crockery.

Malmö Modern HOMEWARES
(☑040-30 00 86; www.malmomodern.se; Skeppsbron 3; ☺11am-6pm Mon-Fri, to 3pm Sat) Scandinavian design really does have that certain
something. Check out the homewares, fabrics, clocks, clothes and all sorts of idiosyncratic and thought-provoking dust collectors
for your shelves back home.

Formargruppen HANDICRAFTS
(040-780 60; www.formargruppen.se; Engelbrektsgatan 8; 11am-6pm Mon-Fri, to 4pm Sat) Representing a dynamic collective of Swedish artists, artisans and designers, this central shop-gallery stocks striking wares, from ceramics and pottery to jewellery and textiles.

Information

EMERGENCY

Akutklinik (1813; entrance 36, Södra Förstadsgatan 101) Emergency ward at the general hospital.

Police Station (040-114 14; Porslinsgatan 6)

MEDICAL SERVICES

You can call the dentist and doctor on duty on 1177.

Apotek Gripen (0771-45 04 50; Bergsgatan 48; 8am-10pm) After-hours pharmacy.

MONEY

Banks and ATMs are found on Södergatan.

TOURIST INFORMATION

Malmö Airport Visitor Centre (www.malmoairport.se; Sturup airport; 8am-6pm, varies slightly according to flight arrival times) Helpful tourist office. You can also purchase Flygbuss tickets here.

Tourist Information (040-34 12 00; www.malmotown.com; Skånegårdsvägen 5; 9am-5pm Mon-Fri, 10am-2.30pm Sat & Sun) On the E20, 800m from the Öresund bridge tollgate.

Tourist Office (040-34 12 00; www.malmotown.com; Skeppsbron 2; 9am-7pm Mon-Fri, 10am-4pm Sat & Sun) Across from the Centralstationen.

Tourism in Skåne (www.skane.com) Regional website with lots of information, tips, maps and booking service.

Getting There & Around

TO/FROM THE AIRPORT

Flygbuss (www.flygbussarna.se) runs from in front of Centralstationen to Sturup airport (adult/child Skr109/89 one way) roughly every 40 minutes on weekdays, with six services on Saturday and seven on Sunday; a taxi shouldn't cost more than Skr450. You can pay for your ticket on the bus, but only with a credit card. Alternatively, buy your ticket at the Malmö Airport Visitor Centre or at the Centralstationen customer desk.

AIR

Sturup airport (010-109 45 00; www.swedavia.se) is 33km southeast of Malmö. Located here is the Malmö Airport Visitor Centre, left-luggage lockers (small/large Skr15/25 per 24 hours), as well as money exchange.

SAS (0770-72 77 27; www.sas.se) has up to eight nonstop flights to Stockholm Arlanda daily. **Malmö Aviation** (www.malmoaviation.se) flies as often as 11 times daily to Stockholm Bromma airport (from Skr410, one hour and five minutes).

Trains run directly from Malmö to Copenhagen's main airport (Skr105, 35 minutes, every 20 minutes), which has a much wider flight selection.

BUS

Local & Regional

Skånetrafiken (p180) operates Skåne's efficient local bus and train networks (the latter known as Pågatågen).

Its buses operate in zones, with a single journey costing Skr22 within the city of Malmö. Note that (aside from the Flygbuss) you can't buy a ticket on the bus. Instead, purchase a reusable **Jojo** card at the Skånetrafiken customer-service centres at Centralstationen or Triangeln and load it with an amount to cover your estimated local bus travel. Alternatively, purchase a 24- or 72-hour Timmarsbijett bus pass.

Most long-distance regional buses leave from the bus station on Spårvägsgatan, while a few go from in front of Centralplan. Bus 146 is a useful service to the ferries departing from Trelleborg (Skr65, 40 minutes); this service runs once or twice hourly. Bus 100 to Falsterbo (Skr65, one hour) is equally useful.

Long-Distance

There are two bus terminals with daily departures to Swedish and European destinations. **Travelshop** (Malmö Buss & Resecenter; 33 05 70; www.travelshop.se; Carlsgatan 4A), north of Centralstationen, sells tickets for several companies, including **Swebus Express** (0771-21 82 18; www.swebus.se), which runs two to four times daily direct to Stockholm (from Skr539, 8½ hours), four times to Jönköping (from Skr239, 4½ hours) and up to 10 times daily to Göteborg (from Skr139, three to four hours); five continue to Oslo (from Skr219, eight hours).

> **BUS PASS**
>
> If you are planning on travelling around Malmö by bus, consider buying a 24- or 72-hour **Timmarsbijett** (Skr65/165) bus ticket, which may be purchased at the tourist office or at Skånetrafikens customer-service centres. You can also purchase tickets via the Skånetrafiken (p180) app.

The second long-distance bus terminal, **Öresundsterminalen** (☎040-59 09 00; www.oresundsterminalen.se; Terminalgatan 10) is reached via bus 35 from Centralstationen towards Flansbjer (Skr25, 30 minutes). From here **Svenska Buss** (☎0771-67 67 67; www.svenskabuss.se) runs a service to Stockholm (Skr420, 11 hours) via Karlskrona, six times weekly.

Eurolines also runs services from here to several European destinations.

Trains are your best option for journeys to Copenhagen and beyond.

CAR & MOTORCYCLE

Several of the larger car-hire companies, such as **Avis** (☎778 30, airport 50 05 15; www.avisworld.com; Stormgatan 6) and **Hertz** (☎040-33 07 70; www.hertz-europe.com; Jörgen Kocksgatan 1B), are represented at Sturup airport and directly opposite Centralstationen.

Parking in the city is expensive: typical charges start at Skr15 per hour or Skr110 per day (24 hours). Most hotels also charge for parking.

Malmö's taxis are notorious for overcharging so agree on the fare with the driver before hopping in. The tourist office recommends **Taxi Skåne** (☎040-33 03 30) and **Taxi 97** (☎040-97 97 97).

TRAIN

Pågatågen (local trains) operated by **Skånetrafiken** (www.skanetrafiken.se) run regularly to Helsingborg (Skr103, one hour), Landskrona (Skr84, 40 minutes), Lund (Skr48, 15 minutes), Simrishamn (Skr103, 1½ hours), Ystad (Skr84, 50 minutes) and other towns in Skåne. Bicycles are half-fare but are not allowed during peak times of the day except from mid-June to mid-August.

The Malmö to Copenhagen central station train leaves every 20 minutes (Skr105, 35 minutes).

X2000 (from Skr342, 2½ hours) and regional (from Skr235, 3¼ hours) trains run several times daily to/from Göteborg. X2000 (from Skr750, 4½ hours, hourly) and Intercity (from Skr795, 6½ hours, infrequently) trains run between Stockholm and Malmö.

There are baggage lockers at Centralstationen for Skr30 to Skr50 per 24 hours.

Lund

☎046 / POP 105,300

Centred on a striking cathedral (complete with a giant in the crypt and a magical clock), learned Lund is a soulful blend of leafy parks, medieval abodes and coffee-sipping bookworms. The city buzzes with students during the school year and remains busy through the summer when visitors meander the cobblestone streets and enjoy the dense selection of top-notch museums.

Lund is Sweden's second-oldest town, founded by the Danes around 1000 and once the seat of the largest archbishopric in Europe. It's also the birthplace of the ink-jet printer!

Sights

Numerous galleries and small, special-interest museums and archives are dotted around town, many attached to university departments – inquire at the tourist office.

★ Domkyrkan CHURCH

(Kyrkogatan; ⏲8am-6pm Mon-Fri, 9.30am-5pm Sat, to 6pm Sun) FREE Lund's twin-towered Romanesque cathedral, Domkyrkan, is magnificent. Try to pop in at noon or 3pm (1pm and 3pm on Sunday and holidays) when the marvellous astronomical clock strikes up *In Dulci Jubilo* and the wooden figures at the top whirr into action. Within the crypt, you'll find Finn, the mythological giant who helped construct the cathedral, and a 16th-century well carved with comical scenes.

★ Skissernas Museum ARTS CENTRE

(Sketch Museum; ☎046-222 72 83; www.skissernasmuseum.se; Finngatan 2; admission Skr50; ⏲noon-5pm Tue-Sun, to 9pm Wed) The exhibition rooms here with their visual feast of paintings and sculpture are designed for maximum impact and art immersion. Several sculptures and installations are huge, including the 6m-high *Women by the Sea* by Ivar Johnsson. Formerly a private collection, it includes works by some of the world's greats, including Joan Miró, Henri Matisse, Raoul Dufy, Sonia Delaunay and Fernand Léger. A sculpture park includes pieces by Henry Moore, and a Mexican gallery space will be completed by early 2015.

★ Kulturen MUSEUM

(www.kulturen.com; Tegnerplatsen; adult/child Skr90/free; ⏲10am-5pm May-Aug, noon-4pm Tue-Sat Sep-Apr; 👪) Kulturen, opened in 1892, is a huge open-air museum filling two whole blocks. Its 30-odd buildings include everything from the meanest birch-bark hovel to grand 17th-century houses. Permanent displays encompass Lund in the Middle Ages, vintage toys, ceramics, silver and glass (among many others); ask about guided tours in English. The popular outdoor cafe flanks several rune stones.

Historiska Museet MUSEUM

(History Museum; www.luhm.lu.se; Kraftstorg; admission Skr50; ⌚11am-4pm Tue-Fri, noon-4pm Sun) Behind the cathedral, the Historiska Museet has a large collection of pre–Viking Age finds, including a 7000-year-old skeleton. It's joined with **Domkyrkomuseet**, which explores the history of the church in the area; the rooms filled with countless statues of the crucified Christ are supremely creepy.

Drottens Arkeologiska Museum MUSEUM

(☎046-14 13 28; www.kulturen.com; Kattesund 6A; ⌚9am-6pm Mon-Thu, 10am-6pm Fri & Sat) FREE Subterranean Drottens Arkeologiska Museum contains the foundations of an 11th-century church, as well as a grisly collection of skeletons that build a picture of the Middle Ages through their diseases and amputations. Entrance is through the Gattostretto restaurant.

Botanical Gardens GARDENS

(☎046-222 73 20; www.botaniskatradgarden.se; Östra Vallgatan 20; ⌚6am-9.30pm) FREE The 8-hectare Botanical Gardens, east of the town centre, feature around 7000 species and nine climate zones. Also on site are tropical **greenhouses** (Östra Valgatan 20; ⌚11am-3pm) FREE

Lundskonsthall GALLERY

(www.lundskonsthall.se; Mårtenstorget 3; ⌚noon-5pm Wed, Fri, Sat & Sun, to 8pm Tue & Thu) FREE This contemporary art space has cutting-edge exhibitions, including Tate Modern–style installations and other forms of creative art.

University Building UNIVERSITY

(cnr Kyrkogatan & Paradisgatan) The main university building, topped by four sphinxes representing the original faculties, is worth a peek.

Apoteket Svanen HISTORIC BUILDING

(Kyrkogatan 5) Check out the aesthetically restored pharmacy, opposite the tourist office.

Sleeping

The tourist office can arrange a private room from Skr300 per person plus a Skr50 booking fee.

Winstrup Hostel HOSTEL €

(☎0723-29 08 00 08; www.winstruphostel.se; Winstrupsgatan 3; dm Skr275, breakfast Skr65, dinner Skr75; wi-fi) The dorm accommodation here is imaginatively designed for added privacy; beds are essentially cubby hole–style spaces, accessed by a respective short ladder. The whole place has a sparkling contemporary look.

Lilla Hotellet i Lund HOTEL €€

(☎046-32 88 88; www.lillahotellet.com; Bankgatan 7; s/d Skr1350/1450; P wi-fi) Partly housed in an old shoe factory, this homely spot offers cosy rooms (think patchwork quilts and Laura Ashley–style wallpaper), as well as a sunny courtyard and guest lounge. Prices drop considerably on Friday and Saturday.

Hotell Oskar BOUTIQUE HOTEL €€

(☎046-18 80 85; www.hotelloskar.com; Bytaregatan 3; s/d Skr995/1195; @ wi-fi) Tucked away in a petite 19th-century townhouse, this central hotel has superb rooms reflecting sleek Scandi design. It's also well equipped, with DVD players, kettles and stereos, plus it has a pretty back garden. The adjacent cafe is handy for coffee and cake.

Hotel Ahlström HISTORIC HOTEL €€

(☎046-211 01 74; www.hotellahlstrom.se; Skomakaregatan 3; s/d with shared bathroom Skr670/850, r with bathroom Skr1100; wi-fi) Lund's oldest hotel is friendly and affordable, and on a quiet, central street. Rooms have parquet floors, cool white walls and washbasins (most bathrooms are shared). Breakfast is brought to your door. On the downside, some readers have complained of a whiff of drains.

★ **Hotel Duxiana** BOUTIQUE HOTEL €€€

(☎046-13 55 15; www.lundhotelduxiana.com; Sankt Petri Kyrkogatan 7; s/d 1695/1895; @ wi-fi) Top tip is that all rooms are priced the same, despite various levels of luxury, including a private sauna in one, a small kitchenette in another and still another which is split level with a sitting room. The decor is slickly contemporary and there is an oasis of a courtyard out the back, as well as a restaurant and bar.

Grand Hotel HOTEL €€€

(☎046-280 61 00; www.grandilund.se; Bantorget 1; s/d Skr1275/1775; P @ wi-fi) Lund's most luxurious establishment is the Grand, which opened in 1899 and is resplendent with gilt and chandeliers. Rooms are smallish but decorated in grand style with heavy wooden beds, Persian carpets and cherub wallpaper. Extras include a sauna and upmarket dining at Gambrinus.

Lund

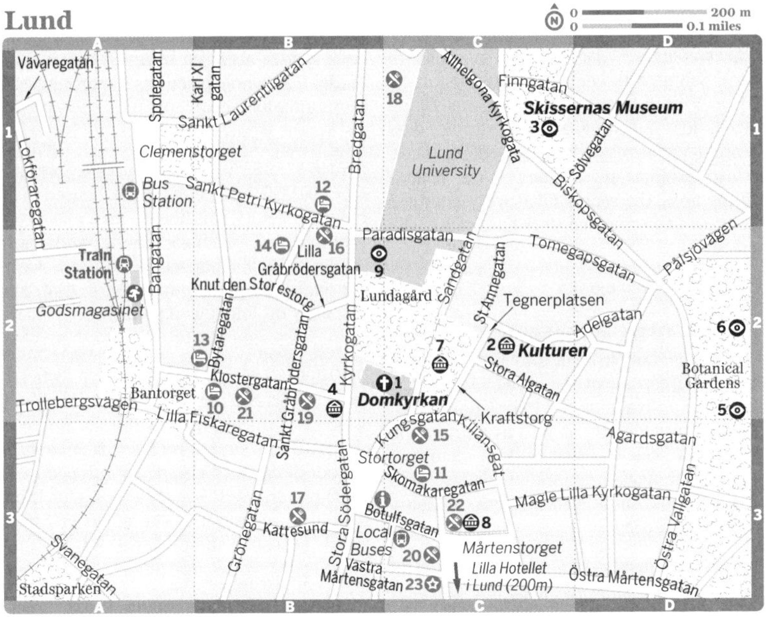

Eating & Drinking

★ St Jakobs Stenugnsbageri BAKERY €
(046-13 70 60; www.stjakobs.se; Klostergatan 9; baked goods Skr15-50; 8am-6pm Mon-Fri, to 4pm Sat, to 3pm Sun) Mouthwatering is the only way to describe the selection of stone-baked breads, knotted cardamom rolls, melt-in-your-mouth coconut-lemon towers and crisp sugar cookies overflowing from the countertops and baking trays at St Jakobs. During the summer you're likely to see an enormous bowl of strawberries at the centre of it all, served with fresh cream, of course.

Saluhallen FOOD HALL €
(www.lundssaluhall.se; Mårtenstorget; snacks from Skr35; 10am-6pm Mon-Wed, to 7pm Thu & Fri, 9.30am-3pm Sat) A mouthwatering market hall, it sells reasonably priced grub, from fresh fish and piping-hot pasta to Thai, kebabs and croissants. Six additional restaurants recently opened in a brand-new extension, making Saluhallen a still more serious dining option in Lund.

Café Ariman CAFE €
(www.ariman.se; Kungsgatan 2B; mains from Skr70; 11am-midnight Mon, to 1am Tue, Wed & Thu, to 3am Fri & Sat, 3-11pm Sun;) Head to this hip, grungy hang-out for cathedral views, strong coffee and fine cafe fare such as ciabattas, salads and burritos. It's popular with left-wing students: think nose-rings, dreads and leisurely chess games. From September to May, DJs hit the decks on Friday and Saturday nights.

Govindas VEGETARIAN €
(046-12 04 13; Bredgatan 28; lunch Skr70; 11.30am-3.30pm Mon-Fri, closed Jul;) In a quiet, leafy cobbled courtyard, vegetarian Govindas is a hit with krona-conscious students and anyone craving a spicy curry and cool raita. Much of the produce is organically grown by the charming owner.

Coffee Break CAFE €
(046-211 21 00; www.coffeebreak.nu; Sankt Petri Kyrkogatan 3; sandwiches from Skr35; 8am-8pm Mon-Fri, from 9am Sat & Sun;) Small rooms give this place a classic teashop feel, plus there's a flower-filled garden, tasteful funky local art on the walls and a menu of home-made scones, bagels, ciabattas or baguettes with a wide choice of fillings. There are magazines for browsing, and a chillout soundtrack. Kick back and relax; it's that kind of place.

Ved SWEDISH €€
(046-13 05 65; www.restaurangved.se; Mårtenstorget 3; mains from Skr120; 10am-6pm Mon-Wed, 9.30am-3pm Sat, 10am-7pm Thu & Fri;)

Lund

Top Sights

1 Domkyrkan ... C2
2 Kulturen ... C2
3 Skissernas Museum ... C1

Sights

4 Apoteket Svanen ... B2
5 Botanical Gardens ... D2
Drottens Arkeologiska Museum ... (see 17)
6 Greenhouses ... D2
7 Historiska Museet ... C2
8 Lundskonsthall ... C3
9 University Building ... B2

Sleeping

10 Grand Hotel ... B2
11 Hotel Ahlström ... C3
12 Hotel Duxiana ... B1
13 Hotell Oskar ... B2
14 Winstrup Hostel ... B2

Eating

15 Café Ariman ... C3
16 Coffee Break ... B2
Gambrinus ... (see 10)
17 Gattostretto ... B3
18 Govindas ... C1
19 Klostergatans Vin & Delikatess ... B2
20 Saluhallen ... C3
21 St Jakobs Stenugnsbageri ... B2
22 Ved ... C3

Entertainment

23 SF Bio Filmstaden ... C3

Opened in 2014 and on the verge of expanding when we visited, this moodily lit bar and restaurant dishes up good-looking plates of Swedish-fusion dishes. Plates are intentionally midsized, so they're cheaper than you may expect, and the place hums with city-slick sophistication.

Klostergatans Vin & Delikatess FRENCH, DELI €€
(046-14 14 83; www.klostergatan.se; Klostergatan 3; lunch mains from Skr85, dinner mains from Skr125; 11am-3pm & 5-9pm Mon-Thu, to 11.30pm Fri, noon-4pm Sat) A French-style wine bar and delicatessen, ideal for a quick bite or for a longer meal, complete with crisp white tablecloths and a glass of the house wine. The menu definitely has a Gallic influence, using local ingredients. Its adjacent sister bakery, Patisseriet, has lovely cakes, coffees and sandwiches.

Gattostretto ITALIAN €€
(www.gattostretto.se; Kattesund 6A; lunch Skr80, mains from Skr139; 11.30am-9pm Mon-Sat) Located over medieval ruins and co-run by an affable Roman chef, this breezy cafe-restaurant serves a tasty slice of *dolce vita.* Guzzle down proper Italian espresso and a slice of *torta rustica,* or long for Rome over hearty *ragù* or tri-coloured bruschetta.

Gambrinus EUROPEAN €€€
(046-280 61 00; Bantorget 1; lunch/dinner mains from Skr125/235; 11.30am-midnight;) The star turn at the Grand Hotel's gourmet nosh spot is the Lund menu, featuring creative interpretations of regional classics using seasonal local produce. While the speciality is sweetbreads, there's a vegetarian menu for herbivorous guests.

Entertainment

Pick up the local monthly events calendar from the tourist office for entertainment info.

SF Bio Filmstaden CINEMA
(0856-26 00 00; Västra Mårtensgatan 12) Mainstream flicks.

Information

Banks, ATMs and other services line the main street (Stora Södergatan, changing to Kyrkogatan).

Read about the **university** (www.lu.se; Sandgatan) online, and check out www.lund.se for information about the town.

Tourist Office (046-35 50 40; www.lund.se; Botulfsgatan 1A; 10am-6pm Mon-Fri, to 2pm Sat) At the southern end of Stortorget.

Getting There & Away

Flygbuss (0771-77 77 77; www.flygbussarna.se) runs regularly to/from Malmö's Sturup airport (Skr109).

Long-distance buses leave from outside the train station. Most buses to/from Malmö run via Lund.

It's 15 minutes from Lund to Malmö by train, with frequent Pågatågen departures (Skr48). Some trains continue to Copenhagen (Skr135, one hour). Other direct services run from Malmö to Kristianstad and Karlskrona via Lund. All long-distance trains from Stockholm or Göteborg to Malmö stop in Lund.

Getting Around

Skånetrafiken (0771-77 77 77) local town buses operate with the prepaid **Jojo** card, which you can purchase at the terminal on Botulfsplatsen, west of Mårtenstorget, the tourist office or at Pressbyrån stores. For bike hire, head to **Godsmagasinet** (☎046-35 57 42; Bangatan; per day/week Skr20/130; ⊙6.30am-9.30pm Mon-Fri), a bicycle lock-up in the northernmost train-station building. Phone **Taxi Skåne** (☎046-33 03 30) for a taxi.

Falsterbo Peninsula

☎040

This fishtail-shaped peninsula 30km south of Malmö lures sun lovers with its sandy beaches and ornithologists with its impressive posse of feathered creatures. Eclectic extras include the Foteviken Viking Reserve and the offbeat amber museum.

Höllviken

Sights

★Foteviken Viking Reserve HISTORIC SITE
(☎040-33 08 00; www.fotevikensmuseum.se; Muselvägen 24, Höllviken; adult/child Skr90/30; ⊙10am-4pm Jun-Aug, shorter hours rest of year; P 👪) If you mourn the passing of big hairy men in longboats, find solace at the fascinating Foteviken Viking Reserve, an evocative 'living' reconstruction of a late-Viking Age village. Around 22 authentic reconstructions of houses with reed or turf roofs have been built, near the site of the Battle of Foteviken (1134). Amazingly, the reserve's residents live as the Vikings did, eschewing most modern conveniences and adhering to old traditions, laws and religions – even after the last tourist has left.

The houses you see belong to various tradespeople, like the town's jarl (commander of the armed forces), juror and scribe; and the chieftain, whose home has wooden floorboards, fleeces and a Battle of Foteviken tapestry. There's even a shield-lined great hall (the Thinghöll), a lethally powerful war catapult and nifty Viking-made handicrafts to buy. Viking Week is usually held in late June, and culminates in a Viking market, complete with agile warriors in training.

The Viking Reserve is located about 700m north of Höllviken.

Bärnstensmuseum MUSEUM
(Amber Museum; ☎040-45 45 04; www.brost.se; Södra Mariavägen 4, Höllviken; adult/child Skr25/10; ⊙11am-5pm mid-May–end-Sep, shorter hours rest of year; P) Trapped in sticky resin 40 million years ago, insects fight, mate and feed in pieces of amber at the Bärnstensmuseum. The museum is near Höllviken's southern edge, just off the coast road towards Trelleborg.

Information

The town has banks and supermarkets.

Tourist Office (☎040-42 54 54; www.vellinge.se; Videholms Allé 1A, Höllviken; ⊙10am-6pm Mon-Fri, to 2pm Sat & Sun mid-Jun–mid-Aug, shorter hours rest of the year) The area's major tourist office is in the same building as the Höllviken library, just off Falsterbovägen.

Falsterbo & Skanör

Informally known as the Swedish Rivera, Falsterbo's long, white-sand **beach** with its colourful beach huts is popular with locals and Malmö leisure-seekers; a sense of serenity is enhanced by a ban on jet skis and motorboats here.

The hook-shaped island of **Måkläppen** is a nature reserve, off limits to the public from March to October.

Sights & Activities

Falsterbo Museum MUSEUM
(☎040-47 22 42; www.kulturbron.com/falsterbomuseum.htm; Sjögatan; adult/child Skr40/10; ⊙10am-6pm mid-Jun–Aug) Little Falsterbo Museum, at the southern tip of the peninsula, is a pleasing jumble: a small Naturum, old shops and smithies, WWII mines and the remains of a 13th-century boat.

Falsterbo Fågelstation BIRDWATCHING
(☎040-47 06 88; www.falsterbofagelstation.se; Sjögatan; 1hr guided tours per person Skr40; ⊙Apr, May & Aug-Oct, advanced booking required) Residents of Måkläppen include seals and over 50 species of bird, including little terns, Kentish plovers (rare in Sweden) and avocets; in the autumn, between one and three million migrating birds rest their wings here. Located near Falsterbo Museum, this observatory studies the feathery visitors.

Sleeping & Eating

Ljungens Camping CAMPGROUND €
(☎040-47 06 88; www.ljungenscamping.mamutweb.com; Strandbadsvägen; sites with/without electricity Skr250/210; ⊙Apr-Sep; P) This super-friendly campground is a couple of kilometres from Falsterbo; amenities include mini golf.

Skanörs Gästgifvaregård HOTEL €€€
(☎040-47 56 90; www.skanorsgastis.com; Mellangatan 13; r Skr1895; P 📶) A superb hotel with plushly decorated and eminently comfort-

able rooms combined with a stellar restaurant (which also offers cookery classes).

Da Aldo ITALIAN €
(040-47 40 26; www.aldo.se; Mellangatan 47; gelato from Skr30, piadine Skr65; 8.30am-10pm) Calabrian expat Aldo makes sublime gelato here on Skanör's main street using strictly Italian ingredients and no added egg, cream or butter. Lunch options, from frittata and salads to *piadine* (Italian flat-bread sandwiches) and stuffed aubergine, are well priced and equally authentic. As for the coffee...*buonissimo!*

★ **Skanörs Fiskrögeri** SEAFOOD €€€
(040-47 40 50; www.rogeriet.se; Skanörs Hamn; mains Skr218-393; restaurant noon-11pm Mon-Sat, to 10pm Sun Jun-Aug, deli 10am-9pm) By the harbour, this marine-chic place is a must for seafood lovers, as its harbourside location and white smokehouse chimneys attest. The fish soup is exquisite and there's a gourmet seafood deli for stocking that beachside picnic.

Getting There & Away

Bus 100 (Skr60, one hour, every 30 minutes Monday to Saturday, less frequently on Sunday) runs from Malmö to Falsterbo and Skanör.

Trelleborg

0410 / POP 41,000 /

Trelleborg is the main gateway between Sweden and Germany, with frequent ferry services. It's not really on the tourist trail: if you're entering Sweden from here, consider heading on to Malmö or Ystad.

Sights

Trelleborgen HISTORIC SITE
(0410-73 30 21; www.trelleborgen.se; Västra Vallgatan 6; visitors centre adult/child Skr30/free; 10am-4pm Jun-Aug, 1-5pm Mon-Thu rest of year; P) FREE Trelleborgen is a 9th-century Viking ring fortress, discovered in 1988 off Bryggaregatan (just west of the town centre). It's built to the same pattern as Danish fortresses of the same era, showing the centralised power of Harald Bluetooth at work. A quarter of the palisaded fort and a wooden gateway have been re-created, as has a Viking farmhouse and a medieval house built within the walls. An on-site **visitors centre** showcases finds from the archaeological digs, including Viking jewellery, grooming implements and a c 10th-century skull illustrating the ancient trend of teeth filing.

Trelleborgs Museum MUSEUM
(0410-73 30 50; museum@trelleborg.se; Östergatan 58; admission Skr30; noon-4pm Tue-Sun) Just east of the town centre, this museum covers a wide range of themes, including a 7000-year-old settlement discovered nearby.

Axel Ebbe Konsthall GALLERY
(0410-73 30 56; Hesekillegatan 1; admission Skr30; noon-4pm Wed-Sun mid-Jun–Aug) By the town park, Axel Ebbe Konsthall features nude sculptures by Scanian Axel Ebbe (1868–1941). For a preview, check out the fountain **Sjöormen** (literally 'the sea monster') in Storatorget.

Sleeping & Eating

The tourist office can book private rooms from Skr300.

Night Stop MOTEL €
(0410-410 70; www.hotelnightstop.com; Östergatan 59; s/d/tr Skr300/400/500; P) Simple and functional with shared bathrooms, Night Stop has the cheapest beds in town. Open 24 hours, it's about 500m from the ferry (turn right along Hamngatan after disembarking), diagonally opposite the museum. Breakfast costs Skr50.

Hotel Duxiana Dannegården HOTEL €€
(0410-481 80; www.dannegarden.se; Strandgatan 32; r from Skr1175; P @) Trelleborg's most beautiful slumber spot is this old sea captain's villa. Run with quiet confidence by the Duxiana hotel chain, rooms here are discreetly luxurious, the breakfast is generous and the staff is pleasant. Extras include a reputable restaurant, a sauna and hot tub, plus gorgeous gardens.

Vattentornet Café & Bistro CAFE €
(0410-254 84; Stortorget 2; sandwiches from Skr35; 9am-6pm Mon-Thu, to 8pm Fri & Sat, 11am-4pm Sun) On the ground floor of the splendid 58m-high water tower (1912), selling sandwiches, cakes and other yummy snacks; snag an outdoor table in the fabulous courtyard here with its thought-provoking murals.

Restaurang & Pizzeria Istanbul TURKISH €
(0410-44 44 44; Algatan 30; mains from Skr65; 11am-11pm) This bustling place has a huge menu of pasta, pizza, salad and kebabs, plus pricier local fish and meat dishes.

Information

Banks and ATMs line Algatan.

Tourist Office (☎0410-73 33 20; www.trelleborg.se/turism; Kontinentgatan 2; ⏲9am-6pm Mon-Fri, 10am-6pm Sat, 10am-5pm Sun Jun-Aug, 9am-5pm Mon-Fri Sep-May) Across from the ferry terminal.

Getting There & Away

Bus 146 runs roughly every half-hour between Malmö (Skr60, 45 minutes) and Trelleborg's bus station, some 500m inland from the ferry terminals. Bus 165 runs frequently Monday to Friday (five services Saturday and four services Sunday) from Lund (Skr70, one hour and five minutes).

There are international train services from Malmö to Berlin via Trelleborg.

Stena Line (www.stenaline.com) ferries connect Trelleborg to Sassnitz (twice daily each way, from Skr190) and Rostock (two or three daily, from Skr315). **TT-Line** (☎0450-280 181; www.ttline.com) ferries shuttle between Trelleborg and Travemünde (from Skr310) and Rostock (from Skr450) three to four times daily. Buy tickets inside the ferry building.

Smygehuk

☎0410

Thanks to the power of geography – it's Sweden's most southerly point (latitude 55° 20' 3") – diminutive Smygehuk has become something of a tourist magnet, despite its modest attractions.

Sights

Köpmansmagasinet GALLERY
A renovated 19th-century warehouse east of the harbour, with local exhibitions of handicrafts and art (for sale).

Lime Kiln HISTORIC SITE
This huge 19th-century kiln near Köpmansmagasinet gallery recalls the bygone lime industry; it smoked its last in 1954.

Lighthouse LIGHTHOUSE
West of the harbour, scramble to the top of the now-defunct 19th-century **lighthouse** (17m), and visit the tiny maritime museum inside **Captain Brinck's Cabin** (donation appreciated; ⏲mid-May–mid-Sep). (Note that the lighthouse is managed by the hostel warden, so opening hours are erratic.) A soothing **coastal path** features prolific bird life.

Sleeping & Eating

STF Vandrarhem Smygehuk HOSTEL €
(☎0410-245 83; www.smygehukhostel.com; s/d Skr375/520; ⏲mid-May–mid-Sep; P) STF Vandrarhem Smygehuk is a comfortable, well-equipped hostel in the old lighthouse-keeper's residence, next to the lighthouse. Book ahead outside high season.

Smyge Fisk Rökeri SEAFOOD €
(www.smygerokeri.se; Skepparevägen 3; sandwiches from Skr45; ⏲9am-6pm Tue-Fri, 10am-4pm Sat & Sun) Packs people like sardines into its tiny shop. The smoke house's salmon baguettes and crayfish cakes on brown bread are worth the crush.

Information

Smygehuk Tourist Office (☎0410-240 53; www.smygehuk.com; ⏲10am-7pm Jul, to 6pm Jun & Aug) East of the harbour, this **tourist office** with cafe sits inside Köpmansmagasinet gallery.

Getting There & Away

The Trelleborg to Ystad bus service stops in Smygehuk.

Ystad

☎0411 / POP 28,000

Medieval market town Ystad has an intoxicating allure thanks to its half-timbered houses, rambling cobbled streets and the haunting sound of a nightwatchman's horn. Fans of writer Henning Mankell know it as the setting for his best-selling Inspector Wallander crime thrillers, while fans of drums and uniforms head in for the spectacular three-day **Military Tattoo** (www.ystadtattoo.se; ⏲mid-Aug) in August.

Ystad was Sweden's window to Europe from the 17th to the mid-19th century, with new ideas and inventions – including cars, banks and hotels – arriving here first. Now a terminal for ferries to the Danish island of Bornholm and to Poland, the port's transitory feel doesn't spread to the rest of Ystad: settle in for a few days and let the place work its magic.

Sights

Half-timbered houses are scattered liberally round town, especially on Stora Östergatan. Most date from the latter half of the 18th century, although **Pilgrändshuset** on the corner of Pilgrand and Stora Östergatan is Scandi-

INSPECTOR WALLANDER'S YSTAD

Fans of crime thrillers most likely know the name of Henning Mankell (1948–), author of the bestselling Inspector Wallander series. The books are set in the small, seemingly peaceful town of Ystad. The gloomy inspector paces its medieval streets, solving gruesome murders through his meticulous police work...but at a cost to his personal life, which is slowly and painfully disintegrating. The first book is *Faceless Killers*, but it's generally agreed that Mankell really hit his stride in number four, *The Man Who Smiled*. Impressively, Mankell's nail-biting stories have been translated into 41 languages.

Between 2005 and 2006, 13 Wallander films were shot in and around Ystad, starring Krister Henriksson in the lead role. In 2008 a further 13 Wallander films were shot here, alongside a BBC-commissioned TV series starring Kenneth Branagh as Wallander. In 2014, Branagh was on the brink of returning to film three follow-up episodes.

Interactive film centre **Cineteket** (☎0411-57 70 57; www.ystad.se/cineteket; Elis Nilssons väg 8; adult/child Skr150/100; ⏰10am-4pm Mon-Thu, Sat & Sun mid-Jun–Aug, times vary rest of year) runs guided tours between 10am and 4pm Monday to Thursday and at weekends (adult/child Skr150/100) of the adjoining Ystad Studios, where sets include forensic detective Leif Nyberg's laboratory and the inspector's own apartment.

The Ystad tourist office provides a free map with featured locations in town. There's even an iPhone app. For a quirkier excursion around Wallander's Ystad, the volunteer fire brigade runs 45-minute tours starting at Stortorget on a veteran fire engine at 1pm and 4.45pm from late June to mid-August (Skr70). Contact the tourist office for details.

Mankell has spent much of his time in Maputo, Mozambique, where he juggled writing, running a theatre company and carrying out his AIDS education work. His wife, Eva Bergman, is the daughter of the late film director Ingmar Bergman.

navia's oldest half-timbered house and dates from 1480. Take a peek, too, at the facade of beautiful **Änglahuset** on Stora Norregatan, which originates from around 1630.

★**Sankta Maria Kyrka** CHURCH
(Stortorget; ⏰10am-6pm Jun-Aug, to 4pm Sep-May) FREE Among the church's highlights is a magnificent 17th-century baroque pulpit. This is also, famously, the place from where the nightwatchman sounds his horn. **Latinskolan**, next to Sankta Maria Kyrka, is a late-15th-century brick building and the oldest preserved school in Scandinavia.

★**Klostret i Ystad** MUSEUM
(www.klostret.ystad.se; St Petri Kyrkoplan; adult/child Skr40/free; ⏰noon-5pm Tue-Fri, noon-4pm Sat & Sun) Klostret i Ystad, in the Middle Ages Franciscan monastery of Gråbrödraklostret, features local textiles and silverware. The monastery includes the 13th-century deconsecrated Sankt Petri Kyrkan (now used for art exhibitions), which has around 80 gravestones from the 14th to 18th centuries. Also included is the **Ystads Konstmuseum** (☎0411-57 72 85; www.konstmuseet.ystad.se; St Knuts Torg; ⏰10am-5pm Mon-Fri, noon-4pm Sat & Sun Jul–mid-Aug, noon-5pm Tue-Fri, noon-4pm Sat & Sun mid-Aug–Jun) FREE. In the same building as the tourist office, its superb collection of southern Swedish and Danish art includes work by the great Per Kirkeby.

★**Per Helsas Gård** ARTS CENTRE
(Besökaregränd 3; ⏰11am-5pm Jun-Aug, shorter hours rest of year) Housed in one of Ystad's most iconic (and magnificent) half-timbered buildings, dating from the 1500s and set around a courtyard; the central cobbles here are flanked by craft workshops, art galleries and a cafe.

Charlotte Berlins Museum MUSEUM
(☎0411-188 66; Dammgatan 23; adult/child Skr20/free; ⏰noon-5pm Mon-Fri, to 4pm Sat & Sun Jun-Aug, tours hourly from 11am) For fetching interiors, pop into Charlotte Berlins Museum, which is a late-19th-century middle-class abode.

Sleeping

Travellers with their own wheels can select from the B&B and cabin options along the scenic coastal roads on either side of Ystad. The tourist office can also arrange B&B accommodation for around Skr600 to Skr800 per double room.

★**Sekelgården Hotel** HOTEL €€
(☎0411-739 00; www.sekelgarden.se; Långgatan 18; s/d Skr995/1395; P@) A romantic

Ystad

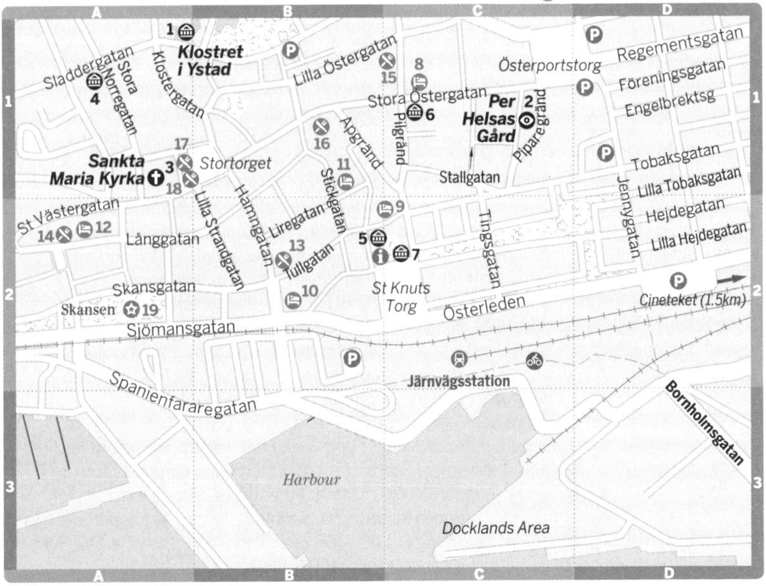

family-run hotel in a superb half-timbered house (1793); staying here is a bit like staying with your (affluent) country cousins. Rooms are set around a delightful garden and are all different, although typically decorated with a combination of William Morris–style wallpaper and pastel paintwork combined with colourful quilts, rugs and fabrics.

Hotell Klara B&B €€
(☎0702-94 52 55; www.ystadhotell.se; Stickgatan 17; s/d Skr795/895; 📶) Next to a large playground, so a good option for families with tots, the half-timbered building contrasts sharply with the 12 modern and crisply renovated apartments with their well-equipped kitchenettes and small dining space.

Hotel Tornvaktaren HOTEL €€
(☎0411-79 59 95; Stora Östergatan 33; s/d Skr795/995; @📶) An inviting place to stay, with pleasant homey rooms sporting embroidered cushions, oriental rugs and charmingly mismatched furniture. Request room number 8 with its balcony overlooking the main pedestrian street. There's a sitting room with a small kitchen for the use of guests, plus an interior courtyard.

Hotell Bäckagården GUESTHOUSE €€
(☎0411-198 48; www.backagarden.nu; Dammgatan 36; s/d from Skr695/995; 📶) Exuding a warm and homely feel, this cosy guesthouse occupies a 17th-century home one block behind the tourist office. The lovely walled garden is perfect for sunny breakfasts.

Hotell Continental HISTORIC HOTEL €€€
(☎0411-137 00; www.hotelcontinental-ystad.se; Hamngatan 13; s/d Skr1490/1690; P@📶) On the site of the old customs house, the Continental is reputedly Sweden's oldest hotel, dating from 1829. It's loaded with old-world charm (think grand chandeliered foyer and marble staircase), but its rooms are more business-style with light wood furnishings, parquet floors and smart, if small, slate-grey-and-cream bathrooms.

Eating & Drinking

Most budget eating places are on Stora Östergatan, the main pedestrian street.

Host Morten CAFE €
(☎0411-134 03; Gåsegränd; mains from Skr75; ⏰11am-5pm Mon-Fri, to 3pm Sat, 12.30-5pm Sun) Plunge into that Henning Mankell novel at this fabulous cafe – serving light meals like filled baked potatoes, focaccias and piled-high salads – then pluck a book from one

Ystad

of the shelves and plan to stay awhile. In summer the 18th-century cobbled courtyard is a delight, especially when there's live music.

Maltes Mackor SANDWICHES €
(☎0411-101 30; Stora Östergatan 12; baguettes Skr60; ⊙10am-6pm, to 3pm Sat) Short on space but long on choice, the baguettes and wraps here are made with only the freshest locally sourced produce. Even if you're not peckish, grab a coffee; it's reputed to be the best in town.

Upperllerner EUROPEAN €
(www.uppellerner.se; Stortorget 11; mains from Skr90; ⊙5pm-11 Mon-Fri, 8pm-late Sat & Sun) A brick-clad dining space combined with subtle lighting creates a soothing rustic ambience for enjoying mainly meat and fishes, including classics like steak tartare and a gut-busting mixed grill. There's terrace seating overlooking the square.

Store Thor INTERNATIONAL €€
(☎0411-185 10; www.storethor.se; Stortorget 1; mains from Skr105, tapas Skr39; ⊙11.30am-4pm & 5pm-late Mon-Sat) Described as one of Ystad's best restaurants by Kurt Wallander in the movie *Täckmanteln*, Store Thor occupies the monastic arched cellar of the old town hall (1572). Nibble on such tapas as jalapeño peppers with cheese, tuck into succulent grilled meats or enjoy the cognac raw-spiced salmon with dill-stewed potatoes. The square-side terrace is a hit with summertime night owls.

Bröderna M BISTRO €€
(☎0411-191 99; www.brodernam.se; Hamngatan 11; mains from Skr175, pizzas from Skr58; ⊙11.30am-11pm Mon-Fri, from noon Sat & Sun) Relaxed and contemporary, Bröderna M serves up Ystad's best pizza, ranging from classic margheritas to posh thin-crusted pies topped with prosciutto, rocket and pecorino. Main dishes are solid bistro fare: steak with red-wine sauce or fish soup.

Bryggeriet SWEDISH €€
(☎0411-699 99; www.ystadbryggeriet.se; Långgatan 20; mains from Skr125; ⊙11.30am-9pm Tue-Fri, to 10pm Sat, to 7pm Sun) Unique Bryggeriet is a relaxed meat-leaning restaurant-pub in an old brewery. The courtyard is an excellent spot to linger over a well-cooked meal and Ystad Färsköl, a beer brewed on the premises. The chocolate truffle with raspberry sorbet comes plumply recommended.

Entertainment

Ystads Teater THEATRE
(☎0411-57 77 98; www.ystadsteater.se; Sjömansgatan 13; tickets around Skr300) The extraordinary Ystads Teater dates back to 1894; its repertoire spans operas, musicals, tango and big-band gigs. Guided tours (usually in Swedish) of the building take place daily from late June to August. Contact the tourist office for details.

Information

Banks and other services line Hamngatan.

Tourist Office (☎0411-57 76 81; www.ystad.se; St Knuts Torg; ⊙9am-7pm Mon-Fri, 10am-6pm Sat & Sun mid-Jun–mid-Aug; wi-fi) Just opposite the train station with free internet access.

Getting There & Away

BOAT

Unity Line (☎0411-55 69 00; www.unityline.se; adult one way Skr386) and **Polferries** (☎040-12 17 00; www.polferries.se; adult one way Skr353) operate daily crossings between Ystad and Swinoujscie, Poland.

Faergen (www.faergen.dk; adult one way Skr240) runs frequent ferries and catamarans between Ystad and Rønne, on the Danish island of Bornholm.

THE NIGHTWATCHMAN'S HORN

Ever since 1250 a nightwatchman has blown his bugle through the little window in the clock tower of Ystad's Sankta Maria Kyrka church (every 15 minutes from 9.15pm to 3am). The tradition was apparently introduced to help thwart fires, a hazardous side effect of the flammable thatched-roof houses. If a blaze started, the watchman would blow his horn repeatedly, which was a signal for locals to rush to the scene and extinguish the blaze. It was a serious role: if the nightwatchman had the audacity to doze off while on duty, he was unceremoniously beheaded.

BUS

Buses depart from outside Ystad train station. Bus 190 runs from Ystad to Trelleborg (Skr72, one hour) via Smygehuk 14 times daily on weekdays, six times on Saturday and twice on Sunday. The direct bus to Simrishamn (Skr54, 40 minutes) via Löderup runs hourly in the summer.

SkåneExpressen bus 5 runs to Lund (Skr96, 1¼ hours, hourly weekdays, infrequently on weekends).

TRAIN

Pågatågen trains run roughly hourly (fewer on weekends) from Malmö (Skr84, 50 minutes). Other local trains run daily to Simrishamn (Skr54, 40 minutes).

Getting Around

Local bus services depart from outside the tourist office. Try **Taxi Ystad** (720 00) for a taxi or for bike hire try **Roslins Cykel** (www.roslinscykel.se; Norra Zinkgatan 2; per day/week Skr65/325; 9.30am-6pm Mon-Fri, to 3pm Sat year-round, plus 11am-3pm Sun Apr-Aug), located about 3km northeast of the city centre.

Around Ystad

Löderups Strandbad

0411

The Baltic resort of Löderups Strandbad, 4km east of Ales Stenar, has an inviting long, white sandy beach that is perfect for relaxing (school holidays aside...).

On the edge of the Hagestad Nature Reserve, **Löderups Strandbads Camping** (0411-52 63 11; www.loderupsstrandbadscamping.se; sites Skr200, cabins from Skr500; mid-Apr–Sep) is a pleasant spot in a pine forest next to the beach. The family hotel **Löderups Strandbad Hotell** (0411-52 62 60; www.loderupsstrandbad.com; s/d Skr990/1290; P @) is a popular summer spot, complete with sauna, heated outdoor pool and restaurant. It also rents cabins, most with sea views (by the week only in high season; Skr7900) and bicycles. Near Strandbad, beside the main road, the helpful **STF Vandrarhem Backåkra** (0411-52 60 80; www.backakra.se; dm/s/d Skr250/360/500; mid-Jun–mid-Aug; P @) has simple cheery rooms and a great garden and is a short stroll from the beach.

Österlen

0414 / POP 19,400

Softly lit Österlen is an alluring area of waving wheat fields, tiny fishing villages and glorious apple orchards. Everything moves at a slow, seductive speed: cycling is the best way of fitting in with the local tempo.

Simrishamn

Summer holidaymakers mill around Simrishamn harbour, idly licking ice creams or waiting for the ferry to the Danish island of Bornholm.

Sights & Activities

The quaint pastel-hued houses on **Lilla Norregatan** are worth a look, as is nearby **Sankt Nikolai Kyrka**. Petrol-heads should visit **Autoseum** (0702-03 94 20; www.autoseum.se; Fabriksgatan 10; adult/child Skr100/60; 11am-5pm daily Jul & Aug, to 5pm Sat & Sun Apr-Jun, Sep & Oct) with its booty of classic cars.

The region is great for cycling and there is a variety of routes to choose from, ranging from a 66km spin covering major food highlights to the 136km-long Österlen Trail. The Simrishamn tourist office has free biking maps, or contact **Österlenguiderna** (705-18 33 29; www.osterlenguiderna.se), which rents bikes and runs organised tours.

Sleeping & Eating

STF Vandrarhem Simrishamn HOSTEL €
(0414-105 40; www.simrishamnsvandrarhem.se; Christian Barnekowsgatan 10C; s/d from Skr400/500; Apr–mid-Nov; P @) Pick up a map: this

recommended hostel is tucked away near the hospital. It offers spotless, homely lodgings with bathroom and TV in every room.

Maritim Krog & Hotell BOUTIQUE HOTEL €€
(☎0414-41 13 60; www.maritim.nu; Hamngatan 31; s/d from Skr1050/1450; P @) The old blue building by the harbour is a wonderful boutique hotel with stylish decor, lashings of white linen and sea views. It's also home to a fine restaurant (mains Skr170 to Skr295) specialising in fish dishes.

★ **Gärdens Café & Vedugn** PIZZA €€
(☎0414-161 61; Storgatan 17; pizza from Skr120; 11am-10pm Mon-Sat, noon-8pm Sun;) Head for the outside terrace with its mini maze, riot of flowers and pretty tiled tables. A former cafe (the cinnamon rolls still sell out fast), the thin crispy-based pizzas are Neapolitan-authentic and fabulous. Try the white pizza with its earthy topping of potatoes, caramelised onions, cheese and baby spinach.

En Gaffel Kort MODERN EUROPEAN €€€
(☎0414-44 80 70; www.engaffelkort.se; Storgatan 3; mains from Skr240; 5-10pm Wed-Sat) A dress-for-dinner style of place with terrific innovative dishes with just enough foam and drizzle to set it apart from the mainstream-style joints that line the other side of this pretty pedestrian street.

Information

Banks and other services line Storgatan.

Tourist Office (☎0414-81 98 00; www.visitystadosterlen.se; Varvsgatan 2; 9am-7pm Mon-Fri, 10am-6pm Sat & Sun Jul & Aug, 9am-5pm Mon-Fri rest of year) Has information on the whole of Österlen.

Getting There & Around

SkåneExpressen bus 3 runs hourly on weekdays (less frequently on weekends) from Simrishamn train station to Kristianstad (Skr66, 1¼ hours) via Kivik (Skr22, 24 minutes). Bus 5 to Lund (Skr103, 1½ hours) runs up to 12 times on weekdays (and up to five times on weekends). There's a direct bus to Ystad via Löderup (Skr60, one hour) three to 13 times daily.

Local trains run up to 12 times daily from Simrishamn to Ystad (Skr54, 40 minutes), with connections from Ystad to Malmö and Lund.

For bike hire, try **Hotell Turistgården** (Storgatan 21; per day first/subsequent days Skr100/70; Mon-Sat) or ask at the Simrishamn tourist office. Call **Taxi Österlen** (☎0414-177 77) for a taxi.

Glimmingehus & Skillinge

Sights

Glimmingehus CASTLE
(☎0414-186 20; adult/child Skr60/free; 10am-6pm Jun–mid-Aug, 11am-4pm mid-Apr–May & mid-Aug–Sep, noon-4pm Sat & Sun Oct & early Apr; P) Located around 5km inland, the striking, five-storey Glimmingehus dates from the early 1500s and is one of the best-preserved medieval castles in Sweden. Features include an all-encompassing moat and 11 resident ghosts! Guided tours in English are at 3pm daily in July and August (less frequently the rest of the year). In summer there's a stellar cafe and a program of medieval events and activities: contact the castle for details.

Sleeping

★ **Sjöbacka Gård** B&B €€
(☎0414-310 66; www.sjobacka.se; s/d from Skr764/864; P) This superb accommodation

ALES STENAR

Ales Stenar (tours adult/child Skr20/10; 24hr) FREE has all the mystery of England's Stonehenge, with none of the commercial fanfare. The 67m-long oval of stones, shaped like a boat, was probably constructed around AD 600 for reasons unknown. Limited excavations at the site have revealed no bones; it's possible that this wasn't a grave but a ritual site, with built-in solar calendar (the 'stem' and 'stern' stones point towards the midsummer sunset and midwinter sunrise).

The enigmatic ship is in the middle of a raised field, with an uncannily low and level 360-degree horizon. In the summer, a diminutive roadside tourist office provides information and runs tours.

Free to visit and always open, Ales Stenar lies 19km east of Ystad at Kåseberga. It's badly served by public transport, although bus 392 from Ystad runs daily in summer. At other times, take bus 570 from Ystad to Valleberga kyrka, and then walk 5km south to Kåseberga.

is located in the countryside west of Skillinge, a picturesque fishing village close to Glimmingehus castle. The B&B occupies an atmospheric Scanian farmhouse complete with fireplace, antiques, heaving bookshelves and a gorgeous cobblestone courtyard with pots of flowers and fragrant herbs. There is occasional live music here in summer.

Getting There & Away

Bus 322 (Skr54, 50 minutes) runs up to four times daily between Skillinge and Ystad from mid-June to mid-August only.

Kivik

Rosy apples and burial cists make for strange bedfellows in sleepy, soothing Kivik (north of Simrishamn).

Sights

★Kiviks Musteri ORCHARD, MUSEUM
(☎0414-719 00; www.kiviks.se; ⏱10am-6pm Jun-Aug, shorter hours rest of year; P 🚸) FREE This is a large-scale commercial operation encompassing a small museum, a vast shop selling everything from apple mustard to apple cake, an apple orchard with numerous varieties of (labelled) trees, and a restaurant and cafe (try the baked apple cobbler with custard). You can taste cider from 11am to 3pm daily (no reservations necessary) for Skr40 to Skr70 depending on whether calvados (apple brandy) is on your tipple list. Or splash out on an evening tasting with snacks (Skr395).

Kiviksgraven HISTORIC SITE
(Kungagraven; ☎0414-703 37; adult/child Skr25/free; ⏱10am-6pm mid-May–Aug; P) Believed to be a site of ancient human sacrifice, Kiviksgraven is Sweden's largest Bronze Age grave, dating from around 1000 BC. It's an extraordinary shield-like cairn, about 75m in diameter, which once contained a burial cist and eight engraved slabs. What you see inside are replicas; the tomb was looted in the 18th century.

The on-site cafe sells delicious sweet treats like raspberry crumble.

Sleeping

STF Vandrarhem Hanöbris HOSTEL, HOTEL €
(☎0414-700 50; www.hanobris.se; Eliselundsvägen 6; r hostel/hotel from Skr700/1000; ⏱Apr-Oct; P @ 📶) Offers clean rooms in a 19th-century dance hall given an unfortunate modernist makeover. More expensive hotel rooms are also available.

★Kivik Strand Logi & Café HOTEL, HOSTEL €€
(☎0414-711 95; www.kivikstrand.se; Tittutvägen; d hostel/hotel from Skr880/980; ⏱Apr-Oct; P 📶) Located down by the beach in a meticulously restored 19th-century schoolhouse is a superlative hostel-B&B combo that's more chic boutique than backpacker bolt-hole (think William Morris–style wallpaper, rustic floorboards and a savvy sprinkling of antiques). The communal kitchen is bright and well equipped, while the cafe serves exceptional espresso (and key lime pie).

Stenshuvud National Park

Just 3km south of Kivik, this enchanting **national park** (www.stenshuvud.se) features lush woodland, marshes, sandy beaches and a high headland. Among its more unusual residents are orchids, dormice and tree frogs. Several superb walks in the area include the hike up to a 6th-century ruined hill fort. The long-distance path **Skåneleden** (www.skaneleden.org) also runs through the park, along the coast; the best section is from Vik to Kivik (two or three hours).

The **Naturum** (Visitor Centre; ☎0414-708 82; ⏱11am-4pm mid-Aug–Sep, shorter hours rest of year) is 2.5km from the main road. Rangers lead regular 1½-hour guided tours of the park (adult/child Skr30/15) covering everything from bird life to swamps. Call ahead to arrange an English-language tour.

Kristianstad

☎044 / POP 77,250

Kristianstad (kri-*shan*-sta) is a handsome town with elegant squares, an exquisite cathedral, quirky street sculptures and a sprinkling of eye-catching 18th- and 19th-century buildings.

Known as the most Danish town in Sweden, its construction was ordered by the Danish king Christian IV in 1614. Its rectangular street network still follows the first town plan, although the original walls and bastions have long gone (aside from the **Bastinonen Konungen** rampart, which has been restored). Both a major transport hub and gateway to Skåne's southern coast, it's also the region's administrative and political centre.

Kristianstad

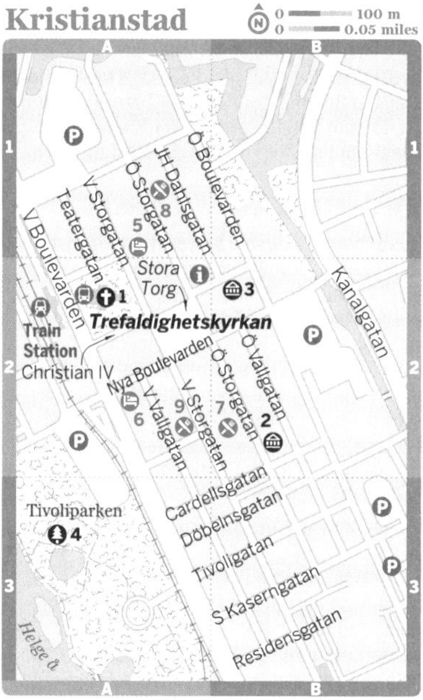

Kristianstad

Top Sights

Sights

Sleeping

Eating

Sights

★Trefaldighetskyrkan CHURCH

(Västra Storgatan 6; 8am-4pm) FREE One of the finest Renaissance churches in Scandinavia, Trefaldighetskyrkan was completed in 1628 when Skåne was still under Danish control. The light-filled interior has many of its original fittings, including wonderfully carved oak pews and an ornate marble-and-alabaster pulpit.

Regionmuseet & Konsthall MUSEUM

(044-13 52 45; www.regionmuseet.se; Stora Torg; 11am-5pm Jun-Aug, from noon Tue-Sun Sep-May) FREE Originally intended as a palace, the building ended up being used as an arsenal. It now houses local-history exhibits and art, handicrafts and silverware displays. **Café Miro** (044-13 60 97; sandwiches & snacks Skr35-75) serves great organic lunches, with herbs and flowers picked from the owner's garden.

Filmmuseet MUSEUM

(044-13 57 29; Östra Storgatan 53; noon-5pm Mon-Fri Jul–mid-Aug, Sun only rest of year) FREE Swedish film-making began in Kristianstad, so it's appropriate that Filmmuseet, Sweden's only film museum, is based here.

Tivoliparken PARK

Riverside Tivoliparken is perfect for a summertime evening stroll or a waffle or two at a waterside cafe.

Tours

Landskapet BOAT TOUR

(044-28 93 95; www.landskapet.se; adult/child Skr195/120; May-Sep;) Organise three-hour guided tours of Kiristianstad's unique wetland area in a safari boat, as well as specialised trips, including goose safaris. Book via phone or website.

Festivals & Events

Kristianstadsdagarna CULTURAL

(www.kristianstadsdagarna.nu) Held annually in July, Kristianstadsdagarna is a week-long festival with music, dance, exhibitions and foodie events, mostly held in Tivoliparken.

Sleeping

Budget accommodation is limited in town.

★Bäckaskog Slott HISTORIC HOTEL €€

(044-530 20; www.backaskogslott.se; Barumsvägen 255, Kiaby; s/d cottage Skr450/700, castle Skr1180/1600; P@) This dreamy castle sits between two lakes 15km north-east of Kristianstad. Built as a monastery in the mid-13th century, it's a stunning spot, with different tiers of accommodation available in various wings and cottages in the grounds. Plus there is a well-priced restaurant. Bus 558 (Skr25, 20 minutes) from Kristianstad bus station to Arkelstorp stops near the castle.

Best Western Hotel Anno 1937 HOTEL €€
(☎044-12 61 50; www.hotelanno.se; Västra Storgatan 17; s/d Skr1095/1345; P @) A rustic beam here, a 17th-century wall there: this hotel has a pleasing sense of pervading history. Opposite the cathedral, its pale-toned rooms are a bit dull, but the amenities are good and include a sauna.

First Hotel Christian IV HISTORIC HOTEL €€
(☎044-20 38 50; www.firsthotels.com; Västra Boulevarden 15; s/d Skr858/975; P @) With parquet floors and stucco ceilings, Hotel Christian IV is certainly grand, if a little worn around the edges. The beautiful turn-of-the-century building was once a bank; one of the vaults is still a place of value: it's home to a vast wine cellar.

Eating & Drinking

The city has a good range of restaurants and cafes.

Conditori Duvander SWEDISH €
(☎044-21 94 18; www.conditoriduvander.se; Hesslegatan 6; mains from Skr90; 7.30am-7pm Mon-Fri, 10am-8pm Sat, 10am-5pm Sun) This historic restaurant and patisserie has a belle époque feel with its marble columns, arched windows, potted palms and classic tilework. Equally enticing for a (Fairtrade) coffee and cake or a light lunch with choices like salads, wraps and pasta plus daily specials.

La Finestra Italiana ITALIAN €
(☎044-20 97 20; www.lafinestraitaliana.se; Vastra Storgatan 30; pasta from Skr70, pizza from Skr75; 11am-4pm Tue-Fri, to 9pm Sat & Sun) Look for the yellow awning and head for the outside terrace (weather permitting), as the interior space is bar stool style and you may be elbowed into a corner by the takeaway crowd. The pizzas and pasta dishes taste pretty authentic for being this far north. Italian espresso also available.

Kippers Källare MEDITERRANEAN €€
(☎044-10 62 00; www.kippers.se; Östra Storgatan 9; mains Skr145-265; noon-3pm & 6-11pm Tue-Sat) Listed in the *White Guide* (Sweden's foodie bible) and sporting a 17th-century arched cellar, this is the most atmospheric restaurant in town. Spanish-style tapas take up much of the menu, but there are more substantial dishes like suckling pig and burgers.

Information

Lilla Torg has banks and ATMs.

Tourist Office (☎044-13 53 35; www.kristianstad.se/turism; Stora Torg; 10am-7pm Mon-Fri, to 3pm Sat, to 2pm Sun mid-Jun–mid-Aug, 10am-5pm Mon-Fri, to 2pm Sat rest of year)

Getting There & Around

Buses depart from the **bus station** (Västra Boulevarden). Frequent SkåneExpressen buses include: bus 1 to Malmö (Skr103, 1½ hours), bus 2 to Lund (Skr103, 1½ hours), bus 3 to Simrishamn (Skr84, 1¼ hours) and bus 4 to Ystad (Skr78, 1½ hours); the latter two services run infrequently on weekends. **Svenska Buss** (www.svenskabuss.se) runs to Karlskrona (Skr120, 1¾ hours), Kalmar (Skr330, three hours and 25 minutes) and Stockholm (Skr420, nine hours and 40 minutes).

Call **Avis** (☎044-10 30 20; Östra Storgatan 10) for car hire.

The train station is across town from the bus station. Trains run daily to Lund (Skr103, one hour) and Malmö (Skr103, 1¼ hours); many services continue on to Copenhagen (Skr200, two hours). Regular trains also run to Helsingborg (Skr103, 1½ hours).

Call **TaxiKurir Kristianstad** (☎044-21 52 70) for a taxi.

Åhus

☎044 / POP 8980

The small coastal town of Åhus (about 18km southeast of Kristianstad) is a popular summer spot thanks to its long sandy **beach**. The area is also known for its **eels**: the Eel Coast runs south from Åhus, and this delicacy is served up boiled, fried, smoked, grilled or cooked on a bed of straw at restaurants and at autumn Eel Feasts throughout the region.

Åhus is home to the **Absolut Vodka distillery** (☎044-28 80 00; www.absolut.com; Köpmannagatan 29), where half a million bottles are produced daily. Free tours run six times daily on weekdays from late June to the end of August. Tickets are available from the company's reception one hour before the tour begins. There is no prebooking and only 19 people are allowed on a single tour.

Landskapet (www.landskapet.se) also runs regular boat trips from Åhus to Kristianstad from late June to the second half of August.

Very close to the harbour is **STF Vandrarhem Åhus** (☎044-24 85 35; www.cigarrkungenshus.se; Stavgatan 3; hostel dm/s/d Skr250/325/500, B&B per person from Skr400; Mar-Nov;

P @), an agreeable youth hostel and B&B based in a 19th-century cigar factory.

The harbour has several good dining options.

The central **tourist office** (044-13 47 77; Järnvägsgatan 7; 10am-7pm Mon-Fri, 9am-5pm Sat, 10am-2pm Sun mid-Jun–Aug, 10am-5pm Mon-Fri mid-Apr–Sep) is well stocked and helpful.

Bus 551 runs several times an hour (roughly hourly on weekends) between Kristianstad and Åhus (Skr40, 30 minutes).

Helsingborg

042 / POP 129,000

At its heart, Helsingborg is a sparkly showcase of rejuvenated waterfront, metro-glam restaurants, lively cobbled streets and lofty castle ruins. With Denmark looking on from a mere 4km across the Öresund, its flouncy, turreted buildings feel like a brazen statement.

It's hardly surprising: Helsingborg's strategic position on the Sound saw it battled over and battered down with tedious regularity during the many Swedish-Danish wars. In 1709 the Danes invaded Skåne but were finally defeated the following year in a battle just outside Helsingborg. One wonders what those armies would make of the over 14 million annual passengers who now traverse the Sound with seasoned nonchalance.

Sights

Town Centre

Small and specialist museums (about the fire brigade, medical history, sport, schools and military defence) dot the town; contact the tourist office for details.

★ **Dunkers Kulturhus** MUSEUM
(www.dunkerskulturhus.se; Kungsgatan 11; exhibitions adult/child Skr75/free; 10am-6pm Mon-Fri, to 8pm Thu, to 5pm Sat & Sun) Just north of the transport terminal, the crisp white Dunkers Kulturhus houses the main tourist office, an interesting town museum and temporary exhibitions (admission includes entry to both), plus a concert hall, an urbane cafe and a design-savvy gift shop. The building's creator, Danish architect Kim Utzon, is the son of Sydney Opera House architect Jørn Utzon.

From here, saunter along **Norra Hamnen** (North Harbour), where apartments, restaurants and bars meet yachts and preened locals in one rather successful harbour-redevelopment project.

> **KULTURKORT**
>
> If you are planning on visiting Helsingborg's main sights, consider investing Skr120 in a **Kulturkort** (www.mittkulturkort.se), which can save you close to Skr200 in admission costs over two days. Purchase at the tourist office.

★ **Kärnan** RUIN
(adult/child Skr40/20; 10am-6pm Jun-Aug, closed Mon rest of year) Dramatic steps and archways lead up from Stortorget to the square tower Kärnan (34m), all that remains of the medieval castle. The castle became Swedish property during the 17th-century Danish-Swedish War, and was mostly demolished once the fighting stopped. The tower was restored from dereliction in 1894, and the view is regal indeed. There are plans to mount a permanent exhibition about the history of the castle.

Mariakyrkan CHURCH
(042-37 28 30; Mariatorget; 8am-6pm Mon-Fri, 9am-6pm Sat & Sun) FREE In the old town, the 15th-century Gothic brick Mariakyrkan has a magnificent interior, including a triptych dating from 1450 and an ornate Renaissance pulpit.

Rådhuset HISTORIC BUILDING
(Town Hall; Stortorget; 9am-1pm Mon-Fri) FREE The mighty Rådhuset was completed in 1897 in neo-Gothic style and contains stained-glass scenes illustrating Helsingborg's history.

Fredriksdal & Sofiero

Just 2km northeast of the centre, the Fredriksdal area is well worth a visit. Take bus 8 to the Zoégas bus stop.

★ **Fredriksdals Friluftsmuseum** MUSEUM
(www.fredriksdal.se; off Hävertgatan; May-Sep adult/child Skr70/free, Oct-Mar free; 10am-6pm May-Sep, shorter hours rest of year; P) One of Sweden's best open-air museums, based around an 18th-century manor house (not open to the public), the houses and shops you see here once graced the streets of central Helsingborg; they were moved here, brick for brick, in the 1960s. Thankfully, this is no contrived theme park; the whole place

Helsingborg

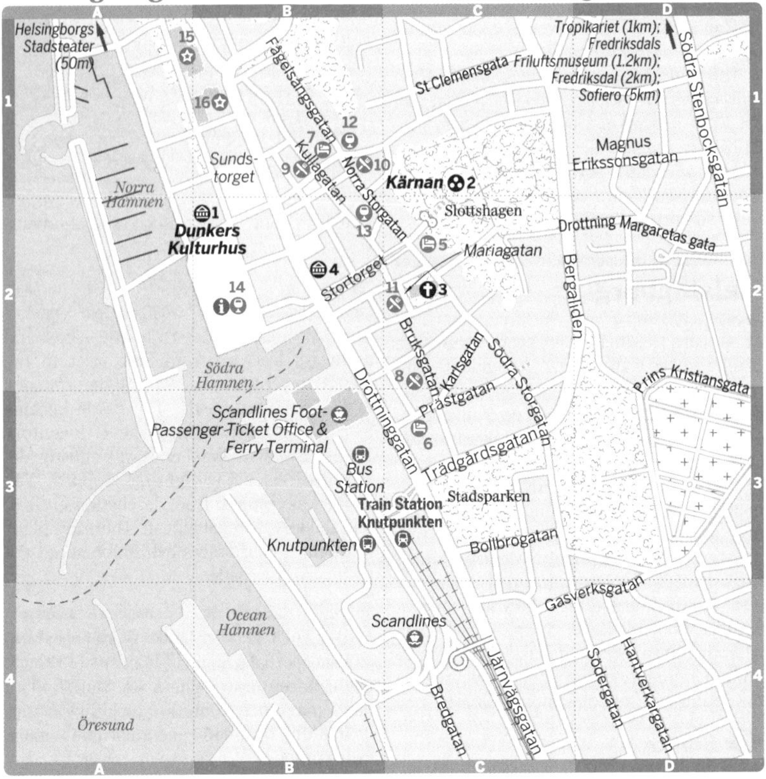

is charming and there's plenty of scope for souvenir shopping at the art and craft workshops. There are also herb, rose and vegetable gardens and blissfully leafy grounds.

Local wildflowers grace the beautiful botanic gardens, and there's a summer program of activities and performances in the French baroque open-air theatre. The museum entrance, located just off Hävertgatan, is an easy 250m walk south of the Zoégas bus stop on Ängelsholmsvägen.

Sofiero GARDENS

(042-13 74 00; www.sofiero.se; Sofierovägen; adult/child Skr100/free; park 10am-6pm, palace & orangery 11am-6pm; P) About 5km north of the town centre, Sofiero is an impressive former royal summer residence and park with wonderful rhododendrons (best seen in full bloom in May and June) and top-notch summer concerts by the like of Bob Dylan (in 2014). Bus 8 runs out here.

Tropikariet ZOO

(042-13 00 35; www.tropikariet.com; Hävertgatan 21; adult/child Skr110/55; 11am-5pm Tue-Sun; P) Tropikariet is a semi-zoo, with a reptile house, an aquarium and exotic furry critters housed in faux-natural habitats.

Sleeping

Råå Vallar Camping CAMPGROUND €

(042-18 26 00; http://raavallar.nordiccamping.se; Kustgatan; sites/cabins Skr195/460; P) About 5km south of the city centre, by Öresund, this is a great place to hammer down those tent pegs: huge and well equipped, with shop, cafe and sandy beach. Take bus 8 from the town hall.

★ **Clarion Collection Hotel Helsing** HOTEL €€

(042-37 18 00; www.choice.se; Stortorget 20; s/d Skr800/1050; P @) In an elegant, early-20th-century building at the foot of the stairs

Helsingborg

to the Kärnan tower, Hotel Helsing boasts distinct, boutique-style rooms with underfloor heating, a spa and a popular restaurant and nightclub. A buffet dinner is included in the room cost, a standard and great-value perk of the Clarion Collection chain.

Try for a room on the southwest corner for a grand view down Stortorget and across to Denmark.

Hotel Maria HOTEL €€
(042-24 99 40; www.hotelmaria.se; Mariagatan 8A; s/d from Skr800/1050; P @ wifi) Tucked away behind Olsons Skafferi restaurant, Hotel Maria is utterly inspired, with each room flaunting a different historical style. Themes include national romantic, art deco and '70s disco. Beds are divinely comfy, the staff is friendly and there's a tapas bar downstairs.

Hotell Viking HOTEL €€
(042-14 44 20; www.hotellviking.se; Fågelsångsgatan 1; s/d from Skr940/1250; P @ wifi) Trendy and urbane, this hipster hotel sets the tone from the get-go with velvet cushions, modern bookshelves and brass candlesticks decorating the lobby. Rooms are similarly chic and stylish, although they do vary considerably: some are swing-a-cat size, while the most luxurious has a hot tub.

Hotell Linnéa HOTEL €€
(042-37 24 00; www.hotell-linnea.se; Prästgatan 4; s/d Skr700/1395; P @ wifi) Linnéa is super central and has a pretty, small courtyard for catching the rays, as well as a cosy library. The carpeted, mildly corporate-looking rooms are spacious and well equipped with kettle and minibar.

Eating

Helsingborg boasts an appetising selection of restaurants and cafes, although a fair few close on Sunday.

For quick snacks, try the Knutpunkten (p198) complex on the seafront.

★ **Holy Greens** HEALTH FOOD €
(042-12 40 40; Nedre Långvinkelsgatan 7; mains from Skr69; 7.30am-6.30pm Mon-Fri, 11am-4pm Sat;) The key word here is fresh. Choose from set salad combos like Asian Greens, Green Mexican, Salmon & Avocado and Nutty Chicken with various dressing choices. Then boost up the healthy-eating factor a notch by ordering a fresh fruit smoothie with ingredients like avocado, blackberries and mango (but not combined!).

Koppi CAFE €
(042-13 30 33; www.koppi.se; Norra Storgatan 16; sandwiches/salads Skr60/70; 9am-6pm Mon-Fri, 10am-5pm Sat) This hip cafe-microroastery is your best bet for top-notch coffee. The savvy young owners sell their own roasted beans, alongside scrumptious edibles like fresh salads and gourmet ciabatta.

Globe Trotter ASIAN €€
(042-37 18 00; Clarion Collection Hotel Helsing, Stortorget 20; tapas Skr39, mains from Skr100; 5-10pm Sun-Thu, to 1am Fri & Sat; wifi) These beautifully presented gastro-Asian tapas and mains hit the spot and, combined with the mood music and superb Stortorget people-watching potential from the terrace, make it hard to get a table at weekends.

Ebbas Fik CAFE €€
(www.ebbasfik.se; Bruksgatan 20; mains from Skr115; ⏰9am-6pm Mon-Fri, to 4pm Sat; 👪) It's still 1955 at this kitsch-tastic cafe, complete with jukebox (Skr1), retro petrol pump and hamburgers made to Elvis' recipe. You can also buy '50s memorabilia here, ranging from vinyl records to Enid Blyton books (in Swedish!). The extensive cafe menu also includes sandwiches, baked potatoes, Coca-Cola floats and American-style pie.

Pålsjö Krog EUROPEAN €€
(☎042-14 97 30; www.palsjokrog.com; Drottninggatan 151; mains from Skr190; ⏰11.30am-2.30 & 6-10pm Mon-Fri, from noon Sat & Sun) Located near Sofiero, around 3km north of the city centre in the Pålsjö area, this is a great old seaside inn revamped into an elegant nosh spot. There's a fabulous verandah with stirling views, accompanied by tasty, bistro-style dishes like fish soup or pepper steak.

Olsons Skafferi ITALIAN €€€
(☎042-14 07 80; www.olsonsskafferi.se; Mariagatan 6; mains from Skr225; ⏰11am-5.30pm & 7.30-11pm Mon-Sat) Olsons is a super little spot, with alfresco seating on the pedestrian square right in front of Mariakyrkan. It doubles as an Italian deli and cafe, with rustic good looks, spangly chandeliers and pasta that would make Bologna proud. Be sure to finish things off in proper Italian fashion with Vino Santo and *cantuccini* (almond biscotti). Lunch is more economical.

Drinking & Nightlife

There are several good pubs and bars around town.

Madame Mustache BAR
(www.madamemoustache.se; Norra Storgatan 9; ⏰5pm-1.30am Thu-Sat) Classic bar in a historic half-timbered building; sitting rooms are suitably 'period' with chintzy furniture, shelves of antiquated books, museum-piece wirelesses and similar. Too stuffy sounding? Then head out to the streetside courtyard centred on a bubbling fountain.

Bara Vara BAR
(☎042-24 52 52; www.baravara.eu; Fågelsångsgatan 2; ⏰11.30am-2pm & 5.30pm-1am Tue-Fri, 6pm-1am Sat; 📶) A fashionable bar with outside seating, punchy colourful decor and a great wine list. Also a reputable restaurant.

Helsing COCKTAIL BAR
(www.helsingbar.se; Södra Storgatan 1; ⏰11am-10pm Mon-Thu, to midnight Fri & Sat) Chic bar with an extensive selection of cocktails and an ideal people-watching location.

Tivoli CLUB
(www.thetivoli.nu; Kungsgatan 1; ⏰11pm-late Wed-Sat) Down by the harbour, this is an enduring nightclub attracting a younger foot-tapping crowd with occasional live music.

Entertainment

Helsingborgs Stadsteater THEATRE
(☎042-10 68 10; www.helsingborgsstadsteater.se; Karl Johans gata 1) Helsingborgs Stadsteater has regular drama performances. Info and tickets are available from the tourist office.

Konserthus CLASSICAL MUSIC
(☎042-10 42 70; www.helsingborgskonserthus.se; Drottninggatan 19) Regularly plays host to Helsingborg's Symphony Orchestra. Information and tickets are available from the tourist office.

Information

The **Knutpunkten** (Drottninggatan) complex on the seafront has currency-exchange facilities and ATMs, as well as left-luggage lockers. For banks, head to Stortorget.

Tourist Office (☎042-10 43 50; www.helsingborg.se; Kungsgatan 11; ⏰10am-6pm Mon-Fri, to 8pm Thu, to 5pm Sat & Sun) Well stocked with a gift shop and conveniently located in the Dunkers Kulturhus museum.

Getting There & Away

The main transport hub is the waterfront Knutpunkten complex.

BOAT

Knutpunkten is the terminal for the frequent **Scandlines** (☎042-18 61 00; www.scandlines.se) car ferry to Helsingør (one way with 6m car Skr420, no bookings without a vehicle).

BUS

The bus terminal is at ground level in Knutpunkten. Regional Skånetrafiken buses dominate, but long-distance services are offered by **Swebus Express** (☎0771-21 82 18; www.swebus.se).

Swebus runs north to Göteborg, continuing on to Oslo, and south to Malmö. It also operates services northeast to Stockholm via Jönköping and Norrköping. Fares to Stockholm cost around Skr539 (7½ hours), to Göteborg Skr130 (three hours) and to Oslo Skr379 (seven hours).

TRAIN

Underground platforms in Knutpunkten serve SJ, Pågatågen and Öresundståg trains, which depart daily for Stockholm (Skr695, five to seven hours), Göteborg (Skr285, 2½ to three hours) and nearby towns including Lund (Skr84, 25 minutes), Malmö (Skr103, 40 minutes), Kristianstad (Skr103, one hour and 20 minutes) and Halmstad (Skr125, one hour), as well as Copenhagen (Denmark) and Oslo (Norway).

❶ Getting Around

Bike hire (per day/week Skr120/550) is available at **Travelshop** (☑ 042-12 70 20; www.travelshop.se; Knutpunkten; ☺ 9.30am-7pm), located at the bus station at Knutpunkten. Town buses cost Skr17 and run from Rådhuset (the town hall). Contact **Avis** (☑ 042-15 70 80; www.avisworld.com; Angelholmsvagen 36) for car hire, and **Taxi Helsingborg** (☑ 042-18 02 00) for cabs.

KULLA ON HORSEBACK

One great way to experience the broad fields, woodlands and coastal scenery of the Kulla Peninsula is on horseback. There are a few farms to choose from, running trips ranging from a few hours to several days. **Kullabergs Islandshäster** (☑ 042-33 52 44; www.kullabergsislandshastar.com) does 1½- and 2½-hour trips (Skr500/650), or there's a four-hour lunch expedition to Mölle (Skr1050). **Hippo Tours** (☑ 042-88 04 66; www.hippotours.se) focuses on luxury weekend getaways (Skr3500), including a night at the historic boutique Hotel Rusthållargården (p200) in the picture-perfect fishing village of Arild. Both farms use smooth-gaited Icelandic horses.

Kulla Peninsula

☑ 042

A seductive brew of golden light, artisan studios and sleepy fishing villages, Skåne's northwest coast is a perfect place to spend a few soothing days.

❶ Getting There & Away

Bus 220 runs at least hourly from Helsingborg to Höganäs (Skr48, 40 minutes). From there, bus 222 runs every hour or two to Mölle (Skr32, 20 minutes), while bus 223 runs to Arild (Skr32, 20 minutes).

Höganäs

Gateway to the Kulla Peninsula, the coal-mining town of Höganäs (21km north of Helsingborg) harbours a few cultural gems that are worth stopping for.

◉ Sights

Pick up the free guide to Höganäs' impressive posse of public art, liberally sprinkled around town, at the Höganäs Tourist Office (p200). Two of the most entertaining works are a family of pigs on Storgatan and a levitating dog on Köpmansgatan.

★ **Krapperups Slott** HISTORIC BUILDING
(☑ 042-34 41 90; www.krapperup.se; Krapperups Kyrkovägen 13; ☺ garden year-round, cafe 11am-5pm daily mid-Jun–mid-Aug, 11am-5pm Sat & Sun rest of year, closed Jan; P 🚻) **FREE** One of Sweden's oldest estates and home to an exquisite garden, the manor has an exterior

inlaid with giant white stars representing the coat of arms of the Gyllenstierna family, who lived here for centuries. One-hour tours of the building (Skr100; Easter to late June and mid-September to mid-October) can be booked by emailing kulturintendenten@krapperup.se. The grounds also house an art gallery and local museum, a cafe and a gift shop.

The converted stables play host to the annual **Musik i Kullabygden** (☑ tickets 0771-70 70 70; www.musikikullabygd.se; ☺ Jul), a week-long music festival spanning folk, jazz, classical and opera.

Höganäs Saltglaserat ARTS CENTRE
(☑ 042-32 76 55; www.hoganassaltglaserat.se; Bruksgatan 36; ☺ 10am-6pm Mon-Fri, 11am-4pm Sat & Sun Jun-Aug, 10am-4pm Fri, 11am-3pm Sat & Sun rest of year; P) This is Sweden's most famous pottery factory, established in 1835. Its trademark brown salt-glazed pottery is a veritable national icon and its famous Höganäskrus (little jug) is mentioned in the opening line of August Strindberg's novel *Natives of Hemsö*.

Höganäs Museum & Konsthall MUSEUM
(☑ 042-34 13 35; www.hoganasmuseum.se; Polhemsgatan 1; adult/child Skr50/free; ☺ 1-5pm Tue-Sun, closed Jan) Art lovers should head to this fascinating museum where the highlight is a brilliant collection of witty, exquisitely humane sculptures from home-grown artist Åke Holm.

Information

Höganäs Tourist Office (042-33 77 74; www.hoganas.se; Centralgatan 20; 9am-6pm Mon-Fri, 10am-2pm Sat & Sun mid-Jun–Aug, shorter hours rest of year) The small tourist office is a good source of information on the town, as well as the entire Kullabygden area.

Mölle & Surrounds

The steep, picket fence–pretty village of **Mölle** is the area's main tourist centre. It also enjoys a scandalous past. In the 19th century it was one of the first seaside resorts to encourage mixed bathing, much to the horror of the country...and to the delight of racy Berliners, who flocked here on a direct rail link from the German capital.

A novel way of exploring the area around Mölle is on an **Icelandic horse**, one of the world's gentlest, most smooth-gated equine breeds.

Five kilometres east of Mölle, the fishing village (and artists' colony) of **Arild** lays on the charm with its petite pastel houses, teeny-tiny harbour and supporting cast of roses, hollyhocks, butterflies and coastal nature reserves.

It is worth noting that accommodation in the area generally isn't cheap and fills up fast.

Sights & Activities

Kullaberg Nature Reserve NATURE RESERVE
(http://k.inventit.dk; road toll Skr40) This magnificent nature reserve occupies the tip of the Kulla Peninsula and houses Scandinavia's brightest lighthouse, **Kullens fyr** (042-34 70 56; www.kullensfyr.se; Kulla Peninsula; adult/child Skr20/10; 11am-5pm), the light of which can be seen from 50km away. The reserve offers a dramatic spectacle of plunging cliffs, windswept vegetation and incredible sunsets, and a number of **hiking trails** crisscross the area, leading to ancient caves, tide pools and secluded swimming spots.

The reserve's website is a good place to get an idea of the available activities.

Kullabergsguiderna ADVENTURE SPORTS
(073-988 10 77; www.kullabergsguiderna.se; Kullens fyr, Mölle; daily Jul–mid-Aug, less frequently rest of year;) This company organises a wide range of activities. You can go on a one-hour **caving expedition** (adult/child Skr150/50) with experienced guides (starting from Naturum at the Kullaberg Nature Reserve) or opt for **abseiling** (Skr200) down the primordial cliffs. Alternatively, why not take to the seas with a **porpoise safari** (adult/child Skr395/265)?

Kullen Dyk DIVING
(0411-34 77 14; www.kullendyk.nu; dives from Skr600) The helpful crew at Kullen Dyk, 2km southeast of Mölle (adjacent to the First Camp Mölle campground), can get you flippered and submerged.

ZANY SCULPTURES

Looking like a cubby house gone mad, the driftwood sculpture **Nimis** and its younger concrete sibling **Arx** stand on a beach on the Kulla Peninsula's northern side. Created without permission by eccentric artist Lars Vilks, their existence has sparked several court cases between Vilks and the county council, not to mention the odd fire and chainsaw attack. In 1996 the crafty Vilks founded micronation **Ladonia** (www.ladonia.org) at the site, effectively turning his works into protected 'national monuments'. In 2011 the coronation of Queen Carolyn I took place. If you are interested in applying for citizenship (as 4000 Pakistanis apparently were...), check out the website.

Sleeping & Eating

First Camp Mölle CAMPGROUND €
(042-34 73 84; www.firstcamp.se/molle; Möllehässle; powered sites from Skr275, 4-person cabins from Skr590; P) This friendly campground is a good bet. It's 2km southeast of Mölle, and you can hire bikes here for exploring the area (Skr60 per day).

Strand Hotell HOTEL €€
(042-34 61 00; www.strand-arild.se; Stora Vägen 42, Arild; d from Skr1250; P@) A civilised option in picture-perfect Arild that oozes old-world appeal. Four of the elegant rooms in the old building boast balconies with sea views, while the modern annexe features long, narrow rooms with terraces and sea views for all. There's a fine in-house restaurant here, too.

★**Hotel Rusthållargården** HISTORIC HOTEL €€€
(042-34 65 30; www.rusthallargarden.com; Utsikten 1, Arild; d from Skr1950; P@) This lovely hotel has been managed by the same family since 1904 and is housed in a charming white and blue-trimmed farm building

that dates back to 1675. Rooms in the main building are comfortable and quaint – think flowered wallpaper and wooden floors – and half have sea views. There's a swimming pool and an excellent, mostly organic, breakfast.

Grand Hotel Mölle HOTEL €€€
(☑042-36 22 30; www.grand-molle.se; Bökebollsvägen 11, Mölle; s/d from Skr1350/1790; ⓟ @ 🛜) Exuding faded grandeur, this majestic hotel sits regally above Mölle. Rooms are an agreeable blend of modern Scandi style and nautical undertones. Go for the splurge with a room in the main building sporting a sea view, balcony and hot tub (doubles Skr3790). There's also an in-house gourmet restaurant.

★ Flickorna Lundgren CAFE €
(☑042-34 60 44; www.fl-lundgren.se; Flickorna Lundgren pa Skäret, Skäretvägen 19; pastries from Skr30; ⊙10am-6pm Jun-Aug, to 8pm mid-Jul–mid-Aug; ⓟ) Signposted off the main road between Arild and Jonstorp, this is a huge, justifiably famous cafe in a gorgeous garden setting. Grab a large plate of pastries and your copper kettle, and lose yourself in a cloud of flowers. It's wildly popular, so be prepared for crowds during the peak months of July and August.

Ellens Café i Ransvik CAFE €
(☑042-34 76 66; www.ransvik.se; sandwiches from Skr50; ⊙11am-5pm) A longstanding favourite, this casual place overlooks a popular bathing spot about 1km beyond the Kullaberg toll booth. Munch happily on sandwiches, salads and the scrumptious carrot cake before taking a dip from the rocks.

Mölle Krukmakeri & Café CAFE €
(☑042-34 79 91; www.mollekrukmakeri.se; Mölle Hamnallé 9; sandwiches from Skr75; ⊙10am-6pm Wed-Sun mid-Jun–late Aug, Sat & Sun late Aug–mid-Jun) Just up from the harbour in Mölle, this cosy cafe and ceramics gallery is run by potter Lisa Wohlfart. Stock up on her sleek, contemporary wares or simply tuck into fantastic homemade grub like tomato and spinach soup and hazelnut cinnamon scrolls.

ⓘ Information

Naturum (☑042-34 70 56; ⊙11am-6pm daily Jun-Aug, shorter hours rest of year) Located in the Kullaberg Nature Reserve, Naturum has information on the area's flora, fauna and geology and can also arrange guided walks.

BLEKINGE

With its long coastline and safe harbours, Blekinge's past and present are faithfully fastened to the sea. Sweden and Denmark once squabbled over the area, a trump card in power games over the Baltic. The region's own prized possession is the Unesco-lauded naval town of Karlskrona, famed for its baroque design. The region's second-largest town, Karlshamn, was the exit point for thousands of 19th-century emigrants bound for America. Beyond the urban centres is a low-key landscape of fish-filled rivers and lakes, brooding forests and a stunning archipelago fit for lazy island-hopping.

Karlskrona

☑0455 / POP 62,340
This handsome military-base town is included on the Unesco World Heritage list for its impressive collection of 17th- and 18th-century naval architecture.

It was the failed Danish invasion of Skåne in 1679 that sparked Karlskrona's conception, when King Karl XI decided that a southern naval base was needed for better control over the Baltic Sea. Almost immediately, it became Sweden's third-biggest city. Much of the town is still a military base, so for many sights you'll need to book a tour at the tourist office.

◉ Sights & Activities

★ Fortifications HISTORIC BUILDING
Karlskrona's star is the extraordinary offshore **Kungsholms Fort** (guided tours adult/under 17yr Skr210/50; ⊙10am-2pm Jun-Aug), built in 1680 to defend the town. Two-hour guided **boat tours** (adult/child Skr220/free; ⊙10am mid-Jun–Aug) depart from Fisktorget, the tourist office or the Marinmuseum. Tickets must be prebooked through the tourist office. Another option is the boat operated by **Affärsverken** (www.affarsverken.se; adult/child Skr90/50; ⊙Jul & Aug), which runs from Fisktorget and circles the fort in June, July and August (adult/child Skr90/50); inform the tourist office of your visit in advance if you choose this second option.

Bristling with cannons, the tower Drottningskärs Kastell on the island of Aspö was described by Admiral Nelson of the British Royal Navy as 'impregnable'. You can visit it on an Äspoleden, a free car ferry

Karlskrona

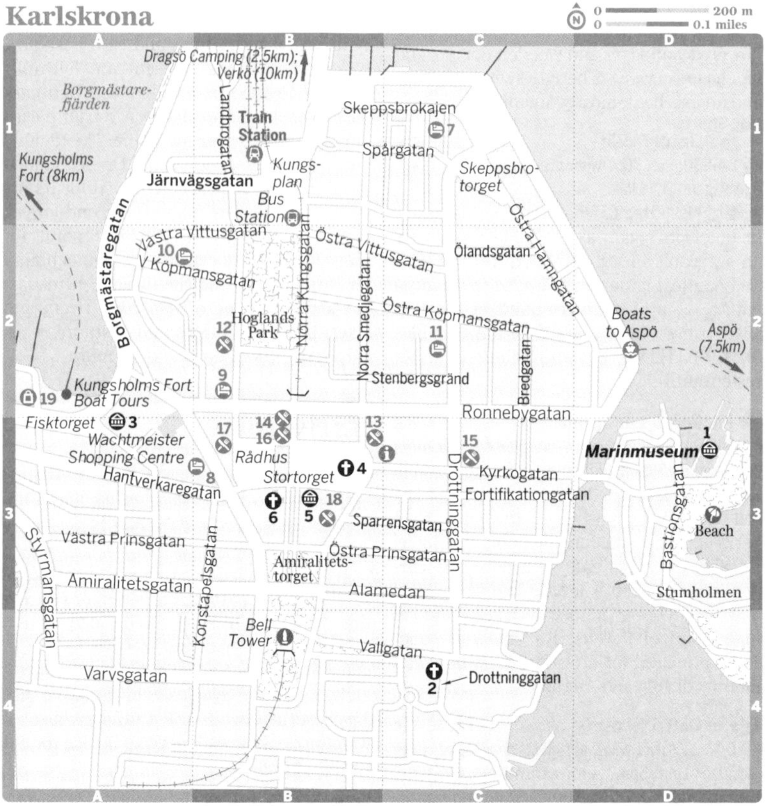

that runs up to twice hourly in July and August from Handelshamnen, north of the Marinmuseum.

★ Marinmuseum MUSEUM
(www.marinmuseum.se; Stumholmen; adult/child Skr100/free; ⏲10am-6pm Jun-Aug, shorter hours rest of year; P) The striking Marinmuseum is the national naval museum. Dive in for reconstructions of a battle deck in wartime, a hall full of fantastic figureheads, piles of model boats, and even some of the real thing – such as a minesweeper, the HMS *Västervik* and Sweden's royal sloop. There is also a pleasant **restaurant** (mains from Skr100).

Blekinge Museum MUSEUM
(www.blekingemuseum.se; Fisktorget; adult/child Skr60/free; ⏲10am-6pm Jun-Aug, noon-5pm Tue-Sun rest of year) This evocative museum explores the local fishing, boat-building and quarrying trades. The most captivating part is Grevagården, an impressively preserved 18th-century abode crammed with thousands of vintage objects, from fans and fashion to bizarre wax models of syphilis-plagued faces. Topping it off is a petite baroque garden and an inviting cafe.

Museum Leonardo da Vinci Ideale MUSEUM
(Kulenovic Collection; www.museumldv.com; Stortorget 5; ⏲10am-6pm Mon-Sat, 11am-6pm Sun) FREE Showcases the famous Kulenovic private collection of original art. There's also a great cafe that hosts live music in summer.

Stortorget SQUARE
Karlskrona's monumental square, Stortorget, was planned to rival Europe's best. Alas, the funds ran out, resulting in a somewhat odd mix of grand architectural gestures and humble stand-ins. Dominating the square are the courthouse, along with the baroque church **Fredrikskyrkan** (⏲11am-4pm Mon-Fri, 9.30am-2pm Sat) FREE and **Trefaldighet-**

Karlskrona

skyrkan (Trinity Church; ⊙11am-4pm Mon-Fri, 9.30am-2pm Sat) **FREE**, inspired by Rome's Pantheon.

Amiralitetskyrkan CHURCH
(Vallgatan 11; ⊙11am-4pm Mon-Fri, 9.30am-2pm Sat) **FREE** Sweden's oldest wooden church is the stocky Amiralitetskyrkan, with a gorgeous pastel interior. Outside, the wooden statue Old Rosenbom raises his hat to charitable visitors.

🏳 Tours

Pick a sunny summer afternoon for a tour around Karlskrona's archipelago, made up of almost 1000 islands. A three-hour tour costs Skr150/70 per adult/child. Book through the tourist office or log onto the Affärsverken (p201) website for timetables and information.

Enquire at the tourist office about two-hour guided tours around the old naval shipyard at Lindholmen or of the museums.

🛏 Sleeping

Dragsö Camping CAMPGROUND **€**
(☑0455-153 54; www.dragso.se; Dragsövägen; sites/d/2-bed cabins from Skr250/500/575; ⊙Apr–mid-Sep; P) This large, good-looking campground, 2.5km northwest of town, is situated on a scenic bay. Facilities include boat and bicycle hire, plus a Karlskrona-themed mini-golf course. Bus 7 stops about 1km short of the campground.

STF Vandrarhem Trossö Karlskrona HOSTEL **€**
(☑0455-100 20; www.karlskronavandrarhem.se; Drottninggatan 39; dm/s/d from Skr160/280/370;

📶) Modern, clean and friendly, this hostel has a laundry, a TV room, a backyard for kids to play in and handy parking across the street.

Hotell Aston HOTEL **€€**
(☑0455-194 70; www.hotellaston.se; Landbrogatan 1; s/d Skr795/995; P📶) Third-floor Hotell Aston and its sister, Hotell Conrad (☑0455-36 32 00; www.hotelconrad.se; Västra Köpmansgatan 12; s/d Skr750/895; 📶), are both smart central options. Aston has spacious rooms, with simple, modern furnishings (but six flights of stairs). Conrad is flashier, and takes up three buildings, with decorations based on the era of the building: '70s, '80s and 'culture' from the late 1700s. Both serve an excellent breakfast.

First Hotel Ja HOTEL **€€**
(☑0455-555 60; www.firsthotels.se; Borgmästaregatan 13; s/d Skr790/990; P@📶) Karlskrona's top slumber spot boasts fashionable rooms with stripey wallpaper and decorative fabrics. Hotel perks include a sauna, a bar-restaurant and a full-blown breakfast buffet served in a pleasant atrium. There are also several more decorative 'Ladies Rooms', exclusively for women.

Clarion Collection Hotel Carlscrona HOTEL **€€**
(☑0455-36 15 00; www.hotelcarlscrona.se; Skeppsbrokajen; s/d incl evening buffet Skr1020/1275; P📶) Handy for the train station, this chain hotel combines original rustic beams and slinky furniture in the bar, and navy blues, greys and handsome wooden furnishings in its stately rooms.

Eating & Drinking

The ICA supermarket and Systembolaget are in the **Wachtmeister Galleria** (www.wachtmeistergalleria.se; Borgmästaregatan 13; ⏲9am-6pm) shopping centre.

Nya Skafferiet DELI €
(☎0455-171 78; www.nyaskafferiet.se; Rädhusgatan 9; buffet Skr90; ⏲9am-6pm Mon-Fri, to 3pm Sat) Worldly Mediterranean cafe right behind the main square. There is a superb lunch buffet, as well as a well-stocked deli offering a bounty of cheeses, charcuterie, breads and excellent coffee.

Glassiärens Glassbar ICE CREAM €
(Stortorget 4; cones from Skr25; ⏲9am-6pm May-Sep) The queues at this legendary ice-cream parlour are matched by the mammoth serves, piled high in a heavenly waffle cone. Go for three flavours if you can. Memories are made of this...

Lennarths Konditori BAKERY €
(☎0455-31 03 32; Norra Kungsgatan 3; cakes from Skr25; ⏲8am-6pm Mon-Fri, to 3pm Sat) Old-school bakery with a fantastic tubular retro ceiling, two outdoor terraces, and calorific treats; try the delectable (if unfortunately named) *munk* – think doughnut meets apple strudel.

Café Tre G CAFE €
(☎0455-31 03 33; Landbrogatan 9; snacks from Skr75; ⏲7am-9pm Mon-Fri, 9am-6pm Sat & Sun; 👪) This cafe is a hit with everyone from prim pensioners to indie types. Fill up on such offerings as baked potatoes, quiche and pasta salads, plus perfect pralines, pastries and muffins. It also has a raw-food menu with beetroot burgers (and similar), and there are good choices for kids.

Montmartre ITALIAN €
(Ronnebygatan 18; pizza from Skr75, pasta from Skr79; ⏲4-11pm Mon-Fri, from 1pm Sat & Sun) The atmospheric Montmartre evokes a French bistro with its wine-red drapes, tasselled lampshades and oil paintings. The menu hops over the border, however, with excellent pastas and 36-plus choices of pizza.

Nivå INTERNATIONAL €€
(☎0455-103 71; www.niva.nu; Norra Kungsgatan 3; mains from Skr190; ⏲5-11pm Mon-Thu, 4pm-1am Fri, noon-1am Sat) Just off Stortorget, this steakhouse has a variety of light, well-priced dishes (nachos, burgers, salads), as well as heartier meals from the grill and some veggie options like a tasty haloumi burger. It's also a popular evening bar; the doors stay open until at least 1am.

Två Rum & Kök EUROPEAN €€€
(☎0455-104 22; www.2rok.se; Södra Smedjegatan 3; fondue minimum 2 people Skr279, mains Skr200-298; ⏲5-10.30pm Mon-Sat) This gourmet dinner spot is best known for its magnificent fondue, with flavours ranging from French to barbecue.

Information

ATMs are in the Wachtmeister Galleria on Borgmästeregatan.

Tourist Office (☎0455-30 34 90; www.visitkarlskrona.se; Stortorget 2; ⏲9am-7pm Jun-Aug, shorter hours rest of year) Internet access and super-helpful staff.

Getting There & Around

Ronneby airport (☎010-109 54 00; www.swedavia.com) is 33km west of Karlskrona; the Flygbuss leaves from Stortorget (adult/child Skr90/45). SAS flies to Stockholm Arlanda daily, and **Blekingeflyg** (☎0457-62 99 99; www.blekingeflyg.se) flies to Stockholm Bromma (from Skr495, 50 minutes) between one and four times daily.

Stena Line (p332) ferries to Gdynia (Poland) depart from Verkö, 10km east of Karlskrona.

The bus and train stations are just north of central Karlskrona. **Blekingetrafiken** (☎0455-569 00; www.blekingetrafiken.se) runs public transport in the Blekinge region.

Svenska Buss (www.svenskabuss.se) runs daily from Malmö to Stockholm, calling at Kristianstad (Skr420, 2¼ hours) and Karlskrona (Skr420, 3½ hours).

Direct trains run at least 13 times daily to Karlshamn (Skr85, one hour) and Kristianstad (Skr158, two hours), at least 10 times to Lund (Skr222, two hours and 40 minutes) and Malmö (Skr221, three hours).

For a taxi, call **Zon Taxi** (☎0455-230 50; www.zontaxi.se).

Karlshamn

☎0454 / POP 31,000

You'd never guess that quiet Karslhamn, with its quaint cobbled streets, old wooden houses and art-nouveau architecture, was once so wicked. Alcoholic drinks, tobacco, snuff and playing cards were produced in great quantities here, and it was a major 19th-century smugglers' den. It was also the port from where many Swedes left for

America. One of the biggest free festivals, the **Baltic Festival** (Östersjöfestivalen; www.ostersjofestivalen.se; ⏲Jul) sees a quarter of a million people roll in for bands and a carnival parade.

Sights

Utvandrar-Monumentet MONUMENT
This poignant monument commemorates all America-bound emigrants. Its figures are characters from Vilhelm Moberg's classic *The Emigrants:* Karl Oscar, looking forward to the new country, and Kristina, looking back towards her beloved Duvemåla.

Karlshamns Kulturkvarter MUSEUM
(☎0454-148 68; Vinkelgatan 8; admission Skr20; ⏲1-5pm Tue-Sun Jun-Sep, noon-4pm Mon-Fri rest of year) The 'culture quarter' museum has interesting information about Karlhamn's history of producing tobacco and *punsch* (strong alcoholic punch), as well as a replica of the city's liquor factory, complete with barrels, bottles and machinery. Beautiful 18th-century houses include manor and merchant house **Skottsbergska Gården** (admission Skr20) and **Holländarhuset** (Dutchman's house).

Sleeping & Eating

Hotell Bode HOTEL €
(☎0454-315 00; www.hotellbode.se; Fogdelyckeg 28; r from Skr750; 📶) A sound, central choice providing you don't mind the lack of lift or sharing a shower (rooms have en-suite toilets). The homey rooms are spacious, with comfy chairs, good lighting and leafy plants.

First Hotel Carlshamn HOTEL €€
(☎0454-890 00; www.firsthotels.com; Varvsgatan 1; s/d Skr999/1099; P @ 📶) Rooms are spotlessly clean and comfortable, if stuck in the 1980s. The best offer harbour views. Other positives include a hot tub, sauna and restaurant.

Taj Mahal INDIAN €
(☎0454-156 78; www.karlshamntajmahal.se; Drottninggatan 75; mains from Skr85; ⏲11am-10pm Mon-Sat, noon-9pm Sun; ✎) An authentic Indian restaurant, particularly recommended for homesick Brits pining for their corner curry house back home. All the standard dishes are here and vegetarians have their usual meat-free choice.

★ **Fiskstugan** SEAFOOD €€
(Vägga Fiskhamn; ☎0454-190 35; www.delikatess-rokeri.se; sandwiches Skr54-79, mains from Skr100; ⏲11am-8pm mid-Apr–mid-Sep) A 25-minute stroll southeast of the centre, this unpretentious seafood restaurant sits on a picturesque small harbour. Choose from the delicious array of seafood from the deli-style counter, then head to the terrace and enjoy seamless maritime views while your dish is prepared.

Gourmet Grön BUFFET €€
(☎0454-164 40; Östra Piren, Biblioteksgatan 6; lunch buffet Skr95; ⏲11.30am-3pm Mon-Fri; ✎) This waterside award-winner serves wonderful buffets with a strong emphasis on organic and vegetarian food. You can nibble on ciabattas, tapas-style goodies or inventive Med-inspired spreads.

Information

Most services line Drottninggatan.

Tourist Office (☎0454-812 03; www.karlshamn.se; Pirgatan 2; ⏲10am-7pm Mon-Fri) Can help with information and bookings.

Getting There & Away

The bus and train stations are in the northeastern part of town.

DFDS Seaways (www.dfdsseaways.se) sails once a day between Karlshamn and Klaipėda (Lithuania; one way from Skr650, 14 hours).

The Southeast & Gotland

Includes ➜

Best Places to Eat

- ➜ Surfers (p240)
- ➜ Bröd & Sovel (p221)
- ➜ Saltmagasinet (p229)
- ➜ Krakas Krog (p244)
- ➜ Café Berget (p212)

Best Places to Stay

- ➜ Villa Sol (p232)
- ➜ Kosta Boda Art Hotel (p225)
- ➜ Hotell Västanå Slott (p218)
- ➜ Clarion Collection Hotel Packhuset (p223)
- ➜ Clarion Hotel Wisby (p239)

Why Go?

Southeastern Sweden is a treasure trove of stoic castles, storybook towns and magical islands.

Carved by the epic Göta Canal, Östergötland boasts lovable, lakeside Vadstena: St Birgitta's terrestrial stomping ground and home to a hulking Renaissance castle.

Further south, Småland sparkles with its ethereal forests, preserved pastel towns and show-off Kalmar castle. Snoop through Astrid Lindgren's childhood home in Vimmerby, pig out on peppermint rock in sweet-smelling Gränna or blow glass in the world-renowned Glasriket (Kingdom of Crystal).

Öland has a beguiling mix of beaches, windswept fields, windmills, ring forts and Iron Age burial sites. Unsurprisingly, much of the island sits on the Unesco World Heritage list.

Yet the real ace of spades is the island of Gotland. It's a mesmerising spectacle of rune stone–scattered landscapes, hauntingly beautiful medieval churches and the walled Hanseatic town of Visby.

When to Go

Visby

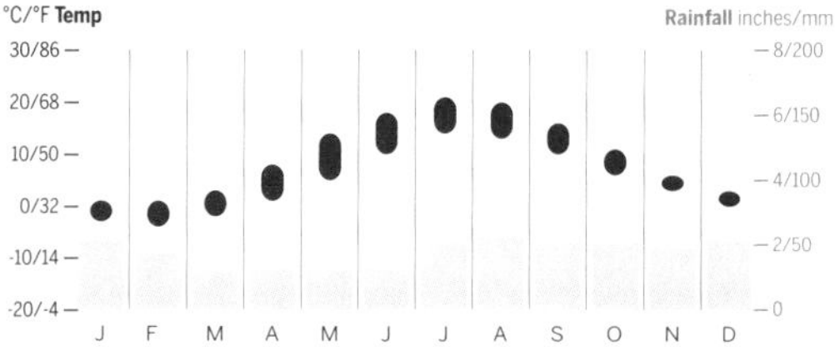

Jun–Aug Visitors drawn by warm days, canal boat trips and Gotland's medieval week.

May & Sep Less predictable weather but often as nice as summer. Easier to find places to stay.

Dec Christmas markets abound across Småland.

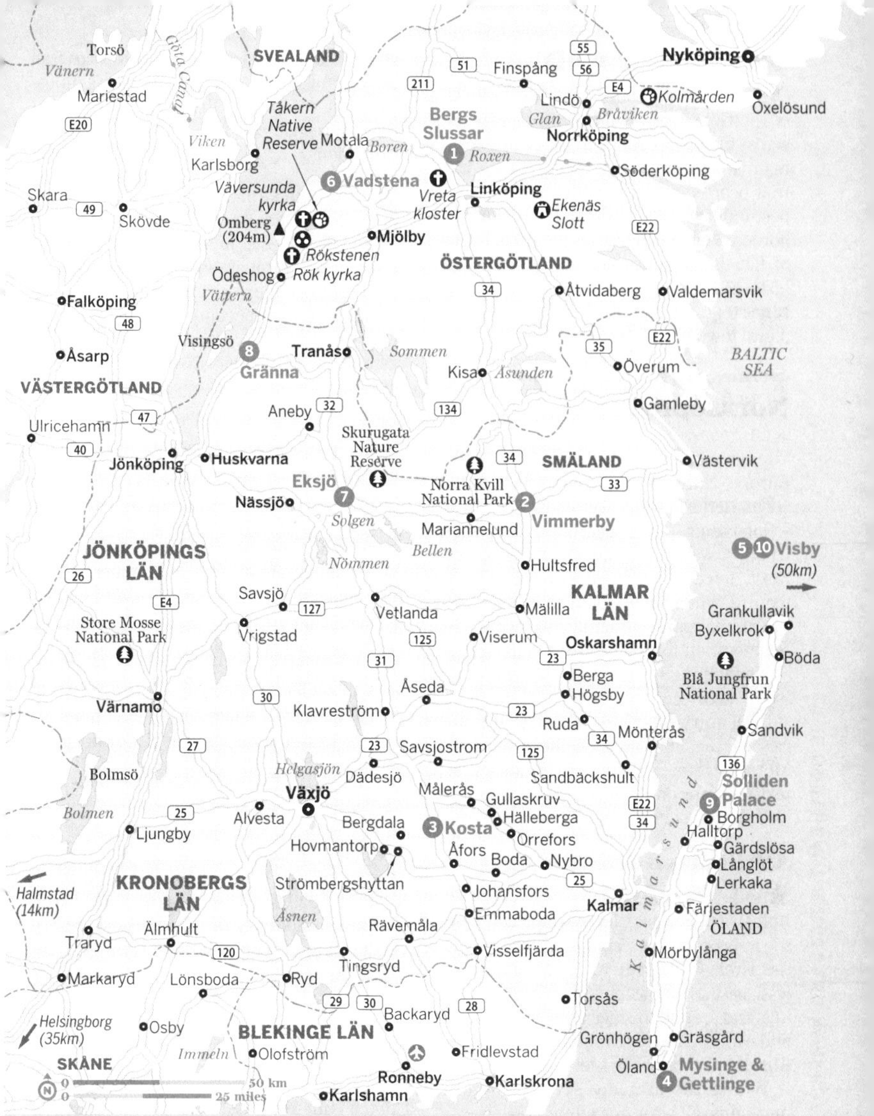

The Southeast & Gotland Highlights

1. Observing captains at **Bergs Slussar** (p213).
2. Getting literary at **Astrid Lindgrens Näs** (p230) or **Astrid Lindgrens Värld** (p230).
3. Browsing and also blowing glass at **Kosta Boda** (p225).
4. Visiting the grave fields of **Mysinge & Gettlinge** (p235).
5. Exploring Visby's **medieval churches** (p237).
6. Following in pilgrims' footsteps at the **Sancta Birgitta Klostermuseum** (p214).
7. Exploring the history of the wooden town of Eksjö at the **Fornmin-nesgårdens Museum** (p219).
8. Watching traditional sweet-makers at Gränna's **Grenna Polkagriskokeri** (p217).
9. Smelling the roses in the royal gardens of **Solliden Palace** (p232).
10. Attending a concert in the evocative surroundings of the **Sankta Maria kyrka** (p237).

ÖSTERGÖTLAND

Östergötland harbours gems on both sides of the Göta Canal, which threads diagonally across the region. Along its banks, the region's main towns are mostly 19th-century industrial heartlands, laced with some impressive post-industrial conversions. The region's west, bordered by the mighty lake Vättern, is a treat of flat, lush countryside steeped in ancient history. This is where you'll find Sweden's rune-stone superstar and the unmissable medieval town of Vadstena.

Norrköping

011 / POP 130,050

The envy of industrial has-beens all across Europe, Norrköping has cleverly regenerated its defunct mills and canals into a posse of cultural and gastronomic hang-outs fringing waterfalls and locks. Retro trams rattle down streets lined with eclectic architecture, while some 30km to the northeast, the animal park at Kolmården swaps urban regeneration for majestic Siberian tigers.

Norrköping's industrial identity began in the 17th century but took off in the late 19th century when textile mills and factories sprang up alongside the swift-flowing Motala ström. Seventy per cent of Sweden's textiles were once made here, with the last mill shutting shop in the 1970s.

Sights & Activities

★Industrilandskapet HISTORIC SITE

Industrilandskapet, Norrköping's star turn, is the impeccably preserved industrial area near the river. Pedestrian walkways and bridges lead past magnificent former factory buildings and around the ingenious system of locks and canals. The most thunderous waterfall is **Kungsfallet**, near the islet Laxholmen.

Within the area are several interesting museums, all with free admission.

The innovative **Arbetets Museum** (www.arbetetsmuseum.se; Laxholmen; 11am-5pm, to 8pm Tue) FREE documents working life. The seven-sided building, completed in 1917 and dubbed the 'flat iron', is a work of art in itself. The restaurant (6th floor) has stunning views.

The **Holmens Museum** (011-12 89 92; 9am-12.30pm Tue & Thu) exhibits cover the history of Louis de Geer's paper factory, which was founded in the early 17th century.

Over the bridge, **Stadsmuseum** (City Museum; www.norrkoping.se/stadsmuseet; Holmbrogränd; 11am-5pm Tue-Fri, to 8pm Thu, noon-5pm Sat & Sun) FREE delves into the town's industrial past, complete with still-functioning machinery, a great cafe and dynamic temporary exhibitions.

★Konstmuseum MUSEUM

(www.norrkoping.se/konstmuseet; Kristinaplatsen; noon-4pm Tue-Sun, to 8pm Wed Jun-Aug) FREE Over near Vasaparken, Konstmuseum is Norrköping's impressive art museum. Its collection boasts important early-20th-century works, including modernist and cubist gems, as well as one of Sweden's largest collections of graphic art.

★Kolmården ZOO

(www.kolmarden.com; adult/child Skr399/299; 10am-7pm mid-Jun–mid-Aug; P) This zoo is Scandinavia's largest, with some 750 residents from all climates and continents. There is a safari park, marine world and tiger world, plus dolphin shows and a separate, superb **Tropicarium** (011-39 52 50; www.tropicarium.se; adult/child Skr120/60; 10am-8pm daily Jul-mid–Aug, 10am-6pm Mon-Fri, to 7pm Sat & Sun May-Jun, shorter hours rest of year) with its motley crew of spiders, sharks, alligators and snakes.

You'll need a whole day to fully appreciate the zoo. Kolmården lies 35km north of Norrköping, on the north shore of Bråviken. Take bus 432 or 433 from Norrköping (Skr80, 40 minutes).

★Louis de Geer Konserthus CULTURAL CENTRE

(011-15 50 30; www.louisdegeer.com; Dalsgatan 15) A modern addition to the riverside scenery is the extraordinary 1300-seat Louis de Geer Konserthus concert venue, located in a former paper mill. Still containing the original balconies, it's a superb setting for concerts.

Bronze Age Rock Carvings ARCHAEOLOGICAL SITE

Two kilometres west of the city, near the river, await fine examples of Bronze Age rock carvings, with an adjacent museum, **Hällristningsmuseet** (011-16 55 45; www.ffin.se; Himmelstalund; 5.30-6.30pm Tue, 11am-3pm Sat & Sun May-Aug) FREE. The site is a 30-minute walk along the river.

Sleeping

STF Vandrarhem Abborreberg HOSTEL €

(011-31 93 44; www.abborreberg.se; dm/s/d Skr250/300/500; Apr–mid-Oct; P; 116) Stunningly situated in a coastal pine wood

5km east of town, this sterling hostel offers accommodation in huts scattered through the surrounding park. The associated ice-cream parlour is a hit with gluttons. Take bus 116 to Lindö (Skr35).

★**Strand Hotell** BOUTIQUE HOTEL €€
(☎011-16 99 00; www.hotellstrand.se; Drottninggatan 2; s/d from Skr995/1295, apt Skr2100; @📶) A real gem in the heart of town, the Strand takes up the 2nd floor of a gorgeous 1890 building overlooking the Motala river and Drottninggattan. It's operated as a hotel since the 1930s, and the furniture and fabrics make the most of the building's existing features, such as cut-glass chandeliers and big bay windows.

An additional 20 rooms recently opened, plus a sumptuous two-bedroom apartment.

Hotell Hörnan HOTEL €€
(☎011-16 58 90; www.hotellhornan.com; cnr Hörngatan & Sankt Persgatan; r with/without bathroom Skr865/665; ❄📶) These spacious rooms were fully renovated in 2013 and are excellent value. Glossy parquet floors, comfortable chairs, colourful rugs and scarlet drapes contrasting with dazzling white linen make a contemporary, comfortable look. Pick up the key to your room in the adjacent pub.

Hotel Centric HOTEL €€
(☎011-12 90 30; www.centrichotel.se; Gamla Rådstugugatan 18; s/d Skr560/925; @📶) Conveniently located near the Industrilandskapet, 3rd-floor Hotel Centric is Norrköping's oldest hotel. Rooms are spacious, furniture solid and staff welcoming.

BUS TICKETS

You cannot pay cash on the bus throughout Östergötland. The best way to pay for your ticket is to buy a **Resekortet** travel card, which you can then load with a minimum of Skr100. Check the www.osgotatrafiken.se website for a list of sales agents and venues where you can purchase the card.

Eating & Drinking

Jolla Choklad & Dessert DESSERTS €
(☎011-12 61 61; www.jolla.se; Prästgatan 3; ⊙noon-6pm Mon-Wed, 10am-6pm Thu-Sat) Head to this chocolate shop–cafe for exquisite homemade ice cream and chocolates (try the namesake Jolla with cognac, orange and lime).

★**Bryggeriet** SWEDISH €€
(☎011-10 30 20; www.gamlabrygg.se; Sandgatan 1; mains from Skr196; ⊙4-10pm Mon-Fri, to 11pm Sat & Sun) Enjoying a dreamy position overlooking the water, the menu here includes finely crafted game dishes with fillet of deer and wild boar, while lunch is more along the lines of posh burgers and pasta. The atmosphere is elegant – don't turn up in flip-flops.

Lagerqvist EUROPEAN €€
(☎011-10 07 40; www.restauranglagerqvist.se; Gamla Torget 4; mains Skr125-285; ⊙5-11pm Tue-Sun) This popular restaurant-pub has a great summer garden courtyard and a snug vaulted cellar. Meat dishes are the speciality, with innovative sides like green beans with truffle butter. There are also platters for sharing.

KVARTERET KNÄPPINGSBORG

Some of Norrköping's best restaurants, cafes and shops are all tucked into this cleverly modernised block of warehouses and factory buildings at **Kvarteret Knäppingsborg** (www.knappingsborg.se). It's hard to go wrong here. Try to swing by on a Wednesday at 7pm, when there's live music ranging from blues to swing.

Housed in a converted 19th-century *snus* (snuff) factory, urbane **Fiskmagasinet** (☎011-13 45 60; www.fiskmagasinet.se; Skolgatan 1; lunch Skr90, mains Skr135-285; ⊙11.30am-2pm & 5-10pm Mon-Fri, noon-10pm Sat) combines an intimate bar with a casually chic dining room serving modern seafood dishes. Alternatively, cheese lovers should find something to salivate over at adjacent **Norins** (www.norinsost.se; Storgatan 54; ⊙10am-6pm Mon-Fri, to 4pm Sat): there are 200-plus varieties to choose from…

Mimmi's Visthus (www.mimmisvisthus.se; Skolgatan 1B; lunch Skr89; ⊙10am-6pm Mon-Fri, to 4pm Sat, noon-4pm Sun; 🖉) 🍃 is an organic deli with delicious wraps, frittatas and salads. **Bagarstugan** (☎011-470 20 20; Skolgatan 1A; sandwiches Skr40-49, salads Skr59-65; ⊙7.30am-8pm Mon-Wed, to 10pm Sat) is a stylish bakery-bistro with two shops (the second branch is on Knäppingsborgsgatan); both sell freshly baked cookies, cardamom buns, muffins and scones, as well as salubrious salads and sandwiches.

Norrköping

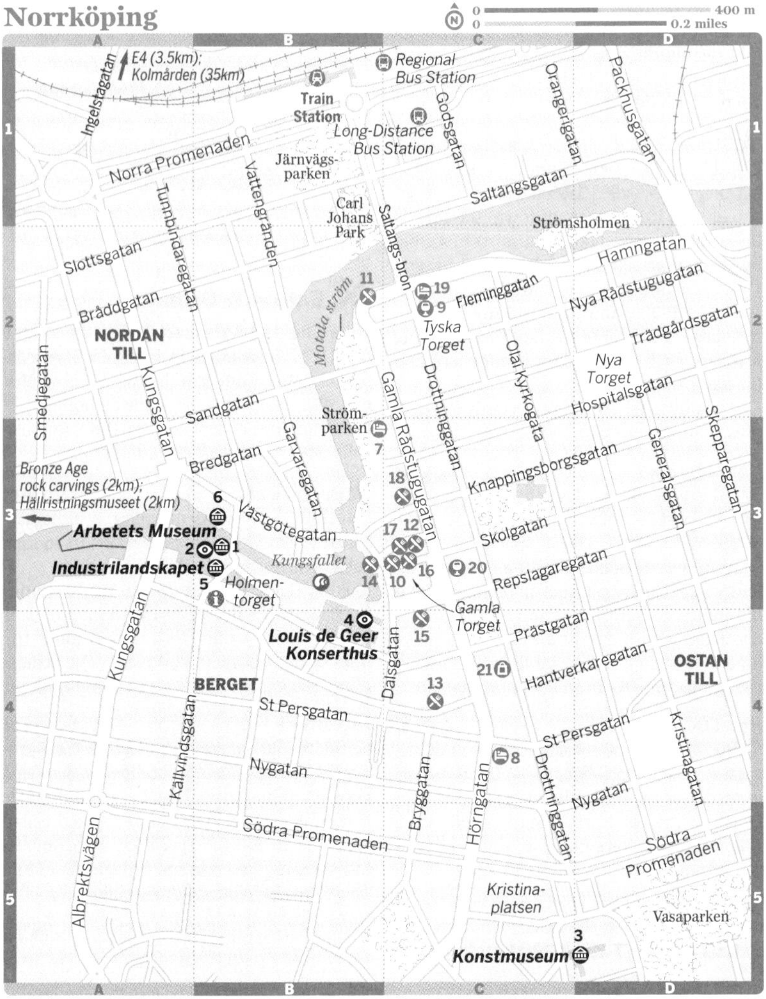

Pappa Grappa Bar & Trattoria ITALIAN €€
(www.pappagrappa.se; Gamla Rådstugugatan 26-28; pizzas from Skr83, mains from Skr165; 4-10pm Mon-Fri, noon-late Sat, to 9pm Sun, pizzeria also 4-11pm Sun) Gobble up a brilliant wood-fired pizza or slip into the vaulted restaurant for scrumptious antipasto.

Pub Wasa PUB
(011-18 26 05; Gamla Rådstugugatan; 6pm-3am Tue-Sat) Favourite post-work drinking spot.

Bishop's Arms PUB
(011-36 41 20; Tyska Torget 2; 4pm-midnight Mon-Thu, to 1am Fri, 3pm-1am Sat, 4-10pm Sun) Located at the Grand Hotel, this is a good English-style pub with a great river view.

Shopping

The blocks between Drottninggatan and Olai Kyrkogata contain shopping centres that are packed with chain stores, supermarkets, and a **Systembolaget** (Drottninggatan 50B).

Information

Banks and ATMs line Drottninggatan.

Tourist Office (011-15 50 00; www.norrkoping.se; Källvindsgatan 1; 10am-6pm daily Jul–mid-Aug, shorter hours rest of year) The

Norrköping

Top Sights

1	Arbetets Museum	B3
2	Industrilandskapet	B3
3	Konstmuseum	D5
4	Louis de Geer Konserthus	B4

Sights

5	Holmens Museum	B3
6	Stadsmuseum	B3

Sleeping

7	Hotel Centric	B3
8	Hotell Hörnan	C4
9	Strand Hotell	C2

Eating

10	Bagarstugan	C3
11	Bryggeriet	B2
12	Fiskmagasinet	C3
13	Jolla Choklad & Dessert	C4
14	Kvarteret Knäppingsborg	B3
15	Lagerqvist	C4
16	Mimmis Visthus	C3
17	Norins	C3
18	Pappa Grappa Bar & Trattoria	C3

Drinking & Nightlife

19	Bishop's Arms	C2
20	Pub Wasa	C3

Shopping

21	Systembolaget	C4

tourist office runs free one-hour walking tours of the industrial area in summer.

Getting There & Away

Sweden's third-largest airport, **Stockholm Skavsta** (www.skavsta.se) is 60km away. To get there take the train to Nyköping, then catch a local bus. **Norrköping Airport** (011-15 37 22; www.norrkopingflygplats.se) has direct flights from Copenhagen, Munich and Helsinki.

The regional bus station is next to the train station, and long-distance buses leave from a terminal across the road. **Swebus Express** (www.swebus.se) has frequent services to Stockholm (Skr149, 2¼ hours) and Jönköping (Skr219, 2½ hours), and several services daily to Göteborg (Skr299, five hours) and Kalmar (Skr269, four hours).

Norrköping is on the main north–south railway line, and **Sveriges Järnväg** (SJ; www.sj.se) trains depart every one to two hours for Stockholm (from Skr230, 1½ hours) and Malmö (from Skr370, 3¼ hours). Trains run roughly every hour north to Nyköping (from Skr93, one hour) and every 20 minutes south to Linköping (from Skr84, 25 minutes).

Getting Around

The main sights, aside from Kolmården, are within easy walking distance of the centre. Taxis can be booked with **Norrköpings Taxi** (30 00 00).

Linköping

013 / POP 145,000

Most famous for its mighty medieval cathedral, Linköping fancies itself as Norrköping's more upmarket rival. Its most infamous claim to fame is the 'bloodbath of Linköping'. Following the Battle of Stångebro (1598), many of King Sigismund's defeated Catholic army were executed here, leaving Duke Karl and his Protestant forces in full control of Sweden.

While quite the modern, industrial city today (manufacturer Saab is the major employer), pockets of its past survive in its churches, castle and museums and in the picture-perfect streets around Hunnebergsgatan and Storgatan.

Sights & Activities

★ Gamla Linköping & Valla Fritidsområde HISTORIC SITE

(www.gamlalinkoping.info; P) FREE Located 2km west of the city, this is one of the biggest living-museum villages in Sweden. It's a gorgeous combo of cobbled streets, picket-fenced gardens and around 90 19th-century houses. Take bus 12 or 19 (Skr25).

Just 300m through the forest is Valla Fritidsområde, a recreation area with domestic animals, a children's playground, mini golf, small museums and vintage abodes.

Highlights at Gamla Linköping include about a dozen themed museums (most free, with various opening times), an artisan shop, horse and carriage rides and even a small chocolate factory.

Domkyrka CHURCH

(9am-6pm) FREE Made from blocks of hand-carved limestone, the enormous Domkyrka was the country's largest and most expensive church in the Middle Ages. Its foundations were laid around 1250 and its 107m spire and vast interior still impress. Inside, the contemporary stained-glass windows may also catch your eye; they're the work of famous British stained-glass artist Brian Clarke.

There are organ concerts on Thursday in summer.

Östergötlands Länsmuseum GALLERY
(www.ostergotlandsmuseum.se; Vasavägen; adult/
child Skr70/free; ⊙11am-4pm Tue-Sun) Has a
decent European art collection (Cranach's
painting of Eden, *Original Sin,* is wonderful,
with a smiling Eve twiddling her toes), and
Swedish art dating from the Middle Ages.

Sankt Lars Kyrka CHURCH
(Storgatan; ⊙11am-4pm Mon-Sun) `FREE` The
concrete floor of Sankt Lars Kyrka was built
in 1802 above the previous medieval church
crypt. There are tours of the crypt on Tuesday at 3pm, where fascinating finds include
11th-century gravestones, a teenager's skeleton (complete with fatal blow to the skull)
and fragments of the medieval church's
painted roof tiles.

Ekenäs Slott CASTLE
(www.ekenasslott.se; tours adult/child Skr80/40;
⊙guided tours on the hour 1-3pm Tue-Sun Jul,
Sat & Sun Jun & Aug; P) Built between 1630
and 1644, this is one of the best-preserved
Renaissance castles in Sweden. Features include three spectacular towers, a moat, and
furnishings from the 17th to 19th centuries.
It's located 20km east of Linköping; you'll
need your own transport to get there.

Kinda Canal CRUISE
While it's upstaged by the Göta Canal,
Linköping boasts its own canal system, the
90km Kinda Canal. Opened in 1871, it has
15 locks, including Sweden's deepest. Cruises include evening sailings, musical outings
and wine-tasting trips. For a simple day excursion, from late June to early August the
M/S Kind (☑0141-23 33 70; www.kindakanal.
se; adult/child Skr375/185; ⊙May-Sep) leaves
Tullbron dock at 10am on Tuesday, Thursday and Saturday, and travels to Rimforsa
(return by bus or train).

🛏 Sleeping

City Hotel &
STF Vandrarhem HOSTEL, HOTEL €
(☑013-35 90 00; www.lvh.se; Klostergatan 52A;
hostel s/d Skr585/649, hotel s/d Skr690/1090;
P@🛜; ⊒30, 52, 59, 72, 78) This slickly modern hostel has hotel-style accommodation
too, mostly with kitchenettes. All rooms
have TV and private bathroom – rooms for
the hotels and hostels are similar, but the
hotel price includes breakfast and linen.

Park Hotel HOTEL €€
(☑013-12 90 05; www.fawltytowers.se; Järnvägsgatan 6; s/d Skr1145/1345; P@🛜) Disturbingly

billed as Sweden's 'Fawlty Towers', this smart
family-run establishment resembles that
madhouse in appearance only (yes, there's
an elk head at reception). The public spaces
sport chandeliers, oil paintings and clean,
parquet-floored rooms, while the rooms are
crisply modern.

There is a classic English afternoon
tea (Skr195) and a hearty breakfast buffet
served in the hotel's pleasant dining room
(but thankfully not by Manuel!).

It's close to the train station.

Hotell du Nord HISTORIC HOTEL €€
(☑013-12 98 95; www.hotelldunord.se; Repslagare-
gatan 5; s/d from Skr680/850; P🛜) Located
across from the beautiful Järnvägsparken,
Hotell du Nord is appropriately leafy and
tranquil. The main dusky-rose 19th-century
building looks like a doll's house, staff are
friendly and the rooms are light filled and
welcoming (those in the aesthetically chal-
lenged rear building are freshly renovated
and larger). There's a patio for outdoor summer breakfasts.

Best Western Hotel Linköping HOTEL €€
(☑013-79 27 52; www.hotellinkoping.se; Hantver-
karegatan 1; s/d Skr895/1035; P@🛜) Right
off Stora Torget, this hotel is within a few
minutes' walk of the city's main sights, restaurants and shopping. Rooms are all pale
wood and scarlet fabrics with good-size
bathrooms and fridges. The breakfast is
generous and there is an Italian cafe plus
Spanish-style tapas bar.

🍴 Eating & Drinking

Most places to eat (and drink) are found
around the main square or nearby streets,
especially along buzzing Ågatan.

★Café Berget BAKERY €
(www.cafeberget.com; Klostergatan 38; cakes from
Skr35; ⊙10am-6pm Mon-Fri, to 4pm Sat) Up a
narrow set of stone stairs you'll find a sunny terrace, resplendent with flowers and ivy,
which serves as the doorstep to this glorious
little bolt-hole bakery. Café Berget serves
up classic Swedish baked goodies – vanilla
cream hearts and blueberry tartlets – as
well as coffee, tea and sandwiches, in lovingly restored rooms in this 1905 building.

Tropikhuset CAFE €
(www.tropikhuset.nu; Trägårdsföreningen; sandwiches from Skr79; ⊙9am-6pm Mon-Fri, 10am-
5pm Sat, 11am-5pm Sun; P🚼) Grab a slice of
cake and park yourself under a palm tree

inside the pyramid greenhouse or enjoy the outdoor tables overlooking this gorgeous park. It's just south of the centre with a handy car park across the road.

Yellow Fellow ASIAN **€€**
(913-12 22 26; Stora Torget 7; mains from Skr100; 11am-11pm Mon-Thu, to 1.30am Fri & Sat, noon-9pm Sun) Overlooking the main square and making a change from the ubiquitous cafes, this Thai restaurant is great for a cold beer and a spicy curry. Check out the lavish frond-filled interior.

Stångs Magasin SWEDISH **€€€**
(www.stangsmagasin.se; Södra Stånggatan 1; lunch Skr115, mains Skr145-505; 11.30am-2pm Mon-Fri, 6pm-midnight Tue-Fri, 5pm-midnight Sat Jul & Aug;) In a 200-year-old warehouse down near the Kinda Canal docks, this elegant award-winner fuses classic Swedish cuisine with continental influences – think stuffed trout with beet aioli. There is an extensive wine list and a sommelier on hand to help you choose.

Information

There are banks and other services around Stora Torget.

Tourist Office (013-190 0070; www.visitlinkoping.se; Storgatan 15; 10am-6pm Mon-Fri, to 4pm Sat, to 6pm Sun) Across from Sankt Lars Kyrka.

Getting There & Away

Linköping City Airport (013-18 10 30; www.linkopingcityairport.se) is only 2km east of town. There's no airport bus, but taxi company Taxibil (p213) charges around Skr160 for the ride.

Regional and local buses, run by **Östgöta Trafiken** (0771-21 10 10; www.ostgotatrafiken.se), leave from the terminal next to the train station.

Up to five express buses per day go to Vadstena (Skr135, one hour); otherwise change at Motala.

Long-distance buses depart from a terminal 500m northwest of the train station. **Swebus Express** (www.swebus.se) runs 10 to 12 times daily to Jönköping (Skr169, 1½ hours) and seven to eight times daily to Göteborg (Skr289, four hours), and north to Norrköping (Skr59, 45 minutes).

Linköping is on the main north–south railway line. Regional and express trains run to Stockholm roughly every hour; express trains go to Malmö. Frequent regional trains run north to Norrköping (from Skr84, 25 minutes).

Getting Around

Most city buses depart from Centralstationen. For bike hire contact **Cykelaventyr** (www.cykelaventyr.se; Linköping; per day Skr165), with locations in Borensberg (on the canal 10km north of Bergs Slussar) or Motala (15km north of Vadstena). For a taxi, ring **Taxibil** (013-14 60 00).

Vadstena

0143 / POP 7383

Sublimely situated beside Vättern lake, Vadstena is a legacy of both church and state power, and today St Birgitta's abbey and Gustav Vasa's castle compete with each other for admiration. The atmosphere in the old town, with its wonderful cobbled lanes, intriguing small shops and wooden buildings, makes it an especially satisfying place to end a day of touring along the Göta Canal.

Sights

Both the old courthouse **rådhus** (town hall), on the town square, and **Rödtornet** (Sånggatan) are late-medieval constructions.

BERGS SLUSSAR

Bergs Slussar, 12km northwest of Linköping, is one of the most scenic sections of the Göta Canal: there are seven locks with a height gain of 19m – very impressive in canal terms! The nearby ruin **Vreta kloster**, Sweden's oldest monastery, was founded by Benedictine monks in 1120. While it's worth a look, the adjacent 13th-century **abbey church** is actually more interesting.

There's a small **tourist office** (9.30am-5pm May-Aug) in the same building as the beautifully located **STF Vandrarhem** (013-603 30; www.bergsslussar.com/vandrarhem; Bergs Slussar; dm Skr275; May-Aug) near the locks, with a cafe, mini golf and bike hire. You'll find a couple of cafes and restaurants out this way, including **Kanalkrogen** (Stenbordsvagen 10; mains Skr120; 11.30am-6pm Mon-Sat), with a great range of meals and lock-side views.

Buses 521 and 522 run regularly from Linköping.

★ **Vadstena Slott** CASTLE
(www.vadstenadirect.se; Slottsvägen; tours adult/child Skr80/60; ⏲11am-4pm, to 6pm Jun–early Aug) Overlooking the lake, and considered one of the finest early Renaissance buildings in the Nordic region, Vadstena Slott was the family project of the early Vasa kings; their gloomy portraits are on view, along with a modest historical display. The furnished upper floors are the most interesting, and be sure to visit the chapel, with its incredible 17-second echo! There are guided tours (in English) mid-July to mid-September; call ahead for times.

★ **Sancta Birgitta Klostermuseet** MUSEUM
(www.sanctabirgitta.com; Lasarettsgatan; adult/child Sk60/30; ⏲10.30am-5pm Jul–mid-Aug, 11am-4pm Jun & rest of Aug) The Sancta Birgitta Klostermuseet is in Bjälboättens Palats (a royal residence that became a convent in 1384) and tells the story of St Birgitta's roller-coaster life and those of all her saint-and-sinner children. Artefacts include the coffin that carried her back from Rome.

Klosterkyrkan CHURCH
(Abbey Church; ⏲9am-8pm Jul, to 7pm Jun & Aug) 'Of plain construction, humble and strong', Klosterkyrkan was built in response to one of St Birgitta's visions. After the church's consecration in 1430, Vadstena became *the* top pilgrimage site in Sweden. Step inside for medieval sculptures and carved floor slabs.

Sleeping

Chain hotels don't get a look-in here – pretty and personal is the rule. Book well in advance.

Pensionat Solgården B&B €
(☎0143-143 50; www.pensionatsolgarden.se; Strågatan 3; s/d from Skr540/790; ⏲May-Sep; P 📶) Set in a classic 1905 wooden house, this family-run hotel boasts lovingly decorated rooms; some have private bathrooms and all have an art/artist connection. They're each *very* different – check the photos on the website to choose your favourite (number 25 is particularly grand).

27ans Nattlogi B&B €
(☎0143-134 47; www.27ansnattlogi.se; Storgatan 27; s/d from Skr590/790; P 📶) Wooden floors, pretty wallpaper and fresh flowers provide a welcoming, homey vibe to the six rooms (some with views of Klosterkyrkan). More expensive rooms have private bathrooms. Breakfast costs an extra Skr64.

Vadstena Klosterhotel HISTORIC HOTEL €€
(☎0143-315 30; www.klosterhotel.se; r from Skr1475; P @ 📶) History and luxury merge at this wonderfully atmospheric hotel in St Birgitta's old convent. The bathrooms are a wee bit dated, but the medieval-style rooms are great, with chandeliers and high wooden beds. Most boast lake views. The hotel also has simpler rooms with shared bathrooms and showers in a nearby cottage (singles/doubles Skr790/990).

Eating & Drinking

★ **Restaurant Munkklostret** EUROPEAN €€
(☎0143-130 00; lunch mains from Skr125, dinner mains from Skr169; ⏲noon-11pm daily Jun-Aug, from 6pm rest of year; P 📶) The Klosterhotel's ravishing restaurant is the best dining spot in town. Seasonal, succulent steak, lamb, game and fish dishes are flavoured with herbs from the monastery garden, and served in the monks' old dorms.

Rojas BISTRO €€
(☎0143-123 43; Storgatan 20; mains from Skr115; ⏲10am-10pm Sun-Mon, to 11pm Wed-Sat) The interior here is cosily cluttered with a 1950s theme, kickback sofas and an eclectic display of art and antiques, while the terrace sprawls invitingly into the square. The menu has an interesting range of dishes, including excellent tacos.

Rådhuskällaren INTERNATIONAL €€
(www.radhuskallaren.com; Rådhustorget; mains from Skr150; ⏲noon-10pm Mon-Tue, to 11pm Wed, to 1am Thu & Fri, to 10pm Sat) Under the old courthouse, this affable 15th-century cellar restaurant dishes out simple but satisfying burger, pasta and fish meals. Its outdoor area is a favourite afternoon drinking spot in summer.

Shopping

Storgatan is the main shopping street, with a healthy mix of tourist-geared and local shops.

Wadstena Spetsar ARTS, CRAFTS
(☎0143-103 10; Storgatan 23; ⏲10am-6pm Mon-Fri, to 4pm Sat) The oldest shop in town, selling exquisite, finely woven embroidery from patterns dating back some 200 years.

Information

You'll find banks and other services east of the castle, on Storgatan and around Stora Torget.

Tourist Office (☎0143-315 70; www.vadstena.se; ⏲10am-6pm daily Jul, 10am-6pm Mon-Sat, to 4pm Sun Jun & early Aug, to 2pm Mon-Sat rest of year) Located in the Rödtornet (Sånggatan). A great place to get details about town walks, boat tours and festivals.

Getting There & Around

Only buses run to Vadstena – take bus 610 to Motala (for trains to Örebro), or bus 661 to Mjölby (for trains to Linköping and Stockholm). **Blåklints Buss** (0142-121 50; www.blaklintsbuss.se) runs one to three services daily from the Viking Line Terminal in Stockholm to Vadstena (Skr250).

Cykelaventyr (www.cykelaventyr.se), in Borensberg (on the canal 10km north of Bergs Slussar) and Motala (15km north of Vadstena), has bikes for rent (Skr150 per day).

Around Vadstena

Rök

Sweden's most famous rune stone, the 9th-century **Rökstenen**, is near the church at Rök (just off the E4 on the road to Heda and Alvastra). It's a monumental memorial stone raised to commemorate a dead son and features the longest runic inscription in the world. It's an ancient, intricate verse so cryptic that scholars constantly scrap over its interpretation. The outdoor exhibition and stone are always open.

Buses are virtually nonexistent, though the scenic flatlands around Vättern make for perfect cycling.

Väversunda

The Romanesque 12th-century limestone **Väversunda kyrka**, situated 15km southwest of Vadstena, is a bizarre-looking church, and contains restored 13th-century wall paintings. The adjacent **Tåkern Nature Reserve** pulls in a diverse cast of birds; there's a birdwatcher's tower near the church.

Buses are hopeless; pedalling is your best option.

SMÅLAND

The region of Småland is one of dense forests, glinting lakes and bare marshlands. Historically it served as a buffer zone between the Swedes and Danes; the eastern and southern coasts in particular witnessed territorial tussles. Today it's better known for the **Glasriket** (Kingdom of Glass), a sparsely populated area in the central southeast dotted with crystal workshops. Småland is broken up into *län* (smaller counties): Jönköpings in the northwest, Kronobergs in the southwest and Kalmar in the east.

Jönköping & Huskvarna

036 / POP 123,710

Whenever you hear the scratching of matches on sandpaper, spare a thought for Jönköping – birthplace of the safety match. You can visit the restored production area here to learn more about this undervalued necessity.

Fairy-tale illustrator John Bauer was inspired by the deep-green forests around Jönköping, and the town museum shows off his superb otherworldly drawings of trolls, knights and princesses.

Sights & Activities

Jönköping

Tändsticksmuseet MUSEUM
(036-10 55 43; www.matchmuseum.se; Tändsticksgränd 27; adult/child Skr40/free, Nov-Feb free; 10am-5pm Mon-Fri, to 3pm Sat & Sun Jun-Aug, shorter hours rest of year) Apparently 'the only match museum in the world', Tändsticksmuseet, in an old match factory, deals with this practical Swedish invention. It's quite an eye-opener: the industry was initially based on cheap child labour, workers frequently suffered from repulsive 'phossy jaw', and it was common knowledge that phosphorus matches were good for 'speeding up inheritance and inducing abortions'.

Radio Museum MUSEUM
(036-71 39 59; www.radiomuseet.com; Tändsticksgränd 16; admission Skr20; 10am-5pm Mon-Fri, to 2pm Sat, 11am-3pm Sun Jun–mid-Aug, closed Sun & Mon mid-Aug–May) Near the Tändsticksmuseet, the Radio Museum boasts over 1000 radio sets and related memorabilia.

Jönköpings Läns Museum MUSEUM
(036-30 18 00; www.jkpglm.se; Dag Hammarskjöld Plats 2; adult/child Skr40/free; noon-7pm Mon-Fri, 11am-3pm Sat & Sun Jul & Aug, shorter hours rest of year) Exhibits cover local history and contemporary culture, but the real reason for coming here is to see the haunting fantasy works of artist John Bauer (1882–1918).

Cruises CRUISE
(☎070-637 17 00; www.rederiabkind.se) From May to October, you can choose various cruises on Vättern lake aboard the M/S *Nya Skärgården*. There's a lunch-buffet trip (Skr495) complete with local delicacies, while several other similarly priced trips combine dinner and live music. The boat departs from Hamnpiren (the harbour pier); bookings can be made at the tourist office or directly.

Huskvarna

From Jönköping, take bus 1 to Huskvarna (Skr25), 7km away.

Husqvarna Fabriksmuseum MUSEUM
(☎036-14 61 62; www.husqvarnamuseum.se; Hakarpsvägen 1; adult/child Skr50/20; ⏲10am-5pm Mon-Fri, noon-4pm Sat & Sun May-Sep, shorter hours rest of year) Square-jawed men going hunting while their wives snuggle up to their sewing machines: the Husqvarna Fabriksmuseum conjures up a vivid 1950s world. The factory began as an arms manufacturer before diverting into motorbikes, chainsaws, cooking ranges and microwave ovens. The atmospheric museum charts the company's rise.

Sleeping

Jönköping

Elite Stora Hotellet HOTEL €€
(☎036-10 00 00; www.elite.se; Hotellplan; s/d Skr850/950; P@🛜) The Elite is Jönköping's harbourside show-stopper. Rooms are chic, with either pastel, Carl Larsson–inspired undertones or a more contemporary combo of black-and-white photographs and natural hues. There's a sauna, a pool table and a slinky restaurant, as well as a banqueting hall fit for royalty.

City Hotel HOTEL €€
(☎036-71 92 80; www.cityhotel.se; Västra Storgatan 25; s/d from Skr795/995; @🛜) Dowdy, tired halls give way to rooms that are bright, clean and modern – think flat-screen TVs, giant photos of Jönköping, and oak-toned functionalist furniture – at this midrange, family-run hotel. Some rooms have stunning sea views.

Grand Hotel HOTEL €€
(☎036-71 96 00; www.grandhotel-jonkoping.se; Hovrättstorget; s/d Skr690/890; @🛜) In a stately early-20th-century building, this homey central choice offers budget, standard and superior rooms. All are clean and comfy, many are spacious, and several look out over the square.

Huskvarna

STF Vandrarhem Huskvarna HOSTEL €
(☎036-14 88 70; www.hhv.se; Odengatan 10; s/d per person Skr275/400; @🛜) Standards are high at this sizeable year-round hostel. All rooms are sparkling and have a TV; breakfast is an additional Skr65. By the time you read this, more deluxe hotel rooms will be available; check the website for an update.

Eating

For bobbing boats and tasty seafood, head straight for Jönköping's Hamnpiren pier. For cheaper alternatives, try inside the Juneporten transport and shopping complex.

Kafé Braheparken VEGAN €
(☎036-12 60 20; www.kafebraheparken.se; Kyrkogatan 16; mains Skr85; ⏲11am-7pm Mon-Fri; ✎) Really tasty organic vegan dishes and a generous lunchtime buffet with tofu 'cheese', hummus and more green crunchy veg than you can shake a carrot stick at, plus a hot special. Also sells delicious pies, cakes and cookies.

Pescadores SEAFOOD €€
(www.pescadores.se; Svavelsticksgränd 23; mains from Skr110; ⏲4-11.30pm Wed-Sat, shorter hours Sat & Sun) A family-run fish restaurant located in one of the quirky brick buildings that once belonged to the match-making empire. The father and son owners were previously commercial crayfishermen, so they know their stuff. The menu features all the classics, from fish and chips to gravlax and mussel soup.

Mäster Gudmunds Källare EUROPEAN €€
(☎036-10 06 40; www.mastergudmund.se; Kapellgatan 2; lunches Skr75, mains Skr149-219; ⏲11.30am-2pm & 6-10pm Mon-Fri, noon-10pm Sat, to 5pm Sun, closed Sun summer) This much-loved restaurant sits in a 17th-century cellar, with beautiful vaulted ceilings and good-value lunches. Evening mains are mainly meaty and fishy local dishes, with a few nods to French fare.

Information

You'll find banks along Östra Storgatan.

Tourist Office (☎036-10 50 50; www.destinationjonkoping.se; ⏲9.30am-7pm Mon-Fri, to 3pm Sat & Sun mid-Jun–mid-Aug, shorter hours rest of year) In the Juneporten complex at the train station.

Getting There & Around

Jönköping Airport (036-31 11 00; www.jonkopingairport.se) is located about 8km southwest of the town centre. **SAS** (www.flysas.com) operates several daily flights on weekdays to/from Copenhagen. Bus 18 serves the airport, or else a taxi costs around Skr250.

Most local buses leave from opposite Juneporten on Västra Storgatan. Local transport is run by **Jönköpings Länstrafik** (www.jlt.se; Juneporten; 7.30am-6pm Mon-Fri); there's an office with information, tickets and passes in Juneporten.

The long-distance bus station is next to the train station. There are at least eight daily Swebus Express (p213) services to Göteborg (from Skr89, two hours) and Stockholm (from Helsingborg Skr329, 4½ hours); at least three to Helsingborg (from Skr249, three hours) and Malmö (from Skr279, 4½ hours); and two to Karlstad (from Skr299, four hours). **Svenska Buss** (www.svenskabuss.se) also operates a daily service each way between Göteborg and Stockholm.

Jönköping is on a regional train line; you'll need to change trains in either Nässjö or Falköping to get to or from larger towns. Train tickets can be purchased online through **Tågkompaniet** (www.tagkompaniet.se).

Taxi Jönköping (34 40 00; www.taxijonkoping.se) is the local taxi company.

Gränna & Visingsö

0390

All that's missing from Gränna are Oompa-Loompas. The scent of sugar hangs over the village, and shops overflow with the village's trademark red-and-white peppermint rock *(polkagris)*. It's a bit touristy, but the steep streets, lakeside location and excellent polar exhibition redeem the place.

Across the water and 6km west is peaceful Visingsö. Connected by frequent ferries and home to Sweden's largest oak forest, it's a great place to cycle and relax.

Sights & Activities

Gränna

Grenna Museum: Andréexpedition Polarcenter MUSEUM
(www.grennamuseum.se; adult/child Skr50/20; 10am-6pm daily mid-May–Aug, to 4pm Sep–mid-May; P) In the same building as the tourist office, Grenna Museum: Andréexpedition Polarcenter describes the disastrous attempt of Salomon August Andrée to reach the North Pole by balloon in 1897. It's riveting stuff, particularly the poignant remnants of the expedition: cracked leather boots, monogrammed handkerchiefs, lucky amulets, and mustard paper to ward off those polar winds.

Grenna Polkagriskokeri CONFECTIONER
(0390-100 39; www.polkagris.com; Brahegatan 39; 8am-9pm Mon-Fri, 9am-8pm Sat & Sun) Several sweet-makers in Gränna have kitchens where you can watch the town's trademark red-and-white peppermint rock *(polkagris)* being made. However, this place, directly opposite the tourist office, is the best known, and uses an authentic 19th-century recipe that is refreshingly natural, using solely sugar, water, vinegar and natural peppermint oil.

Grenna Ballongresor BALLOONING
(0390-305 25; www.flyg-ballong.nu; per person Skr2000) Take to the skies in a hot-air balloon for a one-hour scenic trip.

Visingsö

Visingsö has a 17th-century **church**, **castle** and **aromatic herb garden**. An extensive network of footpaths and bicycle trails leads through tranquil woods.

The beautiful lakes of Bunn and Ören, and their dark forests, inspired local artist John Bauer to paint his trolls and magical pools (you can see his work at Jönköpings Läns Museum (p215)). In summer you can take a **boat tour** (070-791 78 10; www.trolska.se; adult/child Skr180/90; tours 12.30pm Sat & Sun Jun, daily Jul–mid-Aug) to the lakes, departing from Bunnströms badplats, 2.5km from Gränna.

Sleeping & Eating

Gränna

The tourist office arranges private rooms from Skr140 to Skr250 per person per night (plus Skr100 booking fee). For a choice of food in a great waterside setting, head down to the harbour (1.5km), where half a dozen restaurants sell everything from Greek, French and Italian fare to Swedish dishes (most places are open in summer only).

Strandterrassens Vandrarhem HOSTEL €
(0390-418 40; www.strandterrassen.se; Hamnen; dm Skr270; P) This hostel offers simple, bright, clean rooms in long wooden cabins, as well as a cafe.

THE GÖTA CANAL

Not only is the Göta Canal Sweden's greatest civil-engineering feat, idling along it on a boat or cycling the towpaths is one of the best ways to soak up Gotland's gorgeous countryside.

The canal connects the North Sea with the Baltic Sea, and links the great lakes Vättern and Vänern. Its total length is 190km, although only around 87km is human made – the rest is rivers and lakes. Built between 1802 and 1832 by a burly team of some 60,000 soldiers, it provided a hugely valuable transport and trade link between Sweden's east and west coasts.

The canal has two sections: the eastern section from Mem (southeast of Norrköping) to Motala (north of Vadstena on Vättern); and the western section from Karlsborg (on Vättern) to Sjötorp (on the shores of Vänern). The system is then linked to the sea by the Trollhätte Canal, in Västergötland. Along these stretches of the canal are towpaths, used in earlier times by horses and oxen pulling barges. Nowadays they're the domain of walkers and cyclists.

Boat trips are obviously a favourite way to experience the canal. You can go on a four- or six-day cruise of its entire length, travelling from Stockholm to Göteborg (or vice versa) and stopping to enjoy the wayside attractions. Shorter, cheaper boat trips along sections of the canal are also available – any tourist office in the area should be able to give you the low-down.

A good website for ideas is www.gotakanal.se.

★Hotell Västanå Slott HISTORIC HOTEL €€
(0390-107 00; www.vastanaslott.se; d from Skr1490; May-Dec; P Wi-Fi) This stately manor house, 6km south of town, is perfect for regal relaxation. Count Per Brahe owned it in the 17th century, although today it's decorated according to its 18th-century past, with chandeliers, brooding oil paintings and suits of armour. Some rooms even have copper bathtubs. The surrounding woods are ideal for hikers and there's an adjacent golf course.

Grännagården HOTEL €€
(0390-100 91; www.grannagarden.se; Hamnvägen 2; s/d Skr650/950; P Wi-Fi) Just nudging into the midrange bracket, this hotel is right in the centre of town in a handsome 18th-century building. Rooms have kept up with the times and are slick and modern with a fashionable grey-and-white colour scheme.

Hotel Amalias Hus BOUTIQUE HOTEL €€€
(0390-413 23; www.amaliashus.se; s/d from Skr1350/1690; P @ Wi-Fi) Once owned by Amalia Eriksson, the creator of Granna's famous peppermint rock, this hotel is just a doily short of being overly kitsch. Rooms are furnished with antique furniture, old-fashioned wallpaper and lacy drapes.

Fiket BAKERY €
(0390-100 57; Brahegatan 57; sandwiches from Skr45; 8.30am-8pm) The pick of Gränna's eateries is this time-warp bakery-cafe, complete with retro jukebox, chequered floor and record-clad walls. Tackle tasty grilled baguettes, quiches, salads and pastries, either indoors or on the breezy balcony.

Visingsö

STF Vandrarhem Visingsö HOSTEL, HOTEL €
(0390-401 91; www.visingso-vandrarhem.se; dm/s/d per person Skr190/400/600, breakfast Skr75; May-Oct) This hostel and hotel lies in an oak wood around 3km from the ferry pier and has excellent facilities and modern, comfortable rooms.

Restaurant Solbacken SWEDISH €€
(0390-400 29; www.restaurang-solbacken.se; mains Skr90-220; May-Aug) Local fish find themselves on the menu at this lively restaurant, pub and pizzeria at Visingsö harbour. The fish is smoked at the owners' own farm and the kitchen is certified by Sweden's organic and sustainability label Krav.

Information

Brahegatan, the main street of Gränna, has a bank and an ATM.

Gränna Tourist Office (036-10 38 60; www.destinationjonkoping.se; Grenna Kulturgård, Brahegatan 38; 10am-6pm daily mid-May–Aug, to 4pm Sep–mid-May) In the same building as the Grenna Museum.

Visingsö Tourist Office (☑ 036-10 38 89; www.visingso.net; ◷ 10am-5pm daily May-Aug, shorter hours rest of year) At the harbour. Offers bicycle hire (Skr50/80 per three hours/day).

ⓘ Getting There & Around

Local bus 101 runs hourly from Jönköping to Gränna (Skr75, one hour). Bus 120 runs several times Monday to Friday from Gränna to the mainline train station in Tranås (Skr75, one hour). Daily **Swebus Express** (www.swebus. se) destinations include Göteborg, Jönköping, Linköping, Norrköping and Stockholm. Swebus Express services stop 3km outside Gränna. Catch bus 121 into town or walk (30 minutes).

The Gränna–Visingsö **ferry** (☑ 0390-410 25) runs half-hourly in summer (less frequently the rest of the year). Return tickets for foot passengers are Skr50 per adult, and Skr25 for those aged between six and 15 years; a bicycle is Skr30 and a car plus driver is Skr165.

Eksjö

☑ 0381 / POP 16,440

Eksjö is one of the most exquisitely preserved wooden towns in Sweden. The area south of Stora Torget was razed to the ground in a blaze in 1856, paving the way for beautiful neoclassical buildings. To the north of the square, buildings date back to the 17th century. Both sides will have you swooning over the jumble of candy-coloured houses and flower-filled courtyards.

⊙ Sights

★ Eksjö Museum MUSEUM
(☑ 0381-361 60; Österlånggatan 31; admission Skr50; ◷ 11am-6pm Mon-Fri, to 3pm Sat & Sun Jul & Aug, shorter hours rest of year) Award-winning Eksjö Museum tells the town's story from the 15th century onward. The top floor is devoted to local Albert Engström (1869–1940), renowned for his burlesque, satirical cartoons. Eksjö was once known as the 'Hussar Town', and the region's longstanding military connections are also explored at the museum. The town hosts a tattoo (www.eksjotattoo.se) in early August, complete with plenty of military pomp and circumstance.

Fornminnesgårdens Museum MUSEUM
(☑ 0381-148 39; Arendt Byggmästares gatan 22; admission Skr20; ◷ noon-3pm Mon-Sat mid-Jun–mid-Aug) Check out the 17th-century buildings at Fornminnesgårdens Museum. Exhibits here chart the history of the area from the Stone Age to modern times.

Skurugata Nature
Reserve NATURE RESERVE
The Skurugata Nature Reserve, 13km northeast of Eksjö, is centred on a peculiar 800m-long fissure in the rocks. Its sides tower to 56m, yet in places the fissure is only 7m wide. In times past, the ravine was believed to harbour trolls and thieves. The nearby hill of Skuruhatt (337m) offers impressive forest views. You'll need your own transport to get here.

Höglandsleden HIKING
Try some berry picking or just enjoy woodland tranquillity on the well-maintained Höglandsleden, which passes through the Skurugata Nature Reserve; ask the tourist office for details of this walking trail.

🛏 Sleeping

STF Vandrarhem Eksjö HOSTEL €
(☑ 0381-361 70; www.eksjovandrarhem.se; Österlånggatan 31; dm/s/d Skr200/345/500; @ 🗟) 🖋 In the heart of the old town, this hostel is based in a supremely quaint wooden building, with a gallery running round the upper floor. Reception is at the tourist office.

Eksjö Camping CAMPGROUND €
(☑ 0381-395 00; www.eksjocamping.se; sites Skr195, 2-/4-bed cabins from Skr350/500; P 🗟) This friendly nook by picturesque Husnäsen, about a kilometre east of town, has a restaurant and cafe, plus mini golf. There's also a hostel (dorm beds Skr300).

★ Hotell Vaxblekaregården B&B €€
(☑ 0381-140 40; www.vaxblekaregarden.com; Arendt Byggmästares gata 8; s/d Skr995/1195; P @ 🗟) Set in a converted 17th-century wax-bleaching workshop, this boutique number features stylish, pared-back rooms with wooden floorboards, Carl Larsson–inspired wallpaper and wrought-iron bedheads. The lounge-laced backyard hosts barbecues and live-music gigs on Saturday evening from mid-June to mid-August.

🍴 Eating & Drinking

Lennarts Konditori BAKERY €
(☑ 0381-61 13 90; www.lennartskonditori.se; Stora Torget; snacks from Skr50; ◷ 8am-6pm Mon-Fri, 9am-4pm Sat, 11am-4pm Sun) With an outdoor terrace and views of dramatic Stora Torget, the place to go for cakes, crêpes and quiche is this old-school *konditori* (bakery-cafe) dating from 1947.

Lilla Caféet CAFE **€**
(Norra Storgatan 24; cakes from Skr25; ⊙8am-6pm Mon-Fri, 9am-3pm Sat) Lovely cakes and coffee at this quaint little shop on Norra Storgatan.

Sunrise MONGOLIAN **€€**
(☑0381-121 20; Norra Storgatan 19; mains Skr100; ⊙noon-11pm Tue-Sun) The Mongolian barbecue is the star turn here, prepared fresh on the griddle with a selection of 12 sauces, plus a vegetarian option.

❶ Information

The **tourist office** (☑361 70; www.visiteksjo.se; Norra Storgatan 29; ⊙8am-8pm daily Jul–mid-Aug, 10am-6pm Mon-Fri, 10am-2pm Sat rest of year) can arrange English-language guided town tours or audio guides for Skr40 and Skr45, respectively, from Monday to Saturday from late June to early August. Bicycle hire (Skr65/230 per day/week) is also available.

❶ Getting There & Around

The bus and train stations are in the southern part of town. The tiny *länståg* (regional train) runs up to seven times daily to/from Jönköping. Local buses run to Nässjö (Skr40, hourly to 6pm, then less frequently Monday to Friday, three to four at weekends). Swebus Express runs one bus daily from Jönköping to Eksjö.

Växjö

☑0470 / POP 82.000

A venerable old market town, Växjö (*vak-choo*, with the 'ch' sound pronounced as in the Scottish 'loch'), in Kronobergs *län,* is an important stop for Americans seeking their Swedish roots. **Karl Oscar Days** (www.karloskardagarna.se; ⊙mid-Aug) commemorates the mass 19th-century emigration from the area, and the Swedish-American of the year is chosen during the festival. The town's glass museum, packed with gorgeous works of art and plenty of history, is another highlight.

⊙ Sights & Activities

Enquire at the tourist office about guided summer **walking tours** (5.30pm Tuesday and Thursday; Skr50) of town.

★ **Smålands Museum** MUSEUM
(www.kulturparkensmaland.se; Södra Järnvägsgatan 2; adult/child Skr70/free; ⊙10am-5pm Tue-Fri, to 4pm Sat & Sun) Among the varied exhibits at Sweden's oldest provincial mu-

seum is a truly stunning exhibition about the country's 500-year-old glass industry, with objects spanning medieval goblets to cutting-edge contemporary sculptures. It even houses a Guinness World Records collection of Swedish cheese-dish covers – 71 in total. There's a great cafe and the ticket price covers the adjacent House of Emigrants.

House of Emigrants MUSEUM
(Utvandrarnas Hus; www.utvandrarnashus.se; Vilhelm Mobergs gata 4; adult/child Skr70/free; ⊙10am-5pm Tue-Fri, to 4pm Sat & Sun) Boasts engrossing displays on the emigration of over one million Swedes to America (1850–1930) and includes a replica of Vilhelm Moberg's office and the original manuscripts of his famous emigration novels.

Växjö Konsthall MUSEUM
(☑0470-414 75; Västra Esplanaden 10; ⊙noon-6pm Tue-Fri, to 4pm Sat & Sun) **FREE** Opposite the library, Växjö Konsthall showcases contemporary work by local and national artists; expect anything from minimalist ceramics to mixed-media installations.

Domkyrkan CHURCH
(Linnégatan; ⊙9am-5pm) Looking like an ode to Pippi Longstocking, the bizarre Domkyrkan has been struck by lightning and repeatedly ravaged by fire – the latest renovation was in 1995. Inside is a fine 15th-century altar and a whimsical contemporary sculpture by Erik Höglund. Don't miss the Viking rune stone in the eastern wall.

Kronobergs Slott CASTLE
(adult/child Skr25/free; ⊙11am-7pm, to 9pm Fri & Sat) In 1542 Småland rebel Nils Dacke spent Christmas in Kronobergs Slott, now a ruin. The 14th-century castle is on a small island (reached by footbridge) in Helgasjön, about 8km north of the town. **Boat trips** (☑0470-630-00; www.ryttmastaregarden.se; adult/child Skr185/110; ⊙Wed, Sat & Sun Jun-Sep) on S/S *Thor*, Sweden's oldest steamship, built in 1887, leave from below the ruins. Take bus 1B from town.

🛏 Sleeping

Växjö Vandrarhem HOSTEL **€**
(☑0470-630 70; www.vaxjovandrarhem.nu; Brandts väg 11, Evedal; dm/s/d Skr200/450/550; ⊙reception 5-8pm Jun-Aug; 🅿@🛜) Located at the lakeside recreation area of Evedal, 6km north of the centre, this former spa hotel dates from the late 18th century. All

Växjö

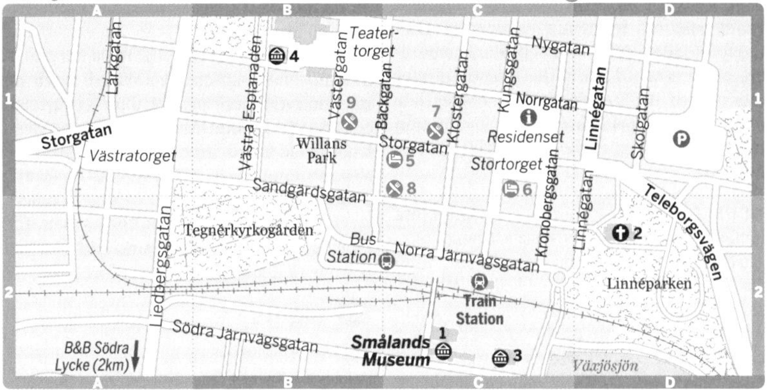

rooms have washbasins, and there's a big kitchen, a laundry and a wonderful lounge in the attic. You can also hire canoes and bikes.

★B&B Södra Lycke B&B €€
(0706-76 65 06; www.sodralycke.se; Hagagatan 10; s/d Skr500/800; P) This charming B&B in an atmospheric mid-19th-century family house is in a residential area 10 minutes' walk southwest from the centre via Södra Järnvägsgatan (check online for a map). There are three rooms and an appealingly overgrown garden complete with vegetable plot, wildflowers, greenhouse and black hens.

Elite Stadshotellet HOTEL €€
(0470-134 00; www.elite.se; Kungsgatan 6; s/d Skr850/1190; P@) Right on Stortorget and tastefully renovated, this hotel couples crisply modern rooms with the glamour of a 19th-century building. Single rooms aren't particularly roomy, but all are smart and comfortable, and there's an English pub here too if you're 'hopping' for some real draught ale.

Clarion Collection Cardinal HOTEL €€
(0470-72 28 00; www.choice.se; Bäckgatan 10; s/d Skr820/920; P@) A jump up in quality, the central Cardinal offers simple, stylish rooms with Persian rugs and the odd antique touch. There's also a small fitness centre, a bar and a restaurant serving modern Nordic cuisine. Note that, as with all Clarion Collection hotels, a buffet dinner (as well as breakfast) is generously included in the room price.

Växjö

Top Sights
1 Smålands Museum ... C2

Sights
2 Domkyrkan ... D2
3 House of Emigrants ... C2
4 Växjö Konsthall ... B1

Sleeping
5 Clarion Collection Cardinal ... C1
6 Elite Stadshotellet ... C1

Eating
7 Bröd & Sovel ... C1
8 Kafe de Luxe ... C1
9 PM & Vänner ... B1

Drinking & Nightlife
Loft & Terrassen ... (see 9)

Eating & Drinking

★Bröd & Sovel BAKERY €
(www.pmrestauranger.se; Storgatan 12; sandwiches from Skr55; 7.30am-7pm Mon-Fri, 9am-5pm Sat, noon-7pm Sun; P) Voted the country's best pastry shop in 2014 by Sweden's prestigious foodie bible, the *White Guide*, this bakery offers a vast array of buttery pastries, creamy cakes, freshly made sandwiches and homemade sweets. At the very least pick up half a dozen of the chocolate-covered macadamia nuts to go (you *will* return for more...)!

Kafe de Luxe INTERNATIONAL €€
(0470-74 04 09; Sandgärdsgatan 19; mains from Skr155; 11am-midnight Mon-Thu, to 2am Fri & Sat, 10am-1am Sun;) An urban-boho vibe,

great music (live at weekends) and '50s- to '60s-style decor, including an adjacent candy-coloured ice-cream parlour, contribute to the special feel of this place. The burgers are renowned, as is the eclectic dinner menu with its French-inspired dishes like entrecôte with a classic *béarnaise* sauce and its innovative veggie choices: nettle gnocchi, anyone?

★ **PM & Vänner** SWEDISH €€€
(☎0470-70 04 44; www.pmrestauranger.se; Storgatan 22; restaurant tasting menu Skr995, bistro mains Skr209-365; ⊙11.30am-1.30pm Mon-Sat, plus 6-10pm Wed-Sat) A stylish bistro complete with black-and-white tiled floors and wicker chairs, PM & Vänner serves up new-school Swedish flavours with global twists. Local produce sparkles in dishes ranging from grilled cod with summer chanterelles to Småland veal. It also runs popular cocktail and lounge bar **Terrassen** (www.pmrestauranger.se; Västergatan 10; ⊙6pm-midnight), which has live music Wednesday and Thursday.

Information

Pedestrianised Storgatan has banks and other services.

Tourist Office (☎0470-73 32 80; www.turism.vaxjo.se; Stortorget, Residencet; ⊙9.30am-6pm Mon-Fri, 10am-2pm Sat Jun-Aug) On the main square.

Getting There & Away

Småland Airport (☎0470-75 85 00; www.smalandairport.se) is 9km northwest of Växjö. **SAS** (☎0770-72 77 27; www.flysas.com) has direct flights to Stockholm; **Fly Smaland** (☎0900-20 71 720; www.flysmaland.com) flies to Stockholm, Berlin and Visby; and **Ryanair** (☎0900-20 20 240; www.ryanair.com) goes to Düsseldorf Weeze. An airport bus (Flygbussen) connects with flights (Skr25); otherwise, take a **taxi** (☎135 00) (fares from Skr240).

Länstrafiken Kronoberg (☎0470-72 75 50; www.lanstrafikenkron.se) runs the regional bus network, with daily buses to Halmstad, Jönköping and Kosta. Long-distance buses depart beside the train station. **Svenska Buss** (www.svenskabuss.se) runs one or two services daily to Eksjö (Skr250, 1½ hours), Linköping (Skr320, 3¼ hours) and Stockholm (Skr420, 6½ hours).

Växjö is served by **SJ** (www.sj.se) trains running roughly hourly between Alvesta (on the main north–south line; from Skr50, 15 minutes) and Kalmar (Skr146, 1¼ hours). A few trains run daily directly to Karlskrona (Skr163, 1½ hours) and Malmö (from Skr195).

Kalmar

☎0480 / POP 64,000

Not only is Kalmar dashing, it claims one of Sweden's most spectacular castles, with an interior even more perfect than its turreted outside. Other local assets include Sweden's largest gold hoard, from the 17th-century ship *Kronan*, and the cobbled streets of Gamla Stan (Old Town) to the west of Slottshotellet.

The Kalmar Union of 1397, when the crowns of Sweden, Denmark and Norway became one, was agreed to at the castle.

Sights

★ **Kalmar Slott** CASTLE
(www.kalmarslott.kalmar.se; adult/child Skr120/100; ⊙10am-6pm daily Jul–mid-Aug, shorter hours rest of year; 👪) Fairy-tale turrets, a drawbridge, a foul dungeon and secret passages…yes, Kalmar Slott has everything that a proper castle should. This powerful Renaissance building was once the most important in Sweden, and it's fortified accordingly. It also boasts one of the best-preserved interiors from the period.

For more information, join one of the **guided tours** (⊙in English at 11.30am, 1.30pm & 2.30pm Jun–mid-Aug, 11.30am only mid-Aug–early Oct), included in the admission price. There are also children's activities here in summer.

King Erik's chamber is a real scene-stealer. Erik's rivalry with his brother Johan caused him to install a secret passage in the loo! There's also a superb suspended ceiling in the **Golden Hall**; mesmerising wall-to-wall and floor-to-ceiling marquetry in the **Chequered Hall**; an elaborate **bed**, stolen as war booty then carefully vandalised so that no Danish ghosts could haunt it; and a delightful **chapel**, one of Sweden's Most Wanted for weddings.

★ **Kalmar Länsmuseum** MUSEUM
(County Museum; www.kalmarlansmuseum.se; Skeppsbrogatan; adult/child Skr80/free; ⊙10am-4pm Mon-Fri, to 8pm Wed, 11am-4pm Sat & Sun) The highlight of this fine museum, in an old steam mill by the harbour, are finds from the 17th-century flagship *Kronan*. The ship exploded and sank just before a battle in 1676, with the loss of almost 800 men. It was rediscovered in 1980, and over 30,000 wonderfully preserved items have been excavated so far, including a spectacular gold hoard, clothing and musical instruments.

Kalmar Sjöfartsmuseum MUSEUM
(☎0480-158 75; www.kalmarsjofartsmuseum.se; Södra Långgatan 81; adult/child Skr50/20; ⊙11am-

Kalmar

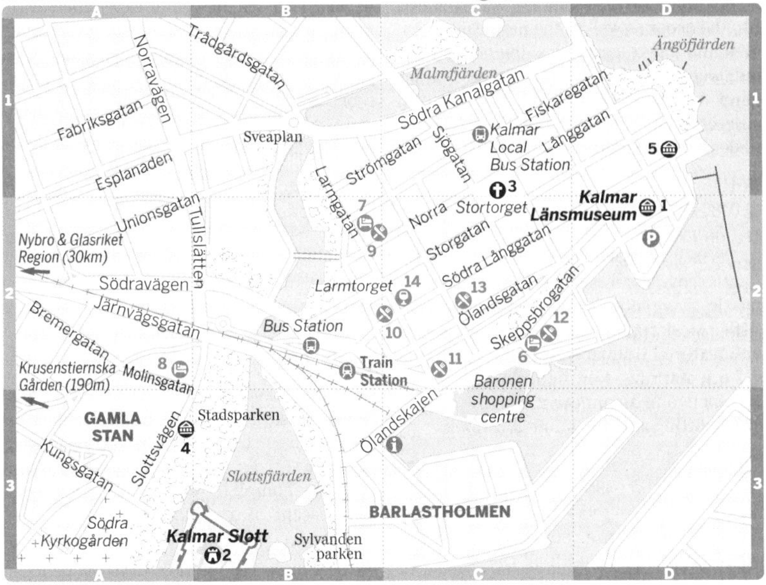

4pm daily mid-Jun–mid-Sep;) Houses an eccentric maritime collection, with bottled ships, foghorns and things made out of knots and armadillos.

Domkyrkan CHURCH

(Cathedral; www.kalmardomkyrka.se; Stortorget; 8am-3.30pm Mon-Fri, to 6.30pm Wed, 9am-4pm Sat & Sun) Home to a spectacular pulpit, the baroque Domkyrkan was designed by Tessin, King Karl X Gustav's favourite architect.

Krusenstiernska Gården GARDENS

(0480-41 15 52; www.krusenstiernskagarden.se; Stora Dammgatan 11; tours adult/child Skr30/10; 11am-6pm Mon-Fri, noon-5pm Sat & Sun Jun-Aug, closed Sat Jul, shorter hours rest of year) FREE Krusenstiernska Gården is a stuck-in-time 19th-century middle-class home around 500m from the entrance to Kalmar Slott. Tours of the house are on the hour, but entry to the beautiful gardens and cafe is free.

Kalmar Konstmuseum MUSEUM

(www.kalmarkonstmuseum.se; Stadsparken; adult/child Skr50/free; noon-5pm Tue-Sun, to 7pm Wed) The striking Kalmar Konstmuseum, in the park near the Kalmar Slott, dishes out brilliant temporary exhibitions featuring local and global art-scene 'It' kids.

Kalmar

Top Sights

1	Kalmar Länsmuseum	D2
2	Kalmar Slott	B3

Sights

3	Domkyrkan	C1
4	Kalmar Konstmuseum	A3
5	Kalmar Sjöfartsmuseum	D1

Sleeping

6	Clarion Collection Hotel Packhuset	C2
7	Kalmarsund Hotel	B2
8	Slottshotellet	A2

Eating

9	Athena	B2
10	Da Ernesto	C2
11	Gröna Stugan	C2
12	Hamnkrogen	C2
13	Restaurang Källaren Kronan	C2

Drinking & Nightlife

14	Lilla Puben	C2

Sleeping

★ **Clarion Collection Hotel Packhuset** HOTEL €€

(0480-570 00; www.choicehotels.se; Skeppsbrogatan 26; s/d Skr1320/1420; P) The seafaring theme here extends from the 1950s-era trunks and suitcases that are incorporated into the decor as well as the nautical barometers and gauges, grainy 'ship-ahoy' photos and wood-panelled rooms (request a sea view). A lavish dinner buffet is included in the accommodation price, along with home-made cakes at teatime.

Slottshotellet HOTEL €€
(☑ 0480-882 60; www.slottshotellet.se; Slottsvägen 7; r/ste from Skr1395/1795, annexe s/d Skr795/995; P @ 🖎) This wonderfully romantic, cosy hotel is housed in four buildings in a gorgeous green setting near the castle. Most rooms have antique furniture with textured wallpaper, crystal chandeliers and oriental rugs. New budget accommodation opened in an annexe across the road in 2013 sporting a white, minimalist look.

Kalmarsund Hotel HOTEL €€
(Best Western; ☑ 0480-48 03 80; www.kalmar sundhotel.se; Fiskaregatan 5; s/d Skr1295/1495; P @ 🖎) Tidy midsize rooms are painted in muted earth colours with all the extras, including kettle, hairdryer, fridge and even a pillow menu. There's a sauna and parking and the breakfast buffet is five-star standard; you won't go hungry.

🍴 Eating & Drinking

Kalmar has plenty of good food and a variety of scenes to choose from, whether you want showy sailboats, a view of the castle or to people-watch on Larmtorget.

Athena GREEK €
(☑ 0480-280 88; Norra Långgatan 8; mains from Skr90; ⊘ 11am-10pm Mon-Thu, to 11pm Fri & Sat, 1-9pm Sun) Faux Acropolis-style busts, statues and murals adorn the interior of this Greek restaurant with a nod towards Italy (there's pasta and pizza on the menu), but the Greek dishes, like moussaka and *keftedes* (meatballs), are your best bet.

Hamnkrogen FRENCH €€
(☑ 0480-41 10 20; Skeppsbrogatan 30; mains from Skr120; ⊘ 11.30am-2pm Mon-Frii, plus 5-9pm Sat) This renowned former seafood restaurant has morphed into an excellent upmarket French brasserie with dishes like steamed mussels, *bouillabaisse* and French onion soup on the menu.

Restaurang Källaren Kronan SWEDISH €€
(☑ 0480-41 14 00; www.kallarenkronan.com; Ölandsgatan 7; mains Skr135-275; ⊘ noon-2pm &

6-10pm Tue-Sun) Six cellars have been transformed into a high-calibre experience, with meals served under a cosy vaulted ceiling. There's even a 1660s menu, with mains like salmon poached in wine with crayfish and root vegetables. Otherwise, the menu is replete with Swedish classics like meatballs and gravlax.

Da Ernesto ITALIAN €€
(www.ernestokalmar.se; Larmtorget 4; mains from Skr130; ⊘ 5-11pm Mon-Fri, noon-midnight Sat, 1-10pm Sun) Run by a real-deal Neapolitan, this Italian cafe, restaurant and bar attracts scores of people with its baristi, extensive menu (including Neapolitan-style pizzas) and well-mixed drinks.

Gröna Stugan EUROPEAN €€€
(www.gronastuganikalmar.se; Larmgatan 1; mains Skr210-285; ⊘ 5-11pm Mon-Sat, to 9pm Sun) Located in an unassuming sage-green building complete with round windows reminiscent of a ship, this gem of a restaurant serves up dishes that are gorgeous on the plate and even better to eat. Leave space for the blueberry pancakes with raspberry panna cotta.

Lilla Puben PUB
(☑ 0480-42 24 22; Larmgatan 24; ⊘ 5pm-1am Tue-Sat) Thirsty? This bar is almost obscenely decorated with shelf after shelf of every imaginable brand of beer, some 700 varieties, plus a choice of 120 whiskies.

ℹ Information

You'll find banks and other services on Storgatan.

Tourist Office (☑ 0480-41 77 00; www.kalmar. com; Ölandskajen 9; ⊘ 9am-9pm Mon-Fri, 10am-5pm Sat & Sun Jun-Aug, shorter hours rest of year) Handy for information on the region.

ℹ Getting There & Around

Kalmar Airport (☑ 0480-45 90 00; www.kal marairport.se) is located 6km west of town. **SAS** (☑ 0770-72 77 27; www.flysas.com) flies several times daily to Stockholm Arlanda, while **Kalmarflyg** (www.kalmarflyg.se) flies to Stockholm Bromma and Prag. The Flygbuss airport bus (Skr50) provides connections to central Kalmar. A taxi to/from the airport costs about Skr150.

Roughly three **Swebus Express** (☑ 0771-21 82 18; www.swebus.se) services daily run north to Norrköping (Skr289, four hours); and one to three services daily run south to Karlskrona (Skr69, 1¼ hours) and Malmö (Skr229, 4½ hours), among other destinations. **Svenska**

Buss (☎0771-67 67 67; www.svenskabuss.se) has similar routes and prices.

SJ (p222) trains run every hour or two between Kalmar and Alvesta (from Skr167, 1¼ hours), where you can connect with the main Stockholm–Malmö line and with trains to Göteborg. Trains run to Linköping up to nine times daily (from Skr333, three hours), also with connections to Stockholm.

Taxi Kalmar (☎44 44 44) can help you get around town.

Glasriket

With its hypnotic glass-blowing workshops, the **'Kingdom of Crystal'** (www.glasriket.se) is Sweden's third-biggest drawcard after Stockholm and Göteborg. There are at least 11 glass factories (look for *glasbruk* signs), most with long histories: Kosta, for example, was founded in 1742. The region is also immensely popular with Americans tracing their ancestors, many of whom emigrated from this area at the end of the 19th century.

The glassworks have similar opening hours, usually 10am to 6pm Monday to Friday, 10am to 4pm Saturday and noon to 4pm Sunday. Expert glass designers produce some extraordinary avant-garde pieces, often with a good dollop of Swedish wit involved. Factory outlets have substantial discounts on seconds (around 30% to 40% off), and larger places can arrange shipping to your home country.

There's a **Glasriket Pass** (Skr95), allowing free admission into 'hot shops' and museums, and discounts on purchases and *hyttsill* parties (where you eat traditional-style dishes on communal tables). It's a good deal if you want to try glass-blowing and *hyttsill* and buy some pieces, but skip it if you're just browsing.

Getting There & Around

Apart from the main routes, bus services around the area are practically nonexistent. The easiest way to explore is with your own transport (beware of elk). Bicycle tours on the unsurfaced country roads are excellent; there are plenty of hostels, and you can camp almost anywhere except near the military area on the Kosta–Orrefors road.

Kalmar Länstrafik's bus 139 runs from mid-June to mid-August only and calls at a few of the glass factories. The service operates four times per day on weekdays and once on Saturday, and runs from Nybro to Orrefors and Målerås. Year-round bus services connect Nybro and Orrefors (up to nine weekdays), and Kosta is served by regular bus 218 from Växjö (two or three daily).

Buses and trains run from Emmaboda to Nybro and Kalmar (roughly hourly); trains also run to Karlskrona, Växjö and Alvesta, from where there are direct services to Göteborg and Stockholm.

Kosta

☎0478

The small town of Kosta is where Glasriket first fired up, way back in 1742.

Sights & Activities

Kosta Boda GLASSWORKS

(☎0478-345 00; www.kostaboda.se; Stora vägen 96; ⏲shops 10am-6pm Mon-Fri, to 5pm Sat & Sun, glass-blowing demonstrations 9am-3.30pm Mon-Fri, 10am-4pm Sat & Sun, exhibition gallery 10am-5pm Mon-Fri, to 4pm Sat & Sun; P) One of the first glassworks in Sweden, today the Kosta Boda complex (established 1742) pulls in coachloads of visitors, who raid the vast discount outlets. It's touristy, but the Kosta Boda Art Hotel, exhibition gallery, glass-blowing demonstrations and great cafes make it a good base for exploration. There are plenty of glass-blowing demos in the old factory quarters.

Inside the factory's outlet store, the Kosta Boda Art Café serves tasty quiches and grilled sandwiches for around Skr60.

Grönåsens Älgpark WILDLIFE RESERVE

(☎0478-507 70; www.moosepark.net; admission Skr60; ⏲10am-6pm daily Apr–mid-Sep, to 5pm mid-Sep–Oct; P) For a close encounter with a beautiful bandy-legged elk, head for Sweden's biggest elk park, located 3km west of Kosta towards Orrefors. You can admire these gentle creatures on a 1.3km walk in the forested enclosure. Ironically, you can also buy elk sausages to roast on the outdoor barbecue or purchase an elk-skin baseball cap.

Sleeping & Eating

★**Kosta Boda Art Hotel** HOTEL

(☎0487-348 30; www.kostabodaarthotel.com; Stora vägen 75; s/d Skr1100/2590; P) As befitting the best hotel in the Glass Kingdom, Kosta Boda Art Hotel showcases inspired glasswork in unusual ways – like a designer glass bar. Each of the 102 rooms also features glasswork and textiles by Kosta Boda artists. Even if you don't stay the night, drop in for the mouth-watering buffet lunch at the hotel's **Linnéa Art Restaurant** (www.kostabodaarthotel.com; buffet Skr245; ⏲noon-3.30pm).

Alternatively, inside the factory's outlet store (and open the same hours), the Kosta Boda Art Café has quiches and grilled sandwiches for around Skr60.

Nybro

0481 / POP 19,640

Quiet Nybro has two lovely glassworks and was once a centre for hand-blown light bulbs (!). The town's tourist office (0481-450 85; www.nybro.se; Stadshusplan; 9am-5pm Mon-Fri, noon-4pm Sun) is within the town hall.

Sights & Activities

Pukeberg GLASSWORKS
(www.pukeberg.se; Pukebergarnas väg; 10am-5pm Mon-Fri, to 2pm Sat, noon-4pm Sun; P) Of the two glassworks in Nybro, the unfortunately named Pukeberg, just southeast of the centre, is perhaps more interesting for its historic setting (dating from 1871).

Nybro GLASSWORKS
(www.nybro-glasbruk.se; Herkulesgatan; 10am-5pm Mon-Fri, to 3pm Sat, 11am-2pm Sun; P) Nybro is a small glassworks specialising in quirky items (think Elvis Presley glass platters).

Sleeping

Joelskogens Camping CAMPGROUND €
(0481-450 86; www.laget.se/nybroifcamping; Grönvägen 51; sites/cabins Skr170/370; May–mid-Sep; P) Campers should head for this lakeside ground just out of the centre.

DON'T MISS

HOMESTEAD MUSEUM

Madesjö Hembygdsgård (admission Skr50; 1-5pm daily mid-May–mid-Sep; P) No one has counted, apparently, but there are probably upwards of 35,000 objects on display at this fascinating ethnological museum housed in the former stables of Nybro's village church. Various tableaus illustrate the social history of the region over the last 100 years; the mannequins will make you smile – there are plenty of bad hair days here. Exhibits range from coffins to a fantastic (ice-)cycle. You can also buy honey and flour produced on the premises.

Nybro Lågprishotell & Vandrarhem HOSTEL €
(0481-109 32; www.nybrovandrarhem.se; Vasagatan 22; dm/s/d Skr300/400/500, hotel s/d Skr550/850; P) This local STF hostel, near Pukeberg, is clean and comfortable, with a kitchen on each floor as well as a sauna. More expensive 'hotel' rooms have cable TV, non-bunk beds and private showers and toilets. You can also rent bicycles.

Orrefors

0481

This small town is home to arguably the most famous glassworks in Sweden.

Sights & Activities

Orrefors GLASSWORKS
(www.orrefors.se; Stora vägen 96; 10am-6pm Mon-Fri, noon-4pm Sat & Sun; P) Established in 1898, this huge site is home to a factory and a large shop with a shipping service. The ubersleek museum-gallery showcases a range of stunning glassware spanning 1910 to the present day, and houses stylish bar-cafe Kristallbaren (sandwiches Skr60; 9am-6pm Mon-Fri, to 3pm Sat).

Sleeping & Eating

Orrefors Bed & Breakfast B&B €
(0481-301 30; www.bnb.nu; Silversparregatan 17; s/d Skr550/650; Jun-Aug; P) Located in an aesthetically renovated 19th-century cottage with simple yet comfortable rooms and shared facilities. The friendly owners run short summer courses in glass-blowing (three hours, Skr350) at the nearby Riksglasskolan (National School of Glass; 0481-302 64; www.riksglasskolan.se).

Orrefors Värdshus SWEDISH €
(0481-300 59; mains Skr95; 11.30am-4pm Mon-Sat; P) Located in the Orrefors factory grounds, the inn Orrefors Värdshus serves good lunches with an emphasis on local produce.

Other Glassworks

0481

Don't miss the glassworks at Gullaskruv, about 6km northwest of Orrefors. Here, Uruguayan-born artist Carlos R Pebaqué (0481-321 17; www.carlosartglass.com; Glasblasarvärgen 6, Gullaskruv; 11am-6pm Mon-Fri, to 5pm Sat, to 4pm Sun) creates extraordinary vases in his one glass oven.

The large and popular **Mats Jonasson factory** (☎0481-314 00; www.matsjonasson.com; Industrigatan 20, Målerås; ⊙10am-6pm Mon-Fri, to 4pm Sat, 11am-4pm Sun), 8km further northwest in Målerås, features work by the famous glass-blower who is especially well known for his skilled glass painting. There's also a restaurant for a post-shopping refuel.

A kilometre or so southeast of Gullaskruv, **Hälleberga Bed & Breakfast** (☎0481-320 21; www.halleberga.se; Hälleberga 108; s/d incl breakfast Skr350/650; P), a youth hostel turned B&B, boasts a tranquil, rustic setting. Rooms all have washbasins, and linen is included in the price.

Oskarshamn

☎0491 / POP 26,300

Oskarshamn is useful for its regular boat connections to Gotland. A few sights help to kill time.

Sights

Döderhultarmuseet MUSEUM

(☎0491-880 40; adult/child Skr60/free; ⊙9am-6pm Mon-Fri, 10am-4pm Sat & Sun Jun-Aug, 9am-6pm Mon-Fri, 10am-2pm Sat rest of year) Upstairs in the Kulturhuset cultural centre, Döderhultarmuseet features around 200 works by home-grown artist Axel Petersson 'Döderhultarn' (1868–1925), who captured local characters and occasions in vigorous and funny woodcarvings. Also upstairs, with the same opening hours, **Sjöfartsmuseet** showcases local maritime exhibits. One admission price covers entry to both museums.

Blå Jungfrun National Park NATURE RESERVE

(Blue Maiden) Blå Jungfrun, a 1km-long granite island, is known as the 'Witches' Mountain' because, according to tradition, this is where they gather every Easter to meet the devil. The island is a nature reserve with fantastic scenery, gnarled trees, blue hares and bird life, and the curious stone maze **Trojeborg**.

Between mid-June and August a local launch, **M/S Solkust** (www.solkustturer.se; adult/child Skr250/125; ⊙mid-Jun–Aug), departs up to five times weekly (usually not Monday and Tuesday) from Brädholmskajen, the quay at the head of the harbour in Oskarshamn, allowing passengers 3½ hours to explore the island. Book online or contact the tourist office.

Sleeping & Eating

There are no outstanding eateries, but there are a couple of pleasant ones.

Vandrarhemmet Oscar HOSTEL €

(☎0491-158 00; www.forumoskarshamn.com; Södra Långgatan 15-17; hostel dm/s/d Skr180/305/410, hotel s/d Skr790/1060; P@📶) This shiny hotel-hostel hybrid is a convenient budget option. Rooms have TV, fans and bathrooms – only the kitchen for self-caterers gives it away as a hostel.

Steakhouse Oscar STEAK €€

(☎0491-772 28; www.steakhouseoscar.se; Östra Torggatan 2; mains from Skr195; ⊙11.30am-2pm Mon-Fri, 5pm-midnight Tue-Fri, 3pm-midnight Sat) Carnivores flock to this place with its meaty choices including rib-eye steak, pork tenderloin and fillet of beef. There's a Skr99 lunch menu with just one choice, but you can bet it's a good one (unless you're vegetarian).

Pub Kråkan PUB

(☎0491-770 84; www.krakan.se; Kungsgatan 2; mains from Skr100; ⊙noon-11pm Tue-Fri, to midnight Sat & Sun; 📶) The oldest pub in town, with a suitably welcoming atmosphere and a superb range of ales on tap and whiskeys. Also dishes up typical pub grub like burgers (and even the occasional curry).

Information

There are ATMs at the Flanaden shopping centre.

Tourist Office (☎0491-770 72; www.oskarshamn.se; Hantverksgatan 3; ⊙9am-6pm Mon-Fri, 10am-3pm Sat & Sun) Helpful tourist office with plenty of information about the town and region.

Getting There & Away

Boats to Visby depart from the Gotland Ferry Terminal near the now-disused train station daily in winter and twice daily in summer. The M/S *Solsund* **ferry** (www.olandsfarjan.se) to Byxelkrok, Öland (adult/child Skr150/100), departs twice daily in summer from the ferry terminal off Skeppsbron.

Long-distance bus services stop at the very central bus station. Regional **KLT** (www.klt.se) bus services run up to six times daily from Oskarshamn to Kalmar (Skr64, 1½ hours).

Swebus Express has four daily buses between Stockholm and Kalmar, calling in at Oskarshamn. The closest train station is in Berga, 25km west of town. Here, regional trains run from Linköping and Nässjö. Local buses connect Berga and Oskarshamn.

Västervik

☎0490 / POP 36,460

Västervik is a bustling, picturesque coastal summer resort, with cute cobbled streets, a buzzing nightlife, sandy beaches just east of town, and 5000 islands on the doorstep. Harried by the Danes in its early years, it bloomed into a major shipbuilding centre between the 17th and 19th centuries. **VisFestivalen** (www.visfestivalen.se; ⏲mid-Jul), Västervik's famous folk-song festival, is held in summer.

Sights & Activities

★Historic Buildings HISTORIC BUILDINGS

The tourist office has a town-walking brochure that leads you round the best of Västervik's beautiful old buildings. **St Petri Kyrka** (Östra Kyrkogatan 67) is a dramatic mass of spires and buttresses, while the calmer **St Gertruds Kyrkan** (Västra Kyrkogatan) dates from 1433 and has taken lightning strikes and riots in its stride.

Nearby, **Aspagården** (Västra Kyrkogatan 9), dating from the 17th century, is the oldest wooden house in town. Other abodes from the 1740s are the picture-perfect former ferrymen's cottages at **Båtmansstugorna** (Båtmansgatan).

★Västerviks Museum MUSEUM

(☎049-211 77; www.vastervikmuseum.se; Kulbacken; adult/child Skr50/free; ⏲11am-4pm Mon-Fri, 1-4pm Sat & Sun Jun-Aug, closed Sat rest of year) Displays at this museum, just north of the tourist office, cover the town's history. You'll also find **Unos Torn**, an 18m-high lookout tower with archipelago views, here.

Archipelago Boat Trips CRUISE

(☎070-265 09 01; www.vastervikskargardsturer.se; return adult/child Skr200/100; ⏲mid-Jun–end Aug) Archipelago tours depart from Skeppsbron daily from mid-June to the end of August. Buy tickets directly at the Skärgårdsterminalen pier kiosk, at the tourist office or via the website.

For a full day of touring on the archipelago, bikes can be rented on the island of **Hasselö** and from **Handelsboa** at **Hasselö Sand**.

There are also shrimp cruises with a meal of unlimited shrimps on board, sailing trips on a schooner, diving and speedboat trips and several boat taxis.

Sleeping

The town bursts at the seams in summer, so book your accommodation ahead.

Akrells i Båtmansgränd HISTORIC HOTEL €

(☎0490-194 03; Strömsgatan 42; cottages per person Skr400) While they're a little run-down, there is something to be said for spending a night in one of these 18th-century fishermen's cottages, located in the atmospheric old part of town. Most sleep four and have their own kitchen, though bathrooms are shared.

Västerviks Stadshotell HISTORIC HOTEL €€

(Best Western; ☎0490-820 00; www.stadshotellet.nu; Storgatan 3; s/d Skr1050/1350; P@📶) Major renovations in 2014 have added another floor to this elegant central hotel, which is now under the Best Western umbrella. Rooms are spacious and modern, plus there's sauna, hot tub and gym. The breakfast buffet is particularly lavish.

Hotel Fängelset HOTEL €€

(☎076-136 89 66; www.hotellfangelset.se; Fängelsetorget 1; s without bathroom Skr570, d with/without bathroom Skr990/690; P@📶) Housed in a magnificent building, this former prison (until 2007) has a lingering institutional feel, with rooms in the cells (with bars still on the windows). Space is tight, even in the doubles, where the bathrooms are similarly cellsize. The quirkiness continues with the on-site craft brewery – you can taste the results in the bar.

Eating & Drinking

Västervik's fast-food speciality is French fries, mashed potato and shrimp salad (Skr25); look out for it at stands along the waterside.

Waterside Fiskaretorget is a hive of activity, studded with several restaurant-bars that have popular summer terraces.

Guldkant INTERNATIONAL €€

(☎0490-216 00; www.restaurangguldkant.se; Grönsakstorget 6; mains from Skr185, set lunch Skr80; ⏲10am-10pm Mon-Thu, to 2am Fri & Sat, noon-10pm Sun) A bar, a deli, a restaurant and a waterfront terrace with one of the best views of Västervik...OK, the interior is a bit of a dated decor disaster, but the food, ranging from Thai curry to Swedish meatballs, is well prepared and tasty. The lunch is a good deal, too, and includes salad and coffee.

Västervik

Västervik

Top Sights

1 Aspagården A3
2 St Petri Kyrka A3
3 Västerviks Museum B1

Sights

4 Båtmansstugorna B3
5 St Gertruds Kyrkan A3

Sleeping

6 Akrells i Båtmansgränd B4
7 Hotel Fängelset B4
8 Västerviks Stadshotell B3

Eating

9 Dolce e Salato B3
10 Guldkant A3
11 Restaurang Smugglaren B3
12 Saltmagasinet B1

Dolce e Salato ITALIAN €€
(☎0490-368 85; www.dolceesalato.se; Strömsgatan 7; mains Skr115; ⏲11.30am-3.30pm Mon-Thu, to 10pm Fri & Sat; 📶) Italian owned and run, this is the best Italian restaurant in town. The pasta dishes may stand out, but the ice cream is in another realm altogether: home made on the premises as only Italianos know how... (sorry, Mr Whippy, you don't count).

★ **Saltmagasinet** SWEDISH €€€
(www.saltmagasinet.se; Kulbaken; mains Skr250-345; ⏲lunch 11.30am-3pm, dinner from 5pm Mon-Sat) 🌿 Located on the same hill as the Unos Torn tower, Saltmagasinet boasts great views and was named the city's best restaurant for four years running in the *White Guide*, Sweden's food bible. It's also among the top 10 best places in Sweden to enjoy organic and fair-trade cuisine. Smoked fish, beet soup, lamb: everything is beautifully presented and prepared.

It also runs a brilliant bakery, located in the same building as the restaurant.

Restaurang Smugglaren EUROPEAN €€€
(☎0490-213 22; www.smugglaren.se; Smugglaregränd 1; mains Skr250-345; ⏲from 6pm Mon-Sat) In a cosy wooden building tucked down an alley off Strandvägen, Smugglaren dresses up Swedish classics such as beef with lingonberries or salmon tournedos. Model ships, paraffin lamps and the odd elk head crank up the eccentricity.

Information

Västervik Tourist Office (☎0490-875 20; www.vastervik.com; ⏲10am-6pm Mon-Fri, to 2pm Sat May–late Jun, shorter hours rest of year)

Getting There & Away

Long-distance buses stop outside the train station, at the eastern edge of the town centre. Trains run between Västervik and Linköping up to 10 times daily (Skr150, 1¾ hours). Daily bus services run roughly every hour to 90 minutes to Vimmerby (Skr90, one hour), and every two hours to Oskarshamn (Skr98, one hour) and Kalmar (Skr105, 2¾ hours).

Svenska Buss runs to Stockholm, Kalmar, Karlskrona and Malmö four times per week. Swebus Express runs a Västervik–Vimmerby–Eksjö–Jönköping–Göteborg route.

Vimmerby

0492 / POP 15,600

Vimmerby is the birthplace of Astrid Lindgren, and home to one of Sweden's favourite drawcards – a theme park based on the Pippi Longstocking books. Almost everything in town revolves around the strongest girl in the world – there's little escape!

Sights & Activities

Astrid Lindgrens Värld AMUSEMENT PARK
(0492-798 00; www.alv.se; adult/child/family Skr395/280/1295; 10am-6pm daily Jun-Aug, to 5pm Sat & Sun Sep; P) Young children and Pippi Longstocking aficionados shouldn't miss Astrid Lindgrens Värld, on the northern edge of town. Actresses dressed as Pippi (complete with gravity-defying pigtails) sing and dance their way around the 100 buildings and settings from the books. Prices drop outside peak season, as there are fewer activities and theatre performances. The theme park is a 15-minute walk from central Vimmerby.

There's a reasonably priced restaurant, a fast-food joint and coffee shops in the park. Dedicated fans can crash at the on-site campground.

Astrid Lindgrens Näs MUSEUM
(tours 0492-76 94 00; www.astridlindgrensnas.se; Prästgården 24; adult/child Skr120/free, tours adult/child Skr95/50; 10am-6pm mid-Jun–end Aug, shorter hours rest of the year; P) Near Astrid Lindgrens Värld you'll find Astrid Lindgrens Näs, a fascinating cultural centre set on the farm on which Lindgren grew up. There's a permanent exhibition about the writer's life and temporary exhibitions inspired by Lindgren's stories and legacy. The true highlight, however, is the 30-minute **guided tour** (adult/child Skr95/50; daily in summer, by appointment only rest of year) of Lindgren's faithfully restored childhood home. Call for tour times.

Guides bring the place to life with entertaining anecdotes, which you can ponder over a decent coffee and a book at the centre's cafe and gift shop. New in 2014 are the beautiful gardens now open to the public. When you've reached ginger-plait overload, wander down Storgatan for a fix of quaint 18th- and 19th-century wooden abodes.

Sleeping & Eating

There's plenty of accommodation in town, much of it offering theme-park packages; ask at the tourist office for details.

Vimmerby Vandrarhem HOSTEL €
(0492-100 20; www.vimmerbyvandrarhem.nu; Järnvägsallén 2; r from Skr520; P @) This cheerful hostel, based in a fine wooden building, is right near the train station. There are more expensive doubles available, with proper (non-bunk) beds, plus a garden and barbecue.

Campground CAMPGROUND €
(0492-798 00; www.alv.se; Astrid Lindgrens Värld; sites/4-bed cabins from Skr380/1795; mid-May–Aug; P) For those who are visiting the theme park, these sites and cabins are on the premises.

Vimmerby Stadshotell HOTEL €€
(Best Western; 0492-121 00; www.vimmerbystadshotell.se; Stora Torget 9; s/d Skr1195/1395; P @) You can't miss this dashing pink building on the town square. Rooms aren't as grand as the exterior implies, but they're comfortable, with cable TV and minibar. Staff members are friendly and the in-house restaurant serves some of the better food in town.

Konditori Brödstugan BAKERY €
(0492-104 21; Storgatan 42; meals around Skr65; 8am-5pm Mon-Fri, to 2pm Sat) A busy lunch spot, this bakery-cafe has a wide choice of quiches, salads, baked potatoes and hot dishes.

Information

Tourist Office (0492-310 10; www.vimmerbyturistbyra.se; Rådhuset 1, Stångågatan 29; 9am-8pm daily late Jun–mid-Aug, to 6pm Mon-Fri, to 2pm Sat & Sun late Jun & end Aug, shorter hours rest of year) Facing Stora Torget is Vimmerby's helpful tourist office.

Getting There & Away

All bus and train services depart from the Resecentrum, downhill past the church from Stora Torget. Swebus Express runs to Eksjö, Jönköping and Göteborg, and in the other direction to Västervik (Skr79, 1¼ hours). Svenska Buss operates daily between Stockholm, Linköping and Vimmerby.

South of Vimmerby, bus services continue on to Oskarshamn, Åseda, or Kalmar and Nybro.

Trains run several times daily south to Kalmar and north to Linköping.

ÖLAND

0485 / POP 25,000

Like a deranged vision of Don Quixote, Öland is *covered* in old wooden windmills. Symbols of power and wealth in the mid-18th century, they were a must-have for

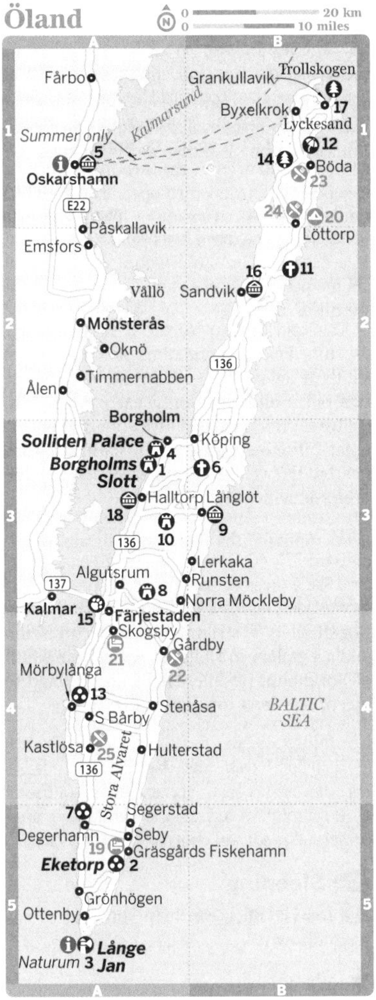

Öland

Top Sights

1 Borgholms Slott A3
2 Eketorp A5
3 Långe Jan A5
4 Solliden Palace A3

Sights

5 Döderhultarmuseet A1
6 Gärdslösa Kyrka B3
7 Gettlinge A5
8 Gråborg A3
9 Himmelsberga B3
10 Ismantorp A3
11 Källa kyrka B2
12 Lyckesand B1
13 Mysinge Hög A4
14 Neptuni Åkrar Nature Reserve B1
15 Ölands Djurpark A3
16 Sandvikskvarn B2
17 Trollskogen Nature Reserve B1
18 VIDA Museum & Konsthall A3

Sleeping

19 Gammalsbygårdens Gästgiveri A5
20 Neptuni Camping B1
21 STF Vandrarhem Ölands Skogsby A4
Vandrarhemmet Oscar .... (see 5)

Eating

22 Gärdby Kafe A4
23 Kaffestugan B1
24 Lammet & Grisen B1
25 Restaurang & Pizzeria Linda A4
Steakhouse Oscar .... (see 5)

Drinking & Nightlife

Pub Kråkan .... (see 5)

every aspiring man about town and the death knell for many of Öland's oak forests. Today 400 or so remain, many lovingly restored by local windmill associations.

At 137km long and 16km wide, the island is Sweden's smallest province. Once a regal hunting ground, it's now a hugely popular summer destination for Swedes – the royal family still has a summer pad here. The island gets around two million visitors annually, mostly in July. Around 90% of them flock to the golden shores fringing the northern half of the island to bask and bathe. Behind the beaches, fairy-tale forests make for soulful wanders.

South of Färjestaden, the entire island is a Unesco World Heritage Site, lauded for its unique agricultural landscape, in continuous use from the Stone Age to today, and peppered with runic stones and ancient burial cairns.

There are surprisingly few hotels, but you can stay in innumerable private rooms (booked through the tourist offices), more than 25 campgrounds and at least a dozen hostels (book ahead). Camping between Midsummer and mid-August can cost up to Skr300 per site.

Locals like to think of the island as Sweden's Provence and food-linked walking tours and farmers markets abound. **Ölands Skördefest** (www.skordefest.nu; late Sep), the island's three-day harvest festival, is Sweden's biggest.

Information

The bridge from Kalmar lands you on the island just north of Färjestaden, where there's a well-stocked **tourist office** (☎485-89 000; www.olandsturist.se; ⊙9am-7pm Mon-Fri, to 6pm Sat, to 5pm Sun Jul–mid-Aug) at the Träffpunkt Öland centre. Staff can book island accommodation (for a Skr195 booking fee) and organise themed packages, including cycling, spa and gourmet getaways. There is also a small history and nature exhibit.

There's a smaller tourist office in Borgholm.

Getting There & Around

BICYCLE

There are no bicycle lanes on the bridge between Öland and Kalmar, so cyclists should exercise caution! Bicycles aren't allowed on the bridge in summer – instead there's free Cykelbuss or Cykelfärjeservices to get you across (roughly hourly; enquire at the tourist office in Kalmar). If you fancy pedalling your way across Öland, check **Cykla på Öland** (www.cyklapaoland.se) for cycling routes and other handy information.

BOAT

From mid-June to mid-August, **M/S Solsund** (www.olandsfarjan.se) sails twice daily from Byxelkrok (northwest Öland) to Oskarshamn (on the mainland 60km north of Kalmar). One-way tickets are Skr150/100 per adult/child seven to 16 years. A car and up to five passengers costs Skr600, and a bicycle is free.

BUS

Silverlinjen (www.silverlinjen.se) runs one to two daily direct buses from Öland to Stockholm (adult/child Skr320/220, 6½ hours), calling at Kalmar; reservations are essential.

KLT (www.klt.se) buses connect all the main towns on the island to Kalmar; they run every hour or two to Borgholm (Skr56, one hour) and Mörbylånga (Skr40, one hour). A few buses per day (including bus 106) run to Byxelkrok and Grankullavik (both Skr96, around 2¼ hours), in the far north of the island. Services to the south are poor, with some improvement May to August.

Borgholm & Around

Öland's 'capital' and busiest town, Borgholm has a pleasant centre 'grid' of pedestrian streets lined with shops and restaurants that can get packed out in midsummer. The most dramatic (and satisfying) sight is the enormous ruined castle on its outskirts.

Sights

★Solliden Palace PALACE

(Sollidens Slott; www.sollidensslott.se; adult/child Skr75/45; ⊙11am-6pm mid-May–mid-Sep) Sweden's most famous 'summer house', Solliden Palace, 2.5km south of Borgholm town centre, is still used by the Swedish royals. Its exceptional gardens are open to the public and are well worth a wander. The idyllic cafe is ideal for a post-garden break.

★Borgholms Slott CASTLE

(www.borgholmsslott.se; adult/child Skr70/40; ⊙10am-6pm Jun-Aug) Northern Europe's largest ruined castle, Borgholms Slott, looms just south of town. This epic limestone structure was burnt and abandoned early in the 18th century, after life as a dyeworks. There's a great museum inside and a nature reserve nearby, as well as summer concerts, children's activities and a cafe.

VIDA Museum & Konsthall MUSEUM

(☎0485-774 40; www.vidamuseum.com; adult/child Skr50/free; ⊙10am-6pm daily Jul–early Aug, shorter hours rest of year; P) VIDA Museum & Konsthall is a strikingly modern museum and art gallery in Halltorp, about 9km south of Borgholm. Its finest halls are devoted to two of Sweden's top glass designers.

Gärdslösa Kyrka CHURCH

(⊙11am-5pm daily mid-May–mid-Sep) FREE On the east coast, about 13km southeast of Borgholm, is Gärdslösa kyrka, the best-preserved medieval church (1138) on Öland.

Sleeping

The tourist office can help you find rooms around town.

★Villa Sol B&B €

(☎0485-56 25 52; www.villasol.nu; Slottsgatan 30; s/d without bathroom from Skr450/800;) The sunny yellow exterior sets the tone for this delightful accommodation located on a quiet residential street near Borgholm's centre. Rooms in the main house share two bathrooms, a fully equipped cottage-style kitchen and a homey living room, complete with board games and books. The marginally more expensive garden rooms are in separate chalets overlooking the flower-filled garden.

Ebbas Vandrarhem & Trädgårdscafé HOSTEL €

(☎0485-103 73; www.ebbas.se; Storgatan 12; dm/s/d Skr300/375/580; ⊙May-Sep;) Look for the classic 1950s Morris Minor 1000 out front here. Five of the lemon-yellow rooms overlook the gorgeous rose-laced garden, and four the bustling Borgholm main street. There's a kitchen for self-caterers…or just pop downstairs to the cafe for decent hot and cold grub (lunch Skr100), served until 9pm in summer.

Hotell Borgholm HOTEL €€€
(☎0485-770 60; www.hotellborgholm.com; Trädgårdsgatan 15-19; s/d Skr1335/1535; ❄@🛜) Cool grey hues, bold feature walls, pine wood floors and smart functionalist furniture make for stylish slumber at this urbane hotel. Rooms are spacious, with those on the top floor (Skr1885) especially chic. Owner Karin Fransson is one of Sweden's top chefs, so a table at the restaurant here is best booked ahead (tasting menu Skr1075).

Eating & Drinking

Nya Conditoriet BAKERY €
(Storgatan 28; ⏰8am-5pm Mon-Fri, to 3pm Sat) This busy old-fashioned bakery-cafe in Borgholm serves yummy sandwiches and pastries.

Robinson Crusoe EUROPEAN €€
(www.robinsoncrusoe.se; Hamnvägen; lunch buffet Skr130, mains from Skr150; ⏰noon-10pm Apr-Sep) Slouch back on the plush purple terrace sofas for a cocktail or an (excellent) coffee, or make a date for the daily buffet. The setting is sublime, overlooking the bobbing boats in Borgholm harbour.

Information

Tourist Office (☎0485-890 00; Storgatan 1; ⏰9am-6pm Mon-Fri, to 5pm Sat, 10am-4pm Sun Jul, 9am-6pm Mon-Fri, 10am-4pm Sat late May–Jun, shorter hours rest of year) Located at the marina end of Storgatan in Borgholm.

Northern Öland

The north of the island has a wild beauty and is home to some of the best beaches.

Sights

Atmospheric **Källa kyrka**, at a little harbour about 36km northeast of Borgholm, off Rd 136, is a fine example of Öland's medieval fortified churches. The broken **rune stone** inside shows the Christian cross growing from the pagan tree of life.

Grankullavik, in the far north, has sandy beaches and summer crowds; **Lyckesand** is one of the island's best beaches, and the strangely twisted trees and ancient barrows at the nearby **Trollskogen Nature Reserve** (Trolls' Forest) are well worth a visit. On the far north's western edge is the beautiful **Neptuni Åkrar Nature Reserve**, famed for its spread of blue viper's bugoss flowers in early summer.

Sandvikskvarn HISTORIC BUILDING
(www.sandvikskvarn.se; adult/child Skr20/free; ⏰noon-8pm daily May-Sep, to 10pm mid-Jun–mid-Aug; P) At Sandvik on the west coast, about 30km north of Borgholm, this Dutch-style windmill is one of the largest in the world. In summer, you can climb its seven storeys for good views across to the mainland. The rustic restaurant serves the local speciality, *lufsa* (baked pork and potato; Skr75); and there's an adjacent pizzeria (pizzas from Skr80).

Sleeping & Eating

Neptuni Camping CAMPGROUND
(☎0485-284 95; www.neptunicamping.se; Småskogsvägen; sites Skr200, cabins from Skr400; P) This campground just north of Löttorp is a wild and grassy place with good amenities.

Kaffestugan CAFE €
(☎0485-221 27; www.kaffestuganiboda.se; Böda; sandwiches Skr45-50; ⏰7am-6pm daily Jun-Aug, 8am-5pm Fri-Sun May-Sep) Located on the main road in tiny Böda, this is a clued-up cafe that micro-roasts its own Fairtrade coffee and bakes everything from luscious berry tarts and cakes to organic breads and moreish lavender-and-chocolate biscotti.

Lammet & Grisen SWEDISH €€
(☎0485-203 50; www.lammet.nu; Löttorp; buffet Skr395; ⏰from 4.30pm; P 👪) Just 10km south of Böda, come here for all-you-can-eat evenings, with whole spit-roasted lamb and pork on the menu, plus live entertainment. The restaurant is particularly family-friendly.

Central Öland

Fortresses, a zoo and a charming farm village are central Öland's star attractions. The largest settlement is Färjestaden (Ferry Town), where you'll find banks, services and a Systembolaget liquor store. The town lost its purpose in life after the bridge was built, although an effort has been made to rejuvenate the old jetty.

Sights & Activities

The largest Iron Age ring fort in Sweden, **Gråborg** was built as the Roman Empire was crumbling. Its impressively monumental walls measure 640m around, even though much of the stonework was plundered for later housing. After falling into disuse, the fort sprang back to life around 1200, when the adjacent **St Knut's chapel** (now a ruin) was built. The Gråborg complex is about 8km east of Färjestaden; you need your own transport to get there.

The vast **Ismantorp fortress**, with the remains of 88 houses and nine mysterious gates, is deep in the woods, about 20km northeast of Ölands Djurpark. Drive north to Rälla and take a right on Högsrumsvägen; keep following this road for about 10km to reach the fortress. It's an undisturbed fortress ruin, illustrating how the village's tiny huts were encircled by the outer wall. (Eketorp (p234), in southern Öland, is an imaginative reconstruction of similar remains.) This area, just south of the Ekerum–Långlöt road, can be visited at any time.

A 17km **hiking trail** leads from Gråborg to Ismantorp fortress.

Himmelsberga MUSEUM
(0485-56 10 22; www.himmelsbergamuseum.com; Himmelsberga; adult/child Skr80/60; 11am-5.30pm daily Jun–mid-Aug, shorter hours rest of year) This is the best open-air museum on Öland; basically a traditional farming village on the east coast at Långlöt, its quaint cottages are fully furnished. There's hay in the mangers and slippers by the door; it's so convincing you'd swear the inhabitants just popped out for a minute. Extras include a dinky cafe and modern art gallery.

Ölands Djurpark ZOO
(0485-392 22; www.olandsdjurpark.com; Färjestaden; admission Skr350; 10am-5pm daily mid-May–mid-Aug, 11am-4pm Apr–mid-May & mid-Aug–Oct; P) A zoo, amusement park and water park combined. Free admission for children under 1m.

Sleeping & Eating

STF Vandrarhem Ölands Skogsby HOSTEL
(0485-383 95; www.vandrarhskogsby.se; s/d per person Skr180/320; mid-Apr–Sep; P @) This charming STF hostel claims to be Sweden's oldest (it dates from 1934). It's based in a flowery old wooden house 3km southeast of Färjestaden. The Färjestaden–Mörbylånga bus 103 (Skr30) runs past at least five times daily.

Gärdby Kafe CAFE €
(0485-330 06; Gärdby; snacks from Skr50; 10am-5pm Mon-Fri, to 4pm Sat & Sun) Take a sidestep to this heartwarming cafe, which dates from the 1920s and oozes old-fashioned charm with its dazzling white stripped-back tearooms and expansive garden with well-weathered sculptures and randomly placed tables and chairs. Savoury snacks, traditional sweets, locally produced deli items and superb coffee are on offer.

Outhouses have been resurrected into small stores selling clothes and tasteful homewares, plus there's a playhouse for children.

Southern Öland

The southern half of the island has made it onto Unesco's World Heritage list. Its treeless, limestone landscape is hauntingly beautiful and littered with the relics of human settlement and conflict. Besides linear villages, Iron Age fortresses and tombs, this area is also a natural haven for plants and wildlife.

Sights & Activities

★**Eketorp** ARCHAEOLOGICAL SITE
(www.eketorp.se; adult/child Skr120/80; 11am-5pm daily May-Jun & late Aug, 10.30am-6pm Jul–mid-Aug; P) If you can't picture how the ring forts looked in their prime, take a trip to Eketorp. The site has been partly reconstructed to show typical fortified villages in medieval times. Children will love the scampering pigs, and the fort is particularly fun when there are re-enactment days – phone for details. Excavations at the site have revealed over 26,000 artefacts, including 3 tonnes of human bones; some of the finds are on display at the little **museum** inside.

There's a free daily tour in English from late June to the end of August (11.15am, 1.15pm and 2.15pm). The fort is 6km northeast of Grönhögen; there are several buses (summer only) from Mörbylånga.

Stora Alvaret NATURE RESERVE
Birds, insects and flowers populate the striking limestone plain of Stora Alvaret. Birdwatching is best in May and June, which is also when the Alvar's rock roses and rare orchids burst into bloom. The plain occupies most of the inland area of southern Öland,

and can be crossed by road from Mörbylånga or Degerhamn.

Mysinge and Gettlinge ARCHAEOLOGICAL SITE

The ancient grave fields of **Mysinge** and **Gettlinge**, stretching for kilometres on the ridge alongside the main Mörbylånga–Degerhamn road, include burial sites and standing stones from the Stone Age to the late Iron Age. The biggest single monument is the Bronze Age tomb **Mysinge Hög**, 4km east of Mörbylånga, from where there are views of almost the whole World Heritage Site.

Gräsgårds Fiskehamn HARBOUR

On the east coast, about 5km north of Eketorp, Gräsgårds Fiskehamn is a delightful little fishing harbour. A little further north, there's an 11th-century rune stone at **Seby**, and in **Segerstad** there are standing stones, stone circles and over 200 graves.

Öland's Southernmost Point LANDMARK

Öland's southernmost point is a stark, striking spectacle of epic sky, sea and rock-strewn pastures. A nature reserve almost surrounded by sea, it's justifiably popular with birdwatchers. There's a free **Naturum** (nature park; ☎0485-66 12 00; www.ottenby.se; ⏲10am-6pm daily Jul–mid-Aug, 11am-5pm May, Jun & mid-Aug–Sep, 11am-4pm Apr, Oct & Nov, 11am-4pm Fri-Sun Mar) FREE, a great cafe-restaurant and, at 42m, Scandinavia's tallest lighthouse, **Långe Jan** (adult/child Skr30/10) to climb.

Sleeping & Eating

You'll find supermarkets in Mörbylånga.

Gammalsbygårdens Gästgiveri B&B €€

(☎0485-66 30 51; www.gammalsbygarden.se; s/d Skr700/900; ⏲closed Christmas–Easter; P @) This country farmhouse sits on the hauntingly beautiful southeastern coast, 5km north of Eketorp. The picture-perfect lounge is complemented by cheerful rooms with whitewashed walls and cosy floor heating. A couple have private balconies. The restaurant serves fish, venison, lamb and heavenly desserts. Booking ahead is essential.

Mörby Vandrarhem & Lågprishotell HOSTEL €

(☎0485-493 93; www.morbyhotell.se; Bruksgatan; hostel s/d Skr350/550, hotel s/d Skr650/850; ⏲May-Aug; P @ 🛜 🏊) In the small village of Mörbylånga, this place has a mixture of hostel- and hotel-style accommodation. The big, anonymous building is a bit hospital-like, but there's a pool and plenty of space, with a park and beaches nearby, as well as bikes for hire.

Restaurang & Pizzeria Linda PIZZA €

(☎0485-410 79; Torget; pizzas from Skr70; ⏲11.30am-8pm Mon-Thu, to 9pm Fri, noon-9pm Sat, to 8pm Sun) Overlooking Mörbylånga's main (albeit modest) square with a cosy stone-clad dining room, flower-flanked terrace and grassy seating out back; the pizzas are piled high and tasty.

GOTLAND

☎0498

Gorgeous Gotland has much to brag about: a Unesco-lauded capital, truffle-sprinkled woods, A-list dining hot spots, talented artisans and more hours of sunshine than anywhere else in Sweden. It's also one of the country's richest historical regions, with around 100 medieval churches and countless prehistoric sites.

The island lies nearly halfway between Sweden and Latvia, in the middle of the Baltic Sea, roughly equidistant from the mainland ports of Nynäshamn and Oskarshamn. Just off its northeast tip lies the island of Fårö, most famous as the home of Sweden's

Gotland

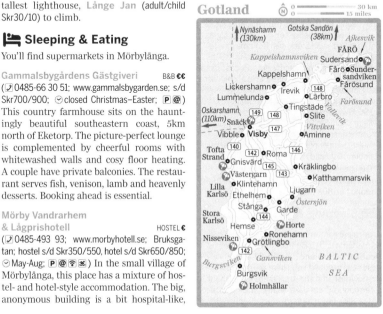

THE ISLAND OF CHURCHES

Gotland boasts the highest concentration of medieval churches in northern Europe. A God-pleasing 92 churches inhabit villages outside Visby; more than 70 still harbour medieval frescoes and a few also contain extremely rare medieval stained glass. Visby alone has a dozen church ruins and a fairy-tale cathedral.

A church was built in most villages between the early 12th century and the mid-14th century, Gotland's golden age of trading. After 1350, war and struggle saw the money run out and the tradition end. Ironically, it was the lack of funds that helped keep the island in an ecclesiastical time warp: the old churches weren't demolished, and new ones weren't constructed until 1960. Each church is still in use, and the posse of medieval villages still exist as entities.

Most churches are open 9am to 6pm daily from mid-May to late August. Some churches have the old key in the door even before 15 May, or sometimes the key is hidden above the door. *The Churches in the Diocese of Visby* is an English-language brochure available from tourist offices containing a map of the churches throughout the island, historical background and a thoughtprovoking quote from Bishop Sven-Bernhard Fast that begins: 'You can hear 700 years of silence as you sit in a pew beneath the vault of this early medieval church...'

directing great, the late Ingmar Bergman. The island national park of Gotska Sandön lies 38km further north, while the petite islets of Stora Karlsö and Lilla Karlsö sit just off the western coast.

Information on the island abounds; both www.gotland.net and www.guteinfo.com are good places to start.

Getting There & Away

AIR

The cheaper local airline is **Gotlands Flyg** (☎22 22 22; www.gotlandsflyg.se), with regular flights between Visby and Stockholm Bromma (one to eight times daily) and daily flights (June to September) between Visby and Malmö. Prices start at Skr346 one way to Stockholm and to Malmö; book early for discounts, and enquire about stand-by fares. Another budget airline, **NextJet** (☎0771-90 00 90; www.nextjet.se), operates two to three daily flights from Stockholm Arlanda to Visby (June to September). Prices start at Skr445 one way. Popular summer-only routes include Göteborg, Hamburg, Oslo and Helsingfors (Helsinki).

The island's **airport** (☎26 31 00) is 4km northeast of Visby. Catch a taxi into/from town (around Skr180); there is an airport bus during summer.

BOAT

Year-round car ferries between Visby and both Nynäshamn and Oskarshamn are operated by **Destination Gotland** (☎0771-22 33 00; www.destinationgotland.se). There are departures from Nynäshamn one to six times daily (about three hours). From Oskarshamn, there are one or two daily departures in either direction (three to four hours). **Gotlandsbåten** (www.gotlandsbaten.se) runs one or two daily ferries (June to August) from Västervik to Visby (from Skr250, about three hours).

Regular one-way adult tickets for the ferry start at Skr260, but from mid-June to mid-August there is a far more complicated fare system; some overnight, evening and early-morning sailings in the middle of the week have cheaper fares.

Transporting a bicycle costs Skr50; a car usually starts at Skr345, although, again, in the peak summer season a tiered price system operates and advance reservations are recommended.

Getting Around

There are over 1200km of roads in Gotland, typically running from village to village through picture-perfect landscapes. Cycling on these is heavenly, and bikes can be hired from a number of places in Visby. The forested belt south and east of Visby is useful if you bring a tent and want to take advantage of the liberal camping laws.

Many travel agents and bike-hire places on the island also rent out camping equipment. In Visby, hire bikes from Skr100 per 24 hours at **Gotlands Cykeluthyrning** (☎0498-21 41 33; www.gotlandscykeluthyrning.com; Skeppsbron 2), at the harbour. It also rents tents (Skr100/500 per day/week), or for Skr340 per day (Skr1500 per week) you can hire the 'camping package': two bikes, a tent, a camping stove and two sleeping mats.

Kollektiv Trafiken (☎0498-21 41 12; www.gotland.se) runs buses via most villages to all corners of the island. The most useful routes, which have connections up to seven times daily, operate between Visby and Burgsvik in the far south, Visby and Fårösund in the north (also with bus connections on Fårö), and Visby and Klintehamn. A maximum-distance one-way ticket will not cost you more than Skr75 (although if you take a bike on board it will cost an additional Skr40), but enthusiasts will find a monthly ticket good value at Skr740.

A few companies and service stations offer car hire. **Avis** (☎0498-21 98 10; www.avisworld.com; Donners Plats 2) in central Visby or **Europcar** (☎21 50 10; www.europcar.com; Visby flygplats) at the airport offer rentals starting from Skr700 per day.

Visby

POP 22,593

The medieval port town of Visby alone warrants a trip to Gotland. Within its sturdy city walls await twisting cobbled streets, fairytale wooden cottages, evocative church ruins and steep hills with impromptu Baltic views. The wining and dining options are similarly superb, while the leafy oasis of lush botanical gardens offers a tranquil respite, especially in high season.

A Unesco World Heritage Site, Visby swarms with holidaymakers from mid-June to mid-August and cars are banned in the old town. For many, the highlight of the season is the costumes, performances, crafts, markets and re-enactments of **Medeltidsveckan** (Medieval Week; www.medeltidsveckan.com; Aug), held during the first or second week of August. Finding accommodation during this time is almost impossible unless you've booked ahead.

Sights & Activities

The town, with its 13th-century wall of 40 towers, is a noble sight – savour it for a few hours while walking around the perimeter (3.5km). Also take time to stroll around the Botanic Gardens and the narrow roads and scandalously cute lanes just south of here. Pick up a map and the *Welcome to World Heritage Visby* booklet to help guide you around the town.

The tourist office organises free two-hour tours at 11am daily from June to the end of August from outside the tourist office. No reservations are necessary.

★Medieval Churches CHURCH

Founded by Franciscans in 1233, **St Karins Kyrka** (Stora Torget) is one of the most stunning of Visby's medieval churches, with a beautiful Gothic interior. Other ruins include the magnificant **St Nicolai Kyrka**, built in 1230 by Dominican monks. The **Helge And Kyrka** ruin is the only stone-built octagonal church in Sweden. It was built in 1200, possibly by the Bishop of Riga; the roof collapsed after a fire in 1611.

★Sankta Maria kyrka CHURCH

(Cathedral of St Maria; www.visbydf.se; Norra Kyrkogatan 2; 9am-9pm Jul & Aug, to 5pm rest of year) Visby's church ruins contrast with the stoic Sankta Maria kykra. Built in the late 12th and early 13th centuries and heavily touched up over the years, its whimsical towers are topped by baroque cupolas. Soak up the beautiful stained-glass windows, carved floor slabs and ornate carved reredos. The cathedral is used for intimate **music concerts** in summer. Check the tourist-office website for details.

★Gotlands Museum MUSEUM

(www.gotlandsmuseum.se; Strandgatan 14; adult/child Skr100/80; 10am-6pm) Gotlands Museum is one of the mightiest regional museums in Sweden. While highlights include amazing 8th-century pre-Viking picture stones, human skeletons from chambered tombs and medieval wooden sculptures, the star turn is the legendary Spillings horde. At 70kg it's the world's largest booty of preserved silver treasure. Included in the ticket price is entry to the nearby **Konstmuseum** (☎0498-29 27 75; Sankt Hansgatan 21; adult/under 20yr/senior Skr50/free/40; noon-4pm Tue-Sun, closed for Midsummer), which has a small permanent collection mainly focusing on Gotland-inspired 19th- and 20th-century art, plus temporary exhibitions showcasing contemporary local artists.

The museum is excellently laid out and explanations are in English as well as Swedish. Read about the Black Death ravaging the island in 1350, the Vikings' old Norse religion, the fossils and coral reefs that surround the island, and the astonishing 1999 discovery of all that silver on a farm in northern Gotland.

Sleeping

Wisby Jernvägshotellet HOSTEL €

(☎0498-20 33 00; www.gtsab.se; Adelsgatan 9; 2-/4-bed r from Skr495/595; year-round;) Run by the same folks as Hotel Villa Borgen next door, this is an excellent budget choice. The spotless rooms are more spacious than some swing-a-cat hostels in these parts, and the kitchen-dining room is airy and bright, with an outside terrace.

Visby

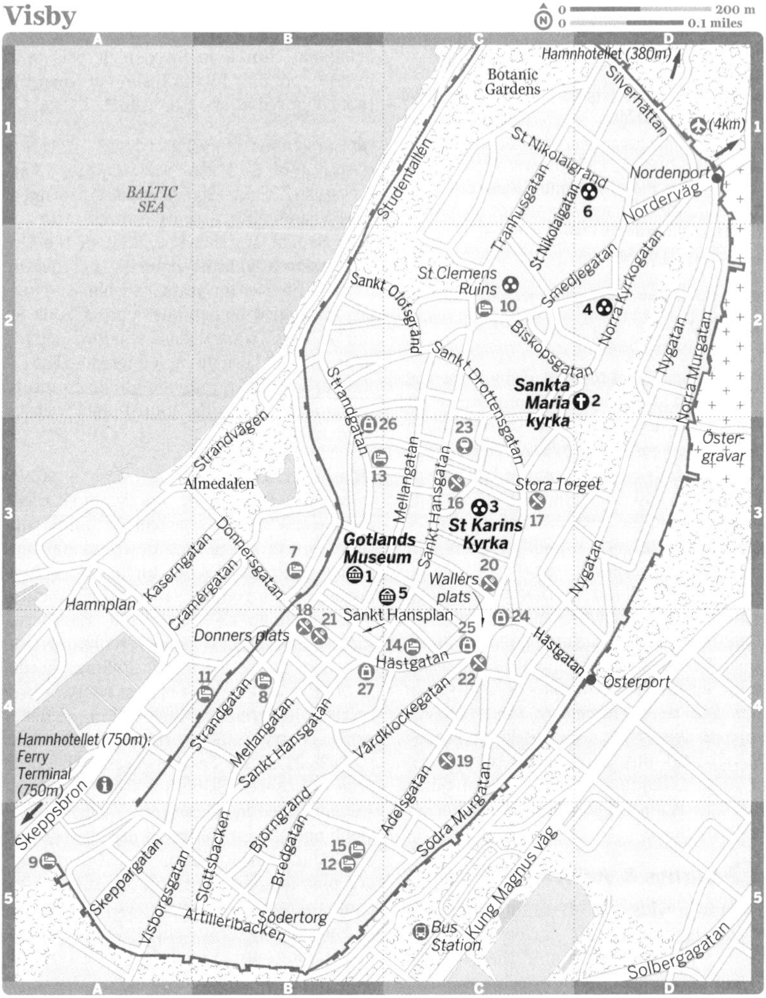

Fängelse Vandrarhem HOSTEL €
(☎0498-20 60 50; www.visbyfangelse.se; Skeppsbron 1; dm/s/d from Skr300/400/500;) This hostel offers beds year-round in the small converted cells of an old prison. It's in a handy location, between the ferry dock and the harbour restaurants, and there's an inviting terrace bar in summer. Reception is open from 9am to 2pm, so call ahead if you are arriving outside these times.

Take a look at the historic poster listing the crimes you could be imprisoned for in Sweden during the mid-19th century: 'Noise, illegal bathing and being dressed as an Easter witch...'!

Hotel St Clemens HOTEL €€
(☎0498-21 90 00; www.clemenshotell.se; Smedjegatan 3; r from Skr1295-1450, ste from Skr2195;) Located at the southeastern corner of the botanical garden, this family-run hotel is just a stone's throw away from the vine-covered ruins of the ghostly St Clemens kyrka. It takes up five historical buildings and has two gardens and a summery floral theme in the rooms.

Visby

Hotel Stenugnen HOTEL €€
(☎0498-21 02 11; www.stenugnen.nu; Korsgatan 6; s/d Skr950/1250, annexe r Skr999; P) At this inviting small hotel, bright, whitewashed rooms are designed to make you feel as if you're sleeping in a yacht and the location is practically on top of the medieval wall. Plenty of rainy-day distractions are provided for kids and the homemade bread is just delicious. Cheaper doubles come with shared bathrooms in the annexe.

Visby Logi & Vandrarhem HOSTEL €€
(☎0498-52 20 55; www.visbylogi.se; Hästgatan 14 & Sankt Hansgatan 31; r Skr950;) Petite hostel located in two historic houses – one from the 16th century, one from the 17th – on Sankt Hansgatan and Hästgatan. Rooms are simple, decorated in white and grey, and there's a rustic courtyard at Hästgatan.

Hotel Villa Borgen BOUTIQUE HOTEL €€
(☎0498-20 33 00; www.gtsab.se; Adelsgatan 11; s/d/apt Skr1050/1195/2000; @) This place has attractive rooms with lashings of white linen, pale grey walls and scarlet cushions. Accommodation is set around a pretty, quiet courtyard, and the intimate breakfast room with French doors and stained glass contributes to that boutique feeling. There is also a self-contained apartment that sleeps six.

Almedalens B&B B&B €€
(☎0498-771 30 09; www.almedalens.se; Tage Cervinsgata 3B; s/d Skr800/1000;) The light-filled rooms here share a central large living room and small well-equipped kitchenette. The traditional Scandinavian bleached timber provides a fresh, contemporary look and a pretty private garden is available for guests. The owners run the downstairs cafe, which is excellent for lunchtime snacks.

Värdshuset Lindgården HOTEL €€
(☎0498-21 87 00; www.lindgarden.com; Strandgatan 26; s/d Skr1250/1450; @) This is a sound central option, with rooms set facing a soothing garden beside a popular restaurant. Dine outdoors and listen to music in the romantic courtyard in summer.

Hamnhotellet HOTEL €€
(☎0498-20 12 50; www.visbyhamnhotell.se; Färjeleden 3; s/d incl breakfast Skr1400/1500; P @) Close to the ferry terminal, Hamnhotellet offers clean, comfortable rooms and a decent buffet breakfast. Opt for the cheaper annexe rooms (about Skr300 less), which are perfectly adequate with private bathroom and TV.

★ **Clarion Hotel Wisby** HOTEL €€€
(☎0498-25 75 00; www.clarionwisby.com; Strandgatan 6; s/d from Skr1870/2170; P @) Top of the heap in Visby is the luxurious, landmark Wisby. Medieval vaulted ceilings and sparkling candelabras contrast with funky contemporary furnishings. The gorgeous pool (complete with medieval pillar) occupies a converted merchant warehouse. Don't miss the 11th-century chapel, just inside the entrance.

Eating & Drinking

There are more restaurants per capita in Visby than in any other Swedish city. Most are clustered around the old-town squares, on Adelsgatan or at the harbour. Wherever you choose, do not pass up a chance to try *saffranspankaka* (a saffron pancake with berries and cream), the island's speciality. You'll find it at many cafes in Visby and around the island, usually for around Skr60.

Serious foodies should pick up the *Regional Culinary Heritage* map from the tourist office, which maps traditional restaurants, farm shops and bakeries throughout the island. Alternatively, check the www.culinary-heritage.com website.

Visby Crêperie & Logi CREPERIE €
(www.creperielogi.se; Wallérs plats; galettes from Skr98, crepes from Skr45; 11am-midnight Mon-Sat, to 4pm Sun May-Aug, shorter hours rest of year;) Cheapish, cheerful and a hit with the boho-arty crowd, this lovable corner bolthole serves scrumptious savoury galettes and sweet crêpes, ranging from a moreish lamb, chèvre, honey, rocket and almond combo to a wicked chocolate composition further enhanced up with white-chocolate chunks and ice cream. The recommended tipple is cider, with 10 varieties to choose from.

Gula Cafe CAFE €
(Tranhusgatan 2; cakes from Skr45; noon-5pm) Sit in this enchanting cottage garden surrounded by pots of flowers, herbs, butterflies and birdsong. The homemade cakes are fabulous and include local specialties, like *saffranspankaka* (Skr55). Freshly made sandwiches are also available.

Skafferiet SWEDISH €
(www.skafferietvisby.se; Adelsgatan 38; sandwiches from Skr85; 11am-5pm Mon-Fri, 10am-6pm Sat, noon-4pm Sun;) This casual lunch spot with wooden floors and a cosy atmosphere offers salubrious sandwiches, homemade soups, a variety of salads and delicious cakes and pastries. There's a pretty garden out back.

★ **Surfers** ASIAN €€
(0498-21 18 00; www.surfersvisby.se; Södra Kyrkogatan 1; dishes Skr80; 5pm-2am) Not your normal Chinese restaurant abroad, the speciality here is Szechuan finger food designed to share and ranging from Chinese dumplings to traditional twice-cooked pork. There's plenty of heat in the dishes, which are complemented by the other Surfers' speciality: zingy cocktails (from Skr100) made with fresh fruit and juice – they're good for you. Honest.

Vinäger RESTAURANT €€
(0498-21 11 68; www.vinager.se; Hästgatan 34; tapas Skr65, mains from Skr135; 11am-5pm & 6-10pm) Sporting a slick, ethno-chic interior, this hip cafe-bar puts the emphasis on fresh food, whether it's pumpkin ravioli, red-pepper salad or sinfully good carrot cake. The outdoor resto-bar cranks up the X factor with a dazzling white, glam alfresco lounge for enjoying those super-smooth cocktails.

Bakfickan SEAFOOD €€
(www.bakfickan-visby.nu; Stora Torget; lunch specials Skr95, mains Skr139-235) White-tiled walls, merrily strung lights and boisterous crowds define this foodie-loved bolt-hole, where enlightened seafood gems might include *toast skagen* (shrimps, dill and mayonnaise), pickled herrings on Gotland bread or Bakfickan's fish soup. Delicious!

Bolaget FRENCH €€
(www.gamlabolaget.se; Stora Torget 16; mains Skr179-229; 1pm-2am) Take a defunct Systembolaget shop, chip the 'System' off the signage, and reinvent the space as a buzzing, French bistro–inspired hot spot (fried frog legs, anyone?). Staff members are amiable and the summertime square-side bar seating is perfect for a cool break.

Donners Brunn EUROPEAN €€€
(Donners plats; 0498-27 10 90; www.donners-brunn.se; mains Skr260-325) A longstanding favourite for a luxury meal, Donners Brunn blends Swedish and global flavours. The alfresco summer bar is a fine spot for a peaceful beer or well-shaken cocktail overlooking Donners plats.

Gutekällaren BEER HALL
(www.gutekallaren.com; Stora Torget; 10pm-2am Jun-Sep) A restaurant-bar with seemingly infinite levels of seating, from cellars to balconies; also home to nightclubs loved by summer revellers.

Shopping

Gotlandssmychken ARTS, CRAFTS
(0706-15 88 85; www.gotlandssmychken.se; Strandgatan 32; 10am-7pm Mon-Fri, to 1pm Sat) Forty-three million years ago, Gotland was covered by tropical seas and coral reefs. The result, today, is that it is a paradise for fossil

hunters. This small shop specialises in selling jewellery made from fossils and has a fascinating fossil display.

The owner can also organise fossil-hunting trips (Skr200 per person) of around three hours' duration.

Gotländsk Konst & Form ARTS, CRAFTS
(☎0498-21 03 49; Wallérs plats 5; ⏰10am-7pm Mon-Fri, to 2am Sat) Cool local art and handicrafts are the focus at this artisans' cooperative, with stock ranging from textiles and threads to ceramics, pottery, jewellery, glassware and painting.

Bröderna Wikströms FOOD
(Wallérs plats; ⏰10am-6pm Mon-Sat, to 4pm Sun) A fabulous, niffy cheese shop with plenty of local Gotland varieties. Also sells gourmet goodies, like local preserves made from *salmbärssylt* (a wild berry indigenous to Gotland).

Kränku DRINK
(☎0498-21 74 81; Sankt Hansplan 4; ⏰10am-6pm Mon-Fri, to 4pm Sat) Tea fiends head here for local blends, which make for soothing, civilised souvenirs.

Information

Tourist Office (☎0498-20 17 00; www.gotland.info; Donners plats; ⏰8am-7pm summer, to 4pm Mon-Fri, 10am-4pm Sat & Sun rest of year) The tourist office is located at Donners plats.

Around Visby

There's not much but forest and farmland until you're at least 10km from Visby. If you're heading northeast, visit the remarkable **Bro church**, which has several 5th-century picture stones in the south wall of the oratory, beautiful sculptures and interior lime paintings.

Heading southeast on Rd 143, on your way to Ljugarn, pull over to check out the 12th-century Cistercian monastery ruin **Romakloster** (☎0498-501 23; guided tour per group Skr800; ⏰10am-6pm daily May-Sep, shorter hours rest of year) FREE, a kilometre from the main road. Summer theatre performances here start at Skr250 (tickets are available from Visby tourist office, or book online at www.romateatern.se). The 18th-century manor house is also impressive.

Dalhem, 6km northeast of the Cistercian monastery, has a large church with some 14th-century stained glass (the oldest in Gotland) and magnificent (albeit restored) wall and ceiling paintings; take note of the scales of good and evil. There's also a historic **steam railway** (www.gotlandstaget.se; adult/child Skr50/30; ⏰11.15am-3.45pm Wed, Thu & Sat Jul-early Aug, Sun only Jun & rest of Aug) and museum in Dalhem.

The town of Klintehamn has a good range of services. From the town's harbour, you can catch a passenger-only boat to the island nature reserve **Stora Karlsö** (www.storakarlso.se) one to three times daily from May to early September (adult/six to 15 years return Skr345/155, 30 minutes). Remote as it is, the island is home to extensive bird life, including thousands of guillemots and razorbills, as well as the *maculinea arion* (large blue butterfly), and is well worth the time it takes to get there. You can visit the island as a day trip (with 3½ hours ashore) or stay overnight.

STF Stora Karlsö (☎0498-24 04 50; www.storakarlso.se; hostel r Skr500, beach-house d Skr845; ⏰May-Aug), Stora Karlsö's simple STF hostel, is a really special choice if you want to get away from it all. Visitors can opt to stay in a beach house near the old lighthouse. There's a nature exhibit and museum where you can learn about ongoing research projects on the island, plus a restaurant and cafe. The owners regularly organise birdwatching trips and wild-orchid walks. Book ahead.

In Klintehamn and under new ownership since 2014, enticing **Warfsholm** (☎0498-24 00 10; www.warfsholm.se; sites Skr100, s/d from Skr490/690; ⏰hotel May-Sep, apt/cottages year round; P ❄ @ ᯤ) has several accommodation options, plus a beautiful waterside location,

GOTLAND'S BEST BEACHES

- **Snäck** A few kilometres north of Visby with shallow water and good facilities. Popular with families and also good for fossil hunting.
- **Tofta Strand** Located 18km south of Visby and another family favourite with shallow waters for paddling tots.
- **Sundersandviken** A pristine sandy bay with good facilities in the far northeast on the island of Fårö.
- **Holmhällar** Located in the far southeast, surrounded by lush countryside and limestone *raukar*.
- **Ljugarn** Superb family-geared sandy beach at this east-coast resort. Avoid Sundays in August!

a pleasant restaurant and a cosy bar. There are rooms in the atmospheric 19th-century main house, as well as apartments and cottages in the grounds. The former hostel is now only rented out to groups. Alternatively, for the ultimate in pampering, check out one of Gotland's latest top luxury sleeps, also in Klintehamn: **Djupvik Hotel** (0498-24 42 72; www.djupvikhotel.com; Eksta Bopparve; r incl breakfast from Skr2390; P ❄ @ ᯤ ≈).

Northern Gotland, Furillen & Fårö

It's hard to imagine a better way to absorb the area than by cycling up to Fårö and following the bike trails around the beautiful, windswept little island. There's an **information centre** (0498-22 40 22; www.faroframtid.se; Fårö; 10am-5pm daily Jul & Aug, 10am-5pm Fri-Sun May–mid-Jun & Sep) with internet access in Fårö town.

The **grotto** (0498-27 30 50; www.lummelundagrottan.se; adult/child Skr130/70; May-Sep) south of Lummelunda is the island's largest. The temperature here is a cool 8°C, so rug up. The impressive *raukar* (limestone formations) at nearby **Lickershamn** are up to 12m high; look out for **Jungfru** (signposted), with its haunting legend of witches, toads and serpents.

Step back in time at the **Bungemuseet** (0498-22 10 18; www.bungemuseet.se; adult/under 16yr Skr100/free; 11am-6pm daily Jul–mid-Aug, 10am-5pm Jun & late Aug, 11am-4pm early Sep), an open-air museum with 17th- to 19th-century houses, picture stones dating from AD 800 and a historic 'themed' playground. It's near Gotland's northeastern tip, about 1km south of where the ferry connects to Fårö. Across the road is a cute cafe with superlative saffron pancakes.

The frequent ferry to **Fårö** is free for cars, passengers and cyclists. This island, once home to Ingmar Bergman, has magnificent *raukar* formations; watch the sunset at **Langhammarshammaren** if you can. At the island's eastern tip, the rocks by Fårö lighthouse are laced with fossils. British troops who fought in the Crimean war are

BERGMAN WEEK

The wild, mysterious landscape of Fårö is not easily forgotten, as anyone who has visited can testify. The tiny island just off the northern tip of Gotland particularly haunted Ingmar Bergman (1918–2007), the legendary Swedish director, who first visited Fårö in 1960 while scouting locations for *Through a Glass Darkly*. Bergman ended up living and working on Fårö for 40 years, shooting seven films there, and he is now buried on the island.

Since 2004 Fårö has been home to **Bergman Week** (www.bergmanveckan.se), a celebration of Bergman's life and work, and a meeting place for people who share Bergman's passion for film. The event consists of screenings of Bergman's films, as well as new premieres; guest speakers (recently including fellow filmmakers Jan Troell, Ang Lee, Bille August and Noah Baumbach); master classes; and tours of film locations around the island.

The **Bergmancenter** (www.bergmancenter.se; 10am-6pm summer, noon to 4pm May & Sep) was inaugurated in 2014 and hosts exhibits, lectures, workshops and screenings, as well as a library and cafe. The centre can set you up with your very own Bergman guide (Skr125 for one hour), or try a Bergman bus safari (tours every other Saturday in July and August from 3pm to 5pm, Skr325, or, during Bergman Week in late June, 5.30pm to 9pm, Skr495).

Jannike Åhlund, one of the people behind Bergman Week who knew Bergman, describes the director as curious, with a quick intellect and a great sense of humour, as well as being childish and a lover of gossip. Her two favourite Bergman films are *Autumn Sonata* and *Wild Strawberries*.

To get the most out of Fårö, Åhlund recommends: walking along the wild and magnificent Norsta Aura beach; renting a bike and pedalling the 7km-long *rauk* (column formation) road to enjoy the huge limestone stacks up close; eating lunch at **Crêperie Tati** (Friggars; snacks from Skr35); checking out the '50s memorabilia at **Kutens Bensin** (www.kuten.se; Broskogs) or listening to a rockabilly concert on a summery Friday or Saturday night; and riding an **Icelandic horse** (70 690 0432, 22 14 44; fia@faroislandshastar.se).

buried at Ryssnäs in the extreme south; obey signs posted along roads here, as this area is still used for military exercises.

South of here, the small island of Furillen until recently was mainly known by ornithologists, thanks to its large population of waterfowl and waders. These days, an eco-friendly hotel and top restaurant are the main draws.

Sleeping & Eating

Lummelunda Hostel HOSTEL €
(☎0498-27 30 43; www.lummelundavandrarhem.se; Lummelunda; r with shared bathroom Skr500, cabins with shared/private bathroom Skr700/900; ⏲May-Sep; P) This rustic-style accommodation has a choice of doubles in the main building, plus cabins that range from very basic (bathroom and kitchen in the main house) to fully equipped with small terraces.

Tjauls Gård B&B €€
(☎0736-15 57 53; www.tjaulsgard.se; Lummelunda Tjauls 188; r incl breakfast Skr995; P) This homely farmhouse is a great place to stay, with a hot tub and the option of horse riding, bike hire and offroad-motorbiking tours (owners are keen bikers). Rooms are spacious and comfortable.

Fabriken Furillen HOTEL €€€
(☎0498-22 30 40; www.furillen.com; Lärbro; r from Skr2145; ⏲Jun-Sep; P) In the unlikely setting of an old limestone factory, this extraordinary hotel combines a raw industrial environment with cutting-edge Scandinavian design. There are even hermit huts for those really wanting to get away from it all, with hand-built Hästens beds and a copy of Thoreau's *Walden*. The restaurant (mains from Skr295) is Michelin-chef standard and uses only local products and produce.

Lickershamnskrogen SWEDISH €€
(☎0498-27 24 25; www.lickershamnskrogen.se; mains Skr159-295; ⏲8am-9pm May-Aug) Near the Jungfru trailhead at Lickershamn, this place serves both local and Med-style dishes and tapas, and there's a hut selling smoked fish.

Gotska Sandön National Park

Isolated Gotska Sandön (www.gotskasandon.se), with an area of 37 sq km, is an unusual island with lighthouses at its three corners, 30km of beaches, sand dunes, pine forest and a church. There's a fantastic network of trails right around the island.

There is a hostel (☎0498-24 04 50; info@resestugan.se; r from Skr500; ⏲mid-May–early Sep); facilities are basic, so bring all supplies with you.

Boats (☎0498-24 04 50; ⏲mid-May–early Sep) run from Fårösund and Nynäshamn three to four times weekly when operating (Skr895/1095 return from Fårösund/Nynäshamn).

Eastern Gotland

Ancient monuments here include Bronze Age ship setting Tjelvars grav, 1.5km west of Rd 146 (level with Visby), and its surrounding landscape of standing stones. Gothem church is one of the most impressive in Gotland; the nave is decorated with friezes dating from 1300. Torsburgen, 9km north of Ljugarn, is a partly walled hill fort (the largest in Scandinavia) measuring 5km around its irregular perimeter.

Ljugarn is a small seaside resort. There are impressive *raukar* formations at Folhammar Nature Reserve, 2km north. Southwest of Ljugarn and the village of Alskog, the imposing Garde church has four extraordinary medieval lich gates and an upside-down medieval key in the door; the original 12th-century roof is still visible.

Around 20km north of Ljugarn, in the hamlet of Kräklingbo, Leonettes Konst & Keramik (☎0498-533 40; www.leonette.com; Hajdeby) is home to Californian expat Dan Leonette and his highly regarded, idiosyncratic ceramics and art, created using techniques like Japanese raku and sawdust firing. In summer you can watch the master fire his wares (call ahead for times). Workshops are also held according to demand.

Truffle-hunting safaris (www.tryffelsafari.se; ⏲Oct & Nov) in the area are a unique way for foodies to discover more about this delicacy and local produce in general. Check the website for package prices, which include a five-star dinner (featuring truffles, of course) and an accommodation option.

Sleeping & Eating

There's a Konsum supermarket in Ljugarn, and some fine-dining options in the area.

TF Hostel Ljugarn HOSTEL €
(☎0498-49 31 84; ljugarn@gotlandsturist.se; dm from Skr200; ⏲mid-May–Aug) This place has a

fine spot down by the water at the eastern end of Ljugarn village.

Bruna Dörren PIZZA €
(☎0498-49 32 89; www.brunadorren.nu; Strandvägen 5, Ljugarn; pizzas from Skr70, mains Skr95-189; ⏲noon-10pm May-Aug; P) A casual restaurant and pizzeria, with a spacious outdoor courtyard and beachside location.

★ **Krakas Krog** SWEDISH €€€
(☎0498-530 62; www.krakas.se; Kräklings 223, Katthammarsvik; mains Skr280-325; ⏲4-10pm Wed-Sun early Jun–Sep) The owners of Krakas Krog make a point of sourcing their ingredients from Gotland's fields, woods and sea, including frogs' legs direct from the garden. Meals are served on the porch and in the petite dining room. The menu is replete with local delicacies: eggs with morels and beets, turkey in truffle broth or Baltic Sea turbot with sage butter.

Smakrike Krog & Logi SWEDISH €€€
(☎0498-49 33 71; www.smakrike.se; Claudelins väg 1, Ljugarn; mains Skr245-345; ⏲noon-4pm & 5.30-10pm mid-Jun–Aug; P) Meals at Smakrike Krog capture the essence of a true Swedish summer. The restaurant's menu follows the seasons and the affable owners also operate a stylish bed and breakfast upstairs (singles/doubles Skr1650/1995).

Southern Gotland

As you head south, stop off at **Lojsta** to see the deepest lakes in Gotland, the remains of an early medieval fortress and a fine church. **Hemse** is a commercial centre, with good services (such as supermarkets, banks and a bakery). About 10km south, the **Hablingbo** church boasts three lavishly carved doorways, a votive ship, carved floor slabs and rune stones. The red-brick **STF Vandrarhem Hablingbo** (☎0498-48 71 61; www.gutevin.se; Hablingbo; dm Skr280; ⏲May-Sep; @) is next to Gute Vingård, Gotland's only commercial vineyard, which also has a good restaurant.

Maria's Hästeri (www.mariashasteri.se; Grötlingbo Skradarve 209; per person from Skr400; ⏲Jun-Sep), 9km south in Grötlingbo (another 10km south from Hablingbo), is a friendly stable that organises horse-riding tours lasting from a couple of hours to a full day complete with lunch. In Björklunda, 10km further south, **B&B Björklunda** (☎0498-49 71 90; www.bjorklundabb.se; hostel s/4 Skr300/500, B&B s/d Skr500/1000, 2-/4 bed apts Skr1500/1900; P) vaguely recalls a Greek villa with its whitewashed buildings and blue trim. Furnishings and decorations are somewhat dated, but rooms are clean and comfy. You can choose among double rooms, hostel-style rooms with shared facilities and apartments. There is also a restaurant and 'rock pub' with live bands at weekends in summer.

The small town of **Burgsvik** is another convenient commercial centre further south. Just north of town, the **Öja church** dates from 1232 and has Gotland's highest church tower (67m). It has a magnificent cross, and the wall and ceiling paintings are remarkably detailed. Look for the inscribed stone slabs under the covered shelter just outside the churchyard.

Seven kilometres south of Burgsvik, in the old Vamlingbo *prästgård* (vicarage) on Rd 142, **Museum Lars Jonsson** (☎0498-20 26 91; www.larsjonsson.se; adult/under 18yr Skr40/free; ⏲11am-5pm daily May–mid-Sep, call ahead to check hours rest of year) showcases delicate paintings and watercolours by local artist Lars Jonsson, famed for his depictions of Gotland's bird life and coastal landscapes. There's also a cinnamon-scented cafe, Naturum and soothing garden.

On the eastern coast near Ronehamn, **Uggarderojr** is a huge, late-Bronze Age cairn with nearby traces of settlement. The cairn, probably a navigation marker, is now a long way inland due to postglacial uplift.

Östersund & the Bothnian Coast

Includes ➜

Best Places to Eat

- Hemmagastronomi (p267)
- Fäviken Magasinet (p252)
- Innefickan Restaurang & Bar (p249)
- Matildas (p255)
- Lörruden (p259)
- Havvi i Glen (p252)

Best Places to Stay

- Treehotel (p263)
- Hulkoffgården (p267)
- Stora Hotellet Umeå (p264)
- STF Tänndalen/ Skarvruets Fjällhotel (p253)
- Copperhill Mountain Lodge (p251)

Why Go?

The north of Sweden seems to have it all. There are endless pristine forests where the odds of encountering elk, reindeer and bear are high and the hiking is splendid. Plus, there are jagged mountains that provide Sweden's best skiing in winter, and host the best mountain biking in summer, along with every other mountain sport you can imagine.

On the other hand, you are never too far from the bright lights of civilisation: you can go lake-monster spotting in Östersund, party with locals and visit quality museums in the student towns of Gävle, Umeå and Luleå, or just enjoy the laid-back rhythm of life in the pretty coastal towns, rich in historical sights and medieval churches. Slow down even further by lingering in the tiny fishing villages and sampling the fresh catch, or strike out for Höga Kusten's remote islands and wonder why the Swedes invented *surströmming* (fermented herring).

When to Go

Sundsvall

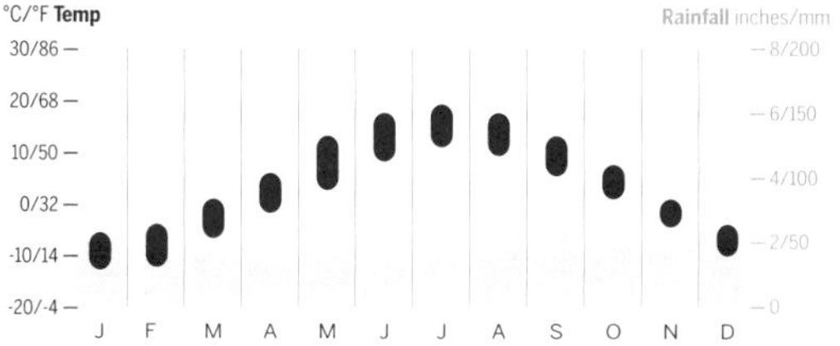

Mar & Apr Days are longer and warmer, but still plenty of snow for snow sports.

Jul The best time for hiking and island-hopping.

Aug (last week) Fill your belly with crayfish on Höga Kusten's islands.

Östersund & the Bothnian Coast Highlights

1. Travelling along **Höga Kusten**, northern Sweden's beautiful coastline, and sampling *surströmming* (p260).
2. Hitting **Umeå's** lively scene and visiting its superb museums and sculpture park (p262).
3. Staying in a spaceship, bird's nest or mirror cube at the incredible **Treehotel** (p263).
4. Skiing, biking, rafting and zorbing in **Åre** (p250) Sweden's outdoor-adventure central.
5. Driving the Bothnian Coast's scenic **Kustvägen** (p259).
6. Going in search of the Storsjöodjuret (Lake Monster) in **Östersund** (p247).
7. Trying to burn down the goat in **Gävle** (p254).
8. Visiting Sweden's largest church town near **Luleå** (p266).
9. Hiking the wilderness of **Tänndalen** (p252).

JÄMTLAND

Östersund

063 / POP 44,327

Sitting on the shore of the enormous Storsjön (Great Lake), Östersund is the largest town in the area, particularly famous for the local answer to the Loch Ness Monster: Storsjöodjuret. The best way to appreciate Östersund is to take the footbridge across to the adjacent island of Frösön and gaze back at the city in profile, ideally around sunset. Seen in that light, this fun-loving town is hard to resist. Dedicated sightseers will stay busy, but what Östersund really encourages is relaxation: in summer, people flock to the terrace bars and cafes at the water's edge or idly wander the pedestrianised shopping streets in the stroll-friendly centre.

Sights & Activities

★Jamtli MUSEUM

(www.jamtli.com; adult/under 18yr Skr250/free; 11am-5pm;) Jamtli, 1km north of the centre, consists of two parts. One is an open-air museum comprising painstakingly reconstructed wooden buildings, complete with enthusiastic guides wearing 19th-century period costume.

The stars of the indoor museum are the **Överhogdal Tapestries**, the oldest of their kind in Europe – Christian Viking relics from AD 1100 that feature animals, people, ships and dwellings. Another fascinating display is devoted to Storsjöodjuret, including taped interviews with those who've seen the monster, monster-catching gear and a pickled monster embryo.

Outside, you can stroll the paths around the bakery, smithy, woodman's cottage and 18th-century farm, and take part in milking, baking, tree felling and more. Kids can get acquainted with different farm animals, run wild in the playground or ride a children's railway.

Frösön ISLAND

Large and peaceful Frösön island sits just across the bridge from central Östersund, reachable by road and by footbridge from Badhusparken. The island takes its name from Frö, the pagan god of fertility, worshipped by the Vikings originally resident here.

Just across the footbridge, outside Landstingshuset and near the Konsum supermarket, is Sweden's northernmost **rune stone**, which commemorates the 1050 arrival of Austmaður or 'East Man', the first Christian missionary on Frösön.

Frösöns Kyrka CHURCH

(8am-8pm; 3) Five kilometres west of the centre of Östersund is the restored, late-12th-century Frösöns kyrka, with its distinctive separate bell tower, built on a sacrificial site to the ancient gods (*æsir*) and incredibly popular for midsummer weddings. Catch bus 3.

Exercishallen Norr GALLERY

(Infanterigatan 30; noon-4pm Thu-Sun) FREE A worthwhile contemporary art museum, Exercishallen Norr lives across the E14 motorway from Jamtli. It's a cavernous room with an ambitious curatorial scope and always something curious on show, from installations, painting and sculpture to photography and soundscapes.

Storsjöhyttan GLASSWORKS

(www.storsjohyttan.com; Sjötorget; 10am-7pm Mon-Thu, to 4pm Fri, 11am-3pm Sat) At Sweden's first Économusée (a concept originating in Quebec), you can observe the three masters of glass at work as they transform white-hot melted putty into original, striking creations. Immerse yourself in different glassmaking techniques and the history of glass or take some glassy goodies home with you.

Badhusparken BEACH

(www.vinterparken.se; mobile sauna & hot tub 6-8pm Tue & Thu mid-Jan–mid-Mar) The waterfront park is the town's most popular stop for sunbathing and a brisk swim. In winter the

OFF THE BEATEN TRACK

GLÖSA PETROGLYPHS

Stone Age Rock Carvings (Alsensjön lake; 24hr, souvenir shop & guided tours 11am-4pm Tue-Sun Jul & Aug) Glösa, 40km northwest of Östersund and by the Alsensjön lake, has some of Sweden's finest Stone Age petroglyphs. The carvings, on rock slabs beside a stream, feature large numbers of elk and date from 5000 BC. There's also an excellent reconstruction of a Stone Age hut and replicas of skis, snowshoes, a sledge and an elk-skin boat.

It's best to get out here with your own wheels as the public-transport connections are atrocious.

Östersund

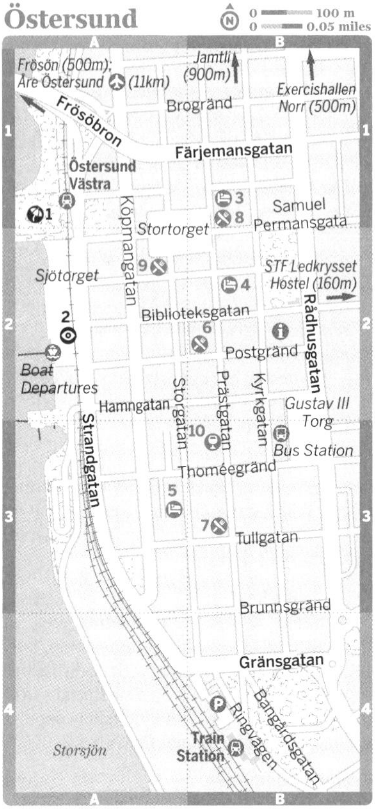

Östersund

⊙ Sights
1 Badhusparken .. A1
2 Storsjöhyttan ... A2

🛏 Sleeping
3 Clarion Grand Östersund B1
4 Hotel Emma ... B2
5 Hotel Jämteborg A3

🍽 Eating
6 Innefickan Restaurang & Bar B2
7 Lilla Siam ... B3
8 Sir Winston .. B1
9 Törners Konditori A2

🍸 Drinking & Nightlife
10 Jazzkoket ... B3

lake turns into Sweden's largest ice-skating rink (rent your skates here; Skr160 per day) and you also can swim in the specially cut hole in the ice further south along the waterfront before making a spirited dash to the nearby mobile sauna and hot tub (Skr140).

🎉 Festivals & Events

Storsjöyran MUSIC
(Great Lake Festival; www.storsjoyran.se) A gigantic, raucous annual three-day music festival, Storsjöyran is held in the town centre in late July or early August and features a range of local and international artists, from The Prodigy to Blondie. Some 55,000 people attend.

🛏 Sleeping

Book in advance during the Storsjöyran festival, as budget accommodation in particular fills up quickly.

STF Ledkrysset Hostel HOSTEL €
(☑ 063-10 33 10; www.ostersundledkrysset.se; Biblioteksgatan 25; dm/s/d Skr170/300/460; 🛜🐾) This well-run, central hostel is in a converted old fire station and is your best shoestring bet.

★ Hotel Emma HOTEL €€
(☑ 063-51 78 40; www.hotelemma.com; Prästgatan 31; s/d Skr950/1095; 🅿🛜) The individually styled rooms at super-central Emma nestle in crooked hallways on two floors, with homey touches like squishy armchairs and imposing ceramic stoves; some rooms have French doors facing the courtyard. The breakfast spread is a delight. Reception hours are limited, so call ahead if arriving late or early.

Hotel Jämteborg HOTEL €€
(☑ 063-51 01 01; www.jamteborg.se; Storgatan 54; hostel d/tr Skr590/840, B&B s/d/tr Skr590/690/890, hotel s/d from Skr1065/1250; 🅿🛜) Just imagine: you're travelling with friends but you're all on different budgets. Hotel Jämteborg comes to the rescue, with its catch-all combo of hostel beds, B&B rooms and hotel rooms in several buildings next to each other. The cheerful hotel rooms come in cream-and-crimson, defying Sweden's 'earth tones only' rule.

Clarion Grand Östersund HOTEL €€
(☑ 063-55 60 00; www.clarionostersund.se; Prästgatan 16; s/d from Skr960/1060; 🅿🛜♨) Östersund's most luxurious option has an excellent restaurant featuring sophisticated northern Swedish and international cuisine, and the plushest of the rooms come with their very own marbled hallways.

Eating & Drinking

Törners Konditori CAFE €
(www.tornerskonditori.se; Storgatan 24; sandwiches Skr60-70; 7.30am-7pm Mon-Fri, 9am-5pm Sat, 11am-5pm Sun;) This large, cafeteria-style cafe seems perpetually filled with locals, who come for the cakes (Skr 35), chunky sandwiches – from open-faced prawn to toasted pulled-pork baguettes – as well as salads and daily lunch specials ranging from goulash to chicken curry.

Sir Winston SWEDISH €€
(063-10 68 00; www.sirwinston.se; Prästgatan 19; mains Skr169-269; 11am-2pm Mon-Fri, 4pm-midnight daily) Though named after a British Prime Minister and decked out to look like a British pub, the menu at Sir Winston strays into more adventurous territory with bouillabaisse and platters marked 'A Taste of Jämtland' that showcase local ingredients. The beer menu spans the world: from Red Stripe and Newcastle Brown Ale to Sol and locally brewed Bärnsten.

Lilla Siam THAI €€
(www.lillasiam.com; Prästgatan 54A; lunch Skr95, mains Skr149-169; 11am-9pm Mon-Fri, from noon Sat, 4-8pm Sun;) Reasonably authentic Thai restaurant with a good lunch buffet and an extensive dinner menu full of Thai stir-fries, noodle dishes and curries.

★ **Innefickan Restaurang & Bar** FUSION €€€
(063-12 90 99; www.innefickan.se; Postgränd 11; mains Skr210-295; 5pm-late Tue-Sat) With a cosy cellar ambience – all exposed brick and contemporary-art pieces – Innefickan packs a great deal of creativity into its succinct 13-item menu. We're floored by the carpaccio with wasabi and coriander, the veal with chanterelles and pumpkin puree is expertly seared, and rhubarb is transformed into something far greater than the raw material in their capable hands.

Jazzkoket PUB
(063-10 15 75; www.jazzkoket.se; Prästgatan 44; 7.30-10am Mon-Fri, 5pm-1am Tue-Sat) Jazzkoket wears many hats: she's a buzzy bakery and breakfast joint on weekday mornings, a relaxed loosen-your-tie-after-work venue, and a sultry, stormy bacchanale on weekend nights, when her walls reverberate with the sounds of live jazz and rock. The menu's a bit hit-and-miss, but the charcuterie and cheese platters from local producers are a sure bet.

Information

Tourist Office (063-14 40 01; www.visitostersund.se; Rådhusgatan 44; 9am-5pm Mon-Fri, 10am-3pm Sat & Sun) The tourist office is opposite the town hall, and has free internet access.

Getting There & Around

AIR

Åre Östersund Airport (063-19 30 00; www.swedavia.se/ostersund) The Åre Östersund Airport is on Frösön, 11km west of the town centre. The airport bus (adult/child Skr80/30) leaves regularly from the Östersund bus terminal to meet Stockholm flights. Destinations include Stockholm, Göteborg, Luleå, Umeå and Malmö.

STORSJÖODJURET – THE LAKE MONSTER

Just imagine...you're sitting by Storsjön lake at dusk when you notice a dark shadow rise out of the water. Could it be just ripples in the wake of a passing boat? Perhaps a couple of elk swimming? Or maybe it's the head of **Storsjöodjuret** (www.storsjoodjuret.com) – the monster that dwells somewhere in the dark waters of the 91m-deep lake.

Sightings of the only monster of its kind in Sweden were made as early as 1635, when the description of a strange animal with a black serpentine body and catlike head first appeared in a folk tale. The Frösö Runestone does, in fact, depict a serpentlike creature and the Lake Monster has had such a grip on the public imagination that in 1894 a hunt for it was organised by a special committee put together by King Oscar II. However, the Norwegian whalers specially hired for the job came back empty-handed. Every summer there are claims of new sightings, and the monster was granted protected status as an 'endangered species' in 1986, only for that status to be revoked in 2005.

Through the Östersund tourist office you can book a spot on the popular two-hour monster-spotting cruise aboard the 1875 steamship **S/S Thomée** (adult/child Skr120/60; tours Tue-Sun Jun-early Sep).

BUS

Daily bus 45 runs north at 7.15am from Östersund to Gällivare (Skr507, 11¼ hours) via Arvidsjaur (Skr440, seven hours) and Jokkmokk (Skr507, 9½ hours) and south to Mora (Skr269, 5¼ hours, two daily).

TRAIN

In summer the daily 7.05am Inlandsbanan train heads north to Gällivare (Skr1194, 14½ hours) via Arvidsjaur (Skr728, nine hours) and Jokkmokk (Skr993, 12½ hours). Inlandsbanan also runs south to Mora (Skr 494, six hours, one daily at 7.45am). SJ departures include two trains daily to Stockholm (Skr670, five hours) via Uppsala and up to six daily trains heading west to Åre (Skr181, 1¼ hours).

Åre

☎0647 / POP 1417

Beautifully situated in a mountain valley by the shores of Åresjön lake, Åre is Sweden's most popular **skiing resort**: 30,000 people invade the village during the December-to-May skiing season. In July Åre hosts the **Åre Bike Festival** (www.arebikefestival.com) and the hardcore **Åre Extreme Challenge** (www.areextremechallenge.se) that has its competitors running, paddling and biking for the grand prize. Besides traditional sports, winter and summer bring a bewildering array of mountain-related activities that you can try your hand at.

Sights & Activities

★**Kabinbanan** CABLE CAR, VIEWPOINT

(adult/child Skr150/110; ⏲10am-4pm daily late Jun-late Sep) Taking you almost to the top of Mt Åreskutan, the only gondola in Scandinavia is worth taking for the awesome views alone. The seven-minute ride departs from behind Åre's main square and whisks you up to a viewing platform (1274m) complete with Åre's most expensive cafe.

★**Åre Bike Park** MOUNTAIN BIKING

(www.arebikepark.com) In summer the slopes of Mt Åreskutan become an enormous playground dedicated to downhill biking. More than 30 trails span 40km of track, ranging from beginner to extreme (the trails are graded using the same system as ski slopes). The Kabinbanan cable car, the Bergbanan funicular, and the VM6:an and Hummelliften chairlifts are fitted with bike racks.

Hiking HIKING

Popular short hikes include the 30-minute scramble to the top of Mt Åreskutan from the Kabinbana viewing platform and the two-hour hike down to the village from the same spot. The tourist office stocks booklets and maps detailing multiple hikes in the area.

The area west of Åre is popular among fell walkers, and there's a network of STF wilderness huts and lodges here for enthusiasts, especially around Sylarna, one of Sweden's finest mountains for trekking and climbing.

DON'T MISS

EXTREME FUN IN ÅRE

Come summer, come winter, there's always something to test your mettle and push your boundaries in Åre if you thrive on adrenalin.

JoPe Fors & Fjäll (☎0647-314 65; www.jope.se) Challenging white-water rafting and mountain tours in summer; ice climbing and heliskiing in winter with Nature's Best operator.

Åre Mountainboard (☎0707-60 74 70; www.aremountainboard.se) Mountainboarding – think snowboarding with wheels.

Camp Åre (☎0647-525 25; www.campare.se) Guided snowmobile safaris, driving on ice, dogsledding, ziplining and more.

Åre Sleddog Adventures (☎0647-303 81; www.aresleddog.se; Grimsta 135) Dogsledding tours ranging from two hours (Skr850) to seven-day expeditions with overnights in cabins (Skr14,400).

Skysport (☎0647-511 85; www.skysport.se; Årevägen 173B) Tandem paragliding and hang-gliding flights.

Åre Hillcart (☎0707-60 74 70; www.arehillcart.se) Hillcarting – like gocarting, but down, down, down, on grass or snow!

INLANDSBANAN

Inlandsbanan (Inland Railway; www.inlandsbanan.se; ⊙late Jun–mid-Aug, reduced service to late Sep) The 1000km Inlandsbanan between Gällivare and Mora, now a privately preserved heritage railway route, is covered by a combination of *rälsbuss* (railcar) and steam train. There's one daily train from Östersund south to Mora and one north to Gällivare. The average speed is 50km/h, making it a wonderfully relaxing way to appreciate northern Sweden.

The journey is accompanied by commentary from onboard guides, with stops in places of interest and particularly picturesque spots, meaning that the timetable is only loosely adhered to.

You can buy a single ticket from, say, Östersund to Gällivare and stop in as many towns en route as you like, though you have to pay a Skr30 supplement per stretch to reserve your seat. An **Inlandsbanan Card** (Skr1795) is valid for 14 days of unlimited travel along the line.

To find out more about the history of Sweden's most entertaining railway, stop off at the Inlandsbanemuseet (p274).

Mt Åreskutan SKIING
(www.skistar.com/are; one-day ski pass Skr425) The Mt Åreskutan (1420m) ski area boasts 45 ski lifts, 100 pistes and 1000 vertical metres of skiable slopes, including a 6.5km downhill run, with runs suitable for all abilities. The ski season is between December and mid-April, though skiing conditions are best from February, when daylight hours increase.

Åre Bikes MOUNTAIN BIKING
(☎0647-500 96; www.arebikes.se; Årevägen 138; ⊙9.30am-5pm Jun-Sep) Rents mountain bikes and protective equipment and arranges guided mountain-biking excursions.

Sleeping

Accommodation fills up quickly in winter, so plan well ahead.

STF Åre Torg HOSTEL €
(☎0647-515 90; www.svenskaturistforeningen.se/aretorg; Kabinbanevägen 22b; dm/s/d Skr295/540/690; ❄📶) This large, renovated hostel sits right on the main square. All rooms are identical windowless cubes with four glossy darkwood bunks, ventilated from the inside. All open onto an enormous common space, with an indoor 'patio' with picnic tables in front of each room and a cafe serving light bites during the day. Spotless guest kitchen and bathrooms.

Fjällgården HOTEL €€
(☎0647-145 00; www.fjallgarden.se; s/d from Skr745/1390; P) On the hillside, this is as much activity centre as hotel. It offers fishing, mountain biking, golf, horse riding, paddling and a chance to try the zipline, which lets you fly across the valley on a tiny string. Rooms are large, plush and full of light, and decorated in faux-rustic, après-ski style. The stylish suites come with stand-alone tubs.

★ **Copperhill Mountain Lodge** LODGE €€€
(☎0647-143 00; Åre Björnen; r from Skr2400; P📶) Beautifully constructed of wood and stone with copper accents, this lodge looks down on Åre from its lofty mountain perch. Its stylish, contemporary rooms are grouped according to precious metals; the Gold Suites come equipped with Playstation 3 for après-ski gaming. Its spa offers facials, massages and mineral baths and the three-course seasonal dinner menu (Skr395) is a worthy splurge.

Eating & Drinking

Åre Bageri BAKERY, SWEDISH €€
(www.arebageri.se; Årevägen 55; mains Skr165-235; ⊙7am-4pm & 5-10pm; 🖉) This sprawling organic cafe and stone-oven bakery does an enormous all-you-can-eat breakfast spread for Skr89 (7am to 10.30am), great coffee, pastries and huge sandwiches. In the evenings, the upstairs restaurant serves the best of Norrland's seasonal cuisine.

Broken AMERICAN €€
(www.broken-are.com; Torggränd 4; mains Skr115-196; ⊙noon-11pm) Just off the main square, this American-style diner is where all the hungry bikers and skiers converge to replenish burned calories by hoovering down Philly cheese steak, fajitas the size of your head, rib platters and jumbo hamburgers, washed down with frozen margaritas.

Vinbaren Åre BAR
(www.vinbaren-are.com; Stationsvägen; ⊙4pm-late Nov-Apr) Its vast wine list spans the world, and you have to get here early to get a seat,

WORTH A TRIP

WILDERNESS CUISINE

The remote mountains and fells of Jämtland and Härjedalen are responsible for some of the most exciting back-to-nature cooking in Sweden. But to taste it, you have to travel the extra mile...

Fäviken Magasinet (☎0647-401 77; www.favikenmagasinet.se; taster menu Skr1750; ⏲7pm-late Tue-Sat) Stellar chef Magnus Nillson has gone back to his countryside roots at this intimate 12-seat mountain restaurant. His culinary alchemy draws strictly on seasonal Jämtland produce and traditions such as drying, pickling and salting, and multi-course menus may include moose carpaccio with bone marrow and lobster with rosehip. It's off the E14, 15km east of Åre. Book well ahead.

Havvi i Glen (☎070-600 64 76; www.havviiglen.se; Glen 530; mains Skr165-265, tasting menus Skr595-1095; ⏲noon-5pm Mon-Tue, Thu-Fri & Sun, to 9pm Wed & Sat early Jul–late Aug) A proud standard bearer for the Slow Food Sápmi movement, Havvi i Glen initiates you into the richness of mountain Sami cuisine, with game, mushrooms and berries featuring prominently on its seasonal menu. Expect the likes of thinly sliced reindeer steak with blueberry chutney, smoked Arctic char with sea buckthorn and cloudberry sorbet with candied angelica. Website provides directions.

as the skiing clientele packs this place to the rafters in the evenings. The tapas don't let the side down either: think fish tacos, cheese fondue, pulled pork and mini burgers.

ℹ Information

Tourist Office (☎0647-163 21; www.visitare.se; St Olafsväg 35; ⏲10am-6pm Mon-Fri, to 3pm Sat & Sun) Inside the public library in the train-station building. Plenty of info on the area, including maps of hiking trails and brochures on outdoor activities.

ℹ Getting There & Away

Åre has eastbound trains for Östersund (Skr181, 1¼ hours, six daily) and overnighters to Stockholm (Skr845, 10¼ hours, 8.12pm daily). To get to Trondheim, Norway (Skr220, 2½ hours, two daily), change at Storlien (Skr125, 45 minutes, two daily).

Storlien & Around

☎0647

Storlien, a microvillage near the Norwegian border, is a small ski resort, as well as the starting point for the Southern Kungsleden (p253) trail.

Hiking is the main draw here, particularly the main multiday hike south to Tänndalen that passes by Sweden's southernmost glacier on the flank of Mt Helagsfjället.

Storvallens Fjällgården (☎0647-700 58; www.storliensfjallgard.se; Vackerlidsvägen 9; dm/s/d Skr180/390/400), just off the E14 about 4.5km east of Storlien, in Storvalen, provides hikers with top-quality accommodation in the form of comfortable dorms and rooms with warm, wood-panelled common areas, guest kitchens, sauna and good hiking advice. Besides the huge breakfast spread, the restaurant fattens you up with steak, club sandwiches and hearty fish soup.

From Storlien, trains run east to Åre (Skr125, 45 minutes, two daily) and west to Trondheim, Norway (Skr135, 1½ hours, two daily).

HÄRJEDALEN

Funäsdalen & Around

☎0684 / POP 980

Funäsdalen is a small, narrow mountain village arranged along a single road – because that's the only place flat enough to be accessible when the area is buried in snow for half the year. Dominated by the impressive peak Funäsdalsberget, the village and surrounding area are popular with hikers, skiers and other outdoor-sports enthusiasts. Beyond Funäsdalen, Rte 84 leads uphill to diminutive **Tänndalen**, an even better destination for hikers, while the highest road in Sweden leads north to beautiful Ljungdalen village, surrounded by mountains.

👁 Sights & Activities

Härjedalens Fjällmuseum MUSEUM
(www.fjallmuseet.se; Rörovägen 30; adult/child Skr100/free; ⏲11am-5pm mid-Jun–late Sep; 👪) Härjedalens Fjällmuseum has displays cov-

ering the South Sami, who still herd their reindeer in from the nearby Mittådalen and Brändåsen villages, and settlement of this area by local farmers and miners. There's a fun play area for kids that includes a secret tunnel, and the adjacent Fornminnesparken open-air section features 19th-century buildings from this area.

Rock Paintings ARCHAEOLOGICAL SITE

These remarkably well-preserved 4000-year-old rock paintings (*hällmålningar*), depicting reindeer and other animals, are located near the hamlet of Messlingen, on the high, desolate Flatruet plateau between Funäsdalen and Ljungdalen. Turn right in Mittådalen for Messlingen, walk east along a Ruvallen-bound track and take the signposted 6km footpath. Bus 621 connects Funäsdalen and Messlingen (Skr67, 35 minutes, three daily).

Route 535 SCENIC ROUTE

The narrow, serpentine 100km road that connects Ljungdalen and Åsarna runs through some of the remotest mountain landscape in Sweden, but its appeal lies not only in its glorious isolation but also in the pristine wilderness all around you (with the exception of tiny logging villages en route). It's a beautiful drive, but you can also take daily bus 613 (Skr204, 1¾ hours) between the two towns.

★ **Southern Kungsleden** HIKING

Tänndalen is the starting point for the **Southern Kungsleden**, which runs north to Storlien. Twenty kilometres from Tänndalen, the trail passes along the ski slopes of **Ramundberget** before the steep terrain takes you up to Sweden's southernmost glacier on **Helagsfjället** (1797m), the highest peak in the area.

From Helagsfjället you can either tackle a challenging, mountainous 50km stretch to Storlien via the STF-run *fjällstation* at Sylarna and Blåhammaren, or else head down to Ljungdalen (18km) to catch bus 613 to Östersund.

Sleeping & Eating

★ **STF Tänndalen/Skarvruets Fjällhotel** HOTEL, HOSTEL €

(☎0684-221 11; www.skarvruet.com; Skarvruvägen 20; hostel dm/s/d Skr300/350/600, hotel s/d Skr595/1190; P) This mountain hotel and hostel on a steep hillside in Tänndalen certainly looks the part: stuffed stags' heads and log fire in the snug lounge-bar, and Home Sweet Home rugs in the homiest rooms imaginable. The hostel is spread over several red cottages with awesome views of the mountains across the valley. Take bus 623 from Funäsdalen.

Funäsdalen Berg & Hotell HOTEL €

(☎0684-214 30; www.hotell-funasdalen.se; dm/d from Skr245/575; P) This is the go-to accommodation in Funäsdalen: a large, modern hotel with attractive hotel rooms in three levels of fanciness, plus hostel beds, overlooking the lake. It's open all year and has a good restaurant (the daily lunch buffet draws the locals) and a hot tub. Winter bookings for no fewer than three nights.

STF Vandrarhem Ljungdalen HOSTEL €

(☎070-210 48 73; www.svenskaturistforeningen.se; dm/d Skr185/500;) Ljungdalen's hostel makes a good stopover for shoestring travellers as most of its rooms are compact dorms. Guest kitchen, sauna and swimming pool available.

STF Sylarna LODGE €€

(☎010-190 23 60; www.svenskaturistforeningen.se; sites/dm/d/q Skr90/150/1120/1620; ⏲mid-Feb–Apr & late Jun–late Sep;) Attractive mountain lodge with sauna, provisions shop and equipment rental. Dorms are for guests who don't mind bunking with 19 other people.

STF Blåhammaren LODGE €€

(☎010-190 23 60; www.stfblahammaren.com; dm/d/q Skr295/1000/1500; ⏲mid-Feb– late Apr & late Jun–late Sep;) Sweden's highest mountain lodge (1080m) with awesome views from the sauna.

Information

Tourist Office (☎0684-155 80; www.funasdalen.se; Rörosvägen 30; ⏲10am-6pm) The tourist office, inside Funäsdalen's Fjällmuseum, can advise on and arrange all manner of outdoor activities.

Getting There & Around

Härjedalingen (www.harjedalingen.se) runs daily buses between Stockholm and Funäsdalen (Skr469, 8¾ hours) several days a week. From Funäsdalen, local bus 623 runs to Tänndalen (Skr33, 10 minutes, one to three daily except Sunday). Bus 613 runs between Ljungdalen and Åsarna (Skr204, 1¾ hours, daily except Saturday), where you can transfer to bus 164 to Östersund (Skr155, 1½ hours, five daily) or else catch the Inlandsbanan train. Bus 164 runs from Funäsdalen via Åsarna to Östersund (Skr269, 3½ hours, one or two daily).

BOTHNIAN COAST

Gävle

026 / POP 71,033

Infamous among certain naughty youngsters because its name (pronounced *yerv-luh*) sounds a lot like a Swedish swear word, Gävle is a lively university town that's been a prosperous industrial centre since the late 19th century, when it exported local timber and iron. Founded in 1446, Gävle is officially Norrland's oldest town, but not much of its original incarnation remains due to a devastating fire in 1869. A vibrant culinary scene and a host of oddball attractions in and around town appeal to a motley crew of beachgoers, would-be arsonists, whisky connoisseurs and trainspotters and make Gävle linger-worthy for a day or three.

Sights & Activities

★ Sveriges Järnvägsmuseet MUSEUM
(Swedish Railway Museum; www.jarnvagsmuseum.se; Rälsgatan 1; adult/under 19yr Skr100/60; 10am-5pm Jun-Aug; P) Inside Gävle's former engine shed, this excellent museum traces the history of the railway in Sweden through seriously hands-on displays. Besides numerous old locomotives and carriages that you can clamber inside (including the 1859 hunting coach belonging to King Karl XV), there are collections of miniature trains, an X2000 simulator, toy railways, and a small railway for kids to ride.

To get here, walk to the southern end of Muréngatan, and then follow the cycle path to the museum.

Länsmuseum Gävleborg MUSEUM
(www.lansmuseetgavleborg.se; Södra Strandgatan 20; 11am-6pm Tue-Fri, noon-4pm Sat & Sun) FREE The county museum, Länsmuseum Gävleborg, has beautifully designed exhibi-

Gävle

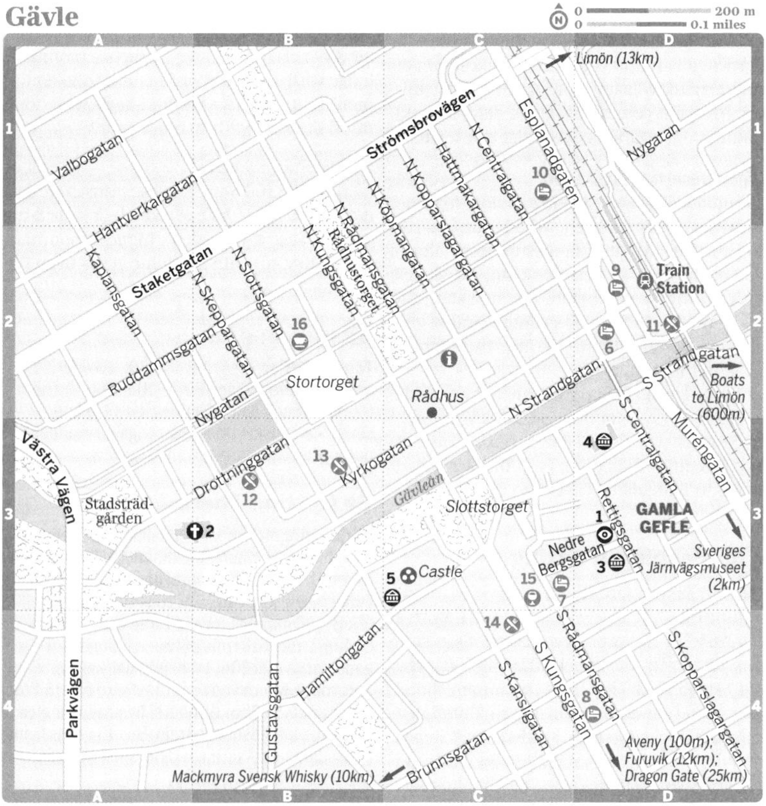

tions on regional culture through the ages, from prehistory to the 'golden era' (mid-19th century) to modern times, with recreated sitting rooms and shopfronts, the life stories of key figures in Gävle's history, and multimedia augmentation. The excellent **Rettig Art Gallery** occupies the top two floors and showcases one of the most important collections of Swedish art, from neoclassicism to super-realism and postmodernism, with a special section dedicated to the Gothenburg Colourists.

Mackmyra Svensk Whisky & Whiskyby DISTILLERY
(☎026-54 18 80; www.mackmyra.se; Kolonnvägen 2; ⊙noon-8pm year-round, tours Jun-Aug) Mackmyra Svensk Whisky, established in 1999 as the first Scandinavian malt-whisky distillery, is set in a historic *bruk* (works) about 10km west of Gävle. It offers tasting sessions (Skr4395) that must be booked in advance via the website. Mackmyra also has the additional Whiskyby distillery and lookout tower just west of Gävle, off the E4, which can be visited separately (10am to 5pm).

Gamla Gefle HISTORIC SITE
A fire in 1869 wiped out most of the colourful old wooden buildings that formed the town's core. Today the little cluster that survived the fire is preserved in the rickety jumble that is Gamla Gefle, just south of the city centre.

Gävle

Sights

1 Gamla Gefle ... D3
2 Heliga Trefaldighets kyrka ... B3
3 Joe Hillgården ... D3
4 Länsmuseum Gävleborg ... D3
5 Sveriges Fängelse Museum ... C3

Sleeping

6 Elite Grand Hotel Gävle ... D2
7 Gefle Vandrarhem ... C3
8 Hotel Aveny ... D4
9 Järnvägshotellet ... D2
10 Scandic-CH ... C1

Eating

11 Bistro Nord ... D2
12 Cafe Pazzo ... B3
13 Church Street Saloon ... B3
14 Matildas ... C4

Drinking & Nightlife

15 Bishop's Arms ... C3
16 Coffee Lounge ... B2

Sveriges Fängelse Museum MUSEUM
(Swedish Prison Museum; Hamiltongatan 3; adult/student Skr80/40; ⊙noon-4pm Wed-Sun, daily Jul & Aug) Duck into underground dungeons, check out ye olde instruments of retribution, peer into the windowless 'punishment' cells, and enjoy the tableaux of slatterns and miscreants getting merry inside one of Sweden's first penitentiaries.

Furuvik AMUSEMENT PARK
(www.furuvik.se; adult/3-12yr Skr199/169; ⊙10am-7pm mid-Jun–mid-Aug; 👪) Families mob Furuvik amusement park in summer, thanks to its roller coasters, Aqua Jungle pool area with water slides, and ape enclosure at the zoo. Furuvik is 12km southeast of Gävle; take a local train to Furuvik stop (seven minutes, every two hours).

Limön ISLAND
(boat tours adult/child each way Skr50/30) From late May to late August up to three daily 45-minute **boat tours** on the M/S *Queen Silvia* run from Södra Skeppsbron to the island of Limön, part of the surrounding archipelago. The island has a **nature trail** and several forested walking paths, and a **mass grave** and **memorial** to the sailors of a ship that was lost here in the early 1800s.

Joe Hillgården MUSEUM
(www.joehill.se; Nedre Bergsgatan 28; ⊙10am-3pm Jun-Aug) FREE One of the houses in Gamla Gefle is a museum marking the birthplace of the US labour-union organiser. Hill was wrongly convicted of a murder and executed in Utah in 1915. Some of his folk songs form part of the memorial here.

Heliga Trefaldighets kyrka CHURCH
(Kaplansgatan; ⊙10am-3pm Mon-Fri) The oldest church in Gävle has an 11th-century rune stone inside, as well as incredible woodcrafter decoration – the work of German craftsman Ewardt Friis.

Sleeping

Hotels are typically booked well ahead Monday to Friday by Stockholm commuters. Prices drop on weekends.

Gefle Vandrarhem HOSTEL €
(☎026-62 17 45; www.geflevandrarhem.se; Södra Rådmansgatan 1; dm/s/d Skr240/410/580; ⊙mid-Jan–early Dec) Set in one of Gamla Gefle's old-style wooden buildings around a flowering courtyard, this quiet hostel with good guest kitchen is popular with travellers of all ages.

The staff are lovely, with the exception of one crochety member. Breakfast buffet costs Skr70.

Hotel Aveny
HOTEL €

(☑026-615 590; www.hotelaveny.eu; Södra Kungsgatan 31; s/d from Skr430/640; P📶) Family-run budget hotel south of the river with terracotta-coloured rooms, minuscule bathrooms and a decent breakfast spread. Online discounts available.

Elite Grand Hotel Gävle
HOTEL €€

(☑026-400 73 00; www.elite.se; Kyrkogatan 28; s/d from Skr729/999; P📶) This beautifully restored Art Deco hotel has a lot going for it, not least its super-central location and bright, contemporary decor. Light sleepers should opt for a room overlooking the river.

Järnvägshotellet
HOTEL €€

(☑026-12 09 90; www.jarnvagshotellet.nu; Centralplan 3; s/d incl breakfast Skr525/695; P📶) Just across the square from the train station, this small, family-run hotel in a historic building largely attracts travellers riding the rails with its individually decorated rooms and ample breakfasts. Good ratio of guests to shared bathrooms.

Scandic-CH
HOTEL €€

(☑026-495 84 00; www.scandic-hotels.se; Nygatan 45; s/d from Skr864/961; P❄📶) This business-friendly hotel overcomes its chaininess with cheery staff and small perks like bicycles for guests to borrow. Rooms are typical Scandinavian: Ikea-style furniture and bedding, flat-screen TVs and eco-conscious wall art.

Eating

Cafe Pazzo
ITALIAN €

(www.pazzo.se; Drottninggatan 6; mains Skr89-119; ☺11am-9pm) This self-styled 'bistro' may look like a canteen, but it has a good stab at cooking up large portions of pizza and pasta as well as lighter bites (focaccia, salads, grilled sandwiches).

★ Matildas
FUSION €€

(www.matildas.nu; Timmermansgatan 23; ☺5pm-late Tue-Sat) The menu at this small, stylish bistro is short, sweet and seasonal, with a real depth of flavour to the dishes, wonderful attention to presentation and a relaxed ambience. Feast on lobster tacos, oysters paired with champagne, crispy pork belly and homemade black pudding with lingon-

berry. The home-brewed beer, served by the delightful owners, goes down very smoothly.

Bistro Nord
FUSION €€

(☑026-10 91 01; www.bistronord.se; Centralplan 1; mains Skr195-285; ☺4pm-late Mon-Sat; 🍴) Tucked away by the railway station, Nord has a modest entrance that belies its stylish, contemporary interior and edgy dishes. The chanterelle pizza and spinach risotto win the vegetarian vote, and the calf's-liver and lamb dishes tickle the taste buds of the carnivorously inclined. The service is warm and polished and the wine selection impressive and reasonably priced.

Church Street Saloon
TEX-MEX €€

(☑026-12 62 11; Kyrkogatan 11; mains Skr190-513; ☺5pm-midnight Mon-Fri, noon-1am Sat; 🍴) Locals stampede this Wild West–themed saloon, encrusted with cowboy kitsch, looking to rustle up some Tex-Mex. The steaks (including the 'ridiculous size' 900g ribeye), enchiladas, ribs, buffalo wings and Macho Nachos arrive on plates the size of serving platters, so come ravenous. On weekends after 10pm the bar wenches hitch up their skirts and dance the can-can on the bar.

🍷 Drinking

Bishop's Arms
PUB

(www.bishopsarms.com/Gavle/Presentation; Södra Kungsgatan 7; ☺4pm-midnight Mon-Fri, 1pm-1am Sat, 4-10pm Sun) It's rather like drinking in an antiques shop, albeit one with the widest selection of beers and microbrews in town. We dig the conversation-friendly ambience, too.

Coffee Lounge
CAFE

(www.coffee-lounge.se; Nygatan 21; ☺9am-5pm) Bright cafe with filled bagels and sandwiches accompanying the signature latte art and good, strong, lava-thick coffee.

ℹ️ Information

Tourist Office (☑026-17 71 17; www.visitgavle.se; Drottninggatan 22; ☺10am-7pm Mon-Fri, to 4pm Sat, noon-4pm Sun) Off the main pedestrian drag.

ℹ️ Getting There & Away

BUS

Long-distance bus services leave from behind the train station. For Ybuss departures, take a 'Busstaxi' from the train station to Gävlebro.

Ybuss (www.ybuss.se) runs daily to Sundsvall (Skr240, 2¾ to 3¼ hours, three to six daily) and Umeå (Skr390, 6½ to 7½ hours, three daily).

SGS Bussen (www.sgsbussen.nu) serves Stockholm (Skr150, two hours, five to seven daily).

TRAIN

There are numerous daily services to Stockholm (Skr247, 1½ to 2¼ hours) via Uppsala (Skr97, 45 minutes to 1¼ hours), Sundsvall (Skr112, 2¼ hours, roughly hourly), one or two trains to Kiruna (Skr763, 14¼ hours, two daily), via Luleå (Skr691, 11¼ hours, daily), and three to Östersund (Skr232, 3½ hours).

Hudiksvall

0650 / POP 15,015

Hudiksvall is one plucky little town. Not only has it survived 10 major fires that left it in piles of ashes but also it has weathered a Russian rampage in 1721 (check out the cannonball-pockmarked Jacobs Kyrka (10am-4pm) just southwest of the centre). Its cute harbour, surrounded by red wooden fishermen's storehouses (Möljen), has a sedate appeal, as does the grander Fiskarstan, further along Hamngatan. 'Fishermen's Town' consists of partly preserved, elegantly wood-panelled merchants' yards and winter dwellings of local fishermen, dating back to the early 19th century.

A block from the waterfront, the highlights of Hälsinglands Museum (www.halsinglandsmuseum.se; Storgatan 31; noon-4pm Mon & Sat, 10am-4pm Tue-Fri) FREE include eerily illuminated medieval church art, the Malsta rune stone from around AD 1000, engraved with the Helsinge runic script, and an early cubism exhibition by Swedish artists John Sten and Dick Beer.

Your best bet for lodgings in central Hudik is the somewhat weathered First Hotell Statt (0650-150 60; www.firsthotels.se; Storgatan 36; r from Skr798; P), in which the town's timber barons used to carouse in the 19th century (and which looks like it hasn't changed its decor since). More carousing can done at the on-site O'Leary's bar. Four kilometres east of Hudik, lakeside Malnbadens Camping & STF Hudiksvall (0650-132 60; www.malnbadenscamping.com; Linsänkevägen 15; sites from Skr160, s/d/q Skr345/410/795; P) has tree-shaded camping spots, rustic hostel cottages, canoes for rent and a decent lakeside restaurant; it's best to have your own wheels.

Waterside Hot Chilli (www.hotchilli.se; Hamngatan 5; mains Skr79-158; 11am-8pm Mon-Fri, noon-8pm Sat & Sun;) specialises in stir-fry and noodle dishes of a Chinese/Thai persuasion, while the menu at Sigges Bistro & Bar (0650-333 33; Hamngatan 6; mains from Skr115-269; 5pm-late) runs the gamut from herring platters with all the trimmings to homemade cheeseburgers and Caesar salads. On weekends, the bar morphs into a small nightclub.

The tourist office (0650-191 00; www.hudiksvall.se/turism; Storgatan 33; 10am-4pm Mon-Fri) is next door to the museum.

Getting There & Away

The **bus station** is next to the main train station, by the harbour. **Ybuss** (060-17 19 60; www.ybuss.se) travels to Gävle (Skr140, 1½ hours to two hours, two to three daily), Stockholm via Uppsala (Skr275, 3¾ to five hours, two to three daily) and Umeå (Skr320, 5¼ hours, daily).

Trains run to Sundsvall (Skr195, 50 minutes, seven daily), Gävle (Skr195, 1¼ hours, hourly) and Stockholm (Skr373, 2¾ hours, seven to 10 daily).

Sundsvall

060 / POP 50,7112

When Sundsvall burned to the ground in 1888 after a spark from the Selånger steamboat set the town brewery alight, civic leaders made a decision to have the old wooden houses rebuilt in stone, separated by wide avenues. This immediately set Sundsvall apart from the other towns along the Bothnian Coast, making them look like poor provincial cousins. This move also forced poorer residents (including the workers who rebuilt Sundsvall) to the city's outskirts, while wealth and power collected in the centre.

Sundsvall's main appeal today lies less in any one specific sight than in the Bothnian Coast's most cosmopolitan city as a whole, complete with highly strollable boulevards and a clutch of great restaurants.

Sights & Activities

★ Kulturmagasinet MUSEUM
(www.sunsvall.se/kulturmagasinet; Sjögatan; 10am-7pm Mon-Thu, to 6pm Fri, 11am-4pm Sat & Sun) FREE Down near the harbour, Kulturmagasinet is a magnificent restoration of some old warehouses and now contains the town library and Sundsvall Museum, which has engaging exhibits of the history of Sundsvall, plus natural history and geology. There's a permanent art exhibition upstairs featuring 20th-century Swedish artists, and the superb temporary exhibitions have recently included

some rather risque photography featuring aged, beautiful burlesque dancers.

Norra Berget HILL
(www.norraberget.se) Norra Berget hill (150m) is crowned with a 19th-century **viewing tower**, from which you get sweeping views of the city, squeezed between the sea and surrounding hills. Nearby, you can also learn to bake *tunnbröd* (soft, thin unleavened bread) at the **Norra Bergets Hantverksmuseum**, an entertaining collection of wooden buildings that make up the open-air museum (open 11am to 5pm, admission Skr25). In July you'll also find yourself knee-deep in blueberries. To get here, take any Norra Berget–bound bus.

Alnö Gamla Kyrka CHURCH
(noon-6pm mid-Jun–mid-Aug) This magnificent church, a mixture of 12th- and 15th-century styles, sits 2km north of the bridge (at Vi) on Alnö island, just east of Sundsvall. The upper wall and ceiling paintings, likely done by one of Albertus Pictor's pupils, have survived intact. Even better is the late-11th-century carved wooden **font** across the road; the upper part combines Christian and Viking symbolism, while the lower part shows beasts that embody evil. Catch bus 1 to Vi (two hourly), then walk.

Sleeping

STF Sundsvall City HOSTEL €
(060-12 60 90; www.sundsvallcityhostel.se; Sjögatan 11; hostel s/d/tr/q Skr400/500/720/920, hotel s/d Skr500/595; P wi-fi) Friendly but rather anonymous hostel in a super-central location. All the rooms are sparsely furnished but bright and en suite; guests have use of the sauna and fully equipped kitchen; and reception is open all day – a miracle in the budget lodging category. 'Hotel' rooms are essentially hostel rooms but with bed linen and breakfast included.

Lilla Hotellet HOTEL €
(060-61 35 87; Rådhusgatan 15; s/d Skr695/795) In a stone building designated a historical monument (since it was built the year after the great fire), this small family-run hotel has a great location and a friendly vibe. The eight spacious rooms with high ceilings have interesting architectural details, such as ceramic tile stoves.

Elite Hotel Knaust HOTEL €€
(060-608 00 00; www.elite.se; Storgatan 13; s/d from Skr990/1290; P wi-fi) In a striking 19th-century building on Sundsvall's main pedestrian drag, this opulent hotel is full of old-world charm. Besides the grand, lobby-dominating (and much photographed) marble staircase, the rooms are decorated in classic Scandinavian style and have high ceilings. The breakfast buffet is excellent. Our only quibble is that wi-fi is still not complimentary.

Best Western Hotel Baltic HOTEL €€
(060-14 04 40; www.baltichotell.com; Sjögatan 5; s/d from Skr690/1090; P wi-fi) Bright, modern room inside an 1880s building, at the water's edge near Kulturmagasinet. Particularly good for solo travellers.

Eating & Drinking

Tant Anci & Fröcken Sara CAFE €
(Bankgatan 15; mains Skr85-115; 10am-10pm Mon-Thu, to 8pm Fri, 11am-5pm Sat;) Humongous bowls of soup or salad are the speciality at this frilly organic cafe, where you can also get hearty sandwiches, giant bowls of pasta and pastries.

★ **Udda Tapas Bar** TAPAS €
(073-098 66 07; http://uddatapasbar.wordpress.com; Esplanaden 17; tapas Skr40-75; 5-11pm Mon-Thu, to 2am Fri & Sat) Head for the roof terrace of this congenial bar on summer evenings to savour the likes of clams with lemongrass, smoked reindeer with Dijon mustard, lamb tacos and yellow beets with honey and feta, along with a glass of wine or a local brew. DJs kick it up a notch on weekends.

7 Kryddor SWEDISH €€
(www.7kryddor.com; Trädgårdsgatan 25; lunch mains Skr95-125, dinner mains Skr165-235; 11am-2pm Mon-Thu, 11am-2pm & 5-11pm Fri, 5-11pm Sat & Sun;) The (Mediterranean) Force is strong with this one: besides the well-conceived platters of meze, there's hummus, saksuka and grilled veg to tempt non-carnivorous customers, while discerning carnivores are treated to superlative kebabs, kofte and grilled meats.

Invito Ristorante Italiano ITALIAN €€€
(060-15 39 00; www.invitobar.se; Storgatan 6-8; 3-/6-/9-course menu Skr450/675/849; 11am-2pm & 5-11pm Mon-Fri, 5pm-2am Sat) Plusses: we love the fusing of Italian and northern Swedish cuisine and the adventurous pairings of ingredients, such as cloudberries and blue cheese and classics, such as lobster risotto. Also, the sommellier really knows his stuff and weekday lunches are a steal at Skr90. Fusses: the service at this fine-dining

WORTH A TRIP

KUSTVÄGEN

If you're driving between Hudiksvall and Sundsvall, the 75km-long **Kustvägen** (www.kustvagen.se) (Coastal Road) is a much lovelier alternative to the parallel stretch of the E4. Narrow, winding and largely unpeopled, Kustvägen meanders through forest and past secluded beaches and tiny working fishing communities.

If coming from Hudiksvall, join the Coastal Road at Jättendal and follow its sinuous curves to the **Sörfjärden** turnoff. From the northern end of the beach, a gorgeous walking path skirts the forested peninsula. Further north, a tiny road branches off east to **Oxsand**, a village with appealing bathing spots. Another turnoff further along takes you to **Galtströms Bruk**, where there's a miniature railway for children and the small but lovely **Vitsand Beach**, just a stroll through the forest, with flat slabs of waterside rock perfect for sunbathing.

Further north still, **Skåtan** is a picture-perfect village with a small yacht marina, and **Skatans Cafe & Krog** (www.skatanscafe.se; mains from Skr125; ⏲11am-9pm Jun–late Aug) that serves mostly fishy delights; there are ship-shape rooms upstairs in sailor stripes should you wish to linger. At the northern end of the Kustvägen there's a T-junction; the eastern branch leads you to Lörruden, while the western one takes you back to the E4 via Njurundabommen. Lörruden's eponymous **restaurant** (☎060-370 98; www.sillmans.se; mains Skr 165-275) sits amidst red fishing cottages right by the water and has a devoted following of Sundsvall customers due to the chefs' passion for locally sourced ingredients. Dishes such as the hearty fish stew and seafood lasagne really stand out, and the perch with chanterelles and truffle puree was out of this world.

establishment is snooty bordering on condescending.

Oscar Matsal & Bar BAR
(www.oscarmatsal.se; Bankgatan 11; ⏲5-11pm Mon-Thu, to 3am Fri & Sat) The hottest watering hole in town with retro decor triples as a sophisticated bistro and a nightclub where you can knock back Tom Collinses while checking out the latest live band.

Information

Tourist Office (☎060-658 58 00; www.visitsundsvall.se; Stora Torget; ⏲11am-7pm Mon-Fri, 10am-4pm Sat, noon-4pm Sun) Inside the Stadhus.

Getting There & Away

AIR

Sundsvall-Timrå Airport (☎070-522 03 12; www.sdlairport.se) Sundsvall-Timrå Airport is 21km north of Sundsvall; flights serve Göteborg, Luleå, Stockholm and Visby (summer only).

BUS

Buses depart from the Sundsvall bus station, near Kulturmagasinet. Ybuss (p257) runs to Gävle (Skr240, 2¾ to 3¾ hours, up to six daily) and Stockholm (Skr300, 4½ to six hours, up to six daily). Länstrafiken Västerbotten buses 10 and 100 run to Umeå (Skr310, 5¼ hours, up to five daily) via other coastal towns.

TRAIN

Trains run west to Östersund (Skr266, 2½ hours, up to eight daily) and south to Gävle (Skr265, 2¼ hours, hourly) and Stockholm (Skr373, 3½ to five hours, up to eight daily). The station is just east of the town centre on Landsvagsalen, which is a continuation of Köpmangatan.

Härnösand

☎0611 / POP 17,556

Once a pre-Viking trading post on the island of Härnön, Härnösand was burned to the ground three times in the 1700s: once when drunken churchgoers set the place on fire by accident, once by schoolboy pranksters, and once when Russian Cossacks flattened it in 1721. Härnösand's Storatorget (main square) is lined with attractive neoclassical 18th-century buildings, and its pretty harbour fills up with yachts in July when Härnösand celebrates its maritime heritage.

Länsmuseet Västernorrland (www.murberget.se; ⏲11am-4pm) FREE showcases historic photographs and Sami handicraft, while equally interesting temporary offerings may include a study of Sweden's attitudes to witchcraft and evil forces, and spectacular weddings dresses that are part of a here-comes-the-bride-through-the-ages' display. The adjacent open-air museum, **Murberget** (www.murberget.se; Varvsallén; 11am-4pm) FREE, is the second largest of its kind in Sweden and features over 80 wooden buildings from Ångermanland from the 18th century onwards. Among the traditional farmhouses, 19th-century inn, smithy, church and school in the style typical of this part of Norrland, you'll find Rysstugan, the only building to survive the marauding Russians. The museums are a 30-minute walk from the centre, or take bus 2 or 52 from Nybrogatan near the Rådhuset.

Directly across the street from the cathedral is a restored wooden building from 1844 that houses the original **STF Mitti Härnösand** (0611-243 00; www.mittiharnosand.com; Franzengatan 14 ; hostel dm/s/d from Skr150/300/400, hotel s/d from Skr545/695; reception 8-10am & 3-5pm; P). The facilities are more modern at Köpmangatan 7 (where, incidentally, the reception is located). 'Hotel' rooms are hostel rooms, with bed linen, towels and breakfast included. A more refined option is **First Hotel Stadt** (0611-55 44 40; www.firsthotels.se; Skeppsbron 9; s/d from Skr840/1040; P), with its harbourside location and Scandinavian-modern rooms.

Run by a hardworking owner, **Kanal Café & Restaurang** (www.kanalcafeet.se; Storgatan 18; mains Skr109-249; 11am-10pm) has a loyal local following, thanks to dishes such as hot-smoked salmon with house mayo, pepper steak 'Fidel Castro style' and tapas platters made for sharing. Located in a darkly atmospheric 19th-century timber building, **Vägg i Vägg** (0611-247 45; www.vaggivagg.com; Brunnshusgatan 1; mains Skr175-235; 6pm-late Tue-Sat) caters to a largely carnivorous clientele. Their offerings range from homemade bacon-and-jalapeño hamburgers and expertly seared steaks to Swedish tapas combos.

The **tourist office** (0611-881 40; www.harnosand.se; Storatorget 2; 9am-6pm Mon-Fri, 10am-3pm Sat & Sun Jun-Aug) is located on the main square and sells guides to the Höga Kusten.

Buses 100 and 201 run to Sundsvall (Skr94, 45 minutes, roughly hourly), buses 100 and 10 serve Umeå (Skr263, three to 4¼ hours, six daily). Ybuss runs daily to Gävle (Skr285, 3¾ hours, up to six daily) and Stockholm (Skr349, 5½ to seven hours, up to six daily).

Höga Kusten

0613

Cross the **Höga Kustenbron**, the spectacular suspension bridge over the Ångerman river – Norrland's answer to the Golden Gate Bridge and one of the longest in the world (1867m) – and you find yourself amid some of the most dramatic scenery on the Swedish coastline. The secret to the Höga Kusten's (High Coast's) spectacular beauty is elevation; nowhere else on the coast do you find such a mountainous landscape, with sheer rocky cliffs – the highest in Sweden – plunging straight down to the sea, as well as lakes, fjords and dozens of tranquil islands, covered in dense spruce and pine forest. The region is recognised as a geographically unique area and was listed as a Unesco World Heritage Site in 2000.

The combined processes of glacial retreat and land rising from the sea (which continues today at a rate of 8mm per year) are responsible for this stunning scenery. Höga Kusten stretches from north of Härnösand to Örnsköldsvik, and it's a wonderful area for scenic drives along the narrow, twisty roads, though you can't really say that you've 'done' the Höga Kusten without visiting its tranquil islands.

Information

Tourist Office (0613-504 80; www.hogakusten.com; 10am-6pm Jun-Aug) Inside Hotell Höga Kusten, just north of Höga Kustenbron suspension bridge. Has a detailed map of the scenic byways, boat timetables and guidebooks on the Höga Kusten trail.

Naturum (0613-700 200; www.naturumhogekusten.se; 9am-7pm late Jun–mid-Aug) Naturum, off the E4, north of the village of Docksta, has exhibitions on the formation of the Höga Kusten and stocks brochures on the area. Adrenalin junkies can tackle the four **via ferrata** routes of varying difficulty (www.via-ferrata.se; from Skr350 per person) along the flanks of **Skuleberget** mountain (285m) behind the visitor centre between May and October.

Högbonden

A tiny island in the southern part of Höga Kusten, Högbonden is only 15 minutes by boat from the villages of Bönhamn and Barsta. It's famous for its 100-year-old lighthouse – its only building – atop the highest point of the rocky plateau that soars above the island's tree line. Högbonden is bisected by a narrow gorge, and its rugged cliffs lend themselves to exploration. Your only option is to come here as a day tripper and bring a picnic, as the island's sole hostel and cafe have now closed down.

Ulvön

0660

The largest island in the Höga Kusten archipelago, Ulvön is famous for its regatta (14 to 18 July) and for the production of *surströmming*. It's possible to purchase the noxious (or delightful, depending on your outlook) stuff in the shops at Ulvöhamn, the island's one-street village. A cycle path leads through the picturesque fishermen's settlement with traditional red-and-white wooden houses drowning in hibiscus blossoms in summer, past the tiny 17th-century chapel decorated with colourful murals, and onwards to the preserved 17th-century fishing village of Sandviken in the northern part of the island.

If you wish to linger overnight, the refined Ulvö Skarrgårdshotell (0660-22 40 09; www.ulvohotell.se; Hamngatan 1; d Skr2190) is conveniently located by the quay; its superb restaurant has a seasonal menu featuring local ingredients. A cheaper spot is the hostel (0522-291 80; www.ulvon.se; Ulvövägen; s/d/tr Skr460/600/900; Apr-Sep; @) with a helluva view and guest kitchen; walk uphill, beyond the chapel. Run by one of Ulvön's *surströmming*-producing giants, Ruben Madsen, flower-festooned Cafe Måsen (mains Skr75-145; 10am-6pm Jun-Aug) serves cakes, sandwiches and light dishes. If you opt for the *surströmming* platter the maestro himself will talk you through the correct way to consume this local delicacy.

Trysunda

A small island with a namesake village consisting of cute fishermen's houses clustered around a little U-shaped bay, Trysunda has an attractive wooden chapel, dating back to 1655 – the oldest along the Bothnian Coast. There are also some great secluded spots for bathing, reachable by the walking paths that run through the woods; just pick your own flat rock by the water or else head to the sandy cove at Björnviken, on the eastern side of the island. You can walk around the whole of Trysunda in an hour or two, but overnight stays are available at Trysunda Gästhamn (0660-430 38; s/d Skr270/550; May-Sep), a guesthouse consisting of a red waterfront building with super-compact doubles and guest kitchen. If you don't feel like cooking up a storm, you can purchase some smoked fish at the village shop, which also stocks free maps of the island.

GETTING AROUND THE HÖGA KUSTEN

Höga Kusten can be tricky to explore if you're relying solely on public transport. The three main islands can be reached by a combination of buses and boats in summer only; arm yourself with bus and boat timetables in advance to plan the multi-legged journey. As for the coast itself, buses reach few of the remote fishing villages, so you're better off with your own set of wheels. That's unless, of course, you wish to walk the Höga Kusten Leden (p262)...

Getting There & Around

BUS

You can reach most departure points for boats by public transport. Buses are infrequent on weekends. Länstrafiken Västerbotten buses 10 and 100 (at least six daily) run between Härnösand and Örnsköldsvik, stopping at Ullånger, Docksta and Bjästa. From Örnsköldsvik, bus 421 runs to Köpmanholmen via Bjästa (Skr 59, 40 minutes, up to nine daily). The villages of Bönhamn and Barsta are not reachable by public transport.

BOAT

M/S Ronja (www.hkship.se; one way/return Skr100/150) Ferry to Högbonden departs Barsta between late June and mid-August at 9.30am, 11.30am, 2.30pm and 5.30pm daily, returning at 10.15pm, 12.15pm. 3.15pm and 6.15pm, while the Bönhamn–Högbonden service runs at 10am, noon, 3pm and 6pm, returning at 9.30am, 11.30am, 2.30pm and 5.30pm. There are reduced services from Barsta from early May to late June and from mid-August to early October.

MF Ulvön & MF Minerva (070-651 92 65; www.ornskolvikshamn.se; return adult/6-19yr Skr150/90) Between mid-June and mid-August, ferries leave Köpmanholmen for Ulvöhamn (adult/six to 19 years Skr150/90 return, 1½ hours, six daily), three of them stopping at Trysunda (adult/six to 19 years Skr120/80, 30 minutes). From late May to mid-June and mid-August to mid-September, reduced services call at Ulvöhamn twice daily and at

THE HIGH COAST TRAIL

The **Höga Kusten Leden** (High Coast Trail) is 129km long and runs the entire length of the Höga Kusten, starting at the northern end of the Höga Kustenbron and finishing at the summit of Varvsberget, the hill overlooking Örnsköldsvik. The trail is divided into 13 sections, each between 15km and 24km in length, with accommodation at the end of each section consisting mostly of rustic cabins. Buses running along the E4 stop at either end of the trail, as well as by the Lappuden, Ullånger, Skoved, Skule Naturum and Köpmanholmen villages along the way, close to the different sections of the trail. The trail is well signposted, but it's best to pick up a detailed booklet and map at the Härnösand tourist office (p260).

Parts of the trail involve an easy ramble, whereas other sections will challenge you with steep, uneven ground. Take food and plenty of drinking water with you.

The trail takes in some of the most beautiful coastal scenery in Sweden, from rocky coastline and sandy coves to lush countryside, dense evergreen forest and deep ravines, including **Slåtterdalskrevan**, a 200m-deep canyon in **Skuleskogen National Park**, through which part of the trail passes. The 26-sq-km park, which lies between Docksta and Köpmanholmen, is a Unesco World Heritage Site due to its wealth of fauna and flora: the park is home to the lynx, roe deer, mink and other shy animals, as well as all four of Sweden's game birds: the black grouse, willow grouse, capercallie and hazel hen.

A recommended detour from the trail is north of Docksta, towards Norrgällsta (1.4km), where you can either hike up Mt Skuleberget or take a **cable car** (per person Skr100; ⏲10am-5pm Jun-Aug) to the top to appreciate the all-encompassing view. The **Skuleberget cave** is another popular attraction – it was once a hideout for bandits. Other worthwhile diversions include Dalsjöfallet (1.5km from the main trail), a **waterfall** that lies halfway between the Skuleberget and Gyltberget mountains, and **lake Balestjärn**, with its crystal-clear waters, in the middle of the small peninsula to the north of Köpmanholmen.

Trysunda once or twice daily. Both destinations are served daily the rest of the year.

M/S Kusttrafik (☎0613-105 50; www.hkship.se) The ferry to Ulvön leaves Ullånger for Ulvöhamn via Docksta daily at 9.30am, returning from Ulvöhamn at 3pm between June and August.

Umeå

☎090 / POP 115,473

With the vibrant feel of a college town (it has around 30,000 students), Umeå is a welcome outpost of urbanity in the barren north. Since the title of Culture Capital of Europe was bestowed on it in 2014, it's really been strutting its stuff, with its museums and other venues showcasing northern and Sami culture.

Umeå is also widely considered the most 'metal' town in Sweden, thanks to its thriving metal and straight-edge music scene. Legendary hardcore band Refused started here, and an annual metalfest, **House of Metal** (www.houseofmetal.se), takes place at Folkets Hus in early February – the darkest time of the year, of course.

Sights & Activities

★ Västerbottens Museum MUSEUM
(www.vbm.se; Gammliavägen; ⏲10am-5pm, to 9pm Wed) FREE The star of the Gammlia museum complex, the engrossing Västerbottens Museum traces the history of the province from prehistoric times to Umeå today. Exhibitions include an enormous skis-through-the-ages collection starring the world's oldest ski (5400 years old), and an exploration of Sami rock art and shaman symbols. Of the temporary exhibitions, a photographic portrayal of a single family through several decades, shot by Latvian photographer Inta Ruka, was particularly moving. Take bus 2 or 7.

Bildmuséet GALLERY
(www.bildmuseet.umu.se; Östra Strandgatan 30B; ⏲11am-8pm Tue, to 6pm Wed-Sun) In its new home next to the Umeå Academy of Fine Arts, this state-of-the-art modern-art museum showcases the likes of *Right is Wrong* – four decades of contemporary art in China, and *A Cry from the Expanses* by Carola Granh, a haunting sound installation that's

all about the Sami presence on the northern Swedish landscape. Take bus 1, 5, 6, or 8.

Umedalens Skulpturpark SCULPTURE
(www.umedalenskulptur.se; Umedalen; 24hr) Perhaps appropriately located in the vast grounds of Umeå's former psychiatric hospital, this contemporary sculpture park features the efforts of Anthony Gormley and Sean Henry, among others. Works range from the eerie *New Perspective* sound installation by Lin Peng and humorous *Eye Benches* by Louise Bourgeois to the baffling *Untitled* by Carina Gunnars that consists of eight half-buried bathtubs. Take bus 1 or 61 to the Löftets gränd stop.

Friluftsmuséet MUSEUM
(Gammliavägen; 10am-5pm) FREE Part of the Gammlia museum complex, this open-air historic village presents a ye olde church, a smokehouse, a windmill, a 17th-century gatehouse and traditional Sami dwellings. Decked out in period costume, staff demonstrate traditional homestead life. Become a baker's apprentice and learn to bake *tunnbröd* (a thin unleavened bread) or else take the kids for a spin in a horse-drawn carriage.

Guitars – The Museum MUSEUM
(www.guitarsthemuseum.com; Vasagatan 18-20; adult/student Skr125/90; 11am-6pm Mon-Fri, to 4pm Sat & Sun) If you're into the six-string, then this result of two brothers' lifelong hobby, a huge collection of vintage guitars, is for you. Want to see a 1959 Les Paul Standard, identical to the one on which Keith Richards played the 'It's All Over Now' riff? They've got it. Or perhaps a 1958 Gibson Flying V, made famous by ZZ Top?

Älgens Hus FARM
(0932-500 00; www.algenshus.se; Västernyliden 23; adult/child Skr120/60; noon-6pm Tue-Sun mid-Jun–mid-Aug;) This elk farm, 70km west of Umeå along Rte 92, near Bjurholm, is your chance to meet the (tame) King of the Forest face to face. There's a museum dedicated to all things elk, and even a small dairy where the ultra-rare elk cheese is produced; at Skr3000 per kilogram, this is the most expensive cheese you'll ever taste. Don't forget to pick up bananas beforehand, as elks love them.

Fiske och Sjöfartsmuseum MUSEUM
(Gammliavägen; noon-5pm mid-Jun–mid-Aug) FREE Nautically themed displays at this small maritime museum – part of the Gammlia museum complex – focus on the history of seal hunting in the Arctic. There are several fishing craft on display, as well as a tug boat that formerly plied the Ume river.

Sleeping

STF Vandrarhem Umeå HOSTEL €
(090-771650; www.umeavandrarhem.com; Västra Esplanaden 10; dm/s/d from Skr170/300/500;) This busy, efficient hostel has rooms of varying quality: try to nab a space in one of the newer rooms with beds, as opposed to the rather basic dorms with bunks. It's in a great location: a residential neighbourhood at the edge of the town centre, and the

WORTH A TRIP

TREEHOTEL

A spaceship suspended high above ground. A mirror cube reflecting sunlight and surrounding spruce branches. A giant bird's nest...The six individually styled tree-rooms that make up the **Treehotel** (070-572 77 52, 0928-104 03; www.treehotel.se; Rte 97; r Skr4700-7200), Sweden's most mind-boggling, award-winning lodgings, sit just off Rte 97 in the midst of pristine forest, with saunas and hot tubs to relax stiff muscles after a day of hiking, kayaking or dogsledding.

The Treehotel came into being in 2010, inspired by the film *The Tree Lover* by Jonas Selberg Augustsen, and its unique rooms were designed by some of Sweden's leading architects, such as Tham & Videgård and Bertil Harström, with an emphasis on minimal environmental impact and ecologically friendly construction. The toilets are a wonder all in themselves. We have only one question: why is the Blue Cone red?

Guided tours of this architectural wonder are available on weekends at 1pm (Skr150) and at other times by prior arrangement. Even if you don't stay in the Treehotel itself, you can lodge at the retro **Britta's Pensionat** (doubles Skr750) by the road and treat yourself to a delicious weekday lunch buffet (11am to 3pm) at the cheerful cafe inside (open early July until the end of August); three-course dinners are available on request.

Umeå

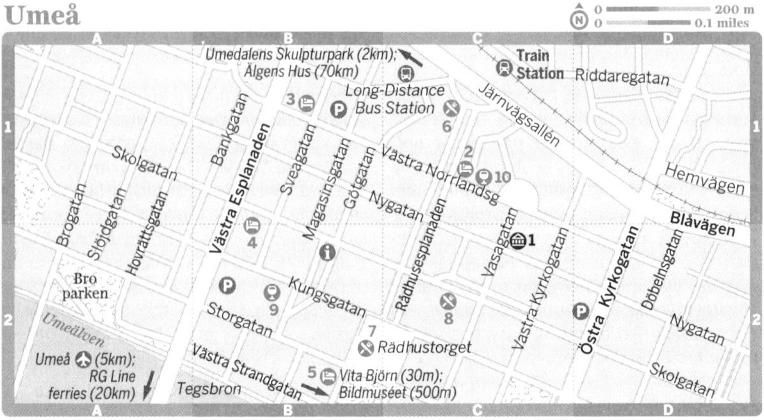

Umeå

Sights

1 Guitars – The Museum C2

Sleeping

2 Hotel Aveny C1
3 Hotell Dragonen B1
4 STF Vandrarhem Umeå B2
5 Stora Hotellet Umeå B2

Eating

6 Gandhi C1
7 Rex Bar och Grill B2
8 Rost Mat & Kaffe C2

Drinking & Nightlife

9 Allstar B2
10 Pipes of Scotland C1

facilities (kitchen, laundry) are very handy for self-caterers. Reception hours are limited.

★ **Stora Hotellet Umeå** BOUTIQUE HOTEL €€
(090-77 88 70; www.storahotelletumea.se; Storgatan 46; s/d/ste from Skr1000/1150/6000; P) We love the muted colours and the plush, old-style furnishings that give you the impression that you're adrift aboard a luxurious ship. Of the six categories of rooms, even the modest 'Superstition' presents you with luxurious queen-size bunks that real sailors could only dream of, while 'Passion' offers grander surroundings, velvet couches and his 'n' hers showers.

Hotel Aveny HOTEL €€
(090-13 41 00; Rådhusesplanaden 14; r/ste from Skr1285/2885; P) Not only does Hotel Aveny take its Green Key eco-credentials seriously, it also has a playful techno-sleek decor scheme, vivid with all the colours of the neon rainbow. Rooms are modern and comfortable; suites contain hot tubs and rain showers. The Scottish pub and Italian restaurant on the premises are a nice bonus.

Hotell Dragonen HOTEL €€
(090-12 58 00; www.hotelldragonen.se; Västra Norrlandsgatan 5; s/d Skr595/850;) With its compact, contemporary rooms with splashes of lime green, Hotell Dragonen conveniently sits on the edge of central Umeå. The free morning sauna slot is a boon for winter guests.

Eating & Drinking

Rost Mat & Kaffe CAFE €
(www.rostmatochkaffe.se; Skolgatan 62; mains Skr83-98; 11am-8pm Mon-Fri, noon-5pm Sat & Sun;) Fresh, imaginative salads, dish-of-the-day lunches with a Mediterranean lean, some of the best coffee in town and scrumptous cakes await at this popular vegetarian cafe.

Vita Björn SWEDISH €€
(www.vitabjorn.se; Kajen 12; mains Skr129-285; 1-9.30pm May-Sep;) Perch yourself on the sunny deck of this boat-restaurant and choose from a casual international menu of caesar salad, veggie burgers, baked salmon and beef tenderloin. For us, however, it gets no better than that simple, moreish Swedish delight – fresh grilled herring.

Gandhi INDIAN €€
(www.gandhi.se; Rådhusesplanaden 17B; mains from Skr135-235; 11am-11pm Mon-Sat, 3-9pm

Sun;) This appealing basement restaurant lures you in with scents of tandoori king prawns, lamb *nawabi* and *paneer* mango masala. Tandoori dishes are the strong point, and vegetarians are well catered for.

Rex Bar och Grill INTERNATIONAL €€€
(090-70 60 50; www.rexbar.com; Rädhustorget; mains Skr175-315; 11am-2pm & 5-11pm Mon-Thu, 11am-2am Fri & Sat) This popular bistro has northern Swedish cuisine meeting international brasserie in a convincing explosion of flavour. Choose the northern menu (bleak roe, smoked Arctic char and reindeer steak) or opt for Iberico pork cheek or grilled courgette with morels. Alternatively, stop by for the American-style pancake-and-bacon weekend brunch. Dinner reservations on weekends recommended.

Pipes of Scotland PUB
(www.pipesofscotland.se; Västra Norrlandsgatan 17; 5pm-late Tue-Sat) Congenial pseudo-Scottish pub where you can buy your lad or lass a wee dram 'o' whisky while enjoying a wholly un-Scottish menu of nachos, pulled beef and veggie burgers.

Allstar SPORTS BAR
(www.allstarbar.se; Kungsgatan 50A; 3-11pm Mon-Thu, noon-2am Fri & Sat, 2-10pm Sun) Umeå's branch of the American-style sports-bar chain is perpetually packed with punters who come to watch the latest game on the big screen.

Information

Tourist Office (090-16 16 16; www.visitumea.se; Renmarkstorget 15; 9am-7pm Mon-Fri, 10am-4pm Sat, noon-4pm Sun) Located on a central square.

Getting There & Around

AIR

Umeå Airport (www.swedavia.se/umea) The airport is 5km south of the city centre. SAS and Norwegian fly daily to Stockholm's Arlanda and Bromma, Malmö Aviation to Göteborg and Stockholm and Direktflyg to Östersund. Airport buses connect it to the city centre (Skr40, 20 minutes).

BOAT

RG Line (www.directferries.co.uk/rg_line.htm) Ferries between Umeå and Vaasa (Finland) run once or twice daily (Skr349 one way, four hours, Sunday to Friday) from Holmsund, 20km south of Umeå.

BUS

The long-distance bus station is directly opposite the train station. Ybuss runs services south to Gävle (Skr435, 6½ to 7½ hours, two daily) and Stockholm (Skr430, 9¼ to 10 hours, two daily), stopping at all the coastal towns.

Buses 20 and 100 head up the coast to Haparanda (Skr356, 6½ to 7¾ hours, up to six daily) via Luleå (Skr310, four to five hours) and Skellefteå (Skr177, two to 2½ hours).

Local buses leave from Vasaplan on Skolgatan.

TRAIN

Departures include five daily trains to Stockholm, including two overnighters (Skr804, nine hours), while the north-bound trains to Luleå (Skr295, five to 5½ hours, two daily) stop in Boden, from where there are connections to Kiruna (Skr647, 7½ to 8½ hours, two daily) and Narvik (Norway; Skr452, 11 hours, daily).

Skellefteå

0910 / POP 71,641

Constructed in 1845, Skellefteå is dominated by the impressive **Bonnstan** (Brännavägen), a *kyrkstad* (church town) consisting of 392 dark log cabins that line several silent streets. Originally built for the faithful coming from afar, they may not be legally altered in any way due to their protected status. In spite of their not having electricity (or running water, or any mod cons whatsoever), many of them are still used as summer houses by locals.

Bonnstan's centrepiece is the striking white neoclassical 19th-century **Landskyrka** (Kyrkvägen; 10am-4pm); on the right, behind the altar, is the 13th-century **Virgin of Skellefteå**, carved out of walnut – the rarest of the church's medieval sculptures. Nearby, the riverside Nordanå park is home to the thought-provoking modern-art exhibitions of **Museum Anna Nordlander** (http://man.skelleftea.org; 10am-7pm Tue, to 4pm Thu-Sun) FREE, such as the recent *Herstory*: installations and paintings by Moncia Sjöö.

Across the road from the church, **Stiftsgården** (0910-72 57 00; www.stiftsgarden.se; Brännvägen 25; hostel s/d from Skr290/480, hotel s/d from Skr950/1200; P) is home to a hotel and Skellefteå's STF hostel. The thimble-size whitewashed rooms are simple yet comfortable, while the hotel rooms are all creams and light wood. The grand yellow building hides an award-winning gourmet restaurant (mains Skr169 to Skr269). In the centre, at **Nygatan 57** (www.nygatan57.se; Nygatan 57;

DON'T MISS

LULEÅ ARCHIPELAGO

This extensive offshore archipelago contains over 1700 large and small islands, most of them uninhabited and therefore perfect for skinny-dipping, berry picking, camping wild... we can go on! The larger islands, decorated with classic red-and-white Swedish summer cottages, are accessible by boat from Luleå. Facilities are limited, so most visitors come as picnicking day-trippers. Here's our island-in-a-nutshell top five:

➜ **Sandön**, the largest permanently inhabited island and the easiest to access from Luleå, features an attractive beach in **Klubbviken bay** and a walking path running across pine moors.

➜ **Junkön's** distinguishing feature is a 16th-century windmill; fishers catch herring and whitefish here in summer.

➜ **Rödkallen**, the southernmost large island, is famous for its numerous bird species and the 1872 lighthouse that was 'retired' a hundred years later and turned into a historical monument.

➜ **Kluntarna**, the all-in-one island, with holiday cottages and all the different bits of scenery you'll find on the other islands – pine forest, seabird colonies and fishing villages.

➜ **Brändöskär** is bleakly beautiful, lashed by the wind and the waves in the outermost archipelago.

Regular boats depart from Södra Hammen in Luleå from late June to mid-August, with a reduced service running until mid-September; check online **timetables** (www.bottenvicken.se). Fares are Skr60 to Klubbviken, Skr430 to Rödkallen and Skr110 to all the other islands.

lunch mains Skr99-110, dinner mains Skr175-295; ⊙ 11am-1.30pm Mon-Fri, 5-10pm Mon-Sat) you may be treated to bouillabasse and home-made burgers at lunchtime, while evenings bring savoury goat's-cheese pie and halibut with hot-smoked pork.

The **tourist office** (☑ 0910-73 60 20; www.skelleftea.se; Trädgårdsgatan 7; ⊙ 10am-6pm Mon-Fri, to 3pm Sat, noon-3pm Sun) is on the corner of the pedestrianised Nygatan and the central square.

Buses 20 and 100 depart for Luleå (Skr158, 2½ hours, five to eight daily) and Umeå (Skr177, two to 2½ hours, six daily).

Luleå

☑ 0920 / POP 46,607

Luleå is the capital of Norrbotten, chartered in 1621, though it didn't become a boom town until the late 19th century when the Malmbanan railway was built to transport iron ore from the Bothnian Coast to Narvik (Norway). The town centre moved to its present location from Gammelstad in 1649 because of the falling sea level (8mm per year), due to postglacial uplift of the land.

A laidback university town and an important high-tech centre, Luleå claims more than its fair share of top-notch restaurants for a town its size, as well as an enticing archipelago of islands off its coast and a sparkling bay with a marina.

◉ Sights

★ **Gammelstad** HISTORIC SITE

(☑ 0920-45 70 10; www.lulea.se/gammelstad) **FREE** The Unesco World Heritage–listed Gammelstad, Sweden's largest church town, was the medieval centre of northern Sweden. The 1492-built stone **Nederluleå church** has a reredos worthy of a cathedral and a wonderfully opulent pulpit. Four hundred and twenty-four wooden houses (where the pioneers stayed during weekend pilgrimages) and six church stables remain.

Guided tours (Skr70) leave from the Gammelstad tourist office at 10am, 11am, 1pm and 3pm (mid-June to mid-August).

Bus 9 runs roughly hourly from Luleå; disembark at the Kyrkbyn stop.

Adjoining the church village is an open-air museum, **Hägnan** (open 11am to 5pm) a recreation of a 19th-century village, staffed by guides and actors in period costume, which houses an 'olde tyme' candy store and where you can have a go at baking bread or assisting the blacksmith.

Norrbottens Museum
MUSEUM

(www.norrbottensmuseum.nu; Storgatan 2; ⊙10am-4pm Mon-Fri, noon-4pm Sat & Sun; 🚻) **FREE** Besides the extensive displays on the history of Norrbotten, Norrbottens Museum is worth a visit for the Sami section alone, with its engrossing collection of photos, tools, and dioramas depicting traditional reindeer-herding Sami life, as well as a nomad tent for kids. The little ones will love the recreated 19th-century playrooms.

Teknikens Hus
MUSEUM

(www.teknikenshus.se; University Campus; adult/under 4yr Skr70/free; ⊙10am-4pm mid-Jun–Aug; 🚻; 🚌4, 5) Curious minds of all ages will love the gigantic educational playground that is Teknikens Hus, within the university campus 4km north of town. The museum has hands-on exhibitions about everything from hot-air balloons and rocket launching to the aurora borealis. Take bus 4 or 5 to Universitetsentrén.

🛏 Sleeping

Citysleep
HOSTEL €

(☑0920-420 002; www.citysleep.se; Skeppsbrogatan 18; dm Skr450) The only budget digs in central Luleå don't come more anonymous than this: book online to get the door code, since there's no reception, then let yourself into a featureless room with two-tiered beds. There are no windows but reasonably good in-room ventilation and a large guest kitchen.

Elite Luleå
HOTEL €€

(☑0920-27 40 00; www.lulea.elite.se; Storgatan 15; s/d from Skr790/990; 🅿❄🛜) One of Luleå's most sumptuous hotels, the grand Elite is more than a hundred years old, with classically decorated and beautifully refurbished rooms. All bathrooms are decked out in Italian marble and the plusher suites come with whirlpool tubs as well. Bargains are to be had on weekends and the breakfast buffet is extensive.

Hotell Aveny
HOTEL €€

(☑0920-22 18 20; www.hotellaveny.com; Hermelinsgatan 10; s/d Skr825/950; 🅿🛜) This quirky hotel has individually designed rooms and corridors decorated to look like avenues and shopping streets (hence the name). Reception has limited opening hours, so make sure you get an access code. Prices drop on weekends.

★ Clarion Sense
HOTEL €€€

(☑0920-45 04 50; www.clarionsense.se; Skeppsbrogatan 34; s/d/ste from Skr2360/2760/7900; ❄) Luleå's sleeping scene has a new top dog in the form of super-central, ultra-modern Clarion Sense. Popular with the business set (and anyone who's not averse to a bit of pampering), it offers generously proportioned rooms, all classic charcoals and creams with contemporary bold splashes of colour. The fitness centre with panoramic views, spa and pool seals the deal.

🍴 Eating & Drinking

Roasters
CAFE €

(Storgatan 43; mains from Skr70; ⊙10am-midnight Mon-Sat, noon-7pm Sun) This perpetually popular cafe serves some of the town's best coffee, salads, sandwiches and a dish-of-the-day lunch, and segues into an after-work drinks hang-out as the day progresses.

★ Hemmagastronomi
FUSION €€

(www.hemmagastronomi.se; Norra Strandgatan 1; tapas from Skr75; ⊙8am-11pm Mon-Fri, to 1am Sat) Is it a bakery? Is it a deli? Is it a bar? Is it a bistro? Hemmagastronomi wears many hats and we love them all. Come for a leisurely breakfast, grab a light bite at lunchtime, or romance your sweetie in the evening under dimmed lights over softshell-crab tapas and seafood platters, complemented by the wide-spanning wine list.

DON'T MISS

HULKOFFGÅRDEN

This luxurious **Hulkoffgården B&B** (☑0922-320 15; www.hulkoff.se; s/d Skr650/1100; 🅿) is located inside a yellow farmhouse, 35km north of Haparanda along Rte 99, amidst the most peaceful countryside imaginable and with wonderfully welcoming proprietresses. Its restaurant is the best in the area, with imaginatively executed northern Swedish specialities made from organic, locally sourced ingredients; order in advance.

Fifteen kilometres north of Haparanda, stop by the scenic spot where the Torneälv river is covered with the white crests of the **Kukkolaforsen rapids**, and watch locals hunt for whitefish using medieval dip nets from the rickety-looking jetties.

Baan Thai THAI €€
(Kungsgatan 22; mains Skr130-250;) All dark wood and gold Buddha images, this authentic Thai restaurant on the main drag is perpetually filled with locals. Dishes such as the *chu chi pla* (deep-fried fish curry) are particularly good, but ask the staff to spice it up if you want the true Thai fire.

Kitchen & Table FUSION €€
(www.kitchenandtable.se; Skeppsbrogatan 34; mains Skr169-295; noon-midnight) You have to give the chef points for the ambitious pairing of carpaccio with kimchi and Nashi pears and scallop ceviche with coconut, even if some combos work better than others. However, the place is a clear winner when it comes to sheer ambience, the huge windows drinking in the bay views, and the 'not-so-classic' cocktails.

Cook's Krog SWEDISH €€€
(0920-20 10 25; www.cookskrog.se; Storgatan 17; mains Skr195-339, Norrland 4-course taster menu Srk695; 6pm-late Mon-Sat) Still *the* choice for discerning carnivores, Cook's Krog is Luleå's top spot for steak, reindeer and other Norrbotten specialities. The worthiest splurge here is the four-course menu that shows off Norrbotten's culinary prowess and includes whitefish, elk carpaccio, reindeer steak with lingonberries and cloudberry-enhanced chocolate fondant.

Bishop's Arms PUB
(Storgatan 15; 4pm-late) With book-filled nooks, this pseudo-English pub is one of Luleå's most popular watering holes. Whisky lovers can sample over 200 kinds of the amber stuff.

Information

Tourist Office (0920-45 70 00; www.visitlulea.se; Skeppsbrogatan 17; 10am-7pm Mon-Fri, to 4pm Sat & Sun) The tourist office is inside Kulturens Hus.

Getting There & Around

AIR

Luleå Airport (010-109 48 00; www.swedavia.se/lulea) The airport is 10km southwest of the town centre. SAS and Norwegian fly daily to Stockholm, while Direktflyg serves Kiruna, Sundsvall, Umeå and Östersund. Bus 4 connects it to the city centre.

BUS

Buses 20 and 100 run north to Haparanda (Skr178, 2½ hours, up to 10 daily) and south to Umeå (Skr310, four to five hours, seven daily), stopping at all the coastal towns. Bus 44 connects Luleå with Gällivare (Skr311, 3½ to 4½ hours) and Jokkmokk (Skr237, three hours) up to five times daily.

TRAIN

There are two overnight trains to Stockholm (Skr829, 14 to 15 hours) via Gävle (Skr829, 11¾ to 12½ hours) and Uppsala (Skr829, 14 hours), while two daily trains connect Luleå with Narvik (Norway; Skr477, 7¼ to 8¼ hours) via Kiruna (Skr292, 3¾ to 4¼ hours, four daily) and Abisko (Skr457, 5½ to 6½ hours).

Haparanda

0922 / POP 4856

Haparanda was founded in 1821 across the river to compensate for the loss of Finnish Tornio, an important trading centre, to Russia in 1809. When both Sweden and Finland joined the EU, the two towns declared themselves a single Eurocity. Still, Sweden drew the short straw: Tornio got the art galleries and the vibrant nightlife, and what did Haparanda get? The world's largest IKEA.

Haparanda's other distinguishing feature is the **Haparanda Kyrka** on Östra Kyrkogatan, built in 1963 and subsequently awarded the prize for 'Sweden's ugliest church'.

Rambling riverside **Haparanda Vandrarhem** (0922-611 71; www.haparandavandrarhem.se; Strandgatan 26; dm/s/d Skr200/325/480; P) is a godsend for shoestring travellers, while **Cape East** (0922-80 07 90; www.capeeast.se; Sundholmen; P) caters to the opposite end of the spectrum, with the world's largest sauna and a gourmet restaurant. It was undergoing renovations when we visited but is due to reopen in September 2015.

The aforementioned **IKEA** (Norrskensvägen 5; mains from Skr25; 10am-7pm) is one of the better places to eat out in Haparanda, as it offers Swedish standards such as meatballs and mash for a wallet-friendly Skr25.

Haparanda's main **tourist office** (0922-262 00; www.haparandatornio.com; Krannigatan 5; 8am-7pm Mon-Fri, 7am-3pm Sat, 10am-4pm Sun) is shared with Tornio in a brand new location, at the new bus station just down the road from IKEA.

Buses 20 and 100 run south to Luleå (Skr178, 2½ hours, up to 10 daily) and Umeå (Skr356, 6½ to 7¾ hours, up to six daily), while bus 53 connects Haparanda to Kiruna (Skr395, six hours, two daily except Saturday).

Lappland & the Far North

Includes ➡

Best for Northern Fun

- Icehotel (p285)
- Lights Over Lapland (p287)
- Snöfestivalen (p283)
- Jokkmokk Guiderna (p278)
- Lapland Lodge (p275)

Best for Sami Culture

- Nutti Sami Siida (p282)
- Båtsuoj Sami Camp (p276)
- Atoklimpen (p271)
- Ájtte Museum (p277)
- Risfjells Sameslöjd (p271)

Why Go?

Lappland is Europe's last true wilderness. With a grand mountain range, endless forest and countless pristine lakes as your playground, it's your chance to be a true explorer. Its great swathes of virgin land are dotted with reindeer – this is Sami country still, and your chance to delve into the reindeer herders' centuries-old way of life.

Travelling in the far north of Sweden can draw you into an unusual rhythm. The long, lonely stretches between towns are often completely deserted apart from the ever-present reindeer. Extreme natural phenomena are at their strongest here – in summer you'll be travelling under the perpetual light of the midnight sun; in winter, under the haunting wraiths that are the northern lights. During the colder months Lappland is a different country: a white wilderness traversed by huskies and snowmobiles and punctuated with colourful Sami winter markets.

When to Go

Kiruna

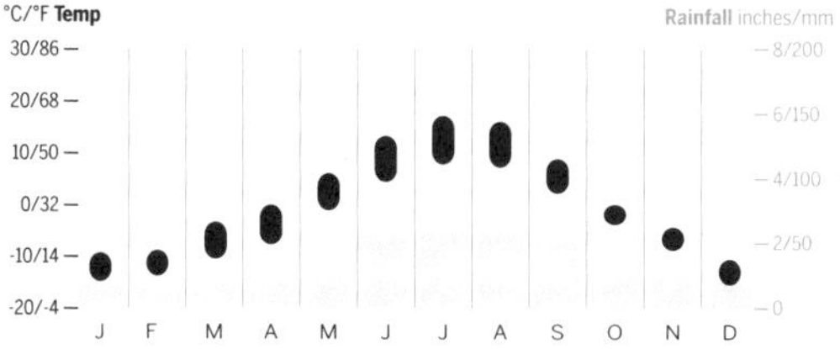

Jan & Feb Kiruna Snow Festival, Sami winter market in Jokkmokk and the northern lights.

Mar & Apr Warmer, longer days perfect for snowmobiling, dogsledding and ice-driving.

Jul & Aug Hit the trails in the national parks during the warmest and driest months.

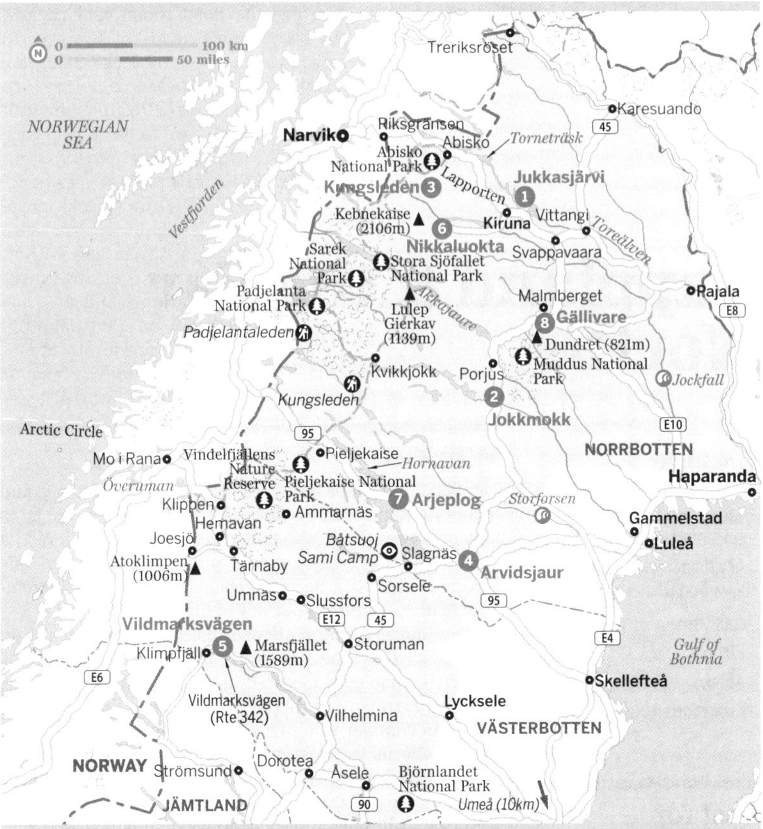

Lappland & the Far North Highlights

1 Residing inside the **Icehotel** (p285), Jukkasjärvi's spectacular ice dwelling.

2 Checking out Sami crafts, reindeer races and revelry at the **Jokkmokk Winter Market** (p277).

3 Tackling the **Kungsleden** (p288), Sweden's longest hiking trail.

4 Driving on frozen lakes and going snowmobiling and husky sledding at **Arvidsjaur** (p274).

5 Driving the **Vildmarksvägen** (p272), Sweden's most beautiful road.

6 Flying over the Arctic tundra and mountains in a helicopter from **Nikkaluokta** (p284).

7 Viewing the largest collection of Sami silver creations at the **Silvermuseet** (p276) in Arjeplog.

8 Descending into the bowels of the earth on a visit to Gällivare's impressive **mines** (p280).

Strömsund

0670 / POP 3589

North of Östersund along the E45, Strömsund is the starting point for the Vildmarksvägen (Rte 342, p272) and the first town of any size – a two-street affair sitting amid some extensive waterways popular with kayakers. If you wish to break your journey here, **Hotel Nordica** (0670-61 10 00; www.hotelnordica.se; Ramselevägen 6; r Skr599; P) offers standard rooms in sedate creams, while its antler-festooned restaurant makes a good pit stop. The **tourist office** (www.stromsund.se; Ramselevägen 6; 9am-noon &

1-4pm Mon-Fri) inside the hotel has some info on the Vildmarksvägen.

Bus 45 passes by daily on the Gällivare-Jokkmokk-Arvidsjaur-Storuman-Östersund route.

Vilhelmina

0940 / POP 3657

The main attraction of quiet little Vilhelmina, in the heart of Lappland's huntin' an' fishin' country, is its restored 18th-century **Kyrkstaden** (Storgatan) (church town), whose 30-plus cottages are now the town's hostel, run by the **tourist office** (0940-398 86; www.vilhelmina.se; Tingsgatan 1; 8am-7pm). **Risfjells Sameslöjd** (0940-152 05; www.sameslojd.se; Storgatan 8; 10am-5.30pm Mon-Fri, to 4pm Sat & Sun) (opposite Vilhelmina's museum) is a good place to pick up leatherwork, woodwork or a knife by husband-and-wife craftsman team Sven-Åke and Doris Risfjell. They're happy to explain the difference between North and South Sami *duodji* (handicrafts) – they're South Sami – and show you the vintage *duodji* in their small museum.

You can stay the night at the appealing **Lilla hotel** (0940-150 59; www.lillahotellet.vilhelmina.com; Granvägen 1; s/d Skr675/880), with its brightly papered walls, flowers everywhere and cracking basement spa.

Martin Bergmans Fisk (0940-250 90; E45 & Vildmarksvägen; mains Skr110-159; 9am-5.30pm Mon-Fri, 10am-5pm Sat), just north of town, is famous for its salmon, smoked three ways, while **Wilhelmina** (0940-554 20; www.hotellwilhelmina.se; Volgsjövägen 16; mains Skr90-285; 10.30am-9pm Mon-Fri, to 8pm Sat, to 7pm Sun) serves upmarket northern Swedish specialities as well as pasta dishes.

Bus 45 passes through daily on the Gällivare-Jokkmokk-Arvidsjaur-Sorsele-Östersund route.

Storuman

0951 / POP 2207

Though it sounds like a villain from *Lord of the Rings*, Storuman is more about harnessing hydroelectric power than spreading darkness over the Shire. This one-street town sits along the 2000km-long **Blåvägen** (Blue Highway; www.blavagen.nu) that runs to Norway's Atlantic coast. Storuman's distinguishing features include the **old railway hotel** building with a wonderfully ornate wooden interior.

The en-suite hotel rooms and cheaper, more basic hostel rooms of the cheerful yellow **Hotell Luspen** (0951-333 80; www.hotelluspen.se; Järnvägsgatan 13; hostel s/d Skr380/480, hotel s/d Skr750/850) by the train station are a good place to break your journey along the E45; breakfast (Skr50) is available to guests. The best place to eat in town is **Toppen** (0951-777 00; www.hotelltoppen.se; Blåvägen 238; mains Skr145-235; 11am-7.30pm Mon-Fri, to 6.30pm Sat, to 5.30pm Sun), with an appropriately game-heavy a la carte menu and a bargain weekday lunch buffet.

Bus 45 runs daily on the Gällivare-Jokkmokk-Arvidsjaur-Sorsele-Storuman-Östersund route. Buses also run west to Tärnaby (Skr169, 1¾ hours, five daily) and east to Umeå (Skr265, 3½ hours, three daily), while the twice-weekly **Lapplandspilen** (0940-150 40; www.lapplandspilen.se) buses ply the route from Hemavan to Stockholm via Storuman (Skr680, 11¾ hours) on Thursday and Sunday. In summer, **Inlandsbanan trains** stop here.

Tärnaby & Hemavan

0954 / POP 704

Tärnaby, an elongated one-street village that sits on the shores of Gäutan lake, is the birthplace of double Olympic gold-medallist skier Ingemar Stenmark. Hemavan, its smaller counterpart 18km north, is the southern entry point to the 500km Kungsleden trail that passes through the Vindelfjällens Nature Reserve, and both are popular bases for fresh-air fiends. From excellent hiking and skiing to checking out holy mountains, descending steep slopes on mountain bikes in a shower of mud and scree and sedate pedalling around lakes – it just depends on your interests, and the moods of the weather gods.

Sights & Activities

★ **Atoklimpen** MOUNTAIN

Atoklimpen (1006m), a monolithic, bare mountain 35km west of Tärnaby, has been regarded as holy by the Sami for centuries. Evidence dating back to the 15th century of sacrificial sites and encampments with hearths is scattered across the area; a 3km trail leads up to the top.

Near the car park (off Rd 1116) is a peat hut and a small cottage, built by a Sami couple in the early 1920s, a time when the government forbade the Sami to build permanent

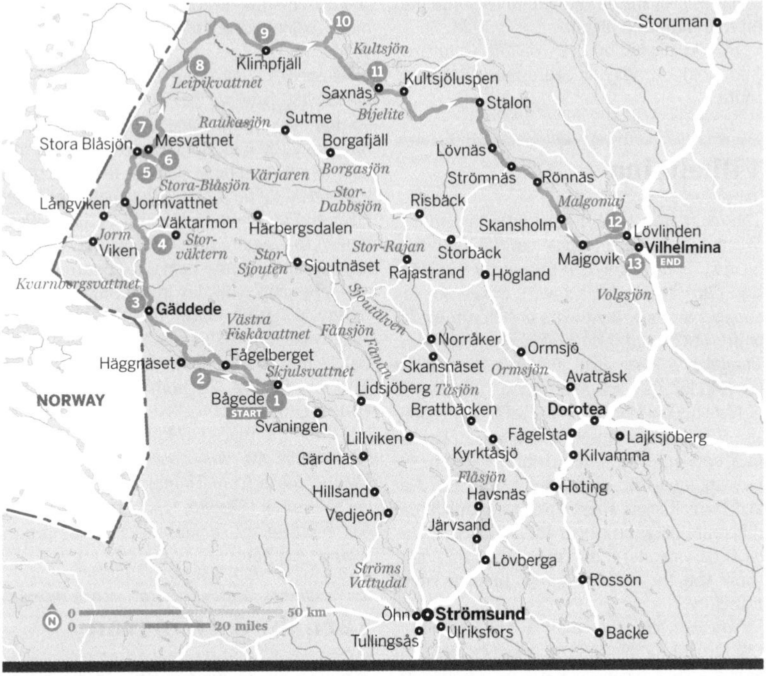

Driving Tour
The Vildmarksvägen

START STRÖMSUND
END VILHELMINA
LENGTH 370KM, EIGHT TO 10 HOURS

Strömsund marks the beginning of Sweden's most spectacular drive. The Vildmarksvägen (Wilderness Rd; Rte 342) runs northwest towards the mountains before skirting the Norwegian border and winding its way back to the E45.

Head north out of Strömsund through through forest, stopping by one of many pristine lakes. If you're lucky, you may spot a bear, a wolverine, an elk or lynx.

Ninety-two kilometres northwest, you reach a worthwhile detour just south of 1 **Bågede**. A rocky track leads towards the 43m 2 **Hällsingsåfallet**, a powerful waterfall that tumbles into an 800m-long canyon. Near the Norwegian border, another 40km west, is 3 **Gäddede**, the only village with a petrol station. At the Gäddede tourist office you can arrange a spelunking tour of the 7 **Korallgrotan** (Coral Cave) – Sweden's longest cave 11km north of 5 **Stora Blåsjön**, a lake 50km north of Gäddede.

Before reaching the lake, you can turn off to the 4 **Mountain Moose Moosepark**, a good stop for elk-viewing. Just past the lake, a small road leads to 6 **Ankarede**, a centuries-old meeting place for the local Sami, who gather at its 1898 chapel for Midsummer celebrations.

Beyond Stora Blåsjon village, Rte 345 climbs up onto the vast, boulder-strewn 8 **Stekkenjokk plateau**, before descending to the tiny village of 9 **Klimpfjäll** (this stretch of road is closed October to early June). A turn-off 13km east leads to the late-18th-century Sami church village at 10 **Fatmomakke**, where you find traditional Sami *kåtor* (wooden dwellings) and log cabins.

Twenty kilometres further east, you reach the fishermen's paradise of 11 **Saxnäs**, a small village set in a scenic spot between lakes.

Another 89km brings you to the Vildmarksvägen/E45 junction. If you get here early enough, you can grab a meal at the excellent 12 **Martin Bergmans Fisk** smokery before driving the final 3km south to 13 **Vilhelmina**.

structures; the ensuing debate over the cottage helped to change the law in 1928.

Laxfjället HIKING

Hike up Laxfjället (820m) for perspective-shifting views of the surrounding lakes and mountains. There are four trails, the steepest and most direct being the 2km trail that runs from Tärnaby Fjällby underneath the ski lift (two to three hours return). At the top, pose for a pic under the precariously balanced Laxfjäll Stone that looks poised to squish you.

Laisaleden Trail HIKING

This spectacular yet not too demanding 9km trail (four to six hours) starts out along Drottningsleden (Queen's Trail) and takes in splendid views of Norwegian peaks before descending to Naturum in Hemavan. Follow signs to a turn-off 15km north of the Tärnaby tourist office along the main road. You can hike in reverse from Hemavan for more of an uphill challenge.

Hemavan Bike Park MOUNTAIN BIKING

(☎0954-305 00; www.bikepark.nu; day pass adult/child Skr210/170; ⏲10am-5pm daily Jul-Sep) In warm weather, Hemavan's ski slopes morph into an extreme playground for mountain bikers. The network of trails varies in difficulty, ranging from green (beginners' slope) to black (a rugged, steep, bumpy descent; for pros), and is spread over five slopes. A chairlift 2km north of central Hemavan is adapted to carry bikes to the top of the mountain.

Ski Areas SKIING, SNOWBOARDING

(www.hemavantarnaby.se; day ski pass Skr350) Tärnaby and Hemavan offer decent downhill skiing and the day ski passes are valid at both resorts. There's a good mix of runs for all abilities at the two, though Tärnaby's are more extensive and there's plenty of opportunity for night skiing. If that's not challenging enough, experienced skiers can go off-piste or arrange heli-skiing trips at the tourist office.

If snowboarding, jumps and tricks are more your bag, there are two fun parks in the area also.

BikeNorth MOUNTAIN BIKING

(☎070-347 82 69; www.bikenorth.se; per day Skr750) This pro bike-hire agency in Hemavan will sort you out with rugged mountain bikes with full suspension and protective gear to boot, and can also organise heli-biking tours of varying difficulty.

Sleeping & Eating

STF Hostel Hemavan HOSTEL €

(☎0954-300 02; www.svenskaturistforeningen.se/hemavan; s/d from Skr330/430; P @ 🏊 🐾) A sprawling complex of a hostel, STF Hemavan is perpetually busy with hikers. The separate blocks are each equipped with a kitchen, and while the rooms are bland and unmemorable, the facilities (cafeteria, swimming pool, climbing wall, lively bar upstairs in the main building) are top notch.

STF Vandrarhem Tärnaby/Åkerlundska Gården HOSTEL €

(☎0954-104 21; www.svenskaturistforeningen.se; Östra Strandvägen 16; dm/s/d Skr195/350/470; ⏲Jan-May & mid-Jun–mid-Sep; P) Cosy hostel with awesome views across the valley and excellent self-catering facilities. If you don't feel like cooking, there's some great food to be had at the restaurant at Tärnaby Fjällhotell (where the hostel reception is).

Tärnaby Fjällhotell HOTEL €€

(☎0954-104 20; www.tarnabyfjallhotell.com; Östra Strandvägen 16; s/d from Skr940/1700) This appealing ski lodge sits just off the main road. Rooms are bright and comfortable, with nice touches such as reading lights; Super G rooms offer more space to throw your gear around. The hunting lodge–style restaurant invests heavily in local, seasonal ingredients, and there are 360-degree views of the surrounding mountains from the sauna.

Information

Tourist Office (☎0954-104 50; www.hemavantarnaby.se; Strandvägen 1; ⏲8.30am-7pm Mon-Fri, 10am-6pm Sat & Sun) On the Blåvägen (Blue Hwy) that runs through the village. Handy booklets on hiking and biking routes available.

Vindelfjallen Naturum (☎0954-380 23; www.vindelfjallen.se; ⏲9am-6pm) Next to Hemavan's entrance to the Kungsleden (p288), Naturum features exhibits on the local flora and fauna. Staff can advise on trekking and day hikes in the area.

Getting There & Away

Länstrafiken bus 45 runs to Mora (5½ hours, two to four daily). Buses 31, 319 and 320 run west from Tärnaby to Hemavan (Skr41, 36 minutes, up to six daily) and southeast to Umeå (Skr265, 5¼ hours, two to three daily).

Sorsele & Ammarnäs

0952 / POP 1277

Railway enthusiasts should pull up at Sorsele for the **Inlandsbanemuseet** (Stationsgatan 19; adult/child Skr30/free; 9am-6pm Mon-Fri, 10am-5pm Sat & Sun), inside the train-station building, that covers the history of the railway. Though supposedly neutral, Sweden allowed Nazi troops to transfer supplies to different parts of occupied Norway using the Inlandsbanan line during WWII. The adjoining **tourist office** (0952-140 90; www.sorsele.se; Stationsgatan 19; 9am-6pm Mon-Fri, 10am-5pm Sat & Sun) can arrange fishing permits and fly-fishing trips.

Sorsele River Hotel (0952-121 50; www.sorseleriverhotel.se; Hotellgatan 2; s/d Skr995/1295; P) is a swish affair of cream shades and quality bed linens. More importantly for travellers just passing through, it also offers a superb weekday lunch buffet (Skr85) and dinner buffet (Skr140) with dish-of-the-day star; *palt* (blood pancake) is our favourite.

From Sorsele, Rte 363 leads to tiny Ammarnäs, nestling in a river valley hemmed in by the Ammarfjället mountains and used by Sami herders for centuries. Even now, a third of the population makes their living from reindeer husbandry. Hikers can tackle the wildest part of the Kungsleden (p288) from here or else embark on easier day hikes, such as the 8km jaunt to the top of Mt Kaissats (984m) that runs from Stora Tjulträsk at the western end of the village.

The only accommodation in the village is **Ammarnäsgården** (0952-600 03; www.ammarnasgarden.se; Tjulträskvägen 1; hostel s/d Skr250/440, hotel s/d Skr595/795; P), a modern hotel with adjoining youth hostel in a superbly picturesque location. There is a sauna and pool in the basement, and the hotel's restaurant (open June to October) serves reindeer stew, fish from nearby rivers and elk burgers alongside international dishes.

The **tourist office** (0952-600 00; www.ammarnas.nu; Ammarnäsgården; 9am-5pm mid-Jun–mid-Sep) on the main road can help organise Icelandic-pony rides in summer and dogsledding and snowmobiling in winter.

Sorsele is served daily by bus 45 along the Gällivare–Östersund route, while bus 341 runs from Sorsele to Ammarnäs (Skr115, 1¼-1¾ hours, one to three daily).

Arvidsjaur

0960 / POP 6529

If you're coming from another town along the E45, Arvidsjaur, with its busy main street, will seem like a bustling metropolis. Established several centuries ago as a Sami marketplace and meeting spot, Arvidsjaur is home to two dozen Sami families who still make a living from reindeer herding.

Between December and April dozens of test drivers from different car companies descend on the town to stage their own version of *Top Gear* – putting fast machines through their paces on the frozen lakes.

Sights & Activities

★ **Lappstaden** HISTORIC BUILDING
(Lappstadsgatan; tours Skr50; tours 6pm mid-Jun–mid-Aug) FREE The first church was built in Arvidsjaur in 1607, and church-attendance

CHASING THE NORTHERN LIGHTS

The otherworldly lights of the aurora borealis, named after the Roman goddess of dawn and the Greek term for the north wind, have captivated the imagination of the people of the north and travellers alike for centuries. The celestial spectacle of the streaks in the sky – from yellowish-green to violet, white and red – are caused by the collision of energy-charged solar particles with atoms in the Earth's magnetic field, and are visible in the north of Sweden between October and March.

Don't expect to see the northern lights every day; it all depends on weather conditions, and if it's cloudy the lights aren't visible. One of Lappland's best spots for aurora borealis viewing is Abisko's Aurora Sky Station (p286), away from the town's light pollution and vastly aided by Abisko's dry climate.

Nutti Sami Siida (p282), the Icehotel (p285), and most tour agencies in Kiruna, Abisko and elsewhere in Lappland organise northern-lights tours, often combined with other outdoor activities, while Lights Over Lapland (p287) teaches you how to capture this otherworldly shining for posterity.

DON'T MISS

WINTER FUN

Arvidsjaur really comes into its own in winter. On the high-octane side of things, snowmobiles whiz along the 600km or so of snowmobile tracks around the town, teams of huskies carry passengers through the snow and driving enthusiasts grapple with the steering wheels of BMWs, Audis and Porsches on special ice tracks marked on frozen lakes. Operators below can help you tap into the snowy thrills:

Lapland Lodge (☎0960-137 20; www.laplandlodge.se; Östra Kyrkogatan 18; 3hr ice-driving Skr5900) This all-rounder teams up with Arctic Car Experience (ACE) to arrange ice-driving (three to six hours) in an Audi TT Quattro, and with Snowmobile Outdoor Adventures to send you on half-day safaris (Skr1490), polar night tours (Skr1390) and two-hour starter trips (Skr790).

Nymånen (☎070-625 40 32; www.nymanen.com) Go dogsledding with one of the largest Siberian-husky kennels in Lappland, certified ecofriendly by Nature's Best.

Super Safari (☎0960-104 57; www.supersafari.info; Idrottsgatan 9A; 2hr tours Skr950) Guided snowmobile tours.

Wildact Adventure Tours (☎0960-160 52; www.wildact.ch; Storberg 4) Based 22km southwest of Arvidsjaur along Rte 94 (turn off towards Hedberg), these guys let you do the Jack London thing with your own husky team, let you ride as a passenger or give you a 30-minute taster. Ski tours and overnight stays in your very own self-built igloo are available or else crash at their own cosy lodge (doubles Skr940).

laws (urged by zealous priests and enforced by the monarchy) imposed a certain amount of pew time upon the nomadic Sami. To make their church visits manageable they built small, square cottages with pyramid-shaped roofs *(gåhties)* for overnighting. Eighty *gåhties* are preserved here, just across Storgatan from the modern church.

During the last weekend in August, Lappstaden hosts **Storstämningshelgen**, an annual feast, party and Sami association meeting.

Steam Train TRAIN RIDES
(adult/child Skr220/free) From mid-July to mid-August an immensely popular 1930s steam train makes return evening trips to Slagnäs on Friday and Saturday, departing at 5.45pm and returning around 10pm. It stops along the way at Storavan beach for a barbecue and swim.

Outdoor Lapland OUTDOORS, SNOW SPORTS
(☎070-260 05 37; www.laplandraftingcafe.se) Offers canoeing and kayaking trips, as well as guided hikes in pristine wilderness in summer and snow-cat safaris and skiing expeditions in winter.

Sleeping & Eating

Silver Cross 45 HOSTEL €
(☎070-644 28 62; www.silvercross45.se; Fjällströmsvägen 16; s/d/tr/f Skr300/500/550/600; P 📶) Doubling as a gallery for glass creations, this family-friendly hostel has cosy wood-panelled rooms and shared facilities. Prices include bed linen, a budget-range anomaly, as is the on-site hot tub and the TV–DVD player in every room, with the exception of the most 'rustic' option – a Sami-style teepee.

★ **Lapland Lodge** B&B, HOTEL €€
(☎0960-137 20; www.laplandlodge.se; Östra Kyrkogatan 18; B&B s/d/f Skr690/850/950, hotel s/d Skr1490/1890; P 📶) Next to the church, this friendly B&B offers a range of room configurations (some en suite) in a pretty yellow house. Contemporary comforts sit amid antique style accented with old wooden skis, antlers and snowshoes. The new hotel wing is all en suite. An outdoor hot tub and sauna are available, and snowmobile, ice-driving and husky-sledding tours run in winter.

Hotell Laponia HOTEL €€
(☎0960-555 00; www.hotell-laponia.se; Storgatan 45; s/d/ste Skr1190/1290/1990; P 📶 🏊) All heavy dark wood inside, Arvidsjaur's only hotel gets booked out by drivers in winter who come to test the Mercedes, BMWs and Porsches on ice. This is also one of the nicer places to eat in town – the bistro-pub serves a very good weekday buffet (Skr85) – and there's a spa.

WORTH A TRIP

BÅTSUOJ SAMI CAMP

Båtsuoj Sami Camp (☎0960-65 10 26; www.batsuoj.se; short tour/long tour/overnight stay Skr290/600/1100) To experience the life of the Forest Sami, visit Båtsuoj, where Tom and Lotta Svensson practise their traditional livelihood full-time. You can watch the reindeer get lassoed, or stay overnight on reindeer skins inside a *kåta* (typical Forest Sámi log hut), learn about Sami shamanic practices, eat grilled reindeer and sip coffee cooked over a wood fire. Book visits in advance.

The Sami camp is near the village of Gasa, 17km north of the village of Slagnäs, on E45.

Hans På Hörnet CAFE €
(Storgatan 21; mains from Skr59; ⏲10am-5pm Mon-Sat) A very local spot, serving inexpensive lunches: salads, sandwiches and pies.

Afrodite GREEK €€
(Storgatan 10; mains Skr75-199; ⏲11am-10pm) The Goddess of Love tempts diners with 'Greek-inspired' dishes, so expect to see chicken souvlaki alongside reindeer in this vaguely Mediterranean set-up.

Laponiakåtan BARBECUE €€
(www.hotell-laponia.se; Storgatan; mains Skr145-325; ⏲4-10pm Mon-Fri, noon-10pm Sat & Sun mid-Jun–Sep) Belonging to Hotell Laponia, this enormous Sami hut on the lakeside delivers on its promise of 'BBQ with a view'. A single concession to vegetarianism aside (gnocchi), this place attracts discerning carnivores with its burgers, troll-sized portions of hickory ribs and tender reindeer steaks. Outside the summer season, the culinary action moves back inside the hotel.

ℹ Information

Tourist Office (☎0960-175 00; www.arvidsjaur.se; Östra Skolgatan 18C; ⏲9.30am-6pm Mon-Fri, noon-4.30 Sat & Sun Jun-Aug) Just off Storgatan, the town's main road.

ℹ Getting There & Around

AIR

Arvidsjaur Airport (☎0960-173 80; www.ajr.nu), 11km east of the centre, has several daily connections to Stockholm Arlanda with **Nextjet** (www.nextjet.se). During the winter season it's served by several weekly flights with **Air Berlin** (www.airberlin.com) from Frankfurt, Hanover, Munich and Stuttgart.

BUS

The bus station is at Västlundavägen, in the town centre behind the large Konsum supermarket. Popular bus routes include bus 45 south to Östersund (Skr440, 7¼ hours, daily) and north to Gällivare (Skr311, 3¾ hours, daily) via Jokkmokk (Skr215, 2¼ hours), as well as daily bus 104 to Arjeplog (Skr130, one hour).

TRAIN

Arvidsjaur is connected by daily Inlandsbanan trains in summer/autumn to Östersund (Skr728, 8¼ hours), Gällivare (Skr420, 5¾ hours) and Jokkmokk (Skr265, 3½ hours).

Arjeplog

☎0961 / POP 3161

Eighty-five kilometres northwest of Arvidsjaur, the one-street Sami town of Arejplog (Árjepluovve, in Sami) sits on the Silvervägen (Silver Rd; E95) surrounded by prime fishing country of 8700 lakes (each local has their favourite).

Arjeplog's star attraction is its excellent **Silvermuseet** (Silver Museum; www.silvermuseet.se; Torget; adult/child Skr80/free; ⏲10am-noon & 1-6pm Mon-Fri, 10am-2pm Sat). Housed in what used to be a nomad school, the tour de force here is the vast collection of Sami silver objects – the most extensive of its kind – including belt buckles, ornate spoons and goblets, and collars that would traditionally have been passed down from mother to daughter. You may also spot a *dásska*, a special bag for a silver spoon, favoured by the Southern Sami; shaman drums; and 2000-year-old skis used by Sami hunters. Other displays trace the history of the town and its main industries – silver mining and logging, and delve into Sami medical lore by focusing on native plants and their traditional uses. Linger in the basement cinema to catch the engaging slideshow and voice-over describing life in Arjeplog through its harsh seasons.

The most central place to stay is the revamped **Hotel Lyktan** (☎0961-612 10; www.hotellyktan-arjeplog.se; Lugnetvägen 4 ; s/d Skr730/900; P📶) that's moved upmarket, introducing appealing doubles with shiny wooden floors and discreet splashes of colour. A sauna, steam room and hot tub are just some of the new perks.

There's one exception to the lacklustre eating scene: the restaurant at **Kraja** (☎0961-315 00; www.silverhatten.se; mains Skr149-269), a catch-all hotel and campground on its own little peninsula just west of town, combines lake views with great local cuisine; try the deluxe elk burger or the reindeer steak with morel sauce.

The helpful **tourist office** (☎0961-145 00; www.polcirkeln.nu; Torget 1; ⏲10am-noon & 1-5pm Mon-Fri, 10am-2pm Sat) inside the Silvermuseet has plenty of info on the surrounding area.

Eastbound buses 26 and 17 run to Arvidsjaur (Skr130, one hour, one to two daily) and Skellefteå (Skr252, 3¼ hours, daily except Sunday). Westbound bus 104 runs to Jäkkvikk (Skr105, 1¼ hours, daily except Saturday).

Jokkmokk

☎0971 / POP 5170

The capital of Sami culture, and the biggest handicraft centre in Lappland, Jokkmokk (meaning 'river bend' in Sami) not only has the definitive Sami museum but also is the site of a huge annual winter market gathering. Just north of the Arctic Circle, it's a tranquil place and the only town in Sweden that has a further-education college that teaches reindeer husbandry, craft making and ecology using the Sami language. Jokkmokk is the jumping-off point for visiting the four national parks that are part of the **Laponia World Heritage Area** (www.laponia.nu) and makes a great base for all manner of outdoor adventures year round.

Sights & Activities

★Ájtte Museum MUSEUM

(www.ajtte.com; Kyrkogatan 3; adult/child Skr80/40; ⏲9am-6pm) This illuminating museum is Sweden's most thorough introduction to Sami culture. Follow the 'spokes' radiating from the central chamber, each dealing with a different theme – from traditional costume, silverware, creatures from Sami folk tales and 400-year-old painted shamans' drums, to replicas of sacrificial sites and a diagram explaining the uses and significance of various reindeer entrails. The beautifully showcased collection of traditional silver jewellery features heavy collars, now making a comeback among Sami women after a long absence.

One section details the widespread practice of harnessing the rivers in Lappland for hydroelectric power and the consequences this has had for the Sami people and their territory, and there is a large fauna section featuring some impressive taxidermied mammals and birds of the Swedish Arctic.

★Sameslöjdstiftelsen Sami Duodji GALLERY

(www.sameslojdstiftelsen.se; Porjusvägen 4; ⏲10am-5pm Mon-Fri) This centrally located Sami gallery and crafts centre is your one-stop shop for diverse, authentic Sami handicrafts of the highest quality: from leatherwork, clothing in Sami colours and silver jewellery to bone-inlaid wood carvings and Sami knives in reindeer-antler sheaths. Most items are available for purchase.

For more on Sami crafts, see p320.

JOKKMOKK WINTER MARKET

Winter travellers shouldn't miss the annual Sami Winter Market, **Jokkmokk Winter Market** (www.jokkmokksmarknad.com), held the first Thursday through Saturday in February. The oldest and biggest of its kind, it attracts some 30,000 people annually; it's the biggest sales opportunity of the year for the Sami traders to make contacts and see old friends, while visitors can splurge on the widest array of Sami *duodji* (handicrafts) in the country and watch the merry chaos of reindeer races on the frozen Talvatissjön lake behind Hotel Jokkmokk.

The event has been going strong since 1605, when King Karl XI decreed that markets should be set up in Lappland to increase taxes, spread Christianity and exert greater control over the nomadic Sami. The Winter Market is preceded by the opening of the smaller Historical Market and several days of folk music, plays, parades, local cinematography, photography exhibitions, food-tasting sessions and talks on different aspects of Sami life – all of which segues into the Winter Market itself. It's the most exciting (and coldest!) time to be in Jokkmokk, with temperatures as low as -40°C, so wrap up warm!

Lappkyrkan CHURCH
(Storgatan; ⏲8am-4pm) The octagonal red wooden church is a 1976, post-fire replacement built in the style of its 1753 predecessor. The colour scheme is inspired by Sami clothing and the design reflects the Sami building style; in winter, the space between the timbers used to hold coffins awaiting the spring thaw, which allowed for graves to be dug.

Jokkmokks Fjällträdgård GARDENS
(www.ajtte.com; Lappstavägen; adult/child Skr30/free, with Ajtté Museum ticket free; ⏲11am-5pm Mon-Fri, noon-5pm Sat & Sun mid-Jun–mid-Aug) Part of the **Ajtté Museum**, this appealing botanical garden introduces local flora, such as glacier crowfoot, moor-king and mountain avens, as well as plants traditionally used by the Sami for medicinal purposes. Follow the signposted path from the museum.

Tours

Jokkmokk Guiderna CANOEING, SNOW SPORTS
(☎0971-122 20, 070-684 22 20; www.jokkmokkguiderna.com) Canoe rental and canoe and hiking tours by a Nature's Best ecotourism operator. It also excels at multi-day dogsledding expeditions in Sarek National Park in winter.

Årrenjarka Fjällby SNOW SPORTS
(☎0971-230 18; www.arrenjarka.com) Mush your own husky team and chase the aurora borealis aboard a dogsled near Kvikkjokk, and stay in rustic wilderness cottages.

Sleeping & Eating

Book weeks in advance for the Winter Market weekend in February or prepare to commute from a neighbouring town.

STF Vandrarhem Åsgård HOSTEL €
(☎0971-55 977; www.svenskaturistforeningen.se; Åsgatan 20; dm/s/d from Skr250/300/600; @ 📶) This family-run STF hostel has a lovely setting among green lawns and trees, right near the tourist office. It's a creaky, cheerful old wooden house with numerous bunk beds, compact private rooms, guest kitchen, TV lounge and basement sauna (Skr30 per person). Walls are on the thin side, so you may feel as if you're in bed with your neighbours.

Hotel Jokkmokk HOTEL €€
(☎0971-777 00; www.hoteljokkmokk.se; Solgatan 45; s/d Skr935/1130; P 📶) Overlooking picturesque Talvatis lake, Jokkmokk's nicest hotel has thoroughly modern, if unmemorable rooms, a superb tiled sauna in the basement and another by the lake (for that refreshing hole-in-the-ice dip in winter). The large restaurant, shaped like a Sami *kåta* (hut), appropriately serves the likes of elk fillet and smoked reindeer with juniper-berry sauce.

Hotell Gästis HOTEL €€
(☎0971-100 12; www.hotell-gastis.com; Herrevägen 1; s/d/tr from Skr950/1195/1300; P) Pleasant central hotel. Meals are served in the attached restaurant shaped like a Sami *kåta*.

★ **Ájtte Museum Restaurant** SWEDISH €€
(www.restaurangattje.se; Kyrkogatan 3; mains Skr95-140; ⏲noon-4pm) This Sami restaurant makes it possible to enhance what you've learned about the local wildlife by sampling some of it – from *suovas* (smoked and salted reindeer meat) to reindeer steak and grouse with local berries. The weekday lunchtime buffet (Skr90) serves home-style Swedish dishes.

Yoik evenings and Sami storytelling events take place here occasionally.

Café Glasskas CAFE €€
(Porjusvägen 7; mains Skr165-295; ⏲4-10pm Mon-Fri) This friendly coffee shop turned gourmet spot delights resident and visiting palates with a succinct menu of local game and fish (think elk burger, grilled Arctic char and reindeer steak with all the trimmings).

Thai Muang Isaan THAI €€
(Porjusvägen 4; mains Skr120-140; ⏲11am-8pm Mon-Fri, noon-8pm Sat; ✎) Central, authentic Thai place fills the spice gap in the local dining scene with noodle, rice and stir-fry dishes, but it's the curries that really hit the spot.

Shopping

Jokkmokk is the best location in Sweden to pick up those Sami creations that'll make your life complete: from contemporary fashion to knives, silver jewellery and more.

Information

Tourist Office (☎0971-222 50; www.turism.jokkmokk.se; Stortorget 4; ⏲10am-6pm Tue-Sat, noon-3pm Sun) Stocks numerous brochures on activities and tours in the area.

Getting There & Away

BUS

Buses arrive and leave from the bus station on Klockarvägen. Daily bus 45 connects Jokkmokk with Östersund (Skr507, 9¾ hours) via Arvidsjaur (Skr215, 2¼ hours), while bus 44 runs northeast to Luleå (Skr237, 2¾ hours, one or two daily) via Gällivare (Skr142, 1½ hours, five daily).

TRAIN

In the summer only, daily Inlandsbanan trains head south to Östersund (Skr993, 12 hours) via Arvidsjaur (Skr129, 3¾ hours) at 9.17am, and north to Gällivare (Skr154, 2¼ hours) at 7.34pm.

Around Jokkmokk

Padjelanta National Park

The largest national park in Sweden, 1984-sq-km Padjelanta gets its name from the Sami name Badjelánnda, meaning 'higher land', and appropriately consists of a vast plateau surrounding two huge lakes: Vastenjávvre and Virihávvre.

The hilly, 139km-long **Padjelantaleden** (Padjelanta Trail) can be hiked in seven to 10 days (use *Fjällkartan BD10* and *Fjällkartan BD7*). At the northern end (by lake Akkajaure), you can start at either of the STF huts, Vaisaluokta or Áhkká (the latter is easier). STF runs the Såmmarlappa, Tarrekaise and Njunjes huts at the southern end of the trail, and the Kvikkjokk hostel (p279), while the rest are maintained by Sami villages. Most huts sell provisions.

To reach the northern end of the trail, take bus 93 from Gällivare to Ritsem (Skr198, 3¼ hours, one daily mid-June to mid-September) and connect with the STF ferry (once or twice daily, late June to mid-September) to Vaisaluokta and Änonjálmme, 1.5km north of the Áhkká STF hut. For details of boats from the end of the Padjelantaleden to Kvikkjokk (one to three daily, late June to mid-September), check with **Båttraffik i Kvikkjokk** (☎070-205 31 93; www.battraffikikvikkjokk.com).

Fiskflyg (☎072-512 77 70; www.fiskflyg.se) has daily helicopter flights (late June to late August) departing Kvikkjokk (12.45pm) for the Padjelanta trail, stopping at the Njunjes, Tarrekaise and Sommarlappa STF mountain huts. It also runs a twice-daily Ritsem-to-Staloluokta taxi flight (Skr1100), departing Ritsem at 7.30am and 3pm and Staloluokta at 8am and 3.30pm.

Kvikkjokk

Tiny Kvikkjokk (Huhttán in Sami), around 100km west of Jokkmokk, is on the Kungsleden and the Padjelantaleden trails, and is an ideal jumping-off point for Sarek National Park.

Several fantastic day walks start from the village, including climbs to the mountain Snjerak (809m; three hours return) and a steeper ascent of Prinskullen (749m; three hours return). Follow signs to a car park at the top of the hill to find the trail; if you instead continue straight ahead until the road ends, you'll find another car park and the **STF Kvikkjokk Fjällstation** (☎0971-210 22; www.svenskaturistforeningen.se/kvikkjokk; dm/s/d Skr295/610/815; ⊙mid-Feb–May & mid-Jun–Oct), a picturesque mountain station on the banks of a roaring river with a restaurant serving Swedish standards, as well as fully equipped guest kitchens.

For transport, see p288 and p279.

Sarek & Stora Sjöfallet National Parks

Experienced and well-kitted trekkers meet their match in **Sarek National Park**. Named after Sarektjåhkkå (2098m), and full of sharp peaks and huge glaciers, the park is rich in wildlife such as bears, wolverines and lynxes. The most challenging section of the Kungsleden trail (p288) passes through the park: there are no tourist facilities, major trails are often washed out or in poor repair, there are

LAPONIA WORLD HERITAGE AREA

The vast **Laponia World Heritage Area** (www.laponia.nu) stretches for 9400 sq km, comprising the mountains, forests and marshlands of Padjelanta, Sarek, Stora Sjöfallet and Muddus National Parks. Unusually for a World Heritage Area, it's recognised both for its cultural wealth and its natural wealth.

Established in 1996, Laponia encompasses ancient reindeer-grazing grounds of both the Mountain and the Forest Sami, whose seven settlements and herds of around 50,000 reindeer are located here. The Sami still lead relatively traditional lives, following the reindeer during their seasonal migrations. The Mountain Sami winter in the forests, where there is lichen for their herds, and move into the mountains in summer, while their Forest counterparts follow their herds through the forests year-round.

rivers to cross, and the extremes of terrain are exacerbated by volatile weather conditions.

Bordering Sarek to the north is the mountainous and thickly forested Stora Sjöfallet National Park (www.storasjofallet.com), dominated by Áhkká (2105m), known as the 'Queen of Lappland' and crowned with 10 glaciers. The Kungsleden dips briefly into the southeastern corner of Sarek and passes through Stora Sjöfallet. At the eastern end of the park you can cross the Stora Lulevatten lake on the STF ferry (summer only) to STF Saltoluokta Fjällstation (☑0973-410 10; www.svenskaturistforeninggen.se/saltoluokta; dm/d/q Skr325/1295/1580; ⊙Mar, Apr & mid-Jun–mid-Sep), a mountain station consisting of a main timber building and five satellite guesthouses. The on-site restaurant serves excellent northern Swedish dishes, and numerous guided wilderness tours are available, including kayaking and a hike up Lulep Gierkav (1139m) for great views of the two parks.

Gällivare

☑0970 / POP 18,425

Gällivare (Váhtjer in Sami) and its northern twin, Malmberget, are surrounded by forest and dwarfed by the bald Dundret hill. After Kiruna, Malmberget (Ore Mountain) is the second-largest iron-ore mine in Sweden. And just like Kiruna, the area's sustaining industry is simultaneously threatening the town with collapse into a great big pit, so buildings are gradually being shifted to sturdier ground. Gällivare's biggest attractions are ore-oriented, and even if you don't descend into the subterranean gloom, a visit to Malmberget casts a melancholy spell: many of its houses have been abandoned in anticipation of their imminent destruction.

The strong Sami presence in Gällivare is reflected in its monuments. The bronze statue in the park next to the church, by local sculptor Berto Marklund, is called *Tre seitar* (*seite* being a Sami god of nature) and symbolises the pre-Christian Sami religion.

◉ Sights & Activities

★LKAB Iron-Ore Mine MINE
(admission Skr340; ⊙tours 9.30am daily) In Malmberget you can descend into the bowels of the earth to marvel at the immense, noisy trucks labouring in the darkness of the underground LKAB iron-ore mine. The tourist office runs daily tours at 9.30am from mid-June to mid-August and the timings allow you to take the Aitik copper-mine tour in the afternoon.

Aitik Open-Pit Copper Mine MINE
(admission Skr340) The Aitik open-pit copper mine in Malmberget is Europe's largest, producing 18 million tonnes of copper ore per year. The view of the pit from the top of the hairpin bends is particularly impressive. The tourist office runs tours of the mine at 2pm on Monday, Wednesday and Friday between mid-June and early August.

Gällivare Museum MUSEUM
(☑0970-186 92; Storgatan 16; ⊙10am-3.30pm Mon-Fri, 11am-2pm Sat mid-Jun–Aug) FREE The Gällivare Museum has exhibitions on the navvies (railway workers), Sami culture and early settlers, plus a collection of local artefacts and the famous Mosquito Museum (relocated from a nearby bog).

Midnight Sun Tour TOUR
(return Skr200) Dundret (823m) is a nature reserve with excellent views of the town, Malmberget and the Aitik copper mine, and a favourite spot for viewing the midnight

VISIT SÁPMI

Visit Sápmi (☑070-688 15 77, 070-346 56 06; www.visitsapmi.com; Östra Kyrkallén 2) Started in 2010, Visit Sápmi is an initiative owned by the Swedish Sami Association with an emphasis on sustainable ecotourism. It aims to be the first port of call for visitors with an interest in any aspect of Sami life, be it staying with reindeer herders, attending a *yoik* (Sami song) session or purchasing *duodji* from the best craftspeople.

So that it can put visitors in touch with relevant Sami operators, Visit Sápmi looks to establish contact with every Sámi entrepreneur in Sweden. It awards the Sápmi Experience quality label to operators who meet its criteria regarding sustainable practices. In time, these guys hope to be in touch with Sami craftspeople, tour operators, musicians, chefs and herders all over Sápmi, transcending Norwegian, Finnish and Russian country borders.

THE MIDNIGHT SUN

Northern Sweden's most spectacular attractions are its natural phenomena. In summer, beyond the Arctic Circle, the sun does not leave the sky for weeks on end. You can see the midnight sun just south of the Arctic Circle as well (Arvidsjaur is the southernmost point in Sweden where this occurs) due to the refraction of sunlight in the atmosphere. The midnight sun can be seen on the following dates in the following places:

TOWN	MIDNIGHT SUN
Arvidsjaur, Haparanda	20/21 Jun
Arjeplog	12/13 Jun to 28/29 Jul
Jokkmokk	8/9 Jun to 2/3 Jul
Gällivare	4/5 Jun to 6/7 Jul
Kiruna	28/29 May to 11/12 Jul
Karesuando	26/27 May to 15/16 Jul
Treriksröset	22/23 May to 17/18 Jul

sun. The tourist office organises special taxi transfers (11pm early June to mid-July, 10pm mid-July to early August) from the train station and the price includes ice cream and waffles at the cafe at the top.

Sleeping & Eating

Gällivare Camping CAMPGROUND €
(☎0970-100 10; www.gellivarecamping.com; Kvarkbacksvägen 2; sites Skr170, dm/s Skr220/270, 2-/4-bed cabins Skr650/900; 📶) This year-round campground shares a lovely riverside spot with the *hembygdsområde*, an old homestead. Cabins are set up more like apartments, with excellent, modern facilities. Campers and hostel guests have sauna access.

Stay In HOSTEL €
(☎070-216 69 65; Lasaretsgatan 3; s/d Skr350/650; 📶) This rambling complex, across the road from the train/bus station, may look a bit institutional, but it's clean, functional, super-central and a godsend to self-caterers: guests share several fully equipped kitchens and TV lounges with more long-term local hospital-staff residents. Reserve in advance to get an access code.

Grand Hotel Lapland HOTEL €€
(☎0970-77 22 90; www.ghl.se; Lasarettsgatan 1; s/d from Skr850/1077; P📶🐾) This modern, business set-oriented hotel opposite the train station was a building site when we visited but should be fully revamped by the time you do, with a new gym, pool and steakhouse to complement its airy, comfortable rooms. The ground-level **Vassara Pub** serves local specialities such as reindeer, Arctic char and cloudberry tiramisu.

Sofias Kök SWEDISH €
(Storgatan 19; mains from Skr70; ⏰8am-1am Mon-Fri, 10.30am-2am Sat & Sun) A very local spot for breakfast and Swedish standards such as chunky pea soup. In the evening, you can nurse a pint with the local barflies.

Nittaya Thai THAI €€
(www.nittayathaicatering.se; Storgatan 21B; mains Skr110-120; ⏰10am-2pm Mon, to 9pm Tue-Fri, 1-9pm Sat & Sun; 🖉) Authentic Thai cuisine in attractive surroundings. The changing weekday lunch buffet (Skr85) is a crowd-pleaser, but we prefer the curries and stir-fried dishes.

Information

Tourist Office (☎0970-166 60; www.gellivarelapland.se; Central Plan 4; ⏰7am-10pm daily late Jun-Aug, 9am-5pm Mon-Fri rest of year) Inside the train station. Can organise mine and midnight-sun tours. Baggage storage available.

Getting There & Away

BUS

Regional buses depart from the train station. Bus 1 to Malmberget departs from directly opposite the Gällivare church.

Daily bus 45 runs to Östersund (Skr483, 11 hours) via Jokkmokk (also covered by bus 44, Skr142, 1½ hours, three daily) and Arvidsjaur (Skr311, 3¾ hours, daily), while buses 44 and 10 serve Luleå (Skr311, 3½ to 4¾ hours, two daily) via Kiruna (Skr178, 1¾ to two hours).

TRAIN

Inlandsbanan runs south to Östersund (Skr507, 11¼ hours, one daily at 9.15am) via Jokkmokk (Skr154, two hours) and Arvidsjaur (Skr420, six hours). Other departures include the westbound train to Narvik (Skr360, 4¾ to 5¼ hours, two daily) via Kiruna (Skr133, one to 1¼ hours, five daily) and Abisko (Skr229, three to 3½ hours, two daily), and the eastbound train to Luleå (Skr247, 2½ to three hours, five daily).

Muddus National Park

Covered in primeval forest, the 500-sq-km Muddus National Park lies around 20km north of Jokkmokk along the E45, accessed from its southern end, via the village of Skaite (turn off or alight at Liggadammen). The gently undulating terrain is ideal for novice hikers, and there are huts at regular intervals along the two trail loops, 24km and 44km long respectively, both of which start and end at Skaite and take in the attractive Muddus Falls. The park is rich in fauna and home to whooper swans, lynxes, elks and bears. Outside the April-to-September season, get the keys to the huts from the tourist office at either Jokkmokk (p278) or Gällivare (p281).

Kiruna

☎0980 / POP 22,944

The citizens of Kiruna (Giron, in Sami) live up to their nickname – the 'No-Problem People' – by remaining unperturbed at the news that their city is on the verge of collapsing into an enormous mine pit. Plans are to move the entire city a couple of miles northwest within the space of 20 years, starting with the town centre in 2016. Check out the model of Kiruna inside the tourist office to see exactly what's going on.

Scarred by mine works, Kiruna may not be the most aesthetically appealing city, but it's a friendly place with the highest concentration of lodgings and restaurants in the northwestern corner of Sweden. Its proximity to great stretches of hikeable wilderness, the iconic Icehotel and the proliferation of winter activities make it an excellent base.

Sights & Activities

LKAB Iron-Ore Mine MINE
(adult/student Skr295/195) Kiruna owes its existence to the world's largest iron-ore deposit, 4km into the ground, and the action happens 914m below the surface. A visit to the depths of the LKAB iron-ore mine consists of being bussed to the InfoMine – a closed-off section of a mine tunnel, where you can hear mind-blowing stats and view jaw-droppingly large mining equipment, such as the mills used to crush ore. Tours leave daily from the tourist office between June and August.

Kiruna Kyrka CHURCH
(Gruvvägen 2; ⏲11am-5pm) Kiruna kyrka, built to look like a huge Sami *kåta* (hut), is particularly pretty against a snowy backdrop (it was voted Sweden's most beautiful building in 2001).

Stadshus BUILDING
(Town Hall; Hjalmar Lundbohmsvägen; ⏲9am-5pm Mon-Fri) FREE The Stadhus, a recipient of Sweden's most beautiful public building prize back in 1964 and very, erm, eye-catching due to its clocktower, houses a modest art collection and an odd display of Sami handicrafts.

Kiruna Guidetur SNOW SPORTS, OUTDOORS
(☎0980-811 10; www.kirunaguidetur.com; Vänortsgatan 8) These popular all-rounders organise anything from overnighting in a self-made igloo, snowmobile safaris and cross-country skiing outings in winter to overnight mountain-bike tours, rafting and quad-biking in summer.

Active Lapland SNOW SPORTS
(☎076-104 55 08; www.activelapland.com; Solbacksvägen 22) This experienced operator offers two-hour dogsled rides (Skr1050), rides under the northern lights, and airport pick-ups by dog sleigh (Skr5200). It'll even let you drive your own dogsled (Skr3200).

Tours

Nutti Sami Siida CULTURAL TOUR, ADVENTURE TOUR
(☎0980-213 29; www.nutti.se) One of Nature's Best (an endorsement given to tour operators who have certain eco-credentials), this specialist in sustainable Sami ecotourism arranges visits to the Ráidu Sami camp to meet reindeer herders (Skr1880), reindeer-sledding excursions (from Skr2750), northern-lights tours (Skr2700) and four-day, multi-activity Lappland tours that take in dogsledding and more (Skr9450).

Kiruna

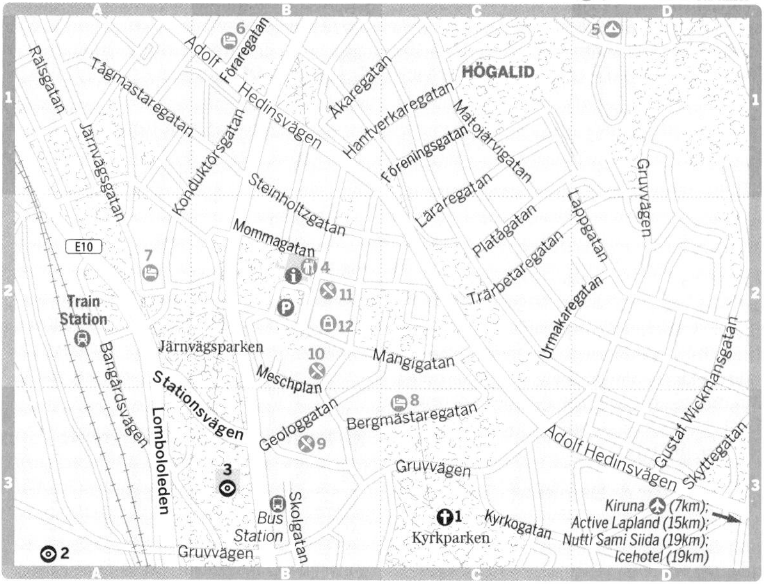

Festivals & Events

Snöfestivalen ART, CULTURAL
(Kiruna Snow Festival; www.snofestivalen.com) Held during the last week of January, this festival is all about snow sculpting. The tradition began in 1985 as a space-themed snow-sculpture contest to celebrate the launching of a rocket *(Viking)* from nearby space base Esrange, and now draws artists from all over to create ever more elaborate and beautiful shapes. The festival also features Sami reindeer-sled racing.

Sleeping

STF Vandrarhem & Hotell City HOSTEL, HOTEL €€
(☎0980-666 55; www.kirunahostel.com; Bergmästaregatan 7; dm/s/d from Skr250/450/500, hotel s/d/tr Skr750/850/1100; P 📶) This catch-all hotel-and-hostel combo has a gleaming red-and-white colour scheme in its modern hotel rooms and cosy dorms. Sauna and breakfast cost extra for hostel guests, but there are handy guest kitchens.

★ **Hotel Arctic Eden** BOUTIQUE HOTEL €€
(☎0980-611 86; www.hotelarcticeden.se; Föraregatan 18; s/d Skr900/1200; P 📶 🏊) At Kiruna's most luxurious lodgings, the rooms are a chic blend of Sami decor and modern technology, there's a plush spa and indoor pool, and the friendly staff can book all manner of outdoor adventures. A fine breakfast spread is served in the morning and the on-site Arctic Thai & Grill is flooded with spice-seeking customers on a daily basis.

Kiruna

Sights

1	Kiruna Kyrka	C3
2	LKAB Iron-Ore Mine	A3
3	Stadshus	B3

Activities, Courses & Tours

4	Kiruna Guidetur	B2

Sleeping

5	Camp Ripan	D1
6	Hotel Arctic Eden	B1
7	Hotel Vinterpalatset	A2
8	STF Vandrarhem & Hotell City	C3

Eating

9	Café Safari	B3
	Camp Ripan Restaurang	(see 5)
10	Landströms Kök & Bar	B2
11	Thai Kitchen	B2

Shopping

12	Ateljé Nord	B2

Camp Ripan CAMPGROUND, HOTEL €€
(☎0980-630 00; www.ripan.se; Campingvägen 5; sites Skr150, cabins from Skr1100; P 📶 🏊) This large and well-equipped campground has hotel-standard chalets and stylish rooms with Sami-inspired art – in addition to its caravan and tent sites. In winter you can bed down in an igloo – a budget version of the Icehotel – and be defrosted in the morning with hot lingonberry drink and a spell in the sauna.

Hotel Vinterpalatset HOTEL €€
(☎0980-677 70; www.vinterpalatset.se; Järnvägsgatan 18; s/d incl breakfast Skr990/1530; P @) Pretty, spacious, individually styled rooms near the train station. Though no palace, in spite of the name, the venerable wooden building is one of Kiruna's oldest, dating to 1904. The decadent breakfast includes cured salmon and roast game.

Eating & Drinking

Thai Kitchen THAI €
(Vänortsgatan 8; mains Skr80-130; ⏰11.30am-9pm; ✎) Don't let the plastic tablecloths fool you – this informal joint cooks up excellent Thai dishes, though if you want authentic spice levels, ask them to kick it up a notch. We particularly love one of the specialities: the sour and spicy glass noodles.

Café Safari CAFE €
(Geologgatan 4; cakes/sandwiches from Skr45/75; ⏰9am-6pm Mon-Fri, 10am-4pm Sat; ✎) A long, skinny cafe serving treacle-thick coffee, outstanding cakes (try the pecan pie), scrummy sandwiches, quiche and baked potatoes.

★ **Camp Ripan Restaurang** SWEDISH €€
(www.ripan.se; Campingvägen; lunch buffet Skr100-125, dinner mains Skr245-355; ⏰11am-2pm & 6-10pm; ✎) The unusually veggie-heavy lunch buffet is good value, but the real draw is the Sami-inspired à la carte menu featuring local, seasonal produce. We're drooling at the very thought of the reindeer steak with bacon and lingonberry sauce, pulled elk with BBQ sauce and rhubarb with licorice meringue. The restaurant's located at the local campground (of all places!).

Landströms Kök & Bar SWEDISH €€
(☎0980-133 55; www.landstroms.net; Föreningsgatan 11; mains Skr165-280; ⏰6-11pm Mon-Thu, to 1am Fri & Sat) Take a stylish, monochrome interior, throw in some reindeer steak, haloumi burgers, racks of lamb and crayfish sandwiches, add a concise, well-chosen wine menu and beers that span the world, and you've got a winning recipe for a perpetually buzzy bistro.

Shopping

Ateljé Nord CRAFTS
(www.ateljenord.com; Lars Janssonsgatan 23; ⏰noon-6pm Mon-Fri, 10am-3pm Sat) This shop is run by a handicraft collective; it's a good place to meet the artisans who specialise in different types of Sami craft.

Information

Tourist Office (☎0980-188 80; www.kirunalapland.se; Lars Janssonsgatan 17; ⏰8.30am-9pm Mon-Fri, to 6pm Sat & Sun) Inside the Folkets Hus visitor centre; has internet access and can book various tours.

Getting There & Around

AIR

Kiruna Airport (☎010-109 46 00; www.swedavia.com/kiruna) Kiruna Airport, 7km east of the town, has flights with SAS and Norwegian to Stockholm (two to three daily), as well as several weekly flights to Luleå and Gällivare. The airport bus (Skr100 one way) is timed to meet Stockholm flights and runs between the tourist office and airport during peak season.

BUS

Daily bus 91 runs to Narvik (Norway; Skr280, 2¾ hours) via Abisko (Skr175, 1¼ hours). Other departures include bus 501 to Jukkasjärvi (Skr40, 30 minutes, two to six daily), and buses 10 and 52 to Gällivare (Skr178, 1¾ hours, two or three daily).

TRAIN

There is a daily overnight train to Stockholm (Skr960, 17½ hours) via Uppsala (Skr960, 16¾ hours) at 3.46pm. Other destinations include Narvik (Norway; Skr227, 3½ to 3¾ hours, two daily) via Abisko (Skr119, 1½ to two hours), Luleå (Skr281, 4¼ hours, five daily) and Gällivare (Skr133, 1¼ hours, five daily).

Nikkaluokta & Kebnekaise

Tiny Nikkaluokta, 66km west of Kiruna, is one of the entrance points to the Kungsleden. It's also the base for those wishing to hike or climb Sweden's highest mountain, Kebnekaise (2106m); the views of the surrounding peaks and glaciers are incredible on a clear day.

For other transport, see p288.

In July and August, the marked trail up the western flank is usually snow-free and no technical equipment is required to reach the southern summit (six to eight hours one way). A considerably shorter but far steeper and harder-to-find trail snakes up the eastern flank and traverses the Björling Glacier, which requires a rope, an ice axe, crampons and a guide (12 to 14 hours one way).

Guided hikes and ice climbing can be arranged at **STF Kebnekaise Fjälstation** (☎0980-550 00; www.svenskaturistforeningen.se/kebnekaise; dm/d/q Skr420/1550/2100; ⊙mid-Feb–early May & mid-Jun–mid-Sep). This large, attractive mountain lodge nestles at the foot of Mt Kebnekaise. A popular entry point to the Kungsleden, it has equipment rental and a gear shop, a sauna and an excellent restaurant serving meals from locally sourced ingredients. The oldest part of the lodge, with fireplaces and characterful bunk rooms, dates to 1907. No guest is ever turned away, with large, basic dorms accommodating the spillover. In winter, the lodge is a good place to view the northern lights and can be reached from Nikkaluokta by snowmobile or reindeer-sled.

Jukkasjärvi

☎0980 / POP 548

The Icehotel has firmly put this one-street village on the world map.

Jukkasjärvi is also home to **Jukkasjärvi kyrka** (Marknadsvägen; ⊙9am-6pm), the oldest church in Lappland (1608). The brightly painted altarpiece by Uppsala artist Bror Hjorth, cut out in teak, depicts scenes with the revivalist preacher Lars Levi Laestadius. In the centre of the birch organ above the entrance hangs a shaman's drum. The organ itself has three sounds: birdsong, drum and reindeer hooves.

Near the church is **Nutti Sámi Siida** (☎0980-213 29; www.nutti.se; Marknadsvägen 84; adult/child Skr150/75; ⊙10am-5pm mid-Jun–mid-Aug, tours 10.30am & 4pm), a reindeer

ICEHOTEL

Every winter, from December onwards, the **Icehotel** (☎0980-668 00; www.icehotel.com; Marnadsvägen 63; s/d/ste from Skr2300/3200/Skr5300, cabins from Skr1900; P) seems to grow organically from ice blocks taken from Torne river, while international artists flock from all over to carve the ice sculptures that make its frozen rooms masterpieces. Besides the experience of sleeping in the world's largest igloo, there's much to tempt active travellers, with warm accommodation available year-round.

From a humble start in 1989 as a small igloo, originally built by Yngve Bergqvist to house an art gallery, the Icehotel has grown into a building comprising an entrance hall and a main walkway lined with ice sculptures and lit with electric lights, with smaller corridors branching off towards the 67 suites. The beds are made of compact snow and covered with reindeer skins, and you are provided with sleeping bags used by the Swedish army for Arctic survival training, guaranteed to keep you warm despite the -5°C temperature inside the rooms (and in winter that's nothing – outside the hotel it can be as low as -30°C).

There are heated bathrooms near the reception, and you leave most of your possessions in lockers so that they don't freeze. Stuff your clothes into the bottom of your sleeping bag, otherwise they'll soon resemble a washboard. Come morning, guests are revived with a hot drink and a spell in the sauna. Guests spend just one night in the Icehotel itself (it's not a comfortable night's sleep for most), so the hotel provides 30 satellite Aurora Houses – bungalows decorated in contemporary Scandinavian style, with skylights for viewing the northern lights.

This custom-built 'igloo' also has an **Ice Church**, popular for weddings (giving new meaning to the expression 'cold feet'!). Outside the winter season the hotel offers 'From River to River' tours (Skr150) that initiate visitors into the process of building this unique hotel, year after year.

Winter adventures on offer include snowmobile safaris, skiing, ice fishing, dogsledding (you can even arrange a dogsled pickup from the airport!), Sami culture tours and northern-lights safaris, while summer activities comprise hiking, rafting, paddleboarding, canoeing, fishing and Ranger all-terrain-buggy tours.

yard that you can tour with a Sami guide to learn about reindeer farming and Sami culture. Here you can book tours, pick up excellent Sami *duodji* (certified handicrafts) and arrange a stay at the nearby **Reindeer Lodge** (☎0980-213 29; www.nutti.se; cabins Skr600) – five cosy two-person cabins in the woods, 3km away from Jukkasjärvi, with a wood-heated sauna and a fully equipped kitchen cabin. In winter, the isolated location is good for viewing the northern lights and a small timber dining room serves elk, reindeer and Arctic char.

Your only eating option outside the winter season, **Old Homestead** (Marknadsvägen; lunch mains Skr75-135, dinner mains from Skr175; 8am-10pm) by the river is nonetheless a good one, with Norrbotten cheese-and-honey sandwiches and meatballs at lunchtime and a game-heavy dinner menu.

The gourmet treat that is the **Icehotel Restaurant** (☎0980-66 800; www.icehotel.se; Marknadsvägen; mains Skr175-355, set menus Skr595-1395; 11.30am-2.30pm & 6-10pm Dec-Apr;) is reserved for winter travellers only. Besides the novelty of dishes served on plates made from Torne river ice, chef Daniel Palmqvist excels when it comes to fusion dishes, such as reindeer steak with shiitake mushrooms and decadent, moreish chocolate souffles with cloudberry puree. You can also sip vodka-based cocktails and champagne served in ice glasses, amidst sculpted ice furniture at the original and best **Icebar** (www.icehotel.com; Marknadsvägen; 1pm-1am Dec-Apr) nearby.

Bus 501 runs between Kiruna and Jukkasjärvi (Skr40, 30 minutes, up to six daily).

Abisko

☎0980

Easy access to spectacular scenery makes Abisko (Ábeskovvu in Sami) one of the highlights of any trip to Lappland. The 75-sq-km **Abisko National Park** spreads out from the southern shore of scenic lake Torneträsk. It's framed by the striking profile of Lapporten, a 'gate' formed by neighbouring hills that serves as the legendary gate to Lappland. This is also the driest part of Sweden and consequently has a relatively long hiking season.

Abisko has two train stops – Östra station puts you in the centre of the tiny, tiny village, while Abisko Turiststation is across the highway from the STF lodge.

Sights & Activities

Aurora Sky Station VIEWPOINT

(www.auroraskystation.se; northern lights Skr595, midnight sun adult/child return Skr220/110; 8pm-midnight Dec-Mar, 9.30am-4pm & 10pm-1am Tue, Thu & Sat mid-Jun–mid-Jul) Across the highway from the STF Turiststation, a chairlift takes you up Mt Nuolja (1169m), where those without vertigo can enjoy epic views from the deck of the Panorama Café, part of the Aurora Sky Station. In summer this is a prime spot from which to see the midnight sun; in winter, to view the northern lights. You can come up on a guided tour (Skr590) and enjoy a three-course dinner with a view (Skr1605).

Hikes HIKING

Hiking is the big draw in the Abisko National Park, aided by the microclimate that makes this one of the driest places in Swe-

OFF THE BEATEN TRACK

TRERIKSRÖSET – WHERE THREE LANDS MEET

Treriksröset, the spot marking the meeting point of Sweden, Norway and Finland, lies 100km northwest of Karesuando.

If driving, cross the bridge from Karesuando to the Finnish Kaaresuvanto, and then take the E8 route northwest to **Kilpisjärvi** (110km). Alternatively, walk across the bridge and take the daily bus departing Kaaresuvanto (1¾ hours, one daily at 2.35pm, plus another one at 4.25pm from June to mid-September) and then hike the 11km woodland trail from the northern side of the village to the small **Goldjärvi lake**, where a yellow concrete 'bell' marks the spot.

To shorten your hike to just 3km each way, hop aboard the **M/S Malla** (☎358-400 66 93 92), which – if it has at least four passengers – sails from Kilpisjärvi to Koltaluokta, an old Sami residence (45 minutes, €28 return, 10am, 2pm, 6pm Finnish time late June to early August). The boat waits at Koltaluokta for two hours.

Check up-to-date bus timetables at www.matkahuolto.fi and don't forget that Finland is one hour ahead of Sweden!

den. Trails are varied in both distance and terrain, and while most people come here to tackle part (or all) of the 450km-long Kungsleden, there are plenty of shorter rambles.

Before you set off, arm yourself with *Fjällkartan BD6* or *Calazo Kungsleden*; both maps are available at the STF lodge and Naturum.

Excellent day hikes include the following: an 8km hike to the Kårsa Rapids, over the Ábeskoeatnu river and then along the left fork of the signposted Kårsavagge (Gorsavággi in Sami) trail through birch and pine forest; and the great 14km, four-hour return hike along Paddus nature trail, past an STF reconstruction of a traditional Sami camp, leading to Báddosdievvá, a former Sami sacrificial site with awesome views of Lapporten and lake Torneträsk.

Longer hikes include the overnight trip to the Gorsajökeln glacier, staying overnight at the STF hut at heart of the Kårsavagge (Gorsavággi) valley, west of Abisko (15km each way), and the 39km-long Rallarvägen (Navvy Rd) to Riksgränsen, running parallel to the railway line and used by railway construction workers in the early 20th century. A good side venture from Rallarvägen is the 10km return trip to the enormous boulders and impressive rock formations of Kärkevagge (Gearggevággi) valley from Låktatjåkka (a short train or bus ride from Abisko) with Trollsjön (Rissájáurre) the 'Sulphur Lake' at the end of the valley, its clear blue waters named after the colour of burning sulphur.

Tours

Lights Over Lapland TOUR
(0760-754 300; www.lightsoverlapland.com; 3hr photography tours Skr1195, 4-day expeditions Skr18,500) If you've always dreamt of chasing the northern lights with a camera in hand, here's your opportunity to learn from professional photographer Chad Blakley. Tours range from nightly photo excursions departing from STF Abisko to four-day expeditions that comprise dogsledding, gourmet meals, Icehotel visits and accommodation at STF Abisko.

Sleeping & Eating

Abisko Fjällturer HOSTEL €
(980-401 03; www.abisko.net; dm/d from Skr225/600; P) This backpackers' delight is spread over two buildings, with comfortable doubles and dorms with wide bunks, sharing guest kitchens and a wonderful wooden sauna. Brothers Tomas and Andreas keep a large team of sled dogs; dogsledding packages (from Skr1200) and northern-lights tours (from Skr600) are not to be missed in winter. Cross the railway tracks 150m east of Abisko Östra station.

STF Abisko Turiststation & Abisko Mountain Lodge HOSTEL €€
(0980-402 00; www.abisko.nu; hostel dm/tw Skr295/885, hotel d Skr1540; year-round; P) This 300-bed place overlooking Torneträsk lake is a massive hiker destination. The dorms, cabins and private rooms are overpriced for what they are, but there's huge demand for the excellent facilities: guest kitchens, a basement sauna, a supply shop and an excellent restaurant to treat yourself to a sumptuous post-hike three-course dinner (Skr395). Guided day treks, caving and tours are available.

Information

Naturum (0980-788 60; www.lansstyrelsen.se; 9am-6pm Tue-Sat early Jul-Sep & Feb-Apr) This information office next to STF Abisko Turiststation has detailed maps and booklets for sale and extensive information on the Kungsleden.

Getting There & Away

Buses and trains stop at Abisko Östra (main village) and Abisko Turiststation – the start of the Kungsleden – five minutes apart. Bus 91 runs east to Kiruna (Skr175, 1¼ hours, two daily) and west to Narvik (Norway; Skr185, 1½ hours, one daily).

Trains run to Kiruna (Skr119, 1¼ hours, two daily) and to Narvik (Skr116, 1¾ hours, two daily).

Riksgränsen

A tiny ski-resort town tucked just inside the border with Norway, 400km north of the Arctic Circle, Riksgränsen is the only place in Sweden where you can ski into Norway and back during Midsummer. The **Riksgränsen** (0980-400 80; www.riksgransen.nu; Riksgränsvägen 15; d/tr/ste from Skr3290/4690/9900; mid-Feb–Midsummer) resort is hugely popular with skiers, and its luxurious spa centre, complete with outdoor hot tubs overlooking Vassijaure lake, is an awesome spot to unwind après-ski. Gear hire costs from Skr350 per day, and day lift passes start at around

Skr400. Exquisite rooms in the intimate **Meteorologen Ski Lodge** (www.riksgransen.se; Riksgränsvägen; s/d Skr1790/3290) next door are available year-round and there's a lively bar to tempt revelers, while the **STF Hostel Riksgränsen** (☎0980-430 88; www.riksgransen.se; Riksgränsvägen 4; d/tr Skr890/1190), a little downhill, is a boon for self-caterers.

Trains stop in Riksgränsen on the way from Kiruna to Narvik, as does bus 91.

Kungsleden

Kungsleden (King's Trail) is Sweden's most important hiking and skiing route. It runs for around 500km from Abisko in the north to Hemavan in the south, through Sami herding lands consisting of spectacular mountainous wilderness that includes Sweden's highest mountain, Kebnekaise (2106m), fringed with forests, speckled with lakes and ribboned with rivers.

The route is split into five mostly easy or moderate sections, with **STF mountain huts** (dm Skr370, sites Skr85; ⏲mid-Feb–early May & late Jun–mid-Sep), each staffed by a custodian, spaced out along the route 10km to 20km from one another (first come, first served), as well as four STF mountain lodges and two hostels en route. Eleven of the 16 mountain huts sell provisions (so you needn't overload your backpack with food), and kitchen facilities are provided, but you'll need your own sleeping bag and there's no electricity. The section between Kvikkjokk and Ammarnäs is not covered by the STF, so you must stay in private accommodation in villages, or camp wild.

Insect repellent is a must in summer to avoid become a walking mosquito buffet, and you have to be prepared for changeable weather.

Abisko to Kebnekaise

From Abisko it's 86km to Kebnekaise Fjällstation (around five days of hiking), and 105km to Nikkaluokta if you're leaving the trail at Kebnekaise (around seven days).

This, the most popular section of the Kungsleden, runs through the dense vegetation of Abisko National Park, mostly following the valley, with wooden boardwalks over the boggy sections and bridges over streams. The highest point along the trail is the Tjäkta Pass (1150m), with great views over the Tjäktavagge valley.

There are five STF huts along the trail: Abiskojaure (in a lovely lakeside setting), Alesjaure (with a sauna and a great view from the mountain ridge), Tjäktja (before Tjäktja Pass), Sälka and Singi. The STF has mountain lodges at Abisko (p287) and **Kebnekaise** (☎0980-550 00; kebnekaise@stfturist.se; dm Skr310, s/d from Skr810/1080; ⏲Mar-Apr & mid-Jun–mid-Sep).

GETTING OUT TO THE KUNGSLEDEN

The Kungsleden is reasonably straightforward to access from its most popular entry points, but if you're aiming for a remoter part of the trail, you may have to contend with limited (or, outside peak season, practically nonexistent) bus services.

Frequent **trains** stop at Abisko en route from Kiruna to Narvik (Norway). Inlandsbanan trains stop at Jokkmokk in summer.

The **bus** routes to other starting points along the Kungsleden are:

- Kiruna to Nikkaluokta on bus 92 (Skr110, 1¼ hours, two daily)
- Gällivare to Ritsem via Kebnats and Vakkotavare on bus 93 (Skr198, 3¼ hours, one daily)
- Jokkmokk to Kvikkjokk on bus 47 (Skr178, 2¾ hours, daily)
- Arjeplog to Jäkkvik on bus 104 (Skr105, 1¼ hours, one daily on weekdays)
- Sorsele to Ammarnäs on bus 341 (Skr115, 1¼ to 1¾ hours, one to three daily)
- Umeå via Tärnaby to Hemavan on bus 31 (Skr261, six hours, one to three daily)

Kallax Flyg helicopters (☎0980-810 00; www.kallaxflyg.se; adult/2-11yr Skr850/500) transport hikers twice daily (9am and 5pm) between Nikkaluokta and Kebnekaise from late June to late August, and daily (9am) until late September, while Fiskflyg (p279) has helicopter flights from Kvikkjokk and between Ritsem and Staloluokta. If you wish to be dropped off in a wilderness location of your choice, that can also be arranged.

Kebnekaise to Saltoluokta

This section is 52km (three to four days) from Kebnekaise Fjällstation and 38km from Singi to Saltoluokta.

South of Singi, 14km from Kebnekaise, this quieter section of the trail runs through peaceful valleys and beech forest. Row yourself 1km across Teusajaure lake and then cross the bare plateau before descending to Vakkotavare through beech forest.

A bus runs from Vakkotavare to the quay at Kebnats, where there's an STF ferry across Langas lake to Saltoluokta Fjällstation. STF has a mountain lodge at Saltoluokta (p280), and four huts en route, at Singi, Kaitumjaure, Teusajaure and Vakkotavare.

Saltoluokta to Kvikkjokk

This section is 73km, or four days of hiking. From Saltoluokta, it's a long and relatively steep climb to Sitojaure (six hours), where you cross a lake using the boat service run by the hut's caretaker, followed by a boggy stretch with wooden walkways. At Aktse (an excellent base for side trips into Sarek National Park), on the shores of Laitaure Lake, you are rewarded with expansive views of the bare mountainous terrain, before you cross the lake using the rowboats provided and pass through pine forest to reach Kvikkjokk.

STF has a lodge at Kvikkjokk (p279), and huts at Sitojaure, Aktse and Pårte.

Kvikkjokk to Ammarnäs

This is the wildest and most difficult section of the park, recommended for experienced hikers only. It stretches for 157km, or eight to 10 days of hiking. Bring your own tent, as accommodation is very spread out.

KUNGSLEDEN IN WINTER

The Kungsleden can be tackled in winter, on cross-country skis or snowshoes; the trail is well marked with red 'x' signs. It's a challenge, since most accommodation (with the exception of year-round STF Abisko, Hemmavan and Ammarnäs options) closes from late September to mid-February and you have to be entirely self-reliant. However, all accommodation en route keeps a single room unlocked all winter, providing emergency shelter if need be.

WHICH MAP?

When arming yourself with maps for different sections of the Kungsleden, you have a choice of either the detailed Fjällkartan (www.lantmetariet.se; 1:100,000) or the Calazo (www.calazo.se) series. Fjällkartan maps cover a slightly wider area around the Kungsleden and are one sided, whereas Calazo maps are double sided and water-resistant.

The best maps for each section of the Kungsleden are as follows:

- **Abisko to Kebnekaise**: *Fjällkartan BD6* or *Calazo Kungsleden*
- **Kebnekaise to Saltoluokta**: *Fjällkartan BD8* or *Calazo Kebnekaisefjällen*
- **Saltoluokta to Kvikkjokk**: *Fjällkartan BD10* or *Calazo Sarek & Padjelanta*
- **Kvikkjokk to Ammarnäs**: *Fjällkartan BD14* (north) and *BD16* (south) or *Calazo Kvikkjokk-Ammarnäs*
- **Ammarnäs to Hemavan**: *Fjällkartan AC2* or *Calazo Ammarnäs-Hemavan*

Take the boat across Saggat lake from Kvikkjokk before walking to Tsielejåkk, from where it's 55km to the next hut at Vuonatjviken. Then cross Riebnesjaure lake and another one from Hornavan to the village of Jäkkvikk, from where the trail runs through Pieljekaise National Park. From Jakkvikk it's only 8km until the next hut, followed by another stop at the village of Adolfström. Cross Iraft lake before making for the cabins at Sjnjultje. Here the trail forks: either take the direct 34km route to Ammarnäs or take a 24km detour to Rävfallet followed by an additional 20km to Ammarnäs.

You'll find private accommodation at Tsielejåkk, Vuonatjviken, Jäkkvikk, Pieljekaise, Adolfström, Sjnjultje, Rävfallet and Ammarnäs (p274).

Ammarnäs to Hemavan

This section is 78km, or four days' hike. Much of the southern section of the Kungs -leden runs through Vindelfjällens Nature Reserve. This trail is the easiest of the five sections, mostly consisting of a gentle ramble through beech forest and wetlands, and over low hills. There's a long, steep climb (8km) through beech forest between Ammarnäs and Aigert, but at the top you are rewarded with an impressive waterfall.

To reach Syter, cross the wetlands using the network of bridges, stopping at the hut by Tärnasjö lake for a spell in the sauna. The hike up to Syter peak (1768m) from Syter hut is greatly recommended and the view on the way down to Hemavan, taking in Norway's Okstindarnas glaciers, is particularly spectacular.

The STF has a hostel at Hemavan (p273), and five huts en route at Aigert, Serve, Tärnasjö, Syter and Viterskalet.

Karesuando

☎0981 / POP 303

The one-elk town of Karesuando (Gárasavvon in Sami) is the northernmost church village in Sweden, and it feels that way: utterly remote and lonely. This Sami reindeer-herder community revels in the romance of extremes: the midnight sun shines here from late May to mid-July, but in winter the temperature hits -50°C. Karesuando's frontier feel is reflected in the four languages spoken by the locals (sometimes all at once): Swedish, Finnish, Northern Sami and Norwegian.

Karesuando boasts Sweden's northernmost **church** (🕙10am-2pm & 3-6pm mid-Jun–Aug), built in 1816. The wooden altar sculpture represents local revivalist preacher Lars Levi Laestadius. Nearby **Vita Huset** (guided tours Skr25; 🕙7am-3pm Mon-Fri) showcases evocative photos depicting Finnish civilians fleeing the retreating German forces in 1944; many of the refugees were rowed to safety across the river by local Olga Raattamaa. West of the tourist office is **Laestadius Pörte** (🕙24hr), the compact log cabin that was home to Lars Levi Laestadius, his wife and their 14 children (yes, it's rather like squeezing a dozen people into a Mini) between 1826 and 1849.

When we visited, both the hostel and the hotel had closed down, so you a) pitch a tent beside the mosquito-plagued river at **Karesuando Camping** (☎070-605 1124, 0981-201 39; www.karesuandokamping.blogspot.com; Laestadiusvägen 153; sites/cabins Skr140/500; 🕙Jun-Aug), b) cross the bridge to Finland's marginally more happenin' Kaaresuvanto or c) stop for a burger or an Asian-style fry-up at the **Arctic Lunch & Grill** (mains Skr45-75; 🕙11am-6pm) and then make tracks south towards Kiruna or east along the wonderfully unpeopled E400 that skirts the Finnish border en route to Pajala.

The **tourist office** (☎0981-202 05; www.karesuando.se; 🕙10am-5pm Mon-Fri) is next to the bridge to Finland.

Bus 50 runs once daily at 6.40am from Karesuando to Kiruna (Skr237, three hours).

Pajala

☎0978 / POP 1958

Tiny riverside Pajala, made famous in the hugely popular Swedish novel and film *Popular Music*, is a place with deeply rooted Torne Valley culture, where the locals speak Tornedalsfinska (Torne Valley Finnish).

The **Pajala Fair** (one week in July), attended by over 40,000 people each year, is the place to pick up some excellent handmade Sami knives, reindeer-skin bags, smoked fish and more.

The **tourist office** (☎0978-100 15; www.pajalaturism.bd.se; 🕙8am-4pm Mon-Fri) is overlooked by a giant wooden model of a great grey owl – the town's symbol. Nearby is one of the world's largest circular **sundials**. Towards the river is **Laestadius Pörtet** (www.laestadiusfriends.se; Laestadiusvagen 36; admission Skr65; 🕙10am-6pm mid-Jun–mid-Aug), home of fiery preacher Lars Levi Laestadius from 1849 until his death; it contains an exhibition dedicated to his life and work.

Central **Snickarbacken Lägenhetshotell** (☎0978-100 70; www.snickarbacken.se; Kirunavägen; s/d Skr790/990, 2-person apt Skr890; P 📶) offers fully equipped apartments, simple rooms and a good weekday dinner buffet. Overlooking the giant sundial, **Thai Dan Sai** (www.thaidanssai.se; Medborgarvägen 3; mains Skr89; 🕙11am-9pm Tue-Thu, to 2am Fri, 4pm-2am Sat) has won many local fans with the proprietress's spice-laden dishes from her native northern Thailand.

Bus 55 serves Luleå (Skr281, 3½ hours, one to two daily). Bus 53 runs east to Haparanda (Skr248, three to 3½ hours, one to three daily) and west to Kiruna (Skr248, 2¾ to three hours, two daily on weekdays).

w

Understand Sweden

Sweden Today

A generally prosperous and peaceful country, Sweden seems able to weather its storms rather easily. Of course there are always internal tensions and occasional threats to smooth sailing, whether they're economic challenges or political battles. But, overall, a visitor to Sweden gets the sense that the system works quite well. The Swedish word *lagom* means not too much and not too little but just right. Sweden strives to embody this concept. It's not perfect, but it's reassuringly consistent.

Best on Film

The Seventh Seal (1957) Ingmar Bergman pits man against Death in a cosmic chess game.
Let the Right One In (2008) Tomas Alfredson's icy, preteen take on the vampire romance is palpably set in Norrland.
Together (2000) Lukas Moodysson aims his lens at a Swedish commune in 1975.
I Am Curious (Yellow) (1967) Vilgot Sjöman's hugely influential political satire took swings at the young king.
Songs from the Second Floor (2000) Roy Andersson's bleak meditation on modern humanity.

Best in Print

Gösta Berling's Saga (1891) Nobel Prize winner Selma Lagerlöf's debut novel.
Faceless Killers (1997) Henning Mankell's detective series, with Kurt Wallander, starts here.
Tomas Tranströmer The Swedish poet won the 2011 Nobel Prize for literature.
The Girl with the Dragon Tattoo (2009) Stieg Larsson's Millennium Trilogy has been a global phenomenon.

Change in the Weather

Despite its middle-way steadiness over the long term, recently Sweden has seen changes in the economy and the political mood that have led some people to question their assumptions. For decades the country was viewed by left-leaning outsiders as an almost utopian model of a socialist state, a successful experiment that gave hope to progressives everywhere. This is still more or less true. Inevitably, though, as the country has grown, it has had to adjust to modern realities – both economic and sociopolitical – and some cracks have begun to appear in the facade.

The Social Democrats, who held a majority of the government (and therefore shaped national policy, most notably the famous 'cradle to grave' welfare state) for most of the past 85 years, have begun to see their influence wane. The first big blow came in 2006, when the long-entrenched party lost its leadership position in the Swedish parliament. The centre-right Alliance Party (made up of four centre-right parties – the Moderates, the Liberals, the Christian Democrats and the Centre Party) won the election, with Prime Minister Fredrik Reinfeldt campaigning on a 'work first' platform. Reinfeldt's government lowered tax rates and trimmed certain benefits, hoping to jump-start the economy and reduce unemployment.

The 2010 election saw the Social Democrats' worst result since 1921: they won just over 30% of the seats in parliament. The Alliance Party won again (173 of the 349 seats), meaning Reinfeldt continued as prime minister. Unemployment remained high, though, and by 2012 the Social Democrats had regained some favour. In the September 2014 general election, Reinfeldt failed to secure a third term as prime minister; instead, Social Democrat leader Stefan Löfven will lead in a coalition government with the Green party. In the election's most startling result, the far-right nationalist Sweden Democrats doubled their proportion of the vote, becoming the third-largest party in parliament. This is sure to cause friction as the other parties have all said they will not work with the Sweden Democrats.

People & Immigration

Sweden's population is relatively small given the size of the country – with 9.72 million people spread over the third-largest country in Western Europe, it has one of the lowest population densities on the continent. Most Swedes live in the large cities of Stockholm, Göteborg, Malmö and Uppsala. Conversely, the interior of Norrland is sparsely populated.

About 30,000 Finnish speakers form a substantial minority in the northeast, near Torneälven.

Swedish culture strongly values socially progressive ideas such as gender and racial equality, gay rights, a free press and free expression, transparency in government, environmental protection and workers' rights. At the same time, racial and religious tensions have increased in recent years, as the number of foreign-born Swedes has grown. Currently around 15% of the population was born outside Sweden. Equality is a straightforward enough goal in a small, homogenous society, but Sweden's relatively sudden diversity has required some adjustment, and it hasn't always gone smoothly. Resistance to immigration by fringe groups and nationalist political parties has led to some ugly clashes. And immigration is on the rise.

Sweden first opened its borders to mass immigration during WWII. At the time it was a closed society, and new arrivals were initially expected to assimilate and 'become Swedish'. But in 1975 parliament adopted a new set of policies that formally recognised the freedom to preserve and celebrate native traditional cultures, paving the way for a broader outlook on immigration.

In recent years, Sweden has been a leader in welcoming immigrants and refugees from Middle Eastern and African countries. In 2007, for example, the small town of Södertälje, 30km south of Stockholm, welcomed 1268 Iraqi refugees – more than what was accepted that year by the US and Canada combined. In 2014 the Swedish government announced that it would take unlimited numbers of Syrian refugees for permanent residence.

Views on immigration – whether it should be restricted or kept relatively open – are now the number one factor as Sweden's many political parties and coalitions grapple for power.

POPULATION: **9.72 MILLION**

GDP: **$393.8 BILLION**

GDP PER CAPITA: **$40,900**

UNEMPLOYMENT: **8.1%**

ADULT LITERACY: **99%**

if Sweden were 100 people

89 would be Swedish
3 would be Finn & Sami (Lapp)
1 would be Iranian
6 would be Other

belief systems

(% of population)

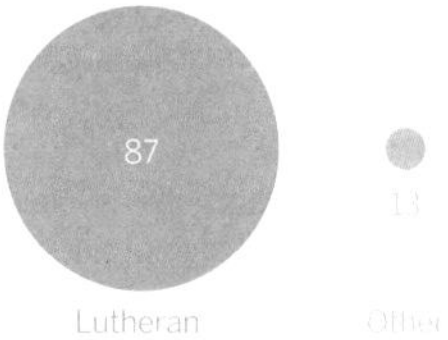

population per sq km

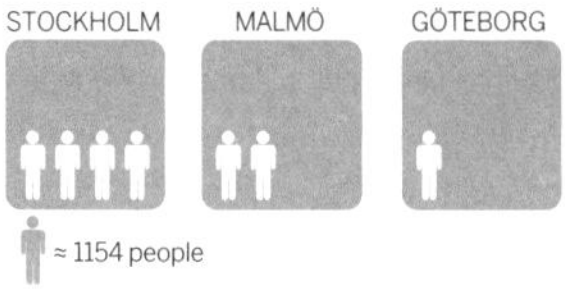

History

Imagine Sweden's history as a play in three acts. There's plenty of action, from the blood and gore of the Viking raids to medieval battles, cross-dressing, and assassinations galore.

Top Five World Heritage Sites in Sweden

Hanseatic town of Visby (p237)

Naval port of Karlskrona (p201)

Gammelstad church village (p266), Luleå

Höga Kusten (p260)

Laponia (p277)

Act I: in the beginning, there is only ice. As the ice slowly melts and retreats, with a clatter of hooves, reindeer tentatively set foot on stage, pursued by fur-clad hunter-gatherers – the predecessors of the Sami. Curious Greek explorers and Roman traders are minor characters who venture into the land of the midnight sun and the Arctic night. Then in a flash of steel and fearsome yells, the Vikings charge on stage to raid and plunder, eventually settling down to more peaceful pursuits.

Act II: the action is split between the court and the battlefield, and the bloody, intrigue-filled plot is worthy of Shakespeare. Royal dynasties follow one another in rapid succession; nobles conspire against the king; another king's brother commits fratricide by poisoned pea soup; an androgynous girl-king ascends the throne only to flee, dressed as a man; a king is assassinated at a masked ball and another during battle. Skirmishes are fought on frozen lakes, at sea and in the mountains. Sweden's territory expands and then rapidly contracts.

Act III: Sweden's dreams of greatness lie in tatters following military defeats and the loss of its colonies. The peacetime population grows. Railways are laid, mines are dug, trees are felled, cities expand. Sweden is largely untouched by the turmoil of the World Wars and improves the lives of its own citizens before turning its sights to the rest of the world. An international player and a member of the UN, Sweden welcomes scores of refugees; the homogenous-looking cast quickly becomes a diverse one. And just when a happy ending is near, a dramatic plot twist brings murder and tragedy, closely followed by international scandal and controversy.

TIMELINE

10,000–6000 BC

Ice sheets melt and hunter-gatherer tribes, the ancestors of the Sami, follow reindeer into a newly uncovered Sweden. The oldest human settlement is founded near Arjeplog.

1800–500 BC

Hällristningar (petroglyphs) illustrating Bronze Age beliefs appear in many parts of Sweden, such as Dalsland and Bohuslän. The sun, hunting scenes and ships are common themes.

500 BC

The runic alphabet arrives, probably from the Germanic region. It is used to carve inscriptions onto monumental rune stones (there are around 3000 in Sweden) well into medieval times.

TRACING YOUR (SWEDISH) ANCESTORS

Around a million people emigrated from Sweden to the USA and Canada between 1850 and 1930. Many of their 12 million descendants are now returning in search of their roots.

Luckily, detailed parish records of births, deaths and marriages have been kept since 1686 and there are *landsarkivet* (regional archives) around the country. The national archive is **Riksarkivet** (☎010-476 70 00; http://sok.riksarkivet.se/svar-digitala-forskarsalen); its newly digitised system allows you to search the National Archives Database and to use SVAR, the Digital Research Room.

Utvandrarnas Hus (p220) (Emigrant House) in Växjö is a particularly good museum dedicated to the mass departure.

Also worth a look is *Tracing Your Swedish Ancestry,* by Nils William Olsson, a free do-it-yourself genealogical guide. Download the latest version from the New York Consulate-General of Sweden's website: www.swedenabroad.com (under Visit Sweden in the menu) or get it free from Amazon.com.

The First Arrivals

In the grip of the last ice age Sweden was an inhospitable place, but perhaps less so than Siberia, where the first hunter-gathers originated 10,000 to 6000 years ago. As the ice retreated, tribes from central Europe migrated into the south of Sweden, and ancestors of the Sami people hunted wild reindeer into the northern regions.

Between 1800 BC and 500 BC, Bronze Age cultures blossomed. Huge Bronze Age burial mounds, such as Kiviksgraven in Österlen, suggest that powerful chieftains had control over spiritual and temporal matters.

After 500 BC, the Iron Age brought about technological advances, demonstrated by archaeological finds of agricultural tools, graves and primitive furnaces, but as the climate worsened again, the downturn in agriculture coincided with the arrival of the Svea – powerful tribes who ended up settling much of Sweden. By AD 600, the Svea people of the Mälaren valley (just west of Stockholm) had gained supremacy, and their kingdom, Svea Rike, gave the country of Sweden its name: Sverige.

The Vikings, by Magnus Magnusson, is an extremely readable history book, covering Viking achievements in Scandinavia (including Sweden), as well as their wild deeds around the world.

Vikings & Christians

Scandinavia's greatest impact on world history probably occurred during the Viking Age, when hardy pagan Norsemen set sail for other shores. The Swedish Vikings were more inclined towards trade than their Norwegian or Danish counterparts, but their reputation as fearsome warriors was fully justified. At home it was the height of paganism; Viking leaders claimed descent from Freyr, 'God of the World', and celebrations at Uppsala involved human sacrifices.

98

The Svea tribe that effectively rules what is now Sweden is first mentioned by Tacitus; they are referred to as Suinoes.

c 800

Birka, founded on Björkö (an island in Mälaren lake), becomes a powerful Svea trading centre. Byzantine and Arab coins have been found here, confirming the existence of trade routes.

1008

Sweden's first Christian king, Olof Skötkonung, is baptised at St Sigfrid's Well in Husaby, but worship continues in Uppsala's pagan temple until at least 1090.

1252

The city of Stockholm is founded by king's statesman Birger Jarl, who has been running the country since 1229.

The Vikings sailed a new type of boat that was fast and highly manoeuvrable, but still sturdy enough for ocean crossings. Initial hit-and-run raids along the European coast were followed by major military expeditions, settlement and trade. The well-travelled Vikings settled part of the Slavic heartland, giving it the name 'Rus' and ventured as far as Newfoundland, Constantinople (modern-day Istanbul) and Baghdad, setting up trade with the Byzantine Empire.

Christianity only took hold when Sweden's first Christian king, Olof Skötkonung (c 968–1020) was baptised. By 1160, King Erik Jedvarsson (Sweden's patron saint, St Erik) had virtually destroyed the last remnants of paganism.

Rise of the Swedish State

By the 13th century, royal power disintegrated over succession squabbles between the Erik and Sverker families, with medieval statesman Birger Jarl (1210–66) rising to fill the gap.

His son, King Magnus Ladulås (1240–90) granted numerous privileges to the church and the nobility, including freedom from taxation. At the same time, he forbade the aristocracy from living off the peasantry when moving from estate to estate.

After deposing his eldest son, Birger (1280–1321), for fratricide, the nobility looked to Norway for their next ruler, choosing the infant grandson of King Haakon V. When Haakon died without leaving a male heir, the kingdoms of Norway and Sweden were united (1319).

The increasingly wealthy church began to show its might in the 13th and 14th centuries, commissioning monumental buildings such as the Domkyrka (Cathedral) in Linköping (founded 1250) and Scandinavia's largest Gothic cathedral in Uppsala (founded 1285).

However, in 1350 the rise of state and church endured a horrific setback when the Black Death swept through the country, carrying off around a third of the Swedish population.

The leather jacket (complete with original bloodstains) that Gustav II Adolf was wearing when killed in battle, as well as his stuffed horse Streiff, can be seen in the Royal Armoury (Livrustkammaren; p44) in Stockholm.

The Birth & Death of a Union

The Black Death created a shortage of candidates for the throne. In 1364 the nobles installed Albrecht of Mecklenburg as their ruler but baulked at his attempts to wield his own power. Their revolt was aided by Danish regent Margareta, and the Union of Kalmar (1397) united Denmark, Norway and Sweden under one crown.

Erik of Pomerania, Margareta's nephew, held that crown until 1439, his rule marred by a constant struggle against the Hanseatic League – a group of well-organised merchants who established walled trading towns in Germany and maintained a strong presence in the young city of Stockholm.

1350s
Following the Black Death scourge, St Birgitta (1303–73) founds a nunnery and cathedral in Vadstena, which becomes Sweden's most important pilgrimage site.

1434
High taxation imposed by the Kalmar Union to fund wars against the Hanseatic League make Erik of Pomerania deeply unpopular; the peasantry rise in the Engelbrekt revolt.

1439–70
Following the short-lived replacement of Erik of Pomerania, succession struggles begin again: two powerful Swedish families, the unionist Oxenstiernas and the nationalist Stures, fight for supremacy.

1520
After granting a full amnesty to Sture followers, Danish King Christian II goes back on his word: over 80 nobles and clergy are arrested, tried and butchered in the 'Stockholm Bloodbath'.

Out of the chaos following Erik's deposition, Sten Sture the Elder (1440–1503) eventually emerged as 'Guardian of Sweden' in 1470, going on to fight and defeat an army of unionist Danes at the Battle of Brunkenberg (1471) in Stockholm.

In a move of retaliation that sounded the union's death knell, Christian II of Denmark invaded Sweden and killed the regent Sten Sture the Younger (1493–1520), adding a massacre in Stockholm's Gamla Stan to his list of accomplishments.

Queen Kristina was immortalised in August Strindberg's 1901 play, her life was chronicled in Veronica Buckley's biography *Christina, Queen of Sweden*, and she was fictionalised in the 1933 film *Queen Christina*, starring Greta Garbo.

The Vasa Dynasty

The brutal 'Stockholm Bloodbath' sparked off an insurrection in 1520 under the leadership of the young nobleman Gustav Ericsson Vasa (1496–1560). Having failed to raise enough support, Gustav was fleeing for the Norwegian border when two exhausted skiers caught him up to tell him that the people had changed their minds. This legendary ski journey is celebrated every year in the Vasaloppet race between Sälen and Mora.

Gustav I ruled from 1523 to 1560, leaving behind a powerful, centralised nation state. He introduced the Reformation to Sweden and passed the power on to his descendants though the 1544 parliament act that made the monarchy hereditary.

After Gustav Vasa's death in 1560, bitter rivalry broke out among his sons. His eldest child, Erik XIV (1533–77), held the throne for eight years in a state of not-unjustified paranoia. After committing a trio of injudicious murders at Uppsala Slott, Erik was deposed by his half-brother Johan III (1537–92) and dispatched to the afterlife via poisoned pea soup at Örbyhus Slott.

The last of the male Vasa rulers, 17-year-old Gustav II Adolf (1594–1632) proved to be a military genius, recapturing southern parts of the country from Denmark and consolidating Sweden's control over the eastern Baltic. He was killed in battle on 6 November 1632, a day remembered for centuries in Sweden as a moment of national trauma.

Gustav II Adolf's daughter Kristina was still a child in 1632, and her regent continued her father's warlike policies. In 1654 Kristina abdicated in favour of her cousin Karl X Gustav, ending the Vasa dynasty.

In 2009 experts sought to establish the chemical composition of the bullet that killed King Karl XII and solve the 18th-century whodunit once and for all. Sadly, permission to have his body exhumed was denied, as it had already been plucked from its resting place three times since 1917.

Rise & Fall of the Swedish Empire

The zenith and collapse of the Swedish empire happened remarkably quickly. During Karl XI's reign, successful battles were waged against Denmark and Norway, the latter resulting in the seizure of Bohuslän, Härjedalen and Jämtland, and the empire reached its maximum size when Sweden established a short-lived American colony in what is now Delaware.

Inheritor of this huge and increasingly sophisticated country was 15-year-old King Karl XII (1681–1718), an overenthusiastic military adventurer

1523
Gustav Vasa becomes the first Vasa king after the Kalmar Union between Denmark, Sweden and Norway breaks up; he marches into Stockholm and is crowned on 6 June, now the country's national day.

1527
Reformation parliament passes a law that transfers the property of the church to the state, and places the church under the state's direct control (repealed in 2000).

1563–70
During the Vasa brothers' reigns, there are wars against Lübeck and Poland, and the Danes try and fail to reassert sovereignty over Sweden in the Northern Seven Years War.

1618–48
Devout Lutheran Gustav II Adolf intervenes in the Thirty Years War between Protestants and Catholics, invading Poland and defeating his cousin King Sigismund III, but dying in battle in 1632.

KRISTINA, QUEEN OF CONTROVERSY

Queen Kristina (1626–89) lived an eccentric and eventful life. Her father, Gustav II, expecting great things from her, instructed that the girl be raised as a prince. He then promptly went off and died in the Battle of Lützen, leaving his six-year-old successor and his country in the hands of the powerful Chancellor Oxenstierna.

Kristina received a boy's education, becoming fluent in six languages and skilled in the art of war, and she took her oath as king, not queen, earning her the nickname 'Girl King'. Childish spats with Oxenstierna increased as she grew older. After being crowned queen in 1644, she defied him even when he had the country's best interests at heart.

In 1649 Kristina made public her desire not to marry, and named her beloved cousin Karl X Gustav her heir to the throne. Kristina's ever-erratic behaviour culminated in her abdication in 1654. Disguised as a man, she rode through Denmark on horseback; tense relations between the two countries would not have allowed her true self safe passage. Kristina ended up in Rome, where she converted to Catholicism – a scandalous act for a daughter of Protestantism's champion. To this day, she is the only woman to be buried in the basilica of St Peter's in Rome.

A strong female character known for her bisexuality, in modern times Kristina has become a lesbian icon, while her cross-dressing has made her a favourite of the transgender community.

who spent almost all of his reign at war. Karl XII cost Sweden its Latvian, Estonian and Polish territory, with the Swedish coast sustaining damaging attacks from Russia, and he perished by a mystery sniper's hand in 1718.

Although not history textbooks, Vilhelm Moberg's four novels about 19th-century Swedish emigration are based on real people and bring this period to life. They're translated into English as *The Emigrants*, *Unto A Good Land*, *The Settlers* and *The Last Letter Home*.

The Age of Liberty

In the 18th century, intellectual enlightenment streaked ahead and Sweden produced some celebrated writers, philosophers and scientists. Anders Celsius gave his name to the temperature scale; Carl Scheele discovered chlorine; and Carl von Linné (Linnaeus) was the great botanist who developed theories about plant reproduction.

Gustav III (1746–92) was a popular and sophisticated king who granted freedom of worship and was surprisingly successful in the maritime battle in the Gulf of Finland against Russia in 1790. Still, his costly foreign policy earned him enemies in the aristocracy and led to his assassination.

His son Gustav IV Adolf (1778–1837) was forced to abdicate after getting drawn into the Napoleonic Wars and permanently losing Finland (one-third of Sweden's territory) to Russia. His rule ended unrestricted royal power with the 1809 constitution.

Out of the blue, Napoleon's marshal Jean-Baptiste Bernadotte (1763–1844) was invited by a nobleman, Baron Mörner, to take the Swedish

1658
The last remaining parts of southern Sweden still in Danish hands are handed over at the Peace of Roskilde, after Swedish troops successfully invade Denmark across the frozen Kattegatt.

1697–1718
Karl XII holds the throne. Russia, Poland and Denmark form an anti-Sweden alliance; the Swedish army is crushed by the Russians at Poltava in 1709 – a battle that ends Sweden's time as a superpower.

1789
The coup d'etat mounted by Gustav III curtails parliamentary powers and reintroduces absolute rule.

1792
At a masked ball in 1792, Gustav III is surrounded by conspirators and shot in the back of the head by Jacob Johan Anckarström, the captain of the king's regiment.

throne – which he did, along with the name Karl Johan. Judiciously changing sides, he led Sweden, allied with Britain, Prussia and Russia, against France and Denmark.

Emigration & Industrialisation

Industry arrived late in Sweden (during the second half of the 19th century), but when it did come it eventually transformed the country from one of Western Europe's poorest to one of its richest.

Significant Swedish inventions, including dynamite (Alfred Nobel) and the safety match (patented by Johan Edvard Lundstrom), coupled with efficient steel-making and timber exports and a thriving textiles industry, added to a growing economy and the rise of a new middle class.

Coupled with discontent in the countryside and exacerbated by famine early in the process, industrialisation led to enormous social changes – from mass emigration to the rapid growth of labour and social movements such as unionisation.

In 1979 hundreds of Swedes called in sick to work on account of 'being gay' to protest homosexuality being treated as a medical disorder at the time.

MURDERS MOST MYSTERIOUS

Assassination has been a common enough cause of death for so many Swedish heads of state as to qualify as 'natural causes'. King Karl XII (1681–1718) was mysteriously shot dead while inspecting his troops during a winter siege in Trondheim, Norway. While Norwegians take credit for the killing, the theory that Karl XII had been shot by one of his own men, disgruntled because the king's many military losses cost Sweden its rank as a great power, has persisted among historians.

Less than a century later, in March 1792, King Gustav III was assassinated at a masked ball in the foyer of the Royal Opera House. The assassination – later the subject of a Verdi opera – was the result of a conspiracy hatched by nobles alarmed at the king's autocratic ways. His principal assailant, Jacob Johan Anckarström, was stripped of his lands and titles before being flogged and decapitated.

This trend of unsolved high-profile deaths has continued to the present day. In 1986, Social Democrat Prime Minister Olof Palme (1927–86) was shot dead by a mystery man as he walked home from the cinema with his wife on a frigid February night. Palme's wife, who behaved strangely throughout the murder investigation, eventually identified Christer Pettersson as the murderer. Pettersson was acquitted on appeal, as there was a great deal of doubt as to whether the murderer could have been accurately identified from a single glimpse on a dark night. Questions remain unanswered as to why the police investigation was so bungled, why strong leads weren't followed up and conspiracy theories abound. Palme's murderer is still at large, though in recent years some evidence has emerged that implicates the South African secret service, which may have targeted Palme due to his strong anti-apartheid stance.

1814

After Napoleon's defeat, Sweden forces Denmark to swap Norway for Swedish Pomerania. The Norwegians object, and Swedish troops occupy most of the country, with the forced union lasting until 1905.

1921

In the interwar period, a Social Democrat–Liberal coalition government takes control and introduces reforms, including an eight-hour working day and universal suffrage for adults aged over 23.

1944

Diplomat Raoul Wallenberg rescues nearly 100,000 Hungarian Jews from the SS by hiding them in Swedish 'neutral houses' in Budapest.

1953

Dag Hammarskjöld is elected Secretary-General of the UN. Under his guidance, the UN resolves the 1956 Suez Crisis.

Sweden (Not) at War

Sweden declared itself neutral in 1912, and remained so throughout the bloodshed of WWI. Swedish neutrality during WWII was ambiguous: letting German troops march through to occupy Norway and selling iron ore to both warring sides certainly tarnished Sweden's image, leading to a crisis of conscience at home and international criticism.

On the other hand, Sweden was a haven for refugees from Finland, Norway, Denmark and the Baltic states; downed Allied air crew who escaped the Gestapo; and thousands of Jews who escaped persecution and death.

Blood on the Snow by Jan Bonderson explores the killing of Olof Palme with a reconstruction of the night of the murder, along with details of the peculiar police conduct and the various conspiracy theories – in addition to suggesting an alternative theory.

Beyond the Wars

After WWII and throughout the 1950s and '60s, the Social Democrats continued with the creation of *folkhemmet* (the welfare state). The idea of a socially conscious society with financial security for all began with the coalition of 1936 between the Social Democrats and the Farmers' Party and introduced unemployment benefits, child care, paid holidays and much more. The standard of living for ordinary Swedes rose rapidly, with poverty virtually eradicated.

Sweden began to take an active (peaceful) role in world affairs in the second half of the 20th century, offering asylum to those fleeing from political oppression worldwide. Prime Minister Olof Palme (1927–86) was deeply involved in questions of democracy, disarmament and third-world issues when he was assassinated on the streets of Stockholm in 1986.

In the last 30 years, Sweden has become an affluent country with a strong economy and one of the most comprehensive welfare systems in the world. This is in spite of the fact that it suffered greatly from economic recession and unemployment in the early '90s, and that its export-led economy continues to be vulnerable to global economic depression. Additionally, as cuts have had to be made to the welfare state over the last two decades, many Swedes feel that the problem is compounded by the country's immigration policies. They argue that the dramatic increase in population renders the existing welfare system unsustainable.

In 2003 Foreign Minister Anna Lindh (1957–2003) was fatally stabbed while shopping at the Nordiska Kompaniet department store in central Stockholm. Her mentally ill murderer, Mijailo Mijailovič, was caught using DNA evidence; the attack doesn't appear to have been politically motivated.

Sweden opted to join the EU in 1995 by a very narrow margin and, while nonaligned militarily, Sweden's troops continue to take part in numerous NATO peacekeeping missions.

Recently, Sweden has been embroiled in the extradition scandal involving WikiLeaks founder Julian Assange. Though wanted by the United States for making classified information public, Assange first and foremost lost an appeal against a court ruling in 2011 that would have him extradited to Sweden on sexual-assault charges. As the Swedish courts cannot guarantee that he would not then be given over to the Americans, Assange has since taken refuge in the Ecuadorian embassy in London.

1974

ABBA triumph in the Eurovision Song Contest in England, kick-starting a hugely successful pop career.

1995

Reluctantly, Sweden joins the European Union.

2001

Parliament votes 260 to 48 against abolition of the monarchy, even though the monarch ceased to have any political power in 1974.

2014

Umeå is named a European Capital of Culture, with the spotlight falling on northern Sweden and Sami art and culture.

Food & Drink

Sweden has come a long way from the days of all-beige fish-and-potato platters. Not only has immigration and membership in the EU introduced new flavours to the Swedish menu, a new wave of bold young chefs has been experimenting with traditional Swedish fare and melding it with various other influences. The result is an exciting dining scene on par with some of the best food cities in Europe.

Classic Cuisine

Traditional Swedish cuisine is based on simple, everyday ingredients known generally as *husmanskost* (basic home cooking). The most famous example of this, naturally, is Swedish meatballs. Other classic *husmanskost* dishes, largely based on fish and potatoes, include various forms of pickled and fried herring, cured salmon, and *pytt i panna* (potato hash served with sliced beets and a fried egg on top), which may be the ultimate comfort food. Open-face shrimp sandwiches are everywhere, piled high with varying degrees of art. And of course, the most thorough introduction to all the staples of Swedish cooking is the smörgåsbord, commonly available during the winter holidays.

One speciality food that not many visitors (and not all that many Swedes, either) take to immediately is *surströmming*. It's a canned, fermented Baltic herring opened and consumed ritually once a year, during late August and early September. It may be wrapped in *tunnbröd* (soft, thin, unleavened bread like a tortilla) with boiled potato, onions and other condiments, all washed down with ample amounts of *snaps* (a distilled alcoholic beverage, such as vodka or aquavit). *Surströmming* may be an acquired taste, but it has a legion of hardcore fans, mostly in northern Sweden. It even boasts its own festival in the village of Alfta. Cans of it make excellent souvenirs, as long as you wrap them well to avoid the truly nightmarish possibility of a leak into your suitcase. (And check with your airline first – flying with *surströmming* is not always allowed.)

The prevalence of preserved grub harks back to a time when Swedes had little choice but to store their spring and summer harvests for the long, icy winter. The landscape similarly influences menus in various parts of the country; you'll find regional specialities wherever you travel, from Västerbotten pie to saffron pancakes (both delicious!).

Wild game features strongly in Swedish cuisine, particularly in the northern part of the country. Traditional Sami cooking relies heavily on reindeer, whether cured, dried, roasted or preserved as sausage or jerky. Elk (moose) are also fairly common. Particularly in Sami cooking, game is often served with rich sauces that incorporate wild berries.

Other northern specialities include *ripa* (ptarmigan) and Arctic char, a cousin of salmon and trout. (The mild-flavoured char makes a seasonal appearance on menus all over Sweden in summer, and is absolutely worth a try, especially for the various inventive methods of preparing it. A chefs' favourite, the sturdy fish is a blank canvas that can handle all kinds of interesting treatments.)

MUST-TRY PLACES

➡ Mathias Dahlgren (p75) Does obscenely fine things to local produce at what has become Stockholm's new epicurean mecca.

➡ Grands Verandan (p74) Another Dahlgren creation, and the place to go for a traditional Swedish smörgåsbord.

➡ Ájtte Museum Restaurant (p278) Enhance what you learn about the local wildlife by sampling some of it, prepared in traditional Sami fashion.

➡ Salt & Brygga (p177) Stylish slow-food restaurant with all-organic Swedish cuisine in an allergy-free space with minimal environmental impact.

Speaking of berries, another uniquely Scandinavian taste is that of the *hjortron* (cloudberry). These grow in the marshes of Norrland and look a bit like pale raspberries, but their flavour is almost otherworldly, and Swedes consider them a delicacy. They're often served as a warm sauce over ice cream. If they strike your fancy, you'll find any number of places selling jars of cloudberry jam to take home. (There's also a sweet *hjortron* liqueur.)

Other traditional foods worth trying include *toast skagen* (toast with bleak roe, crème fraiche and chopped red onion), the classic *köttbullar och potatis* (meatballs and potatoes, usually served with lingonberry jam, known as *lingonsylt*), and *nässelsoppa* (nettle soup, traditionally served with hard-boiled eggs). Pea soup and pancakes are traditionally served on Thursday. Seafood staples include caviar, gravad or rimmad lax (cured salmon), and the ubiquitous *sill* (herring), eaten smoked, fried or pickled and often accompanied by Scandi trimmings like capers, mustard and onion. Tucking into a plate of fresh-fried Baltic herring with new potatoes and lingonberry sauce, at an outdoor table overlooking the sea, is a quintessential – and easily achieved – Swedish experience.

Swedes are devoted to their daily coffee ritual, *fika*, which inevitably also includes a pastry – often *kanelbullar* (cinnamon buns) or *kardemummabullar* (cardamom rolls). Almond paste (marzipan) is a common ingredient in pastries, such as the princess torte, a delicate cake with a lime-green marzipan shell commonly available at bakeries. Gourmet *konditori* (old-fashioned bakery-cafes) and cafes offer their own variations on all the standard cakes and cookies – best to sample several.

Contemporary Tendencies

Essentially, contemporary Swedish cuisine melds global influences with local produce and innovation: think baked wood pigeon with potato-and-apple hash or cauliflower 'cornet' with white chocolate and caviar. Locals have rediscovered the virtues of their own pantry. The result is an intense passion for seasonal, home-grown ingredients, whether apples from Kivik or bleak roe from Kalix. Equally important is the seasonality of food; expect succulent berries in spring, artichokes and crayfish in summer, and hearty truffles and root vegetables in the colder months.

Another growing obsession is a predilection for sustainable farming, small-scale producers and organic produce. Increasingly, restaurants and cafes pride themselves on serving organically grown and raised food, as well as actively supporting ethical, ecofriendly agricultural practices. Practically all the coffee served in big chain hotels is certified organic (labelled *krav* or *ekologisk*), for example, as is most of what you'll find alongside it on the breakfast buffet.

Not surprisingly, this newfound culinary savvy has affected the tourist trade. Gastro-themed itineraries and activities are on the rise, with everything from Gotland truffle hunts to west-coast lobster safaris, while numerous tourist boards stock culinary guides to their respective regions.

Festive Flavours

Around Christmas, many restaurants start offering a *julbord,* a particularly gluttonous version of Sweden's world-famous smörgåsbord buffet. Among the usual delicacies of herring, gravlax, meatballs, short ribs and *blodpudding* (blood pudding) are seasonal gems like baked ham with mustard sauce and *Janssons frestelse* (hearty casserole of sweet cream, potato, onion and anchovy). *Julmust* (sweet dark-brown soft drink that foams like a beer when poured) and *glögg* (warm spiced wine) are also Yuletide staples. The best accompaniment to a warm cup of *glögg,* available at kiosks everywhere in winter, is a *pepparkaka* (gingerbread biscuit) or a *lussekatt* (saffron bun).

During Sweden's short, intense summers, many people hit the countryside for lazy holidays and alfresco noshing. Summer lunch favourites include various *inlagd sill* (pickled herring) with *knäckebröd* (crispbread), strong cheese like the crumbly *Västerbottens ost,* boiled potatoes, diced chives and cream, strawberries, plus a finger or two of *snaps* and some light beer 'to help the fish swim down to the stomach'. Towards the end of summer, Swedes celebrate (or commiserate) its passing with *kräftskivor* (crayfish parties), eating *kräftor* boiled with dill, drinking *snaps* and singing *snapsvisor* (drinking songs).

For those with a sweet tooth, the lead-up to Lent means one thing: the *semla* bun. A wickedly decadent concoction of a wheat-flour bun crammed with whipped cream and almond paste, it was traditionally eaten on *fettisdagen* (Fat Tuesday). These days, it undermines diets as early as January.

Drinks

In the early days, when Stockholm was a rough port town full of stumbling sailors, alcohol taxes were levied according to where you happened to be when you fell down drunk or threw up. (These days, the same method can be used to decide which bars to frequent – or avoid.) Liquor laws and customs have changed a bit since those days, motivated not least by Sweden's need to conform more closely to EU standards. But there are still a few guidelines to navigate when pursuing adult beverages in Sweden.

Öl (beer) is ranked by alcohol content; the stronger the beer, the higher its price and, generally speaking, the more flavour it has. Light beers (*lättöl;* less than 2.25%) and 'folk' beers (*folköl;* 2.25% to 3.5%) account for about two-thirds of all beer sold in Sweden; these can be bought in supermarkets. Medium-strength beer (*mellanöl;* 3.5% to 4.5%) and strong beer (*starköl;* over 4.5%) can be bought only at outlets of the state-owned alcohol store, Systembolaget, or in bars and restaurants. 'Systemet', as it's often called, is also the only place (other than bars and restaurants) to buy hard liquor or wine.

Much like North American domestic brews, the everyday Swedish beer produced by mass breweries like Falcon, Åbro, Pripps and Spendrups is notable only for its complete lack of distinctive flavour. Happily, the range of good microbrews available has drastically improved in recent years. (Look for Jämtlands brewery's Fallen Angel bitter, anything from Nynäshamns Ångbryggeri or the Wisby line from Gotlands brewery.) Imports from the rest of Europe are also much easier to find than in pre-EU days. In bars and restaurants, domestic brews such as Spendrups, Pripps or Falcon cost anywhere from Skr50 to Skr70 a pint, and imported beer, wine or mixed drinks closer to Skr98 to Skr120. Ultra-sweet pear and apple ciders are also common, frequently in light-alcohol or alcohol-free versions.

Sweden's trademark spirit is *brännvin*, of which Absolut Vodka is the most recognisable example. A particularly Scandinavian subsection of *brännvin*, called aquavit and drunk as *snaps*, is a fiery and strongly flavoured drink that's usually distilled from potatoes and spiced with herbs. (A small shot of aquavit is sometimes called a *nubbe*, and it's often accompanied by *snapsvisor*.)

The legal drinking age in Sweden is 18 years; this applies to buying beer in grocery stores and any kind of alcohol in bars and restaurants. The minimum age to buy alcohol at a Systembolaget store is 20 years. Many bars and restaurants impose higher age limits for admission.

Of course, the beverage you're most likely to encounter in Sweden isn't even alcoholic. Coffee is the unofficial national drink, with an ever-increasing number of cafes ditching the percolated stuff for Italian-style espresso. The daily ritual of coffee and a pastry *(fika)* is an easy and rewarding one to adopt during your visit. (Tea is also readily available.) And *saft* is cordial commonly made from lingonberries, blueberries or elderflowers, though the word can refer to ordinary apple or orange juice as well.

Practical Info

Where to Eat

Hotels and hostels offer *frukost* (breakfast) buffets that typically include yoghurt and cereal, several types of bread, pastries, crispbread and/or rolls, with *pålägg* (toppings) including butter, sliced cheese, boiled eggs, sliced meat, liver pâté, Kalles caviar (an iconic caviar spread), pickled herring, sliced cucumber and marmalade. Several coffee chains (Wayne's Coffee, Espresso House) now dot the landscape, offering reliably decent cappuccinos and lattes along with breakfast pastries and more substantial fare.

A hearty lunch has long been a mainstay of the work force, with cafes and restaurants usually serving a weekday lunch special (or a choice of several) called *dagens rätt* at a fixed price (typically Skr85 to Skr125) between 11.30am and 2pm Monday to Friday. It's a practice originally supported and subsidised by the Swedish government with the goal of keeping workers happy and efficient, and it's still one of the most economical ways to sample top-quality Swedish cooking. The *dagens rätt* usually includes a main course, salad, beverage, bread and butter, and coffee.

For a lighter lunch, head to a *konditori* (small cafe), where staples include substantial pastries and the delectable *smörgås* (open sandwich), an artfully arranged creation usually topped with greens, shrimp or salmon, roe, boiled egg and mustard-dill sauce. Most cafes and coffee shops these days serve hearty, great-value salads that include grains or pasta with lettuce and veggies, plus various other exotic goodies in an enormous bowl (typically costing Skr85 to Skr100).

RESOURCES

- **Culinary Skåne** (http://matupplevelser.skane.org/en) is a network of restaurants and growers that produces a regional guide to produce, cuisine and epicurean events.
- **Swedish Institute** (www.sweden.se) provides a detailed discussion of Swedish food; follow the 'Lifestyle' tab.
- **Äkta Sylt** (www.aktasylt.se) is a website devoted to lingonberry jam, its preservation and marketing; in Swedish.
- *Vår Kokbok* is a classic Swedish cookbook from the '50s, akin to Betty Crocker's books in the US.

Etiquette

For the most part, table manners in Sweden are the same as those in the rest of Europe. On very formal occasions, wait for the host to welcome you to the table before beginning to eat or drink. Aside from a proper *skål,* don't clink glasses (it's considered vulgar), and refrain from sipping your wine outside of toasts until the host has declared that everyone may drink freely. Don some decent socks when dining in someone's home, as you'll generally be expected to take off your shoes in the foyer. (It's not uncommon to bring along a pair of house shoes to change into.) Swedes are typically quite punctual, so make an effort to arrive at the agreed-upon time rather than 'fashionably late'. And don't go empty-handed: a bottle of wine or flowers will make the right impression.

Cheap Eats

Street snacks are the cheapest, quickest way to fill up in Sweden, particularly in cities but also on beaches, along motorways and in campgrounds. A snack kiosk with a grill is known as a *gatukök* (literally, 'street kitchen'). In the world of Swedish street food, hot dogs reign supreme – the basic model is called a *grillad korv med bröd,* grilled sausage with bread (hot dog in a bun), although you can also ask for it boiled *(kokt).* Adventurous souls can request a mind-boggling variety of things done to the *korv,* chiefly involving rolling it up in flatbread with accompaniments from shrimp salad to mashed potatoes or coleslaw to fried onions. Kebab restaurants are another good bet for tasty, quick and cheap eats.

Opening Times

Restaurants generally open from 11am to 2pm for lunch, and from 5pm until 10pm for dinner. Cafes, bakeries and coffee shops are likely to be open all day, from around 8am until 6pm.

Tipping

Tipping is becoming a little more common in Sweden, though it isn't expected outside of fine-dining restaurants. A service cost is figured into the bill, but if you've had excellent service, a 10% to 15% tip is a suitable complement.

Self-Catering

Easily found in Swedish towns and villages, the main supermarket chains are ICA, Konsum and Hemköp. Plastic carrier bags usually cost Skr2 to Skr5 at the cashier.

Supermarkets across Sweden have prepared foods for quick snacks, but making your own meals is easy enough if you're hostelling or camping. Produce in standard supermarkets is often uninspiring, but fresh, seasonal fruit and vegetables are readily available at market squares such as Hötorget in Stockholm as well as at rural farm shops and roadside stands.

Vegetarians & Vegans

Vegetarian and vegan restaurants are common; excellent veggie buffets are easy to find in major cities, and even in rural areas restaurants generally have a herbivorous main-course option.

People & Culture

As is true of most places, Sweden's pop culture reflects its people's collective psyche – in this case, with an enthusiastic embrace of both the grim and the frivolous. Swedish humour is a quirky thing indeed; it can be easily overlooked by the untrained eye, or even misperceived as grumpiness. Swedish literature and cinema tend to favour a weighty, Gothic sense of drama blended with gallows humour and stark aesthetics – in other words, the opposite of its best-known pop music.

The National Psyche

Blonde, blue-eyed, cold and reserved: while these four elements may make up the prevailing stereotype of Swedes, the reality is, perhaps unsurprisingly, much more complex and contradictory. Dark hair, impish stature and random acts of friendliness are not as uncommon as you may think, while a widespread passion for travel and trends can make for curious locals and enlightening conversations.

Two vital concepts in the typical Swedish mindset are *lagom* and *ordning och reda*. *Lagom* means 'just right' – not too little, not too much. A good example is *mellanöl* (medium ale) – it's not strong, but it's not as weak as a light ale. An exception to *lagom* is the smörgåsbord.

Ordning och reda connotes tidiness and order: everything in its proper place in the world. A good example is the queuing system; almost every transaction in Sweden requires participants to take a number and stand in line, which everyone does with the utmost patience. An exception to *ordning och reda* is Stockholm traffic.

Lifestyle

Swedes are a friendly sort. *Var så god* is a common phrase and carries all sorts of expressions of goodwill: 'Welcome', 'Please', 'Pleased to meet you', 'I'm happy to serve you', 'Thanks' and 'You're welcome'. And Swedes are so generous with their use of 'thank you' (*tack*) that language texts make jokes about it.

It wasn't until the 1930s that urban Swedes surpassed the number of rural Swedes, and even the most seasoned urbanites commonly retain a strong affinity with nature. The rural *sommarstuga* (summer cottage) is almost de rigueur, at least as an aspiration; there are around 600,000 second homes in Sweden, but no Swede doesn't want a little wooden cottage in the country or on an island in the archipelago. As it is, Sweden boasts the highest number of holiday cottages per capita in the world, and most of the people you'll run across in campgrounds on summer holidays are Swedes themselves, enjoying the natural wonders of their own country.

Another common sight that surprises and delights many visitors to Sweden is the large number of men pushing baby strollers. Gender equality has advanced further in Sweden than in most countries. The government has a Minister for Integration and Gender Equality, as well as the Office of the Equal Opportunities Ombudsman, the latter ensuring that all employers and institutions of learning actively promote gender equality and prevent sexual discrimination. Women make up nearly half of parliament members in the Riksdag and enjoy enviable childcare services, and both parents are assured of plenty of childcare leave from employers.

The new TV sitcom *Welcome to Sweden* offers a goofball take on the many eccentricities of Swedish culture from an outsider's point of view; created by Greg Poehler, the series follows the various misadventures of an American who quits his job in New York and moves to Sweden to be with his Swedish fiancee and her family.

Swedish Cinema

Sweden led the way in the silent-film era of the 1920s, with such masterpieces as *Körkarlen* (The Phantom Carriage), adapted from a novel by Selma Lagerlöf and directed by Mauritz Stiller. In 1967 came Vilgot Sjöman's notorious *I Am Curious (Yellow)*, a subtly hilarious socio-political film that got more attention outside Sweden for its X rating than for its sharp commentary (and its in-jokes about the king, which foreign audiences, unsurprisingly, failed to get).

With a few exceptions, though, one man has largely defined modern Swedish cinema to the outside world: Ingmar Bergman. With deeply contemplative films such as *The Seventh Seal, Through a Glass Darkly* and *Persona*, the beret-topped director explored human alienation, the absence of god, the meaning of life, the certainty of death and other light-hearted themes. Love him or don't, it's basically impossible to discuss or think about Swedish cinema without considering Bergman and his influence.

More recently, the Swedish towns of Trollhättan and Ystad have become film-making centres, the former drawing the likes of wunderkind director Lukas Moodysson, whose *Lilya 4-Ever*, *Show Me Love* and *Tillsammans* have all been both popular and critical hits. Moodysson went through a dark phase for a few years but has found himself back on the international-cinema radar with his newest film, 2014's *We Are the Best!*, a thrilling and heartwarming movie about three high-school girls in 1980s Stockholm who form a punk band out of spite. It's based on a semi-autobiographical graphic novel by Moodysson's wife, Coco, called *Aldrig Godnatt* ('Never Goodnight'), and it's an excellent portrait of the texture of urban Swedish life in this period.

Lebanese-born Josef Fares *(Jalla! Jalla!, Kopps, Zozo, Leo)* is part of a new guard of second-generation immigrant directors. Alongside

FEEL-BAD SWEDISH FILMS

The Swedish film industry is active and varied, but most people associate it with the godfather of gloom, Ingmar Bergman. Many filmmakers have followed in his grim footsteps:

- *Songs from the Second Floor* (Roy Andersson; 2000) A post-apocalyptic urban nightmare in surreal slow motion; it's not for everyone.
- *Lilya 4-Ever* (Lukas Moodysson; 2002) A grim tale of human trafficking.
- *Ondskan* (Evil; Mikael Håfström; 2003) Violence at a boys' boarding school.
- *Zozo* (Josef Fares; 2005) A Lebanese orphan makes his way to Sweden alone, then has culture shock.
- *Darling* (Johan Kling; 2007) Harsh economic realities bring together a shallow, privileged party girl and a sweet old man in an unlikely friendship.
- *Let the Right One In* (Tomas Alfredson; 2008) An excellent, stylish, restrained take on the horror-film genre that gets at what it's like to be a lonely preteen in a cold, hostile world.

Iranian-born directors Reza Bagher *(Wings of Glass)* and Reza Parsa *(Before the Storm)*, Fares has turned a spotlight on the immigrant experience in Sweden. His uncharacteristically dark 2007 feature, *Leo*, also marked Fares' on-screen debut.

Another Swedish award-winner is director Roy Andersson, once dubbed a 'slapstick Ingmar Bergman'. His film *Du levande* (*You, the Living*) scooped up three prizes (including best picture) at Sweden's prestigious Guldbagge Awards in 2008.

That year also saw the well-deserved success of Tomas Alfredson's odd, quietly unsettling teenage-vampire story, *Let the Right One In*, based on a best-selling Swedish novel. Its American remake was also well received.

But of course the big news in contemporary Swedish cinema recently has been the film version of Stieg Larsson's runaway hit series of crime novels, starting with *The Girl with the Dragon Tattoo* (2009). Starring Michael Nyqvist and Noomi Rapace, the Swedish trilogy was a huge commercial success, and the first installment has been remade in English by director David Fincher, with Daniel Craig as journalist Mikael Blomkvist, mostly on location in Sweden.

Swedish Literature

Historically, the best known of Sweden's artistic greats have been writers, chiefly the poet Carl Michael Bellman (1740–95), influential dramatist and author August Strindberg (1849–1912) and children's writer Astrid Lindgren (1907–2002).

During WWII some Swedish writers took a stand against the Nazis, including Eyvind Johnson (1900–76) with his *Krilon* trilogy, completed in 1943, and poet and novelist Karin Boye (1900–41), whose novel *Kallocain* was published in 1940. Vilhelm Moberg (1898–1973), a representative of 20th-century proletarian literature and a controversial social critic, won international acclaim with *Utvandrarna* (The Emigrants; 1949) and *Nybyggarna* (The Settlers; 1956).

Contemporary literary stars include playwright and novelist Per Olov Enquist (1934–), who achieved international acclaim with his novel *Livläkarens besök* (The Visit of the Royal Physician; 2003), in which King Christian VII's physician conspires with the queen to seize power.

Readers interested in deepest Norrland, with its strange and uniquely remote vibe, should investigate the work of Swedish Academy member Torgny Lindgren, particularly his novel *Pölsan* (Hash; 2004), or the short stories in *Merab's Beauty* (1989).

Mikael Niemi's (1959–) novel *Populärmusik från Vittula* (Popular Music; 2003), a coming-of-age story of a wannabe rock star in Sweden's remote north, became an international cult hit, as well as a 2004 film directed by Iranian-born Swedish director Reza Bagher.

Nonfiction author Sven Lindqvist (1932–) is recognised for his hard-hitting, sometimes controversial titles. His most famous offering is arguably *Utrota varenda jävel* (Exterminate All the Brutes; 1992), exploring the Holocaust-like devastation European colonists wrought on Africa. More recently, his book *Terra Nullius* (2005, translated into English in 2007) is a powerful, moving history of colonial Australia and the attempted destruction of Aboriginal culture.

The unlikely publishing phenom of 2013 in Sweden was *A Man Called Ove*, a novel about a grumpy old man in a Swedish suburb who struggles (comically) to deal with the changes modernity has brought to his country and, more importantly, to his parking area; the book was a surprise hit domestically for journalist and blogger Fredrik Backman and has been widely translated into other languages. It's a light read but offers an insightful view of life in a modern Swedish apartment community.

Crime Fiction

The massive success of the Millennium Trilogy, by the late journalist Stieg Larsson (he was the second-best-selling author in the world for 2008), has brought new and well-deserved attention to Swedish crime fiction, which was already a thriving genre domestically. *The Girl with the Dragon Tattoo* (2005) – originally entitled *Män som hatar kvinnor* (Men Who Hate Women) – is the tip of the iceberg when it comes to this genre; Swedish crime writers have a long and robust history.

A few names to start with include Håkan Nesser, whose early novels *The Mind's Eye* (1993) and *Woman with Birthmark* (1996) have at last been translated into English; and Sweden's best-known crime-fiction writer, Henning Mankell, whose novels are mostly set in Ystad and feature moody detective Kurt Wallander. Johan Theorin's quartet of mysteries (starting with *Echoes from the Dead*, 2008) is set on the island of Öland. Other writers to seek out include Karin Alvtegen (dubbed Sweden's 'queen of crime'), Kerstin Ekman, Camilla Läckberg and Jens Lapidus.

Jazz is huge among Swedes; for a primer, look for records by Lars Gullin, Bernt Rosengren and Jan Johansson.

Must-Reads

One of the best ways to get inside the collective mind of a country is to read its top authors. Some popular works by Swedish authors include *The Long Ships* (1954) by Frans Gunnar Bengtsson, *The Wonderful Adventures of Nils* (1906–07) by Selma Lagerlöf, *The Emigrants* series (1949–59) by Vilhelm Moberg, *Marking* (1963–64) by Dag Hammarskjöld, *Röda Rummet* (1879) by August Strindberg and *The Evil* (1981) by Jan Guillou.

Swedish Music

Any survey of Swedish pop music should probably start with ABBA, the iconic, extravagantly outfitted winner of the 1974 Eurovision Song Contest (with 'Waterloo'). You can immerse yourself in ABBA completely at the Stockholm museum (p53) dedicated to the group and its history; one wing of the ABBA museum houses the Swedish Music Hall of Fame, which offers an efficient primer on the history of Swedish popular music.

More current Swedish successes are pop icon Robyn, indie melody-makers Peter Björn & John, and the exquisitely mellow José González, whose cover of the Knife's track 'Heartbeats' catapulted the Göteborg native to international stardom.

Other artists of note include the Field, aka Alex Wilner, and Kristian Matsson, the singer-songwriter who goes by the Tallest Man on Earth, as well as home-grown stalwarts such as the massively popular Kent, the Hives, the Shout Out Louds and Håkan Hellström, who is much lauded for his original renditions of classic Swedish melodies.

Swedish songwriters and producers are sought-after commodities: Denniz Pop and Max Martin have penned hits for pop divas such as Britney Spears and Jennifer Lopez, while Anders Bagge and Bloodshy & Avant (aka Christian Karlsson and Pontus Winnberg) co-created Madonna's 2005 album *Confessions on a Dance Floor*.

ABBA is the fourth-best-selling musical act in history, after Elvis, the Beatles and Michael Jackson – the group has sold over 380 million records worldwide.

Multiculturalism

Over the past couple of decades, immigration has noticeably altered the makeup of the Swedish people. Around 15% of Swedes today are foreign-born, and that number is on the rise as immigration continues to expand. Swedish musician José González, celebrity chef Marcus Samuelsson and film director Josef Fares are testament to Sweden's increasingly multicultural composition. Some 200 languages are now spoken in the country, as well as variations on the standard – the hip-hop crowd, for example, speaks a mishmash of slang, Swedish and foreign phrases that's been dubbed 'Rinkeby Swedish' after an immigrant-heavy Stockholm suburb.

As hip-hop artist Timbuktu (himself the Swedish-born son of a mixed-race American couple) once told the *Washington Post*, 'Sweden still has a very clear picture of what a Swede is. That no longer exists – the blond, blue-eyed physical traits. That's changing. But it still exists in the minds of some people'.

Religion

Christianity arrived fairly late in Sweden and was preceded by a long-standing loyalty to Norse gods such as Odin, Thor and their warlike ilk. Some of the outer reaches of Sweden, particularly in the far north, were among the last areas to convert to Christianity in Europe.

According to the country's constitution, Swedish people have the right to practise any religion they choose. Complete separation of church and state took effect in 2000; prior to that, Evangelical Lutheranism was the official religion. There are also about 100,000 members of Christian Orthodox churches, 20,000 Jews and an estimated 100,000 Muslims in Sweden.

Only about 10% of Swedes regularly attend church services, but church marriages, funerals and communions are still popular.

Sport

Football

Football is the most popular sporting activity in Sweden. There are over 3000 clubs with about a million members. The domestic season runs from April to early November. The national arena, Råsunda Stadium in Solna, a suburb in Stockholm's northwest, can hold up to 37,000 roaring spectators.

Two of Sweden's best-known Swedish football players are Gunnar Nordahl (1921–95), who helped Sweden win gold at the 1948 Olympics and went on to be the all-time top scorer at AC Milan, and Malmö-born Zlatan Ibrahimović (1981–).

Ice Hockey

There are amateur ice-hockey teams in most Swedish communities. The national premier league, Elitserien, has 12 professional teams; there are also several lower divisions. Matches take place from autumn to late spring, up to four times a week in Stockholm, primarily at Globen arena.

Skiing

Alpine skiing competitions are held annually, particularly in Åre. Vasaloppet, the world's biggest nordic (cross-country) skiing race, takes place on the first Sunday in March.

Swedish skiing stars include four-time Olympic gold-medal winner Gunde Svan and giant-slalom icon Ingemar Stenmark, who won a total of 86 races in the Alpine Ski World Cup.

Other Sports

Swedish men have excelled at tennis; superstars include Björn Borg, Mats Wilander and Stefan Edberg. Borg won the Wimbledon Championships in England five times in a row.

Golf is hugely popular, with more than 400 courses throughout the country. Sweden's Annika Sörenstam is ranked as one of the game's leading players.

Bandy, a team sport similar to ice hockey, is played on an outdoor pitch the size of a football field; watching a match is a popular winter social activity in many Swedish cities. (In Stockholm, they're held at Zinkensdamms Idrottsplats.)

Sailing is very popular, around Stockholm in particular, where yacht ownership is extremely common, as well as in smaller villages along both coastlines.

Environment

Sweden is often listed among the world's most eco-friendly, sustainable countries. Its scenic beauty and natural resources are a major part of what make the place such a rewarding destination, and Swedes tend to cherish what they have. Getting outdoors is a popular activity here and, relatedly, 'green' practices such as recycling and conservation are the norm. Even in large cities, Swedes display a deep connection to and reverence for the natural world.

The Land

Geography

Physically, Sweden is long and thin – about the size of California, with a surface area of around 450,000 sq km. It's mostly forest (nearly 60% of the landscape) and is dotted with about 100,000 inland lakes. This includes Vänern, Western Europe's largest lake, at 5585 sq km. There's also 7000km of coastline, plus scads of islands – the Stockholm archipelago alone has around 24,000 of them. The largest and most notable islands are Gotland and Öland on the southeast coast.

Sweden is a long, drawn-out 1574km from north to south, but averages only about 300km in width.

From its position on the eastern side of the Scandinavian peninsula, Sweden borders Norway, Finland and Denmark – the latter a mere 4km to the southwest of Sweden and joined to it by a spectacular bridge and tunnel. The mountains along the border with Norway are graced with alpine and Arctic flowers, including mountain avens (with large, white, eight-petalled flowers), long-stalked mountain sorrel (an unusual source of vitamin C), glacier crowfoot, alpine aster and various saxifrages. Orchids grow on Öland and Gotland. Up north are forests of Scots pine, Norway spruce and firs; the southern part of the country is now mostly farmland.

Geology

Between 500 and 370 million years ago, the European and North American continental plates collided, throwing up an impressive range of peaks called the Caledonian Mountains, which were as tall as today's

HOW'S THE WEATHER?

Sweden has a mostly cool, temperate climate, but the southern quarter of the country is warmer than the rest. The average maximum temperature for July is 18°C in the south and around 14°C in the north. Long hot periods in summer aren't unusual, with temperatures soaring to over 30°C. The west coast is warmer than the east, thanks to the warming waters of the Gulf Stream.

The harsh Lappland winter starts in October and ends in April, and temperatures can plummet as low as -50°C. Snow can accumulate to depths of several metres in the north, making for superb skiing, but snow depths in the south average only 20cm to 40cm. It usually rains in winter in the far south (Skåne).

Norway's mountain ranges act as a rain break, so yearly rainfall is moderate. Swedish summers are generally sunny, with only occasional rainfall, but August can be wet.

Himalayas. Their worn-down stubs form the 800km-long Kjölen Mountains along the Norwegian border – among which is Kebnekaise (2106m), Sweden's highest mountain.

Parts of Skåne and the islands of Öland and Gotland consist of flat limestone and sandstone deposits, probably laid down in a shallow sea east of the Caledonian Mountains during the same period.

Lake Siljan, in the central south, marks the site of Europe's largest meteoric impact: the 3km-wide fireball hurtled into Sweden 360 million years ago, obliterating all life and creating a 75km ring-shaped crater.

The lemming is the smallest but most important mammal in the Arctic regions – its numbers set the population limits for everything that preys on it.

Wildlife

Thanks to Sweden's geographical diversity, it has a great variety of European animals, birds and plants. And its relatively sparse population means you're likely to see some in the wild.

Sweden's big carnivores – the bear, wolf, wolverine, lynx and golden eagle – are all protected species. Wolf hunting was banned in the 1970s, after the wolf population had been hunted nearly to extinction, but in 2010 the Swedish parliament authorised a cull to bring the newly resurgent species' numbers back down. Most of the country's wolf population is in Dalarna and Värmland.

The Swedish Environmental Protection Agency (p314) has detailed information on Sweden's policies regarding endangered animals.

The wolverine, a larger cousin of the weasel, inhabits high forests and alpine areas along the Norwegian border. There are an estimated 680 in Sweden, mostly in Norrbotten and Västerbotten.

Brown bears were persecuted for centuries, but recent conservation measures have seen numbers increase to about 3200. Bears mostly live in forests in the northern half of the country but are spreading south.

The fearsome-looking brown bear's favourite food is... blueberries!

Another fascinating forest dweller is the lynx, which belongs to the panther family and is Europe's only large cat. Sweden's 1200 to 1500 lynx are notoriously difficult to spot because of their nocturnal habits.

Not all of Sweden's wild creatures are predatory, of course. The iconic elk (moose in the USA) is a gentle, knobby-kneed creature that grows up to 2m tall. Though they won't try to eat you, elk are a serious traffic hazard, particularly at night: they can dart out in front of your car at up to 50km/h.

Around 260,000 domesticated reindeer roam the northern areas under the watchful eyes of Sami herders. Like elk, reindeer can be a major traffic hazard.

Lemmings are famous for their extraordinary reproductive capacity. Every 10 years or so the population explodes, resulting in denuded landscapes and thousands of dead lemmings in rivers and lakes and on roads.

Bird Life

Sweden is home to all kinds of bird life. Some of the best birdwatching sites are on Öland, including the nature reserve at its southernmost tip, as well as Getterön Nature Reserve, Tåkern Nature Reserve, Hornborgasjön, between Skara and Falköping in Västergötland, and the national parks Färnebofjärden, Muddus and Abisko.

Swedish elk are slightly smaller than their closely related American counterparts, called moose.

The golden eagle is one of Sweden's most endangered species. Found in the mountains, it's easily identified by its immense wingspan.

Coastal species include common, little and Arctic terns, various gulls, oystercatchers, cormorants, guillemots and razorbills. Territorial Arctic skuas can be seen in a few places, notably the Stockholm archipelago and the coast north of Göteborg.

Look for goldcrests in coniferous forests. A few spectacular waxwings breed in Lappland, but in winter they arrive from Russia in large numbers and are found throughout Sweden. Grouse or capercaillie strut the forest floor, while ptarmigan and snow buntings hang out above the treeline along the Norwegian border.

Sweden has a wide range of wading and water birds, including the unusual and beautiful red-necked phalaropes, which only breed in the northern mountains. Other waders you're likely to encounter are majestic grey herons (southern Sweden), noisy bitterns (south-central Sweden), plovers (including dotterel, in the mountains) and turnstones.

For more details about birdwatching, contact **Sveriges Ornitologiska Förening** (Swedish Ornithological Society; ☎08-612 25 30; www.sofnet.org).

A great resource for twitchers is *Where to Watch Birds in Scandinavia* by Johan Stenlund.

Sea Life

Sprats and herring are economically important food sources. Among other marine species, haddock, sea trout, whiting, flounder and plaice are reasonably abundant, particularly in the salty waters of the Kattegatt and Skagerrak, but the cod is heading for extinction due to overfishing.

Indigenous crayfish were once netted or trapped in Sweden's lakes, but overfishing and disease have driven them to extinction.

Grey and common seals swim in Swedish waters, although overfishing has caused a serious decline in numbers. Common dolphins may also be observed from time to time.

The North and, particularly, the Baltic Seas are suffering severe pollution, and vast alga blooms, caused partly by nitrogen run-off from Swedish farms. As a result, herring, sprats and Baltic salmon contain higher than average levels of cancer-causing dioxins; the Swedish National Food Agency has recommended that children and women of child-bearing age eat Baltic fish no more than two or three times a year.

Overfishing of these waters is also a huge cause for concern, with cod and Norwegian lobster on the verge of extinction. Fishing quotas are determined by the EU as a whole, and there's been a constant struggle to achieve balance between sustainable fish stocks and consumer demand.

You can swim – and fish for trout and salmon – in the waters by Stockholm's city centre.

National Parks

Sweden was the first country in Europe to set up a national park (1909). There are now 29, along with around 2600 smaller nature reserves; together they cover about 9% of Sweden. The organisation Naturvårdsverket oversees and produces pamphlets about the parks in Swedish and English, along with the excellent book *Nationalparkerna i Sverige* (National Parks in Sweden).

Four of Sweden's large rivers (Kalixälven, Piteälven, Vindelälven and Torneälven) have been declared National Heritage Rivers in order to protect them from hydroelectric development.

The right of public access to the countryside *(allemansrätten)* includes national parks and nature reserves.

Four of the national parks in Lappland – Muddus, Padjelanta, Sarek and Stora Sjöfallet – are Unesco World Heritage Sites.

Northern Sweden

- **Abisko** Northern gateway to the Kungsleden hiking track.
- **Haparanda Skärgård** Beaches, dunes and migrant bird life.
- **Muddus** Ancient forests and muskeg bogs, superb birdwatching.
- **Padjelanta** High moorland; great hiking.
- **Pieljekaise** Moorlands, birch forests, flowering meadows and lakes.
- **Sarek** Wild mountain ranges, glaciers, deep valleys; expert hiking.
- **Stora Sjöfallet** Famous waterfall; hydroelectric development.
- **Vadvetjåkka** Large river delta containing bogs, lakes, limestone caves.

Central Sweden

- **Ängsö** Tiny island; meadows, deciduous forest, bird life, spring flowers.
- **Björnlandet** Natural forest, cliffs and boulder fields.
- **Färnebofjärden** Bird life, forests, rare lichens and mosses.
- **Fulufjället** Contains Njupeskär, the country's highest waterfall at 93m.
- **Garphyttan** An 111-hectare park; fantastic springtime flowers.
- **Hamra** Only 800m by 400m; virgin coniferous forest.
- **Kosterhavet** The sea and shores surrounding the Koster Islands.
- **Sånfjället** Natural mountain moorland with extensive views.
- **Skuleskogen** Hilly coastal area, good hiking.
- **Tresticklan** Natural coniferous forest, fine bird life.
- **Tyresta** Stockholm's own national park.
- **Töfsingdalen** Wild and remote; boulder fields, pine forest.

Southern Sweden

- **Blå Jungfrun** Island with granite slabs, caves, labyrinth.
- **Dalby Söderskog** Forest, wildlife.
- **Djurö** Bird life and deer on an archipelago.
- **Gotska Sandön** Sandy isle featuring dunes, dying pine forest.
- **Norra Kvill** An 114-hectare park; ancient coniferous forest.
- **Söderåsen** Deep fissure valleys, lush forests; hiking and cycling.
- **Stenshuvud** Coastal park; beaches, forest, moorland.
- **Store Mosse** Bogs with sand dunes, bird life.
- **Tiveden** Hills, forests, lakes, boulder fields, beaches.

Environmental Issues

Ecological consciousness in Sweden is very high and reflected in concern for native animals, clean water and renewable resources. Swedes are fervent believers in recycling household waste. Most plastic bottles and cans can be recycled – supermarket disposal machines give Skr0.50 to Skr2 per item.

True North: The Grand Landscapes of Sweden, by Per Wästberg and Tommy Hammarström, contains stunning images by some of Sweden's top nature photographers.

Two organisations that set standards for labelling products as ecologically sound are the food-focused **KRAV** (www.krav.se), a member of the International Federation of Organic Agriculture Movements, and **Swan** (www.svanen.se), which has a wider scope and certifies entire hotels and hostels.

Linked to environmental concerns is the challenge of protecting the cultural heritage of the Sami people. The harnessing of rivers for hydroelectric power can have massive (negative) impact on what has historically been Sami territory, whether by flooding reindeer feeding grounds or by diverting water and drying up river valleys. In general, the mining, forestry and space industries have wreaked havoc on Sami homelands.

Environmental Organisations

Naturvårdsverket (www.swedishepa.se) Useful website of the Swedish Environmental Protection Agency.

Svenska Ekoturismföreningen (www.ekoturism.org) Promotes environmentally friendly tourism.

Svenska Naturskyddsföreningen (Swedish Society for Nature Conservation; ☎08-702 65 00; www.naturskyddsforeningen.se) Excellent website on current environmental issues.

Design & Architecture

Stuart Harrison

While it can be hard to separate modern Swedish design from the success of general Scandinavian design, it is the predominantly Swedish embrace of modernity and craft that has fostered admiration around the world for decades.

History

Along with a scattering of Romanesque and Gothic imports from mainland Europe, Sweden's architecture has a classical sensibility, as seen in the grand streets of Stockholm. The Renaissance was embraced at the peak of Sweden's power in the 16th and 17th centuries, and set up the nation's core historic architecture.

Magnificently ornate baroque architecture arrived (mainly from Italy) during the 1640s, while Queen Kristina held the throne. This is perhaps best seen in the buildings at Kalmar, a historical centre of power and where the first union of Denmark, Norway and Sweden was formed in 1397. Kalmar's Domkyrkan (Cathedral), designed in 1660, the adjacent Kalmar Rådhus (Town Hall) and Drottningholms Slott (1662) were all designed by the court architect Nicodemus Tessin the Elder. Tessin the Younger designed the vast 'new' Kungliga Slottet (Royal Palace) in Stockholm after the original palace was gutted by fire in 1697.

Pre-Renaissance examples include the Romanesque Domkyrkan in Lund, consecrated in 1145 and still dominating the city centre with its two imposing square towers. Fine Gothic churches can be seen at the Mariakyrkan in Sigtuna (completed in 1237) and Uppsala's Domkyrkan, consecrated in 1435. The island of Gotland, however, is your best bet in Sweden for ecclesiastical Gothic architecture, with around 100 medieval churches scattered across the ancient landscape.

Stuart Harrison hosts 'The Architects' radio show on Melbourne's RRR, interviewing and talking about design and architecture from around the world. He also designed and built a suite at the Icehotel with artist Lucas Ihlein in 2005.

FROZEN ART & DESIGN

The Icehotel, in the small village of Jukkasjärvi just outside of Kiruna, not only started the global trend of ice hotels and bars but also has become a focus for collaboration between artists and designers from Sweden and around the world. The Icehotel now boasts an open submission process for creatives to come to Sweden to design and build a suite in the ephemeral hotel, which opens typically in late December and then melts entirely by the following April.

The hotel is made from both snow and ice, the superstructure built in a manner similar to rammed earth, with snow blown and compacted onto Gothic archlike steel forms that produce simple vaulted spaces. Artists then create suite interiors using a combination of malleable snow with ice, which is far more like stone in the way it is treated – a heavy material cut into smaller usable blocks using chainsaws and then chiselled and crafted into shape.

A wide range of artists come to the Icehotel. Regulars include fourth-generation stonemason Mats Nilson and younger designer Jens Thoms Ivarsson. Theirs is a very Swedish practice, drawing on crafted tradition and also embracing contemporary design.

Modernity was, as elsewhere, born in the 19th century out of urban and social upheaval, the move to cities and industrialisation. From the harsh conditions of expanding Stockholm and Göteborg (Gothenburg) a social state emerged, the basis for modern Sweden.

The movements were sequential but overlapping. The transitional National Romanticism was an often decorative classical free-style with Arts and Crafts influences. Known locally as Jugendstil, it has strong similarities to the more continental art nouveau. Following this period, abstracted and more international modernism took hold, and Stockholm's 1930 exhibition introduced modern design and the Swedish architects of the 20th century.

Contemporary design and architecture generally follow global trends, but the characteristically Swedish interests of nature and craft are evident when cruising through blogs such as the snappy emmas designblogg (www.emmas.blogg.se).

Key Architects

The transition to modernity through the early 20th century can be seen particularly in the world of Erik Gunnar Asplund (1885–1940), Sweden's most important architect. The best of Asplund's work is in the capital, such as Stockholm's Stadsbiblioteket (City Library; 1932) with its plutonic forms wrestling classical and modernist tendencies. A little further out of the centre at the graceful Skogskyrkogården (Woodland Cemetery) you'll find perhaps the greatest collection of work from the Swedish master; many of the pavilions are collaborations with the less prolific Sigurd Lewerentz (1885–1975).

Asplund was typical of the Swedish approach. He travelled widely as a young designer, returning to his homeland to make an architecture both of its time and true to Swedish tradition. His work contrasted with the more aggressive radical modernism of France and Germany, and set the tone for Finnish master Alvar Aalto.

Asplund and Lewerentz were profoundly influential on English-born architect Ralph Erskine (1914–2005), who formed a practice in Sweden in 1939. The adopted son of Swedish architecture embodied social ideas into a layered form of modernism, typical of the Nordic outlook. His Ort-

FLATPACK FURNITURE TAKES OVER THE WORLD

Ingvar Kamprad was 17 years old when he created Ikea in the city of Älmhult, in the craft-focused province of Småland – and he has gone on to become one of the world's richest men.

The Ikea name (a combination of Kamprad's initials and those of the farm and village where he grew up) was officially registered in 1943. Initially selling pens, watches and nylon stockings, the company added furniture to its products four years later, gradually evolving into the Ikea-designed flatpack creations so familiar today.

There was almost an early end to the Ikea empire when the first Stockholm shop and all its stock burned down in 1970. But, besides his devotion to work and obsession with cost cutting, Kamprad also seems to have thrived on adversity – Ikea bounced back.

Seeking to bring simple, good design to the whole world, in an affordable way, Ikea has had enormous influence. Cheap and innovative products were born out of Swedish modern design – the idea of the house as the starting point of good design, rather than the end.

The clean-cut company was rocked in 1994 by revelations that Kamprad once had links with a pro-Nazi party in Sweden (he later offered a public apology and expressed much regret for this time of his life).

The famously frugal Kamprad has now taken a back seat in terms of running the company, but ownership is still within the family. Control over the empire is now divvied up among Kamprad's three children and divided into a series of complex charity and trust entities. Today Ikea has stores in 40 countries; branches first opened in Australia in 1975, Saudi Arabia in 1983, the US in 1985, Britain in 1987, China in 1998 and Russia in 2000.

drivaren housing project in the northern iron ore-mining city of Kiruna dates from the early 1960s and has held up incredibly well.

Kiruna faces an uncertain future as land subsidence from the mine has prompted the need to move the town, with all buildings to be demolished except possibly the imposing Stadshus (Athur von Schmalensee; 1963) and the well-liked Kiruna kyrka (Gustaf Wickman; 1912), an early example of an attempted fusion between local Sami forms and the Gothic tradition, built in timber.

Standout architectural firms include the established Wingårdh, but emerging practices such as Elding Oscarson show a restrained international influence. Lund & Valentin in Göteborg (Gothenburg) have, since 1952, been a good index of architectural tastes, as seen in their postmodern GöteborgsOperan (1994).

Design Hubs

One hot spot of design and innovation in recent times has been the post-industrial city of Malmö. The old docks northwest of Gamla Staden (Old Town) were converted into ecologically focused housing for the new century. Its landmark Turning Torso (2005) – a twisting residential tower designed by Catalan architect Santiago Calatrava – is an arresting sight dominating the skyline.

Close by is the Öresund bridge (Georg KS Rotne; 2000) connecting the two metropolitan areas of Malmö and Copenhagen, effectively joining them in one trans-country city. Malmö has become a commuter base for Danish residents in Copenhagen as result of this remarkable piece of infrastructure – after it reaches the end of the bridge section the road and rail lines literally disappear into the water, to become a tunnel until it emerges next to Copenhagen airport. It's quite a sight from the air, especially when seen next to Copenhagen's magnificent series of aero-generators that line its side of the Öresund strait.

Within Stockholm, contemporary design and culture found a robust home in 1974 in the excellent Kulturhuset, a large modernist pavilion holding a wide range of cultural activities. Designed by Peter Celsing, it's like a big set of drawers offering their wares onto the large plaza outside, Sergels Torg; the *torg* (town square) is the modern heart of Stockholm, and standing at its centre is Kristallvertikalaccent (Crystal Vertical Accent), a wonderful, luminescent monument to modernity and glassmaking traditions. Designed by sculptor Edvin Öhrström, it was the result of a 1962 competition. Sergels Torg itself has a distinctive triangular ground pattern, a modern backdrop for protests and markets, with the T-Centralen metro station underneath.

Key Turn-of-the-Century Buildings in Stockholm

Fredrik Lilljekvist's Royal Dramatic Theatre (1908)

Ferdinand Boberg's Rosenbad (1902)

Ragnar Östberg's Stockholm City Hall (1911)

Craft

The Swedish tradition of craft can be seen in all forms of design: architecture, textiles, fashion, stonemasonry, carpentry and particularly glass. In the southern province of Småland you'll find many of Sweden's craft traditions, and glassmaking has been here for well over 100 years. The cluster of glass-blowing factories – among them well-known brands Orrefors and Kosta Boda – has consolidated over time. A high point of glass design was in the 1960s, when traditional figurative forms were met with abstracted patterning as young designers were given the chance to compete with more established figures.

The Sami

Europe's only indigenous people, the ancestors of the Sami, migrated to the north of present-day Scandinavia, following the path of the retreating ice. They lived by hunting reindeer in the area spanning from Norway's Atlantic coast to the Kola Peninsula in Russia, collectively known as Sápmi.

Sápmi & Modern Sweden

By the 17th century, the depletion of reindeer herds had transformed the Sami's hunting economy into a nomadic herding economy. Until the 1700s, the Sami lived in *siida* (village units or communities), migrating for their livelihoods, but only within their own defined areas. Those areas were recognised and respected by the Swedish government until colonisation of Lappland began in earnest, and the Sami found their traditional rights and livelihoods threatened both by the settlers and by the establishment of borders between Sweden, Norway, Finland and Russia.

The Sami Information Centre in Östersund (www.samer.se) is a treasure trove of information on all aspects of Sami life – from history and present-day culture to politics and food.

Who Is a Sami?

In Sweden today, the stereotype of the nomadic reindeer herder has been replaced with the multifaceted reality of modern Sami life. According to the Sámediggi (Sami parliament) statutes, a Sami is a person who feels oneself to be Sami, who either knows the Sami language or who has had at least one parent or grandparent who spoke Sami as their mother tongue.

The Sami population of Sápmi numbers around 100,000, out of whom around 45,000 live in Norway, 27,000 or so in Sweden, slightly fewer in Finland and some 2000 in Russia. These numbers are approximate, as a census has never taken place. Famous people of Sami descent include Joni Mitchell and Renee Zellweger.

Fewer than half of all Sami can actually read and speak Sami. The most common language is North Sami, spoken by around 18,000 of the 50,000 Sami speakers. Sami languages are mutually unintelligible: Kildin Sami speakers from Vilhelmina can communicate with Russia's Kola Sami but not Kiruna Sami.

Sami Language

Particularly precise when it comes to describing natural phenomena, the landscape and reindeer, Sami is not a single language. There are, in fact, 10 Sami languages spoken across Sápmi, which belong to the Finno-Ugric language group and are not related to any Scandinavian language.

Sweden officially recognises the Sami languages as minority languages and international law decrees that Sami children are entitled to mother-tongue education in Sami. In practice, however, it hasn't always proved possible to find Sami-speaking teachers, and some municipalities feel that it costs too much to provide education in Sami.

However, the Centre for Sami research (CeSam) in Umeå conducts research into Sami language and Sami language courses can be taken at Umeå and Uppsala universities.

Sami Religion & Mythology

Sami beliefs have traditionally revolved around nature, and Shamanism was widespread until the 17th century. The *noaidi,* or shamans, bridged the gap between the physical world and the spiritual world; when in a trance, it was thought that they could shape-shift and command natural phenomena.

Sami folklore features many myths and legends concerning the underworld. Forces of nature, such as the wind and the sun play an important role in Sami myths and legends: Sápmi is said to have been created by a monstrous giant named Biogolmai, the Wind Man. Sami creation stories feature the Son of the Sun as their ancestor, while the Daughter of the Sun is said to have brought the Sami their reindeer.

In 1685 it was decided by the monarchy and the church that the Sami must be converted to Christianity. Idolatry trials were held, shaman drums burned and sacred sites desecrated. However, not all effects of Christianity were negative: Laestadianism helped to alleviate the poverty and misery of the Sami in 19th-century Lappland.

Gällivare-based Visit Sápmi (p280) pools resources from all over Sápmi and aims to connect travellers with specific aspects of Sami culture – from Sami tour companies to Sami culinary experiences and craftsmen.

'A Lapp Must Remain a Lapp'

From the 1800s onward, Sweden's policies regarding the Sami were tinted with social Darwinist ideas, deeming the Sami to be an inferior race fit only for reindeer husbandry. The nomadic Sami were prevented from settling lest they become idle and neglect their reindeer. A separate schooling system was set up, with Sami children denied admission to regular public schools. Under the *Nomad Schools Act* of 1913, they were taught in their family's tent *(lávvu)* for three years by teachers who moved between Sami settlements in summer. After three more years of limited schooling in winter, they were considered sufficiently educated without becoming 'civilised'.

Despite demands that nomad schools should meet the same standards as regular Swedish schools, the situation did not improve until after WWII, when the Sami began to actively participate in the struggle for their rights, forming numerous associations and pressure groups.

Sami Government

The Sami in Sweden are represented by the Sámediggi (Sami parliament), comprising 31 members. Funded by grants from the Swedish government, it oversees many aspects of Sami life, from representing reindeer-herding interests and promoting Sami culture and organisations to appointing the board of directors for Sami schools. While it acts in an advisory capacity to the Swedish government, the Sámediggi does not have the power to make decisions regarding land use.

The Swedish Sami also take part in the Sámirađđi, the unifying body for the Sami organisations across Sápmi and international Sami interests. Sámirađđi is an active participant in the WCIP (World Council of Indigenous Peoples).

The red, blue, green and yellow of the Sami flag, designed by Norway's Astrid Båhl in 1986, correspond to the colours of the traditional Sami costume, the *kolt*, while the red and blue halves of the circle represent the sun and the moon, respectively.

Sami Rights & Today's Challenges

The Sami claim the right to traditional livelihoods, land and water, citing *usufruct* (age-old usage) and the traditional property rights of the Sami *siidas* (villages or communities), which are not formally acknowledged by Sweden. The Swedish state is yet to ratify the International Labour Organization's Convention 169, which would recognise the Sami as an indigenous people with property rights, as opposed to just an ethnic minority.

While the Swedish state supports Sami efforts to preserve their unique reindeer-herding heritage, with an allowance of 300 to 500 reindeer per family, there is one condition: herding units, or *sameby*, may not engage in any economic activity other than reindeer herding. Currently, around 10% of Sweden's Sami are full-time reindeer herders.

In theory, the *Reindeer Husbandry Act* gives reindeer herders the right to use land and water for their own maintenance and that of their reindeer. In practice, a large chunk of land allocated to the herders for grazing is unsuitable for that purpose, and tourism and extractive industries such as mining also continue to pose a threat to that traditional Sami occupation.

Sami Duodji

Sami crafts combine practicality with beauty. 'Soft crafts', such as leatherwork and textiles, have traditionally been in the female domain, whereas men have predominantly pursued 'hard crafts', such as knife making, woodwork or silverwork.

Traditional creations include wooden *guksi* (drinking cups) or other vessels, made by hollowing out a burl and often inlaid with reindeer bone; knives, with abundantly engraved handles made of reindeer or elk antler and equally decorative bone sheaths; and silverwork – anything from exquisitely engraved spoons, belt buckles and brooches to earrings and pendants.

Designs differ depending on whether an item hails from northern or southern Lappland: northern knife sheaths are typically more steeply curved and decorated with patterns of stars and flowers, while southern craftsmen use abstract square patterns. Northern leatherwork and embroidery often feature cloth appliques, while Southern Sami favour leatherwork combined with beadwork.

Recurring symbols are found in Sami silver jewellery. These include the sunwheel that graces women's belts; animal motifs that were once painted on sacred shaman's drums: beavers, reindeer, elk; and *komsekule*, silver filigree balls that once graced Sami collars but were then used as an anti-goblin charm when hung on children's cradles. The heavy silver collars worn by women often feature the Gothic letter 'M'. In the Middle Ages, such 'M's were a pilgrim sign that symbolised the Virgin Mary.

In the 1970s there was a revival of Sami handicraft; since then, genuine Sami work that uses traditional designs and materials has borne the Sámi Duodji trademark.

Traditional Sami clothing, or *gákti*, comes with its own varied and distinctive headgear and is one of the most distinct symbols of Sami identity. The Sami can tell at a glance which part of Sápmi another is from, or whether the wearer is unaccustomed to wearing Sami garments.

People of the Eight Seasons

For centuries, Sami life revolved around reindeer. Thus the Sami year traditionally has eight seasons, each tied to a period of reindeer herding:

Gidádálvve (springwinter; early March to late April) Herds are moved from the forests to calving lands in the low mountains during the spring migration.

Gidá (spring; late April to late May) Calves are born. Leaves and grass are added to the reindeer's diet.

Gidágiesse (springsummer; end of May to Midsummer) Herds are moved to find more vegetation for calves and their mothers. Reindeer mostly rest and eat. Herders repair temporary homes.

Giesse (summer; Midsummer to end of August) Reindeer move to higher ground to avoid biting insects. Herders round them up and move them into corrals for calf marking.

Tjaktjagiesse (autumnsummer; end of August to mid-September) Reindeer build up fat for the winter. Some of the uncastrated males *(sarvss)* are slaughtered in specially designated corrals. Meat is salted, smoked and made into jerky.

Tjaktja (autumn; mid-September to mid-October) Reindeer mating season. The reindeer stay mostly in the low mountains, where they feed on roots and lichen.

Tjaktjadálvve (autumnwinter; mid-October to Christmas) Reindeer are divided into grazing groups *(sijdor)* and taken to winter grazing grounds in the forest. Surplus reindeer are slaughtered.

Dálvve (winter; Christmas to the end of February) Herders frequently move the reindeer around the forests to make sure the reindeer get enough lichen to eat.

Survival Guide

Directory A–Z

Accommodation

Accommodation in Sweden is generally of a high standard. The below room prices are for a double room in the summer season (mid-June through August); standard weekday prices during the rest of the year might be twice as high.

- **€** less than Skr800
- **€€** Skr800–Skr1600
- **€€€** more than Skr1600

Cabins & Chalets

Camping cabins and *stugor* (chalets) are common at camping grounds and scattered through the countryside. Most have four beds, with two- and six-person cabins sometimes available. They're good value for small groups and families, costing between Skr350 and Skr950 per night. In peak summer season, many are rented out by the week (generally for Skr1000 to Skr5000).

The cheapest cabins are simple, with bunk beds and little else (bathroom and kitchen facilities are shared with campers or other cabin users). Chalets are generally fully equipped with their own kitchen, bathroom and even living room with TV. Bring your own linen and clean up yourself to save cleaning fees of around Skr500.

Pick up the catalogue *Campsites & Cottages in Sweden* from any tourist office, or check out www.stuga.nu.

Camping

Camping is wildly popular in Sweden, and there are hundreds of camping grounds all over the country. Most open between May and September. The majority are busy family-holiday spots with fantastic facilities, such as shops, restaurants, pools, playgrounds, canoe or bike rentals, minigolf, kitchens and laundry facilities. Most also have cabins or chalets.

Camping prices vary (according to season and facilities) from around Skr150 for a small site at a basic ground to Skr250 for a large site at a more luxurious camping ground. Slightly cheaper rates may be available if you're a solo hiker or cyclist.

You must have a Camping Key Europe card to stay at most Swedish camping grounds. Buy one online through **Sveriges Camping & Stugföretagares Riksorganisation** (www.camping.se); otherwise pick one up at your first campground. One card (Skr150 per year) covers the whole family.

Hostels

Sweden has well over 450 *vandrarhem* (hostels), usually with excellent facilities. Outside major cities, hostels aren't backpacker hangouts but are used as holiday accommodation by Swedish families, couples or retired people. Another quirk is the scarcity of dormitories; hostels are more likely to have singles and doubles of almost hotel quality, often with en suite bathrooms. About half of hostels are open year-round; many others open from May to September, some only from mid-June to mid-August.

Be warned: Swedish hostels keep very short reception opening times: generally from 5pm to 7pm, and 8am to 10am. The secret is to prebook by telephone – reservations are recommended in any case, as good hostels fill up fast. If you're stuck arriving when the front desk is closed, you'll usually see a number posted where you can phone for instructions. Hostel phone numbers are also listed in the free guidebooks published annually by Svenska Turistföreninge (STF) and Sveriges Vandrarhem i Förening (SVIF), and online.

Sleeping bags are usually allowed if you have a sheet and pillowcase; bring your own, or hire them (Skr50 to Skr65). Breakfast is usually available (Skr65 to Skr95). Before leaving, you must clean up after yourself; cleaning materials are provided. Most hostels are affiliated with STF or SVIF, but there are other unaffiliated hostels also with high standards of accommodation.

SVENSKA TURISTFÖRENINGEN

About 320 hostels are affiliated with **Svenska Turistföreningen** (STF; ☎08-463 21 00; www.svenskaturistforeningen.se), part of Hostelling International (HI). STF produces a free detailed guide to its hostels; the text is in Swedish only, but the symbols and maps are easy to understand. Hostel details on its website are in English. All STF hostels have kitchens.

Holders of HI membership cards pay the same rates as STF members. Nonmembers can pay Skr50 extra (Skr100 at mountain lodges) or join up online or at hostels (adult/child Skr295/150 annually). Prices quoted in this book are for STF members. Children under 16 pay about half the adult price.

SVERIGES VANDRARHEM I FÖRENING

Around 200 hostels belong to **Sveriges Vandrarhem i Förening** (SVIF; ☎031-82 88 00; www.svif.se). No membership is required and rates are similar to those of STF hostels. Most SVIF hostels have kitchens, but you sometimes need your own utensils. Pick up the free guide at tourist offices or SVIF hostels.

Hotels

Sweden is unusual in that hotel prices tend to fall at weekends and in summer (except in touristy coastal towns), sometimes by as much as 50%. We list the standard summer rates, as that's when most people will be visiting, but be aware that prices may be nearly double at other times of year. Many hotel chains are now also offering a variety of low rates for online booking. Hotel prices include a breakfast buffet unless noted in individual reviews. Ask at tourist offices for the free booklet *Hotels in Sweden* or visit www.hotelsinsweden.net.

Travellers on a budget should investigate **Ibis** (www.ibishotel.com) hotels, offering simple rooms with private facilities. Breakfast is additional.

There are a number of common midrange and top-end chains. Radisson SAS and Elite are the most luxurious. Scandic is known for being environmentally friendly. The top-end Countryside chain has the most characterful rooms, in castles, mansions, monasteries and spas.

Best Western (www.bestwestern.se)

Countryside (www.countrysidehotels.se)

Elite (www.elite.se)

First (www.firsthotels.com)

Nordic Choice (www.nordicchoicehotels.se)

Radisson SAS (www.radisson.com)

Scandic (www.scandichotels.com)

Sweden Hotels (www.swedenhotels.se)

Your Hotel Worldwide (www.yourhotelsworldwide.net)

BOOK YOUR STAY ONLINE

For more accommodation reviews by Lonely Planet authors, check out http://lonelyplanet.com/hotels/. You'll find independent reviews, as well as recommendations on the best places to stay. Best of all, you can book online.

Mountain Huts & Lodges

Most *fjällstugor* (mountain huts) and *fjällstationer* (lodges) in Sweden are owned by STF. There are about 45 huts and nine mountain lodges, mostly spaced at 15km to 25km intervals along major hiking trails, primarily in the Lappland region. Reception hours are quite long as staff members are always on-site. Basic provisions are sold at many huts and all lodges, and many lodges have hiking equipment for hire.

STF mountain huts have cooking and toilet facilities (none has a shower, but some offer saunas). Bring your own sleeping bag. Huts are staffed during March and April and also from late June to early September. You can't book a bed in advance, but no one is turned away (although in the peak of summer this may mean you sleep on a mattress on the floor). Charges for STF or HI members vary depending on the season, and range from Skr190 to Skr350 (children pay about Skr75), with the highest charges on the northern Kungsleden. Nonmembers pay Skr100 extra. You can also pitch a tent in the mountains, but if you camp near STF huts you are requested to pay a service charge (members/nonmembers Skr60/80), which gives you access to any services the hut may offer (such as kitchen and bathroom facilities).

At the excellent STF mountain lodges, accommodation standards range from hostel (with cooking facilities) to hotel (with full- or half-board options), and overnight prices range from Skr250 to around Skr1200. There are often guided activities on offer for guests, and usually a restaurant and shop.

Private Rooms, B&Bs & Farmhouses

Many tourist offices have lists of rooms in private homes, a great way of finding well-priced accommodation and getting to meet Swedish people. Singles/doubles average Skr350/650.

Along the motorways (primarily in the south), you may see 'Rum' or 'Rum & Frukost' signs, indicating informal accommodation (*frukost* means 'breakfast') from Skr300 to Skr400 per person.

The organisation **Bo på Lantgård** (☎035-12 78 70;

www.bopalantgard.org) publishes a free annual booklet on farmhouse accommodation (B&B and self-catering), available from any tourist office. B&B prices average Skr300 per person in a double room. Prices for self-caterers range from Skr300 to Skr850 per night, depending on the time of year, facilities and number of beds.

Customs Regulations

The duty-free allowance for bringing alcohol into Sweden from outside the EU is 1L of spirits or 2L of fortified wine, 4L of wine and 16L of beer. The tobacco allowance is 200 cigarettes, 100 cigarillos, 50 cigars or 250g of smoking tobacco. You must be at least 20 years old to bring in alcohol and 18 to bring in tobacco.

The limits on goods brought into Sweden with 'tax paid for personal use' from within the EU are more generous and somewhat flexible; tax is assessed on a case-by-case basis.

Going through customs rarely involves any hassles, but rules on illegal drugs are strictly enforced; you may be searched on arrival, especially if you're travelling from Denmark. Live plants and animal products (meat, dairy etc) from outside the EU, and all animals, syringes and weapons must be declared to customs on arrival. For the latest regulations, contact **Swedish Customs** (☎0771-23 23 23; www.tullverket.se).

Discount Cards

City Summer Cards

Göteborg, Malmö, Stockholm and Uppsala have worthwhile tourist cards that get you into their major attractions and offer parking, travel on public transport and discounts at participating hotels, restaurants and shops.

Hostel & Student Cards

A Hostelling International (HI) card means cheaper beds in STF hostels, mountain stations and cabins. You can join the STF at hostels and tourist offices in Sweden (membership adult/16 to 25 years/six to 15 years/family Skr295/150/30/450); membership is good for one year.

The most useful student card is the **International Student Identity Card** (ISIC; www.isic.org; fee $25), which offers discounts on many forms of transport (including some airlines, international ferries and local public transport) and on admission to museums, sights, theatres and cinemas.

Seniors

Seniors normally get discounts on entry to museums and other sights, cinema and theatre tickets, air tickets and other transport fares. No special card is required to receive this discount, but show your passport if you are asked for proof of age (the minimum qualifying age is generally 60 or 65 years).

Electricity

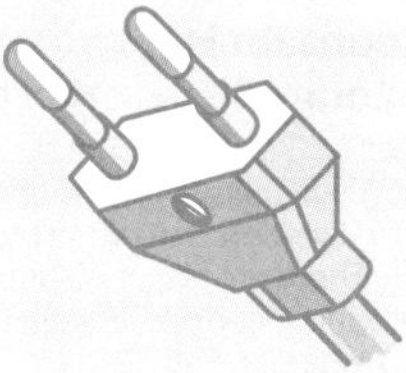

230V/50Hz

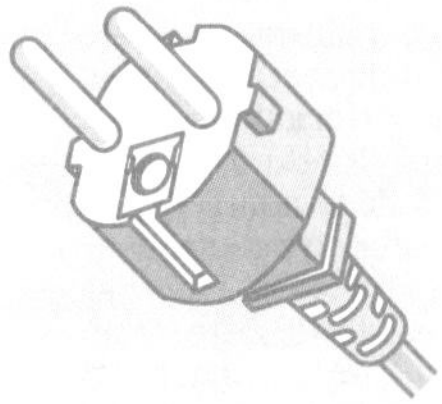

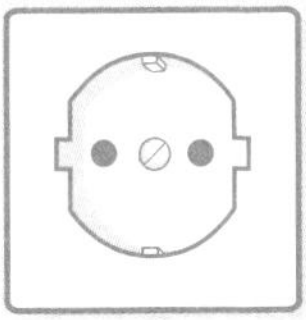

230V/50Hz

Embassies & Consulates

A list of Swedish diplomatic missions abroad (and links) is available at **Sweden Abroad** (www.swedenabroad.com). Most diplomatic missions are in Stockholm, although some neighbouring countries also have consulates in Göteborg, Malmö and Helsingborg.

Food

The following price categories for eating listings refer to the average price of a main dish, not including drinks.

- **€** less than Skr100
- **€€** Skr100–Skr200
- **€€€** more than Skr200

For more on Food in Sweden, see p301

Gay & Lesbian Travellers

Sweden is a famously liberal country; it was a leader in establishing gay and lesbian registered partnerships, and since 2009 its gender-neutral marriage law has given same-sex married couples the same rights and obligations as heterosexual married couples. The national organisation for gay and lesbian rights is **Riksförbundet för Sexuellt Likaberättigande** (RFSL; ☎08-5016 2900; www.rfsl.se; Sveavägen 57-59).

There are gay bars and nightclubs in the big cities, but ask local RFSL societies or your home organisation for up-to-date information. The *Spartacus International Gay Guide*, published by Bruno Gmünder Verlag (Berlin), is an excellent international directory of gay entertainment venues, but it's best used in conjunction with more up-to-date listings in local papers; as elsewhere, gay venues in the region can change with the speed of summer.

Another good source of local information is the free monthly magazine *QX*. You can pick it up at many clubs, shops and restaurants in Stockholm, Göteborg, Malmö and Copenhagen (Denmark). The magazine's website (www.qx.se) has excellent information and recommendations in English.

One of the capital's biggest parties is the annual **Stockholm Pride** (www.stockholmpride.org/en/), a five-day festival celebrating gay culture, held between late July and early August. The extensive program covers art, debate, health, literature, music, spirituality and sport.

Insurance

Depending on the type of policy you choose, insurance can cover you for everything from medical expenses and luggage loss to cancellations or delays in your travel arrangements.

In Sweden, EU citizens pay a fee for all medical treatment (including emergency admissions), but showing an EHIC (European Health Insurance Card) form will make matters much easier. Enquire about the EHIC well in advance at your social-security office, travel agent or local post office. Travel insurance is still advisable, however, as it allows treatment flexibility and will also cover ambulance and repatriation costs.

If you do need health insurance, remember that some policies offer 'lower' and 'higher' medical-expense options, but the higher one is chiefly for countries that have extremely high medical costs, such as the USA. Everyone should be covered for the worst possible scenario, such as an accident requiring an ambulance, hospital treatment or an emergency flight home. You may prefer a policy that pays health-care providers directly, rather than your having to pay on the spot and claim later.

Worldwide travel insurance is available at www.lonelyplanet.com/bookings. You can buy, extend and claim travel insurance online any time – even if you're already on the road.

Internet Access

If you plan to carry a notebook computer or tablet, remember that the power-supply voltage in Sweden may vary from what you have in your home country. To avoid frying your electronics, use a universal AC adaptor (many laptop adaptors already include this; check the label on your power cord) and a plug adaptor, which will enable you to plug in anywhere.

Most hotels have wireless LAN connections, and some have computers and printers in the lobby or business centre, or even laptops you can borrow. Nearly all public libraries offer free internet

EMBASSIES & CONSULATES IN STOCKHOLM

COUNTRY	TELEPHONE	WEBSITE	ADDRESS
Australia	☎08-613 29 00	www.sweden.embassy.gov.au	8th fl, Klarabergsviaducten 63
Canada	☎08-453 30 00	www.sweden.gc.ca	Klarabergsgatan 23
Denmark	☎08-406 75 00	sverige.um.dk	Jakobs Torg 1
Finland	☎08-676 67 00	www.finland.se/fi, in Finnish & Swedish	Gärdesgatan 9-11
France	☎08-459 53 00	www.ambafrance-se.org, in French & Swedish	Kommendörsgatan 13
Germany	☎08-670 15 00	www.stockholm.diplo.de, in German & Swedish	Skarpögatan 9
Ireland	☎08-54 50 40 40	www.embassyofireland.se	Hovslagargatan 5
Netherlands	☎08-55 69 33 00	www.sweden.nlembassy.org	Götgatan 16A
Norway	☎08-58 72 36 00	www.norge.se	Skarpögatan 4
UK	☎08-671 30 00	www.britishembassy.se	Skarpögatan 6-8
USA	☎08-783 53 00	stockholm.usembassy.gov	Dag Hammarskjölds väg 31

access, but often the half-hour or hour slots are fully booked in advance by locals, and certain website categories may be blocked. Many tourist offices offer a computer terminal for visitor use (usually free or for a minimal fee).

Internet cafes are rarely found outside big cities because most Swedes have internet access at home. Where internet cafes do exist, they're full of teenage lads playing computer games. You will typically be charged around Skr1 per online minute, or Skr50 per hour.

Wireless-internet access at coffee shops is now very common and usually free; ask for the security code when you order. At bus and train stations and airports, you often have to sign up for a paid account to access the wi-fi. Free wi-fi in hotels is now fairly standard, though some places still charge a fee.

Legal Matters

If arrested, you have the right to contact your country's embassy, which can usually provide you with a list of local lawyers. There is no provision for bail in Sweden. Sweden has some of the most draconian drug laws in western Europe, with fines and possible long prison sentences for possession and consumption.

Maps

Tourist offices, libraries and hotels usually stock free local town plans.

The best maps of Sweden are published and updated regularly by Kartförlaget, the sales branch of the national mapping agency, **Lantmäteriet** (☎026-63 30 00; www.lantmateriet.se); they can be bought at most tourist offices, bookshops and some youth hostels, service stations and general stores.

Motorists planning an extensive tour should get the *Motormännens Sverige Vägatlas* produced by Kartförlaget (Skr275, often cheaper online), with town plans and detailed coverage at 1:250,000 as far north as Sundsvall, then 1:400,000 for the remainder.

The best tourist road maps are those of Kartförlaget's *Vägkartan* series, at a scale of 1:100,000 and available from larger bookshops. Also useful, especially for hikers, is the *Fjällkartan* mountain series (1:100,000, with 20m contour interval); these cost around Skr127 apiece and are available at larger bookshops, outdoor-equipment stores and STF mountain stations.

To purchase maps before you arrive, try **Kartbutiken** (Map p48; ☎08-20 23 03; www.kartbutiken.se; Mäster Samuelsgatan 54; ⏲10am-6pm Mon-Fri, 10am-4pm Sat, noon-4pm Sun; Ⓜ T-Centralen).

Money

Sweden uses the krona (plural kronor) as currency. One krona is divided into 100 öre.

Cash & ATMs

The simplest and usually cheapest way to get money in Sweden is by accessing your account using an ATM card from your home bank. Bankomat ATMs are found adjacent to many banks and around busy public places such as shopping centres. They accept major credit cards as well as Plus and Cirrus cards. Note that many ATMs in Sweden will not accept PINs of more than four digits; if your PIN is longer than this, just enter the first four and you should be able to access your account. Be aware that some ATMs withdraw from your cheque account without giving you the option to choose a different account. ATMs in busy locations often have extremely long queues and can run out of money on Friday and Saturday night. Don't neglect to tell your bank you'll be travelling overseas; otherwise your account access may be blocked as fraud protection.

Credit Cards

Visa and MasterCard are widely accepted, American Express, Discover and Diners Club less so. Credit cards can be used to buy train tickets but are not accepted on domestic ferries, apart from sailings to Gotland. Electronic debit or credit cards can be used in most shops.

If your card is lost or stolen in Sweden, report it to your credit-card agency.

American Express (☎336-393 11 11)

Diners Club (☎08-14 68 78)

MasterCard (☎020-79 13 24)

Visa (☎020-79 56 75)

Moneychangers

Banks around the country exchange major foreign currencies.

Forex (☎0771-22 22 21; www.forex.se) is the biggest foreign money-exchange company in Sweden, with good rates and branches in major airports, ferry terminals and town and city centres.

Tipping

Hotels Optional; a small tip (Skr10 per day) for housekeeping is appreciated.

Restaurants and bars Not expected, except at dinner (when 10% to 15% for good service is customary).

Taxis Optional; most people round up the bill to the nearest Skr10.

Travellers Cheques

Banks around the country accept international brands of travellers cheques. They may charge up to Skr60 per travellers cheque, so shop around and compare service fees and exchange rates before handing over your money.

Forex (☎0771-22 22 21; www.forex.se) charges a service fee of Skr15 for each travellers cheque exchanged.

Opening Hours

General opening hours vary (particularly in the largest cities, where hours may be longer).

Banks 9.30am to 3pm Monday to Friday; some city branches 9am to 5pm or 6pm.

Bars and pubs 11am or noon to 1am or 2am.

Department stores 10am to 7pm Monday to Saturday (sometimes later), noon to 4pm Sunday.

Government offices 9am to 5pm Monday to Friday.

Restaurants Open for lunch from 11am to 2pm, and dinner between 5pm and 10pm; often closed on Sunday and/or Monday.

Shops 9am to 6pm Monday to Friday, 9am to 1pm Saturday.

Supermarkets 8am or 9am to 7pm or 10pm.

Systembolaget 10am to 6pm Monday to Friday, 10am to 2pm (often until 5pm) Saturday, sometimes with extended hours on Thursday and Friday evenings.

Tourist offices Usually open daily Midsummer to mid-August, Monday to Friday only the rest of the year.

PRACTICALITIES

- **Weights and measures** Sweden uses the metric system. Some shops quote prices followed by '/hg', which means per 100g. Watch out for *mil*, which Swedes may translate into English as 'mile' – a Swedish *mil* is actually 10km.
- **Newspapers** Domestic papers (including the Göteborg and Stockholm dailies and evening tabloids) are in Swedish only. A good selection of English-language imports is sold at major transport terminals, Press Stop, Pressbyrån and tobacconists – even in small towns.
- **Radio** Try National Swedish Radio (variable stations around the country, see www.sr.se for a directory) for classical music and opera, pop and rock.
- **TV** National channels TV1 and TV2 broadcast mainly about local issues, mostly in Swedish. TV3, TV4 and TV5 have lots of shows and films in English.
- **DVDs** Sweden uses the PAL format.

Photography

Camera supplies are readily available in all the large cities. Expert, a chain of electrical-goods shops, sells a wide range of photography gadgets.

It's particularly important to ask permission before taking photos of people in Sami areas, where you may meet resistance. Photography and taking videos are prohibited at many tourist sites, mainly to protect fragile artwork. Photographing military establishments is forbidden. Observe signs, and when in doubt, ask permission.

Technical challenges include the clear northern light and glare from water, ice and snow, which may require use of a UV filter (or skylight filter) and lens shade; and the cold – most cameras don't work below -20°C.

Lonely Planet's *Travel Photography*, by Richard I'Anson, contains some handy hints.

Post

Swedish postal service **Posten** (☎020-23 22 21; www.posten.se) has a network of around 3000 counter services in shops, petrol stations and supermarkets across the country. Look for the yellow post symbol on a pale-blue background, which indicates that postal facilities are offered.

If your postal requirements are more complicated (such as posting a heavy parcel), ask at the local tourist office. Package services are offered at certain office-supply stores.

Mailing letters or postcards weighing up to 20g within Sweden costs Skr6; it's Skr10.50 to Skr12.50 to elsewhere in Europe and beyond. Airmail will take a week to reach most parts of North America, perhaps a little longer to Australia and New Zealand.

Public Holidays

Midsummer brings life almost to a halt for three days: transport and other services are reduced, and most shops and smaller tourist offices close, as do some attractions. Some hotels close between Christmas and New Year. Upscale restaurants in larger cities often close for a few weeks in late July and early August.

School holidays vary from school to school, but in general the kids will be at large for Sweden's one-week sports holiday (February/March), the one-week Easter break, Christmas, and from June to August.

Many businesses close early the day before and all day after official public holidays.

Nyårsdag (New Year's Day) 1 January

Trettondedag Jul (Epiphany) 6 January

Långfredag, Påsk, Annandag Påsk (Good Friday, Easter Sunday and Monday) March/April

Första Maj (Labour Day) 1 May

Kristi Himmelsfärdsdag (Ascension Day) May/June

Pingst, Annandag Pingst (Whit Sunday and Monday) Late May or early June

Midsommardag (Midsummer's Day) Saturday between 19 and 25 June

Alla Helgons dag (All Saints Day) Saturday, late October or early November

Juldag (Christmas Day) 25 December

Annandag Jul (Boxing Day) 26 December

Note also that Midsommarafton (Midsummer's Eve), Julafton (Christmas Eve; 24 December) and Nyårsafton (New Year's Eve; 31 December) are not official holidays but are generally nonworking days for most of the population.

Telephone

Swedish phone numbers have area codes followed by a varying number of digits. Look for business numbers in the **Yellow Pages** (www.gulasidorna.se). The state-owned telephone company, Telia, also has phone books, which include green pages (for community services) and blue pages (for regional services, including health and medical care).

Public telephones are usually to be found at train stations or in the main town square. They accept phonecards or credit cards (although the latter are expensive). It's not possible to receive return international calls or make international collect calls on public phones.

For international calls dial ☎00, followed by the country code and then the local area code. Calls to Sweden from abroad require the country code (☎46) followed by the area code and telephone number (omitting the first zero in the area code).

Mobile-phone codes start with ☎010, ☎070, ☎076, ☎073 and ☎0730. Toll-free codes include ☎020 and ☎0200 (but toll-free numbers can't be called from public telephones or abroad).

Emergency services (112) Toll free.

International directory assistance (118 119)

Swedish directory assistance (118 118)

Mobile Phones

It's worth considering bringing your mobile phone from your home country and buying a Swedish SIM card, which gives you a Swedish mobile number and avoids racking up huge roaming charges on your regular number. Local SIM cards are readily available (around Skr95); you then load them with at least Skr100 worth of credit. You can purchase top-ups at many stores, including petrol stations and Pressbyrån shops. Your mobile may be locked onto your local network in your home country, so ask your home network for advice before going abroad; most will gladly unlock your phone for travel.

Phonecards

Telia *telefonkort* (phonecards) for public payphones cost Skr50 and Skr120 (for 50 and 120 units, respectively) and can be bought from Telia phone shops and newsagents.

You can make international telephone calls with these phonecards, but they won't last long! For international calls, it's better to buy (from tobacconists) one of a wide range of phonecards, such as a Star phonecard, which give cheap rates for calls abroad. These are generally used in public phone boxes in conjunction with a Telia card: so you might have to put the Telia card into the phone, dial the telephone number shown on the back of your cheap international phonecard, then follow the instructions given. International collect calls cannot be made from payphones.

Time

Sweden is one hour ahead of GMT/UTC and is in the same time zone as Norway and Denmark as well as most of western Europe. When it's noon in Sweden, it's 11am in London, 1pm in Helsinki, 6am in New York and Toronto, 3am in Los Angeles, 9pm in Sydney and 11pm in Auckland. Sweden also has daylight-saving time: the clocks go forward an hour on the last Sunday in March and back an hour on the last Sunday in October.

Timetables and business hours are quoted using the 24-hour clock, and dates are often given by week number (1 to 52).

Toilets

Public toilets in parks, shopping malls, libraries, and bus or train stations are rarely free in Sweden, though some churches and most museums and tourist offices have free toilets. Pay toilets cost Skr5 to Skr10, usually payable by coin only except at larger train stations and department stores (where there's an attendant).

Tourist Information

Local Tourist Offices

Most towns in Sweden have centrally located *turistbyrå* (tourist offices) that provide free street plans and information on accommodation, attractions, activities and transport. Brochures for other areas in Sweden are often available. Ask for the handy booklet that lists addresses and phone numbers for most tourist offices in the country.

Most tourist offices are open long hours daily in summer; from mid-August to mid-June a few close down, while others have shorter opening hours – they may close by 4pm, and not open at all at weekends. Public libraries, hostels or large hotels are good alternative sources of information.

Tourist Offices Abroad

The official website for the **Swedish Travel and Tourism Council** (www.visitsweden.com) contains loads of excellent information in many languages, and you can request that brochures and information packs be sent to you.

Tourist offices can usually assist with enquiries and provide promotional material by phone, email or post (most don't have a walk-in service). In countries without a designated tourist office, a good starting point for information is the nearest Swedish embassy.

Swedish Travel and Tourism Council France (☎01-53 43 26 27; servinfo@suede-tourisme.fr; Office Suédois du Tourisme et des Voyages); Germany (☎040-32 55 13-55; info@swetourism.de; Schweden-Werbung für Reisen und Touristik); UK (☎44-20 7917 6400; info@swetourism.org.uk; Swedish Travel & Tourism Council); USA (☎212-885 9700; usa@visit-sweden.com; Swedish Travel & Tourism Council)

Travellers with Disabilities

Sweden is one of the easiest countries in which to travel around in a wheelchair. People with disabilities will find transport services, ranging from trains to taxis, with adapted facilities; contact the operator in advance for the best service.

Public toilets and some hotel rooms have facilities for those with disabilities; **Hotels in Sweden** (www.hotelsinsweden.net) indicates whether hotels have adapted rooms. Some street crossings have ramps for wheelchairs and audio signals for visually impaired people, and some grocery stores are wheelchair accessible.

For further information about Sweden, contact **De Handikappades Riksförbund** (☎08-685 80 00; www.dhr.se), the national association for the disabled.

Also, contact the travel officer at your national support organisation; they may be able to put you in touch with tour companies that specialise in travelling with disabilities.

Visas

Citizens of EU countries can enter Sweden with a passport or a national identification card (passports are recommended) and stay indefinitely. *Uppehållstillstånd* (residence permits) are no longer required for EU citizens to visit, study, live or work in Sweden.

Non-EU passport holders from Australia, New Zealand, Canada and the US can enter and stay in Sweden without a visa for up to 90 days. Australian and New Zealand passport holders aged between 18 and 30 can qualify for a one-year working-holiday visa. For longer stays, you'll need to apply for a visitor's permit instead of an entry visa. These must be applied for before entering Sweden. An interview by consular officials at your nearest Swedish embassy is required – allow up to eight months for this process. Foreign students are granted residence permits if they can prove acceptance by a Swedish educational institution and are able to guarantee that they can support themselves financially.

Citizens of South Africa and many other African, Asian and some eastern European countries require tourist visas for entry to Sweden (and any other Schengen country). These are only available in advance from Swedish embassies (allow two months); there's a nonrefundable application fee of €60 for most applicants. Visas are good for any 90 days within a six-month period; extensions aren't easily obtainable.

Migrationsverket (☎0771-23 52 35; www.migrationsverket.se) is the Swedish migration board and handles all applications for visas and work or residency permits.

Work

Non-EU citizens require an offer of paid employment prior to their arrival in Sweden. They need to apply for a work permit (and residence permit for stays over three months), enclosing confirmation of the job offer, completed forms (available from Swedish diplomatic posts or over the internet), two passport photos and their passport. Processing takes six to eight weeks, and there's a nonrefundable application fee of Skr2000 (Skr1000 for athletes, performers and a few other job categories).

Australians and New Zealanders aged 18 to 30 years can qualify for a one-year working-holiday visa. Full application details are available online through **Migrationsverket** (☎0771-23 52 35; www.migrationsverket.se).

Work permits are only granted if there's a shortage of Swedish workers (or citizens from EU countries) with certain in-demand skills; speaking Swedish may be essential for the job. Students enrolled in Sweden can take summer jobs, but these can be hard to find and such work isn't offered to travelling students.

Plenty of helpful information can be found online from the **Arbetsförmedlinga** (AMV; Swedish National Labour Market Administration; www.arbetsformedlingen.se)

Transport

GETTING THERE & AWAY

Flights, tours and rail tickets can be booked online at lonelyplanet.com/bookings.

Entering the Country

Sweden's main airport is Stockholm Arlanda. Entry is straightforward; most visitors simply need to fill out and hand over a brief customs form and show their passport at immigration.

Air

Airports & Airlines

Stockholm Arlanda (☎10-109 10 00; www.swedavia.se/arlanda) links Sweden with major European and North American cities. **Göteborg Landvetter** (www.swedavia.se/landvetter) is Sweden's second-biggest international airport. **Stockholm Skavsta** (☎0155-28 04 00; www.skavsta.se), 100km south of Stockholm, near Nyköping, and **Göteborg City** (www.goteborgairport.se) both serve budget airline Ryanair. Scandinavian Airlines System (SAS) is the regional carrier.

Continental Europe

SAS offers numerous direct services between Stockholm and European capitals including Amsterdam, Brussels, Geneva, Moscow, Paris and Prague. Many services are routed via Copenhagen (Denmark). Similar routes leave from Göteborg (Gothenburg).

Air Berlin flies from Göteborg Landvetter to Berlin several times weekly; also from Landvetter, Air France goes to Lyon, and Lufthansa goes to Frankfurt and Munich.

Finnair has direct flights from Helsinki to Stockholm (around 15 daily) and Göteborg (up to four services daily).

Ryanair has frequent flights from Stockholm Skavsta to Barcelona, Brussels, Düsseldorf, Frankfurt, Hamburg, Milan, Paris, Riga and Rome.

UK & Ireland

Ryanair flies from London Stansted to Stockholm Skavsta, Göteborg City and Malmö's Sturup airport; Glasgow Prestwick to Stockholm Skavsta and Göteborg City; London Luton to Västerås; and Shannon to Stockholm Skavsta.

Between London Heathrow and Stockholm Arlanda, several commercial airlines have regular daily flights, including SAS, British Airways and BMI.

SAS flies at least four times daily from Stockholm Arlanda to Manchester and Dublin via London or Copenhagen. SAS also flies daily between London Heathrow and Göteborg.

BMI Regional and British Airways fly twice weekly from Göteborg Landvetter to Birmingham and Manchester.

USA

Icelandair has services from Baltimore-Washington, Boston,

CLIMATE CHANGE & TRAVEL

Every form of transport that relies on carbon-based fuel generates CO_2, the main cause of human-induced climate change. Modern travel is dependent on aeroplanes, which might use less fuel per kilometre per person than most cars but travel much greater distances. The altitude at which aircraft emit gases (including CO_2) and particles also contributes to their climate change impact. Many websites offer 'carbon calculators' that allow people to estimate the carbon emissions generated by their journey and, for those who wish to do so, to offset the impact of the greenhouse gases emitted with contributions to portfolios of climate-friendly initiatives throughout the world. Lonely Planet offsets the carbon footprint of all staff and author travel.

New York, Minneapolis and Orlando via Reykjavík to Stockholm. SAS's North American hub is New York City's Newark Airport, with direct daily flights to/from Stockholm. SAS also flies daily from Chicago to Stockholm. Lufthansa has daily flights from Newark Airport to Stockholm.

Land

Border Crossings

Direct access to Sweden is possible from Norway, Finland and Denmark (via the Öresund toll bridge). Border-crossing formalities are nonexistent.

Train and bus journeys between Sweden and the continent go directly to ferries.

For info on visas, see p329.

Eurolines (☎031-10 02 40; www.eurolines.com) Has an office inside the bus terminals in Sweden's three largest cities: Stockholm, Göteborg and Malmö. Full schedules and fares are listed on the website.

Nettbuss Express (☎0771-15 15 15; www.nettbuss.se) Long-distance buses within Sweden and to Oslo (Norway) and Copenhagen.

Sveriges Järnväg (SJ; ☎0771-75 75 99; www.sj.se) Train lines with services to Copenhagen.

Swebus Express (☎0200-21 82 18; www.swebusexpress.se) Long-distance buses within Sweden and to Oslo and Copenhagen.

Denmark

BUS

Eurolines runs buses between Göteborg and Copenhagen (Skr370, 4½ hours, daily). Swebus Express and Nettbuss Express both run regular buses on the same route. All companies offer student, youth (under 26) and senior discounts.

CAR & MOTORCYCLE

You can drive from Copenhagen to Malmö across the Öresund bridge on the E20 motorway. Tolls are paid at Lernacken, on the Swedish side, in Danish or Swedish currency (single crossing per car/motorcycle Skr435/225), or by credit or debit card.

TRAIN

Öresund trains operated by **Skånetrafiken** (www.skanetrafiken.se) run every 20 minutes from 6am to midnight (and once an hour thereafter) between Copenhagen and Malmö (one way Skr105, 35 minutes) via the bridge. The trains usually stop at Copenhagen airport. From Copenhagen, change in Malmö for Stockholm trains.

Frequent services operate between Copenhagen and Göteborg (Skr447, four hours) and between Copenhagen, Kristianstad and Karlskrona.

Finland

BUS

Bus services run from Haparanda to Tornio (Skr15, 10 minutes). **Tapanis Buss** (☎0922-129 55; www.tapanis.se) runs express coaches from Stockholm to Tornio via Haparanda twice a week (Skr675, 15 hours). **Länstrafiken i Norrbotten** (☎0771-10 01 10; www.ltnbd.se) operates buses as far as Karesuando, from where it's only a few minutes' walk across the bridge to Kaaresuvanto (Finland).

There are also regular regional services from Haparanda to Övertorneå (some continue to Pello, Pajala and Kiruna) – you can walk across the border at Övertorneå or Pello and take a Finnish bus to Muonio, with onward connections from there to Kaaresuvanto and Tromsø (Norway).

CAR & MOTORCYCLE

The main routes between Sweden and Finland are the E4 from Umeå to Kemi and Rd 45 from Gällivare to Kaaresuvanto; five other minor roads also cross the border.

Germany

BUS

Eurolines runs services from Göteborg to Berlin (Skr1500, 15 hours, five weekly).

TRAIN

Hamburg is the central European gateway to Scandinavia, with direct trains daily to Copenhagen and a few on to Stockholm. Direct overnight trains and Swebus Express buses run daily between Berlin and Malmö via the Trelleborg–Sassnitz ferry (www.berlin-night-express.com; from Skr449, nine hours).

Norway

BUS

Nettbuss runs from Stockholm to Oslo (from Skr632, 7½ hours, five daily) via Karlstad, and from Göteborg to Oslo (from Skr209, four hours, several daily). Swebus Express has the same routes with similar prices. In the north, buses run once daily from Umeå to Mo i Rana (eight hours) and from Skellefteå to Bodø (nine hours, daily except Saturday); for details, contact **Länstrafiken i Västerbotten** (☎0771-10 01 10; www.tabussen.nu) and **Länstrafiken i Norrbotten** (☎0771-10 01 10; www.ltnbd.se).

CAR & MOTORCYCLE

The main roads between Sweden and Norway are the E6 from Göteborg to Oslo, the E18 from Stockholm to Oslo, the E14 from Sundsvall to Trondheim, the E12 from Umeå to Mo i Rana, and the E10 from Kiruna to Bjerkvik.

TRAIN

SJ trains run twice daily between Stockholm and Oslo (Skr433 to Skr588, six to seven hours), and at night to Narvik (Skr916, about 20 hours). You can also travel from Helsingborg to Oslo (Skr837, seven hours, twice daily), via Göteborg.

UK

BUS

Eurolines has regular routes to the UK from Sweden.

TRAIN

Connections from the UK go through the Channel Tunnel

to Continental Europe. You usually have to book each section separately. From London, a 2nd-class single ticket (including couchette) costs around £300 to Stockholm. For reservations and tickets, contact **Deutsche Bahn UK** (☎08718 808066; www.bahn.co.uk).

Sea

Ferry connections are frequent. Most lines offer substantial discounts for seniors, students and children. Most prices quoted are for single journeys at peak times (weekend travel, overnight crossings, mid-June to mid-August); other fares may be up to 30% lower.

Denmark

GÖTEBORG–FREDRIKSHAVN

Stena Line (☎031-704 00 00; www.stenaline.se) Three-hour crossing. Up to six ferries daily. Pedestrian/car with passengers/bicycle Skr180/1060/238.

Stena Line (Express) Express two-hour crossing. Up to three ferries daily. Pedestrian/car and five passengers/bicycle Skr184/1157/165.

HELSINGØR–HELSINGBORG

This is the quickest route and has frequent ferries (crossing time around 20 minutes).

HH-Ferries (☎042-19 80 00; www.hhferries.se) A 24-hour service. Pedestrian/car and up to nine passengers Skr36/465. Pedestrians can bring bicycles along at no extra charge.

Scandlines (☎042-18 63 00; www.scandlines.se) A 24-hour service. Pedestrian/car and up to nine passengers Skr36/465. Pedestrians can bring bicycles along at no extra charge.

VARBERG–GRENÅ

Stena Line (☎031-704 00 00; www.stenaline.se) Four-hour crossing. Three or four daily. Pedestrian/car and five passengers/bicycle Skr180/1096/238.

YSTAD–RØNNE

BornholmsTrafikken (☎0411-55 87 00; www.bornholmstrafikken.dk) Conventional and fast services (1½ hours, 80 minutes, two to nine times daily). Pedestrian/car with five passengers from Skr242/1420.

Eastern Europe

To/from Estonia, **Tallink** (☎08-666 60 01; www.tallink.ee) runs the routes Stockholm–Tallinn and Kapellskär–Paldiski.

Scandlines operates ferries between Nynäshamn and Ventspils (Latvia) around five times per week.

To/from Poland, **Polferries** (☎040-12 17 00; www.polferries.se) and **Unity Line** (☎0411-55 69 00; www.unityline.pl) have daily Ystad–Swinoujscie crossings. Polferries also runs Nynäshamn–Gdańsk. **Stena Line** (☎031-704 00 00; www.stenaline.se) sails Karlskrona–Gdynia.

Finland

Helsinki is called Helsingfors in Swedish, and Turku is Åbo.

Stockholm–Helsinki and Stockholm–Turku ferries run daily throughout the year via the Åland islands. These ferries have minimum-age limits; check before you travel.

STOCKHOLM–ÅLAND ISLANDS (MARIEHAMN)

Viking Line also goes to Åland from Stockholm and Kapellskär two or three times daily.

Eckerö Linjen (☎0175-258 00; www.eckerolinjen.fi) Runs to the Åland islands from Grisslehamn (passenger/car/bicycle Skr35/125/20).

STOCKHOLM–HELSINKI

Tallink & Silja Line (Map p48; ☎08-22 21 40; www.tallinksilja.com) Around 15 hours. Ticket and cabin berth from about Skr1195.

Viking Line (☎08-452 40 00; www.vikingline.fi) Ticket and cabin berth from about Skr920.

STOCKHOLM–TURKU

Silja Line (Map p48; ☎08-22 21 40; www.silja.com) Eleven hours. Deck place Skr138, cabins from Skr478; prices are higher for evening trips. From September to early May, ferries also depart from Kapellskär (90km northeast of Stockholm); connecting buses operated by Silja Line are included in the full-price fare.

Viking Line (Map p48; ☎08-452 40 00; www.vikingline.fi) Operates routes to Turku from Stockholm and, in high season, also from Kappelskär.

Wasaline (☎090-18 52 00; www.wasaline.com) Runs the Umeå–Vaasa route. One-way foot passengers Skr330; cars Skr475 to Skr505.

Germany

GÖTEBORG–KIEL

Stena Line (Denmark) (www.stenaline.se) Nearest to central Göteborg, the Stena Line Denmark terminal near Masthuggstorget (tram 3, 9 or 11) has around six daily departures for Frederikshavn in peak season (one way/return from Skr499/998).

TRELLEBORG–ROSTOCK & TRELLEBORG–TRAVEMÜNDE

TT-Line (☎0410-562 00; www.ttline.com) Seven hours. Two to five daily. Car and up to five passengers Trelleborg–Rostock Skr490, Trelleborg–Travemünde Skr790. Berths are compulsory on night crossings.

Norway

There's a daily overnight **DFDS Seaways** (☎031-65 06 80; www.dfdsseaways.com) ferry between Copenhagen and Oslo (from €109 per passenger plus €83 per vehicle), via Helsingborg. Passenger fares between Helsingborg and Oslo (14 hours) cost from Skr1100, and cars Skr475, but the journey can't be booked online; you'll need to call.

A **Color Line** (☎0526-620 00; www.colorline.com) ferry between Strömstad and Sandefjord (Norway) sails two to six times daily (2½ hours) year-round. Tickets cost from €19; rail-pass holders get a 50% discount.

GETTING AROUND

Public transport is heavily subsidised and well organised. It's divided into 24 *länstrafik* (regional networks) but with an overarching **Resplus** (www.samtrafiken.se) system, where one ticket is valid on trains and buses. Timetables are available online.

Air

Airlines in Sweden

Domestic airlines in Sweden tend to use **Stockholm Arlanda** (☎10-109 10 00; www.swedavia.se/arlanda) as a hub, but there are 30-odd regional airports. Flying domestic is expensive, but discounts are available on internet bookings, student and youth fares, off-peak travel, return tickets booked in advance, and low-price tickets for accompanying family members and seniors.

The following is a selection of Sweden's internal flight operators and the destinations they cover.

Malmö Aviation (☎040-660 28 20; www.malmoaviation.se) Göteborg, Stockholm, Malmö, Östersund, Halmstad, Kalmar, Ronneby, Sundsvall, Visby, Växjö, Ängelholm and Umeå.

SAS (☎0770-72 77 27; www.flysas.com) Arvidsjaur, Borlänge, Gällivare, Göteborg, Halmstad, Ängelholm-Helsingborg, Hemavan, Hultsfred, Jönköping, Kalmar, Karlstad, Kiruna, Kramfors, Kristianstad, Linköping, Luleå, Lycksele, Malmö, Mora, Norrköping, Oskarshamn, Oskersund, Skellefteå, Stockholm, Storuman, Sundsvall, Sveg, Torsby, Trollhättan, Umeå, Vilhelmina, Visby, Västerås, Örebro and Örnsköldsvik.

Air Passes

Visitors who fly SAS to Sweden from North America or Asia can add on a Visit Scandinavia Airpass, allowing one-way travel on direct flights between any two Scandinavian cities serviced by SAS and its partner airlines. A coupon for use within Sweden costs from US$50 (Stockholm–Kiruna is higher); international flights between Sweden, Denmark, Norway and Finland cost US$50 to US$226. For the latest, call SAS at ☎800-221-2350 or check www.flysas.com.

Bicycle

Cycling is a very common mode of transport for Swedes. Most towns have separate lanes and traffic signals for cyclists. Helmets are compulsory for all cyclists under age 15.

Boat

Canal Boat

The canals provide cross-country routes linking the main lakes. The longest cruises, on the Göta Canal from Söderköping (south of Stockholm) to Göteborg, run from mid-May to mid-September, take at least four days and include the lakes between.

Rederiaktiebolaget Göta Kanal (☎031-80 63 15; www.gotacanal.se) operates three ships over the whole distance at fares from Skr12,295 to Skr17,125 per person for a four-day cruise, including full board and guided excursions.

Ferry

An extensive boat network and the five-day Båtluffarkortet (Boat Hiking Pass; Skr420) open up the attractive Stockholm archipelago. Gotland is served by regular ferries from Nynäshamn and Oskarshamn, and the quaint fishing villages off the west coast can normally be reached by boat with a regional transport pass; enquire at the Göteborg tourist offices.

Bus

You can travel by bus in Sweden on any of the 24 good-value and extensive *länstrafik* networks or on national long-distance routes.

Express Buses

Swebus Express (☎0771-21 82 18; www.swebus.se) has the largest network of express buses, but only serves the southern half of the country. Generally, tickets for travel between Monday and Thursday, and tickets purchased over the internet or more than 24 hours before departure are cheaper; if you're a student or senior, ask about discounts.

Svenska Buss (☎0771-67 67 67; www.svenskabuss.se) and **Nettbuss** (☎0771-15 15 15; www.nettbuss.se) also connect many southern towns and cities with Stockholm; prices are often slightly cheaper than Swebus Express prices, but services are less frequent.

North of Gävle, regular connections with Stockholm are provided by several smaller operators, including **Ybuss** (☎060-17 19 60; www.ybuss.se), which has services to Sundsvall, Östersund and Umeå.

Regional Networks

The *länstrafik* bus networks are well integrated with the regional train system, with one ticket valid on any local or regional bus or train. Rules vary, but transfers are usually free if they are within one to four hours. Fares on local buses and trains are often identical, though prices can vary wildly depending on when you travel and how far in advance you buy tickets.

Bus Passes

Good-value daily or weekly passes are usually available from local and regional transport offices, and many regions have 30-day passes for longer stays or summer travel. These can be bought online, from most newsagents, and from tourist information offices.

Car & Motorcycle

Sweden has good roads, and the excellent E-class motorways rarely have traffic jams.

Automobile Associations

The Swedish national motoring association is **Motormännens Riksförbund** (☎020-21 11 11; www.motormannen.se).

Bringing Your Own Vehicle

If you're bringing your own car, you'll need vehicle registration documents, unlimited third-party liability insurance and a valid driving licence. A right-hand-drive vehicle brought from the UK or Ireland should have deflectors fitted to the headlights to avoid dazzling oncoming traffic. You must carry a reflective warning breakdown triangle.

Driving Licences

An international driving permit isn't necessary; your domestic licence will do.

Hire

To hire a car you have to be at least 20 (sometimes 25) years of age, with a recognised licence and a credit card.

International rental chains Avis, Hertz and Europcar have desks at Stockholm Arlanda and Göteborg Landvetter airports, and offices in most major cities. The lowest car-hire rates are generally from larger petrol stations (like Statoil and OKQ8).

Avis (☎0770-82 00 82; www.avisworld.com)

Europcar (☎020-78 11 80; www.europcar.com)

Hertz (☎0771 21 12 12; www.hertz-europe.com)

Mabi Hyrbilar (☎08-612 60 90; www.mabirent.se) National company with competitive rates.

OK-Q8 (☎020-85 08 50; www.okq8.se) Click on *hyrbilar* in the website menu to see car-hire pages.

Statoil (☎08-429 63 00; www.statoil.se/biluthyrning) Click on *uthyrningsstationer* to see branches with car hire, and on *priser* for prices.

Road Hazards

In the north, elk (moose, to Americans) and reindeer are serious road hazards; around 40 people die in collisions every year. Look out for the signs saying *viltstängsel upphör*, which mean that elk may cross the road, and for black plastic bags tied to roadside trees or poles, which mean Sami have reindeer herds grazing in the area. Report all incidents to police – failure to do so is an offence.

In Göteborg and Norrköping, be aware of trams, which have priority; overtake on the right.

Road Rules

Drive on and give way to the right. Headlights (at least dipped) must be on at all times when driving. Seatbelts

ROAD DISTANCES (KM)

	Gävle	Göteborg	Helsingborg	Jönköping	Kalmar	Karlstad	Kiruna	Linköping	Luleå	Malmö	Skellefteå	Stockholm	Sundsvall	Umeå	Uppsala	Örebro
Göteborg	520															
Helsingborg	690	220														
Jönköping	450	150	240													
Kalmar	560	350	290	215												
Karlstad	325	250	470	245	455											
Kiruna	1090	1645	1785	1540	1660	1420										
Linköping	365	280	365	130	235	230	1440									
Luleå	755	1300	1440	1210	1310	1080	342	1116								
Malmö	740	280	65	290	290	530	1835	415	1500							
Skellefteå	620	1185	1310	1075	1175	950	470	970	135	1360						
Stockholm	175	480	565	330	415	305	1265	205	930	620	795					
Sundsvall	215	765	890	670	770	540	875	575	540	955	405	390				
Umeå	485	1010	1140	935	1040	810	605	850	270	1230	135	660	270			
Uppsala	110	485	615	380	460	285	1195	250	860	665	725	70	320	590		
Örebro	235	285	450	200	350	115	1340	115	970	495	840	200	445	705	170	
Östersund	385	795	990	790	950	560	815	680	595	1075	470	560	185	370	490	590

are compulsory, and children under seven years old should be in the appropriate harness or child seat.

The blood-alcohol limit in Sweden is 0.02% – having just one drink will put you over. Random checks are not unheard of. The maximum speed on motorways (signposted in green and called E1, E4 etc) is 110km/h, highways 90km/h, narrow rural roads 70km/h and built-up areas 50km/h. The speed limit for cars towing caravans is 80km/h. Police using hand-held radar speed detectors have the power to impose on-the-spot fines of up to Skr1200.

Hitching

Travellers who decide to hitch should understand that they are taking a small but potentially serious risk; consider travelling in pairs, and always let someone know where you're planning to go. Hitching isn't popular in Sweden and very long waits are the norm. It's prohibited to hitch on motorways.

Local Transport

In Sweden local transport is always linked with *länstrafik*. Regional passes are valid both in the city and on rural routes. Town and city bus fares are around Skr20, but it usually works out cheaper to get a day card or other travel pass.

Swedish and Danish trains and buses around the Öresund area form an integrated transport system, so buying tickets to Copenhagen from any station in the region is as easy as buying tickets for Swedish journeys.

Tours

We recommend tours tied to various areas throughout this book, but the hostel organisation STF is also reliably good:

Svenska Turistföreningen (STF, Swedish Touring Association; ☎08-463 21 00; www.svenskaturistforeningen.se) Events and tours are generally affordable, ecologically minded and fun, and mostly based on outdoor activities (eg kayaking and hiking). Equipment rental is often available. Prices are usually lower for STF members.

Train

Sweden has an extensive and reliable railway network, and trains are almost always faster than buses. (Exceptions include local commuter trains in large urban and suburban areas, which make frequent stops.)

Inlandsbanan (☎0771-53 53 53; www.inlandsbanan.se) One of the great rail journeys in Scandinavia is this scenic 1300km route from Kristinehamn to Gällivare. Several southern sections have to be travelled by bus, but the all-train route starts at Mora. It takes seven hours from Mora to Östersund (Skr494) and 15 hours from Östersund to Gällivare (Skr1149). A pass allows two weeks' unlimited travel for Skr1795.

Sveriges Järnväg (SJ; ☎0771-75 75 75; www.sj.se) National network covering most main lines, especially in the southern part of the country.

Tågkompaniet (☎0771-44 41 11; www.tagkompaniet.se) Operates excellent overnight trains from Göteborg and Stockholm north to Boden, Kiruna, Luleå and Narvik, and the lines north of Härnösand.

Costs

Ticket prices vary depending on the type of train, class, time of day, and how far in advance you buy the ticket. Full-price 2nd-class tickets for longer journeys cost about twice as much as equivalent bus trips, but there are discounts available for advance or last-minute bookings. Students, pensioners and people aged under 26 get a discount.

All SJ ticket prices drop from late June to mid-August. Most SJ trains don't allow bicycles to be taken onto trains (they have to be sent as freight), but some in southern Sweden do; check when you book your ticket.

Train Passes

The Sweden Rail Pass, Eurodomino tickets and international passes, such as Inter-Rail and Eurail, are accepted on SJ services and most regional trains.

The **Eurail Scandinavia Pass** (www.eurail.com) entitles you to unlimited rail travel in Denmark, Finland, Norway and Sweden; it is valid in 2nd class only and is available for four, five, six, eight or 10 days of travel within a two-month period (prices start at youth/adult US$276/368). The X2000 trains require all rail-pass holders to pay a supplement of Skr62. The pass also provides free travel on Scandlines' Helsingør to Helsingborg ferry route, and 20% to 50% discounts on the following ship routes.

ROUTE	OPERATOR
Frederikshavn–Göteborg	Stena Line
Grenå–Varberg	Stena Line
Helsinki–Åland–Stockholm	Silja Line
Stockholm–Riga	Silja Line
Stockholm–Tallinn	Silja Line
Turku–Åland–Stockholm/Kappelskär	Silja Line
Turku/Helsinki–Stockholm	Viking Line

Some of the main rail routes across the country:

- Stockholm north to Uppsala–Gävle–Sundsvall–Östersund
- Stockholm west to Örebro–Karlstad–Oslo
- Stockholm west to Örebro–Göteborg
- Stockholm south to Norrköping–Malmö–Copenhagen

Language

As a member of the North Germanic or Scandinavian language family, Swedish has Danish and Norwegian as the closest relatives. It is the national language of Sweden, spoken by the majority of residents (around 8.5 million). In neighbouring Finland it shares official status with Finnish and is a mandatory subject in schools, but it's the first language for only about 300,000 people or 6% of Finland's population.

The standard language or *Rikssvenska* reek·*sven*·ska (lit: kingdom-Swedish) is based on the central dialects from the area around Stockholm. Some of the rural dialects that are spoken across the country are quite diverse – for example, *Skånska* *skawn*·ska, spoken in the southern province of Skåne, has flatter vowels (and sounds a lot more like Danish), whereas *Dalmål* *daal*·mawl, spoken in the central region of Dalarna, has a very up-and-down sound.

Most Swedish sounds are similar to their English counterparts. One exception is fh (a breathy sound pronounced with rounded lips, like saying 'f' and 'w' at the same time), but with a little practice, you'll soon get it right. Note also that ai is pronounced as in 'aisle', aw as in 'saw', air as in 'hair', eu as the 'u' in 'nurse', ew as the 'ee' in 'see' with rounded lips, and ey as the 'e' in 'bet' but longer. Just read our coloured pronunciation guides as if they were English and you'll be understood. The stressed syllables are indicated with italics.

BASICS

Hello.	*Hej.*	hey
Goodbye.	*Hej då./Adjö.*	hey daw/aa·*yeu*
Yes.	*Ja.*	yaa
No.	*Nej.*	ney
Please.	*Tack.*	tak
Thank you (very much).	*Tack (så mycket).*	tak (saw *mew*·ke)
You're welcome.	*Varsågod.*	var·sha·*gohd*
Excuse me.	*Ursäkta mig.*	oor·*shek*·ta mey
Sorry.	*Förlåt.*	feur·*lawt*

How are you?	
Hur mår du?	hoor mawr doo
Fine, thanks. And you?	
Bra, tack. Och dig?	braa tak o dey
What's your name?	
Vad heter du?	vaad *hey*·ter doo
My name is ...	
Jag heter ...	yaa *hey*·ter ...
Do you speak English?	
Talar du engelska?	*taa*·lar doo *eng*·el·ska
I don't understand.	
Jag förstår inte.	yaa feur·*shtawr in*·te

ACCOMMODATION

Where's a ...?	*Var finns det ...?*	var fins de ...
campsite	*en camping-plats*	eyn *kam*·ping·*plats*
guesthouse	*ett gästhus*	et *yest*·hoos
hotel	*ett hotell*	et hoh·*tel*
youth hostel	*ett vandrar-hem*	et *van*·drar·hem

Do you have a ... room?	*Har ni ...?*	har nee ...
single	*ett enkelrum*	et *en*·kel·rum
double	*ett dubbelrum*	et *du*·bel·rum

How much is it per ...?	*Hur mycket kostar det per ...?*	hoor *mew*·ket *kos*·tar de peyr ...
night	*natt*	nat
person	*person*	*peyr*·shohn

SAMI LANGUAGES

Sami languages are related to Finnish and other Finno-Ugric languages. Five of the nine main Sami languages are spoken in Sweden, with speakers of each varying in number from 500 to 5000.

Most Sami speakers can communicate in Swedish, but relatively few speak English. Knowing some Sami words and phrases will give you a chance to access the unique Sami culture.

Fell (Northern) Sami

The most common of the Sami languages, Fell Sami is considered the standard Sami variety. It's spoken in Sweden's far north around Karesuando and Jukkasjärvi.

Written Fell Sami includes several accented letters, but it still doesn't accurately represent the spoken language – even some Sami people find the written language difficult to learn. For example, *giitu* (thanks) is pronounced 'geech-too', but the strongly aspirated 'h' isn't written.

Hello.	*Buorre beaivi.*
Hello. (reply)	*Ipmel atti.*
Goodbye.	
(to person leaving)	*Mana dearvan.*
(to person staying)	*Báze dearvan.*
How are you?	*Mot manna?*
I'm fine.	*Buorre dat manna.*
Yes.	*De lea.*
No.	*Li.*
Thank you.	*Giitu.*
You're welcome.	*Leage buorre.*

1	*okta*
2	*guokte*
3	*golbma*
4	*njeallje*
5	*vihta*
6	*guhta*
7	*cieza*
8	*gávcci*
9	*ovcci*
10	*logi*

DIRECTIONS

Where's the ...?
Var ligger ...? — var *li*·ger ...

What's the address?
Vilken adress är det? — *vil*·ken a·*dres* air de

Can you show me (on the map)?
Kan du visa mig (på kartan)? — kan doo *vee*·sa mey (paw *kar*·tan)

How far is it?
Hur långt är det? — hoor lawngt air de

How do I get there?
Hur kommer man dit? — hoor *ko*·mar man deet

Turn ...	*Sväng ...*	sveng ...
at the corner	*vid hörnet*	veed *heur*·net
at the traffic lights	*vid trafik-ljuset*	veed tra·*feek*·yoo·set
left	*till vänster*	til *ven*·ster
right	*till höger*	til *heu*·ger

It's ...	*Det är ...*	de air ...
behind ...	*bakom ...*	*baa*·kom ...
far away	*långt*	lawngt
in front of ...	*framför ...*	*fram*·feur ...
left	*till vänster*	til *ven*·ster
near (to ...)	*nära (på ...)*	*nair*·ra (paw ...)
next to ...	*bredvid ...*	breyd·*veed* ...
on the corner	*vid hörnet*	veed *heur*·net
opposite ...	*mitt emot ...*	mit ey·*moht* ...
right	*till höger*	til *heu*·ger
straight ahead	*rakt fram*	raakt fram

EATING & DRINKING

What would you recommend?
Vad skulle ni rekommendera? — vaad *sku*·le nee re·ko·men·*dey*·ra

What's the local speciality?
Vad är den lokala specialiteten? — vaad air deyn loh·*kaa*·la spe·si·a·li·*tey*·ten

Do you have vegetarian food?
Har ni vegetarisk mat? — har nee ve·ge·*taa*·risk maat

I'll have ...
Jag vill ha ... — yaa vil haa ...

Cheers!
Skål! — skawl

I'd like (the) ...	*Jag skulle vilja ha ...*	yaa *sku*·le *vil*·ya haa ...
bill	*räkningen*	*reyk*·ning·en
drink list	*drickslistan*	*driks*·lis·tan

menu	*menyn*	me·*newn*
that dish	*den maträtten*	deyn *maat*·reten

Could you prepare a meal without ...?	*Kan ni laga en maträtt utan ...?*	kan nee *laa*·ga eyn *maat*·ret oo·tan ...
butter	*smör*	smeur
eggs	*ägg*	eg
meat stock	*köttspad*	*sheut*·spaad

Key Words

bar	*bar*	bar
bottle	*flaska*	*flas*·ka
breakfast	*frukost*	*froo*·kost
cafe	*kafé*	ka·*fey*
children's menu	*barnmeny*	barn·me·*new*
cold	*kylig*	*shew*·lig
cup	*kopp*	kop
daily special	*dagens rätt*	*daa*·gens ret
dinner	*middag*	*mi*·daa
drink	*dricka*	*dri*·ka
food	*mat*	maat
fork	*gaffel*	*ga*·fel
glass	*glas*	glaas
hot	*varm*	varm
knife	*kniv*	kneev
lunch	*lunch*	lunsh
market	*torghandel*	*tory*·han·del
menu	*meny/ matsedel*	me·*new*/ *maat*·sey·del
plate	*tallrik*	*tal*·reek
restaurant	*restaurang*	res·taw·*rang*
snack	*mellanmål*	*me*·lan·mawl
spoon	*sked*	fheyd
teaspoon	*tesked*	*tey*·fheyd
with	*med*	me
without	*utan*	*oo*·taan

Meat & Fish

chicken	*kyckling*	shewk·*ling*
fish	*fisk*	fisk
herring	*sill*	sil
lobster	*hummer*	*hu*·mer
meat	*kött*	sheut
meatballs	*köttbullar*	*sheut*·bu·lar

Signs

Ingång	Entrance
Utgång	Exit
Öppet	Open
Stängt	Closed
Förbjudet	Prohibited
Toaletter	Toilets
Herrar	Men
Damer	Women

salmon	*lax*	laks
tuna	*tonfisk*	*tohn*·fisk
venison	*rådjur*	*rawd*·yur

Fruit & Vegetables

blueberries	*blåbär*	*blaw*·bair
carrot	*morot*	*moh*·rot
fruit	*frukt*	frukt
mushrooms	*svamp*	svamp
potatoes	*potatis*	poh·*taa*·tis
raspberries	*hallon*	*haa*·lon
strawberries	*jordgubbar*	*yohrd*·gu·bar
vegetable	*grönsak*	*greun*·saak

Other

bread	*bröd*	breud
butter	*smör*	smeur
cake	*kaka*	*kaa*·ka
cheese	*ost*	ost
egg	*ägg*	eg
jam	*sylt*	sewlt
rice	*ris*	rees
soup	*soppa*	*so*·pa

Drinks

beer	*öl*	eul
coffee	*kaffe*	*ka*·fe
(orange) juice	*(apelsin-) juice*	(a·pel·*seen*·) djoos
milk	*mjölk*	myeulk
mineral water	*mineral-vatten*	mi·ne·*raal*·va·ten
red wine	*rödvin*	*reud*·veen
soft drink	*läsk*	lesk
sparkling wine	*mousserande vin*	moo·*sey*·ran·de veen

tea	*te*	tey
water	*vatten*	va·ten
white wine	*vitt vin*	vit veen

EMERGENCIES

Help!	*Hjälp!*	yelp
Go away!	*Försvinn!*	feur·*shvin*

Call ...!	*Ring ...!*	ring ...
a doctor	*efter en doktor*	*ef*·ter en *dok*·tor
the police	*polisen*	poh·*lee*·sen

It's an emergency!
Det är ett nödsituation! — de air et *neud*·si·too·a·fhohn

I'm lost.
Jag har gått vilse. — yaa har got *vil*·se

I'm sick.
Jag är sjuk. — yaa air fhook

It hurts here.
Det gör ont här. — de yeur ont hair

I'm allergic to (antibiotics).
Jag är allergisk mot (antibiotika). — yaa air a·*leyr*·gisk moht (an·tee·bee·*oh*·ti·ka)

Where are the toilets?
Var är toaletten? — var air toh·aa·*le*·ten

Numbers

1	*ett*	et
2	*två*	tvaw
3	*tre*	trey
4	*fyra*	*few*·ra
5	*fem*	fem
6	*sex*	seks
7	*sju*	fhoo
8	*åtta*	*o*·ta
9	*nio*	*nee*·oh
10	*tio*	*tee*·oh
20	*tjugo*	*shoo*·go
30	*trettio*	*tre*·tee
40	*fyrtio*	*fewr*·tee
50	*femtio*	*fem*·tee
60	*sextio*	*seks*·tee
70	*sjuttio*	*fhu*·tee
80	*åttio*	*o*·tee
90	*nittio*	*ni*·tee
100	*ett hundra*	et *hun*·dra
1000	*ett tusen*	et *too*·sen

SHOPPING & SERVICES

Where's the ...?	*Var ligger ...?*	var *li*·ger ...
bank	*banken*	*ban*·ken
post office	*posten*	*pos*·ten
tourist office	*turistinformationen*	too·*rist*·in·for·ma·*fhoh*·nen

Where's the local internet cafe?
Var finns det lokala internet kaféet? — var fins de loh·*kaa*·la *in*·ter·net ka·*fey*·et

Where's the nearest public phone?
Var ligger närmaste telefonautomat? — var *li*·ger *nair*·ma·ste te·le·*fohn* ow·toh·*maat*

I'm looking for ...
Jag letar efter ... — yaa *ley*·tar *ef*·ter ...

Can I look at it?
Får jag se den? — fawr yaa se deyn

Do you have any others?
Har ni några andra? — har nee *naw*·ra *an*·dra

How much is it?
Hur mycket kostar det? — hoor *mew*·ke *kos*·tar de

That's too expensive.
Det är för dyrt. — de air feur dewrt

What's your lowest price?
Vad är ditt lägsta pris? — vaad air dit *leyg*·sta prees

There's a mistake in the bill.
Det är ett fel på räkningen. — de air et fel paw *reyk*·ning·en

TIME & DATES

What time is it?
Hur mycket är klockan? — hur *mew*·ke air *klo*·kan

It's (two) o'clock.
Klockan är (två). — *klo*·kan air (tvaw)

Half past (one).
Halv (två). (lit: half two) — halv (tvaw)

At what time ...?
Hur dags ...? — hur daks ...

At (10) o'clock.
Klockan (tio). — *klo*·kan (*tee*·oh)

in the morning	*på förmiddagen*	paw *feur*·mi·daa·gen
in the afternoon	*på eftermiddagen*	paw *ef*·ter·mi·daa·gen
yesterday	*igår*	ee·*gawr*
tomorrow	*imorgon*	ee·*mor*·ron
Monday	*måndag*	*mawn*·daa
Tuesday	*tisdag*	*tees*·taa
Wednesday	*onsdag*	*ohns*·daa
Thursday	*torsdag*	*torsh*·daa
Friday	*fredag*	*frey*·daa

Saturday	*lördag*	*leur*·daa
Sunday	*söndag*	*seun*·daa
January	*januari*	ya·nu·*aa*·ree
February	*februari*	fe·bru·*aa*·ree
March	*mars*	mars
April	*april*	a·*preel*
May	*maj*	mai
June	*juni*	*yoo*·nee
July	*juli*	*yoo*·lee
August	*augusti*	aw·*gus*·tee
September	*september*	sep·*tem*·ber
October	*oktober*	ok·*toh*·ber
November	*november*	noh·*vem*·ber
December	*december*	dey·*sem*·ber

TRANSPORT

Public Transport

Is this the ... to (Stockholm)?	*Är den här ... till (Stockholm)?*	air den hair ... til (*stok*·holm)
boat	*båten*	*baw*·ten
bus	*bussen*	*bu*·sen

Is this the ... to (Stockholm)?	*Är det här ... till (Stockholm)?*	air de hair ... til (*stok*·holm)
plane	*planet*	*plaa*·net
train	*tåget*	*taw*·get

What time's the ... bus?	*När går ...?*	nair gawr ...
first	*första bussen*	*feursh*·ta *bu*·sen
last	*sista bussen*	*sis*·ta *bu*·sen
next	*nästa buss*	*nes*·ta bus

One ... ticket (to Stockholm), please.	*Jag skulle vilja ha en ... (till Stockholm).*	yaa *sku*·le *vil*·ya haa eyn ... (til *stok*·holm)
one-way	*enkelbiljett*	*en*·kel·bil·*yet*
return	*returbiljett*	re·*toor*·bil·*yet*

At what time does it arrive/leave?
Hur dags anländer/ avgår den? — hoor daks *an*·len·der/ *aav*·gawr deyn

How long will it be delayed?
Hur mycket är det försenat? — hoor *mew*·ket air dey feur·*shey*·nat

Question Words

How?	*Hur?*	hoor
What?	*Vad?*	vaad
When?	*När?*	nair
Where?	*Var?*	var
Who?	*Vem?*	vem
Why?	*Varför?*	*var*·feur

What's the next station/stop?
Vilken är nästa station/hållplats? — *vil*·ken air *nes*·ta sta·*fhohn*/*hawl*·plats

Does it stop at (Lund)?
Stannar den i (Lund)? — *sta*·nar den ee (lund)

Please tell me when we get to (Linköping).
Kan du säga till när vi kommer till (Linköping)? — kan doo *say*·ya til nair vee *ko*·mer til (*lin*·sheu·ping)

Please take me to (this address).
Kan du köra mig till (denna address)? — kan doo *sheu*·ra mey til (*dey*·na a·*dres*)

Please stop here.
Kan du stanna här? — kan doo *sta*·na hair

Driving & Cycling

I'd like to hire a ...	*Jag vill hyra en ...*	yaa vil *hew*·ra eyn ...
bicycle	*cykel*	*sew*·kel
car	*bil*	beel
motorbike	*motor-cykel*	*moh*·tor·sew·kel

air	*luft*	luft
oil	*olja*	*ol*·ya
park (car)	*parkera*	par·*key*·ra
petrol/gas	*bensin*	ben·*seen*
service station	*bensin-station*	ben·*seen*·sta·fhohn
tyres	*däck*	dek

Is this the road to (Göteborg)?
Går den här vägen till (Göteborg)? — gawr den hair *vey*·gen til (yeu·te·*bory*)

I need a mechanic.
Jag behöver en mekaniker. — yaa be·*heu*·ver eyn me·*kaa*·ni·ker

I've run out of petrol/gas.
Jag har ingen bensin kvar. — yaa har *ing*·en ben·*seen* kvar

I have a flat tyre.
Jag har fått punktering. — yaa har fawt punk·*tey*·ring

GLOSSARY

Note that the letters **å**, **ä** and **ö** fall at the end of the Swedish alphabet, and the letters **v** and **w** are often used interchangeably (you will see the small town of Vaxholm also referred to as Waxholm, and an inn can be known as a *värdshus* or *wärdshus*). In directories like telephone books they usually fall under one category (eg *wa* is listed before *vu*).

(m) indicates masculine gender, (f) feminine gender and (pl) plural

aktie bolaget (AB) – company
allemansrätt – literally 'every person's right'; a tradition allowing universal access to private property (with some restrictions), public land and wilderness areas
apotek – pharmacy
ateljé – gallery, studio
avgift – payment, fee (seen on parking signs)

bad – swimming pool, bathing place or bathroom
bakfickan – literally 'back pocket'; a low-profile eatery usually associated with a gourmet restaurant
bankautomat – cash machine, ATM
bastu – sauna
bensin – petrol, gas
berg – mountain
bibliotek – library
biljet – ticket
biljetautomat – ticket machines (eg for street parking)
biluthyrning – car hire
bio, biograf – cinema
björn – bear
brännvin – aquavit
bro – bridge
bruk – factory, mill, works
bryggeri – brewery
butik – shop

centrum – town centre
cykel – bicycle
dag – day
dal – valley
domkyrka – cathedral
drottning – queen
duodji – Sami handicraft
dygnet runt – around the clock
dygnskort – a daily transport pass, valid for 24 hours

ej – not
ej motorfordon – no motor vehicles
expedition – office

fabrik – factory
fest – party, festival
fika – coffee and cake
fiskkort – local permits
fjäll – mountain
fjällstation – mountain lodge
fjällstugor – mountain huts
flod – large river
flyg – aeroplane
flygbuss – airport bus
flygplats – airport
folkhemmet – welfare state
friluft – open-air
fyr – lighthouse
fäbod – summer livestock farm
fågel – bird
färja – ferry
fästning – fort, fortress
förbund – union, association
förening – organisation, association
förlag – company

galleri, galleria – shopping mall
gamla staden, gamla stan – 'old town', the historical part of a city or town
gammal, gamla – old
gatan – street (often abbreviated to 'g')
gatukontoret – municipal parking spaces

gatukök – literally 'street kitchen'; kiosk, stall or grill selling fast food
glögg – mulled wine
gott och enkelt – good and simple
gruva – mine
gräns – border
gákti – traditional Sami clothing
gåhties – cottages
gård – yard, farm, estate
gästhamn – guest harbour, where visiting yachts can berth

hamn – harbour
hembygdsgård – open-air museum, usually old farmhouse buildings
hemslöjd – handicraft
hjörtron – cloudberry
hotell – hotel
hus – house
husmanskost – homely Swedish fare; what you would expect cooked at home when you were a (Swedish) child
hyrbilar – car hire
hällristningar – rock carvings

i – in
idrottsplats – sports venue, stadium

joik – see *yoik*
järnvägsstation – train station

kaj – quay
kanot – canoe
karta – map
Kartförlaget – State Mapping Agency (sales division)
kloster – monastery
kombibiljett – combined ticket
konditori – baker and confectioner (often with an attached cafe)
konst – art
kontor – office
kort – card
krog – pub, restaurant (or both)
krona (kronor) – the Swedish currency unit
kulle – hill
kulturkvarter – culture quarter
kung – king
kust – coast
kyrka – church
kyrkogård – graveyard
kyrkstad – church town
kåta – Sami hut
källare – cellar, vault
kök – kitchen

landskap – province, landscape

lastmoped – motorised bike
lavin – avalanche
lavvu – tent
lilla – lesser, little
linbana – chairlift
län – county
länskort – county pass
länsmuseum – regional museum
länstrafiken – public transport network of a *län*
länståg – regional train

magasin – store (usually a department store), warehouse
magasinet – depot
Midsommardag – Midsummer's Day; first Saturday after 21 June (the main celebrations take place on Midsummer's Eve)
museet – museum
mynt – coins

natt – night
nattklubb – nightclub
naturreservat – nature reserve
naturum – visitor centre at national park or nature reserve
Naturvårdsverket – Swedish Environmental Protection Agency (National Parks Authority)
nedre – lower
norr – north
norrsken – northern lights (aurora borealis)
nyheter – news

och – and

palats – palace
pendeltåg – commuter train
pensionat – pension, guesthouse
P-hus – multistorey car park
polis – police
punsch – strong alcoholic punch
på – on, in

raukar – limestone formations
RFSL – Riksförbundet för Sexuellt Likaberättigande (national gay organisation)
riksdag – parliament
rum – room
rådhus – town hall
rälsbuss – railcar

SAS – Scandinavian Airlines Systems
Schlager – Catchy, camp, highly melodic pop tunes that are big on sentimentality, and commonly featured at the Eurovision Song Contest
siida – Sami village units or communities
sjukhus – hospital
sjö – lake, sea
skog – forest
skål – cheers
skärgård – archipelago
slöjd – handicraft
slott – castle, manor house
smörgås – sandwich
smörgåsbord – Swedish buffet
STF – Svenska Turistföreningen (Swedish Touring Association)
stolen – chair
stor, stora – big or large
stortorget – main square
strand – beach
stuga (stugor/na) – cabin (cabins)
stugby – chalet park; small village of cabins
surströmming – fermented herring
svensk – Swedish
Sverige – Sweden
SVIF – Sveriges Vandrarhem i Förening; hostelling association
Systembolaget – state-owned liquor store
söder – south

teater – theatre
telefonkort – telephone card
torg, torget – town square
torn – tower
trädgård – garden open to the public
tull – customs
tunnelbana, T-bana – underground railway, metro
turistbyrå – tourist office

vandrarhem – hostel
vecka – week
vik – bay, inlet
väg – road
värdshus – inn, restaurant
väst – west (abbreviated to 'v')
västra – western

wärdshus – inn

yoik – a type of traditional Sami singing (also referred to as *joik*)

älv – river

ö – island
öst – east (abbreviated to 'ö')
östra – eastern
övre – upper

Behind the Scenes

SEND US YOUR FEEDBACK

We love to hear from travellers – your comments keep us on our toes and help make our books better. Our well-travelled team reads every word on what you loved or loathed about this book. Although we cannot reply individually to your submissions, we always guarantee that your feedback goes straight to the appropriate authors, in time for the next edition. Each person who sends us information is thanked in the next edition – the most useful submissions are rewarded with a selection of digital PDF chapters.

Visit **lonelyplanet.com/contact** to submit your updates and suggestions or to ask for help. Our award-winning website also features inspirational travel stories, news and discussions.

Note: We may edit, reproduce and incorporate your comments in Lonely Planet products such as guidebooks, websites and digital products, so let us know if you don't want your comments reproduced or your name acknowledged. For a copy of our privacy policy visit lonelyplanet.com/privacy.

OUR READERS

Many thanks to the travellers who used the last edition and wrote to us with helpful hints, useful advice and interesting anecdotes:
Arie van der Vlies, Ben den Dulk, Claudia Kuehn, Daan Symons, Daniel Marsá, Eleanor Vale, Jakob Götesson, Jonas Jeppson, Lorenzo Merli, Lucia Krubasik, Martin Williams, Mary Wood, Nick Dowling, Terence Jagger

AUTHOR THANKS

Becky Ohlsen

Thanks to my dad, Joel Ohlsen, an awesome travel buddy, who joined me for the best part of the trip (the Stockholm archipelago) and against his better judgment let me plan our whole itinerary. Thanks also to co-authors Anna Kaminski and Josephine Quintero for their great work, and especially to editor Gemma Graham, an absolute pleasure to work with. A whiskey-soda and a big hug to Travis Gardner for keeping the cat and tomato plants alive while I was away.

Anna Kaminski

Many thanks to Team Sweden, not least to Gemma for entrusting me with five chapters and Becky for on-the-road banter and Midsommar beer. I'm grateful to everyone who helped me along the way, including Britta at STF Kebnekaise, Joran and the Kallaxflyg team in Nikkaluokta, Ali in Luleå, Amelie, Erik and the other medieval doom metal rockers in Gävle, Nandito in Gothenburg, Doris in Vilhelmina and Sven in Kiruna.

Josephine Quintero

Thanks to all the helpful folk at the various tourist information offices, as well as Fredrik Serger, a valuable contact in Malmö. Thanks too to coordinating author Becky Ohlsen and to all those involved in the title from the Lonely Planet offices, as well as to all my Scandinavian friends here in Spain who provided endless advice, contacts and tips, and to Robin Chapman for looking after Marilyn (the cat).

ACKNOWLEDGMENTS

Climate Map Data (CRMS and Discover titles) Climate map data adapted from Peel MC, Finlayson BL & McMahon TA (2007) 'Updated World Map of the Köppen-Geiger Climate Classification', Hydrology and Earth System Sciences, 11, 1633¬44.

Cover photograph: Local in traditional Sami attire, Lappland, Phillip Lee Harvey, Getty Images.

THIS BOOK

This 6th edition of Lonely Planet's Sweden guidebook was researched and written by Becky Ohlsen, Anna Kaminski and Josephine Quintero. Stuart Harrison wrote the Design & Architecture chapter. The previous edition was written by Becky Ohlsen, Anna Kaminski and K Lundgren. This guidebook was produced by the following:

Destination Editor Gemma Graham

Coordinating Editor Sarah Bailey

Product Editor Stephanie Ong

Senior Cartographer Valentina Kremenchutskaya

Book Designer Jessica Rose

Assisting Editors Jodie Martire, Charlotte Orr

Cartographer Rachel Imeson

Cover Research Naomi Parker

Thanks to Elin Berglund, Ryan Evans, Benjamin Little, Wayne Murphy, Alison Ridgway, Dianne Schallmeiner, Samantha Tyson

Index

Map Pages **000**
Photo Pages 000

Map Pages **000**
Photo Pages **000**

Map Pages **000**
Photo Pages 000

Map Legend

Sights

- Beach
- Bird Sanctuary
- Buddhist
- Castle/Palace
- Christian
- Confucian
- Hindu
- Islamic
- Jain
- Jewish
- Monument
- Museum/Gallery/Historic Building
- Ruin
- Shinto
- Sikh
- Taoist
- Winery/Vineyard
- Zoo/Wildlife Sanctuary
- Other Sight

Activities, Courses & Tours

- Bodysurfing
- Diving
- Canoeing/Kayaking
- Course/Tour
- Sento Hot Baths/Onsen
- Skiing
- Snorkelling
- Surfing
- Swimming/Pool
- Walking
- Windsurfing
- Other Activity

Sleeping

- Sleeping
- Camping

Eating

- Eating

Drinking & Nightlife

- Drinking & Nightlife
- Cafe

Entertainment

- Entertainment

Shopping

- Shopping

Information

- Bank
- Embassy/Consulate
- Hospital/Medical
- Internet
- Police
- Post Office
- Telephone
- Toilet
- Tourist Information
- Other Information

Geographic

- Beach
- Hut/Shelter
- Lighthouse
- Lookout
- Mountain/Volcano
- Oasis
- Park
- Pass
- Picnic Area
- Waterfall

Population

- Capital (National)
- Capital (State/Province)
- City/Large Town
- Town/Village

Transport

- Airport
- Border crossing
- Bus
- Cable car/Funicular
- Cycling
- Ferry
- Metro station
- Monorail
- Parking
- Petrol station
- S-Bahn/S-train/Subway station
- Taxi
- T-bane/Tunnelbana station
- Train station/Railway
- Tram
- Tube station
- U-Bahn/Underground station
- Other Transport

Note: Not all symbols displayed above appear on the maps in this book

Routes

- Tollway
- Freeway
- Primary
- Secondary
- Tertiary
- Lane
- Unsealed road
- Road under construction
- Plaza/Mall
- Steps
- Tunnel
- Pedestrian overpass
- Walking Tour
- Walking Tour detour
- Path/Walking Trail

Boundaries

- International
- State/Province
- Disputed
- Regional/Suburb
- Marine Park
- Cliff
- Wall

Hydrography

- River, Creek
- Intermittent River
- Canal
- Water
- Dry/Salt/Intermittent Lake
- Reef

Areas

- Airport/Runway
- Beach/Desert
- Cemetery (Christian)
- Cemetery (Other)
- Glacier
- Mudflat
- Park/Forest
- Sight (Building)
- Sportsground
- Swamp/Mangrove

OUR STORY

A beat-up old car, a few dollars in the pocket and a sense of adventure. In 1972 that's all Tony and Maureen Wheeler needed for the trip of a lifetime – across Europe and Asia overland to Australia. It took several months, and at the end – broke but inspired – they sat at their kitchen table writing and stapling together their first travel guide, *Across Asia on the Cheap*. Within a week they'd sold 1500 copies. Lonely Planet was born.

Today, Lonely Planet has offices in Franklin, London, Melbourne, Oakland, Beijing and Delhi, with more than 600 staff and writers. We share Tony's belief that 'a great guidebook should do three things: inform, educate and amuse'.

OUR WRITERS

Becky Ohlsen

Coordinating Author, Stockholm & Around, Uppsala & Central Sweden Each time she returns to Sweden, Becky discovers something new. This time it was the world's greatest cardamom bun, encountered at an organic bakery on a remote island in the Stockholm archipelago. A huge fan of Stockholm, Becky has spent enough time in the city to know where to find the no-fee public toilets, but not quite enough to have absorbed any of its impressive fashion sense. Maybe next time. She also loves hiking the northern Swedish woods and stumbling over relics of the Viking age. Though raised in the mountains of Colorado, Becky has been exploring Sweden since childhood, while visiting her grandparents and other relatives. She is easily bribed with ice-cold *snaps* or saffron ice cream.

Read more about Becky at:
lonelyplanet.com/members/BeckyOhlsen

Anna Kaminski

Göteborg & the Southwest, Östersund & the Bothnian Coast, Lappland & the Far North Anna got her first taste of Sweden as a youngster in the Soviet Union through the books of Astrid Lindgren and Selma Lagerlof, and has had a great affinity for it ever since. During this research trip, she roamed both of Sweden's coastlines by boat, drove close to 3000 miles, descended into mines and flew over the Arctic tundra in a helicopter. This is the third time she has researched Sweden for Lonely Planet and this seemingly sedate country never fails to surprise her. Anna also wrote the History and Sami Culture essays.

Josephine Quintero

Malmö & the South, The Southeast & Gotland Josephine has visited Sweden several times and finds that the country continually throws up surprises, although there is one constant: the genuine friendliness of the locals. Highlights during this trip included gazing at evocative art, especially in the galleries in Malmö and Norrköping, and listening to a soul-stirring choral concert in one of Visby's extraordinary ruined churches. She also happily increased both her baking knowledge (and her waist measurement) by sampling endless cardamom buns, but then justified this (sort of) by striding out and exploring Skåne's dramatic northwest peninsula.

Read more about Josephine at:
lonelyplanet.com/members/josephinequintero

Published by Lonely Planet Publications Pty Ltd
ABN 36 005 607 983
6th edition – May 2015
ISBN 978 1 74220 737 7
© Lonely Planet 2015 Photographs © as indicated 2015
10 9 8 7 6 5 4 3 2 1
Printed in China

Although the authors and Lonely Planet have taken all reasonable care in preparing this book, we make no warranty about the accuracy or completeness of its content and, to the maximum extent permitted, disclaim all liability arising from its use.

All rights reserved. No part of this publication may be copied, stored in a retrieval system, or transmitted in any form by any means, electronic, mechanical, recording or otherwise, except brief extracts for the purpose of review, and no part of this publication may be sold or hired, without the written permission of the publisher. Lonely Planet and the Lonely Planet logo are trademarks of Lonely Planet and are registered in the US Patent and Trademark Office and in other countries. Lonely Planet does not allow its name or logo to be appropriated by commercial establishments, such as retailers, restaurants or hotels. Please let us know of any misuses: lonelyplanet.com/ip.